OCÉANO

ATLÁNTICO

Estrecho de la Florida

LAS BAHAMAS

La Habana ⚝ • Matanzas

ar del Río

Cienfuegos • **CUBA**

Canal de Yucatán

umel

Camagüey

Guantánamo

Santiago
de Cuba

**REPÚBLICA
DOMINICANA**

San
Juan

*Islas
Vírgenes*

HAITÍ Mayagüez • ⚝
Ponce

Antigua

Port-au-
Prince Santo
Domingo **PUERTO
RICO**

Guadalupe

Kingston ⚝

Dominica

JAMAICA

Martinica
Santa Lucía

Antillas Menores

Mar Caribe

Barbados
San Vicente

NDURAS

Granada

ucigalpa

Curaçao

*Isla
Margarita*

• Managua

NICARAGUA

Aruba Bonaire

on

Trinidad y
Tobago

L. de Nicaragua

*Canal de
Panamá*

Caracas ⚝

ntarenas

**COSTA
RICA**

Colón •

San José

PANAMÁ

⚝ • Panamá

Río Orinoco

*Golfo
de
Panamá*

VENEZUELA

GUYANA

Río Magdalena

COLOMBIA

⚝ Bogotá

B R A S I L

ECUADOR

PERÚ

ANNOTATED INSTRUCTOR'S EDITION

Fifth Edition

MOSAICOS

Spanish as a World Language

Matilde Olivella de Castells (Late)

Emerita, California State University, Los Angeles

Elizabeth E. Guzmán

University of Iowa

Paloma Lapuerta

Central Connecticut State University

Judith E. Liskin-Gasparro

University of Iowa

Prentice Hall

Upper Saddle River   London   Singapore   Toronto
Tokyo   Sydney   Hong Kong   Mexico City

Dedicamos esta edición de Mosaicos a Matilde Castells, quien puso juntas, una a una, las piezas de este libro con un talento y profesionalismo admirables.

Executive Editor: Julia Caballero
Development Editors: Elizabeth Lantz, Celia Meana
Executive Marketing Manager: Kris Ellis-Levy
Senior Marketing Manager: Denise Miller
Marketing Coordinator: William J. Bliss
Senior Managing Editor: Mary Rottino
Associate Managing Editor: Janice Stangel
Project Manager: Manuel Echevarria
Development Editor for Assessment: Melissa Marolla Brown
Media Editor: Meriel Martínez
Senior Media Editor: Samantha Alducin
Art Manager: Gail Cocker
Illustrator: Andrew Lange Illustration
Cartographer: Peter Bull Studio
Assistant Editor/EditorialCoordinator: Jennifer Murphy
Manufacturing Buyer: Cathleen Petersen

Manager, Print Production: Brian Mackey
Manager, Rights and Permissions: Zina Arabia
Manager, Visual Research: Beth Brenzel
Manager, Cover Visual Research & Permissions: Karen Sanatar
Image Permission Coordinator: Fran Toepfer
Cover Image: Ferran Traite Soler/IStockphoto.com
Photo Researcher: Diane Austin
Designer: Ximena Tamvakopoulos
Creative Design Director: Leslie Osher
Art Director, Interior: John Christiana
Editorial Assistant: Katie Spiegel
Publisher: Phil Miller
Composition/Full-Service Project Management: Macmillan Publishing Solutions
Printer/Binder: Courier Kendallville, Inc.

This book was set in 10/12.5 Sabon.

Credits and acknowledgments borrowed from other sources and reproduced, with permission, in this textbook appear on pages A54–A55.

10 9 8 7 6 5 4 3 2 1

Student Edition ISBN - 10:	0-13-500153-6
Student Edition ISBN - 13:	978-0-13-500153-0
Annotated Instructor's Edition ISBN - 10:	0-205-66392-3
Annotated Instructor's Edition ISBN - 13:	978-0-205-66392-7
Volume 1 ISBN - 10:	0-205-63609-8
Volume 1 ISBN - 13:	978-0-205-63609-9
Volume 2 ISBN - 10:	0-205-63608-X
Volume 2 ISBN - 13:	978-0-205-63608-2
Volume 3 ISBN - 10:	0-205-63607-1
Volume 3 ISBN - 13:	978-0-205-63607-5

Prentice Hall
is an imprint of

PEARSON
www.pearsonhighered.com

BRIEF CONTENTS

SCOPE AND SEQUENCE

Capítulo	Communicative objectives	A primera vista

Funciones y formas	Mosaicos	Enfoque cultural

Capítulo	Communicative objectives	A primera vista

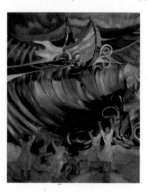

PREFACE

Welcome to the Fifth Edition of *Mosaicos*

Since the publication of its first edition more than a decade ago, *Mosaicos* has been widely acclaimed for its practical, communicative, culturally based approach to first-year Spanish. The approach has been refined over the course of several editions, and for this fifth edition we have been especially thorough in examining all aspects of the Student Text and all components of the *Mosaicos* program. The result is a fresh, twenty-first-century perspective on language teaching and learning in the context of a dynamic introduction to the Hispanic world and its people. We hope that both veteran users and those new to *Mosaicos* will discover a text that is richly contextualized, cognitively engaging, visually attractive, and readily accessible, accompanied by a wide array of resources that support student learning and make each class period valuable and enjoyable.

One of the hallmarks of the *Mosaicos* approach—and the rationale for the title—is the emphasis on the integration of the many different instructional strands that comprise a beginning Spanish course. We have made a special effort to ensure that this fifth edition effectively integrates elements that other programs often treat in isolation. We have gone farther than ever before in our effort to synthesize linguistic content with appropriate cultural contexts. We have refined and improved the open-ended *Situaciones* activities, in which students are asked to integrate their knowledge of grammatical structures and functions with thematically relevant vocabulary. Finally, we have made major revisions to the *Mosaicos* section of each chapter, in which students put linguistic and cultural knowledge together as they develop and practice their listening, speaking, reading, and writing skills.

Mosaicos reflects the wisdom and experience of the many expert language instructors who have used the program and have provided helpful suggestions over the years. But at a deeper level, it is grounded in current theories of language learning and in pedagogical principles embraced by most language instructors today. It presents vocabulary within communicative and cultural contexts. Its grammar sections move from meaning to form, providing an understanding of the language that is both functional and structural. It emphasizes the social aspects of language use by providing an abundance of carefully sequenced pair and group activities. It fosters awareness of the diversity of the Spanish-speaking world through photos, realia, maps, readings, and activities, as well as a new video program. By engaging students in the linguistic, cognitive, and social aspects of language learning, the distinctive *Mosaicos* approach draws on current knowledge about language learning to prepare first-year students to continue their study of Spanish language and culture at the intermediate level.

Highlights of the Fifth Edition

While building on the strengths of earlier editions, the fifth edition of *Mosaicos* incorporates many new and remarkable features. With its focus on learning strategies and communicative functions, it provides students and instructors with more tools than ever before to enhance and enrich the learning experience.

Vocabulary in Context

The *Mosaicos* program features a culturally and communicatively rich format for presenting and practicing new vocabulary. Through the two-page spread at the beginning of each chapter and in the *A primera vista* section that follows, students encounter new words in appropriate linguistic and cultural contexts.

The chapter-opening pages have been completely redesigned to provide a stimulating introduction both to the chapter theme and to the country or region that the chapter targets. New chapter titles highlight the text's active, functional approach to language learning, and abundant annotations on the chapter-opening pages guide instructors in introducing and recycling relevant vocabulary.

In the *A primera vista* section, new vocabulary is presented in contexts that reflect the chapter theme in various ways. Language samples, photos, line drawings, and realia are used to present new material, rather than word lists and translations. The activities that follow foster the use of new and previously learned vocabulary in natural, thematically relevant contexts. Special features include the following:

- Boldface type is used within the language samples to highlight new words and phrases that students will need to learn to use actively. (A convenient list of these words and phrases is provided at the end of each chapter.)

- Audio icons remind students that recorded versions of the language samples are available in the *Mosaicos* audio program.

- *Cultura* boxes (many new to this edition) raise awareness of the cultural contexts in which the language is used and help students learn the skills of close observation and interpretation of cultural products.

- *En otras palabras* boxes (all new to this edition) give examples of regional variations in the language.

Grammar as Function and Meaning

In the newly renamed *Funciones y formas* section of each chapter, grammar is presented as a means to effective communication. The bulleted explanations—clear, concise, and easy to understand—are designed to be studied at home, although their integration into the main body of the text enables students to use them for quick reference as they practice communication in class.

- Visuals and brief language samples are now used consistently to introduce new structures in meaningful contexts. The new structures are highlighted in boldface type.

- Short comprehension-based activities (all new to this edition) draw students' attention to the connection between meaning and linguistic form, providing a bridge from *función* to *forma*. These *Piénselo* activities are designed to help students develop their ability to think about how each structure communicates meaning by means of particular forms.

- A carefully designed sequence of communicative activities (many new or revised for this edition) follow the bulleted grammatical explanations. These activities focus attention on the communicative purpose of the linguistic structures while invoking culturally relevant contexts. All activities require students to process meaning as well as form so that they develop confidence in speaking and skill in using their linguistic knowledge to gather information, answer questions, and resolve problems.

- A large number of open-ended *Situaciones* activities (many new or revised for this edition) prompt students to integrate relevant grammatical structures with contexts drawn from the chapter theme. Two *Situaciones* role-plays are now provided for each grammar topic, and the format of these activities has been standardized so that there are always two roles (Role A and Role B). *En directo* boxes introduce colloquial expressions and encourage students to use them in the *Situaciones* and other communicative activities.

- Strategically placed *Lengua* boxes offer succinct grammatical information when it is needed to support self-expression.

- The grammatical scope and sequence has been modified in order to meet the communicative needs of beginning students more effectively. The *Algo más* boxes used in the fourth edition to present new structures have been eliminated; all essential structures are now given the full range of explanation and activities. Major topics, such as the preterit and imperfect, **ser/estar**, and object pronouns, are recycled to enhance learning, and basic topics such as regular verbs and **gustar** are presented earlier to spread essential structures more evenly over the book's fifteen chapters.

Integrated Culture

The fifth edition of *Mosaicos* builds on the successful integration of culture and language of previous editions. Each chapter focuses on a specific country or region, and numerous references to that country or region appear in the chapter's language samples, photos, maps, and realia. Related cultural content is interwoven throughout the activities and readings.

- A newly designed two-page chapter opener highlights the country or region that is the focus of the chapter. It includes a relevant work of art as well as maps and photos. A new warm-up activity (called *A vista de pájaro*) encourages students to process the visually presented information while accessing relevant prior knowledge. Numerous annotations offer instructors factual, conversational, and linguistic suggestions to pique students' interest and ease them into the chapter.

- The *Enfoque cultural* section of each chapter has new readings and accompanying activities. The first set of activities is available online as well as in the textbook. A final activity asks students to use the reading as a point of departure for expanding and sharing their knowledge. The standardized format of this section makes it possible for students to work with the readings independently so that class time may be devoted to the cultural content.

- Brief *Cultura* boxes found throughout each chapter explain cultural products, practices, and perspectives, making the cultural contexts of the vocabulary and grammatical activities meaningful and accessible to students.

Engaging New Video

A completely new video, entitled *Diarios de bicicleta*, has been scripted and filmed specifically to accompany the fifth edition of *Mosaicos*. Each episode of this engaging, often humorous video reflects the corresponding chapter's communicative objectives, recycling vocabulary and previewing functions and forms. The story line revolves around four recurring characters, but each episode is self-contained and independent of other episodes.

- The video segment for each chapter includes short excerpts that highlight the language functions introduced in the *Funciones y formas* section of the text.

- Pre-viewing, viewing, and post-viewing activities (all new to this edition) are provided in the Student Text in a special section of each chapter entitled *En acción*. Additional activities may be found in the Student Activities Manual.

A Four-Skills Synthesis

Like its predecessors, the fifth edition devotes a prominent section of each chapter to the development and practice of communication skills. These newly streamlined *Mosaicos* sections provide students with a unique opportunity to bring together the chapter's thematic content and vocabulary with its linguistic structures and cultural focus. New features, texts, and activities enhance the effectiveness of this aspect of the program.

- Specific strategies are now presented in each chapter for each of the four skills (listening, speaking, reading, and writing). The strategies build on each other within and across chapters. Activities are designed so that students systematically practice implementing the strategies presented.

- New listening activities have been created for the *A escuchar* sections. The content and genre of the listening texts, as well as the accompanying strategies, consistently support the chapter theme.

- In the *A conversar* sections, specific strategies are now provided for speaking as they are for other skill areas. The speaking activities that follow encourage structured pair interaction and help students develop interpersonal speaking skills.

- The streamlined *A leer* sections now include only one reading each. The reading selections (many new to this edition) are drawn largely from authentic texts. They reflect a variety of discourse types, ranging from expository to journalistic to literary. Activities linked to the reading strategy boost students' comprehension and reading skills.

- The process writing activities in the *A escribir* sections have been revised so that the pre- and post-writing activities now guide students through critical steps in the writing process. Where possible, these activities refer students back to the immediately preceding reading, deepening students' comprehension and awareness of text structure.

Informed by National Standards

The *Standards for Foreign Language Learning: Preparing for the 21st Century*, whose five goal areas have served as an organizing principle for language instruction for more than a decade, inform the pedagogy of the fifth edition of *Mosaicos*. Marginal notes throughout the Annotated Instructor's Edition draw attention to the way specific activities or other elements of the program help students develop proficiency in the five goal areas. A number of general strategies have been followed.

Communication.   Students are prompted to engage in meaningful conversations throughout the text, providing and obtaining information, expressing their opinions and preferences, and sharing their experiences. Readings and listening activities invite them to interpret language on a variety of topics, while *presentaciones* and writing assignments call on them to present information and ideas in both written and oral modes.

Cultures.   Many features of the text, including the maps, photos, *Cultura* boxes, and the readings in the *Mosaicos* and *Enfoque cultural* sections of each chapter, give students an understanding of the relationship between culture and language throughout the Spanish-speaking world.

Connections.   Realia, readings, the *Enfoque cultural* application activities, and conversation activities throughout the text provide opportunities to make connections with other disciplines. Students gain information and insight into the distinctive viewpoints of Spanish speakers and their cultures.

Comparisons. *Lengua* and *En otras palabras* boxes often provide students with points of comparison between English and Spanish (and among the varieties of Spanish spoken in different parts of the world). Readings and activities frequently juxtapose U.S. and Hispanic cultural products, practices, and perspectives.

Communities. The text encourages students to extend their learning through guided research on the Internet and/or other sources, and many of the topics explored in *Mosaicos* can stimulate exploration, personal enjoyment, and enrichment beyond the confines of formal language instruction. Instructors are reminded to encourage students to become acquainted with Spanish-speaking communities in their areas.

The Complete Program

Mosaicos is a complete teaching and learning program that includes a variety of resources for students and instructors, including an innovative offering of online resources.

For the student

Student Text

The *Mosaicos* Student Text is available in a complete, hardbound version, consisting of a preliminary chapter followed by Chapters 1 through 15. New to this edition is the option of three paperback volumes rather than the single hardcover version. Volume 1 of the paperback series contains the preliminary chapter plus Chapters 1 to 5; Volume 2, Chapters 5 to 10; and Volume 3, Chapters 10 to 15. All three volumes include the complete front and back matter.

Student Activities Manual

The Student Activities Manual (SAM), thoroughly revised for this edition, includes workbook activities together with audio- and video-based activities, all designed to provide extensive practice of the vocabulary, grammar, culture, and skills introduced in each chapter. The organization of these materials now parallels that of the student text, with an *A primera vista* section followed by *En acción* video activities, *Funciones y formas*, *Mosaicos*, and *Enfoque cultural*. A new section in each chapter (entitled *Repaso*) provides additional activities designed to help students review the material of the chapter as well as to prepare for tests.

The printed Student Activities Manual is available both in a single volume and in a series of separate volumes, paralleling the paperback volumes of the student text. The contents of the Student Activities Manual and MySpanishLab are also available online.

Answer Key to Accompany Student Activities Manual

An Answer Key to the Student Activities Manual is available separately, giving instructors the option of allowing students to check their homework. The Answer Key now includes answers to all SAM activities.

Supplementary Activities Book

Also available is a Supplementary Activities Book consisting of a range of fun, engaging activities that complement the vocabulary and grammar themes of each chapter. It offers instructors additional materials that can serve to energize and enrich their students' classroom experience.

Audio CDs to Accompany Student Text

A set of audio CDs contains recordings of the *A primera vista* language samples and the end-of-chapter vocabulary lists. It also contains audio material for listening activities included in the student text. These recordings are also available online.

Audio CDs to Accompany Student Activities Manual

A second set of audio CDs contains audio material for the listening activities in the Student Activities Manual. These recordings are also available online.

Video on DVD

Diarios de bicicleta is an original video filmed to accompany the fifth edition of *Mosaicos*. Students see the vocabulary and grammar structures of each chapter in use in realistic situations while gaining a deeper understanding of Hispanic cultures. The video also includes segments highlighting the communicative functions of each chapter. Pre-viewing, viewing, and post-viewing activities are found in the *En acción* sections of the textbook and the Student Activities Manual. The video is available for student purchase on DVD, and it is also available within MySpanishLab.

Meet the Cast

Here are the main characters of *Diarios de bicicleta*, who you will get to know when you watch the video:

Javier

Luciana

Daniel

Gaby

In addition to *Diarios de bicicleta*, two other videos are available for use in conjunction with the *Mosaicos* program. *Entrevistas* consists of interviews in which native speakers use authentic Spanish to address topics related to each chapter's theme. *Vistas culturales* contains nineteen 10–minute vignettes with footage from every Spanish-speaking country. Each of the accompanying narrations, which employ vocabulary and grammar designed for first-year language learners, was written by a native of the featured country or region. All three videos are also available online.

For the instructor

Annotated Instructor's Edition

The Annotated Instructor's Edition contains an abundance of marginal annotations (many newly written or revised for this edition) designed especially for novice instructors, instructors who are new to the *Mosaicos* program, or instructors who have limited time for class preparation. A new format allows ample space for annotations alongside full-size pages of the student text. Marginal annotations suggest warm-up and expansion exercises and activities and provide teaching tips, additional cultural information, and audioscripts for the in-text listening activities. Answers to discrete-point activities are printed in blue type for the instructor's convenience. *Resources* boxes (new to this edition) offer cross-references to related material in other components of the *Mosaicos* program, enabling instructors to see at a glance what material is available for student homework and additional practice, as well as for use in the classroom.

Instructor's Resource Manual

The Instructor's Resource Manual (IRM) now contains complete lesson plans for all chapters, integrated syllabi for regular and hybrid courses, as well as helpful suggestions for new and experienced instructors alike. It also provides additional oral practice activities (similar to the *Situaciones* activities in the student text), videoscripts for all episodes of the *Diarios de bicicleta* video, audioscripts for listening activities in the Student Activities Manual, and a complete guide to all *Mosaicos* supplements. The Instructor's Resource Manual is available to instructors online at the *Mosaicos* Instructor Resource Center.

Testing Program

The Testing Program has been thoroughly revised and expanded for this edition. The testing content correlates with the vocabulary, grammar, culture, and skills material presented in the student text. For each chapter of the text, a bank of testing activities is provided in modular form; instructors can select and combine modules to create customized tests tailored to the needs of their classes. Two complete, ready-to-use tests are also provided for each chapter. The tests and testing modules are available to instructors online at the *Mosaicos* Instructor Resource Center.

Testing Audio CD

A special set of audio CDs, available to instructors only, contains recordings corresponding to the listening comprehension portions of the Testing Program.

PowerPoint™ Presentations

A PowerPoint™ Presentation (new to this edition) is available for each chapter of the text. These dynamic, visually engaging presentations allow instructors to enliven class sessions and reinforce key concepts. The presentations are available to instructors online at the *Mosaicos* Instructor Resource Center.

Situaciones adicionales

The *Situaciones adicionales* provide instructors with additional opportunities for reinforcing and assessing students' speaking skills.

Instructor Resource Center

Several of the instructor supplements listed above—the Instructor's Resource Manual, the Testing Program, the Power-Point™ Presentations, and the *Situaciones adicionales* as well as the Supplementary Activities Book—are available for download at the access-protected *Mosaicos* Instructor Resource Center (www.pearsonhighered.com/educator). An access code will be provided at no charge to instructors once their faculty status has been verified.

Online resources

MySpanishLab™

MySpanishLab is a new, nationally hosted online learning system created for students in college-level language courses. It brings together—in one convenient, easily navigable site—a wide array of language-learning tools and resources, including an interactive version of the *Mosaicos* Student Activities Manual, an electronic version of the *Mosaicos* student text, and all materials from the *Mosaicos* audio and video programs. Readiness checks, chapter tests, and tutorials personalize instruction to meet the unique needs of individual students. Instructors can use the system to make assignments, set grading parameters, listen to student-created audio recordings, and provide feedback on student work. Instructor access is provided at no charge. Students can purchase access codes online or at their local bookstore.

Companion Website

The open-access Companion Website (www.pearsonhighered.com/mosaicos) includes an array of activities and resources designed to reinforce the vocabulary, grammar, and cultural material introduced in each chapter. It also provides audio recordings for the student text and Student Activities Manual, links for Internet-based activites in the student text, and additional web exploration activities for each chapter. All contents of the Companion Website are also included in MySpanishLab.

Acknowledgments

Mosaicos is the result of a collaborative effort among the authors, our publisher, and our colleagues. We are especially indebted to many members of the Spanish teaching community for their time, candor, and insightful suggestions as they reviewed the drafts of the fifth edition of *Mosaicos*. Their critiques and recommendations helped us to sharpen our pedagogical focus and improve the overall quality of the program. We gratefully acknowledge the contributions of the following reviewers:

Rafael Arias, *Los Angeles Valley College*
Alejandra Balestra, *University of New Mexico*
Aymará Boggiano, *University of Houston*
Amanda Boomershine, *University of North Carolina-Wilmington*
Talia Bugel, *Indiana University-Purdue University Fort Wayne*
José Carrasquel, *Florida International University*
Zoila Clark, *Florida International University*
Daria Cohen, *Rider University*
Alyce Cook, *Columbus State University*
Richard Curry, *Texas A&M University*
Marta de la Caridad Pérez, *Florida International University*
Beatrice DeAngelis, *University of Pittsburgh*
Marisol del Teso Craviotto, *Miami University of Ohio*
Angela Erickson-Grussing, *St. John's University/College of St. Benedict*
Juliet Falce-Robinson, *University of California-Los Angeles*
Gayle Fiedler-Vierma, *University of Southern California*
Óscar Flores, *State University of New York-Plattsburgh*
Ausenda Folch, *Florida International University*
Myriam García, *Florida International University*
Rosa María Gómez García-Bermejo, *Florida International University*

Frozina Goussak, *Collin County Community College*
Dawn Heston, *University of Missouri-Columbia*
Casilde Isabelli, *University of Nevada-Reno*
Keith Johnson, *California State University-Fresno*
Linda Keown, *University of Missouri-Columbia*
Ruth Konopka, *Grossmont College*
Lina Llerena Callahan, *Fullerton College*
Susana Liso, *University of Virginia-Wise*
Leticia López, *San Diego Mesa College*
Libardo Mitchell, *Portland Community College-Sylvania*
Dorothy Moore, *Gettysburg College*
Michelle Orecchio, *University of Michigan*
Teresa Pérez-Gamboa, *University of Georgia*
Ana María Pinzón, *Frederick Community College*
Mónica Prieto, *Florida International University*
Nuria Sagarra, *Pennsylvania State University*
Toni Trives, *Santa Monica College*
Clara Vega, *Almance Community College*
Celinés Villalba, *University of California-Berkeley*
Lisa Volle, *Central Texas College*
Sarah Williams, *University of Pittsburgh*
Loretta Zehngut, *Pennsylvania State University*

We are also grateful for the guidance of Elizabeth Lantz, development editor, for all of her work, suggestions, attention to detail, and dedication to the text. Her support and spirit helped us to achieve the final product. Special thanks are due to Celia Meana, development editor, for helping with the art program, with the final pages, and with many other editorial details. We would also like to thank the contributors who assisted us in the preparation of the fifth edition: Daria Cohen, Marisol del Teso Craviotto, Juliet Falce-Robinson, Linda Keown, Gustavo Mejía, Teresa Pérez-Gamboa, Anne Prucha, and Lilián Uribe. Special thanks to Ninon Larché and Debbie King for their assistance in the preparation of the manuscript. We are very grateful to other colleagues and friends at Prentice Hall: Meriel Martínez, Media Editor, for helping us produce such a great video, audio programs, and Companion Website; Melissa Marolla Brown, Development Editor for Assessment, for the diligent coordination among the text, Student Activities Manual, and Testing Program; Samantha Alducin, Senior Media Editor, for managing the creation of *Mosaicos* materials for My SpanishLab™; and Jenn Murphy, Assistant Editor/Editorial Coordinator, for her work in managing the preparation of the other supplements. Thanks to Katie Spiegel, Editorial Assistant, for her hard work and efficiency in obtaining reviews and attending to many administrative details.

We are very grateful to our marketing team, Kris Ellis-Levy, Denise Miller, and Bill Bliss, for their creativity and efforts in coordinating all marketing and promotion for this edition. Thanks, too, to our production team, Mary Rottino, Janice Stangel, and Manuel Echevarria, who guided *Mosaicos* through the many stages of production; to our partners at Macmillan Publishing Solutions, especially Jill Traut, for her careful and professional editing and production services. We also thank our art team, Gail Cocker, Peter Bull, and Andrew Lange, for their amazing creativity and beautiful maps and illustrations. Special thanks to Leslie Osher, John Christina, and Ximena Tamvakopoulos for the gorgeous interior and cover designs. Finally, we would like to express our sincere thanks to Phil Miller, Publisher, and Julia Caballero, Executive Editor, for their guidance and support through every aspect of this new edition.

A Guide to *Mosaicos* Icons

👁	*A vista de pájaro*	This icon indicates a panoramic, quick overview. It accompanies the chapter opener activity and reminds students to activate background knowledge about the country or countries featured in the chapter, as well as to use the information presented in the map.
)))	**Text Audio Program**	This icon indicates that recorded material is available for students in the *Mosaicos* text audio program for students. The audio includes vocabulary and dialogues presented in *A primera vista*, as well as the listening activities presented in the text.
👥	**Pair Activity**	This icon indicates that the activity is designed to be done by students working in pairs.
👥	**Group Activity**	This icon indicates that the activity is designed to be done by students working in small groups.
🌐	**Web Activity**	This icon indicates that the activity involves use of the World Wide Web. Helpful links and activities can be found on the *Mosaicos* Companion Website.

ABOUT THE AUTHORS

Elizabeth E. Guzmán is the Director of the Elementary and Intermediate Spanish Language Program at the University of Iowa. Previously, she served as Language Coordinator at St. John's University/College of St. Benedict, Director of the Spanish Program at Yale University, and Coordinator and Co-Director of the Elementary and Intermediate Language Program at The University of Michigan. In her native Chile, she supervised instructors of English as a Foreign Language. Ms. Guzmán received her B.A. in English from Universidad de Santiago (Chile) and her M.A. in English as a Second Language from West Virginia University, and then pursued doctoral studies at the University of Pittsburgh. She is a co-author of Prentice-Hall's *Identidades* and several earlier editions of *Mosaicos*.

Paloma Lapuerta holds the title of Professor of Spanish at Central Connecticut State University, where she teaches courses in Spanish language, culture, and literature. She has over twenty years of teaching experience at higher institutions around the world, including Spain, Switzerland, South Africa, and the United States, where she has taught at the University of Michigan, Dartmouth College, and the Middlebury College Spanish School. She completed her *Licenciatura* in Spanish Philology at the University of Salamanca, and she holds a Ph.D. in Spanish literature from the University of Geneva, Switzerland. She has published numerous articles and a book on Spanish culture and literature. She is a co-author of *Identidades*, *La escritura paso a paso*, and earlier editions of *Mosaicos*, all published by Prentice Hall.

Judith E. Liskin-Gasparro is a professor of Spanish at the University of Iowa, where she teaches courses in second language acquisition, pedagogy, and Spanish language. She is the co-director of FLARE (Foreign Language Acquisition Research and Education), which offers an interdisciplinary doctoral program in Second Language Acquisition, and she was formerly the Director of the Elementary and Intermediate Spanish Language Program. Previously, she taught at Middlebury College and worked as a test development consultant at Educational Testing Service. She received her B.A. in Spanish from Bryn Mawr College, her M.A. from Princeton University, and her Ph.D. in Foreign Language Education from the University of Texas at Austin. She has published articles and books on language learning and teaching and has led many workshops for language teachers. She is a co-author of *Identidades*, published by Prentice Hall.

Resources

■ Instructor's Resource Manual (IRM): Syllabi & Lesson Plans

Goals. *Bienvenidos* is designed to make students' first exposure to the Spanish classroom a successful, enjoyable experience. Establish a comfortable atmosphere by using a variety of supportive techniques to lower students' anxiety level. Give frequent praise and encouragement. Help students access meanings of unknown words by making frequent use of gestures or visuals, particularly in the beginning stages of learning.

Suggestions for photos. Point to the page or use visuals and ask if students understand the word *bienvenidos*. Introduce the words *hablan* and *lengua*. Then point to photos and ask questions such as the following (you may write questions and answers on the board/transparency): *¿Qué lengua hablan estas personas? Hablan español.* Personalize by asking: *¿Qué lengua habla usted? ¿Habla usted inglés? ¿Estudia español?¿Qué lengua hablamos en clase? ¿Hablamos inglés o español en clase?* Help them come up with answers that use cognates (*porque es una lengua importante, para comunicarse con muchas personas*, etc.).

Bienvenidos

El mundo hispano les da la bienvenida.

In this chapter you will learn how to:

- introduce yourself, greet others, and say good-bye
- use expressions of courtesy
- spell in Spanish
- identify people and classroom objects
- locate people and things

- use numbers from 0–99
- express dates
- tell time
- use classroom expressions
- comment on the weather

Note for A vista de pájaro.
The first activity in each chapter is called *A vista de pájaro*. Explain that this expression is used to indicate a panoramic and quick overview. Encourage students to look at the map and photos that precede *A vista de pájaro* before they do the activity. It is also a good idea to do a warm-up to activate students' prior knowledge about the featured country or countries. The teacher's notes on this page suggest questions you may ask for this purpose.

Suggestions for A vista de pájaro. Ask students questions about the Spanish language using cognates and allow them to answer in English. *¿Qué otras lenguas son similares al español?¿El francés o el ruso?¿El italiano o el chino?¿El portugués o el árabe? ¿El catalán o el alemán?* Introduce the word *mundo*. Point to the map and call attention to the number of Spanish speakers in different countries: *Muchas personas en el mundo hablan español. ¿Cuántas personas hablan español en Estados Unidos? ¿en México?*, etc.

Explain that in Spanish the comma is used in place of the decimal point and vice-versa so that 3,5 is equal to 3.5 in English.

Personas que hablan español (en millones)

Estados Unidos 35
Cuba 11,4
República Dominicana 9,4
Puerto Rico 3,9
México 108,7
Guatemala 12,7
El Salvador 6,9 — Honduras 7,5
Nicaragua 5,7 — Venezuela 26
Costa Rica 4,1 — Colombia 44,4
Panamá 3,2
Ecuador 13,8 — Perú 28,7
Bolivia 9,1
Paraguay 6,7
Chile 16,3
Uruguay 3,4
Argentina 40,3
España 40,4
Guinea Ecuatorial 0,7
Filipinas 2,9

 A vista de pájaro. Relying on your knowledge of the world, look at the map and determine whether each statement is true (**Cierto**) or false (**Falso**).

1. <u>Cierto</u> Más de (*More than*) 350 millones de personas hablan español en el mundo.
2. <u>Falso</u> En Filipinas no se habla español.
3. <u>Cierto</u> En Estados Unidos hablan español más personas que (*more … than*) en Chile.
4. <u>Cierto</u> En Guinea Ecuatorial se habla español.
5. <u>Cierto</u> En Brasil se habla portugués.
6. <u>Cierto</u> El español se habla en 23 países.

3

Resources

■ Student Activities Manual (SAM): P-1 to P-3
■ Supplementary Activities Book (Supp. Activ. Book): *Bienvenidos*

Suggestions. Model *Me llamo* by pointing to yourself and saying your name. Then write *Me llamo* on the board and repeat the sentence. Now ask individual students for their names. Accept answers if they say only their names, but encourage them to use *Me llamo. . .* , pointing to the board to guide them. Introduce yourself to a student, asking his/her name; answer with *Mucho gusto*. Write *Mucho gusto* on the board, and encourage the same response from the student. You can shake the student's hand to make the introduction more realistic. Repeat with another student. Again, encourage the student to say *Mucho gusto* after his or her name; this time respond with *Igualmente*. Repeat it again before asking students to introduce themselves to a classmate. They may refer to the dialogue if needed.

You may wish to spend a few minutes having students introduce themselves to several students sitting near them.

Suggestion. Bring in pictures of people of various ages to quickly compare the uses of *tú* and *usted*. Tell students to use *tú* when addressing each other. Then model the second dialogue by acting it out with a female and a male to show the change in *encantado/a*. Write both forms on the board.

Alternate. Model the third dialogue. Write *amigo/a* on the board. Do the dialogue again with a female student, using *amiga*. Then, in groups of three, one student introduces the other two, using their real names.

Expansion. You may introduce the phrase *Su (Tu) nombre, por favor.* For further practice, have a student ask you your name or the names of two classmates.

Suggestion. When the need arises, use the *Expresiones útiles en la clase*, page 20. Try to speak Spanish as much as possible from the first day of class.

Las presentaciones

CD 1
Track 1

ANTONIO: **Me llamo** Antonio Mendoza. **Y tú, ¿cómo te llamas?**
BENITO: Me llamo Benito Sánchez.
ANTONIO: **Mucho gusto.**
BENITO: **Igualmente.**

LAURA: María, **mi amigo** José.
MARÍA: Mucho gusto.
JOSÉ: **Encantado.**

PROFESOR: **¿Cómo se llama usted?**
ISABEL: Me llamo Isabel Contreras.
PROFESOR: Mucho gusto.

■ Spanish has more than one word meaning *you*. Use **tú** when talking to someone on a first-name basis (a child, close friend, or relative).

Use **usted** when talking to someone you address in a respectful or formal manner; for example, **doctor/doctora; profesor/profesora; señor/señora.** Also use **usted** to address individuals you do not know well.

■ Young people normally use **tú** when speaking to each other.

■ **Mucho gusto** is used by both men and women when they are meeting someone for the first time. A man may also say **encantado,** and a woman, **encantada.**

■ You may respond to **mucho gusto** with either **encantado/a** or **igualmente.**

P-1 Presentaciones. PRIMERA FASE. Complete the following conversation with the appropriate expressions from the box on the right.

ALICIA: Me llamo Alicia. Y tú, ¿cómo te llamas?
ISABEL: Isabel Pérez. <u>Mucho gusto</u>.
ALICIA: <u>Igualmente</u>.
ALICIA: Isabel, <u>mi amigo Pedro</u>.
ISABEL: Mucho gusto.
PEDRO: <u>Encantado</u>.

> Igualmente
> Mucho gusto
> Encantado
> mi amigo Pedro

SEGUNDA FASE. Move around the classroom, introducing yourself to several classmates and introducing classmates to each other.

Resources

■ SAM: P-4 to P-6

Los saludos y las despedidas

Los saludos

CD 1
Track 2

SEÑOR: **Buenos días, señorita** Rivas.

SEÑORITA: Buenos días. **¿Cómo está usted, señor** Gómez?

SEÑOR: **Bien, gracias.** ¿Y usted?

SEÑORITA: **Muy** bien, gracias.

MARTA: **¡Hola,** Inés! **¿Qué tal? ¿Cómo estás?**

INÉS: **Regular,** ¿y tú?

MARTA: **Bastante** bien, gracias.

SEÑORA: **Buenas tardes,** Felipe. ¿Cómo estás?

FELIPE: Bien, gracias. Y usted, ¿cómo está, **señora**?

SEÑORA: **Mal,** Felipe, mal.

FELIPE: **Lo siento.**

■ Use **buenos días** until lunchtime.

■ Use **buenas tardes** from noon until nightfall. After nightfall, use **buenas noches** (*good evening, good night*).

■ **¿Qué tal?** is a more informal greeting. It is normally used with **tú**, but it may also be used with **usted**.

■ Use **está** with **usted** and **estás** with **tú**.

P-2 Saludos. You work as a receptionist in a hotel. Which greeting (**buenos días, buenas tardes, buenas noches**) is appropriate at the following times?

1. 9:00 a.m.   buenos días
2. 11:00 p.m.   buenas noches
3. 4:00 p.m.   buenas tardes
4. 8:00 a.m.   buenos días
5. 1:00 p.m.   buenas tardes
6. 10:00 p.m.   buenas noches

Las despedidas

CD 1
Track 3

adiós	*good-bye*
hasta luego	*see you later*
hasta mañana	*see you tomorrow*
hasta pronto	*see you soon*
chao	*good-bye*

Suggestions. Introduce *buenos días, buenas tardes,* and *buenas noches* with visuals or by drawing the sun and the moon or writing times on the board. You may mention that in Spain people normally use *buenos días* until 2:00 p.m., their usual lunchtime. In other countries it is used until noon. Model and practice each greeting before moving to the next.

Suggestions. Present the first dialogue, modeling the parts of both characters; students follow along in their books. Personalize the dialogue by addressing some students by name. Then pair up students, assign roles, and have them practice the dialogue. Have them change roles for further practice.

Standard 2.1. Students demonstrate an understanding of the relationship between the practices and perspectives of the culture studied. This culture note gives students information about some everyday cultural practices, including both appropriate phrases and appropriate actions. Instructors may wish to have students talk about cultural perspectives (social distance, courtesy, etc.) enacted in these common cultural practices.

Note. Point out the importance of the *Cultura* boxes as a source of information about Hispanic culture.

Warm-up for P-2. Write different times of the day on the board and model possible greeting(s) for each. Students respond *sí* or *no*.

Suggestion. Model the *despedidas*, using hand gestures while speaking. Point out that some Spanish speakers use a different hand gesture when saying goodbye: palm facing out, fingers moving up and down. With a student, model the use of *adiós* meaning "hello" when two people pass each other, but do not stop to talk.

Resources

■ SAM: P-7 to P-9

Suggestion. Model correct pronunciation of the *d* in *adiós*: Students should place the tip of tongue against the back of the upper front teeth. (English d̲ is pronounced with the tip of the tongue on the ridge behind the upper teeth.) Explain that the word has only two syllables: *a-diós*.

Suggestion. Have students move around the room, greeting one another, asking how the other is, and saying good-bye.

Suggestions. Model *por favor*. Give a student a pencil and say *El lápiz, por favor*, indicating that you would like it back. When the student returns the pencil, say *Gracias*. Coach students to reply with *De nada*. Repeat with other classroom objects. Then ask them to continue in small groups or pairs. Write useful words on the board.

Model the difference between *con permiso* and *perdón* by walking in front of a student and saying *con permiso*, and by lightly stepping on a student's toe or bumping into him/her and saying *perdón*. For additional modeling of *con permiso* or *perdón*, bump into chairs and so forth, as you pass through the classroom.

■ **Adiós** is generally used when you do not expect to see the other person for a while. It is also used as a greeting when people pass each other but have no time to stop and talk.

■ **Chao** (also spelled **chau**) is an informal way of saying good-bye. It is popular in South America.

P-3 Despedidas. How would you say good-bye in these situations? Answers may vary
1. You'll see your friend tomorrow. hasta mañana
2. You arrange to meet your classmate at the library in 10 minutes. hasta pronto
3. Your roommate is leaving for a semester abroad. adiós
4. You run into a good friend on campus. chao

Expresiones de cortesía

CD 1
Track 4

por favor	*please*
gracias	*thanks, thank you*
de nada	*you're welcome*
lo siento	*I'm sorry (to hear that)*
con permiso	*pardon me, excuse me*
perdón	*pardon me, excuse me*

■ **Con permiso** and **perdón** may be used before the fact, as when asking a person to allow you to go by or when trying to get someone's attention. Only **perdón** is used after the fact, as when you have stepped on someone's foot or have interrupted a conversation.

P-4 ¿Perdón o con permiso? Would you use **perdón** or **con permiso** in these situations?

1. perdón

2. perdón, con permiso

3. perdón

4. perdón, con permiso

5. perdón, con permiso

P-5 Despedidas y expresiones de cortesía. Which expression(s) would you use in the following situations?

adiós	gracias	lo siento
de nada	hasta luego	por favor

1. Someone thanks you. _de nada_
2. You say good-bye to a friend you will see later this evening. _hasta luego_
3. You ask if you can borrow a classmate's notes. _por favor_
4. You hear that your friend is sick. _lo siento_
5. You receive a present from your cousin. _gracias_
6. Your friend is leaving for a vacation in Costa Rica. _adiós, hasta pronto_

P-6 Encuentros (*Encounters*). You meet the following people on the street. Greet them, ask how they are, and then say good-bye. Switch roles and role play the encounters again.

1. su (*your*) amigo Miguel
2. su profesor/a
3. su amiga Isabel
4. su doctor/a

ᐁ)) Distinguishing Registers

CD 1
Track 5

When you talk to different people, you use different registers, that is, you address them with various degrees of formality, depending on your level of intimacy and the context of the exchange. For example, when you talk to a professor, you probably use more formal language than when you talk to classmates or friends. In Spanish, one way to mark this difference is by using **tú** (informal) and **usted** (formal).

Now you will hear four brief conversations in which people greet each other. Before you listen, complete the following chart with the pronoun you think you would use in each case.

WHEN TALKING TO YOUR ...	TÚ	USTED
1. brother or sister		
2. doctor		
3. coach		
4. parents		

P-7 Conversaciones. As you listen to the four conversations, mark (✓) the appropriate column to indicate whether the greetings are formal (with **usted**) or informal (with **tú**). Do not worry if you do not understand every word.

FORMAL   INFORMAL
1. ✓   ____
2. ____   ✓
3. ✓   ____
4. ____   ✓

Resources
■ SAM: P-10 to P-13

Note. Whenever possible, students should work in pairs, taking turns to answer. This provides additional opportunities to communicate in Spanish. Then the whole class reviews the activity.

Warm-up for P-6. Model the exchange with a student before beginning the activity.

Suggestion. When doing the pre-listening activity explain that in some Spanish-speaking countries children are brought up to address their parents as *usted*.

Note. The listening activity audioscripts appear in the margins for instructors who wish to read them aloud instead of playing the audio CD.

You may wish to use the following procedure: 1) Play (or say) the conversations; students mark their answers; 2) students check their answers with a partner; and 3) play (or say) the conversations again, repeating difficult parts.

Audioscript for Distinguishing Registers
Conversación 1
—Buenos días, señora Gómez. —Buenos días. ¿Cómo está usted, señor Jiménez? —Bastante bien, gracias. ¿Y usted?
—Bien, gracias.

Conversación 2
—¡Hola, Felipe! ¿Qué tal? ¿Cómo estás? —Regular, ¿y tú? —Bien, gracias.

Conversación 3
—Buenas tardes, señora Mena. ¿Cómo está usted?
—Bastante bien, gracias. Y usted, ¿cómo está, señora?
—Regular, regular. —Lo siento.

Conversación 4
—Me llamo Carlos Martínez. Y tú, ¿cómo te llamas?
—Me llamo Cristina Camacho. —Mucho gusto.
—Igualmente.

Notes. The Spanish alphabet included *ch* and *ll* as letters until 1994, when the *Real Academia Española* decided that they would no longer be considered separate letters. Dictionaries published after 1994 alphabetize words starting with *ch* or *ll* as in English. Model the pronunciation of *ch* and *ll* with words students know (e.g., *mucho, llamo, llamas*). Point out that since *b* and *v* are pronounced alike (*be*), many Spanish speakers say *be larga* or *be de burro* for *b* and *ve corta* or *ve de vaca* for *v* when spelling.

Note. Point out the importance of good pronunciation, and remind students of the pronunciation section in the Student Activities Manual.

Note for P-8. Point out that because Spanish is considered a phonetic language, Spanish speakers often do not spell out the whole word, but instead give only the letter(s) that may cause confusion, such as *b* and *v*. However, when they interact with speakers of other languages, they may need to spell out the whole word. Model the activity by using some Spanish last names.

Suggestion for P-9. Have students move around the classroom for this activity.

◜)) El alfabeto

CD 1
Track 6

a	a		o	o
b	be		p	pe
c	ce		q	cu
d	de		r	ere, erre
e	e		s	ese
f	efe		t	te
g	ge		u	u
h	hache		v	ve, uve
i	i		w	doble ve, doble uve
j	jota			uve doble, ve doble
k	ka		x	equis
l	ele		y	i griega, ye
m	eme		z	zeta
n	ene			
ñ	eñe			

En otras palabras

Like English speakers, Spanish speakers have different accents that reflect their region or country of origin. For example, the letter **c** before vowels **e** and **i** and the letter **z** are pronounced like **s**, except in certain regions of Spain, where they are similar to the English *th*.

■ The Spanish alphabet includes **ñ**, a letter that does not exist in English. Its sound is similar to the pronunciation of *ni* and *ny* in the English words *onion* and *canyon*.

■ The letters **k** and **w** appear mainly in words of foreign origin.

 P-8 ¿Cómo se escribe? Ask your classmate how to spell these Spanish last names.

MODELO: Zamora
            E1:   *¿Cómo se escribe Zamora?*
            E2:   *Con zeta.*

1. Celaya   Con ce
2. Montalvo   Con ve
3. Salas   Con ese
4. Bolaños   Con be
5. Henares   Con hache
6. Velázquez   Con ve y con zeta

 P-9 Los nombres. You are at the admissions office of a university in a Spanish-speaking country. Spell out your first or last name for the clerk. Take turns.

MODELO: E1:   *¿Cómo se llama usted?*
          E2:   *Me llamo David Robinson.*
          E1:   *¿Cómo se escribe Robinson?*
          E2:   *ere-o-be-i-ene-ese-o-ene.*

Identificación y descripción de personas

CD 1 Track 7

CARLOS: **¿Quién es ese chico?**

SANDRA: **Es** Julio.

CARLOS: **¿Cómo es** Julio?

SANDRA: **Es** romántico y sentimental.

LUIS: ¿Quién es **esa chica**?

QUIQUE: Es Carmen.

LUIS: ¿Cómo es Carmen?

QUIQUE: Es activa y muy seria.

◼ The verb *ser* is used to identify and describe.

Esa chica **es** Carmen. Ella **es** activa y muy seria.

Rodolfo **es** su amigo. **Es** atractivo.

◼ Here are the forms of *ser* you will be using in this chapter.

SER *(to be)*			
yo	**soy**	*I*	*am*
tú	**eres**	*you*	*are*
usted	**es**	*you*	*are*
él, ella	**es**	*he, she*	*is*

Resources

◼ SAM: P-17 to P-20

Note. The goal of this section is to introduce some forms of the verb *ser* and to preview the notion of gender and its relationship to adjective endings.

Suggestions. Use pictures of well-known people, as well as of your students, to practice *¿Quién es?* Use the pictures again to ask: *¿Cómo es X, serio/a o cómico/a? ¿X es activo/a o inactivo/a? ¿Es sentimental? ¿Es optimista o pesimista?* When presenting cognates with *-o* and *-a* endings, write words on the board, point to a male student using the appropriate adjective, and then point to a female student. Contrast with *¿Cómo está?* (e.g., *¿Cómo es Carmen? Es inteligente y seria. ¿Cómo está Carmen? Está muy bien.*) Model and personalize the short dialogues by pointing to individual students and having classmates respond. (Use only positive traits.)

Note. The verb *ser* is introduced for the first time here although students need only the forms *yo, tú, usted, él,* and *ella* for communication at this stage. The formal presentation of *ser* is in *Capítulo 2.*

Suggestion. Introduce *soy* by pointing to yourself as you describe yourself, sometimes using *yo* and sometimes omitting it: *Yo soy activo/a y serio/a. No soy impulsivo/a. Soy optimista. No soy pesimista.*

Introduce *eres* and *es* by substituting names of students in exchanges like those at the beginning of *Identificación y descripción de personas.*

■ To make a sentence negative, place **no** before the appropriate form of **ser.** When responding negatively to a question, say **no** twice.

Ella es inteligente.	→	Ella **no** es inteligente.
¿Es rebelde?	→	**No, no** es rebelde.

Cognados

Cognados (*cognates*) are words from two languages that have the same origin and are similar in form and meaning. Since English and Spanish have many cognates, you will discover that you already recognize many Spanish words. Here are some cognates that you may use to describe people.

■ The following cognates use the same form to describe a man or a woman.

arrogante	importante	optimista	popular
eficiente	independiente	paciente	responsable
elegante	inteligente	perfeccionista	sentimental
idealista	interesante	pesimista	tradicional

■ The following cognates have two forms. The **-o** form is used to describe a male, and the **-a** form to describe a female.

activo/a	creativo/a	introvertido/a	romántico/a
ambicioso/a	dinámico/a	moderno/a	serio/a
atlético/a	extrovertido/a	nervioso/a	sincero/a
atractivo/a	generoso/a	pasivo/a	tímido/a
cómico/a	impulsivo/a	religioso/a	tranquilo/a

■ Some words appear to be cognates but do not have the same meaning in both languages. These are called false cognates. **Lectura** (*reading*) and **éxito** (*success*) are examples. You will find other examples in future chapters.

 P-10 ¿Cómo es mi compañero/a? Choose from the preceding lists of cognates to ask the person next to you about his/her personality.

MODELO: E1: *¿Eres pesimista?*
　　　　　E2: *No, no soy pesimista. O Sí, soy (muy) pesimista.*

Then find out how your classmate describes himself/herself.

MODELO: E1: *¿Cómo eres (tú)?*
　　　　　E2: *Soy activo, optimista y creativo.*

 P-11 Descripciones. Ask each other about your classmates. Describe them by using cognates from the preceding lists.

MODELO: E1: *¿Cómo es... ?*
　　　　　E2: *Es...*

¿Qué hay en el salón de clase?

Resources
■ SAM: P-26 to P-27

un reloj · una pantalla · una pizarra · un profesor · un televisor · una tiza · un borrador · un DVD · una mesa · una computadora · un libro · un marcador/un rotulador · un escritorio · un cesto · una silla · un estudiante · una estudiante · un cuaderno · una calculadora · un bolígrafo · un lápiz · una mochila · un pupitre

$E = MC^2$

Suggestion. Always strive to present new vocabulary in context. Students can become overwhelmed if too many new vocabulary items are presented at once. We suggest introducing three to four items at a time, checking for understanding before continuing. The vocabulary in this chapter will be recycled in the next few chapters.

Use the images on this page as a springboard for presentation of people and items typically found in the classroom. To check for recognition, mention different objects in the classroom and have students identify them.

Note. You may wish to point out that both *computador* and *computadora* are used (also *ordenador* in Spain). The gender of nouns is presented in *Capítulo 1*; for now, use *un* and *una* without detailed explanation.

Write down the sentence *¿Qué hay en el salón de clase?*, highlighting the verb *hay* and using it in different contexts: *Hay un profesor/una profesora en la clase*; *hay una pizarra*; *hay estudiantes...*

Follow-up. Have students identify additional objects or furniture in the classroom.

P-12 Identificación. With a partner, identify the items on this table.

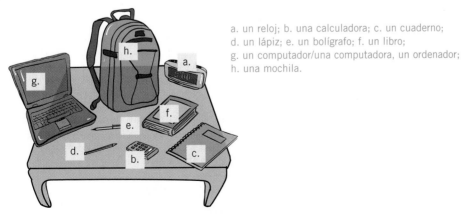

a. un reloj; b. una calculadora; c. un cuaderno;
d. un lápiz; e. un bolígrafo; f. un libro;
g. un computador/una computadora, un ordenador;
h. una mochila.

P-13 Para la clase de español. Write down a list of the things you need for this class. Compare your list with that of your partner.

Suggestion for P-13. Provide additional vocabulary if needed (e.g., *un diccionario*).

Note. Spanish has two words for "in front of." *Marta está delante de Pedro* means that Marta is in front of (ahead of) Pedro when they are facing in the same direction. *Marta está enfrente de Pedro* means that they are facing each other. Also use *enfrente* to express "in front of" with objects or a building. *Los turistas están enfrente de la catedral.* (The tourists are in front of the cathedral.)

Suggestions. Present the contrasting pair *enfrente de/detrás de* by standing in front of a student. Say ¿Dónde está el profesor/la profesora? Está enfrente de... Then move behind a student and ask the same question. *Está detrás de...* Reinforce understanding by asking three students to form a line in front of the class. Make statements about their positions. The remaining students respond with *sí* or *no*, according to whether your statements are correct.

Ask either/or questions about students and objects: *¿Está Manuel enfrente de Carolina o detrás de ella?*

Ask questions using *¿Dónde está... ?* You may want to review *quién*; introduce other expressions such as *encima de, dentro de, a la derecha (de), a la izquierda (de)*. Or preview *están* by asking questions regarding the location of students: *¿Dónde están David y Elena?*

¿Dónde está?

■ To ask about the location of a person or an object, use **dónde + está**.

¿**Dónde está** la profesora?	Está en la clase.
¿**Dónde está** el libro?	Está sobre el escritorio.

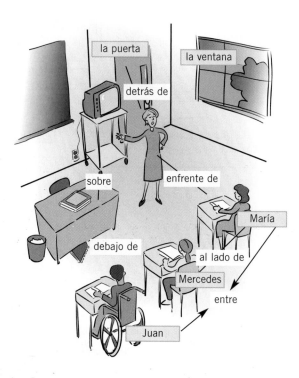

P-14 Localización. PRIMERA FASE. Indicate whether each statement is true (**Cierto**) or false (**Falso**), based on the relative position of people and objects in the drawing.

	CIERTO	FALSO
1. El televisor está detrás de la profesora.	✓	
2. Juan está al lado de la profesora.		✓
3. El libro está sobre el escritorio.	✓	
4. María está entre Mercedes y Juan.		✓
5. Mercedes está enfrente de la ventana.		✓
6. El cesto está debajo de un pupitre.		✓

 SEGUNDA FASE. Now complete the following sentences, based on the relative position of people and objects in the drawing. Compare your answers.

1. La pizarra está ___detrás de___ la profesora.
2. María está ___enfrente de___ la profesora.
3. Mercedes está ___entre___ Juan y María.
4. Juan está ___al lado de___ Mercedes.
5. El cesto está ___enfrente de___ Juan.
6. El televisor está ___entre___ la pizarra y la puerta.

Resources
■ SAM: P-31

◀)) Listening with Visuals

CD 1
Track 8 When you are talking with someone, paying attention to the pictures or objects that the speaker points to or refers to can help you understand what is being said. These objects may be around you, or they may not, in which case you have only a mental representation of them. For example, when a friend describes his/her Spanish classroom, an image of a classroom comes to your mind based on your experience as a student.

In Spanish, make a list of the people and objects you expect to see in a classroom.

Now, as you listen to the statements about the location of people and objects, look at the drawing of the classroom on page 12 to help you understand what the speakers are saying.

Indicate (✓) whether each statement is true (**Cierto**) or false (**Falso**).

	CIERTO	FALSO
1.	✓	
2.	✓	
3.		✓
4.	✓	
5.		✓
6.		✓

P-15 En la clase. Look at the seating chart below, and then follow the instructions.

María	Juan	Ester		Susana	Pedro
Carlos	Cristina	Ángeles		Alberto	Anita
Mercedes	Victoria	Roberto		Rocío	Pablo
		El profesor Gallegos			

ESTUDIANTE 1: Ask where Juan, Pedro, Cristina, Mercedes, Roberto, and Pablo are sitting.

ESTUDIANTE 2: Ask where *María, Ester, Susana, Carlos, Ángeles, Alberto, Anita, Victoria, Rocío,* and *Profesor Gallegos* are sitting.

P-16 ¿Dónde está? Take turns asking where several items in your classroom are. Answer by giving their position in relation to a person or another object.

MODELO: E1: *¿Dónde está el libro?*
E2: *Está sobre el escritorio.*

P-17 ¿Quién es? Based on what your partner says regarding the location of another student, guess who he/she is.

MODELO: E1: *Está al lado de Juan. ¿Quién es?*
E2: *Es María.*

🔗 **Standard 1.2.** Students understand and interpret written and spoken language on a variety of topics. In **Listening with Visuals** the pre-listening activity and the drawing aid comprehension of the spoken word at this early learning stage. Students can understand more than they can say, so instructors should focus on comprehension, rather than limit input to only the words and structures that students can produce orally.

Audioscript for Listening with Visuals.
1. *El televisor está detrás de la profesora.*
2. *El libro está sobre el escritorio.*
3. *María está al lado de Juan.*
4. *La pizarra está al lado de la puerta.*
5. *El cuaderno está debajo del pupitre.*
6. *El cesto está entre la ventana y el escritorio.*

Suggestion for P-15. Start by saying where some of the students are seated (e.g., *Alberto está al lado de Anita*). Students answer *sí* or *no.* Point out that several statements are possible for each name. Then students do the activity.

Alternative for P-15. You may create an information gap activity by preparing two partially filled seating charts (in which version A includes the information missing in version B and vice versa). Pairs of students ask each other questions to fill in their respective charts, e.g., *¿Quién está delante de Ester?*

Warm-up for P-17. Model the activity with students before they pair up. You may wish to introduce the expressions *cerca (de)* and *lejos (de)* and use them in this guessing game: *Está lejos de Susana. Está lejos de Arturo. Está muy cerca de Amelia. ¿Quién es?* Students take turns providing information and guessing.

Resources

■ SAM: P-32 to P-35

Suggestion. Model numbers zero to ten, pointing to numbers written on the board. Have students repeat, first in order, then randomly. Give addresses using numbers from one to ten while pointing to the correct or incorrect number on the board. Students answer *sí* or *no.* Do the same with other numbers.

When presenting sixteen to nineteen, emphasize the *i* sound linking *diez* and rest of number. Point out the written accents (*dieciséis,* etc.). Rules of accentuation are presented in the appendix.

Los números 0 a 99

CD 1 Track 9

0	**cero**	11	**once**	22	**veintidós**
1	**uno**	12	**doce**	23	**veintitrés**
2	**dos**	13	**trece**	30	**treinta**
3	**tres**	14	**catorce**	31	**treinta y uno**
4	**cuatro**	15	**quince**	40	**cuarenta**
5	**cinco**	16	**dieciséis**	50	**cincuenta**
6	**seis**	17	**diecisiete**	60	**sesenta**
7	**siete**	18	**dieciocho**	70	**setenta**
8	**ocho**	19	**diecinueve**	80	**ochenta**
9	**nueve**	20	**veinte**	90	**noventa**
10	**diez**	21	**veintiuno**		

- Numbers from sixteen through twenty-nine are usually written as one word. Note the spelling changes and the written accent on some forms.

  18: **dieciocho** 22: **veintidós**

- Beginning with thirty-one, numbers are written as three words.

  31: **treinta y uno** 45: **cuarenta y cinco**

- The number *one* has three forms in Spanish: **uno**, **un**, and **una**. Use **uno** when counting: **uno, dos, tres...** Use **un** or **una** before nouns: **un borrador, una mochila, veintiún libros, veintiuna mochilas.**

- Use **hay** for both *there is* and *there are.*

Hay un libro sobre la mesa.	*There is one book on the table.*
Hay dos libros sobre la mesa.	*There are two books on the table.*

Suggestion for P-18. Have students hold up one, two, three, or four fingers to represent each number's position. Or have them write each number down on the board, as you read them again.

P-18 ¿Qué número es? Your instructor will read a number from each group. Circle the number you hear. Then compare your responses with those of your partner.

a.	8	4	3	5
b.	12	9	16	6
c.	37	59	41	26
d.	54	38	76	95
e.	83	62	72	49
f.	47	14	91	56

P-19 Para la oficina. You and your partner are student assistants in the Spanish department. You have to check a shipment of equipment and supplies that just arrived. Choose five items and tell your partner how many of each there are. He/She will take notes. Exchange roles.

MODELO: 4-7 mesas: *Hay cuatro mesas.*

a. 6-10 teléfonos
b. 8-12 escritorios
c. 1-2 silla(s)
d. 6-12 calculadoras
e. 10-20 cestos

f. 90-95 bolígrafos
g. 9-15 computadoras
h. 22-24 computadoras portátiles
i. 1-3 reloj(es)
j. ...

P-20 Problemas. Take turns solving the following arithmetic problems. Use **y** (+), **menos** (−), and **son** (=).

MODELO: 2 + 4 =   12 − 5 =
        Dos y cuatro son seis.   Doce menos cinco son siete.

a. 11 + 4 = 15
b. 8 + 2 = 10
c. 13 + 3 = 16

d. 20 − 6 = 14
e. 39 + 50 = 89
f. 80 − 1 = 79

g. 50 − 25 = 25
h. 26 + 40 = 66
i. 90 − 12 = 78

P-21 Los números de teléfono y las direcciones (*addresses*). With your partner, take turns asking each other the phone numbers and addresses of the people listed in the chart below.

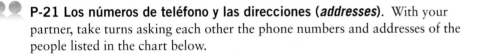

● Cárdenas Alfaro, Joaquín	General Páez 40	423-4837
● Cárdenas Villanueva, Sara	Avenida Bolívar 7	956-1709
● Castelar Torres, Adelaida	Paseo del Prado 85	218-3642
● Castellanos Rey, Carlos	Colón 62	654-6416
● Castelli Rivero, Victoria	Chamberí 3	615-7359
● Castillo Montoya, Rafael	Santa Cruz 73	956-3382

MODELO: Castellanos Rey, Carlos
        E1: *¿Cuál es la dirección de Carlos Castellanos Rey?*
        E2: *Calle Colón, número 62.*
        E1: *¿Cuál es su teléfono?*
        E2: *(Es el) 6-54-64-16*

Cultura

In Spanish-speaking countries, the name of the street precedes the house or building number. Sometimes a comma is placed before the number.

Calle Bolívar 132
132 Bolívar Street

Avenida de Gracia, 18
18 Gracia Avenue

Telephone numbers are generally not stated as individual numbers, but in groups of two, depending on how the numbers are written or on the number of digits, which varies from country to country.

12-24-67:
doce, veinticuatro, sesenta y siete

243-89-07:
dos cuarenta y tres, ochenta y nueve, cero siete

Resources
▪ SAM: P-36 to P-41

Suggestion. Using a Spanish calendar, model days of the week, pointing out that Monday is normally the first day of the week. You may preview ordinal numbers (presented in *Capítulo 5*) by saying *El lunes es el primer* [hold up index finger] *día de la semana. El martes es el segundo día*, etc. Introduce *último: el último día es el domingo*.

Follow-up. Mention that some Spanish calendars show the name of a saint for each day.

Suggestion. Introduce *Hoy es...* and *Mañana es...* by modeling appropriate days. You may also wish to introduce *Ayer fue...*

Note. Point out that the spelling *setiembre* is also correct.

Follow-up. Use a hypothetical class schedule and ask questions: *¿Qué días hay clase de español? ¿Cuándo es la clase de economía? ¿Y la de filosofía?* This will help students practice more cognates and serve as a preview for the vocabulary presented in *Capítulo 1.* You may also use cognates that refer to students' interests: *¿Qué día es el ballet? ¿Cuándo es el concierto?*

Note. You may wish to point out that Roman numerals can also be used to represent the month; for example, 11/X/09.

Note. Mention that the U.S. military also uses this format for writing dates.

))) Los meses del año y los días de la semana

CD 1
Track 10

enero	*January*	mayo	*May*	septiembre	*September*
febrero	*February*	junio	*June*	octubre	*October*
marzo	*March*	julio	*July*	noviembre	*November*
abril	*April*	agosto	*August*	diciembre	*December*

Days of the week and months of the year are not generally capitalized in Spanish, but sometimes they are capitalized in advertisements and invitations.

▪ Monday (**lunes**) is normally considered the first day of the week.

▪ To ask what day it is, use **¿Qué día es hoy?** Answer with **Hoy es...**

▪ To ask about the date, use **¿Qué fecha es?** or **¿Cuál es la fecha?** Respond with **Es el (14) de (octubre).**

▪ Express *on + a day of the week* as follows:

el lunes	*on Monday*
los lunes	*on Mondays*
el domingo	*on Sunday*
los domingos	*on Sundays*

▪ Cardinal numbers are used with dates (e.g., **el dos, el tres**), except for the first day of the month, which is **el primero**. In Spain the first day is also referred to as **el uno**.

Lengua

When dates are written using only numerals, the day normally precedes the month: *11/8* = **el 11 de agosto**.

P-22 ¿Qué día de la semana es? Using the preceding calendar, take turns asking *¿Qué día de la semana es… ?*

1. el 2
2. el 5
3. el 22
4. el 18
5. el 10
6. el 13
7. el 28
8. el…

 P-23 Preguntas. Take turns asking and answering these questions.

1. ¿Qué día es hoy?
2. Hoy es… ¿Qué día es mañana?
3. Hoy es el… de… ¿Qué fecha es mañana?
4. ¿Hay clase de español los domingos? ¿Y los sábados?
5. ¿Qué días hay clase de español?

P-24 Fechas importantes. Working with a partner, tell each other the dates on which these events take place.

MODELO: la reunión de estudiantes (10/9)
E1: *¿Cuándo es la reunión de estudiantes?*
E2: *(Es) el 10 de septiembre.*

1. el concierto de Marc Anthony (12/11)   (Es) el 12 de noviembre
2. el aniversario de Carlos y María (14/4)   (Es) el 14 de abril
3. el banquete (1/3)   (Es) el primero/el 1 de marzo
4. la graduación (22/5)   (Es) el 22 de mayo
5. la fiesta de bienvenida (24/8)   (Es) el 24 de agosto

 P-25 El cumpleaños (*birthday*). Find out when your classmates' birthdays are. Write their names and birthdays in the appropriate space in the chart.

MODELO: E1: *¿Cuándo es tu cumpleaños?*
E2: *(Es) el 3 de mayo.*

CUMPLEAÑOS			
enero	febrero	marzo	abril
mayo	junio	julio	agosto
septiembre	octubre	noviembre	diciembre

Lengua

You may have noticed that the word **tú** (meaning *you*) has a written accent mark, and that the word **tu** (meaning *your*) does not. In *Mosaicos*, boxes similar to this one will help you focus on when to use accent marks. You will find a complete set of the rules for accentuation in the appendix.

Suggestions. Model *¿Qué hora es?* by using a clock with movable hands or pointing to a clock or watch. Answer *Es la una, Son las...* Then give true or erroneous times using a clock with movable hands; students respond *sí* or *no*. Follow with either/or questions (e.g., *¿Son las tres o las cuatro?*) while indicating times. Finally, introduce and practice *y cuarto/y quince, y media/y treinta.*

Suggestions. Point out that there are alternate expressions for the time after the half hour: *son las tres menos diez; son las dos y cincuenta; faltan diez minutos para las tres.*

Present *en punto* and *más o menos* using gestures. Follow with an introduction of *de la mañana/tarde/noche* and indicate *a.m.* or *p.m.* on the board.

Explain that it is also common to say *siete de la tarde* if there is still daylight.

You may introduce the expressions *mediodía* for noon and *medianoche* for midnight.

Warm-up for P-27. Introduce *¿A qué hora es... ?* and *(Es) a la(s) ...* by writing on the board (in appropriate order):

la clase de español	(time)
el almuerzo	12:30 p.m.
la clase de física	1:00 p.m.

Clarify *almuerzo* by using appropriate gestures for eating and by writing *cafetería* on the board. Then model questions and answers for the schedule.

Students will have additional opportunities to practice telling time in *Capítulo 1.*

Cultura

In Spanish-speaking countries, events such as concerts, shows, classes, and professional meetings generally begin on time. Medical appointments are also kept at the scheduled hour. However, informal social functions, such as parties and private gatherings, do not usually begin on time. In fact, guests are expected to arrive at least a half hour after the appointed time. When in doubt, you may ask **¿En punto?** to find out whether you should be punctual.

Lengua

To ask the time at which an event takes place or something happens, use **¿A qué hora es...?** To answer, use **Es a la(s)...** or simply **A la(s)...**

¿A qué hora es la clase de español?
At what time is Spanish class?

(Es) a las nueve y media.
It is at 9:30.

La hora

■ Use **¿Qué hora es?** to inquire about the time. To tell time, use **Es la...** from one o'clock to one thirty and **Son las...** with the other hours.

Es la una.	*It is one o'clock.*
Son las tres.	*It is three o'clock.*

■ To express the quarter hour, use **y cuarto** or **y quince**. To express the half hour, use **y media** or **y treinta**.

Es la una **y media.**	*It is one thirty.*
Es la una **y treinta.**	

Son las dos **y cuarto.**	*It is two fifteen.*
Son las dos **y quince.**	

■ To express time after the half hour, subtract minutes from the next hour, using **menos**.

Son las cuatro **menos** diez.	*It is ten to four.*

■ Add **en punto** for the exact time and **más o menos** for approximate time.

Es la una **en punto.**	*It is one o'clock on the dot/sharp.*
Son las cinco menos cuarto, **más o menos.**	*It is about a quarter to five.*

■ For *a.m.* and *p.m.*, use the following:

de la mañana	(from midnight to noon)
de la tarde	(from noon to nightfall)
de la noche	(from nightfall to midnight)

 P-26 ¿Qué hora es en... ? What time is it in the following cities?

México, p.m.   San Juan, p.m.   Buenos Aires, p.m.   Madrid, p.m.

P-27 El horario de María. Take turns asking and answering questions about María's schedule below. Then write down your own Monday schedule, omitting the time each class meets. Exchange schedules with your partner, and find out what time each of his/her classes starts.

MODELO: E1: *¿A qué hora es la clase de español?*
E2: *Es a las nueve.*

LUNES			
9:00	la clase de español	12:30	el almuerzo
10:00	la clase de matemáticas	1:00	la clase de física
11:00	la clase de psicología	5:00	la clase de tenis
12:00	el laboratorio		

El tiempo

Resources
■ SAM: P-47 to P-48

Hoy hace sol. Hace buen tiempo.   Hoy llueve. Hace mal tiempo.

■ Use **¿Qué tiempo hace?** to inquire about the weather. To answer, you may use the following expressions that start with **hace**:

Hace buen tiempo.   *The weather is good.*
Hace mal tiempo.   *The weather is bad.*

■ To express that it is sunny or that it is raining use the following:

Hace sol.   *It is sunny.*
Llueve./Está lloviendo. *It is raining.*

P-29 ¿Qué tiempo hace hoy? Take turns with your partner asking about the weather in these cities.

MODELO: Miami: ☀
             E1: *¿Qué tiempo hace en Miami?*
             E2: *En Miami hace buen tiempo. Hace sol.*

1. Madrid: ☀
2. Quito: 🌧
3. Lima: 🌧
4. Ciudad de México: ☀
5. Bogotá: 🌧
6. Nueva York: ☀

Suggestion. Explain that *tiempo* is used to talk about weather. Write the word on the board, then point to the window or to the drawing on this page. Say *hace buen tiempo* or *hace mal tiempo*. Ask *¿Qué tiempo hace hoy?* You may need to remind students what the word *hoy* means. Ask this question every day when you arrive in class and after greetings. Students will learn now how to answer simple weather questions as a preview to the weather expressions that they will learn in *Capítulo 7*.

Resources

■ SAM: P-49 to P-52

Suggestions. Use Total Physical Response (TPR) procedures to model the expressions in this section: *escuchen* (cup hand behind ear); *contesten* (make motion of talking); *abran el libro* (open a book); *vayan a la pizarra* (go to the board).

Point to several students, give a command, and have them do it. Write the command. Then point to one student, give the command (without the final *-n*) and cross out or erase the *-n* on the board so students can hear and understand the difference between plural and singular commands: *siéntese/cierren los libros.*

Instructors who feel more comfortable using *tú* when addressing students will want to use informal commands to present these classroom expressions.

Expresiones útiles en la clase

CD 1
Track 11

La tarea, por favor.

Vaya a la pizarra.

Conteste.

Repita.

Levante la mano.

Escriba.

Lea.

■ When asking two or more people to do something, the verb form ends in **-n**: **vaya → vayan, conteste → contesten, repita → repitan.**

■ Although you may not have to use all these expressions, it is useful to be able to recognize them and to respond accordingly. Other expressions that you may hear or say in the classroom include the following:

¿Comprende(n)?	*Do you understand?*
No comprendo.	*I do not understand.*
No sé.	*I do not know.*
Más despacio, por favor.	*More slowly, please.*
Más alto, por favor.	*Louder, please.*
Otra vez.	*Again.*
¿Tienen alguna pregunta?	*Do you have any questions?*
Tengo una pregunta...	*I have a question.*
¿En qué página?	*On what page?*
¿Cómo se dice... en español?	*How do you say ... in Spanish?*
¿Cómo se escribe...?	*How do you spell ... ?*
Vaya(n) a la pizarra.	*Go to the board.*
Conteste(n), por favor.	*Please answer.*
Presente.	*Here (present).*

VOCABULARIO

CD 1
ks 12-18

Las presentaciones — *Introductions*

¿Cómo se llama usted?	*What's your name? (formal)*
¿Cómo te llamas?	*What's your name? (familiar)*
encantado/a	*pleased/nice to meet you*
igualmente	*likewise*
me llamo...	*my name is ...*
mucho gusto	*pleased/nice to meet you*

Los saludos — *Greetings*

bastante	*rather*
bien	*well*
buenas tardes/buenas noches	*good afternoon/good evening, good night*
buenos días	*good morning*
¿Cómo está?	*How are you (formal)?*
¿Cómo estás?	*How are you (informal)?*
hola	*hi, hello*
mal	*bad*
muy	*very*
regular	*fair*
¿Qué tal?	*What's up? What's new? (informal)*

En el salón de clase — *In the classroom*

el bolígrafo	*ballpoint pen*
el borrador	*eraser*
la calculadora	*calculator*
el cesto	*wastebasket*
la computadora	*computer*
la computadora portátil	*laptop*
el cuaderno	*notebook*
el DVD	*DVD; DVD player*
el escritorio	*desk*
el lápiz	*pencil*
el libro	*book*
el mapa	*map*
el marcador/el rotulador	*marker*
la mesa	*table*
la mochila	*backpack*
la pantalla	*screen*
la pizarra	*chalkboard*
la puerta	*door*
el pupitre	*student desk*
el reloj	*clock*
la silla	*chair*
el televisor	*television set*
la tiza	*chalk*
la ventana	*window*

Las personas — *People*

el amigo/la amiga	*friend*
el/chico/la chica	*boy/girl*
él	*he*
ella	*she*
el/la estudiante	*student*

el profesor/la profesora	*professor, teacher*
el señor (Sr.)	*Mr.*
la señora (Sra.)	*Ms., Mrs.*
la señorita (Srta.)	*Ms, Miss*
tú	*you (familiar)*
usted	*you (formal)*
yo	*I*

La posición — *Position*

al lado (de)	*next to*
debajo (de)	*under*
detrás (de)	*behind*
enfrente (de)	*in front of*
entre	*between, among*
sobre	*on, above*

Verbos — *Verbs*

eres	*you are (familiar)*
es	*you are (formal), he/she is*
está	*he/she is, you are (formal)*
estás	*you are (familiar)*
hay	*there is, there are*
soy	*I am*

Palabras y expresiones útiles — *Useful words and expressions*

a	*at, to*
el año	*year*
¿Cómo es?	*What is he/she/it like?*
el día	*day*
¿Dónde está... ?	*Where is ... ?*
en	*in*
ese/a	*that (adjective)*
hoy	*today*
mañana	*tomorrow*
la mañana	*morning*
más o menos	*more or less*
el mes	*month*
mi(s)	*my*
¿Quién es... ?	*Who is ... ?*
la semana	*week*
sí	*yes*
su(s)	*his/her/their*
tu(s)	*your (familiar)*
un/una	*a, an*
y	*and*

See page 5 for expressions for leave-taking.
See page 6 for expressions of courtesy.
See page 10 for cognates.
See pages 14 and 16 for numbers, days of the week, and months.
See page 18 for telling time.
See page 19 for weather expressions.
See page 20 for classroom expressions.

Resources
- Testing Program

Note. Vocabulary lists at the end of each chapter of *Mosaicos* contain the active words and expressions used throughout the chapter, with the exception of obvious cognates.

Note. The 16th-century fresco features the Chariot of Mercury and Virgo. It is located in the cupola of the Old Library at the University of Salamanca.

Suggestion. Point to the fresco and ask if students understand the words *fresco* and *universidad*, which are cognates. (You may have to explain what a fresco is.) Use easily understandable sentences and help students make connections: *Este fresco está en la Universidad de Salamanca, en España.* Using gestures, preview some words that students will learn in the chapter to describe and locate the painting: *El fresco es muy grande; está en la biblioteca de la universidad.* Write down *Universidad de Salamanca. Los estudiantes estudian en la universidad; ustedes son estudiantes;*

En la universidad

Un fresco del siglo XVI en la Universidad de Salamanca

In this chapter you will learn how to:

- exchange information about classes
- identify locations at the university
- talk about academic life and daily occurrences
- ask and answer questions

Cultural focus: España

Museo Guggenheim

FRANCIA

OCÉANO ATLÁNTICO

Santiago de Compostela

Bilbao

Universidad de Salamanca

E S P A Ñ A

Barcelona

Salamanca

Segovia

Paella valenciana

Madrid

PORTUGAL

Valencia

Plaza de toros

Mar Mediterráneo

Córdoba

Sevilla

Granada

La Alhambra

ustedes estudian en una universidad. ¿Cómo se llama su universidad? Point to the map. *¿Dónde está España? ¿Dónde está Salamanca?* Write on the board 1218, the year the *Universidad de Salamanca* was founded. *¿Es una universidad antigua o nueva?* Explain *antiguo/a* and *nuevo/a: la universidad es antigua; el fresco es antiguo; está en la Antigua Biblioteca de la universidad.* Ask students about your college or university: *¿Es antigua o nueva? ¿Cuál es la universidad más antigua de Estados Unidos?*

Standard 3.1. Students reinforce and further their knowledge of other disciplines through the foreign language. The map and photos at the beginning of each chapter reinforce students' general cultural knowledge, remind them of facts about history, art, and geography that they may have learned in the past, and help them to integrate disparate pieces of information into a culturally coherent frame.

Ask what students know about Spain. At this point you may ask this in English and write their answers on the board. Point out the photos on the map and introduce vocabulary as you ask questions. Use gestures to make yourself understood: *¿Qué es este edificio? Es un museo de arte moderno. ¿Conocen la paella? La paella es muy buena,* etc.

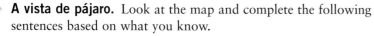

A vista de pájaro. Look at the map and complete the following sentences based on what you know.

1. _b_ España está en…   a. América.   b. Europa.   c. Asia.
2. _b_ La capital de España es…   a. Barcelona.   b. Madrid.   c. Sevilla.
3. _a_ La paella es típica de…   a. Valencia.   b. Salamanca.   c. Madrid.
4. _a_ En la universidad hay…   a. estudiantes.   b. catedrales.   c. toros.
5. _c_ En la plaza de toros hay espectáculos (*shows*)…   a. religiosos.   b. cómicos.   c. populares.

23

Resources

- SAM: 1-1 to 1-10
- Supp. Activ. Book: *A primera vista*

A PRIMERA VISTA

Los estudiantes y los cursos

Me llamo Rosa Pereda. **Estudio sociología** en la **Facultad de Humanidades** de la **Universidad** de Salamanca. Mis clases son muy temprano. **Llego** a la universidad a las ocho y media. Este semestre mis cursos son **economía, ciencias políticas, psicología, antropología** y **estadística.** La clase de economía es mi **favorita.** La clase de antropología es **difícil,** pero el profesor es muy **bueno.** La clase de psicología es **fácil** y muy **interesante.** Por las tardes **trabajo** en una **oficina.**

CD 1
Track 19

CD 1
Track 20

Este chico es mi amigo. Se llama David Thomas. Es **norteamericano** y estudia español en mi universidad. También estudia **literatura, historia** y **geografía.** David es un chico muy responsable y **estudioso.** Generalmente llega a la universidad a las diez. **Habla** español y **practica todos los días** con sus **compañeros** de clase, sus profesores y sus amigos de la universidad. Por la tarde, **escribe** sus **tareas** en la computadora, estudia en el **laboratorio** con uno de sus **compañeros** y **escucha** música o **mira** programas en español en la televisión.

Cultura

Some of Spain's public universities, such as the Universidad de Salamanca, the Universidad de Santiago, and the Universidad Complutense de Madrid, are among the oldest in Europe, dating back hundreds of years. Most private universities in Spain, which are much newer, have higher tuition. To be accepted to a university students take a competitive comprehensive exam, known as **Selectividad.** Many universities offer Spanish language and culture courses for foreign students.

1-1 ¿Qué sabe usted de Rosa? Refer to the information about Rosa to match the information in the right column with the information on the left.

1. __e__ nombre completo
2. __c__ universidad
3. __d__ clase favorita
4. __a__ clase difícil
5. __b__ clase fácil

a. antropología
b. psicología
c. Salamanca
d. economía
e. Rosa Pereda

1-2 ¿Y David? Indicate whether each statement about David is true (**Cierto**) or false (**Falso**).

1. Cierto Es norteamericano.
2. Cierto Habla español.
3. Cierto Estudia literatura, historia y geografía.
4. Falso Llega a la universidad a las nueve.
5. Cierto Practica español con sus amigos.
6. Falso Escucha música por la mañana.

La Universidad de San Marcos, en Lima, Perú, se fundó en 1551.

David y Carmen hablan de sus clases

CD 1
Track 21

DAVID: Hola, Carmen. ¿Cómo estás?

CARMEN: Hola, David. **¿Cómo te va?**

DAVID: Bueno…bastante bien, pero mi clase de historia es muy difícil.

CARMEN: ¿Quién es tu profesor?

DAVID: Se llama Pedro Hernández. Es inteligente y dedicado, pero la clase es **aburrida** y **saco malas notas**.

CARMEN: ¡Vaya! Lo siento. ¿Estudias lo suficiente?

DAVID: Estudio mucho.

CARMEN: **¡Qué lástima!** Mis cinco clases son excelentes. Y tú, **¿cuántas clases tienes?**

DAVID: **Tengo sólo** cuatro.

CARMEN: ¡Uy! Son las once. Tengo un **examen** de economía **ahora**. Hasta luego.

DAVID: Hasta pronto. **¡Buena suerte!**

1-3 ¿En qué clase…? Match the words on the left with the appropriate class on the right.

1. _c_ *Don Quijote* de Cervantes
2. _e_ números
3. _a_ mapa digital
4. _b_ animales
5. _f_ Freud
6. _d_ Napoleón

a. geografía
b. biología
c. literatura
d. historia
e. matemáticas
f. psicología

Suggestion for 1-4. Provide the names of additional courses, using as many cognates as possible. Be prepared to assist students with vocabulary while they write down the subjects they are taking. You may explain the meaning of *contabilidad* and *negocios*.

Suggestion for 1-4 Segunda fase. This activity may be done in groups of three or four. Students listen to each other's answers and compare the information. They may present their information to the class.

Warm up for 1-5. Before doing this activity you may want to have students practice the first-person singular of *-ar* verbs and *tengo*, *tienes*, and *tiene*, which appear in the photo presentations and dialogue at the beginning of this section. Make comparisons with Carmen and David: *Carmen tiene cinco clases. ¿Cuántas clases tiene usted? David saca malas notas, ¿y usted?*

Suggestion. Have students share the information they get with other classmates. You may wish to preview third-person plural forms: *Los estudiantes de esta clase estudian mucho. Trabajan con computadoras y escuchan CDs en el laboratorio. Ustedes estudian español.*

En otras palabras

Words related to computers and computing are often borrowed from English (e.g., **software**, **e-mail**), and they vary from country to country. As you have already learned, one word for *computer* is **la computadora**, used mainly in Latin America, along with **el computador**. *Computer* is **el ordenador** in Spain. *Computer science* is **la informática** in Spain and **la computación** in Latin America.

1-4 Mis clases. PRIMERA FASE. Make a list of your classes. Indicate the days and time each class meets and whether it is easy or difficult, interesting or boring. You will find some subjects in the list below.

economía	comunicaciones	negocios
bioquímica	sociología	historia del arte
física	cálculo	informática
artes plásticas	estadística	seminario de...
contabilidad	astronomía	filosofía

CLASE	DÍAS	HORA	¿CÓMO ES?

SEGUNDA FASE. Tell your partner about your classes. Take turns completing the following ideas.

1. Llego a la universidad a la(s)...
2. Mi clase favorita es...
3. El profesor/La profesora se llama...
4. La clase es muy...
5. Practico español en...
6. En mi clase de español hay...

1-5 Las clases de mis compañeros/as. PRIMERA FASE. Use the following questions to interview your partner. Take notes. Then switch roles.

1. ¿Qué estudias este semestre?
2. ¿Cuántas clases tienes?
3. ¿Cuál es tu clase favorita?
4. ¿Qué día y a qué hora es tu clase favorita?
5. Tu clase de español, ¿cómo es? ¿Es fácil o difícil? ¿Es interesante o aburrida?
6. ¿Trabajas con computadoras? ¿Dónde?
7. ¿Sacas buenas notas?
8. ¿Tienes muchos exámenes?

SEGUNDA FASE. Introduce your partner to another classmate and state one piece of interesting information about him/her. Your classmate will ask your partner about his/her classes.

MODELO: USTED: *Él es Pedro. Estudia ciencias políticas y tiene cuatro clases este semestre.*
SU COMPAÑERO/A: *Mucho gusto. ¿_____?*

La universidad

CD 1
Track 22

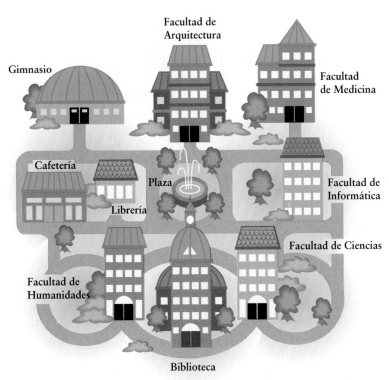

Facultad de Arquitectura

Gimnasio

Facultad de Medicina

Cafetería

Plaza

Facultad de Informática

Librería

Facultad de Ciencias

Facultad de Humanidades

Biblioteca

Carmen

Lorena

Álvaro

Juan

Suggestion. Explain that *facultad* is the equivalent of "school" (e.g., School of Art and Architecture) or "department" in U.S. colleges and universities. Using the campus map on p. 27, point to various buildings, and recycle expressions from *Capítulo preliminar: La Facultad de Humanidades está al lado de la cafetería. La plaza está detrás de la biblioteca.* Remind students: *La librería es donde compramos los libros. La biblioteca es donde estudiamos y consultamos libros.*

Bring in copies of your school's campus map, and have students label buildings in Spanish.

1-6 ¿En qué facultad estudian? PRIMERA FASE. Match the names of the university students pictured at the right with the school where they study.

1. _b_ Juan
2. _a_ Carmen
3. _d_ Lorena
4. _c_ Álvaro

a. Facultad de Medicina
b. Facultad de Arquitectura
c. Facultad de Humanidades
d. Facultad de Ciencias

 SEGUNDA FASE. Exchange the information with a classmate and indicate two classes that each student is probably taking.

MODELO: E1: *¿Dónde estudia Carmen?*
E2: *Carmen estudia en la Facultad de... Probablemente tiene clase de... y de...*

1-7 Mapa de la universidad. Look at the map above and indicate if each statement is true (**Cierto**) or false (**Falso**). If it is **Falso**, correct the information.

1. _Cierto_ La plaza está en el centro del campus.
2. _Cierto_ La Facultad de Humanidades está junto a (*next to*) la biblioteca.
3. _Falso_ La cafetería está detrás del gimnasio.
4. _Cierto_ La Facultad de Ciencias está delante de (*in front of*) la Facultad de Informática.
5. _Cierto_ La librería está al lado de la cafetería.
6. _Falso_ La Facultad de Medicina está al lado del gimnasio.

Expansion for 1-7. Have students work with a partner and ask each other questions to locate places using a map of the university.

Note. Point out that some Spanish speakers say *tomar notas* in place of *tomar apuntes*.

Las actividades de los estudiantes

·)) En la biblioteca

CD 1
Track 23

Unos **alumnos** estudian en la biblioteca. **Toman apuntes** y trabajan en sus tareas. A veces **buscan** palabras en el **diccionario**. Frecuentemente **conversan** sobre sus clases.

·)) Los fines de semana

CD 1
Track 24

Los estudiantes **toman algo** en un **café**.

Miran televisión en **casa**.

Bailan en una **discoteca** con amigos.

Caminan en la **playa**.

Montan en bicicleta.

1-8 Para escoger. Look at the illustrations above. Then choose the word or phrase that completes the sentence logically.

1. Los estudiantes _b_ en la biblioteca.
   a. toman café   **b.** estudian   c. hablan
2. Buscan palabras en _b_ .
   a. el reloj   **b.** el diccionario   c. el laboratorio
3. Miran televisión en _c_ .
   a. la biblioteca   b. la playa   **c.** casa
4. Montan en bicicleta _a_ .
   a. los fines de semana   b. en el café   c. en una discoteca

En la librería

CD 1
Track 25

ESTUDIANTE: **Necesito comprar** un diccionario para mi clase de literatura española.

DEPENDIENTE: **¿Grande** o **pequeño?**

ESTUDIANTE: Grande, y todo en español.

DEPENDIENTE: **Este** diccionario es muy bueno.

ESTUDIANTE: **¿Cuánto cuesta?**

DEPENDIENTE: Cuarenta y ocho **euros.**

1-9 ¿Qué necesita? Complete the following statements, based on the previous conversation.

1. El estudiante necesita... un diccionario
2. Es un diccionario... grande/todo en español/muy bueno/para la clase de literatura española
3. Es para su clase de... español
4. El diccionario cuesta... 48 euros

1-10 ¿Cuánto cuesta? During your semester abroad, you go to the university bookstore. Ask the salesclerk how much the following items cost.

Cultura

Since 2002, the euro has been the official monetary unit of the so-called Eurozone, which includes (as of January 2008) Austria, Belgium, Cyprus, Finland, France, Germany, Greece, Ireland, Italy, Luxembourg, Malta, the Netherlands, Portugal, Slovenia, and Spain. In some other European countries and the United Kingdom, the euro, although not official, is accepted in stores. The euro currency sign is € and the banking code is EUR.

MODELO:

ESTUDIANTE: *¿Cuánto cuesta el mapa?*

DEPENDIENTE/A: *Cuesta cincuenta euros.*

Suggestion. Introduce the new vocabulary in this conversation by describing the photograph: *Estos hombres están en una librería. Hay un estudiante y un dependiente en la foto. El estudiante se llama Alberto García Girón. Necesita comprar un diccionario de español para su clase de literatura española. El diccionario cuesta 48 euros. Alberto busca los 48 euros en su cartera (billetera) y compra el libro.* Show students a wallet to demonstrate the meaning of *cartera*.

Follow-up. Ask short yes/no and either/or questions to check comprehension and to recycle vocabulary. Students can then work in pairs to personalize this dialogue, substituting what they need to buy at the bookstore.

1-11 Entrevista (*Interview*). Ask where and when your classmate does each of the following activities.

MODELO: practicar baloncesto (*basketball*)
    E1: *¿Dónde practicas baloncesto? ¿Y cuándo?*
    E2: *Practico baloncesto en la plaza por las tardes.*

ACTIVIDAD	DÓNDE	CUÁNDO
1. estudiar para un examen difícil		
2. mirar televisión		
3. tomar café/chocolate		
4. bailar salsa		
5. escuchar música		
6. comprar un diccionario/CDs/materiales para tus clases		

1-12 Las actividades de sus compañeros. PRIMERA FASE. Go around the classroom and interview three people. Ask two different questions of each of them. Take notes to report later. Answer the questions of classmates who interview you.

1. ¿Qué haces (*do you do*) los fines de semana?
2. ¿Dónde miras televisión?
3. ¿Qué compras en la librería?
4. ¿Dónde estudias normalmente?
5. ¿Trabajas los fines de semana? ¿Dónde trabajas?

SEGUNDA FASE. Now share your classmates' answers with the rest of the class.

MODELO: *María estudia normalmente en casa. No trabaja los fines de semana.*

1-13 ¿Qué hacen? (*What do they do?*) You will hear three people talking about their activities during the week and on weekends. Before you listen, list your own activities in the chart.

CD 1
Track 26

MIS ACTIVIDADES DE TODOS LOS DÍAS	MIS ACTIVIDADES DEL FIN DE SEMANA

Now pay attention to the general idea of what is said in the recording. As you listen, decide which activities each person is talking about. Then write the number of the speaker (1, 2, 3) next to the appropriate topic.

 _2_ los estudios
 _3_ el tiempo libre (*free time*)
 _1_ el trabajo

EN ACCIÓN

Resources
- Video
- SAM: 1-11 to 1-13

Diarios de bicicleta: La chivita

Antes de ver

1-14 In this video segment, you will be introduced to four college students, some of whom do not know each other. Write down four expressions you think they may use to greet and introduce each other. Answers may vary.

Mientras ve

1-15 As you watch, indicate whether the following statements refer to Javier (**J**), Daniel (**D**), Luciana (**L**), or Gabi (**G**).

1. __J__ Son sus diarios de bicicleta.
2. __L__ Es compañera de Gaby.
3. __J__ Viaja en bicicleta.
4. __D__ Es puntual, simpático y cómico.
5. __G__ Olvida (*forgets*) su teléfono en la cafetería.

Después de ver

1-16 Check off the expressions you prepared in *Antes de ver* that were used in this segment. Answers may vary.

Suggestions for 1-14. You may wish to write students' expressions on the board, since they will be needed for the *Después de ver* activity below.

Give names to the students in the photo before playing the video segment. Ask questions such as the following: *¿Cómo se llaman los dos chicos? Y las dos chicas, ¿cómo se llaman? ¿Quién tiene la bicicleta, Javier o Daniel?*

Note. Explain that *chivita* is a term used for colorful buses typical in Colombia.

Suggestion for 1-16. If time permits, you can expand by asking students to describe the four students, either with whole-class brainstorming or by having students work in pairs and report to the class.

31

Resources

- SAM: 1-14 to 1-18
- Supp. Activ. Book: Present tense of regular -ar verbs
- PowerPoints (PPTs)
- *Situaciones adicionales*

Note. In *Funciones y formas*, structures are presented in context to stress their functions in communication. Each structure is presented first as meaningful input through a visual and a short dialogue or text, and is accompanied by a comprehension-based activity designed to highlight function/form connections. Brief grammar explanations come next and are followed by practice within a focused, contextualized framework. Additional practice is given in the Student Activities Manual (SAM). To use class time efficiently, have students look at the input-oriented visual and introductory dialogue or text, do the comprehension-based activity, and then read the grammar explanations as homework. This way they will come to class ready for the communicative/task-oriented activities. If a grammar point is presented in class, it should take a minimal amount of time.

Suggestion. Review subject pronouns (*Capítulo preliminar*) by pointing to a student or students and having classmates provide the appropriate pronouns.

Note. *Vosotros/as* forms are presented in charts throughout *Mosaicos*; however, activities do not require students to produce *vosotros/as* forms since the majority of Spanish speakers do not use them. Instructors who wish to use *vosotros/as* in class can easily incorporate them into the activities.

Suggestion. To familiarize students with the verb forms, say: *Yo hablo español.* Point to a student or to a picture of

1. Talking about academic life and daily occurrences: Present tense of regular -ar verbs

Sara   Marta

REPORTERO: Perdón. Soy Pablo Brito del canal 11 de televisión. ¿Su nombre, por favor?

SARA: Yo soy Sara y ella es Marta.

REPORTERO: ¿Tienen ustedes una vida muy activa?

MARTA: Sí, nosotras somos (*are*) atletas. **Practicamos** muchos deportes. Sara **participa** en maratones y **practica** el tenis. Yo **practico** el fútbol y el baloncesto.

SARA: Y los fines de semana **montamos** en bicicleta.

REPORTERO: ¡Qué interesante! Gracias, señoritas.

Piénselo. Check (✓) all the statements that are true, based on the reporter's interview with Sara and Marta.

1. ____ Pablo es un reportero de radio.
2. _✓_ Marta y Sara **practican** muchos deportes (*sports*).
3. ____ Marta **participa** en maratones.
4. _✓_ Marta **practica** el fútbol.
5. ____ Sara **practica** el baloncesto.
6. _✓_ Sara y Marta **montan** en bicicleta.

To talk about actions, feelings, and states of being, you need to use verbs. In both English and Spanish, the infinitive is the base form of the verb that appears in vocabulary lists and dictionaries. In English, infinitives are preceded by *to*: *to speak*. Infinitives in Spanish belong to one of three groups, depending on whether they end in **-ar**, **-er**, or **-ir**. Verbs ending in **-ar** are presented here, and verbs ending in **-er** and **-ir** are presented in the next section.

HABLAR (*to speak*)			
yo	hab**lo**	nosotros/as	habl**amos**
tú	habl**as**	vosotros/as	habl**áis**
él, ella, Ud.	habl**a**	ellos, ellas, Uds.	habl**an**

Use the present tense to express what you and others generally or habitually do or do not do. You may also use the present tense to express an ongoing action. Context will tell you which meaning is intended.

Ana **trabaja** en la oficina.
{ *Ana works in the office.*
{ *Ana is working in the office.*

Luis **practica** el piano todos los días.   *Luis practices the piano every day.*

Here are some expressions you may find useful when talking about the frequency of actions.

siempre	*always*	**muchas veces**	*often*
todos los días/meses	*every day/month*	**a veces**	*sometimes*
todas las semanas	*every week*	**nunca**	*never*

Some common **-ar** verbs are **bailar, buscar, caminar, comprar, conversar, escuchar, estudiar, llegar, mirar, montar, necesitar, participar, practicar, sacar, tomar**, and **trabajar**.

1-17 Preferencias. PRIMERA FASE. Rank these activities from 1 to 9, according to your preferences (1 = most interesting, 9 = least interesting).

_____ bailar en una discoteca
_____ mirar televisión en casa
_____ estudiar otras culturas
_____ comprar DVDs y CDs
_____ caminar en la playa
_____ montar en bicicleta cuando hace sol
_____ escuchar música rock
_____ conversar con los amigos con mensajes de texto
_____ bajar (*download*) música de Internet

SEGUNDA FASE. Now compare your answers with those of a classmate. Follow the model.

MODELO: E1: *Para mí, bailar en una discoteca es número 1. ¿Y para ti?*
E2: *Para mí, caminar en la playa es número 1.*

1-18 Mi rutina. PRIMERA FASE. Indicate (✓) the activities that are part of your routine at school.

1. _____ Llego a la universidad a las nueve de la mañana.
2. _____ Converso con mis amigos por teléfono.
3. _____ Tomo notas en todas las clases.
4. _____ Hablo con mis compañeros en la cafetería.
5. _____ Estudio en la biblioteca por las mañanas.
6. _____ Trabajo en mis tareas todas las noches.
7. _____ Miro programas cómicos en la televisión.
8. _____ A veces practico un deporte con mis amigos/as.

SEGUNDA FASE. Now compare your answers with those of a classmate. The expressions in *En directo* will help you react as your classmate tells you about himself/herself. Report your findings to the class.

MODELO: *Daniel y yo somos (muy) similares. Él y yo miramos programas cómicos en la televisión./Daniel y yo somos (muy) diferentes. Yo estudio por las mañanas; él estudia por las tardes.*

En directo

To express disbelief:

¡Qué increíble!

To show surprise at a coincidence:

¡Qué casualidad!

1-19 A preguntar. PRIMERA FASE. Find four different classmates, each of whom does one of the following activities. Write each name on the appropriate line. The expressions in *En directo* will help you carry on the conversation.

MODELO: mirar televisión por la noche
E1: *¡Oye! ¿Miras televisión por la tarde?*
E2: *Sí, miro televisión por la tarde. O*
No, no miro televisión por la tarde.

PERSONA	ACTIVIDAD
_____	estudiar español todos los días
_____	llegar a la universidad a las 9:30 a.m.
_____	escuchar música clásica en casa por la noche
_____	trabajar en una oficina por la tarde

SEGUNDA FASE. Now report to the class your findings about your classmates' activities.

En directo

To get someone's attention:

¡Oye! (to someone your age or younger)

Oiga, por favor. (to someone unknown to you)

To interrupt to ask a question:

Perdón, tengo una pregunta.

To agree to answer:

Con mucho gusto.

1-20 Mis actividades. PRIMERA FASE. Mark (✓) the space that indicates how often you do the following activities:

ACTIVIDADES	A VECES	MUCHAS VECES	SIEMPRE	NUNCA
estudiar con amigos				
sacar buenas notas				
montar en bicicleta los fines de semana				
mirar televisión por la tarde				
bailar los sábados				
tomar café				

SEGUNDA FASE. Now tell each other how often you do these activities, and then ask where your partner does them.

MODELO: E1: *Yo estudio con amigos a veces, ¿y tú?*
E2: *Yo siempre estudio con amigos.*
E1: *¿Dónde estudian ustedes?*
E2: *Estudiamos en la biblioteca.*

1-21 Un día típico en la vida de Luisa. PRIMERA FASE. Describe what Luisa does on a typical day.

MODELO: *Luisa llega a la oficina a las nueve menos diez.*

1. 2. 3. 4.

SEGUNDA FASE. Now, based on a typical day in her life, describe Luisa's personality. Then explain what you normally do on a regular day.

SITUACIONES

1. **Role A.** Your friend works in the afternoon. Ask a) where he/she works; b) the days of the week and the hours that he/she works; and c) if the job (**trabajo**) is interesting/boring/difficult/easy. Then answer your friend's questions about your job.

    Role B. Tell your friend that you work in the afternoon. Answer your friend's questions about your job. Then ask three questions about his/her job (**trabajo**).

2. **Role A.** You need to read *Don Quijote de la Mancha* by Miguel de Cervantes for your World Literature class, so you go to the university library. Tell the librarian that you need a book, and answer the librarian's questions about title (**título**) and author (**autor**).

    Role B. You are a librarian at the university library. A student tells you that he/she needs a book. Ask the title of the book (**¿cuál es el título?**) and the author (**autor**). Comment on the book.

Cultura

A social activity popular with university students and others in Spain is **ir de tapas** (to go out for **tapas**). **Tapas** are small portions of different dishes that are served in most bars with wine or beer. They range from a piece of bread with an anchovy to elaborate appetizers.

Este bar de Madrid tiene una selección de tapas deliciosas.

Suggestion for 1-21. Have students observe the whole series of pictures to infer the context of the scene. Encourage them to describe the setting and action in each picture. Emphasize the importance of guessing when short of vocabulary (e.g., the words in illustrations 1 and 3). Point out that part of the routine of many Spaniards is meeting with friends at a *bar de tapas* after work or school, before going home for dinner (*cena*). Explain that a) many offices close from 1:30 to 4:30 p.m., especially outside the major cities; b) employees usually work until 8:00 p.m.; and c) dinner is late by U.S. standards, about 9:30 p.m.

Note. This activity provides practice telling time, presented in *Capítulo preliminar*.

Note for 1-21, Segunda fase. This is a good opportunity to recycle cognates presented in *Capítulo preliminar* (*eficiente*, *independiente*, *inteligente*, *activa*, *moderna*), as well as others presented in this chapter (*estudiosa*, *interesante*).

Note. Students are given two interactive tasks in *Situaciones*. They are presented in English to ensure that students understand what is requested and that they produce the necessary vocabulary and structures on their own. The *Situaciones* provide students with ample opportunities for practice within realistic contexts and will always appear at the end of each *Funciones y formas* section.

Suggestions for Situaciones. These activities can be organized in a variety of ways. In addition to grouping students in pairs, you may want to divide the class into Group A for *Situaciones* 1 and Group B for *Situaciones* 2. Or you may instruct students in Group A to play all Roles A and Group B to play all Roles B.

Resources

■ SAM: 1-19 to 1-22
■ Supp. Activ. Book: Present tense of regular *-er* and *-ir* verbs

Suggestions. Review *-ar* verbs and person markers (*-s, -mos, -n*). Point out the similarities and differences between *-er* and *-ir* verbs. Contextualize your language as you present the conjugation. *¿Lee usted mucho? ¿Qué libros lee? Y sus amigos, ¿leen mucho también? ¿Lee usted el periódico por la mañana? ¿Lee usted el periódico en Internet o en papel? ¿Dónde vive usted? ¿Vive en una casa o en un apartamento?*

2. Talking about academic life and daily occurrences: Present tense of regular *-er* and *-ir* verbs

REPORTERO: Y ustedes, ¿qué hacen durante el día?

PEDRO: Antonio estudia ciencias en la universidad. **Asiste** a sus clases y luego **corre** al laboratorio, donde trabaja todos los días. Habla con el profesor y **aprende** mucho. Los estudiantes de ciencias **leen** mucho, **escriben** trabajos de investigación y sacan buenas notas. Yo soy un estudiante de arquitectura, y mis compañeros y yo **leemos** y **escribimos** mucho también. Yo casi (*almost*) **vivo** en la biblioteca cuando estudio para los exámenes.

Piénselo. Check (✓) all the statements that are true, based on the reporter's interview with Pedro.

1. _____ Antonio estudia arquitectura.
2. __✓__ Antonio trabaja en el laboratorio y **aprende** (*learns*) mucho.
3. __✓__ Los estudiantes **leen** y **escriben** mucho.
4. _____ Antonio no **asiste** (*attends*) a sus clases.
5. __✓__ Los estudiantes de ciencias sacan buenas notas.
6. __✓__ Pedro estudia arquitectura.
7. __✓__ Pedro **vive** (*lives*) en el laboratorio.

■ You have learned in this chapter that the present tense is used to express activities and ongoing actions. You have also learned the present tense forms for verbs whose infinitives end in **-ar**. Now you will learn those forms for verbs whose infinitives end in **-er** and **-ir**.

■ Note that **-er** and **-ir** verbs have the same endings, except for the **nosotros/as** and **vosotros/as** forms.

APRENDER (*to learn*)			
yo	aprend**o**	nosotros/as	aprend**emos**
tú	aprend**es**	vosotros/as	aprend**éis**
él, ella, Ud.	aprend**e**	ellos, ellas, Uds.	aprend**en**

VIVIR (*to live*)			
yo	viv**o**	nosotros/as	viv**imos**
tú	viv**es**	vosotros/as	viv**ís**
él, ella, Ud.	viv**e**	ellos, ellas, Uds.	viv**en**

- Other common **-er** and **-ir** verbs are **comer** (*to eat*), **comprender**, **correr**, **leer**, **responder** (*to respond*), **asistir**, and **escribir**.

- The verb **ver** (*to see*) has an irregular **yo** form: **veo, ves, ve, vemos, veis, ven.**

  Veo películas los fines de semana.   *I see movies on weekends.*

- Use **deber** + *infinitive* to express that you should/must/ought to do something.

  Los atletas **deben beber** mucha agua.   *Athletes should drink lots of water.*

1-22 Mi profesor/a modelo. PRIMERA FASE. Indicate which of the activities are part of the routine of an ideal instructor inside and outside the classroom.

	SÍ	NO
1. Lee el periódico (*newspaper*) en clase.		✓
2. Escucha los problemas de los estudiantes.	✓	
3. Bebe café y come en la clase.		✓
4. Escribe buenos ejemplos en la pizarra.	✓	
5. Nunca prepara sus clases.		✓
6. Siempre asiste a clase.	✓	
7. Responde a las preguntas de los estudiantes.	✓	
8. Habla con los estudiantes en su oficina.	✓	

SEGUNDA FASE. Compare your answers with those of a classmate. Together write two more activities typical of an ideal instructor and ask your instructor if they are part of his/her academic routine.

1-23 Para pasarlo bien (*To have a good time*). PRIMERA FASE. Indicate which of the following activities your classmates do to have a good time.

1. _____ Leen libros en español todas las semanas.
2. _____ Escriben mensajes de texto.
3. _____ Practican deportes con los amigos.
4. _____ Asisten a clase a las ocho de la mañana.
5. _____ Corren en el gimnasio y en el parque.
6. _____ Ven películas y programas de televisión en casa.
7. _____ Comen en restaurantes elegantes.
8. _____ Beben sólo Coca-Cola en las fiestas.

SEGUNDA FASE. Compare your answers with those of a classmate. Then exchange information with another pair (**pareja**) about the activities you all do to have a good time. Use the expressions in *En directo* to help you react naturally to your classmates' responses.

MODELO: PAREJA 1: *Nosotros bailamos en discotecas para pasarlo bien. ¿Y ustedes?*
              PAREJA 2: *Bebemos café y conversamos con los amigos.*

Suggestion for 1-23. *Pasarlo bien* is introduced as a lexical item. Before the activity, expand on the meaning by giving examples: *Hay muchas maneras de pasarlo bien. Yo, por ejemplo, para pasarlo bien, escucho música, corro en el parque cuando hace buen tiempo, preparo comida mexicana en casa, etc. ¿Y usted, lee o baila para pasarlo bien? ¿Cuáles son sus actividades los fines de semana para pasarlo bien?*

En directo

To react to what someone has said:

¡Qué interesante!

¡Qué divertido!
How funny!

¡Qué aburrido!
How boring!

1-24 Lugares y actividades. Ask what your classmate does in the following places. He/She will respond with one of the activities listed. Then ask what your classmate does not do in those places.

MODELO: en la clase
E1: *¿Qué haces en la clase?*
E2: *Veo películas en español.*
E1: *¿Qué no haces en la clase?*
E2: *No leo el periódico.*

LUGARES	ACTIVIDADES
en la playa	beber cerveza
en un café	tomar el sol
en una discoteca	bailar salsa
en una fiesta	mirar televisión
en el cine	leer el periódico
en la casa	ver películas de horror
en un restaurante	escuchar música clásica
en la biblioteca	comer un sándwich y tomar un café

1-25 A preguntar. PRIMERA FASE. Find four different classmates, each of whom does one of the following activities. Write each name in the chart below.

MODELO: ver películas en casa
E1: *¿Ves películas en casa?*
E2: *Sí, veo películas en casa./ No, no veo películas en casa.*

PERSONA	ACTIVIDAD
_____	asistir a conciertos de música rock
_____	beber café todos los días
_____	vivir en casa con la familia
_____	escribir mensajes de texto por la noche

SEGUNDA FASE. Now report to the class your findings about your classmates' activities.

1-26 ¿Qué deben hacer? Read the situations in the column on the left and select the best advice from the column on the right.

1. _c_ Maricela desea sacar buenas notas.
2. _f_ Carlos corre en el parque.
3. _e_ Luisa y Jorge están (*are*) muy nerviosos.
4. _b_ Los estudiantes desean comer tapas.
5. _d_ Óscar desea aprender a bailar.
6. _a_ Carolina desea preparar tacos, burritos y enchiladas.

a. Debe trabajar en un restaurante mexicano.
b. Deben visitar España.
c. Debe estudiar todos los días.
d. Debe tomar clases de baile.
e. No deben beber café con cafeína.
f. Debe beber mucha agua.

SITUACIONES

1. **Role A.** You see a classmate at a coffee shop with laptop and books spread out on the table. Ask if he/she a) drinks coffee every day; b) often studies in the coffee shop; c) reads the newspaper there; and d) writes on the computer in the coffee shop.

Role B. You are sitting at a table with your laptop and books at your favorite coffee shop. A classmate comes in and walks over. Answer your classmate's questions about what you usually do there.

2. **Role A.** On the way to Spanish class you run into a classmate and ask how he/she is. Your classmate confides that he/she isn't getting good grades in Spanish. Suggest that he/she a) should always attend class; b) must read the chapter every week; c) should study in the library; and d) ought to look for a good dictionary.

Role B. In the hallway you run into the person who sits next to you in Spanish class. When he/she asks how you are, say you're so-so. Explain that you are not getting good grades in Spanish and that you are not learning the vocabulary. Listen to your classmate's advice and thank him/her.

3. Specifying gender and number: Articles and nouns

Resources
■ SAM: 1-23 to 1-28
■ Supp. Activ. Book: Articles and nouns

MANUEL: Hola, Rocío. Tengo **un** plan. ¿Estudiamos español en **la** universidad esta tarde? Necesito **un** diccionario para **la** tarea.

ROCÍO: ¡Buena idea! ¿En **la** biblioteca? **El** profesor de español es bueno, pero es **una** clase difícil. ¿Invitamos a mi amigo Marcos?

MANUEL: Fenomenal. Usamos **la** pizarra y **el** escritorio **del** salón 12 de **la** biblioteca.

Piénselo. Match the words on the right with those on the left. Use the dialogue and the endings of the nouns as clues.

1. _d_ clase
2. _c_ diccionario de español
3. _b_ pizarra
4. _a_ escritorio
5. _b_ universidad

a. el
b. la
c. un
d. una

Suggestions. Write *el/un* on the board or on a visual next to the word *libro*, circling or underlining the *o*. Write *la/una* and the word *tarea*, circling the *a*. Give other examples of vocabulary presented in the chapter. Write *el mapa* and say *excepción*; do the same thing with *el día* and *la mano*. Continue with *la actividad*, *la lección*, and *la televisión*, underlining the endings *-dad*, *-ción*, and *-sión*, pointing out that words with these endings use the articles *la/una*.

As a mnemonic device, write the following words in a vertical column on the board, *el cereal, el libro, el salón, el pupitre, el borrador, el tenis.* Circle the final letters of each word to spell "loners"; point out that words ending in these letters are usually masculine.

Gender

■ Nouns are words that name a person, place, or thing. In English all nouns use the same definite article, *the*, and all singular nouns use the indefinite articles *a* and *an*. Spanish nouns, whether they refer to people or to things, have either masculine or feminine gender. Masculine singular nouns use **el** or **un** and feminine singular nouns use **la** or **una**.

The terms *masculine* and *feminine* are used in a grammatical sense and have nothing to do with biological gender.

	MASCULINE	FEMININE	
SINGULAR DEFINITE ARTICLES	el	la	*the*
SINGULAR INDEFINITE ARTICLES	un	una	*a/an*

■ Generally, nouns that end in **-o** are masculine and require **el** or **un**, and those that end in **-a** are feminine and require **la** or **una**.

el/un libr**o**	**el/un** cuadern**o**	**el/un** diccionari**o**
la/una mes**a**	**la/una** sill**a**	**la/una** ventan**a**

■ Nouns that end in **-dad, -ción, -sión** are feminine and require **la** or **una**.

la/una universi**dad**	**la/una** lec**ción**	**la/una** televi**sión**

■ Nouns that end in **-ma** are generally masculine.

el/un progra**ma**	**el/un** proble**ma**
el/un dra**ma**	**el/un** poe**ma**

■ In general, nouns that refer to males are masculine, and nouns that refer to females are feminine. Masculine nouns ending in **-o** change the **-o** to **-a** for the feminine; those ending in a consonant add **-a** for the feminine.

el/un amig**o**	**la/una** amig**a**
el/un profesor	**la/una** profesor**a**

■ Nouns ending in **-ante** and **-ente** may be feminine or masculine. Gender is signaled by the article (**el/la estudiante**).

■ Use definite articles with titles when you are talking about someone. Do not use definite articles when addressing someone directly.

> **La** señorita Andrade es **la** secretaria en el Departamento de Lenguas Europeas. **El** profesor Campos es **el** director del departamento.
>
> *Ms. Andrade is the secretary in the Department of European Languages. Professor Campos is the chair of the department.*

> Todos los días, el profesor Campos dice "Buenos días, señorita Andrade". Ella contesta, "Buenos días, profesor Campos".
>
> *Every day, Professor Campos says "Good morning, Ms. Andrade." She responds, "Good morning, Professor Campos."*

Number

	MASCULINE	FEMININE	
PLURAL DEFINITE ARTICLES	**los**	**las**	*the*
PLURAL INDEFINITE ARTICLES	**unos**	**unas**	*some*

■ Add **-s** to form the plural of nouns that end in a vowel. Add **-es** to nouns ending in a consonant.

la silla	→ las silla**s**		el cuaderno	→ los cuaderno**s**
la activida**d**	→ las activida**des**		el señor	→ los señor**es**

■ Nouns that end in **-z** change the **z** to **c** before **-es**.

el lápi**z** → los lápi**ces**

■ To refer to a mixed group, use masculine plural forms.

los chic**os**   *the boys and girls*

1-27 Conversaciones incompletas. Complete the dialogues.

1. Supply the definite articles (**el, la, los, las**).
   E1: ¿Dónde está María?
   E2: Está en _la_ clase de _la_ profesora Sánchez.
   E1: ¡Qué lástima! Necesito hablar con ella. Es urgente.
   E2: Bueno, ella está en _el_ salón de clase hasta _la_ una, y por
       _la_ tarde trabaja en _el_ laboratorio.
   E1: ¿Y a qué hora llega?
   E2: Llega a _las_ dos, más o menos.

2. Supply the indefinite articles (**un, una, unos, unas**).
   E1: Necesito comprar _una_ calculadora y _unos_ lápices.
   E2: Y yo necesito _un_ bolígrafo y _un_ diccionario, pero ¿qué diccionario compro?
   E1: Para el curso de español, _unos_ profesores usan _un_ diccionario pequeño y otros usan
       _un_ diccionario grande. ¿Por qué (*Why*) no hablas con tu profesor?

3. Supply the definite or indefinite articles.
   E1: Tengo _un/el_ examen de matemáticas mañana y necesito sacar _una_ buena nota en esa clase.
   E2: ¿Quién es _el_ profesor?
   E1: Es _la_ doctora Solís.
   E2: ¡Ah! Es _una_ profesora excelente.
   E1: Sí, pero _la_ clase es muy difícil. Estudio y escribo _las_ tareas todos
       los días, pero no saco buenas notas.
   E2: ¡Vaya! Lo siento mucho.

1-28 ¿Qué necesitan? Take turns saying what these classmates need.

MODELO: Alicia tiene que buscar unas palabras. *Necesita un diccionario.*   Possible answers:

1. Mónica tiene que tomar apuntes en la clase de historia. un lápiz, un bolígrafo, un cuaderno
2. Carlos y Ana deben hacer la tarea de matemáticas. una calculadora, un cuaderno
3. Alfredo tiene que estudiar para el examen de geografía. un libro, un mapa
4. Isabel tiene que escribir una composición para su clase de inglés. un cuaderno, un bolígrafo, una computadora
5. Blanca y Lucía tienen que encontrar (*find*) dónde está Salamanca. un mapa, una computadora
6. David tiene que escuchar una canción (*song*) para su clase de música. un DVD

SITUACIONES

1. **Role A.** You have missed the first day of class. Ask a classmate a) at what time the class meets; b) who the professor is; and c) what you need for the class.

   Role B. Tell your classmate a) that the class is at 8:00 in the morning; b) the name of the professor and what he/she is like; and c) at least three items that your classmate needs for the class.

2. **Role A.** You work for the student newspaper at your college and have been asked to interview two students to find out how they typically spend their weekends. After introducing yourself, find out a) if they work, and where; b) what they study; and c) what they do (**hacen**) on Saturdays and Sundays.

   Roles B, C. Tell the interviewer a) if you work and, if so, where; b) the classes you take; and c) what you do on weekends, where, and with whom.

Note. Remind students that they have already used two verbs that translate as "to be" in English. Write *ser* and *estar* on the board. Ask students basic questions they practiced in the previous chapter (*¿Cómo está usted? ¿Dónde está...? ¿Cómo es...?*) while pointing to the appropriate verb.

Suggestion. Use photos or illustrations of people in various places to practice forms of *estar*, some of which students have already seen: *Ellos están en un café, y estas chicas están en una oficina* (write *están* on the board). *Pero ustedes están en la clase de español. Yo estoy aquí también. Nosotros* (use gesture) *estamos en la clase de español.*

Cross-reference. The uses of *ser* and *estar* are contrasted in *Capítulo 2.* You have already been using some forms of *estar.* All the present tense forms are presented here.

4. Expressing location and states of being: Present tense of *estar*

ELISA: ¿Humberto? Te habla Elisa.
HUMBERTO: ¡Elisa! ¡Qué sorpresa! ¿Dónde **estás**?
ELISA: **Estoy** en el aeropuerto de Barajas, en Madrid. ¿Y tú?
HUMBERTO: Mi padre y yo **estamos** de vacaciones en Nueva York. En este momento, mi padre **está** en la tienda *Best Buy*. ¿Y cómo **están** todos en tu familia?
ELISA: Todos **estamos** muy bien. ¡Qué bueno escucharte! Lo siento, Humberto, pero el vuelo (*flight*) sale (*leaves*) pronto. Hablamos más mañana. Adiós.

Elisa   Humberto

Piénselo. Indicate whether each statement is true (**Cierto**) or false (**Falso**), based on the conversation. If it is **Falso**, correct the information.

1. <u>Falso</u> Humberto **está** en el aeropuerto.
2. <u>Falso</u> Elisa **está** de vacaciones en Nueva York.
3. <u>Cierto</u> Humberto **está** en una ciudad grande con una persona de su familia.
4. <u>Falso</u> La tienda *Best Buy* de esta conversación **está** en Madrid.
5. <u>Cierto</u> Elisa y Humberto **están** contentos de hablar por teléfono.

■ You have already been using some forms of **estar**. Here are all the present tense forms of this verb.

ESTAR (*to be*)			
yo	**estoy**	nosotros/as	**estamos**
tú	**estás**	vosotros/as	**estáis**
Ud., él, ella	**está**	Uds., ellos, ellas	**están**

■ Use **estar** to express the location of persons or objects.

¿Dónde **está** Humberto?	*Where is Humberto?*
Está en Nueva York.	*He is in New York*

■ Use **estar** to talk about states of health or being.

¿Cómo **está** la familia de Elisa?	*How is Elisa's family?*
Está muy bien.	*They are very well.*

1-29 En la cafetería. In the cafeteria, you run across a former classmate. Complete the conversation, using the correct forms of **estar**. Then indicate in the parentheses if **estar** signals location (**L**) or a state of being (**S**).

ROBERTO: Hola, Carlos. ¿Qué tal? ¿Cómo _estás (S)_?

CARLOS: _Estoy (S)_ muy bien. ¿Y tú?

ROBERTO: Muy bien, muy bien. ¿Y cómo _está (S)_ tu hermana *(sister)* Ana?

CARLOS: Bien, gracias. Ella y mamá _están (L)_ en España ahora.

ROBERTO: ¡Qué suerte! Y nosotros _estamos (L)_ en la universidad, ¡y en la semana de exámenes!

1-30 Horas y lugares favoritos. **PRIMERA FASE.** Ask your classmate his/her favorite time of day or day of the week. Then ask where he/she usually is at that time or on that day.

MODELO: E1: *¿Cuál es tu hora favorita del día?*
E2: *Las 10:00 de la mañana.*
E1: *Generalmente, ¿dónde estás a las 10:00 de la mañana?*
E2: Estoy en... . *¿Y cuál es tu hora favorita?*
E1: ... .
E2: *¿Y dónde estás?*
E1: *Estoy en... .*

SEGUNDA FASE. Compare your responses with those of your partner. Identify any similarities and/or differences in your preferences.

1-31 Conversación. Ask a classmate where the people in these drawings are, how they feel, and what they are doing.

MODELO: E1: *¿Dónde está María Luisa?*
E2: *Está en la biblioteca.*
E1: *¿Cómo está?*
E2: *Está regular.*
E1: *¿Qué hace?*
E2: *Estudia.*

María Luisa

1. Berta Lorena

2. Carlos el Dr. Núñez

3. Marcelo Eduardo

SITUACIONES

1. **Role A.** As editor of the new student handbook, you must give the graphic designer directions for drawing the campus map. First draw a rough sketch of the map, including the places below. Then explain their location to the designer.

   la biblioteca
   la cafetería
   la Facultad de Ciencias
   la Facultad de Humanidades

   Role B. You are a graphic designer. Ask questions about the location of these buildings as you draw the new map. When you have finished, show the map to the editor to check if you have understood his/her explanations.

2. **Role A.** You are a new student at the university and you do not know where the gym is. Introduce yourself to a classmate. Explain that you want to run in the gym and ask where it is located. Thank your classmate for the help (**Gracias por la ayuda**).

   Role B. A new student will greet you and ask questions. Make your answers as complete and specific as possible.

Suggestions for 1-31. Encourage students to guess how to say the location in drawing 2 (*el hospital, la clínica*), telling them only that it is a cognate. Once a student guesses either word, model pronunciation and spelling of both. Do the same thing for *básquetbol* in drawing 3. You may also mention *baloncesto*.

Introduce the phrases *¿Qué hace?* and *¿Qué hacen?*, which students will need in their interactions. Remind them that they have already used the phrase *¿Qué haces?* earlier in the chapter.

Suggestion for Situación 1. Students should switch roles, so they can each play both people. To save time in class, you may ask students to draw the map in *Situación 1*, Role A, in advance.

Suggestion. Encourage students to guess the meanings of the question words in the exchanges between Andrea and her advisor, based on the context as well as on their own experience filling out similar forms.

Suggestions. Ask questions such as the following: *¿Dónde está la pizarra? ¿Y quién(es) está(n) al lado de la pizarra? ¿Cuántos alumnos hay en esta fila? ¿Quiénes son? ¿Cómo es…?* Point out the difference in stress and meaning between *¿por qué?* and *porque.*

To practice asking for definitions, provide students with words such as *lugar* and *objeto*: *¿Qué es una librería? Es un lugar donde compramos libros. ¿Qué es un lápiz? Es un objeto que usamos para escribir.* In small groups, have students practice giving simple definitions (e.g., *oficina, tiza*).

Ask questions using *cuál(es)*: *¿Cuál es la mochila de Alberto? ¿Y cuáles son los libros de Ana y Pedro?*

Point out that intonation rises at the end of yes/no questions. Lift your hand as you raise intonation asking yes/no questions with subjects before and after the verb.

To practice interrogative tags ask several questions of the same student: *Usted es David, ¿verdad? Y usted es norteamericano, ¿no?*

Practice *¿cómo?* to request repetition or clarification.

Some speakers accept *cuál + adjective*, as in *¿Cuál mochila es tuya?*, whereas others do not. *Mosaicos* uses *cuál(es) + ser* (or phrase, as in *¿Cuál de las mochilas es tuya?*).

5. Asking and answering questions: Interrogative words

Andrea Pérez conversa con su consejera (*advisor*) en la universidad. La consejera necesita rellenar (*fill out*) algunos formularios con información sobre Andrea. Aquí están algunas de las preguntas de la consejera y en la columna de la derecha, las respuestas de Andrea.

CONSEJERA

¿**Cómo** se llama la residencia estudiantil donde vives?
¿**Dónde** está?
¿**Cuándo** son tus clases?
¿**Cuánto** cuesta tu transporte por mes?
¿**Quién** es tu compañera de cuarto?
¿**Por qué** deseas (*want to*) estudiar psicología?

ANDREA

Se llama Casa Cervantes.
Está en la Avenida España.
Por la mañana y por la tarde.
Aproximadamente 35 euros.
Cristina Zapatero.
Para ayudar (*help*) a otras personas.

Piénselo. Match Andrea's responses in the left column with the questions her advisor asked her in the right column. **OJO:** You will be able to answer some of the advisor's questions with the information from the conversation above.

1. _c_ Es el profesor Agustín Reyes-Torres.
2. _d_ Se llama Cristina Zapatero.
3. _a_ En la Casa Cervantes.
4. _e_ 400 euros al mes.
5. _b_ Por la tarde.

a. ¿**Dónde** vives?
b. ¿**Cuándo** es tu clase de psicología?
c. ¿**Quién** es tu profesor favorito?
d. ¿**Cómo** se llama tu compañera de cuarto?
e. ¿**Cuánto** cuesta vivir en la residencia?

■ Interrogative words are used to ask questions or to obtain specific information. You have already been using many of these words.

¿**cómo?**	*how/what?*	¿**cuál(es)?**	*which?*
¿**dónde?**	*where?*	¿**quién(es)?**	*who?*
¿**qué?**	*what?*	¿**cuánto/a?**	*how much?*
¿**cuándo?**	*when?*	¿**cuántos/as?**	*how many?*
¿**por qué?**	*why?*	¿**para qué?**	*why?/what for?*

■ If a subject is used in a question, it normally follows the verb.

¿**Dónde** trabaja Elsa?   *Where does Elsa work?*

■ Use **por qué** to ask *why* and **porque** to answer *because.*

¿**Por qué** está Pepe en la biblioteca?   *Why is Pepe at the library?*
Porque necesita estudiar.   *Because he needs to study.*

■ Use **qué + ser** when you want to ask for a definition or an explanation.

¿**Qué es** la sardana?   *What is the sardana?*
Es un baile típico de Cataluña.   *It is a typical dance of Catalonia.*

Lengua

All question words have a written accent over the stressed syllable: **cómo**, **dónde**.

When these words are used in a non-interrogative context, they do not have a written accent.

¿**Dónde está la biblioteca?**
Where is the library?

Esta es la biblioteca donde estudio todos los días.
This is the library where I study everyday.

■ Use **cuál(es) + ser** when you want to ask which one(s).

¿Cuál es tu mochila? *Which (one) is your backpack?*

¿Cuáles son tus papeles? *Which (ones) are your papers?*

■ Questions that may be answered with **sí** or **no** do not use a question word.

¿Trabajan ustedes los sábados? *Do you work on Saturdays?*

No, no trabajamos. *No, we do not.*

■ Another way to ask a question is to place an interrogative tag after a declarative statement.

Tú hablas inglés, **¿verdad?** *You speak English, don't you?*

David es norteamericano, **¿no?** *David is an American, isn't he?*

1-32 Preguntas. First look at the cues in the right column and then complete the questions with **quién, cuándo, cuántos/as, cuál,** or **por qué,** as logical. Use your questions to interview two people as you walk around the room.

1. ¿ _Cuántas/Qué_ clases tomas? Tomo…
2. ¿ _Cuándo_ son tus clases? Por la…
3. ¿ _Cuál_ es tu clase favorita? La clase de…
4. ¿ _Quién_ es tu profesor/a favorito/a? El profesor/La profesora…
5. ¿ _Por qué/Cuándo_ estudias español? Porque…
6. ¿ _Cuántos_ estudiantes hay en tu clase Hay…
   de español?

1-33 Entrevista. Ask your classmate questions to find out the following information. Use the appropriate expressions to show disbelief, coincidence, how interesting the answers are, and so on.

1. número de clases que toma este semestre
2. su clase favorita y razón (y por qué)
3. número de alumnos en la clase favorita
4. nombre del profesor favorito/de la profesora favorita
5. lugar donde estudia generalmente y cuántas horas estudia por (*per*) día
6. lugar donde trabaja

> ### Lengua
>
> To request repetition or clarification of a statement, use **¿Cómo?** or **¿Perdón?** The use of **¿Qué?**, the equivalent of English *What?*, is generally considered rude by native speakers.

Follow-up for 1-32. Have students create more questions using the interrogative words in the directions.

Suggestion for 1-33. Students can interview each other in pairs, and then report to other students in groups of four. Encourage them to be creative and ask additional questions.

SITUACIONES

1. **Role A.** You have just run across a friend you have not seen all year. Inquire about your friend's life in college including a) the location and size of his/her college/university; b) courses this semester; and c) his/her activities.

   Role B. You are talking with a friend you have not seen in a long time. Answer your friend's questions about your life in college. Then ask your friend some questions to get the same information.

2. **Role A.** It is the beginning of the term, and you need to add a psychology class. One of your friends is in a class that looks promising. Ask a) who the professor is; b) if there is a lot of homework; c) when the class meets; and d) if there is an exam soon. Then ask if you should know (**saber**) anything else (**algo más**) about the class.

   Role B. Your friend wants some information about your psychology class. Reply as specifically as possible to all of his/her questions. Then offer some additional information about the class.

Suggestion for Situaciones. You may wish to have students review the phrases in the *En directo* boxes in this chapter to increase the amount of language they produce and to make their exchanges sound more natural.

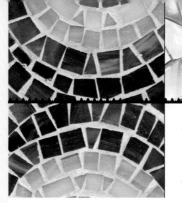

Audioscript for 1-35.

ANA: *Hola, Mario, ¿qué tal? ¿Cómo estás?*
MARIO: *Muy bien, ¿y tú?*
ANA: *Bien, gracias. ¿Estudias aquí este año?*
MARIO: *Sí, sólo este semestre.*
ANA: *¿Y qué clases tomas?*
MARIO: *Matemáticas, inglés, historia y geografía. ¿Y tú?*
ANA: *Yo tomo cinco clases: física, química, matemáticas, biología…*
MARIO: *¿Todas de ciencias? ¿No tomas clases de humanidades?*
ANA: *¡Oh, sí! También estudio literatura. Es una clase muy interesante, pero necesitamos leer mucho. Pasamos horas y horas en la biblioteca.*
MARIO: *¿Y quién es tu profesor?*
ANA: *Es una profesora que se llama Catalina Gómez. Es excelente. Pero mi clase favorita es la de biología. Trabajamos mucho en el laboratorio. ¿Y cuál es tu clase favorita, Mario?*
MARIO: *Pues, la clase de geografía.*
ANA: *¿Geografía?*
MARIO: *Sí, es excelente. Es una clase con computadoras. Visitamos un país diferente en cada clase: España, México, Colombia, Chile, Perú… Es una clase muy popular entre los estudiantes.*
ANA: *¡Qué interesante! ¡Uy! Son las tres menos diez. Mi clase de física es a las tres. Hablamos otro día.*

MOSAICOS

A escuchar

ESTRATEGIA

Listen for the gist

When you are having a conversation or are listening to other people talking in your native language, you may get the gist of what is said without understanding every word or paying attention to every detail. You do this by relying on what you do understand, your knowledge of the topic, and your subconscious expectations of what happens in a conversational exchange. You will find these techniques helpful when listening to Spanish.

Antes de escuchar

1-34 Preparación. You will hear two students talking about their classes. Before listening to the recording, think about the topics they may talk about and make a list of the things you may expect to hear, based on your experience as a student.

Escuchar

1-35 ¿Comprende usted? First read the following statements. Then listen to the conversation between Ana and Mario and indicate whether each statement is true (**Cierto**) or false (**Falso**).

CD 1
Track 27

1. <u>Cierto</u> Mario y Ana estudian en la misma (*same*) universidad este semestre.
2. <u>Cierto</u> Mario toma clases de ciencias y de humanidades.
3. <u>Cierto</u> Ana lee en la biblioteca para sus clases.
4. <u>Cierto</u> Ana toma clases por la tarde.
5. <u>Falso</u> Mario realmente visita otros países en una de sus clases.

Después de escuchar

1-36 Ahora usted. Tell your classmate what you usually do on the following days and times. Your classmate will take notes. Then switch roles. Finally, verify with each other that the notes you took are correct.

LUNES	MARTES	MIÉRCOLES	JUEVES	VIERNES
8:00 a.m.	3:00 p.m.	5:00 p.m.	9:00 p.m.	1:00 p.m.

A conversar

Resources
■ SAM: 1-42
■ *Entrevistas* video

ESTRATEGIA

Ask questions to gather information

Asking questions is a good way to get information, and it is also a way to make conversation, because most people like to talk about themselves. To ask questions, you need to remember question words and common phrases, like **¿Cómo es... ?**, **¿Cuánto cuesta... ?**, **¿Dónde... ?**, **¿Qué... ?**, and **¿Quién... ?**.

Antes de conversar

1-37 Preparación. Write the questions answered by the clerk at your campus bookstore.
Some questions may vary.

1. ¿Cuál es la dirección de la librería?/¿Dónde está la librería?　　La dirección de la librería es Calle Mayor, número 50.
2. ¿Tiene libros de historia de España en español?　　Sí, tengo libros de historia de España en español.
3. ¿Tiene diccionarios en español?　　Sí, tengo diccionarios en español.
4. ¿Cuánto cuesta el diccionario bilingüe?　　El diccionario bilingüe cuesta 40 euros.

Conversar

1-38 Entre nosotros. You are a Spaniard studying in Malaga. Your American friend would like to purchase some gifts to take home: a fancy pen, a book on the history of Spain, a Spanish dictionary, and a map of Spain. Read the following ad and call the bookstore to find out if it has what your friend needs. Your classmate will play the role of the bookstore clerk. Remember to follow the formalities of phone conversations with someone you do not know.

En directo

To answer the phone in Spain:

¿Diga?

To greet someone formally:

Buenos días./Buenas tardes.

To ask if they have what you need:

Necesito/Busco un/una…

LIBRERÍA CERVANTES

Papelería • Impresos • Artículos para escritorio

Libros de texto • Revistas

Casa especializada en estilógrafos y bolígrafos

Plaza Constitución, 3
29005　Málaga
Teléfono　221 19 99

Suggestions for 1-38. Here is some comprehensible input to use as a warm-up for this activity: *Este es un anuncio de una librería de Málaga. Málaga está al sur de España, en la región de Andalucía.* (Point to Málaga on a map of Spain.) *En la Universidad de Málaga, hay un programa muy importante para estudiantes extranjeros: alemanes, ingleses, franceses, norteamericanos, etc. Muchos estudiantes de este programa compran los materiales para sus clases en la Librería Cervantes.*

Point out differences between addresses written in Spanish and in English: placement of the number after the street name (introduced in *Capítulo preliminar*), and placement of the zip code (*código o zona postal*). Clarify words in the ad as necessary.

Have students perform the conversation at least twice so they can switch roles.

Después de conversar

1-39 Un poco más. Call your American friend to explain whether the bookstore has each item he/she needs and the price.

Resources

■ SAM: 1-43 to 1-45

ESTRATEGIA

Identify the format of a text

Even before you start to read, you may draw on your experience with reading texts of different types to support your comprehension. Visual cues, photographs, type size, and the layout will help you make educated guesses about the content and meaning of the text.

A leer

Antes de leer

1-40 Preparación. Indicate which courses from the list students in the following majors (**carreras**) should take.

anatomía
conflictos sociales
depresión
diseño gráfico

drogas tóxicas
estructura del español
fisiología
historia de la lengua

medicinas alternativas
muralistas mexicanos

MEDICINA	BELLAS ARTES	FARMACIA	PSICOLOGÍA	FILOLOGÍA
fisiología	diseño gráfico	drogas tóxicas	conflictos sociales	estructura del español
anatomía	muralistas mexicanos	medicinas alternativas	depresión	historia de la lengua

Leer

1-41 Primera mirada. Circle the letter that completes each statement, based on the information in this web page.

1. Esta es una...   a. página de un libro.   **b.** página web.
2. El logo indica que esta institución es...   a. muy nueva.   **b.** muy antigua.
3. Esta página web presenta una lista de...   **a.** carreras.   b. clases.
4. La información de esta página web es...   a. muy específica.   **b.** muy general.
5. Esta institución tiene...   a. un campus.   **b.** más de un campus.

1-42 Segunda mirada. Answer the following questions, according to the information in the text.

1. Al final (*the bottom*) de esta página web hay varias teclas (*keys*). ¿Qué tecla usan los estudiantes para conversar con personas que trabajan en la Universidad de Salamanca? Aquí está Nuestro Chat
2. Imagínese que usted necesita información sobre su carrera en la Universidad de Salamanca. ¿Qué facultad tiene la información que usted necesita? Answers may vary.

Después de leer

1-43 Ampliación. Explore the **Servicio Central de Idiomas** page on the Universidad de Salamanca website by following the link on the *Mosaicos* website and answer the questions that accompany the link. Be prepared to share your answers with the rest of the class.

A escribir

Antes de escribir

1-44 Preparación. As part of course work in your Spanish class, you have been asked to correspond by e-mail with a university student in Spain. Think about and write down the information you would like to include in your first e-mail. Brainstorm…

1. some basic questions that this Spanish student may have about your college life.
2. some words and ideas that will help you answer those questions.
3. the order in which you will organize these ideas.

Escribir

1-45 Manos a la obra. Now write the Spanish student an e-mail about life at your college or university. Use the information you gathered in *Preparación*. Consider including the following points, if you have not already listed them.

1. introducing yourself
2. telling how things are going for you
3. describing your school and your classes: class number and names, when you are taking them, how interesting (or not) your classes and professors are
4. describing your daily routine at school, what you do after classes and on weekends, where and with whom you do these activities, and so on

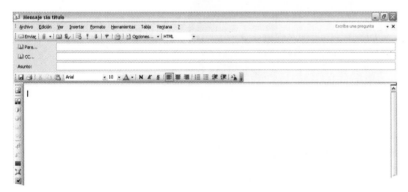

Después de escribir

1-46 Revisión. After writing your e-mail, you may discuss it with a classmate. Then go over it carefully.

1. Make sure you have provided all the information your Spanish friend may need or any other you deem necessary. Pay attention to the content of your message and to the order in which you presented the information.
2. Revise any errors in language use, spelling, punctuation, accentuation, and so on.
3. Finally, make any changes that will help make your email clear and comprehensible to your e-mail pen pal.

ESTRATEGIA

Brainstorm key ideas before writing

Brainstorming stimulates your creativity and helps you access your ideas. To brainstorm, make a note on a blank paper or computer screen of an idea or perspective you may want to emphasize. List words and ideas that will answer any questions that may arise.

Then organize them in the order in which you will use them in your text.

Thinking ahead and jotting down key words and ideas before you start to write your first draft is useful. It helps you think logically, focus on the topic, and put ideas in your own words.

Resources

■ SAM: 1-46 to 1-48

Suggestions for Estrategia. Suggest students set a time limit (10–15 minutes) to relax and let their minds explore the ideas they associate with the topic. Remind students to keep their reader in mind and the questions the reader may have as they read the text.

Note for 1-44. This activity helps students focus on both the rhetorical aspects of their text (i.e., gathering and organizing ideas), as well as on form, accurate use of vocabulary, language structures (tense, agreement), and mechanics of writing in Spanish.

Suggestions for 1-44. You may wish to have students do *Preparación* in pairs. You may also want to model the brainstorming process. Keep input (teacher-talk) as natural and spontaneous as possible so students become comfortable with discussing the writing process. Accept any complete or partial response. Keep in mind that this is probably the students' first formal experience writing in Spanish. Elicit information from them rather than give it yourself. If you decide to have students do the task in pairs, have them approach it as if they were one writer, using the first person singular.

Suggestion for 1-46. You may guide students as to what to pay attention to as they revise their text. At this stage, they should read their text holistically, concentrating on content (quality and quantity), organization, and form. Encourage them to use the knowledge they already possess in English about text organization in writing in Spanish.

ENFOQUE CULTURAL

Escuelas y universidades en España

El sistema escolar español es diferente del sistema de Estados Unidos y está dividido en cuatro partes: Educación Infantil, Educación Primaria, Educación Superior Obligatoria y, finalmente, el Bachillerato. En España, los niños y niñas hacen la Educación Infantil (que no es obligatoria sino voluntaria) hasta los seis años. Después empiezan la Educación Primaria, que es obligatoria y dura seis cursos, de los seis a los doce años de edad.

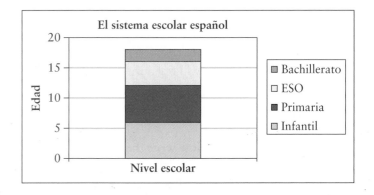

Entre los doce y los dieciséis años, los niños y niñas españoles cursan la Escuela Superior Obligatoria (ESO). La ESO completa la escolaridad obligatoria, pero muchos españoles continúan estudiando dos años más para terminar el Bachillerato, que los prepara para continuar con los estudios universitarios.

Rectorado de la Universidad Complutense

En otras palabras

Expresiones españolas

¡Vamos de tapas!
Let's go out for tapas!

¡Me han **cateado**!
They've flunked me!

Ella es muy **maja**.
She's a very nice person.

Te llamo luego, **¿vale?**
I'll call you later, OK?

¿Dónde está ese **chaval**?
Where is that kid?

En España hay muchas universidades. La Universidad de Salamanca es una de las más antiguas del mundo y una de las más importantes de Europa. Esta universidad tiene un excelente programa de español para extranjeros y sus cursos de verano (durante junio, julio y agosto) tienen mucho prestigio.

De otra parte, la Universidad Complutense de Madrid es la más grande de España y también es muy antigua. Tiene un campus muy grande que se llama Ciudad Universitaria. Este nombre es muy apropiado, porque tiene más de 100.000 estudiantes.

El fútbol es un deporte muy popular en España.

In all the *Enfoque cultural* sections, the *expresiones* in *En otras palabras* are presented as spoken expressions. Students should not be expected to use them in writing.

En general, en las universidades españolas los estudiantes practican muchos deportes, pero la competencia entre universidades no es tan intensa como en Estados Unidos. Los deportes más populares entre los estudiantes universitarios españoles son el fútbol, el baloncesto y el atletismo, pero muchos estudiantes practican otros deportes también.

Los estudiantes universitarios españoles, como los de Estados Unidos, se divierten bailando en discotecas y clubes. Pero la música que escuchan no es necesariamente igual. A los jóvenes españoles les gusta escuchar música de rock en español. Hay muchos grupos de rock españoles. "El canto del loco" y "Fito y Fitipaldi" son dos grupos de rock español muy populares. A muchos jóvenes también les gusta bailar el flamenco, la música tradicional de Andalucía. En Sevilla, por ejemplo, hay clubes donde sólo tocan sevillanas, una música típica de esta ciudad. Finalmente, en su tiempo libre, muchos estudiantes españoles van de tapas y, por ejemplo, la Ciudad Universitaria está cerca de muchos bares de tapas.

Note to Student

In each chapter, the reading in *Enfoque cultural* is followed by two activities, *Comprensión* and *Use la información*. You have the option of doing *Comprensión* here or visiting the *Mosaicos* web page and following the link to that activity to download the worksheet.

1-47 Comprensión. **PRIMERA FASE. Reconocimiento de palabras clave.** Find in the text the Spanish word or phrase that best expresses the meaning of the following concepts:

preschool <u>educación infantil</u>

middle school <u>Educación Superior Obligatoria (ESO)</u>

high school <u>bachillerato</u>

summer school <u>cursos de verano</u>

soccer <u>fútbol</u>

track <u>atletismo</u>

dance <u>bailar</u>

SEGUNDA FASE. Oraciones importantes. Underline the statements that contain ideas found in the text. Then indicate where in the text those ideas appear.

1. Some Spanish students finish school at sixteen, while others continue with their education until they are eighteen.
2. Kindergarten is compulsory in Spain at the age of six.
3. Spanish universities are mostly private institutions.
4. The University of Salamanca has a long history.
5. The University of Madrid is so big that it is like a small city in itself.
6. Spanish universities offer their students the opportunity to practice sports.
7. Fito and Fitipaldi are two famous Spanish Formula drivers.
8. Many Spanish students enjoy dancing to traditional Spanish music.

TERCERA FASE. Ideas principales. Write a brief paragraph in English summarizing the main ideas expressed in the text.

1-48 Use la información. Prepare a poster to present to the class comparing what you have learned about the educational system of Spain to that of your own country. Use visuals to illustrate the different stages of the educational system, a few of the oldest and most important universities, and some of the activities that are popular with students in their free time.

VOCABULARIO

01
28-34

Las materias o asignaturas — *Subjects*

la antropología	*anthropology*
las ciencias políticas	*political science*
la economía	*economics*
el español	*Spanish*
la estadística	*statistics*
la geografía	*geography*
la historia	*history*
la informática/	*computer*
la computación	*science*
la literatura	*literature*
la psicología	*psychology*
la sociología	*sociology*

Los lugares — *Places*

la biblioteca	*library*
el café	*cafe, coffee shop*
la cafetería	*cafeteria*
la casa	*house, home*
la discoteca	*dance club*
el gimnasio	*gymnasium*
el laboratorio	*laboratory*
la librería	*bookstore*
la oficina	*office*
la playa	*beach*
la plaza	*plaza, square*
la universidad	*university*

Las Facultades — *Schools, departments*

de Arquitectura	*of Architecture*
de Ciencias	*of Sciences*
de Humanidades	*of Humanities*
de Informática	*of Computer Science*
de Medicina	*of Medicine*

Las personas — *People*

el alumno/la alumna	*student*
el compañero/	*partner,*
la compañera	*classmate*
el dependiente/	
la dependienta	*salesperson*
ellos/ellas	*they*
nosotros/nosotras	*we*
ustedes	*you* (plural)

Las descripciones — *Descriptions*

aburrido/a	*boring*
antiguo/a	*old*
bueno/a	*good*
difícil	*difficult*
estudioso/a	*studious*
excelente	*excellent*
fácil	*easy*
favorito/a	*favorite*
grande	*big*
interesante	*interesting*
malo/a	*bad*
norteamericano/a	*North American*
pequeño/a	*small*

Verbos — *Verbs*

aprender	*to learn*
asistir	*to attend*
bailar	*to dance*
beber	*to drink*
buscar	*to look for*
caminar	*to walk*
comer	*to eat*
comprar	*to buy*
comprender	*to understand*
conversar	*to talk, to converse*
correr	*to run*
deber	*should*
escribir	*to write*
escuchar	*to listen (to)*
estar	*to be*
estudiar	*to study*
hablar	*to speak*
leer	*to read*
llegar	*to arrive*
mirar	*to look (at)*
montar (en bicicleta)	*to ride (a bicycle)*
necesitar	*to need*
participar	*to participate*
practicar	*to practice*
sacar buenas/malas notas	*to get good/bad grades*
tomar	*to take; to drink*
tomar apuntes/notas	*to take notes*
trabajar	*to work*
ver	*to see*
vivir	*to live*

Palabras y expresiones útiles — *Useful words and expressions*

ahora	*now*
algo	*something*
¡Buena suerte!	*Good luck!*
¿Cómo te va?	*How is it going?*
con	*with*
¿Cuánto cuesta?	*How much is it?*
el diccionario	*dictionary*
este/a	*this*
el examen	*test*
el fin de semana	*weekend*
para	*for, to*
pero	*but*
¡Qué lástima!	*What a pity!*
sólo	*only* (adv.)
también	*also*
la tarea	*homework*
tengo/tienes	*I have/you have*
¿verdad?	*right?*

See page 33 for expressions of frequency.
See page 44 for question words.

53

Resources

■ IRM: Syllabi & Lesson Plans

Note. This painting is by Cristina Cárdenas, an artist of Mexican origin who lives in Tucson, Arizona. (Write or say: *Es de México, pero vive en Estados Unidos.* Introduce *hispano/a* and *latino/a*. Explain *mestizo/a* by writing *origen español + origen indígena = mestizo/a*.) The works of Cárdenas are mostly autobiographical. She often portrays women with complex cultural identities. The title of this work, *Yo soy/Myself*, emphasizes her bilingual and bicultural status in the U.S.

Suggestion. Point out that the girl in this painting holds a very small paintbrush as a tribute to Frida Kahlo, with whom the artist identifies. Show the class some of Kahlo's paintings to compare themes. Then ask questions about *Yo soy/Myself*, recycling vocabulary from previous chapters and introducing other vocabulary,

Mis amigos y yo

Yo soy/Myself, por Cristina Cárdenas, una pintora norteamericana de origen mexicano

In this chapter you will learn how to:

- describe people, places, and things
- state where and when events take place
- express origin and possession
- express likes and dislikes

Cultural focus: Estados Unidos

OCÉANO PACÍFICO

CANADÁ

Un rapero latino, Daddy Yankee

Los actores hispanos Antonio Banderas y Salma Hayek

San Francisco

Chicago

New York
Philadelphia

**E S T A D O S
U N I D O S**

OCÉANO ATLÁNTICO

Los Angeles

Santa Fe

Phoenix

Tucson

Una margarita con guacamole y chips

Houston

San Antonio

Golfo de México

MÉXICO

Miami

Calle Ocho, Miami

El Álamo, San Antonio, Texas

A vista de pájaro. Using the map and photos, as well as what you may already know, provide the following facts about Hispanics.

1. Tres hispanos famosos Answers may vary.
2. El grupo hispano más numeroso en Estados Unidos mexicano
3. La ciudad (*city*) en Estados Unidos con más puertorriqueños Nueva York
4. El estado con más mexicanos California
5. Un producto hispano Answers may vary.
6. Un tipo de música latina Answers may vary.

A PRIMERA VISTA

Mis amigos y yo

¿Quiénes somos?

CD 1
Track 35

Me llamo Mario Quintana. Soy de Puerto Rico y **tengo** veintidós **años. Me gusta** escuchar música y mirar televisión. Estudio en una universidad de Nueva York y **deseo** ser profesor de historia. Los chicos en estas fotografías son mis amigos. Ellos también son **hispanos** y estudian en la universidad. **Todos** somos **bilingües**.

Cultura

Puerto Rico was a Spanish colony for almost four centuries until it was ceded to the United States following the Spanish-American War in 1898. Puerto Rico is a freely associated commonwealth (*estado libre asociado*) of the United States, and its people have been U.S. citizens since 1917. Most Puerto Ricans on the mainland live in New York; New Jersey, Pennsylvania, and Illinois also have large Puerto Rican communities. However, Puerto Rico remains geographically and culturally part of Latin America and almost all of its residents speak Spanish as their primary language. English is also widely spoken. Being bilingual opens doors to better economic opportunities in Puerto Rico and on the mainland.

Esta chica es Amanda Martone. Es **alta, delgada** y **morena.** Tiene los **ojos** de color café y el **pelo negro** y muy **largo.** Amanda es una chica muy **agradable.** Estudia **mucho** y desea ser economista. Su familia es dominicana, pero vive en Estados Unidos.

Esta chica se llama Ana Villegas. No es alta ni baja. Es de **estatura mediana** y usa **lentes de contacto.** Es **pelirroja** y tiene los ojos **oscuros.** Ana es **callada, trabajadora** y muy inteligente. Sus padres son cubanos.

Este chico se llama Ernesto Fernández. Ernesto es moreno y tiene los ojos **castaños** y el pelo **corto.** Es **bajo, fuerte,** muy **conversador** y **simpático. Le gusta usar** la computadora para conversar con sus amigos de aquí y de México.

Esta chica es Marta Chávez Conde. Es española y tiene veintiún años. Es **rubia**, tiene los ojos **azules** y es muy **divertida**. Este año está en Estados Unidos con su familia.

2-1 Asociaciones. To whom do the descriptions on the left refer?

1. _b_ Tiene el pelo largo.
2. _a_ Tiene veintidós años.
3. _e_ Es de España.
4. _c_ Es bajo y fuerte.
5. _d_ Usa lentes de contacto.
6. _c_ Habla mucho.
7. _b_ Tiene los ojos de color café.
8. _b_ Tiene el pelo negro y es muy agradable.
9. _e_ Tiene los ojos azules y el pelo rubio, es muy divertida.
10. _a_ Desea ser profesor de historia.

a. Mario Quintana
b. Amanda Martone
c. Ernesto Fernández
d. Ana Villegas
e. Marta Chávez Conde

2-2 ¿Quién es? PRIMERA FASE. Read the texts on pages 56–57 again and write a list of at least eight expressions that you may use to describe people, including physical appearance (*apariencia*) and personality traits (*personalidad*).

SEGUNDA FASE. Now, without mentioning his/her name, describe a classmate in at least three sentences, using the vocabulary from the *Primera fase*, or any other that you may need. The rest of the group will try to guess who this person is. The group can ask questions if more information is needed to guess the student's identity.

MODELO: E1: *Es de estatura mediana y delgado. Tiene el pelo negro. Es fuerte y callado.*
E2: *¿Es... ?*

Lengua

Depending on the region or country, *moreno/a* or *negro/a* may be used to refer to African ancestry and skin color or to hair color. The word *trigueño/a* (from *trigo*, wheat) is used to describe light brown skin color. *Corto/a* generally refers to length (*pelo corto*), while *bajo/a* refers to height (*Ella es baja*).

2-3 ¿Qué me gusta? Tell your classmate if you like each of the following activities. Then compare your responses.

comer en restaurantes italianos
escribir correos electrónicos
bailar los sábados por la noche

estudiar español
trabajar los fines de semana
tomar café por la noche

practicar tenis/fútbol/béisbol
tener animales en casa

MODELO: estar en casa por las noches
E1: *¿Te gusta estar en casa por las noches?*
E2: *Sí, me gusta. /No, no me gusta.*

Las descripciones

CD 1
Track 36

¿Cómo son estas personas?

fuerte   débil   joven   vieja/mayor   lista   tonto

trabajador   perezoso   simpático   antipático   triste   alegre

pobre   rica   casado   soltero

¿Cómo son estos animales?

CD 1
Track 37

Este perro es **feo** y **gordo**.

Esta gata es **bonita** y **delgada**.

2-4 Opuestos. Complete the following statements about these famous people.

MODELO: *Shakira no es mayor, es joven.*

1. _c_ Penélope Cruz no es gorda, es…
2. _a_ El presidente de la compañía no es perezoso, es…
3. _f_ Jennifer López no es antipática, es…
4. _b_ Madonna no es tonta, es…
5. _d_ Bill Gates no es pobre, es…
6. _e_ Enrique Iglesias no es feo, es…

a. trabajador
b. lista
c. delgada
d. rico
e. guapo
f. simpática

¿De qué color son estas cosas?

CD 1
Track 38

Este auto es **rojo** y es muy bueno.

Esta flor es **amarilla** y **blanca**. Es muy bonita.

La silla **azul** es alta.

La silla **verde** es baja.

Otros colores

CD 1
Track 39

marrón

gris

rosado

morado

anaranjado

negro

Lengua

The word **la pierna** (*leg*) is used with both humans and animals. *Foot* is **el pie** (humans) and **la pata** (animals).

En otras palabras

Depending on the region, Spanish speakers may use **bonita**, **linda**, or **guapa** to refer to a female. **Bien parecido**, **buen mozo**, **guapo** are usually used to refer to a male.

En otras palabras

Depending on the country and what is described, Spanish has various words to express the color brown: **café**, **marrón**, **carmelita**, **castaño/a**, and **pardo/a**. The words **naranja** and **rosa** are also used instead of **anaranjado/a** and **rosado/a**.

Suggestion. Bring photos of people and animals to class or ask students to bring them. Distribute the photos and have students work in groups to describe them. They should describe people by giving both physical characteristics and personality traits. For fun, you may have students assign animals some human personality traits, for example: *el gato es callado y perezoso, el perro es romántico*, etc.

Suggestion. Use the drawings on the previous page to introduce some body parts. Then point to your body or use photos to show: *la cabeza, las piernas, las manos, los pies*. Other parts of the body appear pear in *Capítulo 9*.

Suggestion. Bring in pictures of flowers and describe them to introduce colors. Also use brochures/ads for cars. Ask students about their preferences. Encourage them to describe the cars, giving colors and features. You may also introduce words such as *suéter, blusa, camisa*, and ask: *¿De qué color es el suéter de… ? ¿Y la blusa de… ?*

2-5 ¿De qué color son estas banderas (*flags*)? PRIMERA FASE. Read each description and then write the name of the country under its flag.

1. La bandera de Bolivia es roja, amarilla y verde.
2. La bandera de Estados Unidos es roja, blanca y azul.
3. La bandera de España es roja y amarilla.
4. La bandera de México es verde, blanca y roja.
5. La bandera de Colombia es amarilla, azul y roja.

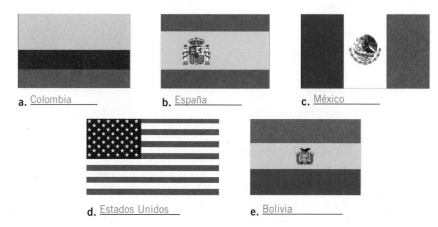

a. Colombia   b. España   c. México

d. Estados Unidos   e. Bolivia

SEGUNDA FASE. Take turns choosing a color and stating how many objects of that color are in the classroom. Your classmate will guess the color.

MODELO: E1: *Hay dos mochilas y ocho pantalones vaqueros (jeans).*
         E2: *Es el azul.*

 2-6 Vamos a describir. Describe the people in these photos.

Suggestion for 2-6. You may wish to introduce the words *mujer/hombre*. Brainstorm with students to get them started by asking questions based on the photos: *¿Cómo es esta mujer? ¿Es joven o mayor? ¿Este hombre es simpático o antipático?* Encourage students to recycle vocabulary by imagining personality traits for the people in the four photos.

Eva   Alicia y Raquel   Alejandro   José Luis

2-7 ¿Quién soy? Write a brief description of yourself including at least three physical traits, two personality traits, and two activities that you like to do. Do not include your name on the paper. Give the paper to your instructor. He/She will ask each student to pick a description, read it, and try to guess who wrote it.

El origen

◄)) **¿De dónde son... ?**

CD 1
Track 40

2-8 Nacionalidades. PRIMERA FASE. Indicate the nationalities of the following people.

MODELO: *Carolina Herrera es una diseñadora famosa de Venezuela.*
   Es <u>venezolana</u>.

1. Albert Pujols es un jugador de béisbol de República Dominicana.
   Es <u>dominicano</u> .
2. Salma Hayek es una actriz de México, protagonista de *Frida.* Es <u>mexicana</u>.
3. Rigoberta Menchú es una activista de Guatemala, Premio Nobel de la Paz, 1992. Es <u>guatemalteca</u>.
4. Julio Bocca es un bailarín de Argentina. Es <u>argentino</u>.
5. Isabel Allende es escritora, originaria de Chile, autora de *La casa de los espíritus.* Es <u>chilena</u>.
6. Oprah Winfrey es una presentadora de televisión de Estados Unidos.
   Es ——————. norteamericana/americana/estadounidense
7. Gabriel García Márquez es un escritor de Colombia, autor de *Cien años de soledad,* Premio Nobel, 1982. Es <u>colombiano</u>.
8. Ricky Martin es un cantante de Puerto Rico. Es <u>puertorriqueño</u>.

En directo

To express some reasons why a person might interest you:

Me gustan sus libros.

Escribe novelas fascinantes.

Trabaja por los pobres.

Es muy guapo/bonita/elegante.

Baila muy bien.

SEGUNDA FASE. Which of the personalities in the *Primera fase* is interesting to you? Why?

MODELO: *Para mí, …es interesante. Es un actor famoso/una actriz famosa.*

 2-9 Adivinanzas (*Guesses*). Think of a well-known person. A classmate will try to guess the identity by asking you questions.

MODELO:
E1: *¿De dónde es?*
E2: *Es estadounidense./Es de Estados Unidos.*
E1: *¿Cómo es?*
E2: *Es de estatura mediana, rubio y muy rico.*
E1: *¿Qué es?/¿En qué trabaja?*
E2: *Es actor.*
E1: *¿Es Brad Pitt?*
E2: *¡Sí!*

 2-10 Entrevista. PRIMERA FASE. Interview a classmate to find out the following information:

1. his/her name
2. his/her age
3. what he/she is like
4. the things he/she likes to do
5. where he/she is from
6. …

SEGUNDA FASE. Write an introduction to the interview and a description of this person, including physical traits. Then share it with the class.

2-11 ¡Hola! PRIMERA FASE. You will hear a student describe himself. Before you listen, mark (✓) in the *Antes de escuchar* column the information you think he may provide.

CD 1
Track 41

Answers may vary.

	ANTES DE ESCUCHAR	DESPUÉS DE ESCUCHAR
1. name		✓
2. age		✓
3. parents' names		
4. physical description		✓
5. country where he was born		✓
6. place where he intends to work		

SEGUNDA FASE. Now, listen and pay attention to the general idea of what is said. Then, in the *Después de escuchar* column, indicate which information the speaker provided.

EN ACCIÓN

Diarios de bicicleta: ¿Una cantante divina?

Antes de ver

2-12 PRIMERA FASE. How well do you remember? Indicate whether the following statements refer to Javier (**J**) or to Daniel (**D**).

1. _D_ Es mexicano.   2. _D_ Es muy puntual.   3. _J_ Es colombiano.

SEGUNDA FASE. In this segment a singer is scheduled to audition for a role in an upcoming musical. Guess what she looks like by underlining one sentence in each pair.

1. Es bonita. Es fea.
2. Es joven. Es vieja.
3. Tiene el pelo corto. Tiene el pelo largo.
4. Tiene los ojos verdes. Tiene los ojos negros.

Mientras ve

2-13 Indicate whether each statement is **cierto** (**C**) or **falso** (**F**) according to the video segment. Correct the statements that are false.

1. _F_ Los amigos están en la cafetería. Los amigos están en un teatro.
2. _C_ Luciana y Gabi necesitan escuchar audiciones para un nuevo musical.
3. _C_ Beatriz Condes canta una canción tradicional mexicana.
4. _C_ Beatriz Condes canta mal.

Después de ver

2-14 At the end of the video segment, a new character appears. Write five sentences in Spanish describing her. Answers may vary.

Note for 2-12. Students are asked to recall information about Javier and Daniel. You may wish to incorporate the characters, settings, and events of the video in class activities or examples.

Suggestion for 2-13. Encourage student self-expression by guiding them to correct the *Falso* statements in simple language and by using the language of the printed statement when possible.

63

FUNCIONES Y FORMAS

Resources

■ SAM: 2-14 to 2-18
■ Supp. Activ. Book: Adjectives
■ PPTs
■ *Situaciones adicionales*

Note. Adjectives and adjective agreement have been previewed in the *A primera vista* section of this chapter. Guide students to notice that adjective endings usually indicate gender and number and that masculine plural adjectives are used for mixed-gender groups.

Suggestions. Use visuals to practice noun-adjective agreement or personalize by describing students: *José es un chico alto y simpático.* Write *chico alto* on the board, underlining the *o*. Do the same with a feminine noun and adjective. Write the plural. Ask yes/no and either/or questions regarding students. Ask about courses with adjectives ending in *-e*, such as *interesante: ¿Es interesante la historia? Y el español, ¿es interesante? Y las ciencias, ¿son interesantes?* Have students work in pairs to find out courses or subject areas that their partners find *interesante(s)* or *aburrido/a(s)* and share opinions with the class. Practice adjectives that end in a consonant and adjectives of nationality: *Antonio Banderas es español. Penélope Cruz es española. Ella es una actriz excelente. Antonio Banderas y Penélope Cruz son muy famosos.* Students in groups find out the programs, sports figures, actors, or singers popular in their groups and compare findings.

1. Describing people, places, and things: Adjectives

Eduardo es alt**o** y atlétic**o**.

Adriana es baj**a** y es muy elegante.

Ana, Patricia y Teresa estudian mucho. Son inteligent**es** y trabajador**as**.

Carlos, Luis y Carmen son sociabl**es** y activ**os**. Conversan y bailan mucho en los clubes.

Piénselo. Complete the descriptions of the people in the drawings by supplying their names.

1. _____Adriana_____ es jove**n** y delgad**a**.
2. _____Ana_____ , _____Patricia_____ y _____Teresa_____ son interesant**es** y estudios**as**.
3. _____Eduardo_____ **es** moren**o** y guap**o**.
4. _____Carlos_____ , _____Luis_____ y _____Carmen_____ son popular**es** y activ**os**.
5. _____Eduardo_____ es colombian**o**.
6. _____Ana_____ , _____Patricia_____ y _____Teresa._____ son español**as**.

■ Adjectives are words that describe people, places, and things. Like articles (**el, la, los, las**) and nouns (**chica, chicas; libro, libros**), they generally have more than one form. In Spanish an adjective must agree in gender (masculine or feminine) and number (singular or plural) with the noun or pronoun it describes. Adjectives that describe characteristics usually follow the noun.

■ Most masculine adjectives end in **-o**, and most feminine adjectives end in **-a**. To form the plural, these adjectives add **-s**.

	MASCULINE	FEMININE
SINGULAR	el chico alt**o**	la chic**a** alt**a**
PLURAL	los chic**os** alt**os**	las chic**as** alt**as**

■ Adjectives that end in **-e** and some adjectives that end in a consonant have the same form for both masculine and feminine. To form the plural, adjectives that end in **-e** add **-s**; those that end in a consonant add **-es**.

	MASCULINE	FEMININE
SINGULAR	un lib**ro** interesant**e**	una revis**ta** (*magazine*) interesant**e**
	un cuadern**o** azu**l**	una mochi**la** azu**l**
PLURAL	unos lib**ros** interesant**es**	unas revis**tas** interesant**es**
	unos cuadern**os** azu**les**	unas mochi**las** azu**les**

■ Other adjectives that end in a consonant add **-a** to form the feminine and **-es** or **-as** to form the plurals.

	MASCULINE	FEMININE
SINGULAR	el alumn**o** español	la alumn**a** español**a**
	el alumn**o** hablador	la alumn**a** hablador**a**
PLURAL	los alumn**os** español**es**	las alumn**as** español**as**
	los alumn**os** hablador**es**	las alumn**as** hablador**as**

■ Adjectives that end in **-ista** are both masculine and feminine. To form the plurals, add **-s**.

Pedro es muy optim**ista**,	*Pedro is very optimistic,*
pero Alicia es pesim**ista**.	*but Alicia is pessimistic.*
Ellos no son material**istas**.	*They are not materialistic.*

2-15 ¿Cómo son estas personas? Choose the correct completion to describe the following people. More than one answer may be possible.

1. Muchos alumnos de mi universidad son…
   - **a.** latinoamericano.
   - (**b.**) hispanos.
   - **c.** norteamericanas.
   - (**d.**) mexicanos.

2. Mi profesora favorita es muy…
   - (**a.**) joven.
   - **b.** activo.
   - (**c.**) inteligente.
   - **d.** delgado.

3. Mi amigo Nicolás es muy…
   - **a.** tonta.
   - (**b.**) fuerte.
   - (**c.**) callado.
   - **d.** antipática.

4. Las dos chicas más inteligentes de la clase son…
   - **a.** activos y sociables.
   - (**b.**) trabajadoras y estudiosas.
   - **c.** altos y morenos.
   - **d.** interesante y optimista.

2-16 Cualidades necesarias. Your school is hiring recent graduates to help recruit students interested in studying other languages and cultures. Mark (✓) the qualities you think these new employees should have and then describe them to a partner, making sure that adjectives agree with nouns. Your partner will mention additional qualities.

MODELO: dos empleados bilingües en inglés y español
   E1: *Los empleados bilingües hablan bien inglés y español. Son activos y extrovertidos.*
   E2: *Sí. Son simpáticos, no son antipáticos. Hablan con los estudiantes y los padres de los estudiantes.*

1. dos especialistas en computadoras para el laboratorio de lenguas

   ____ activo   ____ bilingüe   ____ competente   ____ pasivo
   ____ agradable   ____ callado   ____ extrovertido   ____ trabajador

2. una recepcionista para la Oficina de Admisiones

   ____ eficiente   ____ imparcial   ____ perezoso   ____ simpático
   ____ hablador   ____ interesante   ____ perfeccionista ____ tímido

⊗ **Standard 4.1.** Students demonstrate an understanding of the nature of language through comparisons of the language studied and their own. Students encounter many opportunities to reflect on the different ways that languages accomplish the same function. The characteristics of adjectives in Spanish—different forms for masculine/feminine, singular/plural; placement before/after the noun—can serve as the starting point for reflection on the fact that languages express meanings in different ways.

Note. Point out that *bueno/a*, *malo/a*, *grande* may precede or follow the noun. Explain that *bueno* and *malo* are shortened before a masculine singular noun: *un buen gimnasio, un mal profesor.* Also mention that *grande* is shortened to *gran* before a masculine or feminine singular noun: *una gran casa.*

Note for 2-15. In this activity, students must recognize only the appropriate adjectives according to context. In the activities that follow they will be required to make adjectives agree with nouns.

Expansion for 2-16. Remind students to pay attention to whether they are describing males or females, or one or more persons.

Encourage them to provide additional adjectives. Model or brainstorm adjectives they can use for variety. They may also use the negative with the opposite quality: *La directora de relaciones públicas no es antipática. Por el contrario, es muy simpática.*

Also encourage students to ask questions, such as: *¿Es joven/Son jóvenes? ¿Habla(n) español bien? ¿Cómo se llama(n)?*

2-17 Personas importantes. PRIMERA FASE. With your partner, take turns describing the people in the photos. Use at least three of the following descriptions: *atlético, cómico, extrovertido, guapo, inteligente, liberal, serio, simpático, tiene el pelo…, tiene los ojos…, trabajador, …*

Jimmy Smits es un actor famos**o** de cine (*movies*) y televisión.

Tish Hinojosa es una cantante mexicano-american**a**. Canta y escribe canciones también.

Julia Álvarez es una novelista y poeta dominican**a**. También es profesora.

Alex Rodríguez es un jugador de béisbol muy buen**o**.

 SEGUNDA FASE. Now, take turns describing someone important in your life. Your partner will ask questions to get more information about that person.

En directo

To address someone on the phone about an ad:

Hola, buenos días, llamo por el anuncio…

To respond:

¡Ah, sí, hola! Buenos días…

To greet someone you know on the phone:

Hola, ¿qué tal?

Soy María… /Habla María…

To respond:

Ah, ¡hola!

¿Qué tal, María?/¿Cómo estás?

SITUACIONES

1. **Role A.** You have just rented an apartment near campus and are looking for a roommate (**compañero/a de apartamento**). You receive a call from an interested student. Verify the student's name and ask a) where he/she is from; b) what his/her personality traits are; c) if he/she works and, if so, where; and d) what he/she likes to do in his/her free time (**tiempo libre**).

   Role B. Through an ad (**anuncio**) on a campus bulletin board, you see that someone is looking for a roommate (**compañero/a de apartamento**). You call that person. Answer his/her questions in detail and ask any questions you may have.

2. **Role A.** Your friend calls to tell you that he/she has been dating someone new. Ask a) where your friend's new boyfriend/girlfriend (**novio/a**) is from; b) what he/she is like; c) what he/she studies; d) if he/she has a car and, if so, what it looks like (color, size); and e) at least one other question of your own invention.

   Role B. You call your friend to talk about your new boyfriend/girlfriend. Your friend asks a lot of questions. Answer in as much detail as possible.

2-19 ¿Cómo y dónde? Ask what the following people, places, and objects are like. For your Spanish class, ask when and where it takes place, and for the computer lab, ask where it is located, as well as what the computers are like.

MODELO: tu profesor/a de inglés
E1:   *¿Cómo es tu profesor de inglés?*
E2:   *Es alto, moreno y muy simpático.*

1. tus amigos
2. tu cuarto (*bedroom*)
3. tu compañero/a de cuarto (*roommate*)
4. el auto de tu mejor amigo/a
5. la clase de español
6. el laboratorio de computadoras

2-20 ¿Qué es esto? Take turns to describe an object and its location in the classroom. Your partner will ask you questions and guess what it is.

MODELO: E1:   *Es grande, es de plástico, está al lado de la ventana.*
E2:   *¿De qué color es?*
E1:   *Es roja.*
E2:   *¿Es la mochila de Juan?*

> ### Lengua
>
> **Madera** (*wood*), **plástico**, **tela** (*fabric*), **metal**, **oro** (*gold*), **vidrio** (*glass*) are some words used to describe what something is made of.

2-21 Eventos y lugares. You are working at the university's information booth, and a visitor (your classmate) stops by. Answer his/her questions. Then switch roles.

MODELO: la exposición del club de fotografía

VISITANTE: *Perdón/Disculpe, ¿dónde es la exposición del club de fotografía?*

EMPLEADO/A: *Es en la biblioteca.*

VISITANTE: *¿Dónde está la biblioteca?*

EMPLEADO/A: *Está en la calle Madison, enfrente del edificio (building) de biología.*

1. el concierto de música salsa
2. la conferencia (*lecture*) sobre el arte mexicano
3. el banquete para los estudiantes internacionales
4. la reunión de profesores
5. la fiesta del club de español
6. la ceremonia de graduación

SITUACIONES

1. **Role A.** You meet a student from a Spanish-speaking country in one of your classes. Introduce yourself and find out a) the student's name; b) his/her city and country of origin; c) characteristics of his/her city; and d) what his/her friends are like.

   Role B. You are an international student from a Spanish-speaking country. Answer your classmate's questions and then ask questions to get the same information he/she obtained from you.

2. **Role A.** A friend has invited you to a party at his/her house on Saturday. Ask a) where the house is located; b) what it looks like (so you can find it easily); and c) what time the party is.

   Role B. You have invited a friend to a party at your house on Saturday. Answer your friend's questions. Then explain that the house belongs to your parents (**padres**), and tell your friend why your parents are not at home that weekend.

Follow-up for 2-19. Students change partners. Each new partner should tell the other the information he/she gathered. To facilitate the reporting of information, you may wish to teach and model the following: *X dice que el laboratorio de computadoras es grande. Tiene muchas computadoras.*

Expansion for 2-19. You may ask students to give additional information, using *estar* for location (*Capítulo 1*): *El laboratorio de computadoras está en la biblioteca.*

Warm-up for 2-20. Ask students questions about classroom objects with *¿De quién es/son... ?* and *¿De qué es?* Before students begin the activity, encourage variety by brainstorming questions they may ask their partners.

Note for 2-21. This activity offers a good opportunity to reenter the expressions for location presented in the *Capítulo preliminar.* You may wish to review them before doing the activity.

Follow-up. Students may also ask for the time of the various events, which will give them the opportunity to practice again *¿A qué hora... ?*

Suggestion for Situaciones. Review greetings and introductions presented in the *Capítulo preliminar*, so students can use them to make the conversation sound more natural.

Resources
■ SAM: 2-24 to 2-29
■ Supp. Activ. Book: *Ser* and *estar* with adjectives

Warm-up. Use questions with *ser* to ask for descriptions of people and objects in photos and in the classroom: *¿De qué color es la mochila de Nancy? ¿Cómo es este señor? ¿Es alto o bajo? ¿Es joven o mayor?* Make statements using *estar* and adjectives (*cansado/a, contento/a, furioso/a, triste*) to convey emotional or physical states. Use gestures or visuals to explain meaning as needed.

3. Expressing inherent qualities and changeable conditions: *Ser* and *estar* with adjectives

Todos los estudiantes **están** aburridos porque la profesora **es** aburrida.

Piénselo. Read the statements below and classify them as to whether they describe either a) a personality trait/physical characteristic or b) a feeling or perception that may change.

1. _a_ La profesora **es** aburrida. Sus clases no son interesantes.
2. _b_ Sofía **está** delgada en ese vestido (*dress*) negro.
3. _b_ Los estudiantes **están** nerviosos. Tienen un examen difícil hoy.
4. _a_ Normalmente, las modelos **son** altas y muy delgadas.
5. _b_ Hoy los niños **están** contentos. Van (*They are going*) al parque.
6. _a_ Roberto **es** estudioso y trabajador. Estudia mucho todos los días.

■ **Ser** and **estar** are often used with the same adjectives. However, the choice of verb determines the meaning of the sentence.

■ **Ser +** *adjective* states the norm—what someone or something is like.

Jorge **es** delgado.	*Jorge is thin.* (He is a thin man.)
Sara **es** muy nerviosa.	*Sara is very nervous.* (She is a nervous person.)
El libro **es** nuevo.	*The book is new.* (It is a new book.)

■ **Estar +** *adjective* expresses a change from the norm, a condition, or how one feels about the person or object being discussed.

Jorge **está** delgado.	*Jorge is/looks thin.* (He lost weight recently, or he looks thin in a picture or because of the clothes he is wearing.)
Sara **está** muy nerviosa.	*Sara is very nervous.* (She is feeling nervous.)
El libro **está** nuevo.	*The book is/looks new.* (It is used, but it seems like a brand new book.)

■ The adjectives **contento/a**, **cansado/a**, **enojado/a** are always used with **estar**.

Ella **está contenta** ahora.	*She is happy now.*
Los niños **están cansados**.	*The children are tired.*
Carlos **está enojado**.	*Carlos is angry.*

■ Some adjectives have one meaning with **ser** and another with **estar**.

Ese señor **es** malo.	*That man is bad/evil.*
Ese señor **está** malo.	*That man is ill.*
La chica **es** lista.	*The girl is clever/smart.*
La chica **está** lista.	*The girl is ready.*
La manzana **es** verde.	*The apple is green.*
La manzana **está** verde.	*The apple is not ripe.*
La profesora **es** aburrida.	*The professor is boring.*
La profesora **está** aburrida.	*The professor is bored.*

2-22 ¿Qué pasa aquí? Look at the drawings and then complete the descriptions about each one with the appropriate form of **ser** or **estar**.

1. Esteban ___es___ (1) un joven listo y estudioso. Este semestre saca buenas notas, excepto en la clase de economía. ___Es___ (2) una clase muy difícil. Esteban ___está___ (3) nervioso porque mañana hay un examen sobre la Comunidad Económica Europea, pero él no ___está___ (4) listo. Debe estudiar toda la noche.

2. ¡Pobres niños! (*Poor children!*) La fruta ___es___ (5) buena y saludable (*healthful*), pero estas manzanas ___están___ (6) verdes, no ___están___ (7) buenas. Ahora los niños no ___están___ (8) contentos. Una niña ___está___ (9) mala porque le duele el estómago (*her stomach hurts*).

> ¡Qué asco!
>
> ¡Horrible!

2-23 Cambios (*Changes*). Imagine that you and your partner know the people mentioned below. One of you will describe a person, using an adjective in the list. The other explains how the person has changed and why. Then switch roles.

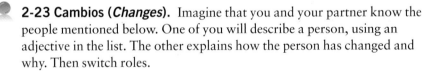

MODELO:	Arturo/fuerte
E1:	*Arturo es fuerte.*
E2:	*Pero por su enfermedad (illness), ahora está muy débil.*

PERSONAS	CARACTERÍSTICAS	RAZONES
1. Ramón	alegre	por sus problemas
2. Laura y Gustavo	callado/a	por la dieta
3. Cristina	conversador/a	por el ejercicio
4. Andrés	débil	por el exceso de estudio
5. Ana y Sofía	extrovertido/a	por la falta (*lack*) de motivación
6. Teresa	feliz	por su depresión
	fuerte	por sus buenas notas
	introvertido/a	
	optimista	
	perezoso/a	
	pesimista	
	trabajador/a	
	triste	

Suggestion. To help students develop their metalinguistic awareness, you may wish to ask why *contento/a*, *cansado/a*, and *enojado/a* are always used with *estar*.

Suggestions. You may wish to remind students to focus on adjective agreement. Have partners exchange roles. Encourage them to use as many adjectives as possible.

Follow-up for 2-23. Brainstorm with the class the conditions that might have prompted the changes in the persons listed by asking questions such as *¿Por qué está delgado ahora Arturo?* (e.g., *dieta*). Focus on the concept that a change of state/condition prompts the switch from *ser* to *estar*.

2-24 Termómetro emocional. PRIMERA FASE. Indicate (✓) how you feel in each situation. Then write two adjectives to further describe how you feel and how you think your classmate feels in these situations.

LUGARES	ABURRIDO/A	CONTENTO/A	TRANQUILO/A	NERVIOSO/A	YO	MI COMPAÑERO/A
en la cafetería con mis compañeros						
en los exámenes finales						
en la oficina de un profesor/una profesora						
en un concierto con mis amigos						
en una fiesta formal						
en mi casa por la noche						

SEGUNDA FASE. Now compare your responses with those of your partner and write down one similarity and one difference between the two of you. Report to the class.

MODELO: en la clase de español
E1: *En la clase de español, yo estoy contento/a. Tú también estás contento/a en la clase de español, ¿verdad?*
E2: *Tienes razón. Yo estoy contento/a. O Estás equivocado/a. Yo estoy aburrido/a.*
E1: [a la clase] *Yo estoy contento/a en la clase de español, pero Amanda está aburrida.*

SITUACIONES

1. **Role A.** You have traveled to another city for a job interview. A friend of a friend who lives in that city has offered to show you around. Make arrangements over the phone to meet this person, whom you do not know. Find out what the person looks like, so you will be able to spot him/her at your meeting place.

   Role B. You have offered to get together with a friend of a friend who has a job interview in your city. You do not know this person, so when you arrange over the phone to meet, you have to find out what the person looks like and something about his/her personality, so you can decide what to show him/her.

2. **Role A.** Show your classmate a photo. Identify the people and explain what they are like. Then respond to your friend's questions and comments about them.

   Role B. After your classmate tells you about the people in the photo, ask and comment about a) how they seem to be feeling, based on their facial expressions or what they are doing and b) where they appear to be.

Suggestion for 2-24 Segunda fase. First introduce *tienes razón* and *estás equivocado/a*. Provide several examples. As students report to the class, you may wish to ask each student alluded to in the report to agree or disagree with what was said about him/her by responding: *Tienes razón* or *Estás equivocado/a*.

Suggestions for Situaciones. Before students begin the first *Situación*, brainstorm with them about the questions they will need to ask.

For the second *Situación*, students will need a photo of two or more people (family, friends, or a magazine photo). If they use a magazine photo, they can invent the information. Students should do this *Situación* twice so that everyone plays both roles.

4. Expressing ownership: Possessive adjectives

Mis amigos y yo

Condorito—the main character of the comic strip magazine of the same name—introduces some of his closest friends. Look at the group portrait to follow what he says.

Condorito y sus amigos

Mi nombre es Condorito. Soy un cóndor simpático, listo y sincero.

Yayita y **su** pequeña hija (*daughter*) Yuyito son **mis** dos grandes amores (*sweethearts*). **La** hija **de** Yayita es muy atractiva, pero es muy dependiente de **su** mamá y de **su** abuelo Don Tremendón. **Nuestra** relación es especial. Nosotros pasamos mucho tiempo juntos.

Mi sobrino (*nephew*) Coné es amoroso, pero un poco llorón (*whiner*). **Su** mejor amiga es Yuyito. La actividad favorita **de ellos** es comer chocolate y jugar en el parque. Finalmente, Doña Tremebunda es la madre de **mi** novia Yayita. Honestamente no me gusta mucho hablar con ella porque es muy materialista. También es dominante y ambiciosa. Y **tu** familia y amigos, ¿cómo son?

Resources
■ SAM: 2-30 to 2-34
■ Supp. Activ. Book: Possessive adjectives

Cultura

Condorito, a comic strip created by the Chilean cartoonist René Ríos (Pepo), is popular throughout Latin America. The main character, Condorito, is an anthropomorphic condor who uses his wit, rather than his work or talents, to solve the problems of everyday life. The multifaceted Condorito, usually in black pants and red shirt, adopts new identities to tell the latest gossip in town. With his ability to transcend social class, nationality, and ideology, he can be a peasant, a scientist, or a beggar, an Egyptian or an Argentinian. The comic strip in which he appears portrays with humor the personality and struggles of the Chilean people. For more information go to the *Mosaicos* web page.

Piénselo. Complete the following statements, using the information in Condorito's description.

1. Condorito tiene una novia. ____ nombre es _____ .
   a. Tu... Yayita   b. Mi... Doña Tremebunda   ⓒ Su... Yayita

2. Condorito dice (*says*): *Nuestra relación es especial.* ¿A qué relación se refiere Condorito en esta afirmación?
   ⓐ La relación de Condorito con Yayita y su familia.
   b. La relación de Yayita con la familia de ella.
   c. La relación entre Coné, Yayita, la familia de Yayita y él (Condorito).

3. Coné es ____ Condorito.
   a. la hija de   ⓑ el sobrino de   c. el hijo (*son*) de

4. Condorito prefiere no pasar tiempo con Doña Tremebunda. ¿Por qué?
   a. por la apariencia física de ella   ⓑ por la personalidad de ella
   c. por el hijo de ella

■ Possessive adjectives modify nouns to express possession. They always precede the noun they modify.

   mi amigo   **tu** familia

Suggestions. Students were introduced to *mi(s)*, *tu(s)*, *su(s)* as lexical items in the *Capítulo preliminar.* You may wish to go over these forms by pointing to objects: *mi libro, mi escritorio, mis lápices, mis bolígrafos.* Use *tu(s)* and *su(s)* by pointing to objects and asking questions to check comprehension. You may also wish to explain to students that *vuestro(s)* and *vuestra(s)* are used only in Spain, whereas *su(s)* is used in Latin American varieties of Spanish.

POSSESSIVE ADJECTIVES	
mi(s)	*my*
tu(s)	*your (familiar)*
su(s)	*your (formal), his, her, its, their*
nuestro(s), nuestra(s)	*our*
vuestro(s), vuestra(s)	*your (familiar plural)*

■ Possessive adjectives change number to agree with the thing possessed, not with the possessor.

   mi *clase*, **mis** *clases*

■ The **nosotros/as** and **vosotros/as** forms must agree also in gender.

   nuestro *profesor*, **nuestros** *amigos*; **nuestra** *profesora*, **nuestras** *amigas*

■ **Su** and **sus** have multiple meanings. To ensure clarity, you may use **de** + *the name of the possessor* or *the appropriate pronoun* instead of *su/sus*. For example, the multiple meanings of *su compañera* can be expressed as follows:

la compañera +
- **de ella** (la compañera de Elena)
- **de él** (la compañera de Jorge)
- **de usted**
- **de ustedes**
- **de ellos** (la compañera de Elena y Jorge)
- **de ellas** (la compañera de Elena y Olga)

En otras palabras

The word for *car* in Spanish varies, depending on the country or region. The most widely accepted word is **el auto**, commonly used in the southern half of South America. In Mexico, Central America, the Caribbean, and the northern countries of South America, **el carro** is frequently used. **El coche** is used in Spain.

2-25 Mi mundo (*world*). PRIMERA FASE. Write down two things that you own (**pertenencias**) and two people whom you value very much. You may use the words in the box or choose others.

Pertenencias:	un carro	una computadora portátil	un iPod
Personas:	un amigo/ una amiga	un profesor ideal/ una profesora ideal	un actor/ una actriz

PERTENENCIAS
1. _____
2. _____

PERSONAS
1. _____
2. _____

SEGUNDA FASE. Take turns describing your selections. Take notes so that you can share with the class the similarities and differences between you and your classmate.

Pertenencias

E1: *Yo tengo un auto. Es rápido y moderno. Y tú, tienes un auto?*
E2: *Sí.*
E1: *¿Y cómo es tu auto?*
E2: *Mi auto es rojo y muy viejo.*

Personas

E1: *Mi madre es importante en mi vida (life). Es muy alegre y activa. Y tu mamá, ¿cómo es?*
E2: *Mi madre es tranquila y muy inteligente.*

2-26 Mi familia. Which of these statements apply to your family and friends? Mark (✓) your answers in the spaces under **Yo**. Then interview a classmate.

	YO	MI COMPAÑERO/A

1. Mi familia es grande.
2. Otros miembros de mi familia viven en nuestro barrio (*neighborhood*).
3. A veces pasamos las vacaciones con mis abuelos (*grandparents*).
4. Siempre conversamos sobre temas políticos.
5. A veces no estamos de acuerdo y discutimos.
6. Nuestros amigos visitan la casa frecuentemente.

2-27 Nuestra universidad. PRIMERA FASE. In preparation for the *Segunda fase*, write some words that generally describe the following aspects of your university.

1. los profesores: _____
2. las clases: _____
3. los estudiantes: _____
4. los equipos (*teams*) de fútbol, baloncesto, béisbol, etc.: _____
5. el campus: _____

SEGUNDA FASE. Now write 1 or 2 sentences about each topic in the *Primera fase*. Be prepared to present your sentences to the class. The class will decide which sentences a) describe the school most accurately and b) present an appealing view of the school for prospective students.

SITUACIONES

1. **Role A.** You are a Spanish professor. You inform a student about a lecture by another professor. Explain that a) the professor is visiting the university; b) there is a lecture by the professor (**una conferencia del profesor**) on Thursday; c) it will take place in the library.

   Role B. Your professor invites you to a lecture. Find out a) the time of the lecture; b) the speaker's name; and c) the topic (**tema**).

2. **Role A.** You are a student from Peru studying in the United States. You phone your parents and ask how they are. Tell about your host parents (**madre americana/padre americano**), brother (**hermano**), and sister (**hermana**). Describe their ages, appearance, personalities, and occupations.

   Role B. You live in Peru, and your child is studying in the United States. When he/she calls, ask about a) the host family schedule (**horario**) and b) activities of the host family.

En directo

To initiate the conversation:
Oye (*Hey*), **mi hermano americano es...**
¿Sabes? (*You know?*) **Mi hermano americano es...**

To acknowledge information by showing surprise:
Ah, ¿sí?
¡No me digas!
Oh, really?, No way!, Wow!

Suggestions for 2-26. This activity has some new words that students should recognize because they are cognates or near cognates. Point out the importance of guessing meaning through context. New words whose meaning will be difficult for students to guess are glossed, as in the case of *barrio*.

Ask questions about students' vacations: *¿Dónde pasa usted las vacaciones? ¿Por qué? ¿Le gusta el lugar? ¿Qué hace usted allí?*

You may wish to gather information about the whole class under categories such as *tamaño de la familia, actividades familiares en la casa, actividades familiares fuera (outside) de la casa, temas de conversación*, etc.

Ask the students to interview each other and complete the table. Students should compare answers, and then write one similarity and one difference between them. Students can share their findings with the class.

Suggestion for 2-27 Segunda fase. You may wish to have each pair of students present two of their sentences, one for each competition listed. The presentations can be oral, or you may wish to have students write them on the board. This second option may lead to more discussion, since the sentences will be available for reference and comparison.

Note. In *A primera vista*, students used *me gusta, te gusta,* and *le gusta* as lexical terms. Here they will find a brief explanation of the forms that they will need for communication at this stage. A detailed grammar explanation is not necessary at this point.

Suggestion. Explain that Mexico City is located in *el Distrito Federal* (*D.F.*) of Mexico.

Suggestions. Be sure to point out that the singular *gusta* is always used with infinitives, even when there is more than one infinitive in the sentence.

Explain that the expression *me cae bien* is often used to refer to people because in some contexts *gustar* may have a sexual connotation.

5. Expressing likes and dislikes: *Gustar*

The following is a transcript of a chat over the Internet between Marisa, a Mexican student living in Mexico City, and Carla, a Mexican American living in El Paso, Texas.

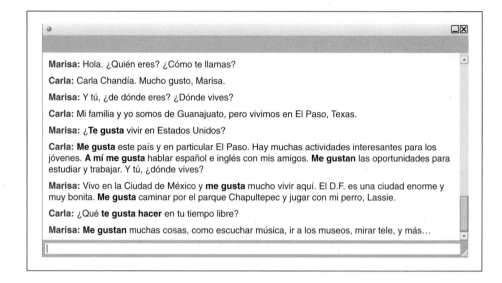

Marisa: Hola. ¿Quién eres? ¿Cómo te llamas?

Carla: Carla Chandía. Mucho gusto, Marisa.

Marisa: Y tú, ¿de dónde eres? ¿Dónde vives?

Carla: Mi familia y yo somos de Guanajuato, pero vivimos en El Paso, Texas.

Marisa: ¿**Te gusta** vivir en Estados Unidos?

Carla: Me gusta este país y en particular El Paso. Hay muchas actividades interesantes para los jóvenes. **A mí me gusta** hablar español e inglés con mis amigos. **Me gustan** las oportunidades para estudiar y trabajar. Y tú, ¿dónde vives?

Marisa: Vivo en la Ciudad de México y **me gusta** mucho vivir aquí. El D.F. es una ciudad enorme y muy bonita. **Me gusta** caminar por el parque Chapultepec y jugar con mi perro, Lassie.

Carla: ¿Qué **te gusta hacer** en tu tiempo libre?

Marisa: Me gustan muchas cosas, como escuchar música, ir a los museos, mirar tele, y más…

Piénselo. Indicate whether each paraphrase best refers to Marisa (**M**) or Carla (**C**).

1. __C__ **Me gustan** las posibilidades académicas que ofrece Estados Unidos.
2. __M__ **Me gusta** vivir en la capital de México.
3. __C__ **Me gusta** ser bilingüe.
4. __M__ **Me gustan** las actividades al aire libre (*open air*).
5. __M__ **Me gusta** el arte.

■ To express what you like to do, use **me gusta** + *infinitive*. To express what you don't like to do, use **no me gusta** + *infinitive*.

Me gusta hablar español.	*I like to speak Spanish.*
No me gusta mirar televisión.	*I don't like to watch television.*
Me gusta practicar deportes y salir con mis amigos.	*I like to play sports and go out with my friends.*

■ To express that you like something or someone, use **me gusta** + *singular noun* or **me gustan** + *plural noun*.

Me gusta la música clásica.	*I like classical music.*
Me gustan las personas alegres.	*I like happy people.*

■ To ask a classmate what he/she likes, use **¿Te gusta(n)… ?** To ask your instructor, use **¿Le gusta(n)… ?**

¿Te gusta/Le gusta tomar café?	*Do you like to drink coffee?*
¿Te gustan/Le gustan los chocolates?	*Do you like chocolates?*

■ To state what another person likes, use **a** + *name of person* + **le gusta(n)…** When you are talking about the preferences of more than one person, use **a** + *name of person* + **les gusta(n)…**

A Diego le gustan las fiestas.	*Diego likes parties.*
A Carlos le gusta el fútbol.	*Carlos likes soccer.*
A Diego y a Carlos les gusta ir de vacaciones con sus padres.	*Diego and Carlos like to go on vacation with their parents.*

2-28 Mis preferencias. PRIMERA FASE. Mark (✓) your preferences in the following chart.

ACTIVIDAD	ME GUSTA MUCHO	ME GUSTA UN POCO	NO ME GUSTA
escribir correos electrónicos en español			
comer en restaurantes de comida mexicana			
bailar salsa			
escuchar música rock en español			
aprender sobre la cultura de otros países			
visitar lugares históricos			

SEGUNDA FASE. Now, compare your answers with those of a classmate. Share with the class one similarity and one difference between you and your partner in terms of your preferences.

2-29 ¿Te gusta… ? PRIMERA FASE. Ask if a classmate likes the following. Be sure to ask follow-up questions as appropriate.

1. el gimnasio de la universidad
2. los teléfonos celulares con conexión a Internet
3. la informática
4. los autos de este año
5. los animales
6. los conciertos de música clásica

SEGUNDA FASE. Write a brief note to another classmate in which you share two pieces of information about yourself and two pieces of information you discovered about your partner.

2-30 ¿Qué te gusta hacer? PRIMERA FASE. Write down some questions that you would ask a classmate to find out the following:

1. what he/she likes to do in his/her free time
2. in what restaurant he/she likes to eat with his/her family

SEGUNDA FASE. Interview two classmates and ask each of them the questions you prepared in the *Primera fase.* Compare their responses and be prepared to share with others your conclusions regarding how your classmates spend their time.

SITUACIONES

1. **Role A:** You are at a park where you hear someone giving Spanish commands to a dog. Break the ice and introduce yourself. Ask a) the person's name; b) the dog's name and age; and c) if the dog is friendly (**manso**). Compliment the dog (smart, strong, very pretty, etc.). Tell the person that you like dogs very much and that you also like cats. Answer the questions this person asks.

   Role B: You are in the park training your dog and someone approaches. Answer this person's questions and ask if he/she has a dog, and if so, what it looks like. Say that you don't like cats because they are not active or fun. Finally, ask where this person is from and where he/she is studying Spanish.

2. **Role A:** You are at Panchero's, a Mexican restaurant. While you are waiting to be seated, you hear someone speaking Spanish to a child. Introduce yourself and ask the child's name and age. Compliment the parent on his/her beautiful child. Also ask the parent if he/she likes Panchero's and likes to eat at American restaurants like McDonald's.

   Role B: You and your two-year-old daughter are waiting to be seated at Panchero's, a Mexican restaurant. Someone asks you about your child. React to the person's comments and answer his/her questions.

Suggestion for 2-28. Tell students about the kind of music you like. Ask about their preferences. Play some traditional music from the Spanish-speaking world (*pasodoble* from Spain, *ranchera* from Mexico, *tango* from Argentina, *son* and *chachachá* from *Cuba*, hip-hop from Puerto Rico/Dominican Republic, Andean music, etc.). Mention that in areas with large Hispanic populations local radio stations play music from Spanish-speaking countries.

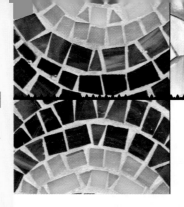

MOSAICOS

A escuchar

ESTRATEGIAS

Listen for specific information

When you ask a person specific questions, he/she may provide not only the answers you need, but also additional information. To listen efficiently, focus on the answers you requested. This will help you obtain the information you need.

Antes de escuchar

2-31 Preparación. You will listen to a student telling her mother about how different her roommates are. Before listening to their conversation, write the name(s) of your own roommate(s) and a sentence that describes each of them.

Escuchar

CD 1
Track 42

2-32 ¿Comprende usted? Listen to the conversation between a student and her mother. Mark (✓) the appropriate column(s) to indicate whether the following statements describe Rita, Marcela, or both.

	RITA	MARCELA
1. Estudia economía.	✓	
2. Le gusta bailar.		✓
3. Es alta, morena y tiene los ojos negros.		✓
4. Es muy seria, baja y delgada.	✓	
5. Estudia arte moderno.		✓

Después de escuchar

2-33 Ahora usted. Complete the following sentences to say how you feel about your roommate(s).

1. Me gusta(n) mi(s) compañero/a(s) de cuarto porque…

2. A veces no me gusta(n) mi(s) compañero/a(s) de cuarto porque…

3. Mi(s) compañero/a(s) de cuarto y yo somos semejantes/diferentes porque…

A conversar

ESTRATEGIAS

Describe a person

Descriptions are most effective when they are well organized. When describing a person, you may want to include demographic information (e.g., age, nationality/origin), physical characteristics, and personality traits. A well-organized description presents information by category, beginning with an introductory phrase to prepare your listener.

Antes de conversar

2-34 Preparación. *Mafalda*, like *Condorito*, featured earlier in this chapter, is a popular comic strip in the Spanish-speaking world. Go to the *Mosaicos* web page, choose one of the characters shown there, and read the description about him/her.

Conversar

2-35 Entre nosotros. Describe the physical characteristics and personality traits of the *Mafalda* character you read about in **2-34**. Your partner will ask questions or comment as appropriate. Then switch roles.

Después de conversar

2-36 Un poco más. Find out about another popular comic character, like those mentioned in the *Cultura* box below, and tell the class about him/her.

Cultura

Mafalda is the name of a character in a comic strip of the same name created by the Argentinian cartoonist Quino. Extremely popular in the Spanish-speaking world, she is a six-year-old girl deeply concerned with political issues and world peace. Her naive yet sharp criticism of society has made her an icon for the defense of human rights. For more information go to the *Mosaicos* web page.

En directo

To introduce information about physical characteristics:

En cuanto a lo físico,... / Físicamente, es...

To introduce information about personality:

Es una persona... /Tiene un carácter...

Suggestion for 2-34. First, describe Mafalda, the main character in the cartoon. Mafalda is a precocious girl who comes from a loving family, and her parents are always present and visible in her life. She often criticizes the world but hopes to change it. Then, assign this activity as homework ahead of time. Students should read the brief description of their chosen character. To avoid having many students choose the same character, you can show a picture of the cartoon characters in class and have students in pairs/small groups make their choices. The characters are Mafalda, Felipe, Manolito, Susanita, Miguelito, Libertad, and Guille.

Suggestion for 2-35. Students should find a partner who has chosen a different character. Brainstorm with students how the listener can ask questions to elicit clarification and details.

Cultura

Many Hispanics who emigrate to other countries maintain connections to their culture by reading and listening to music in Spanish. In areas with large Hispanic populations, Spanish-language newspapers and magazines are available.

These carry some of the many comic strips popular in the Hispanic world, including *Mafalda* (Argentina), *Condorito* (Chile), and *Mortadelo y Filemón* (Spain). You will find information about these comic strips on the Internet.

A leer

Scan a text for specific information

When you read in Spanish, your goal should be to read for ideas, not for the meaning of every word. One way to read for ideas is to search for particular pieces of information that you think will be in the text. Often the comprehension questions after the text will help you decide what information to search for as you read. This approach to reading, called *scanning*, works best if you a) focus on the information you are seeking and b) read the text through quickly at least twice, looking for specific information each time.

Antes de leer

2-37 Preparación. PRIMERA FASE. Read the title of the text and examine its format. (This is the reading strategy you learned in *Capítulo 1*.) What type of text is it?

1. a series of e-mail messages
2. personal ads
3. ads for items for sale

SEGUNDA FASE. Scan the text and use your highlighter to mark the following information in each paragraph.

1. el nombre de la persona
2. la edad (*age*) de la persona
3. la dirección electrónica de la persona

Leer

2-38 Primera mirada. Read the personal ads that follow and scan them for the information needed in the form. In some cases, it may not be possible to provide all the information requested.

	PERSONA 1	PERSONA 2	PERSONA 3	PERSONA 4
nombre				
edad				
nacionalidad				
estado civil				
personalidad (1 ó 2 adjetivos)				
le gusta...				

Suggestion for 2-38. Before the activity, make sure students have deduced that the text is a series of personal ads. Explain that they will now scan the ads for specific information about each person and that they should not worry about words they do not understand.

You may wish to explain the meaning of the following words before students read the ads: *fronteras*, *compromiso*, and *viajo* as follows: *Mi familia y yo viajamos por carro entre... [your state] y... [a neighboring state] para visitar a mis padres. Siempre cruzamos la frontera entre... y... [the two states] durante el día. No nos gusta viajar por la noche.*

Follow-up for 2-38. To check comprehension, students can compare their forms with a partner and report discrepancies. You may wish to teach phrases such as *En su anuncio, Susana dice que...* Make the activity as communicative as possible by having students answer *No sé* or *No se dice* when the information is not provided.

Amigos sin fronteras

Soltera, sin hijos y sin compromiso. Me llamo Susana y tengo 24 años. Soy guatemalteca. Busco amigos extranjeros, solteros, separados o divorciados, jóvenes o mayores. Soy amable, cariñosa y muy trabajadora. Por mi trabajo, viajo mucho, pero me gusta la compañía de otras personas. Soy bilingüe. Hablo español e inglés. Escriban a sincompromiso@comcast.net.

Soy Ricardo Brown. 21 años, sincero, dedicado. Me gustan las fiestas. Soy soltero. Deseo conocer a una chica de unos 23 años, preferiblemente venezolana como yo. Prefiero una mujer activa e independiente. Me gusta practicar deportes y explorar lugares nuevos. Escríbanme a amigosincero@msn.com.

Me llamo Pablo Sosa, tengo 31 años, y soy chileno. Soy agradable y muy trabajador. Me gusta hacer mi trabajo a la perfección, pero soy tolerante. Los autos convertibles son mi pasión. Deseo mantener correspondencia por correo electrónico con jóvenes del extranjero para intercambiar información sobre los convertibles europeos o americanos. Mi dirección electrónica es locoporlosautos@yahoo.com.

Soy Xiomara Stravinsky, decoradora y fotógrafa argentina. Me gusta el arte, especialmente el impresionismo. Tengo 27 años y soy divorciada. Soy dinámica, agradable y generosa, pero tengo pocos amigos porque tengo dos trabajos y paso muchas horas con mis clientes. Necesito un cambio en mi vida. ¿Deseas ser mi amigo/a? Por favor, escríbeme a xiomarastravinsky@hotmail.com.

Lengua

The letter **y** changes to **e** when it precedes a word beginning with **i** or **h**.

inglés y español, but **español e inglés**

inteligente y agradable, but **agradable e inteligente**

Después de leer

2-39 Ampliación. PRIMERA FASE. What qualities do you associate with Susana (**S**), Ricardo (**R**), Pablo (**P**), and Xiomara (**X**)? Why? With a classmate, write the person's initial next to each quality, and support your opinions.

a. _S, R_ sociable
b. _S, X_ simpático/a
c. _R_ divertido/a
d. _P_ perfeccionista
e. _P_ mayor
f. _S, R_ flexible
g. _P, X_ trabajador/a
h. _X_ ocupado/a

SEGUNDA FASE. Find the best match for Susana, Ricardo, Pablo and Xiomara from the following responses received.

1. Tengo 22 años y me gustan todos los deportes. Mis padres viven en Caracas pero yo vivo en Miami. Ricardo
2. Enseño arte en la escuela secundaria. Tengo tiempo para mis amigos los fines de semana. Xiomara
3. Soy de Nicaragua. Soy muy sociable y deseo perfeccionar mi inglés. Susana
4. Trabajo para *Autos de hoy*, una revista de Internet. Pablo

Suggestion for 2-39. Accept any logical, well-supported answer. To review and expand vocabulary, you may ask students to provide synonyms (or related words) and/or antonyms of the descriptive adjectives in the list.

Resources

■ SAM: 2-46 to 2-48

A escribir

ESTRATEGIAS

Consider audience and purpose

Writing is an act of communication between writer and reader. Writers usually have a purpose in mind, such as compiling information, informing the reader, describing something or someone, or expressing a point of view. Readers rely on their prior knowledge and on the quantity and quality of information presented to derive meaning from the text.

As you write, keep in mind your purpose and make the necessary adjustments to form and content to facilitate your audience's comprehension of the message.

Antes de escribir

2-40 Preparación. PRIMERA FASE. Read the following ad written by a movie fan in your local Spanish-language newspaper.

> Fanático del cine necesita amigos para discutir películas los fines de semana. Tengo 24 años y estudio cinematografía. Me fascinan las películas de acción y también las románticas. Soy fuerte, activo, atlético y aventurero. Me gusta practicar deportes, especialmente el tenis y el esquí. Siempre estoy muy ocupado, pero tengo unas horas todas las semanas para conversar sobre películas y hacer deportes. Interesados, favor de enviar correo electrónico a fanaticodelcine@yahoo.com.

SEGUNDA FASE. You decide to respond to the ad. First, think about the following questions and mark (✓) your responses accordingly. Possible answers:

1. What is the purpose that **fanaticodelcine** has in mind when he writes the e-mail?
   a. _____ to find a girlfriend
   b. _✓_ to find someone (male or female) to talk with about movies

2. What would your purpose be if you responded to his personal ad?
   a. _✓_ to share your interest in movies with someone who is knowledgeable about the topic.
   b. _✓_ to date **fanaticodelcine**

TERCERA FASE. Now jot down information that will help you meet the goal of becoming the conversation partner of **fanaticodelcine**.

1. your age
2. your place of origin
3. words (adjectives) that describe you physically
4. expressions (adjectives) that describe your personality
5. activities (verbs) that you like to do that may match the needs of the person in the ad

Escribir

2-41 Manos a la obra. Write an e-mail to *fanaticodelcine* using the information you prepared in the *Tercera fase* of **2-40**.

Suggestion for 2-41. Students who prefer not to talk about themselves can assume a different identity for this activity.

Para:

Asunto: Anuncio

Hola,_____

Respondo a tu anuncio del periódico.(*Provide your name.*)
_____

Primero, aquí tienes alguna información personal.(*Provide personal information.*)_____
_____
_____
_____

En segundo lugar, estas son algunas de las actividades que, al igual que tú, yo hago en mi tiempo libre.(*Provide activities that you, like fanaticodelcine, like to do in your free time.*)_____
_____
_____
_____

En tercer lugar, los fines de semana… (*Tell what you like to do.*)_____
_____
_____
_____

Finalmente, deseo ser tu amigo/a. Por favor, escríbeme un correo electrónico a mi dirección:_____
_____

Hasta pronto.
_____

Después de escribir

2-42 Revisión. After writing your e-mail, read it again and check the following:

1. Did you include all the information *fanaticodelcine* needs? Do you think your information will be interesting to him?
2. Did you use punctuation correctly? Did you verify that there are no spelling or grammatical mistakes that may hinder comunication?
3. Make any necessary changes that will make your e-mail clear and comprehensible to *fanaticodelcine*.

Resources

■ SAM: 2-49 to 2-51
■ Supp. Activ. Book: *Enfoque cultural*
■ *Vistas culturales* Video

Note. For an explanation of the rationale behind the activities in this section, please refer to the note in *Capítulo 1*.

Suggestion. Call students' attention to how the names of the states are spelled in Spanish.

ENFOQUE CULTURAL

Los hispanos y la expansión de Estados Unidos

Inicialmente, Estados Unidos está formado por trece colonias de Inglaterra. Estas trece colonias ocupan principalmente el noreste y la región del Atlántico. Las trece colonias se independizan de Inglaterra en la larga y violenta Guerra de Independencia. George Washington es un líder muy importante de esta guerra. El 4 de julio de 1776, el Congreso Continental firma la Declaración de Independencia en Filadelfia y George Washington es el primer presidente de la nueva república.

La expansión de Estados Unidos

Moneda de 25 centavos en honor de Luisiana, 2002

La primera expansión de las trece colonias hacia el oeste ocurre en 1803 durante la presidencia de Thomas Jefferson. En este año, el gobierno de Estados Unidos compra a Francia el inmenso territorio de Luisiana por 23 millones de dólares. Esta región ocupa unos $2.100.000$ km^2. La compra de Luisiana incorpora todo el valle del Río Misisipi al territorio de Estados Unidos.

En 1810, el presidente James Madison anexa al territorio de Estados Unidos la región de Florida Occidental. Esta región está en la costa norte del Golfo de México y hoy pertenece a los estados de Luisiana, Misisipi, Alabama y Florida. Pero anteriormente, pertenece a España, Francia y también a Inglaterra. Durante un tiempo se llama la República Independiente de Florida Occidental. España disputa esta anexión, pero en 1819 acepta ceder todo el territorio de Florida, incluyendo la península de Florida.

Bonnieblue, la bandera de la República Independiente de Florida Occidental

Dinero de República Independiente de Texas

Entre 1845 y 1853, Estados Unidos anexa extensos territorios mexicanos. La anexión de Texas en 1845 causa la guerra entre México y Estados Unidos. En 1848, México cede otra parte muy grande de su territorio, incluyendo partes de Texas, Colorado, Arizona, Nuevo México y Wyoming, además de toda la extensión de California, Nevada y Utah. En 1853 Estados Unidos compra un área adicional en la frontera de México y el presidente Franklin Pierce paga diez millones de dólares. Los habitantes mexicanos de estas regiones son los ancestros de muchos latinos de Estados Unidos.

En 1898 Puerto Rico se convierte en un protectorado de Estados Unidos a causa de la guerra de Estados Unidos contra España. Los habitantes de Puerto Rico son ciudadanos de Estados Unidos desde 1917.

El escudo de Puerto Rico tiene el símbolo de San Juan y la inscripción en latín: "Su nombre es Juan".

En otras palabras

Expresiones puertorriqueñas:

No le des **cabuya**.
Don't give him/her ammunition to bother you.

Yo no compro la lotería porque tengo una **macacoa** terrible.
I don't buy lottery tickets because I have terrible luck.

Dejó su cuarto hecho un **majarete**.
He/She left his/her room a complete mess.

En otras palabras

Expresiones chicanas (*Mexican-American*):

Ando brujo.
I am broke.

¡Ándale, güero!
Let's go, blondie!

Note. Remind students that *Comprensión* can be done in the text or online.

Answers for 2-43 Segunda fase. 1. *Las trece colonias se independizan de Inglaterra en la larga y violenta Guerra de Independencia.* 2. *El 4 de julio de 1776, el Congreso Continental firma la Declaración de Independencia en Filadelfia.* 6. *La anexión de Texas en 1845 causa la guerra entre México y Estados Unidos.* 7. *Los habitantes de Puerto Rico son ciudadanos de Estados Unidos desde 1917.*

2-43 Comprensión. PRIMERA FASE. **Reconocimiento de palabras clave.** Find in the text the Spanish word or phrase that best expresses the meaning of the following concepts:

1. war   <u>guerra</u>
2. valley   <u>valle</u>
3. ancestors   <u>ancestros</u>
4. border   <u>frontera</u>
5. coat of arms   <u>escudo</u>
6. citizen   <u>ciudadano</u>

SEGUNDA FASE. **Oraciones importantes.** Underline the statements that contain ideas found in the text. Then indicate where in the text those words appear.

1. The colonies became independent after a long and violent war.
2. The Continental Congress signed the Declaration of Independence in Philadelphia.
3. George Washington was a good soldier, but a poor politician.
4. The purchase of the Mississippi Valley turned out to be a poor decision by President Jefferson.
5. Spain gave up its claim to Florida and West Florida without any resistance.
6. The United States and Mexico went to war over the annexation of Texas.
7. Puerto Ricans are citizens of the United States.

TERCERA FASE. **Ideas principales.** Write a brief paragraph in English summarizing the main ideas expressed in the text.

2-44 Use la información. Prepare an oral presentation describing the current flag or a historic flag of one of the states that has a Hispanic heritage. Consult the *Mosaicos* web page where you will find a worksheet and relevant links to collect information about the flag.

VOCABULARIO

Las descripciones — Descriptions

agradable	*nice*
alegre	*happy, glad*
alto/a	*tall*
antipático/a	*unpleasant*
bajo/a	*short* (in stature)
bilingüe	*bilingual*
bonito/a	*pretty*
callado/a	*quiet*
cansado/a	*tired*
casado/a	*married*
contento/a	*happy, glad*
conversador/a	*talkative*
corto/a	*short* (in length)
débil	*weak*
delgado/a	*thin*
divertido/a	*funny, amusing*
enojado/a	*angry*
estatura mediana	*average, medium* (height)
feo/a	*ugly*
fuerte	*strong*
gordo/a	*fat*
guapo/a	*good-looking, handsome*
joven	*young*
largo/a	*long*
listo/a	*smart; ready*
mayor	*old*
moreno/a	*brunette*
nervioso/a	*nervous*
nuevo/a	*new*
oscuro/a	*dark*
pelirrojo/a	*redhead*
perezoso/a	*lazy*
pobre	*poor*
rico/a	*rich, wealthy*
rubio/a	*blond*
simpático/a	*nice, charming*
soltero/a	*single*
tonto/a	*silly, foolish*
trabajador/a	*hardworking*
triste	*sad*
viejo/a	*old*

Las nacionalidades — Nationalities

alemán/alemana	*German*
argentino/a	*Argentinian*
boliviano/a	*Bolivian*
canadiense	*Canadian*
chileno/a	*Chilean*
colombiano/a	*Colombian*
costarricense	*Costa Rican*
cubano/a	*Cuban*
dominicano/a	*Dominican*
ecuatoriano/a	*Ecuadorian*
español/a	*Spanish*
estadounidense	*U.S. citizen*
francés/francesa	*French*
guatemalteco/a	*Guatemalan*
hispano/a	*Hispanic*
hondureño/a	*Honduran*
japonés/japonesa	*Japanese*
marroquí	*Moroccan*
mexicano/a	*Mexican*
nicaragüense	*Nicaraguan*
nigeriano/a	*Nigerian*
panameño/a	*Panamanian*
paraguayo/a	*Paraguayan*
peruano/a	*Peruvian*
polaco/a	*Polish*
portugués/portuguesa	*Portuguese*
puertorriqueño/a	*Puerto Rican*
salvadoreño/a	*Salvadorian*
uruguayo/a	*Uruguayan*
venezolano/a	*Venezuelan*

Los colores — Colors

amarillo/a	*yellow*
anaranjado/a	*orange*
azul	*blue*
blanco/a	*white*
marrón	*brown*
gris	*gray*
morado/a	*purple*
negro/a	*black*
rojo/a	*red*
rosado/a, rosa	*pink*
verde	*green; not ripe*

Verbos — Verbs

desear	*to wish, to want*
ser	*to be*
usar	*to use*

Palabras y expresiones útiles — Useful words and expressions

el auto, el coche, el carro	*car*
de	*of, from*
¿de quién?	*whose?*
del	*of the* (contraction of *de + el*)
la flor	*flower*
le gusta(n)	*you* (formal) *like; he/she likes*
los lentes de contacto	*contact lenses*
me gusta(n)	*I like*
mucho (*adv.*)	*much, a lot*
mucho/a (*adj.*)	*many*
el ojo	*eye*
el pelo	*hair*
te gusta(n)	*you* (familiar) *like*
Tengo… años.	*I am . . . years old.*
tiene	*he/she has; you* (formal) *have*
todos/as	*everybody*

See the English-Spanish and Spanish-English glossaries for other adjectives of nationality.

See page 74 for possessive adjectives.

87

Suggestion. Introduce the word *boda* by pointing to the couple in the painting and the word *casarse*. Ask questions to elicit vocabulary: *¿Qué hacen las personas en una boda normalmente? ¿Comen mucho o poco? ¿Beben? ¿Bailan?* Explain the painting: *El hombre es un aristócrata, es de España; la mujer es una princesa inca. Los incas son indígenas de Perú.* Ask questions to recycle descriptions: *¿Cómo es el hombre? ¿Cómo es la mujer?*, etc.

Standard 2.1. Students demonstrate an understanding of the relationship between the practices and perspectives of the culture studied. This painting depicts a wedding between people from different cultures. Which culture is dominant? Does this appear to be a European or an Inca wedding? Have

El tiempo libre

En este cuadro anónimo del siglo XVIII, vemos la boda de un hombre y una mujer. Ella es la princesa inca Nusta Beatriz y él es un noble español, D. Martín de Loyola.

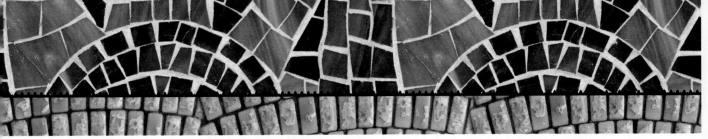

In this chapter you will learn how to:

- discuss daily activities and leisure
- talk about food
- express where you are going
- make plans

Cultural Focus: **Perú**

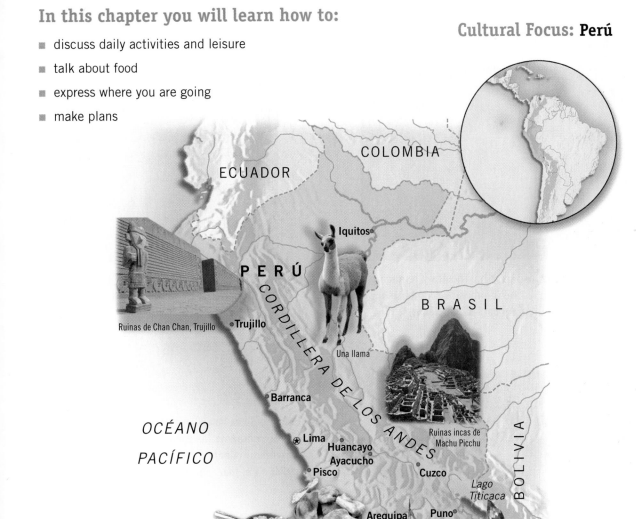

COLOMBIA

ECUADOR

P E R Ú

Iquitos

Ruinas de Chan Chan, Trujillo

Trujillo

Una llama

BRASIL

Barranca

Ruinas incas de Machu Picchu

OCÉANO PACÍFICO

CORDILLERA DE LOS ANDES

Lima

Huancayo

Ayacucho

Pisco

Cuzco

BOLIVIA

Lago Titicaca

Arequipa

Puno

El lago Titicaca

Escabeche de pescado con pan

students reflect on how practices of both cultures are combined (or not) when members of one culture are the conquerors and members of the other culture have been conquered.

Note. Both *Perú* and *el Perú* are widely accepted. In *Mosaicos*, *Perú* is used. Both Cuzco and Cusco are accepted spellings for the Peruvian city that was the capital of the Inca empire.

Warm-up. This activity can be done in pairs or as a class warm-up. Ask questions while students look at the map: *¿Qué países están al norte de Perú? ¿Cuáles están al sur? ¿Y al oeste?* Also ask: *¿Cómo se llama el océano que está al lado de Perú? ¿Qué río está entre Perú y Colombia? ¿Cómo se llaman las montañas de Perú?* Explain *cordillera* by drawing a chain of mountains or by pointing to them on map. Ask questions to check students' general knowledge about Peru. Tell them not to worry if they cannot answer some questions: *¿Cuál es un pueblo indígena de Perú? (los incas) ¿Conocen ustedes alguna ciudad inca? (Machu Picchu). ¿Qué lenguas se hablan en Perú? (español, quechua, aymara)* Pointing to the photos on the map, ask: *¿Dónde está el lago Titicaca? ¿Es un lago grande o pequeño? ¿Qué animal es típico de la región andina de Perú?* Introduce the word *comida*: *La comida de Perú es muy buena y variada. ¿Comen comida peruana alguna vez, nunca, frecuentemente?*

A vista de pájaro. Based on what you know about Peru, indicate if the statement is true (**Cierto**) or false (**Falso**).

1. _Cierto_ Perú está al sur de Colombia.
2. _Falso_ La capital de Perú está en la costa del Atlántico.
3. _Cierto_ La comida de Perú es muy variada.
4. _Cierto_ Algunos peruanos son de origen inca y español.
5. _Falso_ El Amazonas está entre Perú y Ecuador.
6. _Falso_ La llama es un animal débil.

89

Resources

- SAM: 3-1 to 3-10
- Supp. Activ. Book: *A primera vista*

A PRIMERA VISTA

Las diversiones

CD 2
Track 1

En muchos **países** hispanos hay **fiestas** y **reuniones**. Los **jóvenes** bailan, escuchan **música** o conversan. A veces **tocan la guitarra** y **cantan canciones** populares.

Este **hombre** lee el **periódico al aire libre** en un parque de su **ciudad**. Y usted, ¿lee el periódico? ¿Qué periódicos o **revistas** lee?

Estas **mujeres van** a la playa en su **tiempo libre** y también **durante** las **vacaciones**. Allí, caminan y conversan **mientras** otras personas **toman el sol**, **nadan** en **el mar**, corren o **descansan**.

Muchos jóvenes van al **cine**, especialmente los fines de semana. También es común **alquilar películas** para ver en casa.

3-1 Asociaciones. Which leisure activities do you associate with the following places?

1. __c__ la playa   **a.** ver una película
2. __e__ la fiesta   **b.** leer el periódico
3. __a__ el cine   **c.** tomar el sol
4. __b__ la biblioteca   **d.** mirar televisión
5. _a, b, d, e_ la casa   **e.** bailar y conversar

3-2 Nuestro tiempo libre. PRIMERA FASE. What do all of you do in the following places? Take turns asking one another, and take notes on the responses.

MODELO: las fiestas
        E1:   *¿Qué haces en las fiestas?*
        E2:   *En las fiestas bailo mucho. ¿Y tú?*
        E1:   *Bailo y hablo con mis amigos.*
        E2:   *Y tú (E3), ¿qué haces en... ?*

	COMPAÑERO/A 1	COMPAÑERO/A 2	COMPAÑERO/A 3	YO
1. en la universidad después de clase				
2. en la biblioteca pública de tu ciudad				
3. en casa el fin de semana				
4. en un parque de tu ciudad				
5. en la playa durante las vacaciones				
6. en la discoteca con tus amigos				

SEGUNDA FASE. With the other members of your group, prepare a report to share with the class about the activities most popular among group members.

MODELO: *En nuestro grupo, dos personas practican fútbol después de clases.*

3-3 ¿Qué hacen Pedro y Carmen? PRIMERA FASE. Look at the drawings and explain what Pedro and Carmen do on weekends.

SEGUNDA FASE. Write an e-mail to Rafael, your new friend in Peru, explaining what you and your friends do on weekends.

Hola Rafael,

¿Cómo estás? Nosotros estamos muy bien. Los fines de semana mis amigos y yo _____

_____

_____

_____ .

¡Hasta pronto!

_____

Suggestion for 3-2. The expression *¿Qué hacen los estudiantes?* was introduced in *Capítulo 1*. Remind students what *hacer* means by writing on the board *¿Qué hace usted los fines de semana?* Ask questions to review the verb and recycle vocabulary: *¿Qué hace en la universidad? ¿Qué hace Elisa en el gimnasio? ¿Qué hacemos en la clase de español?*

Expansión for 3-2. 7. *en una reunión*; 8. *en el cine*; 9. *en un restaurante elegante*; 10. *en el auto*; 11. *en el centro de la ciudad*; 12. *en el gimnasio.*

Suggestion for 3-3. This is a good opportunity to recycle vocabulary from previous chapters and to use new vocabulary. Before the *Segunda fase*, brainstorm with students the vocabulary related to activities that they have learned (*mirar televisión, practicar básquet-bol/baloncesto, montar en bicicleta*). You may introduce new words, such as *piano, trompeta, violín.*

Note. *Vamos a + infinitive* appears in the dialogue as a lexical item. *Van a + infinitive* appears in the suggested comprehension check that follows. Students will be able to preview other forms of this construction elsewhere in *A primera vista*.

Suggestion for dialogue. Model pronunciation and intonation in the dialogue with a student. Then ask two students to read it aloud and have the class practice it in pairs. Mention that *fabuloso, estupendo*, and *perfecto* express enthusiastic agreement and should be said with emphasis, especially over the phone.

After students read the dialogue you may do this *cierto o falso* comprehension check. 1. *Lola llama por teléfono a Manuel por el cumpleaños de él.* (F) 2. *Manuel y Lola van a ver una película en el cine.* (C) 3. *Lola piensa que las películas de Alfonso Cuarón son malas.* (F) 4. *Lola y Manuel viven juntos.* (F) 5. *Lola acepta la invitación de Manuel.* (C)

Suggestion. You may want to point out that some Spanish speakers use *dar la película/pasar la película* rather than *poner la película.*

Suggestion for 3-4. Before doing the activity you may review the expressions in *En directo* and/or other ways to accept or reject an invitation. Write two columns on the board: *Aceptar: ¡Cómo no! ¡Estupendo! Me gustaría mucho. No aceptar: No puedo. Es que debo estudiar.* You may also brainstorm with students about their plans for the weekend: *¿Qué planes tienen este fin de semana? ¿Van al cine? ¿Van a un concierto? ¿A un partido de béisbol? ¿Van a escuchar música en su casa?*

En otras palabras

Telephone greetings vary from country to country. **¿Diga?** and **¿Dígame?** are used to answer the phone in Spain; **¡Bueno!** in Mexico; **¿Aló?** in Argentina, Peru, and Chile; **¡Oigo!** and **¿Qué hay?** in Cuba. Terms of endearment such as **mi amor, corazón, mi vida, querido/a,** and **mi cielo** also reflect regional preferences.

En directo

To extend an invitation:

Te llamo para ver si quieres (*if you want*) **+ infinitive…**

Tengo una idea. ¿Por qué no + nosotros/as form…of the verb…?

To accept an invitation:

¡Estupendo! ¿Dónde quedamos? *Where do we meet?*

Sí, gracias/¡Ah, qué bien!/ ¡Qué buena idea!

¡Qué bueno!

¡Fabuloso!

To decline an invitation:

Lo siento, pero no tengo tiempo/tengo mucho trabajo/tengo mucha tarea…

Ese día no puedo (*I can't*), **tengo un examen.**

·)) Los planes

CD 2 Track 2 Una conversación por teléfono entre Manuel y Lola

LOLA: ¿Aló?

MANUEL: Hola, mi amor, **¡felicidades** por tu cumpleaños!

LOLA: Ay, gracias, Manuel.

MANUEL: **¿Qué te parece** si **vamos** al cine esta tarde y **después** a un restaurante para **cenar?**

LOLA: Me parece **fabuloso.** ¿Qué película vamos a ver?

MANUEL: Hay una nueva de Alfonso Cuarón.

LOLA: Muy bien. Me gustan mucho sus películas. ¿Dónde **ponen** la película?

MANUEL: **Cerca de** El Jardín Limeño, tu restaurante peruano favorito.

LOLA: **Estupendo,** ¿entonces **luego** vamos a cenar allí?

MANUEL: **¡Claro!** ¿Nos vemos en tu casa a las cinco?

LOLA: Sí, sí, perfecto. ¡Hasta luego!

3-4 Una invitación. PRIMERA FASE. Using the preceding dialogue as a model, role-play a phone call to invite a classmate to join you in a weekend activity. He/She should accept or decline the invitation.

SEGUNDA FASE. Repeat the activity with two other classmates. Then explain to the class your weekend plans and how many people are joining you.

MODELO: *El sábado por la tarde Juan, Verónica y yo vamos al gimnasio para ver un partido de básquetbol.*

Cultura

Traditionally, Mexico, Spain, and Argentina have had important film industries, but films are made in other Spanish-speaking countries as well. Outstanding Spanish-language film directors like Pedro Almodóvar and Icíar Bollaín in Spain, Alfonso Cuarón and Alejandro González in Mexico, Sergio Cabrera in Colombia, and Juan Carlos Tabío in Cuba, among others, are internationally known.

3-5 ¿Adónde vamos? PRIMERA FASE. You and your partner are in a study abroad program in Lima and are looking for something to do together over the weekend. Underline three activities in the cultural section of the newspaper that you find interesting. Then fill in the chart, including the day and time for each activity.

AGENDA CULTURAL
La guía de Lima

Cine

El amor en los tiempos del cólera. Dir. Mike Newell. C.C. Británico. Calle Bellavista 531. Miraflores. 7:30 pm. Libre.

Teatro

La casa de Bernarda Alba. Grupo de Teatro Lorca. C.C. Británico. Av. La Marina 2554. San Miguel. 7:30 pm. Libre.
Entre visillos. Basada en "La cantante calva", de Eugenio Ionesco. Auditorio Municipalidad de San Isidro. La República 455. El Olivar. 8 pm. Boletería.

Música

Los andinos en concierto. Huainos, yaravíes, mulizas. ICPNA. Jr. Cuzco 446. Lima. 7 pm. S/. 10.00.
Noche flamenca. Ballet La flor de Sevilla. ICPNA. Av. Angamos Oeste 120. Miraflores. 7:30 p.m. S/. 25.00.
Amalia Sánchez en concierto. A beneficio del C.C. de Rehabilitación de Ciegos. C.C. Ricardo Palma. Larco 770. Miraflores. 8 pm. S/. 10.00.

Exposición

Maestros en acción. Asociación de Docentes de la ENSABAP. Bellas Artes de La Molina. Av. Rinconada del Lago 1515. 7 pm.

Libro

Lectura de poemas de Óscar Liria. Av. La Paz 646. 7:30 pm. Libre.

Conferencia

La mujer en el arte. Con Lola Reyes. C. C. San Marcos. Parque Universitario. Lima. 6:30 pm. Libre.

Literatura

Perú en la literatura francesa. Con Pierre Brillat. Alianza Francesa. Av. Arequipa 4595. Miraflores. 8 pm. S/.15.00, S/.10.00.

Cultura

Huainos, *yaravíes*, and *mulizas* are Peruvian songs of pre-Columbian origin that are popular in the Andean region of the country. They are often performed and danced in the *peñas*, music clubs that promote traditional (Afro-Andean and Creole) music. In the *peñas* people dance all night long and enjoy excellent regional food.

¿ADÓNDE VAMOS?	¿QUÉ VAMOS A VER/HACER/ESCUCHAR?	¿CUÁNDO?

 SEGUNDA FASE. Explain your plans to another pair. Decide if you can do some of the activities together.

Suggestion for 3-5. This *Agenda cultural* is from a Peruvian newspaper. Ask students to read the *Cultura* box before they do the activity. Go over some key points in the *Agenda cultural* to facilitate comprehension. Write down the abbreviations and ask if students can guess what they mean: *Dir.* (*director*); *C.C.* (*Centro Cultural*); *Av.* (*Avenida*). Ask them to guess the meaning of *Libre* (free, no charge) and *Boletería* (ticket office). Explain that *huainos*, *yaravíes*, and *mulizas* are original dances from Peru (see *Cultura* box) and that *flamenco* is a type of music from Andalucía in the south of Spain. Point out cognates (*docente, narración oral, inicios*) and *S/.*, which stands for *Nuevo Sol*, the Peruvian unit of currency. If you wish, assign students to look up the exchange rate for this currency.

◀)) La comida

CD 2
Track 3 **En el restaurante.** Ahora Lola y Manuel están en el restaurante El Jardín Limeño para **celebrar el cumpleaños** de Lola. Hablan con el **camarero**.

CAMARERO: Buenas noches. ¿Qué desean los señores?

MANUEL: Lola, ¿qué vas a comer?

LOLA: Para mí, una **ensalada** primero y después **pollo** con **verduras**.

MANUEL: Yo, para empezar, **ceviche** de **pescado**. Y luego un **bistec** con **papas**.

CAMARERO: ¿Y para beber?

LOLA: Vamos a beber **vino** blanco. Y también **agua** con gas, por favor.

CAMARERO: ¿Algo más?

MANUEL: Nada más, gracias.

Cultura

Peruvian cooking mostly uses regional ingredients and follows preparation methods inherited from indigenous cultures. Ceviche is a typical dish of Peru and other countries in Latin America. It is generally made with seafood that is not cooked but rather marinated in lime juice and spices.

ESPECIALIDADES DE LA CASA

ENTRADAS

Ensalada de la casa	S/.10
Ceviche de pescado	S/.15
Papa a la huancaína	S/.10
Causa a la limeña	S/.12

PLATOS PRINCIPALES

Chupe de camarones	S/.22
Ají de gallina	S/.18
Lomo saltado	S/.17
Bistec con papas	S/.17
Pollo con verduras	S/.16

POSTRES

Suspiro de limeña	S/.8
Alfajor	S/.8
Mazamorra morada	S/.6

BEBIDAS

Chicha morada	S/.4
Jugo de maracuyá	S/.4
Inca Kola	S/.3

yuca frita · aceitunas · frijoles · ceviche de pescado · adobo de chancho · papas cocidas · tamales · rocotos rellenos

La comida peruana es muy variada. Sobre esta mesa hay ceviche de pescado, tamales, papas cocidas, rocotos (pimientos) rellenos, adobo de chancho (cerdo), yuca frita, frijoles y aceitunas.

En directo

Expressions to take an order:

¿Qué desean los señores?

¿Qué van a tomar/beber?

Expressions to order food:

Para mí, una ensalada, arroz con…

Me gustaría/Quisiera comer/tomar…
I would like to eat/ drink…

Yo quiero/deseo…

Cultura

The *Cultura* box above mentions one of the most typical dishes in Perú, *el ceviche*. Some other typical Peruvian dishes include *papa a la huancaína* (sliced boiled potatoes covered with a spicy creamy cheese sauce); *causa a la limeña* (seasoned mashed potato stuffed with tuna, egg, shrimp, or avocado); *chupe de camarones* (shrimp chowder); *ají de gallina* (shredded chicken casserole with walnuts, parmesan cheese, and Peruvian hot peppers); *suspiro de limeña* (a dessert made with milk and eggs); *alfajor* (two-layer cookies with *dulce de leche* between the layers; *mazamorra morada* (purple corn pudding).

Suggestion. This chapter introduces some Peruvian dishes as part of its cultural content and also presents foods common to students' experience. In *Capítulo 10*, the food theme will be revisited. Introduce the words *pescado, carne, pimientos, papas, plátanos, aceitunas.* Indicate that *pez* refers to a fish before being caught and *pescado* to one already caught. Explain that *vegetales* and *verduras* are used for vegetables.

Suggestion. Explain that *entradas* in a menu is a false cognate, meaning "appetizers," not "entrées." Explain the sections of the menu: *entradas, platos principales, postres.* Write on the board *comidas* and *bebidas* and the related verbs (*comer, beber*). Introduce food vocabulary as you talk about some of the dishes (*queso, huevos, atún, aguacate, pollo, nuez, arroz, leche*) and some methods of cooking (*frito, cocido, estofado*). Explain *relleno.*

Suggestion. Introduce new vocabulary: *El camarero les pregunta a Lola y a Manuel qué desean comer y qué van a beber* [make gestures]. *Ellos van a beber vino para celebrar el cumpleaños de Lola.* Explain that both *beber* and *tomar* mean "to drink." Have students act out the dialogue in groups of three, as if ordering from the menu in a Peruvian restaurant.

Más comidas y bebidas

CD 2
Track 4

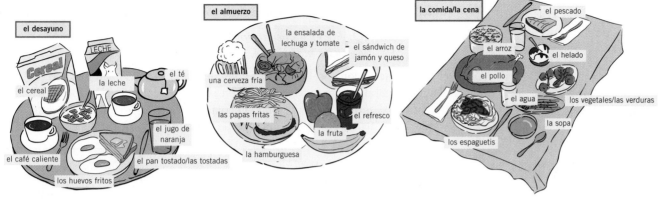

el desayuno

el cereal · la leche · el té · el café caliente · el jugo de naranja · el pan tostado/las tostadas · los huevos fritos

el almuerzo

la ensalada de lechuga y tomate · el sándwich de jamón y queso · una cerveza fría · las papas fritas · la fruta · el refresco · la hamburguesa

la comida/la cena

el pescado · el arroz · el helado · el pollo · el agua · los vegetales/las verduras · la sopa · los espaguetis

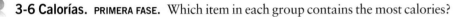

3-6 Calorías. PRIMERA FASE. Which item in each group contains the most calories?

1. la sopa de tomate, una hamburguesa, la sopa de pollo   una hamburguesa
2. el pollo frito, el pescado, la ensalada   el pollo frito
3. los vegetales, las frutas, las papas fritas   las papas fritas
4. la cerveza, la leche desnatada (*skim*), el café   la cerveza
5. el helado de chocolate, el cereal, el arroz   el helado de chocolate

SEGUNDA FASE. Mention items in the *Primera fase* that you eat or drink frequently. Do you both have the same preferences?

MODELO: E1:   *Frecuentemente como ensaladas y bebo cerveza. ¿Y tú?*
          E2:   *Yo frecuentemente como hamburguesas con papas fritas y bebo refrescos.*

3-7 Las comidas. Tell a classmate what you usually have for breakfast, lunch, and dinner. Then find out what he/she usually eats for those meals.

MODELO: *En el desayuno, como tostadas y bebo café. ¿Y tú?*

3-8 Dietas especiales. Which is the best option from this menu for the following people?

1. Su amiga Luisa está un poco delgada y desea subir de peso (*gain weight*). ¿Qué va a comer de este menú?
2. Su mamá es alérgica a los mariscos (*seafood*). ¿Cuál de las ensaladas va a comer?
3. Su amigo José está un poco gordo y quiere bajar de peso (*lose weight*). ¿Cuál de los platos principales no debe comer?
4. El profesor/La profesora de español está enfermo/a (*sick*) del estómago hoy. ¿Qué debe comer?

Cultura

Fast food is popular among young Hispanics, and American-style hamburger places may be found in Hispanic countries. They often adapt to local tastes, and it is not unusual to have hamburgers served with rice and black beans instead of fries. Beer and wine may also be sold in addition to soft drinks.

MENÚ

SOPAS

Sopa de pollo	S/. 9
Sopa de tomate	S/. 7
Sopa de vegetales	S/. 7
Sopa de pescado	S/. 12

ENSALADAS

Ensalada de lechuga y tomate	S/. 8
Ensalada de pollo	S/. 14
Ensalada de atún	S/. 12

PLATOS PRINCIPALES

Bistec con papas y vegetales	S/. 20
Hamburguesa con papas fritas	S/. 16
Pescado con papas fritas	S/. 18
Arroz con vegetales	S/. 15

Note for 3-10. Preview the *ir + a +* infinitive construction with students so that they can use it in this activity.

Suggestions for 3-10. Bring menus to class. Have pairs of students play the roles of diner and server in a restaurant.

Suggestion for 3-11. Review *ir + a +* infinitive to help students talk about their plans. Prepare for this activity by showing photos of Machu Picchu or ask them to read the text in *Enfoque cultural.*

Warm-up for 3-13. Ask students about their weekend plans, favorite restaurants, and favorite foods. Before they listen to the conversation, have them do the *Primera fase* and read aloud the statements they write down.

Audioscript for 3-13
RAFAEL: *Hola, Miguel, ¿cómo estás?*
MIGUEL: *Muy bien, Rafael. ¿Y tú?*
RAFAEL: *Bien, pero cansado. Tomo muchas clases este semestre y estudio mucho porque mi clase de economía es muy difícil. Además trabajo en una librería los martes y jueves por la tarde. Esta semana tenemos exámenes y voy a la biblioteca todos los días.*
MIGUEL: *¿Y qué vas a hacer este fin de semana?*
RAFAEL: *No sé. Me gustaría descansar.*
MIGUEL: *Perfecto. Mira, Rafael, mi familia tiene una casa en la playa. El viernes vamos un grupo de amigos, después del último examen. Vamos a descansar, nadar y tomar el sol. Por la noche vamos a comer en un restaurante. La comida es excelente, especialmente el pescado, y los camareros son muy amables. ¿Por qué no vienes con nosotros? Te va a gustar.*
RAFAEL: *¡Ah! ¡Qué bien! Me gusta mucho descansar en la playa. ¡Y también me gusta la buena comida!*
MIGUEL: *¡Estupendo! Nos vemos el viernes, entonces.*
RAFAEL: *Sí, y gracias, ¿eh?*

 3-9 ¿Qué te gusta más? Using the words below, ask what your partner prefers to drink **por las mañanas, para el almuerzo, por las noches.** Alternate asking questions and taking notes. Then explain your partner's preferences to the class.

MODELO: E1: *¿Qué te gusta beber por las mañanas, té o café?*
E2: *Me gusta más el café.*

el agua mineral con gas	una copa de vino	un refresco
el agua mineral sin gas	una cerveza	el té (helado)
un batido (*shake*)	un chocolate caliente	un vaso (*glass*)
de yogur y fruta	el jugo de naranja	de leche

 3-10 En el café. It is 9:00 on Saturday morning, and you and a friend are in a café in Lima. Ask what your friend wants to order. Then say what you are going to order.

MODELO: E1: *El desayuno es muy bueno aquí. ¿Qué deseas comer?*
E2: _____ *¿Y tú?*
E1: _____ *¿Y qué vas a tomar?*
E2: _____

DESAYUNOS	
café	S/.3
té	S/.3
café con leche	S/.5
jugo de naranja	S/.5
chocolate	S/.6
tostadas	S/.5
pan con mantequilla	S/.5
pan dulce	S/.6
cereal	S/.8
huevos fritos	S/.10

3-11 Un viaje (*trip*). You are in Peru and are planning a day trip to Machu Picchu. Arrange to take some food and beverages with you.

1. Make a list of the food and beverages that you need to take.
2. Talk about the things that you are going to do.

3-12 Nuestro menú. You and your roommate want to have guests over for dinner tonight. Decide whom each of you is going to invite and what you are going to serve. Finally, compare your menu with that of another pair of classmates.

■ Vamos a invitar a _____ .

■ Vamos a servir _____ .

3-13 ¿Qué hacen estos estudiantes? PRIMERA FASE. You will listen to two students, Rafael and Miguel, talk about their activities and weekend plans. Before you listen, write down three activities you normally do during the week, and three that you plan for this weekend.

CD 2
Track 5

actividades de la semana: _____

planes para el fin de semana: _____

SEGUNDA FASE. Now, listen to Rafael and Miguel and pay attention to the general idea of what they say. Then check (✓) the activities they mention they will do during the weekend.

1. ___ estudiar para los exámenes
2. ✓ comer en un restaurante
3. ✓ descansar y tomar el sol
4. ___ trabajar en la librería
5. ___ celebrar el cumpleaños de Rafael

EN ACCIÓN

Diarios de bicicleta: La invitación

Antes de ver

3-14 In this video segment, Javier is at a restaurant. Based on your knowledge of Mexican restaurants in the United States, mark (✓) the sentences that you think describe restaurants in Mexico.

1. _✓_ Hay muchos colores.
2. _✓_ Hay música de mariachis.
3. ___ La comida cuesta mucho dinero.
4. _✓_ Muchos platos tienen chile.

Mientras ve

3-15 Mark (✓) the correct answer according to the information provided.

1. Javier va al restaurante para...
   a. ___ desayunar
   b. _✓_ almorzar
   c. ___ cenar
2. Para comer, Javier pide...
   a. _✓_ pollo con papas fritas y chile habanero.
   b. ___ pollo con papas fritas y chile verde.
   c. ___ sopa azteca.
3. Para beber, Javier pide...
   a. ___ agua mineral bien fría.
   b. ___ un té frío con limón.
   c. _✓_ una limonada bien fría.

Después de ver

3-16 PRIMERA FASE. Mark (✓) the statement that describes the problem that Javier has in this segment.

1. _✓_ Javier no tiene dinero para pagar la cuenta (*bill*).
2. ___ Gabi no puede almorzar con Javier.
3. ___ A Javier no le gusta la comida del restaurante.

SEGUNDA FASE. Write a sentence indicating how Javier's problem is solved. Gabi paga la cuenta.

Warm-up for 3-14. Have students describe their favorite Mexican restaurant to a partner, giving a description of the place as well as the menu.

Note for 3-15. You may wish to preview the *Estrategia* for the *A escuchar* section of the chapter (p. 114) with students, since it deals with using real-life knowledge as a tool for listening comprehension. Students can use their knowledge of restaurants to comprehend the interaction between Javier and the server.

FUNCIONES Y FORMAS

1. Talking about daily activities: Present tense of *hacer, poner, salir, traer,* and *oír*

Unos amigos nuevos conversan sobre sus actividades

CAROLINA: Bueno, para conocernos mejor, ¿por qué no jugamos a *Decir la verdad*? José Manuel, la primera pregunta es para ti. ¿Qué **haces** cuando estás aburrido?

JOSÉ MANUEL: **Pongo** la tele para ver películas. Ahora, Tomás, ¿adónde **sales** cuando tienes tiempo? ¿Y con quién?

TOMÁS: Bueno, **salgo a comer** con mi novia Pilar. Pero cuando tengo exámenes, debo **salir para** la biblioteca. Carolina, cuando **oyes** música salsa, ¿qué **haces**?

CAROLINA: Eso es muy fácil. Siempre bailo cuando **oigo** música salsa. Mi pregunta es para los dos. ¿Qué **hacen** ustedes en casa que no les gusta **hacer**?

TOMÁS: Yo **hago** mi cama porque me gusta el orden.

JOSÉ MANUEL: Mis hermanitos me **traen** su ropa y lavo ropa sucia (*dirty*) todo el fin de semana. La ropa sucia de ellos es repugnante. ¡Qué asco! ¿Y tú, Carolina?

CAROLINA: ¿Yo? Pues, **pongo la mesa** todos los días. ¡Qué lata!

José Manuel   Carolina   Tomás

Piénselo. Match each idea on the left with a logical ending on the right. More than one answer may be possible.

1. _c, e_ **Pongo** la tele…
2. _d_ **Pongo la mesa**…
3. _b, c_ **Oigo** música…
4. _f_ Debo **salir para** la biblioteca…
5. _a, d_ **Hago** mi cama…
6. _d_ Lavo la ropa que **traen** mis hermanos…

a. porque me gusta el orden.
b. cuando **salgo** con mis amigos.
c. para pasarlo bien (*have a good time*).
d. para ayudar (*help*) con el trabajo de casa.
e. porque me gusta ver películas.
f. porque deseo aprender mucho.

- In the present tense, the verbs **hacer, poner, salir, traer,** and **oír** have irregular **yo** forms, but are regular in all other forms.

HACER (*to make, to do*)			
yo	**hago**	nosotros/as	**hacemos**
tú	**haces**	vosotros/as	**hacéis**
Ud., él, ella	**hace**	Uds., ellos/as	**hacen**

- **Hacer** means *to do* or *to make*. It is used frequently in questions to ask in a general sense what someone does, is doing, or likes to do.

¿Qué **haces** para sacar buenas notas?   *What do you do to get good grades?*

Hago la tarea para mis clases todos los días.   *I do the homework for my classes every day.*

PONER (*to put*)			
yo	**pongo**	nosotros/as	**ponemos**
tú	**pones**	vosotros/as	**ponéis**
Ud., él, ella	**pone**	Uds., ellos/as	**ponen**

- **Poner** means *to put*. When used with some electrical appliances, **poner** means *to turn on*; **poner la mesa** means *to set the table*.

Por la mañana **pongo** mis libros en mi mochila.   *In the morning I put my books in my backpack.*

Mi abuelo **pone** la televisión después de la cena.   *My grandfather turns on the TV after dinner.*

Yo **pongo** la mesa a la hora de la cena.   *I set the table at dinner time.*

SALIR (*to leave*)			
yo	**salgo**	nosotros/as	**salimos**
tú	**sales**	vosotros/as	**salís**
Ud., él, ella	**sale**	Uds., ellos/as	**salen**

- **Salir** can be used with several different prepositions. To express that you are leaving a place, use **salir de**; to express your destination, use **salir para**; to express with whom you go out or the person you date, use **salir con**; to express what you are going to do, use **salir a**.

Yo **salgo de** mi cuarto a las 7:15 de la mañana.   *I leave my room at 7:15 in the morning.*

Salgo para la cafetería.   *I am leaving for the cafeteria.*

Mi mejor amiga **sale con** Mauricio.   *My best friend is dating Mauricio.*

Ellos **salen** a bailar los sábados.   *They go out dancing on Saturdays.*

TRAER (*to bring*)			
yo	**traigo**	nosotros/as	**traemos**
tú	**traes**	vosotros/as	**traéis**
Ud., él, ella	**trae**	Uds., ellos/as	**traen**

Yo siempre **traigo** un postre a estas fiestas.   *I always bring a dessert to these parties.*

Suggestion. Present these verbs using images. Talk about the activities of the people in the illustrations, as well as your own activities. For example: *Mi esposo pone la mesa. Yo no pongo* [write *pongo* on the board] *la mesa; yo cocino. Mi hijo pone las películas para nosotros. Y en su casa, ¿quién pone las películas?*

Suggestion. You may want to point out the spelling of *traigo*, as well as the accent mark and the use of *y* in some forms of the verb *oír*.

OÍR (to hear)			
yo	**oigo**	nosotros/as	**oímos**
tú	**oyes**	vosotros/as	**oís**
Ud., él, ella	**oye**	Uds., ellos/as	**oyen**

■ **Oír** means *to hear* in the sense of *to perceive sounds*. Note the spelling and the accent marks in the infinitive, **nosotros/as**, and **vosotros/as** forms.

Yo **oigo** música.	*I hear music.*
— ¿**Oyes** la alarma?	*— Do you hear the alarm?*
— No, no **oigo** nada.	*— No, I don't hear anything.*

Suggestion for 3-17. Have students work in pairs with someone different as often as possible.

3-17 La perfección andante (*Perfection in motion*). PRIMERA FASE. Are you organized, considerate, studious, and/or punctual? Check (✓) the statements that refer to things you do or don't do regularly.

1. _____ Yo **hago** mi cama temprano por la mañana.
2. _____ Cuando **oigo** que un amigo está triste, lo invito a salir.
3. _____ Siempre **pongo** música rock cuando estudio.
4. _____ Generalmente, **traigo** el periódico a la mesa para leer las noticias mientras desayuno.
5. _____ En general, no **traigo** el periódico a la mesa mientras desayuno porque prefiero conversar con mi familia.
6. _____ Por las mañanas, **hago** ejercicio y luego **salgo** para la universidad.

SEGUNDA FASE. Take turns talking about the activities you both do that show off your best qualities.

MODELO: E1: *Yo soy organizado. Siempre hago mi cama temprano. ¿Y tú?*
E2: *Pues, yo también... /No, yo no...*

3-18 ¿Usa usted bien su tiempo libre? PRIMERA FASE. Check (✓) the version of each activity that best describes your habits.

1. _____ Pongo la mesa para cenar.   _____ Como en cualquier lugar de la casa.
2. _____ Hago el desayuno.   _____ Salgo a desayunar fuera de casa.
3. _____ Hago la cama cada día.   _____ Hago la cama una vez por semana.
4. _____ Oigo las noticias en la radio.   _____ Veo las noticias en la televisión.
5. _____ Traigo el periódico a la casa.   _____ Leo el periódico en el cibercafé.
6. _____ Pongo la televisión para ver películas.   _____ Salgo al cine para ver películas.

SEGUNDA FASE. Working with a partner, compare your answers and determine which of you has more fun doing these things. Explain why.

3-19 Mi rutina. PRIMERA FASE. Talk about the activities that you routinely do. Then ask your classmate about his/her activities.

MODELO: tener clases por la mañana/por la tarde
  E1: *Yo tengo clases por la mañana. ¿Y tú?*
  E2: *Yo tengo clases por la mañana y por la tarde./Yo también tengo clases por la mañana.*

1. normalmente salir de su casa temprano/tarde por la mañana
2. generalmente poner la radio/tele para escuchar su música favorita por la mañana
3. hacer la tarea en casa/en la biblioteca
4. frecuentemente salir a comer/ver películas con su familia por la noche
5. con frecuencia traer muchos libros a casa después de las clases

SEGUNDA FASE. Write a brief paragraph comparing your routine with that of your classmate. In your opinion, who has a more interesting routine, and why? Provide a few reasons.

3-20 Para pasarlo bien. PRIMERA FASE. Write a check (✓) next to the activities that, in your opinion, your classmates probably do to have fun.

1. _____ Ponen películas los fines de semana.
2. _____ Oyen música y bailan mientras estudian para los exámenes.
3. _____ Frecuentemente hacen fiestas con sus amigos.
4. _____ Asisten a conciertos y exposiciones de arte.
5. _____ Hacen ejercicio en el gimnasio o en el parque.
6. _____ Escuchan programas en la radio pública.
7. _____ Salen a comer en grupo.
8. _____ ...

SEGUNDA FASE. Using the activities you marked in the *Primera fase* as a starting point, ask if your instructor does the same activities to have fun. Refer to *En directo* to help you express your reactions to your instructor's responses.

MODELO: PAREJA: *Para pasarlo bien, nosotros asistimos a conciertos de música rock. ¿Asiste a conciertos de música rock para pasarlo bien?*
  PROFESOR/A: *No asisto a conciertos de música rock. Para pasarlo bien escucho conciertos de música clásica en la radio pública.*
  PAREJA: *¡Qué aburrido!*

En directo

To react to what someone has said:

¡Qué interesante!

¡Qué divertido!
How funny!

¡Qué aburrido!

SITUACIONES

1. **Role A.** You are interviewing a potential roommate for your two-bedroom apartment. Find out a) if he/she likes things to be neat (**si le gusta el orden**); b) what household chores he/she likes to do and does not like to do; and c) what he/she likes to do at home in his/her free time. Your interviewee will have questions for you also. At the end of the conversation, decide whether to accept this person as a roommate.

   Role B. You are new in town and are being interviewed by someone who has a room to rent in his/her apartment. Answer the questions in as much detail as possible and ask some questions of your own. At the end of the conversation, decide whether you are interested in the room.

2. **Role A.** You have just been hired to take care of a five-year-old boy for the summer. Ask what time the parent leaves the house in the morning and find out a) what the child eats and drinks for breakfast and lunch; b) whether he has to make his bed or set the table; and c) what his favorite activities are.

   Role B. You have just hired a college student to take care of your five-year-old son for the summer. Answer his/her questions. To get to know him/her better, ask a) what he/she studies at school and b) what he/she likes to do in his/her free time.

Alternate for 3-20. Students may ask partners if and when they do some of the activities listed. Then they switch partners and tell each other the information they gathered.

Suggestion for 3-20. *Para pasarlo bien* appeared earlier in the chapter. You may wish to reinforce its meaning: *Hay muchas maneras de pasarlo bien. Yo, por ejemplo, para pasarlo bien, escucho música, voy al cine con amigos, tengo/hago fiestas en mi casa y otras actividades similares. ¿Y usted, lee o baila para pasarlo bien? ¿Qué hace usted para pasarlo bien los fines de semana/durante las vacaciones?*

Suggestion for 3-20 Segunda fase. Encourage students to be creative in their questions about your activities, and use humor to exaggerate similarities and/or differences between students' leisure activities and your own.

Suggestion for Situaciones. Encourage students to make their conversations sound natural and realistic. To help them compensate for possible lack of vocabulary, review greetings and communication strategies, such as asking for repetition, asking questions, and using synonyms/opposite (*Repite, por favor; No comprendo; Más despacio, por favor; ¿Qué significa____?*).

2. Expressing movement and plans: Present tense of *ir* and *ir a + infinitive*

Elena, la chica en el centro, habla de sus amigos

Mis amigos y yo somos diferentes, pero somos muy unidos. Para mi cumpleaños, nosotros **vamos a** un restaurante todos los años. Los sábados, yo **voy a** la casa de mi amiga Estela, y luego ella **va** conmigo **al** gimnasio para hacer ejercicio. A veces Rafael, Humberto y Rodrigo también **van al** gimnasio con nosotras. Mi amiga Teresa, no sale mucho porque prefiere estudiar. Yo siempre bromeo (*joke*) con ella: "Tere, ¿**vas a** la biblioteca a pasarlo bien?" Fernando, es muy tranquilo y artístico y le fascina el silencio. Con frecuencia él y Estela **van a** la librería a comprar libros.

Piénselo. Read the following statements about Elena and her friends. Then indicate (✓) if the statement is **probable** or **improbable**, based on the information Elena provides.

	PROBABLE	IMPROBABLE
1. Elena y sus amigos **van a** lugares juntos para celebrar su cumpleaños.	✓	
2. Fernando **va a** los conciertos de música rock.		✓
3. Estela afirma: "Frecuentemente, yo **voy a** la librería a comprar libros".		✓
4. Teresa comenta: "Fernando y yo **vamos al** museo de arte esta tarde".	✓	
5. Elena no **va a** las fiestas de cumpleaños de sus amigos.		✓

■ After the verb **ir**, use **a** to introduce a noun that refers to a place. When **a** is followed by the article **el**, the two words contract to form **al**.

| Voy **a la** fiesta de María. | *I am going to María's party.* |
| Vamos **al** gimnasio. | *We are going to the gym.* |

■ Use **¿adónde?** when asking *where (to)?* with the verb **ir**.

| **¿Adónde** vas ahora? | *Where are you going now?* |

IR (*to go*)			
yo	**voy**	nosotros/as	**vamos**
tú	**vas**	vosotros/as	**vais**
Ud., él, ella	**va**	Uds., ellos/as	**van**

■ To express a future action or condition, use the present tense of **ir a +** the infinitive form of the verb.

| Mis amigos **van a nadar** después. | *My friends are going to swim later.* |
| ¿**Vas a ir** a la fiesta? | *Are you going to go to the party?* |

■ The expression **vamos a +** *infinitive* can mean *let's*.

| **Vamos a cenar** en mi casa. | *Let's have dinner at my house.* |
| **Vamos a bailar** después. | *Let's go dancing afterward.* |

Lengua

The following expressions denote future time:

después, más tarde, esta noche, mañana, pasado mañana, la próxima semana, el próximo mes/año.

3-21 ¿Adónde van? PRIMERA FASE. Josh and Steve are North American students visiting Peru for their summer vacation. Match the descriptions on the left with the places they plan to see on the right.

1. __c__ Steve estudia historia. Por eso, desea ver la universidad prestigiosa y más antigua de América de Sur. Está en Lima. Él va a…

2. __b__ Los dos amigos van a visitar uno de los lugares más misteriosos del planeta. Allí hay enormes figuras geométricas trazadas (*drawn*) en la tierra que son visibles solamente desde el aire. Ellos van a…

3. __d__ Josh conoce (*meets*) a Susana en Perú. Ella lo invita a un evento folclórico donde las personas oyen poesía, música tradicional y comen y bailan también. Josh y Susana van a…

4. __a__ Steve y Josh van a un lugar histórico imposible de ignorar. Es considerado el símbolo del imperio inca. Está cerca de Cuzco. Steve y Josh van a…

SEGUNDA FASE. Now indicate where you will go to do the following in Peru.

1. Para hacer amigos, conversar y bailar ritmos peruanos, yo voy a
   _____una peña_____ .

2. Voy a _la Universidad de San Marcos_ para tomar fotos de los alumnos y el edificio de una universidad muy antigua.

3. Para escalar unas montañas altas de mucha importancia histórica, voy a
   _____Machu Picchu_____ .

3-22 Intercambio. PRIMERA FASE. Your classmate's friends are busy today. Find out when each friend is leaving the place listed and where he/she is going afterward.

MODELO: E1: *¿A qué hora sale del trabajo tu amigo Armando?*
E2: *(Sale) a las seis de la tarde.*
E1: *¿Adónde va después?*
E2: *Va al cine.*

NOMBRE	HORA	LUGAR
Juan	8:00 a.m.	gimnasio
Alicia	9:30 a.m.	laboratorio de computadoras
Sofía	8:30 p.m.	oficina
Tú	…	…

SEGUNDA FASE. Exchange information with your partner about what each of you does at the times listed in the *Primera fase.*

MODELO: E1: *¿Qué haces a las 8:00 de la mañana?*
E2: *Salgo de mi casa para la universidad.*
E1: *¿Adónde vas cuando llegas a la universidad?*
E2: *Voy a mi clase de español. ¿Qué haces tú a las 8:00 de la mañana?*

a. Machu Picchu

b. las líneas de Nazca

c. la Universidad de San Marcos

d. una peña

Note for 3-21. *Las líneas de Nazca* are a series of figures, including complex hummingbirds, spiders, monkeys, fish, sharks, llamas, and lizards, that were etched into the earth in the Nazca Desert in southern Peru by members of the Nazca culture between 200 B.C. and 700 A.D. The lines can be recognized as coherent figures only from the air, and the question of how and why they were created remains a mystery.

3-23 ¡Qué lío! (*What a mess!*) PRIMERA FASE. Cristina had a party at her house while her parents were out of town, and now her friends are helping her clean up. Match each situation on the left with its probable solution.

1. __b__ Hay muchos platos sucios.
2. __c__ Cristina ve mucha comida en la mesa.
3. __a__ La casa está desordenada.
4. __d__ Cristina y sus amigos necesitan energía para limpiar la casa.
5. __e__ Los amigos de Cristina están cansados después de la fiesta.

a. Dos chicos van a ordenar todo.
b. Algunos amigos van a recoger (*pick up*) los platos.
c. Una amiga va a refrigerar la comida.
d. Una amiga va a preparar café.
e. Van a descansar.

 SEGUNDA FASE. Brainstorm how Cristina's parents are going to react when they find out about her party. Some suggestions may include: *cancelar las tarjetas de crédito, prohibir fiestas/amigos, conversar seriamente, ...*

Suggestion for 3-23 Segunda fase. You may wish to ask students to support their responses. Model as follows: *Los padres van a conversar seriamente con Cristina sobre las fiestas secretas. Creen que no es correcto hacer fiestas secretas, etc.*

Suggestion for 3-24. Before students do the activity, model with a few of them how to issue, accept, and reject invitations. Refer students to the *En directo* box on p. 92.

Expansion for 3-24. Have students prepare their agenda for the upcoming week and then take turns asking questions to find out what their classmates are going to do. Model as follows: *¿Qué vas a hacer la próxima semana? ¿Adónde vas a ir?*

Warm-up for 3-25. Use posters of people engaged in a variety of activities to solicit spontaneous descriptions of what each person is going to do. Then ask students to compare their activities with those shown in the drawings.

SITUACIONES

1. **Role A.** Your friend has invited you to a concert. Call him/her to find out a) where and when the concert is going to be; b) who is going to sing; c) who is going to introduce (**presentar**) the group; and d) how much the ticket (**el boleto/el billete/la entrada**) costs.

   Role B. Your friend calls to find out about a concert you invited him/her to. Answer all the questions with as much information as possible.

2. **Role A.** You call to invite a friend to a café tonight where a mutual friend is going to sing. After your friend responds, ask about his/her plans for later in the evening: a) where he/she is going; b) with whom; and c) what time, etc.

   Role B. A friend calls to invite you to a café tonight where a mutual friend is going to sing. Inquire about the event to find out a) what time and where it will be and b) if other friends are going to go. Accept the invitation and mention your plans for later in the evening.

3-24 Mi agenda para la semana. Invite six classmates individually to do the following activities with you. Each will accept or reject your invitation according to his/her schedule for the week. Indicate the day, the activity and the name of the classmate who accepted your invitation.

MODELO:
estudiar en la biblioteca el lunes
E1: *¿Vamos a estudiar en la biblioteca el lunes?*
E2: *Lo siento, Miguel, el lunes voy a ir al cine con David. Pero, ¿por qué no salimos a comer el martes?*
E3: *Buena idea. Vamos a salir el martes.*

1. ir a un concierto
2. mirar televisión en casa
3. tomar algo en un café
4. estudiar para un examen difícil
5. bailar en la discoteca
6. hacer ejercicio

DÍA	¿QUÉ VA A HACER?	¿CON QUIÉN?
martes	comer en un restaurante peruano	Miguel

3-25 Los planes de Maribel. PRIMERA FASE. Take turns saying what Maribel is going to do at the times indicated.

SEGUNDA FASE. Tell your classmate what you are going to do at those times on Friday.

3. Talking about quantity: Numbers 100 to 2.000.000

Resources

■ SAM: 3-27 to 3-29
■ Supp. Activ. Book: Numbers 100 to 2.000.000

Lengua

In Spanish, numbers higher than one thousand, such as dates or street addresses, are not stated in pairs as they often are in English. For example, 1942 is expressed as **mil novecientos cuarenta y dos**, whereas in English it is almost always given as *nineteen forty-two*.

Piénselo. Your instructor will say a number from each of the following series. Identify each number you hear. The numbers in the last row are dates.

1. 114	360	850	524
2. 213	330	490	919
3. 818	625	723	513
4. 667	777	984	534
5. 1.310	1.420	3.640	6.860
6. 10.467	50.312	100.000	2.000.000
7. 1492	1776	1890	2001

Suggestion for Piénselo. This activity has a different format from the other *Piénselo* activities. The instructor says one number aloud from each row and students identify the number by circling it in their books or by holding up one, two, three, or four fingers to show if the number they hear is the first, second, third, or fourth in the group. As a follow-up, say numbers again in random order and ask students to write each one. (Confirm by writing them on the board.)

Note. Point out the exceptions: *quinientos, setecientos, novecientos.* Also point out that *y* is not used after *cien, ciento, mil,* or *millón,* only between tens and units (*ciento cuarenta y cinco*).

■ You have already learned the numbers up to 99. In this section you will learn numbers to use to talk about larger quantities.

100	cien/ciento	1.000	mil
200	doscientos/as	1.100	mil cien
300	trescientos/as	2.000	dos mil
400	cuatrocientos/as	10.000	diez mil
500	quinientos/as	100.000	cien mil
600	seiscientos/as	150.000	ciento cincuenta mil
700	setecientos/as	500.000	quinientos mil
800	ochocientos/as	1.000.000	un millón (de)
900	novecientos/as	2.000.000	dos millones (de)

- Use **cien** to say 100 when used alone or when followed by a noun. Use **ciento** for numbers from 101 to 199.

100	**cien**
100 chicos	**cien** chicos
120 profesoras	**ciento** veinte profesoras
177 libros	**ciento** setenta y siete libros

- Multiples of 100 agree in gender with the noun they modify.

| 200 periódicos | **doscientos** periódicos |
| 1.400 revistas | **mil cuatrocientas** revistas |

- Use **mil** for *one thousand*. Multiples of 1,000 are also **mil**.

| 1.000 | **mil** alumnos, **mil** alumnas |
| 12.000 | **doce mil** residentes |

- Use **un millón** to say *one million*. Use **un millón de** when a noun follows.

1.000.000	**un millón**
1.000.000 de personas	**un millón de personas**
12.000.000 de dólares	**doce millones de dólares**

- In many Spanish-speaking countries, a period is used to separate thousands, and a comma is used to separate decimals.

| $1.000 | $19,50 |

Note for 3-26. Some Spanish speakers use *el* with the year 2000 and subsequent years: *Voy a visitar Machu Picchu en el 2012. Mosaicos* follows the Royal Spanish Academy (RAE) recommendation not to use *el* in this context. Before students do the activity, introduce and practice the use of *(no) estar de acuerdo.*

 3-26 ¿Cuándo va a ocurrir? Exchange opinions with a classmate about when each of the following events will occur.

MODELO: Todos los libros van a ser electrónicos.
　　　　E1: *En el año 2020.*
　　　　E2: *Estoy de acuerdo.* Or
　　　　　　No estoy de acuerdo. Todos los libros van a ser electrónicos en 2050.

1. Los adultos van a trabajar sólo 20 horas por semana.
2. Los estudiantes no van a ir a clases. Van a estudiar en universidades virtuales.
3. Todos los autos van a ser eléctricos y van a ser muy rápidos.
4. Los turistas van a ir de un país a otro sin pasaporte.
5. La contaminación va a ser muy grande, y las personas van a usar máscaras (*masks*) en los parques y en las calles.
6. Los robots, y no las personas, van a servir la comida en los restaurantes.
7. Las personas van a comunicarse por telepatía.
8. Muchas personas van a comer solamente la comida artificial.
9. Muchos turistas van a viajar (*travel*) al espacio interplanetario.
10. Los viajes en avión van a ser más rápidos y van a costar poco.

3-27 Unas vacaciones. PRIMERA FASE. Your classmate has chosen one of the destinations in the ad for an upcoming vacation. To find out where he/she is going, ask the following questions. Then switch roles.

1. ¿Adónde vas?
2. ¿Qué lugares vas a ver?
3. ¿Cuántos días vas a estar allí?
4. ¿Cuánto cuesta la excursión?

SEGUNDA FASE. Based on your classmate's answers, fill in the information and share it with the class.

1. planes que su compañero/a necesita hacer (sacar un pasaporte, obtener una visa, hacer reservaciones, etc.):

   _____

2. lugar(es) que va a visitar: _____
3. tiempo que va a estar allí: _____
4. costo de la excursión: _____
5. dinero extra que usted cree que su compañero/a va a necesitar: _____

AGENCIA MUNDIAL

A SU SERVICIO SIEMPRE 20 años de experiencia, responsabilidad y profesionalidad.

TODOS LOS PRECIOS INCLUYEN PASAJES AÉREOS Y SERVICIOS TERRESTRES POR PERSONA

PERÚ Y BOLIVIA

LIMA, AREQUIPA, CUZCO, MACHU PICCHU, PUNO, LA PAZ, 15 días. La Ruta del Inca. Hoteles de 3 y 4 estrellas. Desayuno incluido.
$2.760

PERÚ

LIMA, CUZCO, MACHU PICCHU, NAZCA, 12 días. Visite fortalezas incas. Vea las misteriosas líneas de Nazca desde el aire. Hoteles de primera. Desayuno y cena incluidos.
$3.150

LIMA, NAZCA, AREQUIPA, LAGO TITICACA, 10 días. Admire la arquitectura colonial de Lima y Arequipa. Vea las líneas de Nazca desde el aire. Navegue en el lago más alto del mundo. Hoteles de primera.
$2.620

ARGENTINA

BUENOS AIRES, BARILOCHE, MENDOZA, 12 días. Disfrute de una gran metrópoli. Esquíe en uno de los lugares más bellos del mundo. Hoteles de 4 y 5 estrellas. Desayuno y cena.
$3.590

CHILE Y ARGENTINA

SANTIAGO, PUERTO MONTT, BARILOCHE, BUENOS AIRES, 12 días. Excursión a Viña del Mar y Valparaíso. Cruce de los Andes en minibús y barco. Hoteles de 3 y 4 estrellas.
$4.075

CARIBE

JAMAICA, 7 días. Happy Inn, todo incluido. Exclusivo para parejas.
$2.480

PUERTO RICO

SAN JUAN, 5 días. Hotel de 5 estrellas. Excursión a Ponce. Visita con guía al Viejo San Juan. Desayuno incluido.
$1.995

MÉXICO

MÉXICO, TAXCO, ACAPULCO, 7 días. Hoteles de 3 y 4 estrellas. Excursión a Teotihuacán. Desayuno bufet incluido.
$1.800

CANCÚN, 5 días. Hotel de 4 estrellas. Excursión a Cozumel. Visita a ruinas mayas. Las mejores playas.
$1.510

Solicite los programas detallados con variantes de hoteles e itinerarios a su agente de viajes.

Tel. 312-785-4455   Fax: 312-785-4456

Suggestion for 3–27. Students can get information on Peru in *Enfoque cultural*, pages 118–119, and also on the *Mosaicos* web page.

SITUACIONES

1. **Role A.** You have been saving up for a special trip (**viaje**) during the next school vacation, and you are now making plans. Call a friend to explain a) where you plan to go; b) who will travel with you; and c) what you plan to do.

   Role B. Your friend calls to tell you about his/her travel plans for the next school break. Ask a) with whom he/she is planning to go; and b) what places he/she is going to visit. You are curious about the cost of the trip (**viaje**), so you inquire about the cost of the flight (**el vuelo**), the hotel, and the activities your friend plans to do.

2. **Role A.** You have been working hard, and you would like to splurge on a weekend trip to do some special (but expensive) activities, like rent a car, go to a professional sports event or rock concert, eat in good restaurants, and shop (**ir de compras**). Call and invite your friend to go. Explain your plan and be prepared to answer questions about the cost of this weekend adventure.

   Role B. Your friend calls to invite you on an exciting (but expensive) weekend trip. After your friend explains the plan, ask questions to get an idea of the cost. Decide whether you can afford it, and either accept or decline the invitation.

En directo

To call attention to an unusual fact:

¡Fíjate qué noticia!
How about that!

¡Imagínate!

To react to good news:

¡Qué suerte!

¡Qué maravilla!

¡Qué bien!

To convince someone:

¡Ven/Anda, anímate!
Come on, cheer up!

Lo vamos a pasar muy bien.
We are going to have a good time.

Note for Situaciones. Now that students have been doing *Situaciones* for several chapters, you may wish to give them guidance on how to maximize the communicative potential of this activity. Each student should read the instructions for his/her role only, not the partner's instructions. Give them 2 to 3 minutes to prepare for the task. As an oral assessment, you may wish to have students practice the role-play with a partner, and then ask several pairs to perform for the class. (Other pairs may perform for a different role-play in the chapter.) Pay close attention to the use of register (*usted* or *tú*), vocabulary, and negotiation strategies (to clarify meaning, to agree, disagree, refuse politely, etc.) between students.

4. Stating what you know: *Saber* and *conocer*

ALFREDO: Me gustan mucho los músicos y ella **sabe** cantar muy bien.

ELENA: Sí, es una cantante fabulosa.

MARIO: Luisa, **conoces** a Liliana, ¿no?

LUISA: Sí, las dos estamos en la clase de arte de la profesora Ruiz.

Piénselo. Indicate (✓) in the appropriate box whether each sentence refers to knowing a fact, knowing how to do something, knowing a person, or being familiar with a place, an event, or a thing.

	KNOWING A FACT	KNOWING HOW TO DO SOMETHING	KNOWING A PERSON	BEING FAMILIAR WITH A PLACE, EVENT, ETC.
1. **¿Conoces** la música afro-peruana?	___	___	___	✓
2. Me gusta mucho la música, pero no **sé** bailar.	___	✓	___	___
3. **¿Sabes** los nombres de esos grupos musicales?	✓	___	___	___
4. **¿Conoces** a Alfredo Roncal? Toca la guitarra.	___	___	✓	___
5. **¿Sabes** si hay un club de música hispana en la ciudad?	✓	___	___	___
6. Alfredo **conoce** todos los clubes de música en la ciudad.	___	___	___	✓

■ Both **saber** and **conocer** mean *to know*, but they are not used interchangeably.

	SABER	CONOCER
yo	sé	conozco
tú	sabes	conoces
Ud., él, ella	sabe	conoce
nosotros/as	sabemos	conocemos
vosotros/as	sabéis	conocéis
Uds., ellos/as	saben	conocen

■ Use **saber** to express knowledge of facts or pieces of information.

Él **sabe** dónde está el club.　　*He knows where the club is.*

■ Use **saber** + *infinitive* to express knowing how to do something.

Yo **sé** tocar la guitarra.　　　*I know how to play the guitar.*

■ Use **conocer** to express familiarity with someone or something. **Conocer** also means *to meet*. Remember to use the *personal a* when referring to people.

Conozco a los músicos.　　　*I know the musicians.*

Conozco bien ese club.　　　*I am very familiar with that club.*

Ella va a **conocer a** Luis.　　　*She is going to meet Luis.*

> ### Lengua
>
> **Sé**, the **yo** form of the verb **saber**, has a written accent to distinguish it from the pronoun **se**.
>
> Yo **sé** que su hermano **se** llama José.

3-28 Un encuentro entre dos estudiantes. Raúl just arrived on campus, and he asks Sergio some questions. Select the correct words to complete their conversation.

RAÚL:	Soy un estudiante nuevo y no (1) _____ dónde está la biblioteca.	**a.** sé	**b.** conozco
SERGIO:	Es muy fácil. Tú (2) _____ dónde está la cafetería, ¿no? Pues, está al lado.	**a.** sabes	**b.** conoces
RAÚL:	Gracias. ¿Y (3) _____ si hay un club de español?	**a.** sabes	**b.** conoces
SERGIO:	Sí, claro, y (4) _____ que esta noche tiene una reunión.	**a.** sé	**b.** conozco
RAÚL:	Magnífico. Sólo (5) _____ a dos o tres personas en la universidad.	**a.** sé	**b.** conozco
SERGIO:	Pues allí vas a (6) _____ a muchos estudiantes.	**a.** saber	**b.** conocer

3-29 ¿Sabes quién es...? Ask your partner if he/she knows who is being referred to and if he/she knows that person. Take turns asking questions.

MODELO:　　el actor principal de *El ultimátum de Bourne*
E1: *¿Sabes quién es el actor principal de* El ultimátum de Bourne*?*
E2: *Sí, sé quién es. Es Matt Damon.*
E1: *¿Conoces a Matt Damon en persona?*
E2: *No, no conozco a Matt Damon./Sí, conozco a Matt Damon, pero solamente en fotografías.*

1. el/la representante de la Cámara de Representantes (*Congress*) de su distrito
2. el decano/la decana de la facultad
3. su profesor/a de español
4. el rey de España
5. el gobernador de su estado
6. el vicepresidente de Estados Unidos

3-30 Adivina, adivinador. In small groups, take turns reading the descriptions and guessing who is being described.

MODELO:　E1: *Es una chica muy pobre que va a un baile. Allí conoce a un príncipe, pero a las 12:00 de la noche ella debe volver a su casa.*
　　　　E2: *Sé quién es. Es Cenicienta* (Cinderella).

1. Es un gorila gigante con sentimientos (*feelings*) humanos. En una película aparece en el edificio Empire State de Nueva York. King Kong
2. Fue (*She was*) una mujer muy importante en Argentina. Su esposo gobernó (*governed*) ese país por varios años. Hay un musical con su nombre y también una película donde Madonna la representa. Eva Perón/Evita
3. Es una diseñadora de ropa y joyas, hija de un famoso pintor cubista español. Su perfume más famoso lleva su nombre. Paloma Picasso
4. Es un hombre de otro planeta con doble personalidad. Trabaja en un periódico, pero cuando se pone una ropa azul especial, puede volar (*fly*). Superman

Suggestion for 3-31. Use visuals and personalized questions to elicit the use of *saber + infinitive: ¿Sabe bailar esta persona? Y usted, ¿sabe bailar? ¿Sabe bailar muy bien?* Ask some students to name one thing they can do.

Suggestion for 3-32. Students may consult the *Enfoque cultural* (pp. 118–119) or read about Peru on the Internet prior to doing this activity so they will be able to answer the questions. Options for doing this activity: 1. Students close their books, and the instructor asks the questions, calling on the first student to raise his/her hand. 2. In groups of 4 or 5, students spend 5 minutes preparing answers to the questions. Then they close their books and the game proceeds as above, but groups take turns giving the first response to the question.

Answers for 3-32. Top row: *En Perú; Lima; ruinas de los incas* Middle row: Alan García (2008); *Nuevo Sol; el lago Titicaca* Bottom row: Possible answers: *ceviche de pescado, yuca frita, adobo de chancho, chupe de camarones;* answers may vary; answers may vary; *los Andes.*

Suggestion for 3-33. You may wish to give examples of the use of *entonces* and *tampoco.*

Suggestion for Situaciones. Before students do the first role-play, have them make a list of five people, at least some of whom they believe their partner may know personally.

SITUACIONES

1. **Role A.** If you have not already done so, make a list of five people, at least some of whom you think your partner knows personally. Choose three of them and ask a) if your partner knows them and b) what your partner knows about them. Be ready to answer similar questions.

   Role B. If you have not already done so, make a list of five people, at least some of whom you think your partner knows personally. Your partner will tell you the names of three people on his/her list and will ask a) if you know them and b) what you know about them. Answer and then ask your partner the same questions about three of the people on your list.

2. **Role A.** You are looking for a third roommate for your apartment. Your partner knows a student from Peru who is looking for a place to live. Ask your partner a) the Peruvian student's name; b) where in Peru he/she is from; and c) if your partner knows the Peruvian student well. Also find out if the Peruvian student knows how to cook Peruvian dishes and how to play soccer (**fútbol**).

   Role B. Your partner is looking for a third roommate for his/her apartment. Mention that you know a student from Peru who is looking for a place to live. Answer your partner's questions about that person.

3-31 ¿Qué sabes hacer? Ask your partner if he/she knows how to do the following things. If your partner says yes, ask more questions to get additional information.

MODELO: bailar salsa y merengue
E1: *¿Sabes bailar salsa y merengue?*
E2: *Sí, sé bailar salsa y merengue./No, no sé bailar salsa y merengue. ¿Y tú?*

1. tocar un instrumento musical
2. cantar bien
3. preparar ceviche
4. manejar (*drive*) un autobús
5. cocinar platos muy elaborados
6. sacar (*take*) fotos con una cámara digital
7. hablar muchas lenguas
8. …

3-32 Bingo. To win this game of bingo, you have to fill in three boxes (horizontal, vertical, or diagonal) with the names of classmates who answer the answers correctly.

¿Quién sabe dónde está la ciudad de Cuzco?	¿Quién sabe cuál es la capital de Perú ?	¿Quién sabe qué es Machu Picchu?
¿Quién conoce al presidente de Perú?	¿Quién sabe cuál es la unidad monetaria de Perú?	¿Quién sabe el nombre de un lago importante que está entre Perú y Bolivia?
¿Quién conoce unos platos típicos de la cocina (*cuisine*) peruana?	¿Quién conoce algún país hispanoamericano?	¿Quién sabe cómo se llaman las montañas de Perú?

3-33 Saber y conocer. Complete the conversation with the correct forms of **saber** and **conocer.** Review your answers with a partner.

PACO: ¿ __Conoces__ (1) a esa chica?
AUGUSTO: Sí, yo __conozco__ (2) a todas las chicas aquí.
PACO: Entonces, ¿ __sabes__ (3) dónde vive?
AUGUSTO: No, no __sé__ (4) dónde vive.
PACO: ¿ __Sabes__ (5) cómo se llama?
AUGUSTO: Lo siento, pero no __sé__ (6).
PACO: Pero ¿cómo dices que __conoces__ (7) a la chica? Tú no __sabes__ (8) dónde vive y tú no __sabes__ (9) su nombre.

5. Expressing intention, means, movement, and duration: Some uses of *por* and *para*

CARLOS: Papá, necesito tu auto **por** una semana. ¿Está bien?

PADRE: ¿**Por** una semana? ¿**Por** qué?

CARLOS: **Porque** mis amigos y yo vamos a ir la playa **para** las vacaciones de primavera.

PADRE: ¡%$#@!

Piénselo. Indicate whether the following statements are true (**Cierto**) or false (**Falso**) according to the conversation.

1. _C_ Carlos necesita el auto de su padre **por** una semana.
2. _C_ El padre pregunta **por qué** Carlos desea el auto.
3. _C_ Carlos desea ir a la playa **para** las vacaciones de primavera.
4. _F_ Los amigos de Carlos necesitan el auto **para** trabajar.
5. _F_ El padre está alegre **porque** Carlos necesita su auto.

■ **Por** and **para** have different meanings in Spanish, though sometimes they are both translated into English as *for*. The uses presented here include some you have already seen, as well as some new ones.

■ **Para** expresses *for* when you mean *intended for* or *to be used for*. It can refer to a person, an event, or a purpose.

Necesito un diccionario **para** la clase.	*I need a dictionary for the class.*
Este diccionario es **para** David.	*This dictionary is for David.*

■ **Para +** *infinitive* means *in order to.*

Uso el autobús **para** ir a la universidad.	*I use the bus (in order) to go to the university.*
El restaurante hace publicidad **para** traer clientes.	*The restaurant does advertising (in order) to bring in customers.*

■ **Por** appears in expressions such as **por favor**, **por teléfono**, and **por la mañana/tarde/noche**. Other expressions with **por** that you will find useful include the following:

por ciento	*percent*	**por fin**	*finally, at last*
por ejemplo	*for example*	**por lo menos**	*at least*
por eso	*that is why*	**por supuesto**	*of course*

Suggestion. You may remind students that *Caminan para/a la playa* are both used.

■ **Por** and **para** can also be used to express movement in space and time.

Para indicates movement toward a destination.

Caminan **para** la playa.	*They walk toward the beach.*
Vamos **para** el túnel.	*We are going toward the tunnel.*

Por indicates movement through or by a place.

Caminan **por** la playa.	*They walk along the beach.*
Vamos **por** el túnel.	*We are going through the tunnel.*

You may also use **por** to indicate length of time or duration of an action.

Many Spanish speakers omit **por** in this case, or they use **durante**.

Necesito el auto (**por**) tres días.	*I need the car for three days.*

3-34 ¿Por o para? Match each use of **por** and **para** in the following text with the letter of its appropriate meaning from the list on the right.

Mis amigos y yo siempre estamos ocupados los fines de semana. Los viernes **por**¹ la noche, siempre vamos a un cine cerca de nuestro barrio. Cuando vamos **para**² el cine, caminamos **por**³ el parque. Después del cine, a veces hacemos fiestas en casa. Yo compro una pizza y papas fritas **para**⁴ comer con ellos. Si es una fiesta de cumpleaños, compro un regalo especial **para**⁵ mi amigo. **Para**⁶ celebrar, también invito a todos los miembros del grupo. A veces lo pasamos bien **por**⁷ largas horas.

1. <u>d</u>		**a.**	intended for (person)
2. <u>e</u>		**b.**	used for (purpose)
3. <u>f</u>		**c.**	in order to
4. <u>c</u>		**d.**	length of time
5. <u>a</u>		**e.**	movement toward a destination
6. <u>c</u>		**f.**	movement through or by a place
7. <u>d</u>			

 3-35 ¿Para dónde van? Guess where these people are going, and compare your guesses with your classmate's. Then find out where your classmate is going after class, and why.

MODELO: Jorge busca su uniforme de fútbol.
  Va para el estadio.

1. Es la una de la tarde y Pedro desea comer.
2. Sebastián lleva una mochila con sus libros de química y una calculadora.
3. Magdalena y Roberto van a consultar unos libros porque tienen un examen.
4. Gregorio va a comprar un libro para su clase de español.
5. Ana María va a ver una película de su actor favorito.
6. Amanda y Clara están muy elegantes y contentas. En este momento llegan Arturo y Felipe en su auto.

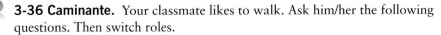 **3-36 Caminante.** Your classmate likes to walk. Ask him/her the following questions. Then switch roles.

1. ¿Te gusta caminar con amigos o solo/a? ¿Por qué?
2. ¿Por dónde caminas cuando quieres estar solo/a?
3. ¿Te gusta caminar por la playa o por un parque?
4. ¿Caminas por la mañana o por la tarde?
5. Cuando sales a caminar, ¿caminas por media hora o por más tiempo?

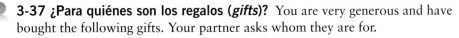 **3-37 ¿Para quiénes son los regalos (*gifts*)?** You are very generous and have bought the following gifts. Your partner asks whom they are for.

MODELO: un disco compacto
        E1: *¿Para quién es el disco compacto?*
        E2: *Es para mi hermana.*

1. tres libros de español
2. dos billetes de avión
3. una revista de deportes
4. cuatro refrescos dietéticos
5. una guitarra española
6. un kilo de helado
7. una computadora portátil
8. un teléfono celular
9. un buen vino chileno
10. una colección de DVDs

Suggestions for 3-37. You may wish to provide words for some family members, so students can use them for gift recipients: *hermano/a, primo/a, tío/a,* etc. This will serve as a warm-up for the presentation of kinship terms in *Capítulo 4.* Have students alternate roles or change roles halfway through. Ask them to elaborate on their responses by identifying the recipient as well as the purpose of the gift.

SITUACIONES

1. **Role A.** You run into a friend on the street who is carrying a large, gift-wrapped box. You are curious about the box, so you ask what it is and whom it is for.

   Role B. You are walking home from the store carrying a large, gift-wrapped package. You run into a friend on the way. Answer your friend's questions and explain why you are giving the gift.

2. **Role A.** You see your neighbor leaving his/her apartment, dragging a big suitcase. You are curious, so you ask a) where he/she is going; b) if the plane leaves in the afternoon or evening; c) how long he/she will be there; and d) why he/she is going.

   Role B. You are about to go on a long international trip, and as you are leaving your apartment with your suitcase you see your nosy neighbor. He/She asks a lot of questions. Answer in as much detail as possible.

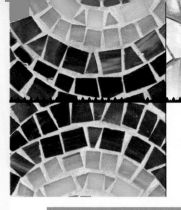

MOSAICOS

Audioscript for 3-39.

Agencia ViajaMás anuncia sus precios especiales de ida y vuelta para las siguientes ciudades desde Miami: Lima, vuelo número 881, sólo sábados y domingos, precio especial: $730. Buenos Aires, vuelo número 479, todos los días, precio: $980. Caracas, vuelo número 963, todos los días, precio especial: $250. Bogotá, vuelo 1247, lunes, martes y sábados, precio: $455. ¡Gracias por llamar a la Agencia ViajaMás y buen viaje!

ESTRATEGIA

Use background knowledge

When you listen to a conversation, you can use your knowledge of the situation to understand what is being said. Relying on the experience and knowledge you bring to the listening experience will enhance your comprehension.

A escuchar

Antes de escuchar

3-38 Preparación. You will listen to an ad for *ViajaMás*, a travel agency, which mentions several destinations in Latin America, the days of the flights, the flight numbers, and the price of a round-trip ticket from Miami. Before you listen, use your knowledge of Latin America and ticket prices to write down the name of one large city in each of the countries below that you think the ad may mention and the likely cost of each ticket.

CIUDADES LATINOAMERICANAS	PRECIO DEL BOLETO DE IDA Y VUELTA DESDE MIAMI
Perú:	
Argentina:	
Venezuela:	

Escuchar

3-39 ¿Comprende usted? Now listen to the ad and complete the chart with the information you hear.

CD 2
Track 6

CIUDAD	VUELO #	DÍAS	PRECIO DEL BOLETO
Lima	881	sábados y domingos	$730
Buenos Aires	479	todos los días	$980
Caracas	963	todos los días	$250
Bogotá	1247	lunes, martes y sábados	$455

Después de escuchar

3-40 Ahora usted. A friend who is studying Spanish wants to visit a capital city in Latin America but is unsure where to go. After listening to the ad, write an e-mail to your friend to suggest a city to visit.

De: _____

Para: _____

Asunto: Una ciudad interesante en América Latina

Hola _____

¡Tengo una información excelente para ti! Hay tarifas (*fares*) fantásticas para visitar _____! ¡Es una ciudad _____! Los vuelos salen los _____. Los boletos cuestan _____.

¿Por qué no hablamos por teléfono este fin de semana? _____

A conversar

Resources
■ SAM: 3-41
■ *Entrevistas* video

ESTRATEGIA

Organize information for a presentation

When preparing for an oral presentation, it is helpful to decide on a plan and then organize your information accordingly. In this section, you will make a presentation on students' food preferences. Organizing your information by meal (i.e., foods students would like to have available for breakfast, for lunch, etc.) is one approach; another is to start with categories of food that students like (e.g., **carnes**, **cereales**) and then list specific items in each category that students would like to see on the cafeteria menus. Both organizational plans will result in effective presentations.

Antes de conversar

3-41 Preparación. A new cafeteria is going to open on campus. You have been hired to survey students' food preferences so that the cafeteria menu will feature the most popular foods. Find out what your classmates like to eat and drink. Write down the names of students who answer **Sí** or **No** in the appropriate column.

MODELO: E1:   *Susana, ¿comes cereal en el desayuno?*
          E2:   *Sí, como cereal en el desayuno./No, no como cereal.*

	DESAYUNO		ALMUERZO		CENA	
	SÍ	NO	SÍ	NO	SÍ	NO
cereal con leche						
café/chocolate caliente						
jugo de naranja/tomate/manzana						
hamburguesas						
ensalada de frutas						
vino						
pan						
…						
…						

Conversar

3-42 Entre nosotros. Analyze the information you collected and write down a proposed menu. Present it to the new cafeteria supervisor (your classmate). Explain what most students (**la mayor parte de los estudiantes**) eat and drink. Be prepared to answer the supervisor's questions.

Después de conversar

3-43 Un poco más. Compare your menu with those of other classmates. Then vote on which menu is the most healthful and the most complete, and explain why.

Cultura

Despite differences from country to country, mealtimes in Hispanic countries generally differ from those in the United States. People typically eat breakfast at 7:00 or 8:00 a.m. It normally consists of **café**, **café con leche** (hot milk with strong coffee), **té**, or **chocolate caliente** with bread, a sweet roll, and sometimes juice or fruit. As this is a light breakfast, people sometimes have a snack in the late morning. Cereals are becoming more popular, especially among children and young adults.

In some countries, the main meal of the day is lunch (**el almuerzo** or **la comida**), eaten between 12:30 and 3:00 p.m. Supper (**la cena** or **la comida**) is served after 7:00 or 8:00 p.m., and sometimes as late as 10:00 p.m.

⚙ **Standard 4.2.** Students demonstrate an understanding of the concept of culture through comparisons of the cultures studied and their own. This culture note presents information on meal times with which many students may already be familiar. Instructors may wish to have students reflect on the connection between meal times and other cultural practices, such as the length of the work day, a long break in the middle of the day to eat the main meal with one's family, and so forth. Students may also be familiar with the U.S. custom of eating the main meal in the middle of the day, although this typically takes place only on weekends and holidays.

Suggestion for 3-41. Have each student survey at least five classmates, and encourage them to ask and answer the questions according to the model. Students should also ask their interviewees about favorite foods that are not included in the grid: *¿Qué más comes en el desayuno/el almuerzo/la cena?*

Suggestion for 3-42. To prepare for this activity, students will organize a presentation and write a menu to present to the cafeteria supervisor (classmates). The menu should be the only aid they have while making their presentations. Then students should switch roles. Remind students that when they take the role of cafeteria supervisor they will need to ask questions for clarification or to request additional information.

Suggestion for 3-42. After students have made their presentations to their partners, they should switch roles and partners for a second round.

Suggestion for 3-44. To make sure that students skim the texts rather than read them for full comprehension, you may give them a time limit to look at the four texts before answering the questions in the *Primera fase*. You may also wish to have them pass their highlighters through the key words they identify in the *Segunda fase*.

Suggestion for 3-45 Primera mirada. You may wish to have each pair of students present a solution to the class, including key words that helped them make their decision. Pairs who have a different solution to the one presented should be encouraged to present their alternative.

Answers for 3-46. Anuncio 1. *Disney, gratis para niños,* etc.; *Senior citizens; people other than children or senior citizens;* Anuncio 2. *Tradicional peruana;* Anuncio 3. *Exquisita, exótica carta, todo tipo de mariscos y camareros profesionales,* etc.; *Reservas.*

A leer

Antes de leer

3-44 Preparación. PRIMERA FASE. The three ads in activity **3-45** come from a newspaper in Lima, Peru. Look them over quickly without reading them. Then mark which ad goes with each of the following descriptions.

1. __3__ un restaurante de comida china
2. __1__ actividades para niños
3. __2__ un restaurante de comida tradicional peruana

SEGUNDA FASE. What word(s) in each ad helped you answer the questions in the *Primera fase*?

Leer

3-45 Primera mirada. Read the ads and offer a solution for the following choices that have to be made. Be prepared to explain your solutions to the class.

1. El señor y la señora Molina tienen cuatro hijos entre tres y ocho años. A los niños les fascinan los animales. ¿Adónde van a ir probablemente? ¿Por qué?
2. Carlos está triste porque se fracturó una pierna y no puede (*he can't*) salir de la casa. Su mamá tiene una sorpresa para él. ¿Qué es?
3. Cuatro médicos franceses visitan el Hospital Central. El Dr. Moreira, director del hospital, desea invitar a sus colegas a cenar en un restaurante cómodo, con comida tradicional peruana. ¿A qué restaurante va a invitarlos? ¿Por qué?

3-46 Segunda mirada. Reread the ads **(3-45)** to answer the following questions.

Anuncio 1: ¿Qué palabras, indican que las actividades son para los niños? ¿Qué significa *3ra edad*? ¿Qué significa *otro público*?
Anuncio 2: Identifique qué expresión indica que este restaurante prepara comida nacional. ¿Cuánto cuesta el menú especial de los fines de semana?
Anuncio 3: ¿Qué expresiones se refieren a la buena calidad del restaurante? ¿Qué palabra significa *reservation*?

Después de leer

👥 **3-47 Ampliación.** With a classmate, answer the following questions about the four ads from Peru.

1. ¿Cuál de las siguientes actividades desean hacer ustedes en Lima: ir a un parque de entretenimiento (*amusement park*), comer comida tradicional peruana, ver teatro o comer comida china? ¿Por qué?
2. ¿Cuál de los dos restaurantes sirve comida que a ustedes les gusta más, Costa Verde o Chifa Lungfung?

1.

NIÑOS

CORPORACIÓN CULTURAL DE LIMA. Santa María y Gálvez. 2209451. A las 12 y 16 horas. Bagdhadas. S/. 12.

TEATRO INFANTIL A DOMICILIO. 2390176. El patito feo. Adaptación del cuento de Andersen. Compañía Arcoiris.

CENTRO LIMA. Av. Grau y Velásquez. A las 12, show especial de Navidad.

FANTASÍA DISNEY. Desde las 15. Niños, S/. 8; adultos, S/. 14. Parque de entretenimientos.

EL MUNDO FANTÁSTICO DE MAFALDA. Desde las 10. Entrada general a todos los juegos. Niños, S/. 12. Calle Domingo Sarmiento 358.

PLANETARIO DEL MORRO SOLAR. A las 12, 17 y 19. Gratis para niños; adultos, S/. 15. Circunvalación, Nuevo Perú. Tel. 5620841.

PARQUE DE LAS LEYENDAS (ZOO). De 9 a 19 hrs. Niños y 3ra edad, S/. 5; S/. 10, otro público. Cerro Tongoy, 3701725.

2.

Costa Verde

Sabrosa comida tradicional peruana
Menú especial los fines de semana

■ Aperitivo
■ Entrada
■ Segundo
■ Postre
■ Café y plus café (crema de café, crema de menta, anisado)

Valor: S/. 75

Carnes, pescados y mariscos preparados por los mejores cocineros del país

Avenida Arequipa 357
Reservas: 428 9654
Fax: 428 9655

3.

El Chifa Lungfung

La más exquisita, variada y exótica carta de comida cantonesa-peruana: finas carnes, pescados y todo tipo de mariscos.

SÁBADOS Y DOMINGOS:

Almuerzos y cenas familiares

...los esperamos

AIRE ACONDICIONADO
MÚSICA AMBIENTAL
CAMAREROS PROFESIONALES
AV. REPÚBLICA DE PANAMÁ 8720
RESERVAS 3817543, 3816532, 3814241

A escribir

Resources
■ SAM: 3-45 to 3-47

ESTRATEGIA

Use appropriate conventions in letter-writing
Writing a casual or formal letter requires observing certain basic conventions, such as including the date, a salutation, an introduction, a body, and a closing, as well as carefully selecting information that will interest your reader. Formalities of writing also require developing one idea per paragraph. Remember to follow these conventions even when writing to a friend.

Antes de escribir

3-48 Preparación. You are visiting a great vacation spot and want to write your friend a letter about it. To prepare to write the letter, do the following:

1. Write a tentative date for the letter: _____ (date) de _____ (month), 20____
2. Choose a salutation and a closing from the *En directo* box.
3. Prepare some information for the introduction. Mention the place where you are: Is it a beach, a park, a city, a historical landmark (**lugar histórico**)?
4. Decide on the information for the body of the letter:
   a. Make a list of words (adjectives) that describe the place: Is it small, big, beautiful, fun, interesting, historical?
   b. Write down some enjoyable activities (verbs) that people do there. Are they outdoor activities, sports (**deportes**), culturally oriented activities such as going to museums (**museos**), excursions (**excursiones**), fairs (**ferias**)?
   c. Indicate some of the activities that others do that you also like.

> **En directo**
>
> Salutations for casual correspondence:
> **Querido/a...**
> **Estimado/a...**
> **Hola...**
>
> Closings for casual correspondence:
> **Tu amigo/a,**
> **Hasta pronto,**
> **Cariños,**
> *Love*

Suggestion for 3-48. Depending on your teaching approach or your students' writing proficiency, you may wish to give this activity a more cultural orientation. To that end, you may ask students to do some research on the Internet. Students may take a virtual tour of a specific place such as a museum, historical landmark, or vacation spot. They should describe the place and indicate its importance.

Escribir

3-49 Manos a la obra. Now write the letter to your friend, telling about your vacation. Use the information you prepared in activity **3-48** and any other that you think may be of interest to your friend.

Después de escribir

3-50 Revisión. After completing your letter, read it at least twice with your friend in mind. Check the following:

1. Did you include the date in your letter?
2. Are your salutation and closing appropriate?
3. Did you include a brief introduction and enough information in the body of the letter to achieve your purpose?
4. Did you check for spelling or grammatical errors?
5. Finally, discuss your letter with one of your peers.

Suggestions for 3-50. If you want students to revise their first drafts in class, have them exchange letters with a peer editor, one whom you appoint or whom they choose. Give students enough time to read their classmate's letter so they can discuss it later. If time is limited, you may assign students to read their partners' text as homework, followed by a class discussion. Remind peer editors to concentrate on content only. They may check that their classmate's letter contains the date, a salutation, and a closing.

ENFOQUE CULTURAL

Breve perfil de Perú

Perú es un país extraordinario por su diversidad y riqueza histórica, geográfica y cultural. En efecto, Perú y México son las dos regiones más importantes durante la época colonial de América Latina. Pero antes de los españoles, en Perú ya existe uno de los imperios indígenas más interesantes del continente. Y, finalmente, en Perú encontramos ruinas espectaculares de las culturas indígenas y de la época colonial, y también ciudades modernas con una mezcla de razas y una diversidad étnica muy grande.

Antes de la llegada de los conquistadores españoles, el imperio de los incas es una de las principales civilizaciones nativas de América. Esta civilización es famosa por su compleja organización social, su avanzada arquitectura y sus sistemas de comunicación. Muchas ciudades conservan restos de esta cultura. Por ejemplo, en Cuzco, la capital del imperio inca, hay espectaculares construcciones, como la gran fortaleza de Sacsayhuamán. Y, naturalmente, una de las ciudades incas más prestigiosas es Machu Picchu.

El Conde de Nieva, virrey de Perú entre 1561 y 1584, depende del rey Felipe II.

La fortaleza de Sacsayhuamán cerca de Cuzco

Cuando los españoles conquistan América, dividen el territorio en tres tipos diferentes de administración. El tipo más importante de administración en el imperio español es el *virreinato*. Esta palabra "vir**re**inato" se relaciona con "rey", porque la autoridad más importante es el virrey. El segundo tipo más importante de administración es la *gobernación*, bajo la autoridad del gobernador. Y el tercer tipo es la *capitanía general*, bajo la autoridad principal del capitán general. México, Perú y la Nueva Granada (la actual Colombia) son los tres virreinatos españoles en el continente americano durante la colonia.

La geografía de Perú es variada y compleja. Tiene una multitud de sistemas ecológicos que forman el hábitat de una infinidad de plantas y animales. Hay tres regiones

La geografía de Perú presenta tres regiones diferentes.

- La selva
- La sierra
- La costa

geográficas principales en Perú. La costa del Pacífico es muy rica en una gran variedad de peces y productos agrícolas. Una de las atracciones más famosas de esta región son las misteriosas líneas de Nazca. La segunda región es la sierra, que está formada por los Andes y que tiene algunas montañas muy altas, tales como el Nevado de Huascarán, el pico más alto de Perú, de aproximadamente 6.700 metros. La tercera región es la selva del Amazonas, al oriente de los Andes. Las grandes selvas tropicales de esta región son una de las fuentes principales de oxígeno en el planeta.

Finalmente, la cultura peruana es el resultado de la mezcla de la cultura indígena de los incas con la cultura española. Muchos peruanos, especialmente entre los habitantes de la sierra, hablan quechua, la lengua original de los incas. Pero Perú también tiene una gran influencia de culturas de origen africano y asiático. En resumen, la comida, el arte, la literatura, y todas las manifestaciones culturales peruanas son realmente únicas.

En otras palabras

Expresiones peruanas

Me conseguí una **chamba**.
I found a job.

José y yo somos **patas**.
José and I are buddies.

¡Juanita es una **chancona**!
Juanita is a nerd!

3-51 Comprensión. PRIMERA FASE. **Reconocimiento de palabras clave.** Find in the text the Spanish word or phrase that best expresses the meaning of the following concepts:

1. profile ___perfil___
2. empire ___imperio___
3. rain forest ___selva___
4. fort, fortress ___fortaleza___
5. fish, fishes ___peces___
6. snow-capped peak ___nevado___
7. east ___oriente___

SEGUNDA FASE. **Oraciones importantes.** Underline the statements that contain ideas found in the text. Then indicate where in the text those ideas appear.

1. Before the arrival of the Spaniards, Cuzco was the capital of the Inca Empire.
2. The viceroyalties of Mexico and Peru were the most important colonies of Spain in the New World.
3. Colombia was one of the three viceroyalties in the Spanish Empire.
4. Peru has some beautiful modern cities, but they are all somewhat run down.
5. The mysterious Nazca drawings are located in the coastal region of Peru.
6. Some mountains, like Peru's highest peak, for example, are capped with snow.
7. A few mountains in the Peruvian Andes are very close to 8,000 meters high.
8. Spanish is not just the main language of Peru; it is the only language spoken there.

TERCERA FASE. **Ideas principales.** Write a brief paragraph in English summarizing the main ideas expressed in the text.

 3-52 Use la información. You are visiting Peru, and you will spend tomorrow visiting Cuzco and its surroundings. Although it is late and you are tired, you take a few minutes to write a postcard to someone you really care about. Explain your plans for tomorrow: a) mention at least one place you plan to visit; b) if the place is in Cuzco or near/far (**cerca/lejos**); c) how you are going to get there; and d) what you are going to see. For help with this activity, go to the web page of *Mosaicos* and use the links provided there to write your postcard.

De...............................

....

....

....

....

....

Para.............................

....

....

....

....

VOCABULARIO

Resource

■ Testing Program

Las diversiones y las celebraciones — *Leisure activities and celebrations*

la boda	*wedding*
la canción	*song*
el cumpleaños	*birthday*
la fiesta	*party*
la guitarra	*guitar*
la música	*music*
la película	*film*
la reunión	*meeting, gathering*
el tiempo libre	*free time*
las vacaciones	*vacation*

Las personas — *People*

el camarero/la camarera	*server, waiter/waitress (restaurant)*
el hombre	*man*
el/la joven	*young man/woman*
la mujer	*woman*

En un café o restaurante — *In a coffee shop or restaurant*

el agua	*water*
el almuerzo	*lunch*
el arroz	*rice*
la bebida	*drink*
el bistec	*steak*
el café	*coffee*
la cena	*dinner, supper*
el cereal	*cereal*
la cerveza	*beer*
el ceviche	*dish of marinated raw fish*
la comida	*food; meal; dinner, supper*
el desayuno	*breakfast*
la ensalada	*salad*
los espaguetis	*spaghetti*
el frijol	*bean*
la fruta	*fruit*
la hamburguesa	*hamburger*
el helado	*ice cream*
el huevo	*egg*
el jamón	*ham*
el jugo	*juice*
la leche	*milk*
la lechuga	*lettuce*
la naranja	*orange*
el pan	*bread*
el pan tostado/la tostada	*toast*
la papa	*potato*
las papas fritas	*French fries*
el pescado	*fish*
el pollo	*chicken*
el queso	*cheese*
el refresco	*soda, soft drink*
el sándwich	*sandwich*
la sopa	*soup*

el té	*tea*
el tomate	*tomato*
el vegetal/la verdura	*vegetable*
el vino	*wine*

La comunicación — *Communication*

el periódico	*newspaper*
la revista	*magazine*
el teléfono	*telephone*

Los lugares — *Places*

el cine	*movies*
la ciudad	*city*
el mar	*sea*
el país	*country, nation*

Las descripciones — *Descriptions*

caliente	*hot*
fabuloso/a	*fabulous, great*
frío/a	*cold*
frito/a	*fried*
rápido/a	*fast*
típico/a	*typical*

Verbos — *Verbs*

alquilar	*to rent*
cantar	*to sing*
celebrar	*to celebrate*
cenar	*to have dinner*
descansar	*to rest*
hacer la cama	*to make the bed*
nadar	*to swim*
poner la mesa	*to set the table*
tocar (un instrumento)	*to play (an instrument)*
tomar el sol	*to sunbathe*

Palabras y expresiones útiles — *Useful words and expressions*

¿adónde?	*where (to)?*
al	*to the* (contraction of **a + el**)
al aire libre	*outdoors*
¡claro!	*of course!*
cerca de	*close to, near*
después, luego	*after, later*
durante	*during*
¡estupendo!	*fabulous!*
felicidades	*congratulations*
mientras	*while*
otro/a	*other, another*
¿qué te parece?	*what do you think?*
si	*if*

See *Lengua* box on page 102 for expressions that denote future time.
See page 105 for numbers from 100 to 2.000.000.
See page 111 for expressions with *por*.

Suggestion. Present *familia, padre, madre, hijo/a, hijos* and ask questions about the family in the painting: *¿Cómo es el padre? ¿Cómo es la madre? ¿Y el hijo mayor?* Show other paintings by Botero that you may find online. Write his name on the board and explain that he features mostly rotund people in his paintings. Compare this painting with *La familia presidencial* and others in which he depicts families. Use cognates to talk about the themes of some of his other paintings: *la injusticia social, la violencia, la tortura, el abuso de poder*, etc.

En familia

Fernando Botero, uno de los pintores contemporáneos más famosos de Colombia, pinta a unos padres con sus hijos en este cuadro titulado *En familia*.

Source: © Fernando Botero, courtesy of Marlborough Gallery, New York.

In this chapter you will learn how to:

- talk about family
- discuss what you have to do
- describe daily routines

Cultural focus: **Colombia**

Las calles de Cartagena de Indias

Mar Caribe

Barranquilla

Cartagena de Indias

PANAMÁ

VENEZUELA

Medellín

Bucaramanga

El Parque Nacional del café, Departamento El Quindío

Pereira

Pieza antigua del Museo del Oro de Bogotá

Cali

⊕ **Bogotá**

COLOMBIA

Popayán

OCÉANO

PACÍFICO

ECUADOR

Río Magdalena

CORDILLERA DE LOS ANDES

Arepas de queso

BRASIL

BRASIL

Cordillera de Los Andes

A vista de pájaro. Complete las siguientes oraciones (*the following sentences*) con la información correcta.

1. Ecuador, ____Perú____ y Brasil están al sur de Colombia.
2. ____Bogotá____ es la capital de Colombia.
3. El ____café____ es el mayor producto de exportación de Colombia.
4. Fernando Botero es un _pintor/artista_ colombiano.

Warm-up for A vista de pájaro. This activity can be done in pairs or as a class warm-up. Brainstorm with students the information they already may know about Colombia. Ask: *¿Qué país está al noroeste de Colombia? ¿Y al nordeste? ¿Con qué mares tiene contacto Colombia? (el Mar del Caribe y el Océano Pacífico) ¿Qué río desemboca (flows into) en Barranquilla? (el Magdalena) ¿Cómo se llaman las montañas que cruzan Colombia? (Cordillera de Los Andes)* Tell them not to worry if they cannot answer some of these questions. *¿Quién es un escritor colombiano muy importante que recibió el premio Nobel? (Gabriel García Márquez) ¿Conocen algún producto que exporta Colombia? (el café, las flores)*

Note. Beginning in *Capítulo 4*, direction lines for activities are in Spanish. Some of these will be glossed. Refer students to the *Expresiones útiles* in the vocabulary pages if the need arises.

123

A PRIMERA VISTA

◄)) Los miembros de la familia

CD 2
Track 15

Una familia colombiana de tres generaciones: **abuelos, hijos** y **nietos**. ¿Cuántos **niños** hay? ¿Hay muchos niños en la familia de usted?

Estos tres niños son **hermanos**. A ellos les gusta **jugar** con el gato. El niño de la **izquierda** se llama Juan y es **el mayor**. La niña se llama Julia y es la segunda. El pequeño, a la **derecha**, se llama Roberto.

En esta foto vemos un **bautizo**. En estas ceremonias participan los **padres**, los **padrinos** y los **ahijados**. Para muchas familias hispanas, el bautizo es un día muy especial.

El árbol familiar de Pablo

don José   doña Olga

Jorge   Osvaldo   Elena

María   Lola   Jaime

Elenita   Ana   Jorgito   Sofía   Inés   Pablo

Pablo habla de su familia

CD 2
Track 16

Me llamo Pablo Méndez Sánchez y vivo con mis padres, mi **hermana** y mis **abuelos** en un apartamento en Bogotá, la capital de Colombia.

Mi **madre** tiene un **hermano**, mi **tío** Jorge. Su **esposa** es mi **tía** María. Tienen tres hijos y viven también en Bogotá. Mi **primo** Jorgito es el **menor**. Mis **primas** Elenita y Ana son **gemelas**. Mis primos son muy simpáticos y **pasamos** mucho tiempo **juntos**.

Mis tíos tienen sólo dos **sobrinos** en Bogotá, mi hermana Inés y yo. Su otra **sobrina**, la hija de mi tía Lola, vive en Cartagena, al norte del país.

La **nieta** favorita de mis abuelos es mi hermanita Inés. Tiene sólo tres años y es la menor de todos sus **nietos**.

4-1 Asociación. Asocie la descripción en la columna izquierda con la expresión correcta en la columna derecha.

1. _c_ la esposa de mi padre
2. _a_ el hermano de mi prima
3. _d_ los padres de mi padre
4. _b_ el hijo de mi hijo
5. _e_ el hermano de mi madre

a. mi primo
b. mi nieto
c. mi madre
d. mis abuelos
e. mi tío

4-2 La familia de Pablo. Complete las siguientes oraciones (*following sentences*) de acuerdo con (*according to*) la información que usted tiene sobre la familia de Pablo.

1. La hermana de Pablo se llama ____Inés____ .
2. Don José y doña Olga son los ____abuelos____ de Pablo.
3. Pablo es el ____hijo____ de Jaime.
4. Jaime es el ____padre____ de Pablo, y Elena es su ____madre____ .
5. Inés y Ana son ____primas____ . Elenita y Ana son ____hermanas gemelas____ .
6. Elena es la ____tía____ de Jorgito, Elenita y Ana.
7. Lola es la ____hermana____ de Jorge y Elena.

Otros miembros de la familia de Pablo

CD 2
Track 17

Paula   Sergio   Lola   Osvaldo

Roberto   Sofía

La única hermana de mi **mamá** es mi tía Lola. Lola y Sergio están **divorciados** y tienen una hija, mi prima Sofía. Ahora la tía Lola está casada con Osvaldo, el **padrastro** de Sofía. Sergio está casado con Paula y tienen un hijo, Roberto. Paula es la **madrastra** de Sofía, y Roberto es su **medio hermano**.

4-3 ¿Cierto o falso? Marque (✓) la columna adecuada de acuerdo con la información sobre la familia de Lola.

	CIERTO	FALSO
1. La tía Lola está casada con Sergio.	____	✓
2. Osvaldo es el papá de Roberto.	____	✓
3. Paula es la madrastra de Roberto.	____	✓
4. Lola es la madre de Sofía.	✓	____
5. Sofía tiene un medio hermano.	✓	____

 4-4 ¿Quién es y cómo es? PRIMERA FASE. Escojan (*Choose*) un miembro de una familia famosa (la familia real [*royal*] española, los Jackson, los Kennedy, los Bush, etc.). Preparen su árbol familiar.

SEGUNDA FASE. Túrnese (*Take turns*) con su compañero/a de clase (*classmate*) para describir el árbol familiar de esta persona.

MODELO: el príncipe Felipe
E1: *Su padre es el rey de España. Su madre es la reina Sofía. Felipe tiene dos hermanas. Está casado con la princesa Letizia.*
E2: *Tiene dos hijas y seis sobrinos. Su hermana Elena tiene un hijo y una hija. Su hermana Cristina tiene tres hijos y una hija.*

4-5 El arte de preguntar. PRIMERA FASE. Prepare las preguntas (*questions*) necesarias para obtener la siguiente información.

1. Tengo cuatro abuelos vivos (*alive*).
2. No, no soy hijo único/hija única.
3. Tengo dos hermanos.
4. Vivo con mi madre y mi padrastro.
5. Mis abuelos no viven con nosotros.
6. Tengo muchos primos.
7. Tengo una media hermana, pero no vive con nosotros.
8. Mi media hermana vive con su madre.

 SEGUNDA FASE. Ahora háganse preguntas (*ask each other questions*) para obtener información sobre la familia de su compañero/a. Después, compartan (*share*) esta información con la clase.

 4-6 Mi familia. PRIMERA FASE. Preparen su árbol familiar individualmente. Luego, intercambien (*exchange*) su árbol.

SEGUNDA FASE. Háganse preguntas sobre su familia para obtener la siguiente información.

1. nombre de los abuelos vivos
2. nombre de los padres (padrastro/madrastra)
3. número y nombre de los hermanos (medios hermanos, hermanastros)
4. número y nombre de los primos
5. descripción de dos parientes (*relatives*)

¿Qué hacen los parientes?

CD 2
Track 18

Mis abuelos viven en una casa al lado del parque. Normalmente, ellos **pasean** por las mañanas y **almuerzan** muy temprano. Después, **duermen la siesta** y por la tarde **visitan** a sus **parientes**.

Jorgito es mi primo favorito. Es un poco menor que yo. Nosotros corremos y jugamos mucho **juntos**. También nos gusta ver el fútbol en la televisión y montar en bicicleta los domingos.

Hace dos años que mi prima Ana tiene **novio**, y **frecuentemente dice** que **quiere casarse** muy pronto. Elenita, su hermana gemela, **piensa** que Ana no debe casarse porque es muy joven.

Mi tío Jorge es un hombre muy **ocupado**. Sale de casa muy **temprano** y **vuelve tarde** todos los días. Mi tía María, su esposa, dice que él **prefiere** el trabajo a su familia. Pienso que en todas las familias hay problemas. En la mía también, pero me gusta mi familia.

> ### Lengua
>
> In Spanish, the direct object of a verb is normally introduced without a preposition. However, the preposition **a** is required when the direct object is a person or a specific animal: **los abuelos visitan a los parientes**; **la hija pasea al perro**.

4-7 ¿Cierto o falso? Conteste (*Answer*) de acuerdo con la información adicional sobre la familia de Pablo.

	CIERTO	FALSO
1. Normalmente los abuelos están muy ocupados.		✓
2. Jorgito y Pablo montan en bicicleta frecuentemente.	✓	
3. Elenita piensa que su hermana es muy joven para casarse.	✓	
4. El tío Jorge cree que Elenita tiene problemas.	✓	
5. El tío Jorge trabaja mucho.	✓	
6. El tío Jorge llega temprano a su casa.		✓

4-8 ¿Y qué hace su familia? Hágale preguntas a su compañero/a para obtener más información sobre su familia. Use la siguiente guía (*guide*).

1. número de personas en la casa, edad (*age*) y relación de parentesco (*kinship*)
2. ocupación y descripción (física y de personalidad) de algunos (*some*) miembros de la familia
3. actividades de estas personas en su tiempo libre
4. nombre del pariente favorito, relación familiar y razón (*reason*) de su preferencia

Suggestion. You may want to point out that *pariente* is a false cognate. Use visuals to practice *pasear* and *almorzar*. Personalize: *Me gusta pasear por el parque por las tardes. ¿Y a usted le gusta pasear? ¿Pasea por las calles o por el parque? ¿Duerme la siesta alguna vez? Yo duermo la siesta en las vacaciones. ¿Visita a sus parientes frecuentemente?* Recycle *correr* and *jugar*. Personalize. Follow a similar procedure for the other illustrations. You may also use additional visual aids.

Suggestion for 4-8. Tell students that if they don't feel comfortable talking about their families they can invent the answers. To ensure students will ask questions accurately, give them a minute or two to write down the questions first. Ask for volunteers to read their questions out loud. Have students work in small groups to list the advantages/disadvantages (*ventajas/desventajas*) of a large family. Have them compare lists.

Follow-up for 4-8. Have students report to the class what a classmate has said about his/her family, reinforcing *él/ella* verb forms: *Mi compañera dice que vive con su familia. Tiene tres hermanos. Su tía vive con ellos.*

Suggestion. The vocabulary of daily routines associated with reflexive verbs is presented here for recognition in the context of family life. Students do not conjugate reflexive verbs at this point. To preview this vocabulary, model the activity by talking about your daily routine with the help of gestures: *Me despierto a las 6:30, me levanto, me ducho, me visto, me lavo los dientes,* etc. Use *temprano* and *tarde: No me acuesto tarde porque me levanto temprano.* Also ask yes/no questions or questions that do not require students to produce structures they have not studied, such as *¿A qué hora se levanta usted? ¿Se levanta usted temprano? ¿Se ducha por las mañanas o por las noches?*

Suggestion. The drawings present an opportunity to preview some vocabulary related to housing that students will learn in *Capítulo 5.* Introduce *cocina* and *cuarto de baño,* then ask: *¿Dónde desayuna la familia? ¿Dónde se lavan?,* etc.

Introduce the expression *Poco después* by comparing it to *luego* and *más tarde.*

Introduce the expression *no sale hasta...* You may also show with gestures what *ropa* means.

Las rutinas familiares

CD 2
Track 19

En casa de Pablo hay mucha actividad por la mañana. Los niños **se despiertan** a las siete. **Se levantan, se lavan** y luego **desayunan** en la cocina con sus padres. Después salen para la escuela.

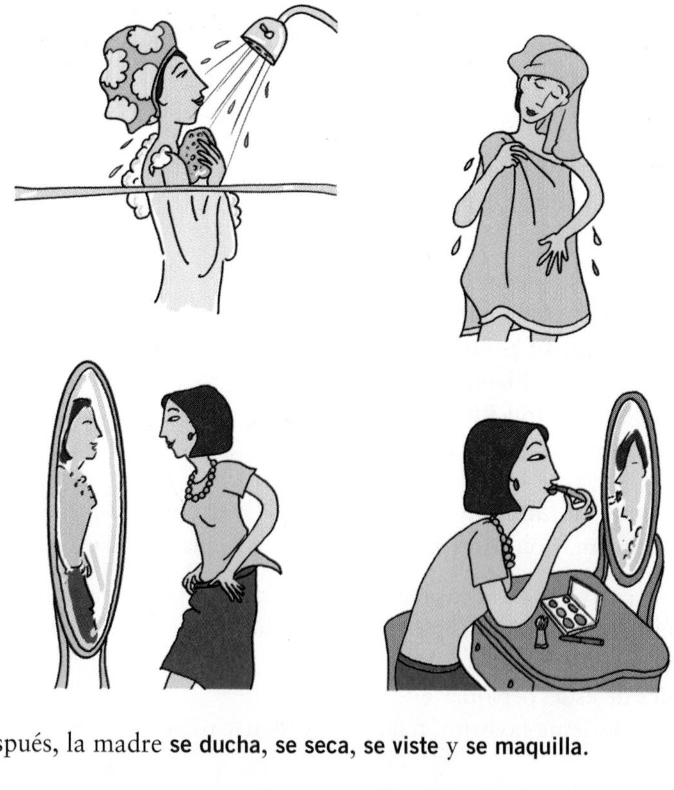

Poco después, la madre **se ducha, se seca, se viste** y **se maquilla.**

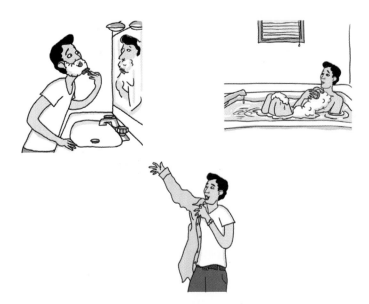

Más tarde, el padre **se afeita**, **se baña** y **se pone la ropa**, pero no sale de casa hasta las nueve.

4-9 Cada cosa a su tiempo. Ponga (*Put*) en orden cronológico las siguientes oraciones según (*according to*) las escenas.

___4___ La madre se maquilla.
___1___ Los niños se despiertan a las siete.
___5___ El padre se baña y luego se pone la ropa.
___3___ La madre se ducha.
___6___ El padre sale de casa a las nueve.
___2___ Los niños desayunan y después salen para la escuela.

4-10 Las rutinas diarias. Conteste las siguientes preguntas sobre la rutina diaria de la familia de Pablo:

1. ¿Con quién desayunan los niños? Con sus padres
2. ¿Quién se maquilla por las mañanas? La madre
3. ¿A qué hora se despiertan los niños? A las siete
4. ¿Quién sale de casa a las nueve? El padre
5. ¿Quién se afeita por las mañanas? El padre
6. ¿Qué hace la madre después de ducharse? Se seca, se viste y se maquilla.

4-11 Mañanas ocupadas (*busy*). Marque (✓) las acciones diarias de los miembros de su familia.

	SE DESPIERTA TEMPRANO	SE DUCHA POR LA MAÑANA	SE PONE ROPA ELEGANTE	DESAYUNA CON LA FAMILIA
Mi padre (padrastro)				
Mi madre (madrastra)				
Mi hermano/a				
Mi abuelo/a				
Mi tío/a				

Lengua

The following are expressions to organize time sequentially: **Primero, luego, poco después, más tarde**, and **por último**.

Warm-up for 4-9 Before doing this activity, explain the expression *Cada cosa a su tiempo* and review the *Lengua* box with students.

Suggestions for 4-10. Students will learn the conjugation of reflexives in *Funciones y formas*. Students may respond to questions with information words only, rather than with complete sentences, e.g., *¿A qué hora se levanta tu madre?* Answer: *A las siete.*

4-12 ¿Y usted? Complete el siguiente párrafo indicando el orden de las acciones en la rutina diaria de usted. Use las expresiones siguientes:

me ducho
me despierto
me levanto
salgo para la universidad
desayuno

Primero ____me despierto____, luego ____me levanto____ . Poco después ____me ducho____, más tarde ____desayuno____. Por último ____salgo para la universidad____.

 4-13 ¿A qué hora? Túrnense para hacerse las siguientes preguntas sobre la rutina diaria.

1. ¿A qué hora se levanta tu madre/padre/hermano?
2. ¿Te duchas por la mañana o por la noche?
3. ¿Quién se levanta temprano en tu familia?
4. ¿Te vistes antes o después de desayunar?
5. ¿Te pones ropa elegante o informal para ir a clase?
6. ¿A qué hora te acuestas durante la semana?
7. ¿A qué hora te acuestas durante los fines de semana?
8. ¿A qué hora te levantas durante los fines de semana?
9. ¿A qué hora tienes la clase de español?
10. ¿Quién se despierta antes los domingos en tu familia?

4-14 Algunas familias hispanas. You will listen to descriptions of four Hispanic families. Before you listen, answer these questions: Is your family large or small? How many brothers and sisters, cousins, aunts, and uncles do you have?

CD 2
Track 20

Now pay attention to the general idea of what is said. As you hear each description, write a check mark (✔) in the corresponding column.

	TIENE UNA FAMILIA GRANDE	TIENE HERMANOS	TIENE MUCHOS TÍOS	TIENE PRIMOS
Pedro	✓	✓	✓	
Alicia	✓	✓		
Magdalena	✓	✓	✓	✓
Alberto		✓		

EN ACCIÓN

Resources
- Video
- SAM: 4-11 to 4-13

Diarios de bicicleta: Nada de bromas

Antes de ver

4-15 En este segmento, Javier se encuentra con Luciana y su familia en el parque. Marque (✓) las actividades que las personas hacen normalmente cuando están en un parque.

1. _✓_ Juegan con una pelota (*ball*).
2. _✓_ Comen sándwiches y beben refrescos.
3. _✓_ Leen el periódico.
4. ___ Buscan trabajo.
5. _✓_ Escuchan música.

Mientras ve

4-16 Ponga en orden cronológico las acciones de Javier cuando la familia de Luciana le hace una broma (*plays a joke*).

_3_ Cierra los ojos.   _6_ Se levanta y se va enojado.
_1_ Se pone el sombrero.   _4_ Levanta los brazos y los mueve.
_2_ Se sienta.   _5_ Abre los ojos.

Después de ver

4-17 ¿Qué ocurre después de esta escena? Marque (✓) todas las actividades que usted cree que son posibles. Answers will vary.

1. ___ Javier come con la familia de Luciana.
2. ___ Javier sale del parque sin despedirse de (*without saying good-bye*) Luciana.
3. ___ La abuela habla con Javier.
4. ___ El padre de Luciana duerme una siesta después del almuerzo.
5. ___ Marcos está enojado y sale del parque.

⚬ **Standard 4.2:** Students demonstrate understanding of the concept of culture through comparisons of the cultures studied and their own. Students' image of a park and what activities people do there are formed by their experience. Activity **4-15**, which asks them to anticipate the context and some of the content of the video clip by referring to their experience, offers instructors the opportunity to help students reflect on their often unconscious assumptions about what life is like in Spanish-speaking cultures.

Suggestion for 4-15. You may wish to have students brainstorm other activities that they or their friends do when they go to a park.

Note for 4-16. Since this is the first time students see the direction lines for the video activities in Spanish, make sure they understand the directions before they watch the video and do the activities.

Suggestion for 4-16. Note that the statements are phrased in simple language that students can understand and produce. You may wish to have students create additional statements that convey the events in the video clip.

Note for 4-17. Asking students to imagine what happens after the scene stretches their imaginations. You may wish to design similar activities for other video clips.

131

Resources

- SAM: 4-14 to 4-19
- Supp. Activ. Book: Present tense of stem-changing verbs
- PPTs
- *Situaciones adicionales*

FUNCIONES Y FORMAS

1. Expressing opinions, plans, preferences, and feelings: Present tense of stem-changing verbs: *e → ie, o → ue*, and *e → i*

Carmen habla

Quiero conversar seriamente con ustedes y les **pido** su ayuda. **Pienso** que mamá y papá **quieren** algunos cambios en casa. Ellos no **pueden** hacer todo. El día **empieza** muy temprano para ellos y **duermen** muy poco. Con frecuencia, **almuerzan** en la oficina, aunque **prefieren** comer en casa. Nosotros necesitamos ayudar. Luis y Ximena, ustedes **vuelven** a casa a las 2:00. Si ustedes le **sirven** el almuerzo a Juanito y **juegan** con él, nuestros padres van a estar muy contentos. **Cuesta** mucho dinero pagar los servicios de una niñera (*babysitter*). ¿**Piensan** ustedes que mis ideas son buenas o **tienen** otras?

Suggestions. To introduce stem-changing verbs, highlight the stem with a different color or use capital letters when writing the stem on the board. Point out that the stem change is in the stressed stem vowel, not in the preceding vowel (e.g., *preferir, almorzar*).

Use visuals and comprehensible input to present some of the verbs: *Este chico almuerza con sus amigos en una cafetería. Ellos almuerzan a la una. Yo no almuerzo a la una, almuerzo a las doce y media. Usted también almuerza a las doce y media, ¿verdad? Ah, entonces nosotros (no) almorzamos a la misma hora. ¿Quién (más) almuerza más temprano/tarde?*

Piénselo. Identifique a la(s) persona(s) que probablemente hace(n) estas actividades en la familia del texto anterior: Los padres (**P**), Luis y Ximena (**LX**), Juanito (**J**) o Carmen (**C**). A veces hay más de una respuesta correcta.

1. __P__ **Almuerzan** fuera de casa.
2. __J__ **Necesita** ayuda para almorzar.
3. __P__ **Prefieren** almorzar en casa.
4. __LX__ **Vuelven** a casa a las 2:00.
5. __LX__ **Sirven** el almuerzo a su hermanito.
6. __C__ **Pide** la colaboración de sus hermanos.

■ Some common verbs in Spanish undergo a vowel change in all forms of the present tense except **nosotros/as** and **vosotros/as**.

PENSAR (e → ie) *(to think)*			
yo	pienso	nosotros/as	pensamos
tú	piensas	vosotros/as	pensáis
Ud., él, ella	piensa	Uds., ellos/as	piensan

VOLVER (o → ue) *(to return)*			
yo	vuelvo	nosotros/as	volvemos
tú	vuelves	vosotros/as	volvéis
Ud., él, ella	vuelve	Uds., ellos/as	vuelven

PEDIR (e → i) *(to ask for)*			
yo	pido	nosotros/as	pedimos
tú	pides	vosotros/as	pedís
Ud., él, ella	pide	Uds., ellos/as	piden

■ Other common verbs that have vowel changes in the stem are:

e → ie	o → ue	e → i
cerrar *(to close)*	**almorzar** *(to have lunch)*	**repetir** *(to repeat)*
empezar *(to begin)*	**costar** *(to cost)*	**servir** *(to serve)*
entender *(to understand)*	**dormir** *(to sleep)*	
preferir *(to prefer)*	**encontrar** *(to meet)*	
querer *(to want; to love)*	**poder** *(to be able to, can)*	

■ Use **pensar +** *infinitive* to express what you or someone else is planning to do.

Pienso estudiar esta noche.   *I plan to study tonight.*

Pensamos comer a las ocho.   *We are planning to eat at 8:00.*

■ Note the irregular **yo** form in the following **e → ie** and **e → i** stem-changing verbs.

tener *(to have)*	**tengo**, tienes, tiene, tenemos, tenéis, tienen
venir *(to come)*	**vengo**, vienes, viene, venimos, venís, vienen
decir *(to say, to tell)*	**digo**, dices, dice, decimos, decís, dicen
seguir *(to follow)*	**sigo**, sigues, sigue, seguimos, seguís, siguen

■ In the verb *jugar* *(to play a game or sport)* **u** changes to **ue**.

Mario **juega** muy bien al tenis, pero   *Mario plays tennis very well, but we*
nosotros **jugamos** regular.   *play so-so.*

4-18 Planes para la boda. Beatriz y Miguel se casan en un mes. Complete la descripción de los planes para la boda con la forma correcta de un verbo apropiado.

empezar	poder	querer	servir
entender	preferir	seguir	volver

Beatriz y Miguel (1) _quieren/prefieren_ tener una boda pequeña, pero elegante. La ceremonia (2) _empieza_ a las 7:00. Los sobrinos y primos jóvenes de los novios no asisten a la ceremonia. Ellos no (3) _entienden_ la ceremonia, y (4) _pueden/prefieren_ jugar con una niñera en otra parte de la iglesia. Después de la ceremonia, todos van a un restaurante, donde los invitados (5) _pueden_ bailar y cenar. Los camareros (6) _sirven_ una cena italiana, porque los padres de Miguel son de Italia. Después de la cena, la familia (7) _vuelve_ a la casa de los padres de la novia. Los invitados (8) _siguen_ en la celebración, pero Beatriz y Miguel salen para su luna de miel (*honeymoon*) a Colombia.

4-19 ¿Qué piensan hacer? Túrnense para decir qué piensa hacer cada (*each*) miembro de la familia en las situaciones siguientes.

MODELO: Mi hermano quiere estar delgado.
E1: *Tu hermano probablemente piensa correr mucho.*
E2: *Él probablemente piensa empezar una dieta.*
E3: *Y probablemente piensa ir al gimnasio todos los días.*

1. Mi hermana tiene un examen de matemáticas mañana.
2. Mi hermana estudia bastante, pero no entiende muchos de los problemas.
3. Mi tía está enferma, por eso se siente muy débil y cansada.
4. Mis abuelos están de vacaciones en Colombia.
5. Mis primos quieren ir a Cartagena para visitar a los abuelos.
6. Mi tío lee y escucha comentarios contradictorios sobre Colombia, por eso, quiere aprender más sobre el país.

4-20 ¿Qué pasa en las reuniones familiares? PRIMERA FASE. Muchas familias se reúnen (*get together*) para las fiestas, los eventos especiales o sólo para reunirse. Describan las reuniones de su familia a su compañero/a. Tomen nota de las semejanzas (*similarities*) y las diferencias.

MODELO: preparar la comida
E1: *En las reuniones de mi familia, mi abuela prepara mucha comida.*
E2: *En las reuniones de mi familia, tenemos mucha comida también. Pero mi madre y mi tía preparan la comida.*

1. venir
2. jugar con los niños
3. servir la comida
4. dormir en el sofá
5. preferir hablar de temas políticos
6. volver a casa

SEGUNDA FASE. Hablen de una semejanza y una diferencia entre las reuniones de su familia. Estén listos (*Be ready*) para compartir la información con la clase.

Lengua

■ **Pensar en** is the Spanish equivalent of *to think of/about someone or something.*

¿Piensas en tu familia cuando estás fuera de casa?
Do you think of/about your family when you are away from home?

Sí, **pienso** mucho **en** ellos.
Yes, I think of/about them a lot.

■ **Pensar de** is used to ask for an opinion. **Pensar que** is normally used in the answer.

¿Qué **piensas de** los planes de ayuda familiar?
What do you think of the plans to help families?

Pienso que son excelentes.
I think they are excellent.

Follow-up for 4-19. Each group chooses the best reply for each item and shares them with the class. You may wish to stage a competition for replies that are the most sensible, the most creative, etc.

Suggestion for 4-20. Encourage students to give their partners as much information as possible so they can identify the similarities and differences between the gatherings in their respective families.

Follow-up for 4-20 Segunda fase. You may wish to have the pairs share their similarity/difference with the class, and then find out which activities, roles, or customs are the most prevalent among your students.

4-21 Entrevista. Túrnense para entrevistarse (*interview each other*). Hablen sobre los siguientes temas (*topics*) y después compartan la información con otro compañero/otra compañera.

1. la hora del almuerzo, qué prefiere comer y dónde
2. los deportes que prefiere practicar o mirar en la televisión
3. a qué hora empieza a hacer la tarea generalmente
4. si duerme una siesta durante el día
5. si vuelve a la casa de sus padres para las vacaciones
6. qué piensa hacer después de la universidad

Suggestion for 4-21. Provide time for students to prepare the questions they are going to ask.

4-22 ¿Cuándo y con quién? PRIMERA FASE. Háganse preguntas para obtener la siguiente información.

1. quiénes son sus amigos y qué actividades hacen juntos durante el año académico, durante la semana y los fines de semana
2. actividades de diversión (o deportivas) que hacen juntos, cuándo y dónde
3. actividades preferidas del fin de semana

Follow-up for 4-22 Primera fase. Encourage students to try to get as much information as possible from their partners.

SEGUNDA FASE. Preparen una lista de sus actividades semejantes o diferentes. Comparen su lista con la de otra pareja (*pair*).

MODELO: *Durante la semana, nosotros almorzamos en la cafetería de la universidad. ¿Y ustedes?*

4-23 Una reunión. En su universidad hay un fin de semana cuando los padres visitan a sus hijos en el campus. Ustedes quieren organizar una reunión para las familias de los miembros de su grupo. Decidan lo siguiente:

1. lugar y hora de la reunión
2. número de niños y adultos que van a participar (especifiquen la relación familiar)
3. comida y bebida que piensan servir
4. actividades y diversiones para los niños y para los adultos

---

En directo

These expressions help maintain the flow of conversation:

¡Cuánto me alegro!
I am so happy for you!

Claro, claro…
Of course . . .

¡Qué bien/bueno!
That's great!

Suggestions for En directo. Model the pronunciation and intonation patterns of the expressions in the box to help students sound more natural.

SITUACIONES

1. **Role A.** You and a member of your family are planning to visit Latin America. Your friend has heard about your plans and calls with some questions. Answer your friend's questions in as much detail as possible.

   Role B. Your friend is planning to go to Latin America with a relative. Call to find out a) when he/she is planning to go; b) with whom; c) what country and cities he/she wants to visit and why; d) if his/her relative prefers to go to other places; and e) when they are returning.

2. **Role A.** The entire family has gathered for a party for the holidays. An elderly aunt/uncle is very curious about your life in college. After commenting on the party and several family members, answer her/his questions politely.

   Role B. You are at a family holiday gathering and you are very happy to see your young nephew/niece who is in college. After commenting on the party and several family members, ask about these aspects of college life: a) his/her classes; b) which class(es) he/she prefers; c) if the food is good; d) when vacation (**vacaciones**) starts; and e) what he/she plans to do after college.

2. Expressing obligation: *Tener que + infinitive*

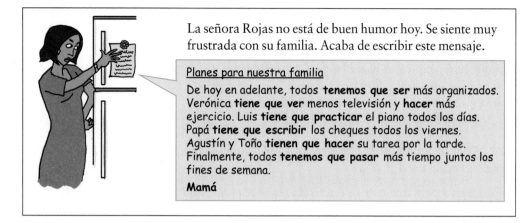

La señora Rojas no está de buen humor hoy. Se siente muy frustrada con su familia. Acaba de escribir este mensaje.

Planes para nuestra familia

De hoy en adelante, todos **tenemos que ser** más organizados. Verónica **tiene que ver** menos televisión y **hacer** más ejercicio. Luis **tiene que practicar** el piano todos los días. Papá **tiene que escribir** los cheques todos los viernes. Agustín y Toño **tienen que hacer** su tarea por la tarde. Finalmente, todos **tenemos que pasar** más tiempo juntos los fines de semana.

Mamá

Piénselo. Según el texto anterior, asocie la situación de la columna izquierda con la obligación de cada persona en la columna derecha.

1. __c__ Verónica mira mucha televisión.
2. __f__ La madre tiene planes para todos.
3. __d__ El padre no se preocupa de los cheques.
4. __e__ Luis no es muy constante con la música.
5. __b__ Agustín y Toño probablemente prefieren practicar deportes y no estudian.
6. __a__ Cada miembro de la familia hace sus actividades independientemente.

a. Todos **tienen que pensar** en la importancia de hacer actividades en familia.
b. **Tienen que dedicar** suficiente tiempo a sus estudios.
c. **Tiene que hacer** más actividades físicas.
d. **Tiene que colaborar** con su esposa.
e. **Tiene que practicar** regularmente.
f. La familia **tiene que organizar** sus actividades.

■ **Tener que +** *infinitive*. Use **tener que** to express what someone *has to*, *needs to*, or *must* do.

Eliana, **tienes que estudiar** más.   *Eliana, you have to study more.*

Tengo que visitar a mis abuelos este fin de semana.   *I have to visit my grandparents this weekend.*

4-24 Mis obligaciones. **PRIMERA FASE.** Marque (✓) las tareas que usted tiene que hacer regularmente. Luego compare sus obligaciones con las de otro compañero/otra compañera.

___ sacar a caminar al perro
___ hacer ejercicio
___ comprar comida
___ hacer la tarea para sus clases
___ revisar el aceite (*oil*) del carro

___ poner los platos sucios en el lavaplatos (*dishwasher*)
___ escuchar los mensajes (*messages*) telefónicos
___ ir a la universidad
___ trabajar por las tardes
___ visitar a mis parientes

SEGUNDA FASE. Ahora dígale (*tell*) a su compañero/a cuándo usted tiene que hacer cada tarea. Luego compare sus obligaciones con las de él/ella.

MODELO: E1:   *Tengo que poner la mesa todos los días. ¿Y tú?*
         E2:   *Yo no tengo que poner la mesa, pero tengo que preparar la comida los domingos.*

Suggestion for 4-24. To preview some new vocabulary, talk about your own (real or imaginary) personal obligations. *Soy una persona con muchas obligaciones y necesidades. Por las mañanas, tengo que preparar el desayuno para mis hijos. También tengo que poner la correspondencia en el buzón antes de salir al trabajo. En la oficina tengo que escribir mucho, ayudar a los alumnos, responder a correos electrónicos, asistir a reuniones, etc. Cuando llego a casa, estoy cansado/a, por eso, necesito descansar. A veces, tengo que acostarme temprano porque tengo que levantarme a las 5:30 de la mañana.* Have students take notes on the similarities and differences between their responsibilities and those of their partners. As a follow-up, you may have them use this information as the basis of a writing activity or report the information to the class.

4-25 Un viaje (*trip*) a Colombia. PRIMERA FASE. Su familia va a viajar a Colombia. Escoja la mejor recomendación para cada persona. Answers may vary.

1. _b_ Mariela quiere visitar un lugar interesante para una persona religiosa.
2. _c_ A mis padres les gustaría ver el trabajo que se hace con metales preciosos en Colombia.
3. _a_ Mi prima Mónica quiere escuchar música colombiana.
4. _d_ Mis abuelitos prefieren las actividades al aire libre.

a. Tiene que asistir a un concierto de Los Príncipes del Vallenato.
b. Tiene que ir a la Catedral de Sal.
c. Tienen que ir al Museo del Oro.
d. Tienen que conocer el Parque Ecológico El Portal.

Cultura

El Portal is an ecological park near Bucaramanga, in the northeastern part of Colombia. With its natural springs and wooded trails, it is a well-known destination for ecotourism. Guests may visit a working sugar mill, and they may also enjoy activities such as horseback riding and mountain biking.

SEGUNDA FASE. Preparen una breve descripción de uno de los lugares o eventos mencionados en la *Primera fase*. Incluyan la localización y las actividades que las personas hacen allí. Luego, compartan la información con la clase.

1. los Príncipes de Vallenato
2. la Catedral de Sal
3. el Museo del Oro
4. el Parque Ecológico El Portal

4-26 Sugerencias. PRIMERA FASE. ¿Qué tienen que hacer (o no) las personas en estas circunstancias?

MODELO: Luis no tiene dinero (*money*).
E1: *¿Qué tiene que hacer Luis?*
E2: *Tiene que leer el periódico para encontrar trabajo.*

1. Mi amigo Juan tiene un examen el lunes.
2. Francisco siempre está cansado.
3. Manuel y Victoria no tienen una buena relación de pareja (*couple*).
4. Mi hermana Marta ve televisión todos los días y saca malas notas en sus clases.
5. Luis y Emilia quieren aprender español.
6. Isabel y Lucía desean visitar un país hispano, pero no hablan español.

SEGUNDA FASE. Escriban individualmente tres circunstancias. Cada persona explica sus circunstancias y su compañero/a dice qué tiene que hacer.

SITUACIONES

1. **Role A.** You run into your cousin downtown. Exchange greetings and explain that today is your father's birthday and that you have to buy a gift (**regalo**). You don't have much time because you have to return home at 5:00. Say that you are thinking of buying a DVD and ask what he/she thinks of the idea. Thank your cousin for the advice (**gracias por los consejos**).

Role B. You run into your cousin downtown. Exchange greetings. Your cousin needs some advice. Listen to his/her concerns and ask pertinent questions. Offer your opinion about whether a DVD is a good idea and, if so, what kind of DVD and where your cousin can find it.

2. **Role A.** You are worried about your bad relationship with your parents. They are angry because a) when you go out, you come home late; b) you do not study much; c) you prefer to spend a lot of time with your friends, but not with your family; d) you never play with your little sister; and e) when you are home you watch a lot of TV. Call a friend for advice. Answer your friend's questions in as much detail as possible.

Role B. A friend calls you to discuss family problems. Listen and ask appropriate questions. Say that he/she a) must return home early in the evenings; b) has to spend more time with family and play with his/her little sister; c) has to study every day to get good grades; and d) must not watch TV before studying.

Resources

■ SAM: 4-24 to 4-28
■ Supp. Activ. Book: Adverbs

3. Expressing when, where, or how an action occurs: Adverbs

Los senderistas (*hikers*) siguen una ruta difícil y tienen que caminar **lentamente**. Si van **rápidamente** van a estar cansados. Cruzan el riachuelo (*creek*) **cuidadosamente**. Hay animales peligrosos en la sierra, pero **afortunadamente** es otoño y **seguramente** no encuentran serpientes.

Sierra de Santa Marta, Colombia

Piénselo. Asocie la expresión en negrita (*bold*) en la columna izquierda con su significado (*meaning*) en la columna derecha.

1. __e__ Los senderistas piensan escalar **poco a poco**.
2. __a__ Si los senderistas suben la montaña **con rapidez**, ellos van a estar cansados.
3. __b__ **Por suerte**, ahora es otoño.
4. __c__ Los senderistas **saben que** no van a encontrar serpientes.
5. __d__ Cruzan el riachuelo **con mucha atención**.

a. rápidamente
b. afortunadamente
c. seguramente
d. cuidadosamente
e. lentamente

Suggestions. Point out secondary stress on *-mente*. Provide practice by saying an adjective and asking for the corresponding adverb. Ask questions to elicit adverbs: *¿Cómo camina usted a clase? ¿Cómo juega al tenis? ¿Cómo habla español?*

You may present the expressions *con frecuencia* and *por lo general* as equivalents of *frecuentemente* and *generalmente*, respectively.

■ Adverbs are used to describe when, where, and how an action/event takes place. You may already be familiar with adverbs referring to time (**mañana, siempre, después**) and place (**allí, abajo, afuera**), and you have used adverbs to express how you feel (**bien, muy mal, regular**). These adverbs can also be used to express how things are done.

Diego nada **bien**, pero yo nado muy **mal**. *Diego swims well, but I swim badly.*

■ Many Spanish adverbs end in **-mente**, an ending that corresponds to the English *-ly*. To form these adverbs, add **-mente** to the feminine singular form of the adjective. With adjectives that do not have a separate feminine form, simply add **-mente** to the singular form.

Abuelita camina **lentamente**. *Grandma walks slowly.*

Mis tíos cantan **alegremente** en las fiestas. *My aunts and uncles sing happily at parties.*

■ When two or more adverbs are used in a series, only the last one has the **-mente** ending. The other adverbs in the series have the same form as the feminine singular form of the adjective.

La profesora habla **clara** y **lentamente**. *The professor speaks clearly and slowly.*

Siempre ganan **rápida** y **fácilmente** el partido. *They always win the game quickly and easily.*

■ Some commonly used adverbs ending in **-mente** are:

básicamente	**lógicamente**	**realmente**	**simplemente**
frecuentemente	**normalmente**	**regularmente**	**tradicionalmente**
generalmente	**perfectamente**	**relativamente**	**tranquilamente**

Lengua

Adjectives with a written accent retain it when forming adverbs ending in **-mente**:
difícil → difícilmente

4-27 ¿Está de acuerdo o no? PRIMERA FASE. Las características de la familia pueden variar entre una comunidad y otra. Indique si usted está de acuerdo (**Sí** o **No**) con las siguientes afirmaciones.

En mi comunidad…

1. _____ los padres frecuentemente hablan con los hijos adolescentes sobre temas importantes.
2. _____ los nietos regularmente visitan a sus abuelos.
3. _____ generalmente los hijos solteros viven con sus padres.
4. _____ los padres siempre hablan lentamente cuando están enojados con sus hijos.
5. _____ idealmente el padre trabaja fuera de casa y la madre trabaja en casa.
6. _____ los hijos adolescentes siempre tratan a sus padres cortésmente.

SEGUNDA FASE. Comparen sus respuestas y digan por qué están de acuerdo.

MODELO: E1: *Estoy de acuerdo con el número uno. Generalmente los padres hablan sobre temas importantes con sus hijos.*

E2: *No estoy de acuerdo. Los padres generalmente hablan sobre educación o dinero, pero no hablan de drogas.*

4-28 ¿Lenta o rápidamente? Escriba tres actividades de la siguiente lista que usted hace rápidamente y tres que hace lentamente. Indique el lugar y/o las circunstancias.

almorzar	escribir composiciones	hablar español	pasear
beber	estudiar	leer el periódico	tomar apuntes

MODELO: *Como rápidamente cuando tengo poco tiempo.*

4-29 ¿Cómo lo hace usted? Primero, individualmente escriba cómo o cuándo usted hace las siguientes actividades. Usando las palabras en la lista u otras, forme adverbios para escribir sus frases. Luego, comparen sus respuestas.

difícil	frecuente	lógico	perfecto
fácil	lento	ocasional	rápido

1. caminar cuando usted está muy cansado/a
2. pensar en la clase de matemáticas
3. respirar (*breathe*) después de una hora de ejercicio en el gimnasio
4. responder en un examen fácil

4-30 Actividades frecuentes. PRIMERA FASE. Hágale estas preguntas a su compañero/a. Después él/ella tiene que hacerle las mismas (*same*) preguntas a usted. Tome apuntes sobre las respuestas de su compañero/a.

1. ¿Qué haces normalmente con tu familia?
2. ¿A qué lugares vas regularmente con tu familia? ¿Y con tus amigos?
3. Generalmente, ¿sales por las noches? ¿Adónde vas y con quién?
4. ¿A quiénes llamas por teléfono más frecuentemente, a tus amigos o a tu familia?

SEGUNDA FASE. Ahora escriba una breve comparación entre usted y su compañero/a con respecto a cada pregunta en la *Primera fase*. ¿Hacen ustedes actividades semejantes o diferentes?

En directo

To express surprise at what you hear:

¡Qué increíble!
Incredible!

¡No me diga(s)!
Really!

SITUACIONES

1. **Role A.** Your class is conducting a survey regarding students' movie habits. Ask a classmate a) when and with whom he/she generally goes to the movies; b) the type of movies he/she normally prefers (**románticas, dramáticas, de ciencia ficción**, etc.); c) what he/she often eats or drinks at the movies; and d) the name of his/her favorite movie.

   Role B. Answer the questions a classmate will ask about your movie preferences.

2. **Role A.** In your Sociology and the Family course, you are helping to conduct a survey about family traditions and activities. Ask a classmate a) if the members of his/her immediate family generally eat together; b) if they visit other family members frequently; and c) which family member normally organizes family gatherings.

   Role B. First answer your classmate's questions about your family. Then ask him/her these questions for the survey: a) Who is generally more organized (**organizado/a**) at home, men or women?; b) Do family members frequently do activities together?; c) Who prepares dinner well in the family?; d) Who talks calmly when angry, your father or your mother?

Follow-up for 4-27 Segunda fase. You may wish to have students write on index cards some traits they consider characteristic of families. Then you can shuffle the cards and read them aloud one at a time. Volunteers can agree or disagree with the statements.

Note for 4-28. You may want to point out the activity title and mention again how to form adverbs that are used in a series.

Alternate for 4-28. Students can work in pairs and then share with the class what they do *lenta o rápidamente* in: 1. *la casa*; 2. *la biblioteca*; 3. *el gimnasio*; 4. *un restaurante*.

Note for 4-30. Although comparatives are presented in *Capítulo 8*, students can use them in this activity since the structures are similar in both languages. Model the use of *y* and *pero* to compare and contrast by talking about yourself: *Mi esposo/a y yo hacemos actividades semejantes por la tarde. Él y yo trabajamos. Pero hacemos algunas actividades diferentes. Regularmente él va a los partidos de fútbol con sus amigos, pero yo voy a los centros comerciales con mis amigas. Mi esposo/a es más sociable y le gusta salir con amigos y hablar por teléfono. Yo prefiero estar en casa y escuchar música.*

Resources

■ SAM: 4-29 to 4-32
■ Supp. Activ. Book: *Hace*
  with expressions of time

4. Expressing how long something has been going on: *Hace* with expressions of time

PATRICIA: Señora, ¿**cuánto tiempo hace que** practico esta sonata? ¡Estoy muy cansada!

SRA. ESCOBEDO: **Hace dos horas que** trabajas en ella. Pero una vez más, por favor, Patricia. El recital es en dos días.

Sra. Escobedo   Patricia

SRA. ESCOBEDO: Les presento a Patricia Suárez. Estudia el violín conmigo **hace cinco años.** Ahora va a tocar la Sonata N° 4 de Mozart.

Piénselo. Diga si las siguientes afirmaciones son lógicas (**L**) o ilógicas (**I**).

1. ⌐⌐ **Hace mucho tiempo que** Patricia toca el violín perfectamente.
2. ⌐⌐ **Hace cinco años que** Patricia no pasa mucho tiempo con sus amigos porque tiene que practicar la sonata.
3. ⌐⌐ Patricia conoce a la profesora de violín **hace cinco años.**
4. ⌐⌐ **Hace sólo un día que** Patricia trabaja en la sonata de Mozart.
5. ⌐⌐ **Hace poco tiempo que** la señora Escobedo toca el violín.
6. ⌐⌐ Los padres de Patricia no le pagan a la profesora por las clases de violín **hace un año.**

■ To say that an action/state began in the past and continues into the present, use **hace** + *length of time* + **que** + *present tense.*

Hace dos horas que juegan. *They have been playing for two hours.*

■ If you begin the sentence with the present tense of the verb, do not use **que.**

Juegan **hace dos horas.** *They've been playing for two hours.*

■ To find out how long an action/state has been taking place, use **cuánto tiempo** + **hace que** + *present tense.*

¿Cuánto tiempo hace que juegan? *How long have they been playing?*

¿Cuántas horas hace que los niños juegan al fútbol? *How many hours have the children been playing soccer?*

4-31 Este soy yo. PRIMERA FASE. Lea esta descripción y conteste las preguntas.

Me llamo Jaime Caicedo y soy de Cali, Colombia. Quiero aprender inglés para poder trabajar en una compañía internacional. Estudio inglés **hace dos años,** pero tengo que estudiar más para hablar correctamente. Siempre miro programas de televisión en inglés. Mis favoritos son *American Idol* y *Grey's Anatomy.* **Hace dos años que** miro estos programas y me gustan mucho. Tengo un auto **hace un año,** y salgo en él con mis amigos y también con mi novia. **Hace seis meses que** somos novios. Somos muy felices.

1. Jaime Caicedo es de...
   a. Estados Unidos.   (b.) Cali.   c. *Grey's Anatomy.*

2. Hace dos años que Jaime...
   a. tiene novia.   b. va al cine.   (c.) mira televisión en inglés.

3. Hace seis meses que Jaime...
   a. va a fiestas.   b. estudia inglés.   (c.) tiene novia.

SEGUNDA FASE. Ahora escriba su propia descripción, siguiendo el modelo en la *Primera fase.* Luego, comparta su descripción con un compañero/una compañera.

Me llamo (1) _____ . Soy de (2) _____ ,
(3) _____ (ciudad y país). Quiero aprender (4) _____
(lengua extranjera) porque (5) _____ . Estudio
(6) _____ (lengua extranjera) hace (7) _____ (período
de tiempo), pero tengo que estudiar más para hablar
correctamente. Miro (8) _____ películas como _____
(películas en español) y escucho la música de (9) _____
(cantante o grupo español) para aprender más.
Mi programa favorito es (10) _____ . Hace
(11) _____ (período de tiempo) que (12) _____
el programa y me gusta mucho. En mi tiempo libre,
(13) _____ . Tengo (14) _____ (vehículo/objeto o
animal) hace (15) _____ . Hace (16) _____ (período
de tiempo) que estudio en (17) _____ (nombre de la
universidad). Espero ser (18) _____ (profesión)
(19) _____ en el futuro.

4-32 ¿Cuánto tiempo hace que...? Túrnense para hacerse las siguientes preguntas. Después compartan la información con otra pareja.

1. ¿Dónde vive tu familia? ¿Cuánto tiempo hace que viven allí?
2. ¿Dónde trabajas? ¿Cuánto tiempo hace que trabajas allí?
3. ¿Cuánto tiempo hace que estudias en esta universidad? ¿Y por qué estudias español?
4. ¿Practicas algún deporte? ¿Cuánto tiempo hace que juegas al...? ¿Juegas bien?

SITUACIONES

1. **Role A.** You live in Queens, New York, and a friend has come to visit. Explain that there are many Hispanic restaurants in this neighborhood (**barrio**). You suggest your favorite Colombian restaurant for dinner. When your friend asks about the Colombian food that they serve, you may want to mention **ajiaco de pollo** (a chicken stew made with potatoes, corn, and cream), **papas chorreadas** (potatoes covered with a sauce made with onions, tomatoes and milk), and **arroz con coco** (rice cooked in coconut milk).

   Role B. You are visiting a friend in Queens, New York. He/She suggests a Colombian restaurant for dinner. Ask a) how long he/she has been living in Queens; b) if he/she knows the restaurant well; c) what Colombian dishes they serve, and what they are like; and d) how much they cost.

2. **Role A.** You go to see your counselor (**consejero/a**) to talk about a personal problem (**un problema**). Greet the counselor and explain your problem. Answer the counselor's questions in as much detail as possible. When the session is over, thank the counselor.

   Role B. You are a student counselor (**consejero/a**). A student comes to you with a problem (**un problema**). Exchange greetings and ask a) how long the student has been at the university; b) how long he/she has been having the problem; and c) what he/she is doing to solve (**resolver**) the problem and for how long. Finally, suggest several things he/she has to do to improve (**mejorar**) the situation.

Suggestion for 4-32. Tell students that those who do not have a job may respond to question 2 with information about a friend or family member: *Yo no trabajo, pero mi amiga Susana trabaja en...*

Note for Situaciones. Tell students that New York City has a large and diverse Hispanic community. The more than two million Hispanics account for close to 30% of the city's total population. The five largest Hispanic groups in New York are Puerto Ricans, Dominicans, Mexicans, Ecuadorans, and Colombians. The residential patterns differ across groups: Most Puerto Ricans live in the Bronx or Brooklyn; Dominicans are concentrated in the Bronx and Manhattan; and Mexican neighborhoods are found primarily in the Bronx, Brooklyn, and Queens. Most of the city's Ecuadorans and Colombians live in Queens.

Suggestion for Situaciones. In preparation for the first *Situación,* you may want to talk about the Colombian dishes mentioned there (*ajiaco de pollo,* a chicken stew made with potatoes, corn, and cream; *papas chorreadas,* boiled potatoes in a sauce made with onions, tomatoes, and milk; *arroz con coco,* rice cooked in coconut milk). Students may also go to the *Mosaicos* web page or the Internet to get additional information about these and other typical Colombian dishes.

For the second *Situación,* you may offer a short list of possible problems students can discuss, e.g., *un compañero/una compañera de cuarto muy desordenado/a, problemas con un curso, falta de amigos/actividades sociales.*

Resources

■ SAM: 4-33 to 4-37
■ Supp. Activ. Book: Reflexive verbs and pronouns

5. Talking about daily routine: Reflexive verbs and pronouns

Suggestions. You may mention that *cepillarse los dientes* is also used.

Write different times on the board and say what you do on a typical morning, using gestures to help students' comprehension: *Por la mañana, a las siete y cuarto más o menos, yo busco el periódico y preparo el café. A las siete y media me baño, me lavo el pelo y me visto. A las ocho desayuno cereal y bebo otra taza de café. A las nueve salgo para la universidad.* Ask questions to check comprehension. Then ask at what time students do each activity: *¿Qué hace usted a las ocho? ¿A qué hora desayuna? ¿Se baña por la mañana o por la noche? ¿A qué hora?*

Suggestions. Remind students that they have been using the reflexive *¿Cómo te llamas? Me llamo... ¿Cómo se llama usted?* since the beginning of the course, as well as many other reflexive forms in *A primera vista*.

Suggestion. Explain the concept of reflexive/nonreflexive actions. Point out that some verbs can be used reflexively or nonreflexively: *La mamá peina a su hija. La mamá se peina. Roberto baña a su perro. Roberto se baña.* If possible, use visuals. You may create a story about a sports figure, for example, using a series of visuals.

Yo **me llamo** Óscar Torres. Mi esposa Rosa y yo tenemos una vida muy ocupada. Nosotros **nos levantamos** a las seis todos los días. Yo **me ducho** mientras Rosa se viste rápidamente. Después, Rosa **despierta** a Carlitos y a Roberto, nuestros hijos. Roberto **se viste**, y Rosa **viste** a Carlitos. Desayunamos y luego todos **nos lavamos** los dientes y a las siete salimos de la casa.

Piénselo. Para cada acción, indique si cada persona hace la acción a sí misma(s) (*him/her/themselves*) o a otra persona.

ACCIÓN	A SÍ MISMO/A	A OTRA PERSONA
1. Óscar **se ducha** por la mañana.	✓	
2. Rosa **despierta** a Carlitos.		✓
3. La madre **viste** al niño porque es muy pequeño.		✓
4. Roberto **se viste** rápidamente.	✓	
5. Nosotros **nos lavamos** los dientes después de desayunar.	✓	
6. Rosa probablemente **se baña** por la noche, porque no tiene tiempo por la mañana.	✓	

■ Reflexive verbs express what people do to or for themselves.

| REFLEXIVE: Mi hermana **se lava**. | *My sister washes (herself).* |
| NONREFLEXIVE: Mi hermana **lava** el auto. | *My sister washes the car.* |

LAVARSE (*to wash oneself*)			
yo	**me lavo**	nosotros/as	**nos lavamos**
tú	**te lavas**	vosotros/as	**os laváis**
Ud., él, ella	**se lava**	Uds., ellos/as	**se lavan**

■ A reflexive pronoun refers back to the subject of the sentence. English sometimes uses the pronouns ending in *-self/-selves* to express reflexive meaning. In many cases, Spanish uses reflexives where English does not.

Yo **me levanto, me ducho, me seco** y **me visto** rápidamente.   *I get up, take a shower, dry myself, and get dressed quickly.*

■ Place reflexive pronouns after the word **no** in negative constructions.

Rosa **no se ducha** por la mañana.   *Rosa does not take a shower in the morning.*

■ The pronoun **se** attached to the end of an infinitive indicates the verb is reflexive.

vestir	*to dress (someone else)*
vestirse	*to get dressed (oneself)*

■ With a conjugated verb followed by an infinitive, place the reflexive pronoun before the conjugated verb or attach it to the infinitive.

Yo **me** voy a levantar a las siete. ⎱
Yo voy a levantar**me** a las siete. ⎰   *I am going to get up at seven.*

■ When referring to parts of the body and articles of clothing, use definite articles rather than possessives with reflexive verbs.

Me lavo **los** dientes.	*I brush my teeth.*
Roberto se pone **la** chaqueta.	*Roberto puts on his jacket.*

■ Some verbs change meaning when used reflexively.

acostar	*to put to bed*	**acostarse**	*to go to bed, to lie down*
dormir	*to sleep*	**dormirse**	*to fall asleep*
levantar	*to raise, to lift*	**levantarse**	*to get up*
llamar	*to call*	**llamarse**	*to be called*
poner	*to put, to place*	**ponerse**	*to put on*
quitar	*to take away*	**quitarse**	*to take off*

4-33 ¿Qué hacemos todos los días? Ponga estas actividades en el orden más lógico.

<u>6</u> Me duermo.   <u>4</u> Salgo para mis clases.   <u>2</u> Me lavo la cara (*face*).
<u>1</u> Me levanto.   <u>5</u> Me acuesto.   <u>3</u> Desayuno.

4-34 ¿Tenemos las mismas rutinas? Hablen sobre sus actividades diarias.

MODELO: despertarse
     E1: *Yo me despierto a las siete. ¿Y tú?*
     E2: *Generalmente, me despierto a las ocho.*

1. levantarse   3. vestirse   5. acostarse
2. ducharse   4. desayunar   6. dormirse

4-35 Los horarios. PRIMERA FASE. Usen la información en la tabla para escribir un párrafo sobre el horario de las hermanas gemelas (*twins*) Alicia y Blanca y su hermanito Carlitos.

	CARLITOS	ALICIA Y BLANCA	YO
despertarse	8:00	7:00	
levantarse	8:15	7:05	
bañarse	8:20	7:10	
vestirse	8:30	7:20	

SEGUNDA FASE. Ahora escriba individualmente sus actividades en la tabla. Luego, hablen de su horario y hagan comparaciones entre su horario y el de las personas de la *Primera fase*.

SITUACIONES

1. **Role A.** A young person in your family has to do a report for school based on an interview of a family member. That person is going to interview you. Exchange greetings and answer his/her questions as completely as possible.

   Role B. You are a middle school student who has to write a report about a family member (your classmate). Greet him/her and explain the purpose of the interview. Then find out a) where he/she lives and for how long he/she has lived there; b) what his/her daily routine is; and c) some differences between the routine of a college student and that of a middle school student.

2. **Role A.** You live in Bogota, and you would like your niece to attend a summer camp (**campamento de verano**) in the United States so she will learn English. Ask the camp director questions to find out a) how many children there are per counselor (**por consejero/a**); b) what time the children get up; c) what sports they play; d) what they eat; e) what they do in the evenings; and f) what time they go to bed.

   Role B. You are the director of the summer camp (**campamento de verano**). Answer the questions of the aunt/uncle of a prospective camper. Add as much information as possible.

Suggestion. You may tell students that *acostarse* literally means to put oneself to bed and that *dormirse* means to put oneself to sleep.

Suggestion for 4-33. Remind students that some reflexive verbs in this activity and the next have stem changes: *dormirse, acostarse, despertarse, vestirse.*

Follow-up for 4-34. You may wish to ask the pairs of students if their routines for any of these activities are the same, so that they respond using *nosotros/as* forms.

Follow-up for 4-35. For the *Primera fase*, have students write portions of their paragraphs on the board to provide input for conversation about the activities of the characters/reflexive forms. For the *Segunda fase*, students can question each other to find out who wakes up the earliest/gets up immediately after awakening/gets dressed before eating breakfast, etc.

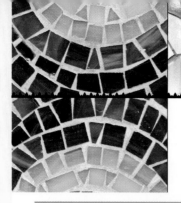

Resources
- SAM: 4-38 to 4-40
- Supp. Activ. Book: *Mosaicos*

MOSAICOS

A escuchar

ESTRATEGIA

Listen for a purpose

Listening with a purpose in mind will help you focus your attention on what is important and relevant to meet your goal. As you focus your attention, you screen what you hear and select only the information you need, letting go of what seems irrelevant to your purpose.

Antes de escuchar

4-36 Preparación. Usted va a escuchar el mensaje de Pedro para Julio sobre una fiesta sorpresa (*surprise*) que está organizando Pedro. Antes de escuchar, escriba el propósito (*purpose*) posible de un mensaje como este. ¿A qué información específica es importante poner atención?

propósito posible: _____

información específica: _____

Escuchar

4-37 ¿Comprende usted? First read the information you will need to have in order to attend the party Pedro is organizing. Then, as you listen, complete the sentences with the rest of the information. Don't worry if you do not understand every word.

CD 2 Track 21

1. La fiesta es para... Josefina
2. La fiesta va a ser en la casa de... Pedro
3. El día de la fiesta es... Domingo
4. Julio debe llevar (*take*)... música típica de Colombia
5. Julio tiene que llegar a la casa a las... ocho y media
6. La dirección es... calle 12, número 127

Después de escuchar

4-38 Ahora usted. Usted va a dar una fiesta sorpresa para un amigo/una amiga en la clase de español y desea invitar a su profesor/a de español. Complete la nota que usted va a poner en el buzón (*mailbox*) de su profesor/a.

Estimado/a profesor/a _____:

Este fin de semana, pienso dar una fiesta sorpresa para _____.

¿Le gustaría venir? Vamos a comer _____ y _____. Vamos a tener refrescos para todos.

La fiesta va a ser el _____ en mi casa a las _____ de la noche.
Mi dirección es _____.

Lo/La espero el _____.

Hasta pronto.

_____

A conversar

Antes de conversar

4-39 Preparación. Complete las siguientes afirmaciones con los nombres de sus parientes, la relación de parentesco y sus actividades.

MODELO: *Mi primo David come* en restaurantes los fines de semana.

1. ... cerveza frecuentemente cuando mira(n) fútbol en la televisión.
2. ... mucho y con frecuencia está(n) cansado/a(s).
3. ... a conciertos de música popular.
4. ... en casa los fines de semana. Descansan, leen, escuchan música, etc.
5. ... ejercicio físico tres o cuatro veces por semana.
6. ... con amigos o con la familia en casa el día de su cumpleaños.
7. ... música romántica a todas horas.
8. ... por el teléfono celular. Llama(n) a sus amigos día y noche.

Conversar

4-40 Entre nosotros. Conteste las preguntas de sus compañeros/as con los nombres de los miembros de su familia para comparar las dos categorías.

MODELO: E1: *¿Quiénes son las personas artísticas en tu familia, las mujeres o los hombres?*
E2: *En mi familia, las mujeres son muy artísticas. Por ejemplo, mi hermana Carlota pinta y escribe poemas. En contraste con las mujeres, los hombres son deportistas. Mi primo Alberto, por ejemplo, practica tenis y fútbol.*

1. ¿Quiénes son las personas activas en tu familia, las mujeres o los hombres?
2. ¿Qué miembros de la familia pasan mucho tiempo en casa, los jóvenes o los mayores?
3. ¿Quiénes son muy sociables, las mujeres o los hombres, los jóvenes o los mayores? ¿Por qué?

Después de conversar

4-41 Un poco más. Completen un pequeño informe (*report*) con la información de su grupo de la actividad **4-40**. Luego compartan la información con el resto de la clase.

1. En nuestras familias (los hombres/las mujeres) _____ son muy activos/as. Por ejemplo, _____. Por otro lado, _____ no son muy activos. Por ejemplo, _____.
2. (Los jóvenes/Los mayores) _____ pasan mucho tiempo en casa porque _____. Por ejemplo, _____ . En cambio, _____ no pasan mucho tiempo en casa porque _____. Por ejemplo, _____ .
3. (Las mujeres/Los hombres/Los jóvenes/Los mayores) _____ son muy sociables. Por ejemplo, _____ . En contraste, _____ no son muy sociables. Por ejemplo, _____ .

ESTRATEGIA

Organize information to make comparisons

In *Capítulo 3*, you practiced organizing information for a presentation. Now you will focus on organizing information for a particular purpose— to compare family members on the basis of different categories (males vs. females, young people vs. elders). Follow these steps in organizing your information.

- List the names of family members you are going to talk about.
- Indicate the family relationships.
- Decide on possible categories of comparison.

En directo

To make comparisons and contrasts:

Por un lado...
On the one hand ...

Por otro lado...
On the other hand ...

En cambio...
On the other hand ...

En contraste...
In contrast ...

Resources
■ SAM: 4-41
■ *Entrevistas* video

Note for Estrategia. The focus here is on organizing information for a purpose. You may wish to introduce as lexical items *más... que, menos... que,* if you think the phrases will help students converse more naturally. (Comparisons are presented in *Capítulo 8*.)

Preparation for 4-39. Make sure students notice that the sample response in the model includes three pieces of information: name (*David*), relationship (*primo*), and activity (*come*). They should follow the model. Encourage them to include more than one family member in each response.

Warm-up for 4-40. Ask questions about students' families: *¿Cuántos hermanos tiene usted? ¿Dónde viven?* Ask other students to recall information given by their classmates.

Suggestion for 4-41. Have students discuss their responses and draw conclusions with the class as a whole.

Resources

■ SAM: 4-42 to 4-44

Follow-up to 4-42. You may wish to have students compare their answers with a classmate and talk about the reasons for their responses. Question 3 lends itself to discussion, since the concept of communication may be interpreted differently in different families. To help students compare responses to question 3, you may write on the board: *Es necesario... ; No es necesario...* and give an example: *Es necesario estar en contacto con la familia. No es necesario hablar por teléfono todos los días.*

Suggestion for 4-43. Remember that students may comprehend more than they can verbalize or write. Therefore, it is advisable not to force them to respond to questions in their own words or paraphrase at this stage. Let them quote their answers directly from the text if they prefer.

Answers for 4-43 Primera mirada. 1. *importancia, comunicación, familiar*; 2. *crisis*; 3. *vital*; 4. *la madre y el padre trabajan largas horas fuera de casa y los hijos están solos mucho tiempo*; 5. *la compañía y la supervisión*; 6. *cierta independencia en los hijos y una distancia emocional.*

ESTRATEGIA

Use title and illustrations to anticipate content

Before you start to read, it is important to gather as much information about the text as possible. The title, section headings, and illustrations can help you anticipate content, so pay special attention to them before you start to read. Verbalize to yourself (aloud or by writing notes) what you think the text is about, and refer to your notes as you are reading, correcting them as necessary. This will help you focus on understanding each section of the text as you read it.

A leer

Antes de leer

4-42 Preparación. Lea el título y los subtítulos del artículo a continuación y observe las fotos. Luego, use la información del título, los subtítulos y las fotos para contestar las siguientes preguntas. Answers may vary.

1. Basándose en el título del artículo, los subtítulos, las fotos y sus leyendas (*captions*), adivine el tema del artículo.
   a. la comunicación entre amigos
   (b.) la comunicación entre los miembros de una familia
   c. la comunicación con los colegas en el trabajo

2. En su opinión, ¿cuáles de las siguientes ideas va a incluir el artículo? (Hay más de una respuesta correcta.)
   a. Hoy en día la comunicación entre padres e hijos es mejor que (*better than*) en el pasado.
   (b.) Los jóvenes no hablan con sus padres sobre sus problemas porque los padres siempre están ocupados.
   (c.) La vida moderna afecta la comunicación entre padres e hijos.
   (d.) La tecnología tiende a reducir la comunicación sobre temas importantes.

3. Marque (✓) las actividades de la siguiente lista que usted asocia usted con una buena relación entre padres e hijos.

   a. ✓ conversar
   b. ✓ pasar tiempo juntos
   c. ✓ hablar por teléfono
   d. ___ pelear (*argue*)
   e. ✓ escribir correos electrónicos a un miembro de la familia que vive lejos (*far*)

   f. ✓ comprar regalos con frecuencia
   g. ✓ expresar cariño (*affection*) verbalmente
   h. ___ no hablar de sus problemas con los padres

Leer

4-43 Primera mirada. Lea los dos primeros párrafos del texto y siga las instrucciones.

Subraye (*Underline*)...

1. las palabras en el título que probablemente indican el tema del artículo.
2. una palabra que describe la condición de la familia de hoy.
3. una palabra que indica la importancia de la comunicación dentro de la familia.

Escriba...

4. una causa de los problemas de comunicación en la familia.
5. dos necesidades de los hijos que tienen padres que trabajan fuera de casa.
6. dos efectos de la ausencia de los padres de la casa.

La importancia de la comunicación familiar

La familia en crisis

Los expertos afirman que la familia de hoy está en crisis por la falta[1] de comunicación entre sus miembros o por la mala comunicación que existe entre ellos. También dicen que la comunicación es vital en todas las relaciones, especialmente en las relaciones familiares.

La comunicación entre padres e hijos sobre temas importantes forma relaciones familiares fuertes y cariñosas.

Ausencia de los padres

¿Por qué hay problemas de comunicación en las familias? Hay varias razones. Una razón es que la madre y el padre trabajan largas horas fuera de casa y los hijos están solos mucho tiempo, sin la compañía y la supervisión de sus mayores. La ausencia casi todos los días de los padres puede crear cierta independencia en los hijos y una distancia emocional que causa dificultades en la comunicación entre padres e hijos.

La tecnología

Un segundo factor es la tecnología. Nuestro mundo está controlado por la tecnología en casa, en el trabajo, etc. Evidentemente la tecnología facilita muchas cosas, pero su uso excesivo puede complicar la vida. Un gran número de hogares[2] están conectados a Internet, así que muchos jóvenes tienen acceso ilimitado al correo electrónico y a la Red, sobre todo a los sitios web de comunicación social y entretenimiento, como MySpace y YouTube. Idealmente, el bajo costo de la conexión debería afectar positivamente la comunicación en la familia, pero la realidad indica que la comunicación moderna (e.g., correo electrónico, mensajes de texto) tiende a ser más breve y más superficial. Los hijos prefieren no discutir sus problemas por correo electrónico o mensajes de texto. Prefieren hablar directamente con sus padres, si es que sus padres tienen el tiempo. Lo mismo ocurre con el teléfono celular. Es cierto que muchos jóvenes usan celulares para llamar a sus padres, pero no muchos usan el celular para conversar largamente con sus padres sobre temas personales importantes. ¡Muy pocos!

La tecnología puede facilitar la comunicación familiar.

Conclusión

En conclusión, el tiempo limitado que los padres pueden dar a sus hijos y la tendencia a usar la tecnología para comunicaciones muy breves pueden afectar negativamente las relaciones familiares. Por eso es importante crear oportunidades para una comunicación real y profunda dentro de la familia. Si usted usa la tecnología de manera positiva para pasar tiempo con sus familiares y para expresar el amor y el cariño que siente por ellos, su familia va a ser más fuerte y unida.

[1]lack [2]homes

4-44 Segunda mirada. Ahora lea el resto del artículo y siga las indicaciones.

En el párrafo sobre la tecnología, el artículo presenta otra razón de la mala comunicación entre padres e hijos.

Indique…

1. una palabra asociada con los problemas de comunicación familiares.
2. por qué la tecnología probablemente afecta las relaciones de la familia.
3. dos ejemplos de cómo la tecnología puede causar problemas en la familia.
4. dos palabras que indican la calidad de la comunicación cuando usamos el correo electrónico o los mensajes de texto.
5. dos formas de usar la tecnología positivamente en la comunicación con la familia.

Después de leer

4-45 Ampliación. Se pueden aplicar las ideas del artículo a la situación de los estudiantes que viven en la universidad y ya no viven en casa con su familia. Hable con su compañero/a sobre el impacto en la comunicación familiar entre los estudiantes universitarios y sus padres. Enfóquese (*Focus*) en los dos temas principales del artículo:

■ la separación física entre los padres y los hijos
■ el uso de la tecnología como medio de comunicación

Answers for 4-44 Segunda mirada. 1. *tecnología*; 2. *el uso excesivo*; 3. *Internet/el correo electrónico, el teléfono celular*; 4. *breve, superficial*; 5. *para pasar tiempo con sus familiares y para expresar el amor y el cariño que siente por ellos.*

Follow-up for 4-45. Students may share their ideas with another pair. Or you may wish to have a class discussion that focuses on making connections between the content of the article and the reality of students' lives: the process of establishing and maintaining communication with family when they are no longer living at home.

Resources

◼ SAM: 4-45 to 4-47

A escribir

ESTRATEGIA

Choose between informal and formal language to express the desired tone

Choosing the appropriate level of formality when you write to someone depends on your relationship to that person. When writing to elders in your family, such as parents or grandparents, a more formal tone may be needed than when writing to friends. The abbreviated format and casual language of computer-based communication may not be the best choice to show your elders love and respect. When you write to them, either in letters or on the computer, choose your language more carefully and write about issues more seriously than you would when corresponding with friends.

The salutation, closing, and forms of address used in letter writing also reflect your degree of closeness and formality. The expressions in *En directo* include some common salutations and forms of address that are appropriate to use when you write to elders in your family.

Antes de escribir

4-46 Preparación. PRIMERA FASE. La madre de Julián, un alumno universitario colombiano, está triste y preocupada porque su hijo estudia en la Universidad de los Andes y vive lejos de casa. Ella le escribe la siguiente carta a su hijo. Lea la carta.

Querido Julián:

¿Qué tal estás? ¿Cómo van tus clases? Hace un mes que no tenemos información sobre ti. ¡No escribes correos electrónicos, no llamas por teléfono! ¿Qué ocurre?

Bueno, es el fin del semestre y debes tener mucho trabajo. ¿Estás muy estresado? ¿Duermes suficiente? ¿Comes bien en la universidad? En tu próxima visita, pienso preparar tus platos favoritos. Tu hermana Mariela, tus abuelos y tíos van a estar con nosotros y vamos a conversar largas horas.

Tengo una sorpresa para ti. Gustavo tiene novia. Se llama Alicia. Pasan mucho tiempo juntos; van al cine, salen a comer por las noches, etc. La semana próxima ambos tienen vacaciones y, para conocerla un poco más, Gustavo piensa ir a Cartagena con ella. Las temperaturas allí están perfectas para nadar y descansar un poco.

Tengo que confesarte que tu padre y yo pensamos mucho en ti. ¿Por qué no escribes? ¿Tienes problemas en tus clases? ¿Trabajas mucho? ¿Estás desconectado de Internet? Por favor, escribe o llama pronto.

Un beso de papá, Mariela y toda la familia.

Abrazos,

Tu madre

SEGUNDA FASE. Usted es Julián. Prepárese para responder a la carta de su madre. Haga lo siguiente:

1. Identifique las preguntas de su madre que usted quiere contestar y escriba algunas ideas que piensa incluir. Seleccione las palabras adecuadas para lograr (*achieve*) el tono adecuado.
2. Escriba algunas preguntas que usted quiere hacerle a su madre: sobre su padre, sus hermanos, sus abuelos, su perro o gato, etc.

Escribir

4-47 Manos a la obra. Ahora responda a la carta de su madre. Use la información de la *Segunda fase* de la actividad **4-46**. Seleccione cuidadosamente las palabras para mostrar respeto a su madre. Recuerde incluir la fecha, un saludo y una despedida (*closing*) apropiados.

Querida madre:

Después de escribir

4-48 Revisión. Revise los siguientes aspectos de su carta.

1. Primero, el grado de intimidad (*intimacy*) y formalidad para comunicarse con su madre. ¿Incluye usted un saludo y una despedida apropiados en la carta? ¿Usa usted el vocabulario adecuado para dirigirse (*address*) a su madre?
2. La coherencia de sus ideas y la cantidad de información que su madre probablemente desea
3. Luego, la precisión gramatical: la estructura de las oraciones, la concordancia, etc.
4. Finalmente, la ortografía, la acentuación

ENFOQUE CULTURAL

La riqueza de Colombia

Normalmente asociamos a Colombia con el café de Juan Valdez, un personaje inventado por las agencias de publicidad, como el representante de Colombia ante el mundo. En realidad, Colombia se conoce en todas partes por la calidad suave de su café y el símbolo de Juan Valdez es una de las imágenes corporativas más famosas del mundo. Sin embargo, Colombia es mucho más que su café. Su diversidad geográfica y climática, y la variedad natural, étnica y cultural de sus regiones hacen de Colombia un país con un inmenso potencial.

Para empezar, Colombia es el único país de América del Sur que tiene costas en los dos mares. La costa Atlántica, que es la región caribeña, tiene playas espectaculares, montañas impresionantes en la Sierra Nevada de Santa Marta, selvas tropicales en el Urabá y un desierto en La

Las cinco regiones de Colombia continental

Guajira. Los habitantes de la costa Atlántica tienen fama de tener un carácter alegre y festivo. La costa Pacífica es la región con mayor biodiversidad del mundo y es la región más lluviosa del planeta. Una gran parte de la población afro-colombiana habita en las dos costas.

En contraste, la Amazonía colombiana forma parte de la zona de selvas tropicales que se extienden a Perú, Brasil y Venezuela para formar el "pulmón del mundo". Se llama así porque es la zona donde se produce la mayor cantidad del oxígeno que respiramos. En esta región se hablan más de cien idiomas indígenas, y hay una gran variedad de animales y plantas. Los indígenas de la región usan muchas de estas plantas como medicinas y muchos científicos investigan los beneficios de estas plantas para la medicina. En la Amazonía, por ejemplo, hay una estación científica para el estudio de la malaria, donde el Dr. Manuel Patarroyo hace investigación para encontrar una vacuna contra esta enfermedad.

La región de los Llanos Orientales está formada por grandes praderas que se extienden a Venezuela. Colombia y Venezuela son dos países hermanos que están unidos por su historia y geografía. La ganadería y la agricultura son las actividades más importantes de esta región. En efecto, los llaneros o habitantes de esta región, son muy aficionados a los caballos y en las fiestas populares practican un deporte similar al rodeo para demostrar sus destrezas. Además, los Llanos Orientales son el hábitat de una gran variedad de aves, reptiles, mamíferos y peces. Esta es la única región de Colombia donde habita el oso hormiguero, un bello animal que come hormigas.

El oso hormiguero habita en los Llanos Orientales de Colombia.

Medellín, conocida como "la capital de la montaña"

La región andina de Colombia es la zona central del país. Precisamente en esta región, cerca de la ciudad de Armenia, se produce el mejor café de Colombia. Está formada por la Cordillera de los Andes y es el lugar donde vive la gran mayoría de los colombianos. Aquí están las ciudades más grandes del país: Bogotá, la capital; Medellín, la ciudad más industrial; Cali, la tercera ciudad más grande de Colombia. La mayoría de la clase media de Colombia vive en las ciudades de la zona central y aquí se encuentran también las universidades más importantes del país, que atraen a jóvenes de todas las regiones colombianas.

Además de las cinco regiones continentales, Colombia tiene una región insular. Las Islas de San Andrés y Providencia están en el Caribe y son un verdadero paraíso tropical. Sus playas blancas, las aguas cristalinas y tranquilas del mar, sus bellas palmeras y sus excelentes restaurantes hacen de estas islas un lugar ideal para el turismo. Las otras islas colombianas están en el Océano Pacífico y son una reserva natural y ecológica. Cerca de la Isla Gorgona se pueden ver ballenas durante gran parte del año.

151

4-49 Comprensión. PRIMERA FASE. **Reconocimiento de palabras clave.** Encuentre en el texto la palabra o expresión que mejor expresa el significado de las siguientes ideas.

1. mild, soft — suave
2. to begin with — para empezar
3. rainy — lluvioso/a
4. lung — pulmón
5. research — investigar
6. vaccine — vacuna
7. ant — hormiga

SEGUNDA FASE. **Oraciones importantes.** Subraye las afirmaciones que contienen ideas que se encuentran en el texto. Luego indique en qué parte del texto están.

1. Juan Valdez was created by a marketing agency.
2. The Pacific coast of Colombia is the rainiest region in the world.
3. Most of the oxygen in the Earth's atmosphere is produced in the Amazon region.
4. Manuel Patarroyo is a Colombian who is searching for a cure for HIV.
5. Spanish is the only language spoken in the Amazonian region of Colombia.
6. The Eastern Prairies (*Llanos Orientales*) of Colombia extend into Venezuela, giving these sister countries a common geography.
7. Different varieties of anteaters can be found all over Colombia.
8. Most Colombians live in the Andean region.

TERCERA FASE. **Ideas principales.** Escriba un párrafo breve en inglés resumiendo (*summarizing*) las ideas principales expresadas en el texto.

4-50 Use la información. Prepare un afiche (*poster*) para hacer una presentación sobre dos colombianos famosos. Elija personas que representen áreas diferentes de la vida colombiana, como la política, las artes, la música, los deportes, etc. Incluya fotos y la siguiente información: lugar donde viven, el trabajo que hacen y otra información de interés. Para preparar esta actividad visite la página web de *Mosaicos* y siga los enlaces útiles.

VOCABULARIO

La familia — *The family*

la abuela	grandmother
el abuelo	grandfather
el ahijado/la ahijada	godchild
la esposa	wife
el esposo	husband
la hermana	sister
el hermano	brother
el hermanastro	stepbrother
la hermanastra	stepsister
la hija	daughter
el hijo	son
el hijo único/la hija única	only child
la madrastra	stepmother
la madre	mother
la madrina	godmother
la mamá	mom
la media hermana	half-sister
el medio hermano	half-brother
la nieta	granddaughter
el nieto	grandson
el niño/la niña	child
la novia	fiancée, girlfriend
el novio	fiancé, boyfriend
el padrastro	stepfather
el padre	father
los padres	parents
el padrino	godfather
el papá	dad
el pariente	relative
el primo/la prima	cousin
la sobrina	niece
el sobrino	nephew
la tía	aunt
el tío	uncle

Verbos — *Verbs*

acostar(se) (ue)	to put to bed; to go to bed
afeitar(se)	to shave; to shave (oneself)
almorzar (ue)	to have lunch
bañar(se)	to bathe; to take a bath
casar(se)	to get married
cerrar(ie)	to close
costar (ue)	to cost
decir (g, i)	to say, to tell
desayunar	to have breakfast
despertar(se) (ie)	to wake (someone up); to wake up
dormir(se) (ue)	to sleep; to fall asleep
dormir (ue) la siesta	to take a nap
duchar(se)	to give a shower to; to take a shower
empezar (ie)	to begin, to start

entender (ie)	to understand
jugar (ue)	to play (a game, sport)
lavar(se)	to wash (oneself)
levantar(se)	to raise; to get up
maquillar(se)	to put makeup on (someone); to put makeup on (oneself)
pasar	to spend (time)
pasear	to take a walk, to stroll
pedir (i)	to ask for; to order
peinar(se)	to comb (someone's hair); to comb (one's hair)
pensar (ie)	to think
pensar (ie) + infinitive	to plan to + verb
poder (ue)	to be able to, can
poner(se) (g) la ropa	to put one's clothes on
preferir (ie)	to prefer
querer (ie)	to want
quitar(se)	to take away; to take off
secar(se)	to dry (oneself)
seguir (i)	to follow, to go on
sentarse (ie)	to sit down
sentir(se) (ie)	to feel
servir (i)	to serve
tener (g, ie)	to have
venir (g, ie)	to come
vestir(se) (i)	to dress; to get dressed
visitar	to visit
volver (ue)	to return

Las descripciones — *Descriptions*

divorciado/a	divorced
gemelo/a	twin
ocupado/a	busy

Palabras y expresiones útiles — *Useful words and expressions*

el bautizo	baptism, christening
la derecha	right
la foto(grafía)	photo(graph)
la izquierda	left
juntos/as	together
el/la mayor	the oldest
el/la menor	the youngest
la noticia	news
tarde	late
temprano	early
un poco	a little

See *Lengua* box on page 129 for time expressions.
See *Lengua* box on page 134 for other expressions with *pensar*.
See page 138 for a list of adverbs.
See page 140 for time expressions with *hacer*.

153

Resources

■ IRM: Syllabi & Lesson Plans

Suggestion. Explain the words *ciudad* and *pueblo* and ask students to describe the painting. Ask questions to introduce these words and to recycle previously learned vocabulary: *¿Qué hay en el cuadro? ¿Esto es un pueblo o una ciudad? ¿Cuántas casas hay? ¿Cómo son las casas? ¿De qué color son? Aparte de casas y árboles, ¿qué más hay en el cuadro? ¿Hay flores/personas/edificios modernos? ¿Qué hacen las personas en este pueblo? ¿Es un pueblo rico o pobre? ¿Por qué? ¿Cree que es bonito o es feo? ¿Por qué? ¿Le gusta el pueblo?*

Mi casa es su casa

Cuadro de un pueblo hondureño, Jorge Fermán, pintor de Honduras

In this chapter you will learn how to:

- discuss housing, furnishings, and architecture
- talk about daily chores and household activities
- talk about activities in progress
- describe physical and emotional states

Cultural focus: Nicaragua, El Salvador, Honduras

Mar Caribe

BELICE

MÉXICO

Ruinas mayas

GUATEMALA

HONDURAS

Copán

Tegucigalpa

El café

EL SALVADOR

San Salvador

NICARAGUA

Mango verde
con limón y sal

León

Managua

Un edificio de arquitectura colonial

El Volcán de Izalco

Granada

OCÉANO PACÍFICO

COSTA
RICA

PANAMÁ

 A vista de pájaro. Mire el mapa y después asocie la información de las dos columnas.

1. _c_ Tegucigalpa…
2. _a_ El mango verde con limón y sal…
3. _f_ Al oeste de El Salvador…
4. _e_ Las ruinas de Copán…
5. _b_ El café…
6. _d_ Granada y otras ciudades de Nicaragua…

a. es un plato típico de El Salvador.
b. es un producto de exportación de los tres países.
c. es la capital de Honduras.
d. tienen arquitectura colonial.
e. son de la civilización maya.
f. está el volcán de Izalco.

Warm-up. Do this activity in pairs or as a class warm-up. Brainstorm with students all the information they already know about Nicaragua, El Salvador, and Honduras. Ask them to locate the countries on the map: *¿Qué países están al norte de El Salvador? ¿Cuál está al sur de Nicaragua?* Highlight the cultural topics, such as food and economic resources, depicted on the map. Explain that *mango verde con limón y sal* is a refreshing snack found all over in these countries, especially in El Salvador. Ask questions to help students make connections: *¿Tienen algún amigo de Honduras/ Nicaragua/El Salvador? ¿Conocen a alguna persona famosa de estos países? ¿Algún escritor importante? ¿Algún músico? ¿Les gusta el mango? ¿Qué otras frutas les gustan? ¿Y ustedes beben café? ¿De dónde es el café que beben? ¿Es de Honduras o de Nicaragua? ¿Es de otro país hispanoamericano?* Recycle adjectives that refer to nationalities: *hondureño, nicaragüense, salvadoreño: Rubén Darío es un escritor nicaragüense muy importante. El clima hondureño es muy bueno.* You may direct the students to the *Enfoque cultural* to broaden their cultural knowledge.

Resources

- SAM: 5-1 to 5-10
- Supp. Activ. Book: *A primera vista*

A PRIMERA VISTA

En casa

CD 2
Track 26
or CD 3
Track 1

En las ciudades de Nicaragua, El Salvador, Honduras, y hay **viviendas** de diferentes **estilos**. La ciudad de Granada, en Nicaragua, tiene **calles** y plazas como esta, con casas coloniales de colores alegres. En Tegucigalpa, la capital de Honduras, hay **edificios** de **apartamentos**. Algunas personas prefieren vivir **cerca** del **centro**. **Creen** que los **barrios** de las **afueras** están muy **lejos** del **trabajo** y de los centros de diversión.

Alquileres	
Categoría:	Alquiler Apartamentos
Ciudad:	Tegucigalpa
Ubicación:	Palmira
Descripción:	PALMIRA ALQUILER DE APARTAMENTO MUY AMPLIO, CÉNTRICO Y ACCESIBLE, 2 HABITACIONES, SALA–COMEDOR, COCINA, 1 BAÑO, ÁREA DE LAVANDERÍA, ESTACIONAMIENTO, TELÉFONO.
Precio:	$ 450,00

En otras palabras

Some words for the parts of a house vary from one region to another in the Spanish-speaking world. Here are some examples:

habitación, dormitorio, cuarto, alcoba, recámara

sala, salón, living

planta, piso

piscina, pileta, alberca

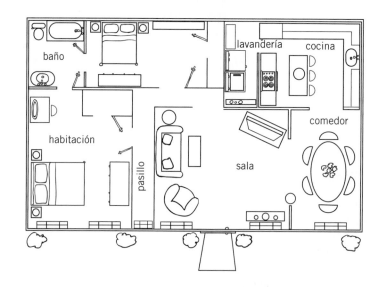

156

El apartamento del anuncio

CD 2
Track 27
and
CD 3
Track 2

MARTA DÍAZ: Hola, buenos días. Me llamo Marta Díaz. ¿Es posible visitar el apartamento del anuncio?

DIEGO LÓPEZ: Sí, claro. Mucho gusto, señorita Díaz. Yo soy Diego López. Pase, pase. Como usted puede ver, el apartamento es muy alegre.

MARTA DÍAZ: ¡Ah, sí! Tiene muchas ventanas.

DIEGO LÓPEZ: Esta es la **sala**. Es muy grande. Junto a la sala hay un **comedor** pequeño y al lado está la **cocina**.

MARTA DÍAZ: ¡La cocina es lindísima!

DIEGO LÓPEZ: Sí, todos los **electrodomésticos** son nuevos. A la izquierda del **pasillo** hay dos **habitaciones** y un **baño**.

MARTA DÍAZ: Esta habitación tiene muy buena **vista** al **jardín**. Además, los **muebles** son de buena calidad. Me gusta el apartamento. ¿Cuánto es el **alquiler**?

DIEGO LÓPEZ: 8.000 lempiras al mes.

MARTA DÍAZ: Pues, señor López, me encantan el apartamento y esta **zona** céntrica. Y el precio es muy bueno. Voy a decidir esta noche y lo llamo mañana.

DIEGO LÓPEZ: Perfecto, señorita Díaz. Hasta mañana.

5-1 Asociación. Indique si las siguientes afirmaciones son ciertas (**C**) o falsas (**F**), según el diálogo anterior.

1. _F_ Marta Díaz quiere comprar el apartamento.
2. _F_ La sala es pequeña.
3. _F_ El apartamento tiene dos baños.
4. _C_ Los electrodomésticos son nuevos.
5. _C_ Los muebles son de buena calidad.
6. _F_ A Marta no le gusta la zona céntrica.

5-2 ¿En qué piso viven? Pregúntele a su compañero/a dónde viven las diferentes personas. Su compañero/a debe contestarle de acuerdo con el dibujo (*drawing*).

MODELO: E1: *¿Dónde viven los Girondo?*
E2: *Viven en el cuarto piso, en el apartamento 4-A.*

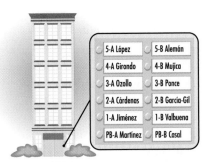

décimo: Rodríguez
noveno: Peralta
octavo: Elizondo
séptimo: Díaz
sexto: Gómez
quinto: Lizaur
cuarto: Sánchez
tercero: Carreras
segundo: Iglesias
primer piso: Olmos
planta baja

5-A López	5-B Alemán
4-A Girondo	4-B Mujica
3-A Ozollo	3-B Ponce
2-A Cárdenas	2-B García-Gil
1-A Jiménez	1-B Valbuena
PB-A Martínez	PB-B Casal

En otras palabras

The Spanish word for *apartment* varies according to the country. **El apartamento** is used in Central America, Colombia, and Venezuela, while **el departamento** is common in Mexico, Argentina, Peru and Chile. The word used in Spain is **el piso**.

En otras palabras

The expressions **Pase(n)** and **Adelante** invite people to enter a room or a house in many Spanish-speaking countries. In others, like Colombia, the expression **Siga(n)** is preferred.

Lengua

Ordinal numbers are adjectives and agree in gender and number with the noun they modify (e.g., **la segunda casa**, **el cuarto edificio**). **Primero** and **tercero** drop the final **-o** when used before a masculine singular noun.

el **primer** apartamento
el **tercer** piso

Cultura

Notice that the first floor is normally called **la planta baja** in most Hispanic countries. The second floor is called **el primer piso**.

Note. The monetary unit of Honduras is *el lempira*, named in honor of Lempira (1497–1537), a Lenca chieftain who fought against the Spanish. House prices are often given in dollars as well as in *lempiras* (Lps). Currently 1 $US = 19 Lps, approximately. You may ask students to find the current rate of exchange.

Standard 4.1. Students demonstrate understanding of the nature of language through the language studied and their own. The information in this *En otras palabras* box shows students that different words are used for the same entity in different parts of the Spanish-speaking world. Instructors may wish to have students brainstorm words they know for apartment in English (flat, rooms) as well as other items (e.g., soda = soft drink, pop; long sandwich with meat, lettuce, etc. = sub, hero, hoagie, grinder, po' boy).

Suggestion. Present the ordinal numbers. Place a number of objects in order and practice ordinals: *primer libro, segundo libro, tercer libro*, etc. Use the photo in the book, or draw a building on the board, showing several floors. Ask questions about the photo to check comprehension: *¿Es este un edificio moderno o antiguo? ¿Tiene piscina/pileta/alberca? ¿En qué planta/piso está la piscina probablemente: en la planta baja o en el piso décimo?¿Hay terrazas en este edificio? ¿Dónde están? En este edificio hay una oficina de administración. ¿En qué piso está probablemente?*

Suggestion for 5-2. Before doing this activity, ask questions to personalize: *¿Quién vive en un edificio de apartamentos? ¿En qué piso vive usted? ¿Le gusta vivir en un edificio de apartamentos muy alto?*

5-3 Un hotel de lujo. Ustedes van a gastar los millones que ganaron (*won*) en la lotería para construir un hotel de lujo en la Bahía de Jiquilisco, cerca de San Salvador. Decidan cómo distribuir los siguientes espacios del hotel.

MODELO: el restaurante
E1: *¿En qué piso vamos a poner el restaurante?*
E2: *Debe estar en la planta baja.*

1. la discoteca
2. la recepción
3. el gimnasio
4. la oficina de seguridad

5. las habitaciones
6. la piscina
7. la cafetería con vista a la playa
8. el salón de computadoras

 5-4 Agentes de bienes raíces (*real estate*). PRIMERA FASE. Los fines de semana ustedes trabajan en una agencia de bienes raíces. Para vender o alquilar la casa del dibujo escriban un anuncio similar al anuncio de la página 156.

Incluyan la siguiente información en su anuncio:

1. número de habitaciones
2. número de baños
3. distribución (*layout*) de los cuartos
4. color de la sala
5. otras características (garaje, jardín, sótano [*basement*], ático, etc.)

6. localización de la casa en relación al centro de la ciudad
7. localización de la casa en relación a la universidad
8. precio de la casa

SEGUNDA FASE. Presenten su anuncio al resto de la clase y contesten las preguntas de sus compañeros sobre la casa que quieren vender o alquilar.

 5-5 Ventajas y desventajas. Discutan los aspectos positivos y negativos de los siguientes temas relacionados con la vivienda. Escriban una ventaja y una desventaja para cada uno de los siguientes puntos. Después compartan sus opiniones con el resto de la clase.

	VENTAJAS	DESVENTAJAS
1. vivir en un apartamento		
2. vivir en una casa		
3. tener una piscina		
4. vivir con un compañero/una compañera de cuarto/casa		

La casa, los muebles y los electrodomésticos

CD 2
Track 28
or CD 3
Track 3

Suggestion. Tell students to imagine that the classroom is a house. Walk around and "identify" the different "rooms." First, whisper to individual students what activities they will charade in each part of the house. Later, you may ask the rest of the class questions: *Mark y Susan están en la cocina. ¿Qué hacen? (Preparan la comida.) Esta es la sala y aquí están María y Carlota. ¿Qué hacen en la sala? (Miran televisión.)* Encourage students to include items from each room in their responses. You may also review colors using the illustration, and/or by having students give the color of rooms in their own house or apartment.

5-6 ¿Aparatos eléctricos, muebles o accesorios? PRIMERA FASE. Escriba cada una de las siguientes palabras en la columna apropiada.

la alfombra   el cuadro   el/la radio
el armario   la butaca   el refrigerador
la cómoda   el horno   las sábanas
las cortinas   el lavaplatos   la silla

En otras palabras

Words for household items often vary from one region to another, for example:

manta, cobija, frazada

armario, clóset

bañera, bañadera, tina

refrigerador, nevera

estufa, cocina

Suggestion. You may introduce some additional vocabulary, such as *pared, congelador, ventilador.*

Note for 5-6. Point out that some Spanish speakers prefer to say *el radio.* In Spain, *la radio* is more common.

APARATOS ELÉCTRICOS	MUEBLES	ACCESORIOS
el refrigerador	el armario	el cuadro
el/la radio	la cómoda	las cortinas
el horno	la silla	la alfombra
el lavaplatos	la butaca	las sábanas

 SEGUNDA FASE. Respondan a las siguientes preguntas relacionadas con la *Primera fase*.

1. Según ustedes, ¿qué aparato eléctrico cuesta más dinero?
2. ¿Qué muebles necesita todos los días un/a estudiante? ¿Necesita un aparato electrónico también? ¿Cuál?
3. ¿Qué accesorios tienen ustedes en su cuarto?
4. ¿En qué parte de la casa generalmente están estos objetos?

Lengua

Here are some electronics that you may have in your house:

la impresora
printer

la consola
game station

el reproductor de DVDs o de CDs
DVD or CD player

el cargador del móvil/celular
cell phone charger

el ipod
iPod

5-7 El curioso. Intercambien preguntas para describir los cuartos de la casa/el apartamento de cada uno/a. Traten (*Try*) de obtener la mayor información posible.

MODELO: E1: *¿Cómo es la sala de tu casa?*
          E2: *Es pequeña. Hay una alfombra verde y un sofá grande. También hay dos sillas modernas y una mesa con una lámpara. ¿Y cómo es tu dormitorio?*

5-8 Preparativos. PRIMERA FASE. Usted va a mudarse (*move*) a una casa muy grande y tiene que comprar muchas cosas. Organice su lista de compras según las siguientes categorías.

	MUEBLES	ACCESORIOS	ELECTRODOMÉSTICOS/ APARATOS ELECTRÓNICOS
para el dormitorio			
para la sala			
para el comedor	—		
para la cocina			

SEGUNDA FASE. Comparta la lista con su compañero/a. Él/Ella le va recordar (*remind you about*) otras cosas que probablemente va a necesitar.

MODELO: E1: *Voy a comprar una cama nueva para el dormitorio.*
          E2: *¿No vas a comprar sábanas y mantas?/¿Y no necesitas un sofá?*

5-9 Por catálogo. Miren las fotos del catálogo y elijan (*choose*) un producto de cada categoría. Intercambien sus preferencias y expliquen en qué lugar de la casa van a poner estos accesorios. Las palabras de la lista los/las pueden ayudar.

barato/a   caro/a   de buena calidad   grande   pequeño/a
bonito/a   confortable   de color...   lindo/a

MODELO: E1: *Me gusta la primera toalla porque no es cara y es muy linda. Es para el cuarto de baño.*
          E2: *Yo prefiero la tercera porque es más grande.*

Las tareas domésticas

CD 2
Track 29
or CD 3
Track 4

Gustavo **lava** los **platos**.

Beatriz **seca** los platos.

Beatriz **cocina**. Ella usa mucho los electrodomésticos.

Gustavo **limpia** el baño y **pasa** la **aspiradora**.

Gustavo **saca** la **basura**.

Gustavo **barre** la terraza.

Beatriz **tiende** la **ropa**.

la lavadora   la secadora

Después la **dobla** cuando está **seca**.

Beatriz **plancha** la ropa.

5-10 Por la mañana. ¿En qué orden hace usted estas actividades por la mañana? Use las siguientes expresiones para indicar el orden: **primero, luego, más tarde, después, finalmente.** Compare sus respuestas con las de su compañero/a.

___ lavar los platos
___ preparar el café
___ salir para la universidad
___ desayunar
___ secar los platos
___ hacer la cama

5-11 Actividades en la casa. Pregúntele a su compañero/a dónde hace estas cosas normalmente cuando está en casa.

MODELO: E1: *¿Dónde ves televisión?*
         E2: *Veo televisión en mi cuarto. ¿Y tú?* O
              No veo televisión. ¿Y tú?

1. dormir la siesta
2. escuchar música
3. planchar
4. lavar la ropa
5. pasar la aspiradora
6. estudiar para un examen
7. tender la ropa
8. hablar por teléfono con amigos/as

Suggestion. Use the drawings to illustrate vocabulary. Personalize questions: *¿Quién limpia su casa? ¿Qué días limpia la casa? ¿Barre usted la terraza? ¿Y pasa la aspiradora también? ¿Quién cocina en su familia? ¿Lava usted los platos? ¿Quién lava la ropa? ¿ ...dobla la ropa? ¿ ...plancha la ropa? ¿ ...saca la basura?*

Point out *colgar/tender la ropa.*

Suggestion for 5-10. Make sure that students use the given expressions to organize their answers and to recycle vocabulary when communicating with each other.

Warm-up for 5-11. Have students name rooms or parts of a house associated with the following activities: *preparar la comida, tener fiestas, pasar tiempo con los amigos, almorzar, cultivar vegetales, conversar, leer el periódico, ver televisión, jugar con el perro.* Expand with other activities: *estacionar el auto (el garaje).*

Follow-up for 5-11. You may introduce some expressions with *tener:* ¿Qué haces cuando tienes sueño?*

Suggestion for 5-12. This activity provides a good opportunity to recycle *ir + a + infinitive*. Students can work together on their lists and then role play their conversation on the distribution of chores in front of the class. As they work on their lists, you may ask questions to elicit some ideas: *¿Quién va a preparar la comida? ¿Quién va a pasar la aspiradora?*, etc.

Audioscript for 5-13.
AGENTE. *Sr. Mena, creo que esta casa es una buena compra. Además, está cerca de su trabajo.*
SRA. MENA: *Sí, pero no me gusta la zona donde está. Nosotros preferimos comprar algo más pequeño, pero en una buena zona, especialmente por los niños.*
AGENTE: *Es que una casa con tres habitaciones, dos baños, sala, comedor y garaje para dos autos en un barrio bueno cuesta bastante... ¿Y un apartamento? Hay unos apartamentos nuevos, muy buenos, en la calle Sol.*
SR. MENA: *Mire, preferimos una casa. Los niños necesitan estar al aire libre para jugar. Por eso queremos una casa con un jardín pequeño.*
AGENTE: *Pues hay una casa en la Colonia La Mascota que no es muy grande, 200 metros cuadrados, pero que tiene dos habitaciones grandes, una tercera habitación más pequeña y dos baños.*
SR. MENA: *La Mascota es un barrio muy bueno, ¿La casa tiene jardín?*
AGENTE: *Sí, uno pequeño.*
SRA. MENA: *¿Y cuánto piden?*
AGENTE: *Déjeme ver... 1.200.000 colones, un buen precio para esa zona.*
SR. MENA: *Pues, creo que debemos verla.*

5-12 ¡A compartir las tareas! PRIMERA FASE. Ustedes van a compartir una casa el próximo año académico. Preparen una lista de todas las tareas domésticas que van a hacer.

SEGUNDA FASE. Discutan qué tareas va a hacer cada uno/a de ustedes según sus gustos. Finalmente, hagan un calendario de tareas y compártanlo con el resto de la clase.

MODELO: *A mí me gusta planchar la ropa pero a mi compañero/a no le gusta. Por eso, yo voy a planchar la ropa los lunes por la tarde.*

5-13 El agente de bienes raíces. PRIMERA FASE. Mr. and Mrs. Mena and their two children live in San Salvador. They have decided to move to a larger place and they are talking to a real estate agent. Before you listen, write down the kind of dwelling and the characteristics of the neighborhood they may be looking for.

CD 2
Track 30
or CD 3
Track 5

SEGUNDA FASE. Now, as you listen, circle the letter next to the correct information.

1. Los señores Mena quieren comprar...
   a. una casa.
   b. un apartamento.

2. El señor y la señora Mena prefieren vivir...
   a. en una buena zona.
   b. lejos de un parque.

3. El agente de bienes raíces...
   a. no sabe cómo ayudarlos.
   b. tiene una casa buena para ellos.

4. El agente dice que la casa del barrio La Mascota...
   a. cuesta mucho.
   b. tiene un buen precio.

5. El señor Mena dice que...
   a. los niños necesitan estar al aire libre para jugar.
   b. los niños no necesitan jugar al aire libre.

EN ACCIÓN

Resources
- Video
- SAM: 5-11 to 5-13

Diarios de bicicleta: El apartamento

Antes de ver

5-14 PRIMERA FASE. En este segmento, Javier está buscando un lugar para vivir. Escriba cuatro muebles o accesorios que probablemente va a necesitar para su habitación o apartamento. *Answers may vary. Most answers will probably include: una cama, un escritorio, un clóset, una silla, una mesa, una lámpara, una computadora/un ordenador.*

SEGUNDA FASE. ¿Qué características le parecen a usted más importantes cuando busca un apartamento o una habitación? Marque (✓) sus respuestas. *Answers may vary.*

1. ___ Está cerca de la universidad o del trabajo.
2. ___ Es barato/a.
3. ___ Tiene mucha luz natural.
4. ___ Es grande.
5. ___ Está amueblado/a.

Note. When referring to a microwave oven, people usually shorten it to *el microondas*, instead of saying *el horno microondas*.

Mientras ve

5-15 Marque (✓) lo que Javier menciona cuando le describe un apartamento a Daniel.

En la sala:
- ✓ la mesa
- ✓ el sofá
- ✓ la silla
- ✓ el televisor
- ___ la lámpara

En la cocina:
- ___ el microondas
- ✓ la estufa
- ___ el lavaplatos
- ✓ el fregadero
- ✓ el refrigerador

En el baño:
- ✓ el inodoro
- ✓ la ducha
- ___ la bañera
- ___ el lavabo
- ___ el jacuzzi

En el cuarto:
- ✓ el clóset
- ✓ la mesa de noche
- ___ la lámpara
- ✓ la cama
- ___ la alfombra

Suggestion for 5-15. You may wish to use the still photos from the video segment as an additional pre-viewing activity by asking students what they see and what they Javier to find when he sees the apartment that he might rent.

Después de ver

5-16 Al final de este segmento, Javier decide compartir casa con Daniel. Imagine cómo es esta casa y escriba cinco oraciones para describirla. *Answers may vary.*

163

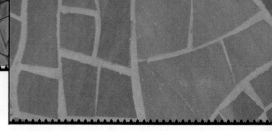

FUNCIONES Y FORMAS

Resources

■ SAM: 5-14 to 5-19
■ Supp. Activ. Book: Present progressive
■ PPTs
■ *Situaciones adicionales*

Suggestions. Use visuals or the board to show the present participle endings. Give additional examples in context referring to your class or to people in illustrations or photos. For example: *Ahora yo estoy hablando y ustedes están escuchando. En esta foto el chico está cocinando y la chica está lavando los platos. Este chico está corriendo y ese chico está bebiendo agua.* Point out that the present participle is invariable, always ending in *-o.* Use the present progressive to ask yes/no and either/or questions based on the visuals.

You may personalize presentation of the present progressive as follows: *Yo estoy hablando español. Y usted, ¿está escuchando o hablando?* (Ask a student to erase the board.) Then say: *Pedro está trabajando en la pizarra. ¿Él está escribiendo o está borrando la pizarra?* (Ask a student to write his/her name on a piece of paper.) Then say: *María está escribiendo en su cuaderno. ¿María está escribiendo la tarea o está escribiendo su nombre?* Then ask: *Yo estoy hablando. Y ustedes, ¿están escuchando? ¿Están contestando preguntas? ¿Están tomando notas?*

1. Expressing ongoing actions: Present progressive

ÓSCAR:	¿Aló?
CATALINA:	Hola, Óscar. Te habla Catalina. ¿Qué **estás haciendo**?
ÓSCAR:	Hola, Catalina. ¡**Estoy trabajando** mucho!
CATALINA:	¿Por qué?
ÓSCAR:	Mis padres **están pasando** sus vacaciones en la playa y vuelven mañana. ¡La casa es un desastre total!
CATALINA:	¿Así que **estás limpiando**?
ÓSCAR:	¡Claro! **Estoy barriendo** el piso, **ordenando** la sala, **recogiendo** la ropa... de mi cuarto. Y tú, ¿qué **estás haciendo**?
CATALINA:	¿Yo?... Nada. **Estoy leyendo** el periódico y **tomando** un café.

Piénselo. Indique las oraciones que son **ciertas** (**C**) o **falsas** (**F**), de acuerdo con la conversación entre Catalina y Óscar.

1. _F_ Catalina y Óscar **están trabajando** juntos.
2. _F_ Óscar **está descansando**.
3. _F_ Óscar **está pasando** sus vacaciones con sus padres en la playa.
4. _C_ Óscar **está limpiando** la casa de sus padres.
5. _C_ Óscar no está contento porque él **está trabajando** mucho en casa.

■ Use the present progressive to emphasize that an action or event is in progress at the moment of speaking, rather than a habitual action.

Óscar **está limpiando** la casa.	*Oscar is cleaning the house.* (at this moment)
Óscar **limpia** la casa.	*Oscar cleans the house.* (habitually)

■ Form the present progressive with the present tense of **estar** + *present participle*. To form the present participle, add **-ando** to the stem of **-ar** verbs and **-iendo** to the stem of **-er** and **-ir** verbs.

ESTAR	PRESENT PARTICIPLE
yo **estoy**	
tú **estás**	hablando
Ud., él, ella **está**	comiendo
nosotros/as **estamos**	escribiendo
vosotros/as **estáis**	
Uds., ellos/as **están**	

■ When the verb stem of an **-er** or an **-ir** verb ends in a vowel, add **-yendo**.

leer → le**yendo**

oír → o**yendo**

■ Stem-changing **-ir** verbs (**o → ue, e → ie, e → i**) change **o → u** and **e → i** in the present participle.

dormir (ue) (**o → u**) d<u>u</u>rm**iendo**

sentir (ie) (**e → i**) s<u>i</u>nt**iendo**

pedir (ie) (**e → i**) p<u>i</u>d**iendo**

■ Spanish does not use the present progressive to express future time, as English does; Spanish uses the present tense instead.

Salgo mañana. *I am leaving tomorrow.*

¿Te levantas temprano mañana? *Are you getting up early tomorrow?*

5-17 Un día ocupado. Hoy es un día muy ocupado para la familia Villa. Asocie las acciones de la columna de la izquierda con las explicaciones de la columna de la derecha para averiguar (*find out*) por qué.

1. <u>d</u> La Sra. Villa está preparando una cena deliciosa y un pastel (*cake*) especial.
2. <u>e</u> Su hijo Marcelo está barriendo la terraza.
3. <u>b</u> Su hija Ana está lavando los platos en el fregadero.
4. <u>c</u> Alicia está decorando la mesa.
5. <u>a</u> Pedro está hablando por teléfono.

a. Está llamando a su mejor amigo para invitarlo a la fiesta.
b. El lavaplatos no está funcionando.
c. Es una ocasión especial.
d. Es el cumpleaños de su esposo.
e. Está muy sucia (*dirty*) y unos amigos vienen a celebrar el cumpleaños.

Note. The infinitive as the subject of a sentence is presented in *Capítulo 14*. Correr es bueno para la salud. *Running is good for one's health.*

Rodrigo   Soledad

5-18 La vida activa. Túrnense para describir lo que está haciendo cada persona en estas escenas. Indiquen en qué lugar de la casa está cada uno de ellos. Luego, imaginen lo que, según ustedes, cada persona va a hacer más tarde.

MODELO: E1: *Rodrigo y Soledad están cantando en una fiesta. Están en la terraza.*
E2: *Después van a bailar y conversar con sus amigos.*

Pepe   Catalina   Arturo   Gonzalo   Carlos

5-19 Lugares y actividades. PRIMERA FASE. Miren las siguientes fotografías de celebraciones y hagan lo siguiente:

SITUACIONES

1. **Role A.** Your best friend calls to invite you to go out. Respond that you and your housemates are busy cleaning the apartment. Explain the chores that each of you is doing.

   Role B. Call your best friend to invite her/him to go out with you. Ask what your friend and her/his roommates are doing. Ask if your friend can go out later (**más tarde**).

2. **Role A.** There is a big family gathering at your aunt's house today, but you are away at school. Call and greet the family member who answers the phone. Explain that you will not be attending, and excuse yourself for not being there. Ask how everyone is and what each family member is doing at the moment.

   Role B. You are at a big family gathering today. A family member calls to say he/she can't attend. Answer the phone. Greet the caller and answer his/her questions. Finally, mention that everyone says hello (**todos te mandan saludos**) and say good-bye.

1.

2.

3.

Asocien las fotos con el país/los países en que probablemente se realiza cada una: Foto **1.** _f_, **2.** _a_, **3.** _c, d_
a. España   c. México   e. Uruguay
b. Estados Unidos d. Ecuador   f. en muchos países

SEGUNDA FASE. Descríbanle a otra pareja dos o tres actividades que las personas están haciendo en la escena de una de las fotos. La otra pareja debe adivinar el nombre del lugar. Luego, entre todos, escriban una descripción completa de una de las fotos. Incluyan el nombre de la fiesta o celebración, su significado cultural y las actividades de las personas en la foto.

2. Describing physical and emotional states: Expressions with *tener*

Resources
■ SAM: 5-20 to 5-24
■ Supp. Activ. Book:
  Expressions with *tener*

Hoy es un día de verano y los Robledo se mudan. **Tienen prisa** porque ya son las tres de la tarde. El señor Robledo y su hija Isabel **tienen calor** porque hace cuatro horas que trabajan bajo (*under*) el sol. Ella **tiene mucha sed** y está bebiendo agua. El bebé, Nicolás, llora porque **tiene hambre**. La señora Robledo le da de comer mientras la abuelita Rosa duerme la siesta. Después de empacar su ropa y todas sus fotografías, libros y plantas, Rosa **tiene mucho sueño**. ¡Qué día para los Robledo!

Suggestion. Personalize these expressions as follows: *¿Tiene usted calor en este momento? ¿Tiene sed? ¿Qué toma usted cuando tiene sed? ¿A qué hora tiene sueño usted generalmente?* Ask other students about their classmates' answers.

Piénselo. Asocie la descripción del estado físico con la(s) persona(s) del dibujo. Escriba el nombre de la(s) persona(s) al lado de la descripción.

_____Nicolás_____	**1.** Va a comer porque **tiene hambre**.
_____Isabel_____	**2.** Está tomando agua porque **tiene sed**.
_____los Robledo_____	**3.** No **tienen frío** porque es verano y hace calor.
_____Rosa_____	**4.** Está cansada y **tiene sueño**.
El señor Robledo e Isabel	**5.** **Tienen calor** porque están trabajando bajo el sol.
_____los Robledo_____	**6.** **Tienen prisa** porque quieren salir pronto.

■ Spanish uses **tener +** *noun* for many conditions and states where English uses *to be* + *adjective*. You have already seen the expression **tener... años: Eduardo tiene veinte años.** Here are some other useful expressions.

Suggestion. You may wish to explain that *mucha prisa* is the Spanish equivalent of being in a rush/great hurry. Provide an example: *Son las ocho menos cinco y Emilio está corriendo por el pasillo para llegar a su clase de español. Hay un examen a las ocho y él no quiere llegar tarde. Emilio tiene mucha prisa.*

Review *ser* and *estar* with *frío* and *caliente* versus *tener frío/calor*. Visuals can be helpful.

TENER + *NOUN*			
	hambre		*hungry*
	sed		*thirsty*
	sueño		*sleepy*
	miedo		*afraid*
	calor		*hot*
tener	cuidado	to be	*careful*
	frío		*cold*
	suerte		*lucky*
	prisa		*in a hurry/rush*
	razón		*right, correct*

■ With these expressions, use **mucho/a** to indicate *very*.

Tengo **mucho** calor (frío, miedo, sueño, cuidado). — *I am very hot (cold, afraid, sleepy, careful).*

Tienen **mucha** hambre (sed, suerte). — *They are very hungry (thirsty, lucky).*

5-20 Asociaciones. Lea las situaciones en que están usted y algunos miembros de su familia. Luego asocie las situaciones con las expresiones de la derecha.

1. Mi hermano siempre tiene ___f___ y, por eso, está comiendo ahora.
2. Mi hermana duerme a todas horas porque siempre tiene ___d___ .
3. En este momento mis primos están visitando la Antártida; probablemente tienen ___e___ .
4. Mis abuelos están bebiendo agua en la cocina porque tienen ___a___ .
5. Mi mamá tiene ___c___ ; siempre gana (*wins*) cuando juega a la lotería.
6. ¡Uf! Todavía estoy planchando mi blusa y mis amigos van a llegar en cinco minutos. Yo tengo ___b___ .

a. sed
b. prisa
c. suerte
d. sueño
e. mucho frío
f. hambre

Suggestion for 5-21. Encourage students to talk about the various illustrations before using the *tener* expressions. Provide additional vocabulary as needed.

5-21 ¿Qué están haciendo, dónde están y cómo se sienten? PRIMERA FASE. Observen a las personas en los dibujos y hagan lo siguiente.

1. Digan qué está(n) haciendo la(s) persona(s) y dónde está(n).
2. Describan su estado físico.

MODELO: *El padre y su hijo están durmiendo en el sofá. Tienen sueño.*

Answers for 5-21. Answers may very. 1. *La familia está comiendo en un restaurante. Tienen hambre y sed.* 2. *Estos niños están en casa solos por la noche. Escuchan un ruido. Tienen mucho miedo.* 3. *Esta mujer está esperando el autobús. Es invierno. Tiene mucho frío.* 4. *Estos hombres están trabajando en la calle. Tienen calor y probablemente tienen sed.*

1.

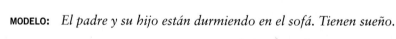

2.

3.

4.

SEGUNDA FASE. Respondan a las siguientes preguntas sobre las escenas de la *Primera fase*. Expliquen. Answers may vary. Have students support their responses.

1. ¿Cuál de los dibujos describe mejor cómo se sienten ustedes en este momento?
2. ¿Qué dibujo refleja (*reflects*) el clima de su región en diciembre?
3. ¿A qué hora se sienten ustedes como las personas del dibujo del modelo?

5-22 ¿Estados de ánimo (*moods*) semejantes o diferentes? PRIMERA

FASE. Primero, termine las siguientes ideas y, luego, compare sus respuestas con las de su compañero/a. Tome apuntes de las respuestas de su compañero/a. Use expresiones con **tener.**

1. En las mañanas de invierno, yo siempre _____ .
2. Cuando mi madre pasa mucho tiempo limpiando nuestra casa, ella

   _____ .
3. Generalmente, cuando mis hermanos y yo hacemos barbacoa, nosotros

   _____ .
4. Cuando yo leo un libro aburrido, siempre _____ .
5. Inmediatamente yo _____ cuando llego a casa y mi esposo está preparando mi plato favorito.

SEGUNDA FASE. Usando sus apuntes de la *Primera fase*, escriba una semejanza y una diferencia entre usted y su compañero/a.

SITUACIONES

1. **Role A.** You share an apartment with a messy friend. Complain to him/her that a) his/her books, backpack, etc., are always all over the living room; b) he/she uses a lot of dishes, but never washes them; c) his/her bottles of soft drinks (**botellas de refrescos**) are always on the table; and d) he/she makes a lot of noise (**ruido**) during the night and you can't sleep.

   Role B. The friend with whom you share an apartment has some complaints about you. Apologize and explain that you a) don't pick up your books or wash the dishes because you are always in a rush to do homework; b) drink a lot of soft drinks because you are always thirsty; and c) go to bed late because you're not sleepy before midnight or later and also because you're scared at night. Say as convincingly as you can that you are going to be more careful in the future.

2. **Role A.** You are a young child. It is a busy Saturday morning at your house, and nobody is paying any attention to you. Go to your parent and say the following: a) You are hungry and want to eat; b) you are thirsty and want some juice; and c) you are bored and want to play outside. What you really want is your parent's attention, so you react negatively to suggestions that you entertain yourself.

   Role B. You are the parent of a young child. You are really busy, and you think your child is old enough to take care himself/herself for awhile. When your child makes demands, say that if he/she a) is hungry, there is fruit in the kitchen; b) is thirsty, there is orange juice in the refrigerator; c) is bored, he/she has a lot of toys (**juguetes**) in his/her room. Explain that you are in a hurry and cannot play outside. Suggest things your child can do while you are busy with your household tasks.

Resources

■ SAM: 5-25 to 5-31
■ Supp. Activ. Book: Direct object nouns and pronouns

Suggestion. Have students identify the direct object nouns in the photos by asking questions using *¿Qué?*, e.g., *Juan lava el auto. ¿Qué lava Juan? (Lava) el auto. Alicia saca la basura. ¿Qué saca Alicia? (Saca) la basura. ¿A quién ayuda la niña? (Ayuda) a su padre.* Ask questions using *¿Quién?* and *¿A quién?* with the photo of the grandmother and child, e.g., *La abuela cuida al niño. ¿Quién cuida al niño? ¿A quién cuida la abuela? (Cuida) al niño.* For additional practice with *¿A quién?*, have one student look at another and ask questions, e.g., *Juan, mire a María. ¿A quién mira Juan? (Mira) a María.*

3. Avoiding repetition in speaking and writing: Direct object nouns and pronouns

A.

¿Qué hacen estas personas?

B.

C.

La abuela cuida (*takes care of*) a la niña. **La** cuida todos los días.

El padre lava los platos y los niños **los** secan.

Las señoras preparan la comida en la cocina del restaurante y después **la** sirven.

Piénselo. Ponga la letra de la foto correcta al lado de la descripción.

1. _A_ La niña está contenta porque su abuela **la** cuida.
2. _B_ El padre trabaja y los niños **lo** ayudan.
3. _C_ Las señoras tienen una parrilla (*grill*) enorme. Ellas **la** usan todos los días.
4. _C_ Las cocineras (*cooks*) están preparando mucha carne en la parrilla. Después, los clientes van a comer**la**.
5. _A_ La abuela está cuidando a la niña. La abuela **la** quiere mucho.
6. _B_ El padre está en la cocina con sus hijos. Él **los** mira con cariño y habla con ellos mientras trabajan.

■ Direct objects answer the question *what?* or *whom?* in relation to the verb.

¿Qué dobla Pedro?	*What does Pedro fold?*
(Pedro dobla) **las toallas.**	*(Pedro folds) the towels.*

■ Direct objects may be nouns or pronouns. When direct object nouns refer to a specific person, a group of persons, or a pet, the word **a** precedes the direct object. This **a** is called the *personal a* and has no equivalent in English. The personal **a** followed by **el** contracts to **al**.

Amanda seca **los platos.**	*Amanda dries the dishes.*
Amanda seca **al perro.**	*Amanda dries off the dog.*
¿Ves la piscina?	*Do you see the swimming pool?*
¿Ves **al** niño en la piscina?	*Do you see the child in the swimming pool?*

■ With the verb *tener* the personal **a** is not needed.

María tiene un hijo.   *María has a child.*

■ Direct object pronouns replace direct object nouns and are used to avoid repeating the noun while speaking or writing. These pronouns may refer to people, animals, or things already mentioned.

DIRECT OBJECT PRONOUNS			
me	*me*	**nos**	*us*
te	*you* (familiar, singular)	**os**	*you* (familiar plural, Spain)
lo	*you* (formal, singular), *him, it* (masculine)	**los**	*you* (formal and familiar, plural), *them* (masculine)
la	*you* (formal, singular), *her, it* (feminine)	**las**	*you* (formal and familiar plural), *them* (feminine)

■ Place the direct object pronoun before the conjugated verb form.

¿Barre **la cocina** Mirta?   *Does Mirta sweep the kitchen?*

No, no **la** barre.   *No, she does not sweep it.*

¿Cuidas **a tu hermanito**?   *Do you take care of your little brother?*

Sí, **lo** cuido.   *Yes, I take care of him.*

■ With compound verb forms (a conjugated verb and an infinitive or present participle), a direct object pronoun may be placed before the conjugated verb, or may be attached to the accompanying infinitive or present participle.

¿Vas a ver **a Rafael**?   *Are you going to see Rafael?*

Sí, **lo** voy a ver mañana.⎫
Sí, voy a ver**lo** mañana.⎭   *Yes, I am going to see him tomorrow.*

¿Están limpiando **la casa**?   *Are they cleaning the house?*

Sí, **la** están limpiando.⎫
Sí, están limpiándo**la**.⎭   *Yes, they are cleaning it.*

■ Since the question word **quién(es)** refers to people, use the *personal* **a** when **quién(es)** is used as a direct object.

¿**A quién** vas a ayudar?   *Whom are you going to help?*

Voy a ayudar **a** Pedro.   *I am going to help Pedro.*

Lengua

You have seen that words that stress the next-to-the-last syllable do not have a written accent if they end in a vowel: **lav<u>a</u>ndo**. If we attach a direct object pronoun, we are adding a syllable, so the stress now falls on the third syllable from the end and a written accent is needed: **lav<u>á</u>ndo<u>lo</u>**.

Suggestion. To practice direct object pronouns, distribute some of your classroom items among the students and then ask questions: *¿Tiene usted mi lápiz? Sí, lo tengo./No, no lo tengo. Y usted, ¿tiene mi libro?* Ask students if they use certain household items, e.g., *¿Usa usted la aspiradora en su casa? Sí, la uso./No, no la uso. ¿Y el horno microondas?* Help them if necessary. You may also ask if they eat certain items, e.g., *¿Come usted cereal en el desayuno... ? Sí, lo como. ¿Y, frutas? Si usted tiene frío, ¿bebe chocolate caliente?* Introduce *me* afterwards by asking *¿Me ve usted? ¿Me escucha?*, and then guide students to ask each other the same questions to practice both *me* and *te*. During the rest of the course be sure to integrate direct object pronouns into regular speech.

5-23 La división del trabajo. Sus compañeros Martín, Pedro y Julio comparten un apartamento y usted le hace las siguientes preguntas a Julio para saber cómo dividen las tareas domésticas entre ellos. Escriba la letra de la respuesta más apropiada de Julio.

1. ¿Quién limpia la nevera?
   a. Yo lo limpio.   **(b.)** Pedro la limpia.   **c.** Nosotros las limpiamos.
2. ¿Quién hace las camas?
   a. Pedro la hace.   **b.** Yo los hago.   **(c.)** Martín las hace.
3. ¿Quién tiende la ropa?
   a. Los tres lo tendemos.   **b.** Pedro los tiende.   **(c.)** Martín la tiende.
4. ¿Quién saca la basura?
   a. Martín lo saca.   **b.** Pedro las saca.   **(c.)** Yo la saco.
5. ¿Quién pasa la aspiradora?
   a. Martín y yo las pasamos.   **(b.)** Pedro la pasa.   **c.** Ellos lo pasan.

5-24 ¿Qué es lógico hacer? PRIMERA FASE. Las afirmaciones de la columna de la izquierda describen la situación doméstica de esta familia. Léalas y, luego, asocie cada afirmación con una acción lógica.

1. _b_ Las camas están sin hacer.
2. _d_ La ropa está seca.
3. _a_ Los dormitorios están desordenados.
4. _f_ El aire acondicionado no funciona.
5. _c_ Las ventanas están sucias.
6. _e_ No pueden poner el auto en el garaje porque hay muchos muebles viejos y cajas con libros.

   a. Los hijos los van a ordenar.
   b. La madre las hace después de leer el periódico.
   c. El padre las va a limpiar.
   d. La hija va a plancharla.
   e. Los hijos lo van a organizar y limpiar.
   f. El hijo mayor lo va a reparar (*fix*).

 SEGUNDA FASE. Dígale a su compañero/a cuál(es) de las afirmaciones de la *Primera fase* describe(n) mejor su apartamento o casa en este momento. Luego, explíquele qué va a hacer usted y cuándo.

5-25 Mis responsabilidades en casa. PRIMERA FASE. Averigüe (*Find out*) si su compañero/a es responsable de las siguientes tareas domésticas en su casa.

MODELO: sacar la basura
E1: ¿*Sacas la basura?*
E2: *Sí, la saco. O No, no la saco. ¿Y tú?*

1. lavar los platos
2. ordenar el garaje
3. tender las cortinas después de lavarlas
4. limpiar la ducha y la bañera
5. lavar las sábanas
6. cortar el césped

SEGUNDA FASE. Ahora, comparen sus respuestas. Después díganle a otra pareja cuáles son las tareas domésticas que ustedes dos hacen y averigüen si ellos las hacen también.

MODELO: E1: *Nosotros no lavamos los platos en casa porque tenemos lavaplatos. ¿Y ustedes los lavan?*
E2: *Sí, nosotros los lavamos y hacemos las camas también.*

5-26 El apartamento de mi compañero/a. Usted va a cuidar el apartamento de su compañero/a por una semana, y quiere saber lo que debe hacer y lo que puede hacer allí.

MODELO: E1: ¿*Debo sacar la basura?*
E2: *Sí, la debes sacar/debes sacarla todos los días.*

¿DEBO O NO DEBO?	SÍ	NO	¿PUEDO O NO PUEDO?	SÍ	NO
regar (*water*) las plantas	____	____	leer los libros	____	____
pasear al perro	____	____	usar los electrodomésticos	____	____
limpiar el apartamento	____	____	invitar a un amigo/una amiga	____	____
poner la alarma	____	____	hacer la tarea en la computadora	____	____
...	____	____	...	____	____

5-27 Los preparativos para la visita. La familia Granados está muy ocupada porque espera la visita de unos parientes. Conteste las preguntas de su compañero/a sobre lo que está haciendo cada miembro de la familia.

MODELO: E1: ¿*Quién está preparando la comida?*
E2: *La abuela la está preparando/está preparándola.*

Suggestion for 5-25. Encourage student 1 to use *también* when answering a question affirmatively if his/her partner has given the same answer previously (e.g., E1: ¿*Sacas la basura?* E2: *Sí, la saco. ¿Y tú?* E1: *Sí, yo la saco también.*). You may wish to preview *tampoco* for negative answers (e.g., E2: *No, no la saco. ¿Y tú?* E1: *No, yo no la saco tampoco.*).

Follow-up for 5-25 Segunda fase. Have students compare their answers and then tell another pair what chores both of them do or do not do in their homes. Also as follow-up, ask students how often they do these tasks—*todos los días, cada tres días*, etc.—and which tasks are their favorites.

Note for 5-26. Many Spanish speakers use *sacar al perro* instead of *pasear al perro*.

Suggestion for 5-26. You may wish to use visuals for this activity, supplementing the actions with additional ones depicted in photos or drawings.

5-28 Una mano amiga. **PRIMERA FASE.** Su compañero/a le va a hacer preguntas sobre sus relaciones con otras personas. Conteste, escogiendo a una de las personas de la lista.

mi madre	mi novio/a	¿...?
mi mejor amigo/a	mi padre	

MODELO: ayudar económicamente
E1: *¿Quién te ayuda económicamente?*
E2: *Mis padres me ayudan económicamente.*

1. querer mucho
2. escuchar en todo momento
3. llamar por teléfono con frecuencia
4. ayudar con los problemas
5. aconsejar (*advise*) cuando estás indeciso/a
6. entender siempre

SEGUNDA FASE. Dígale a su compañero/a lo que usted hace por las siguientes personas. Indique en qué circunstancias lo hace.

MODELO: su esposo/a
E1: *Lo/La ayudo cuando está cansado/a.*
E2: *Y yo lo/la escucho cuando tiene problemas en el trabajo.*

1. su papá
2. su mamá
3. su mejor amigo/a
4. su novio/a
5. sus vecinos (*neighbors*)
6. su compañero/a de cuarto

SITUACIONES

En directo

To assist a customer in a store:

¿Qué desea?
What would you like?
(lit., *What do you desire?*)

¿En qué puedo ayudarlo/a?
How can I help you?

To request a product:

Quisiera...
I would like . . .

¿Podría ver...?
Could I see . . .?

¿Podría mostrarme...?
Could you show me . . .?

1. **Role A.** You are at a furniture store buying a sofa. Tell the salesperson which sofa you want and ask when they can deliver (**entregar**) it. Explain that you are not going to be home at that time, but that you can be home in the afternoon. Agree to the time and thank the salesperson.

   Role B. You are a salesperson at a furniture store. Tell the customer that the sofa he/she wants is a very good one and that you can deliver (**entregar**) it next Monday morning. Mention that you can deliver it between three and five o'clock in the afternoon if the customer prefers.

2. **Role A.** You and your little brother/sister have to do some chores at home. Since you are older, you tell your sibling three or four things that he/she has to do. Be prepared to respond to complaints and questions.

   Role B. You and your older brother/sister have to do some chores at home. Because you are younger, you get some orders from your sibling about what you have to do. You do not feel like working, and you especially do not like being bossed around, so respond to everything you hear with a complaint or a question.

4. Pointing out and identifying people and things: Demonstrative adjectives and pronouns

Resources
■ SAM: 5-32 to 5-35
■ Supp. Activ. Book: Demonstrative adjectives and pronouns

AGENTE: **Esta** casa blanca es muy moderna y el precio es bueno.

CLIENTE: Pero **esa** tiene jardín y **esta** no tiene, ¿verdad?

AGENTE: No, **esta** casa y **aquella** no tienen jardín. Por eso, la casa amarilla es más cara.

Piénselo. En su presentación, el señor Mendoza describe algunos tipos de vivienda para un grupo de salvadoreños que desean comprar una casa. Indique si cada una de las siguientes descripciones se refiere a la vivienda que está cerca (**C**), un poco lejos (**P**) o lejos (**L**) del señor Mendoza.

1. __C__ **Esta** casa de dos pisos está en una ciudad. Tiene muchas ventanas en cada piso, pero no tiene jardín.
2. __L__ **Aquella** casa donde están la madre y su hija es de material sólido y de un color alegre.
3. __P__ **Esa** casa es de construcción sólida y tiene dos pisos y un garaje. Tiene una pequeña área verde enfrente.

Suggestion. To introduce demonstratives, point to objects in class, relating demonstrative adjectives to their location and stressing the demonstrative adjectives as you speak: *Este* libro es mi libro de español. *Ese* cuaderno es su cuaderno de ejercicios, ¿no? *Aquellas* mochilas son de los estudiantes. Walk around the room to show how demonstratives change in relation to the speaker and the person spoken to.

Suggestion. As you walk around the classroom pointing to different objects, you may introduce the words *aquí, acá, allí,* and *allá* along with the corresponding demonstrative adjective.

Note. See Teacher Note on p. 176 regarding the use of accent marks with demonstrative pronouns.

Demonstrative Adjectives

■ Demonstrative adjectives agree in gender and number with the noun they modify. English has two sets of demonstratives (*this, these* and *that, those*), but Spanish has three sets.

this	**este** cuadro **esta** butaca	*these*	**estos** cuadros **estas** butacas
that	**ese** horno **esa** casa	*those*	**esos** hornos **esas** casas
that (over there)	**aquel** camión **aquella** casa	*those (over there)*	**aquellos** camiones **aquellas** casas

■ Use **este, esta, estos,** and **estas** when referring to people or things that are close to you in space or time.

Este escritorio es nuevo.	*This desk is new.*
Traen el sofá **esta** tarde.	*They will bring the sofa this afternoon.*

Lengua

Some Spanish speakers also use the words **este** and **pues** as pause fillers when trying to remember a word while speaking.

Voy a ver la película en el cine... este... Riviera.

What do English speakers do in this situation?

■ Use **ese, esa, esos**, and **esas** when referring to events, people, or things that are not relatively close to you. Sometimes they are close to the person you are addressing.

Esa lámpara es muy bonita.	*That lamp is very pretty.*
Ese amigo de Lola vende su auto, ¿verdad?	*That friend of Lola's is selling his car, isn't he?*

■ Use **aquel, aquella, aquellos**, and **aquellas** when referring to people or things that are more distant, or to events that are distant in time.

Aquel edificio es muy alto.	*That building (over there) is very tall.*
En **aquella** visita los niños jugaron en el parque.	*During that (long ago) visit, the children played in the park.*

Demonstrative pronouns

■ Demonstratives can be used as pronouns to mean *this one/these* or *that one/those*, thus avoiding repetition when speaking or writing.

Compran este espejo y **ese**.	*They are buying this mirror and that one.*
Estas lámparas y **aquellas** son mis favoritas.	*These lamps and those over there are my favorites.*

■ To refer to a general idea or concept, or to ask for the identification of an object, use **esto, eso**, or **aquello**. These forms are invariable.

Trabajan mucho y **eso** es muy bueno.	*They work a lot, and that is very good.*
¿Qué es **esto**?	*What is this?*
Es un espejo.	*It is a mirror.*
Aquello es un edificio de la universidad.	*That (over there) is a university building.*

5-29 Cerca, relativamente cerca o lejos. Decida qué adjetivo demostrativo debe usar de acuerdo con el lugar donde se encuentran los siguientes objetos.

Cerca de usted

1. _a_ mesa es de Honduras.   a. Esta   b. Esa   c. Aquella
2. _a_ cuadros también son de Honduras.   a. Estos b. Esos c. Aquellos

Relativamente cerca de usted

3. _b_ sofá es muy grande.   a. Este   b. Ese   c. Aquel
4. _b_ alfombra tiene unos colores muy alegres.   a. Esta   b. Esa   c. Aquella

Lejos de usted

5. _c_ espejo es nuevo.   a. Este   b. Ese   c. Aquel
6. _c_ lámparas son antiguas.   a. Estas b. Esas c. Aquellas

Note. Since the use of accent marks with demonstrative pronouns is optional (see *Real Academia de la Lengua Española*, 1999), they are not used in *Mosaicos*. You may wish to tell students that they may see demonstrative pronouns with written accent marks in pre-1999 publications.

5-30 ¿Quién es? Coloque (*Place*) sus fotos en la clase de acuerdo con las instrucciones del profesor/de la profesora. Luego pregunte a un compañero/una compañera quién es el sujeto de cada foto.

MODELO: E1: *¿Quién es este/ese/aquel hombre?* (según la distancia de la foto de E1)

E2: *Este/Ese/Aquel hombre es Antonio Banderas.* (según la distancia de la foto de E2)

5-31 En una mueblería en Managua. Usted y su compañero/a van a hacer los papeles de dos amigos/as nicaragüenses que deciden vivir juntos/as. Van a una mueblería para comprar muebles y accesorios. Usen las palabras y frases para hablar sobre lo que ven. Sigan el modelo.

bonito/a   feo/a   (no) me gusta(n)

caro/a   me encanta(n)

MODELO: E1: *¿Te gusta el sofá?*
E2: *¿Cuál? ¿Aquel sofá verde?*
E1: *No, ese sofá azul.*
E2: *Sí, me encanta.* O *No, es muy feo.*

5-32 Descripciones. Cada uno de ustedes va a pensar en tres objetos o muebles y va a decir en qué parte de la casa están. Su compañero/a va a hacerle preguntas para adivinar qué mueble u objeto es.

MODELO: E1: *Este mueble está generalmente en el comedor.*
E2: *¿Es grande?*
E1: *Puede ser grande o pequeño.*
E2: *¿Lo usamos para comer?*
E1: *Sí.*
E2: *Es la mesa.*

SITUACIONES

1. **Role A.** You have a good job and want to move to a nicer apartment. The property manager of several apartment complexes has already shown you pictures of one apartment (**ese apartamento**) and is now showing you pictures of a second one (**este apartamento**). Discuss with the property manager a) the rent (**el alquiler**); b) the number of rooms; and c) the facilities, such as laundry room (**lavandería**), garage, and pool, of both apartments. Say which of the two apartments you want to see and explain why.

   Role B. You are the property manager of several apartment complexes. You have already shown your client pictures of one apartment (**ese apartamento**) and now are showing pictures of a second one (**este apartamento**). Answer his/her questions by saying that a) the rent of the first apartment is $900 dollars per month and the second one is $1,100; b) both apartments have two bedrooms; and c) the first apartment comes with a one-car garage, while this one has a two-car garage. Also tell him/her the advantages of each of the two apartments.

2. **Role A.** You are in a car with a real estate agent, who is showing you some houses for sale in the neighborhood where you hope to live. You are interested in knowing more about one house on the side of the street closer to you (**esta casa**), another house on other side of the street (**esa casa**), and a third house (**aquella casa**) a couple of blocks away.

   Role B. You are a real estate agent driving with a client who is interested in three houses. Answer the client's questions about the three houses.

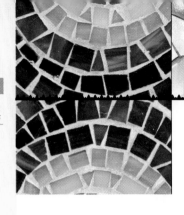

Resources

■ SAM: 5-36 to 5-38
■ Supp. Activ. Book: *Mosaicos*

MOSAICOS

A escuchar

Antes de escuchar

5-33 Preparación. Usted va a escuchar la descripción de una casa. Antes de escuchar, piense en las casas que conoce y haga una lista de cuatro cuartos y de tres objetos (muebles, aparatos eléctricos o accesorios) que usted espera encontrar en cada uno de los cuartos.

Escuchar

5-34 ¿Comprende usted? Now, look at the following drawing, and as you hear the different statements about the location of pieces of furniture and objects, mark (✓) the appropriate column to indicate whether each of the statements is true (**Cierto**) or false (**Falso**).

CD 2 Track 31 or CD 3 Track 6

	CIERTO	FALSO
1.		✓
2.	✓	
3.		✓
4.		✓
5.	✓	
6.	✓	
7.		✓
8.	✓	

ESTRATEGIA

Create mental images
You have already learned that visual cues can increase your listening comprehension. For example, seeing the pictures or objects that a speaker refers to can help you understand what is being said. Even when visuals are not present, you can form images in your mind by using your imagination or by making associations with experiences you have had. As you listen, practice creating mental images to help you develop your listening skills in Spanish.

Audioscript for 5-34. 1. *La casa de los Pérez Esquivel tiene dos dormitorios y un baño.* 2. *En la sala hay un televisor y un sofá grande.* 3. *En el comedor hay una alfombra.* 4. *Un dormitorio tiene una cama grande y dos mesas de noche.* 5. *En los baños de esta casa hay bañadera.* 6. *Hay cuadros en la sala y en el comedor.* 7. *La ventana del comedor no tiene cortinas.* 8. *La cocina está entre un dormitorio y el comedor.*

Después de escuchar

5-35 Ahora usted. Describa su vivienda (número de cuartos, colores, muebles, etc.) a un compañero/una compañera. Él/Ella va a tomar notas para describirle su casa a otra persona de la clase. Verifique si la información es correcta. Luego, intercambien roles.

A conversar

Antes de conversar

5-36 Preparación. Usted necesita alquilar un apartamento. Escriba algunas características esenciales y algunas secundarias del apartamento que usted necesita.

Conversar

5-37 Entre nosotros. Usted y su mejor amigo/a estudian en San Salvador este año y quieren alquilar un apartamento. Van a conversar por teléfono sobre unos apartamentos que se anuncian en el periódico.

PRIMERA FASE. Trabajando individualmente, piense en las características esenciales y secundarias de un buen apartamento. Lea los anuncios y decida qué apartamento prefiere. Organice mentalmente lo que va a decir. Luego, piense en el lenguaje que va a usar para expresarse y para negociar con su amigo/a, por ejemplo, *en mi opinión…*, *entiendo tu punto de vista pero…*, *(no) estoy de acuerdo porque…*

ALQUILERES

1. Se alquila condominio residencial privado, 3er nivel, 2 dormitorios, 1 baño, cuarto y baño, empleada, cocina con despensa, sala y comedor separados, garaje 2 carros, área recreación niños. SVC 4.500 vigilancia incluida. 22 24 46 30.

2. Alquilo apartamento cerca de centro comercial. Transporte público a la puerta. Ideal para profesionales. 1 dormitorio, 1 baño con jacuzzi, con muebles y electrodomésticos, terraza, sistema de seguridad, garaje doble. SVC 7.500. Tfno. 22 65 16 92.

3. Alquilo apartamento, cerca zona universitaria. 3 dormitorios. 1ra planta. Ideal para estudiantes. (SVC 1.800) Contactar al 22 35 37 83.

4. Alquilo preciosa habitación en casa particular. Semi-amueblada. Amplia, enorme clóset, cable gratis. Alimentación opcional. Información al teléfono 22 63 28 07.

SEGUNDA FASE. Hable con su amigo/a por teléfono para llegar a un acuerdo sobre el apartamento que los/las dos quieren alquilar. En su conversación, pueden referirse a algunos de los siguientes temas: el alquiler, la localización, el número de habitaciones y baños, si tiene muebles o no, si tiene aire acondicionado/calefacción.

Después de conversar

5-38 Un poco más. Ya que usted y su compañero/a saben qué apartamento les gusta más, tienen que dar el próximo paso (*next step*). Conversen para decidir lo siguiente:

1. ¿Por qué es este apartamento el favorito de ustedes?
2. ¿Qué preguntas quieren hacerle al dueño del apartamento para obtener más información?

Tomen apuntes, porque van a presentar sus ideas a la clase.

ESTRATEGIA

Plan what you want to say

Speaking consists of more than knowing the words and structures you need. You also have to know what you want to say. Planning what you want to say—both the information you want to ask for or convey and the language you will need to express yourself—before you start to speak will make your speech more accurate and also more coherent.

En directo

To find out who is answering your call:

¿Con quién hablo?
With whom am I speaking?

To request to talk with someone specific:

¿Está… [nombre de la persona], por favor?
Is . . . [person's name] there, please?

Deseo hablar con… [nombre de la persona].
I would like to speak with . . . [person's name].

Resources
■ SAM: 5-39
■ *Entrevistas* video

Suggestion for 5-36. Ask students to review in advance the vocabulary related to the house on p. 187. Encourage them to be as specific as possible as they write their lists. Use visuals to provide an example. Remind them of the word *alquiler* (rent) and introduce *tamaño* (size). Encourage students to speak in full sentences.

As a follow-up, students can compare their lists in pairs. This will help them review vocabulary more thoroughly.

Suggestions for 5-37. Have students read the ads and talk about the apartments with a friend and talk about the apartments with their partner as though they were talking on the phone. You may wish to review the formulaic expressions used in phone conversations.

Review ways to describe different options, for example: *Hay un apartamento que cuesta… Tiene dos habitaciones. También hay otro apartamento que tiene muebles finos.* Point out the meaning of *despensa* (pantry) in the first ad. Direct students to look up the exchange rate between the U.S. dollar and the Salvadoran *colón* (SVC) on the Internet. Students should have two conversations, and each member of the pair must ask and answer questions about two ads. Remind them that the goal is to decide which apartment they want to follow up on.

Suggestion for 5-38. This is a follow-up activity to **5-37** (*Conversar*), so students should work in the same pairs. You may want to have the class vote on the most appealing apartment(s) and give their reasons.

Resources

■ SAM: 5-40 to 5-42

Suggestion for 5-39. To help students learn more about futuristic technologies, you may wish to direct them to the *Mosaicos* web page to read an article in English about digital homes of the future.

Answers for 5-39. Answers may vary. 1. *lámpara, computadora, fotocopiadora, red inalámbrica* 2. *aspiradora, microondas* 3. *ventilador, aire acondicionado central, sensor de temperatura* 4. *teléfono inalámbrico, red inalámbrica, computadora* 5. *televisor, aparato de DVD, computadora, red inalámbrica, música ambiental en todos los cuartos*

Answers for 5-40 Primera mirada. Answers may vary. Students may highlight the following words: *inteligentes, automatizadas, aparatos eléctricos/electrónicos, computadora, avances, dispositivos, sensores, funcionar, electrodomésticos, microondas, ventiladores, aire acondicionado, calefacción, refrigerador, Internet, red, mensajes electrónicos, videoconferencia, video, voz sobre IP, red inalámbrica, banda ancha, satélite, alta definición, contenido digital a petición, servidores.*

Answers for 5-40 Segunda mirada. 1. *Casas con un gran número de aparatos eléctricos y electrónicos, controlados por una computadora, que se comunican entre ellos.* 2. *La casa inteligente incorpora los últimos avances tecnológicos en beneficio de las personas que viven en ella.* 3. *Los sensores abren y cierran cortinas y puertas, hacen funcionar electrodomésticos (cafeteras, microondas, ventiladores, etc.), el aire acondicionado y la calefacción y controlan el movimiento de unos robots.* 4. Answers may vary. 5. Answers may vary. 6. Answers may vary. 7. *Sin embargo, muchos se preguntan si esta abundancia de tecnología va a afectar a nuestra vida positiva o negativamente.*

ESTRATEGIA

Inform yourself about a topic before you start to read

To get acquainted with a topic, you may think about what you already know, read about it (e.g., on the web) in either English or Spanish, or talk with people who are knowledgeable about the topic. Sometimes a combination of approaches will provide the best preparation for reading a new text. The goal is to build your knowledge about a topic before you start to read. Then, when you read the text, try to apply that knowledge to support your comprehension.

A leer

Antes de leer

5-39 Preparación. Muchas casas modernas tienen los aparatos que aparecen en la siguiente lista. Para cada función, escriba el/los aparato(s) correspondiente(s).

aire acondicionado central	red (*network*) inalámbrica
música ambiental en todos los cuartos	reproductor de DVD
computadora	sensor de temperatura
fotocopiadora	teléfono
lámpara	televisor
microondas	ventilador

FUNCIÓN   **APARATOS**

1. para trabajar desde (*from*) casa   _____
2. para hacer trabajos domésticos   _____
3. para controlar la temperatura de la casa _____
4. para comunicarse con otras personas   _____
5. para entretenerse (*have fun*) en casa   _____

Leer

5-40 Primera mirada. El siguiente artículo describe la casa del futuro. Léalo y pase un marcador (*highlighter*) por las palabras en cada párrafo que se asocian con tecnología.

Segunda mirada. Lea el artículo otra vez y haga lo siguiente.

1. En el primer párrafo, el autor del artículo da una definición de una casa inteligente. Escriba la definición.
2. El segundo párrafo contrasta la casa inteligente con la casa tradicional. ¿Cuál es la diferencia? Escríbala.
3. El segundo párrafo también indica algunas formas en que la casa inteligente ayuda a las personas que viven en ella. Indique una función útil para una persona de su familia. ¿Por qué es útil?
4. En el tercer párrafo, se mencionan algunas de las funciones múltiples de los aparatos eléctricos y electrónicos. ¿Cuál de estas funciones múltiples es más beneficiosa para un/a estudiante? ¿Por qué?
5. En el cuarto párrafo se explica cómo la tecnología ayuda a los miembros de la familia a mantenerse en contacto (*to stay in touch*). ¿A su familia le gustaría (*would like*) usar esta tecnología?
6. En el quinto párrafo se mencionan algunos beneficios de la tecnología para divertirse en casa. ¿Cuál de las opciones le gusta más?
7. En el último párrafo, el autor introduce una duda sobre los beneficios de la casa del futuro. Subraye la frase donde se introduce la duda.

La casa inteligente del futuro

Las casas inteligentes o automatizadas ya existen en el presente. Tienen un gran número de aparatos eléctricos y electrónicos, controlados por una computadora, que se comunican entre ellos. Pero, ¿cuáles son las diferencias entre una casa tradicional y una inteligente?

Básicamente, la casa inteligente incorpora los últimos avances tecnológicos en beneficio de las personas que viven en ella. A través de complejos dispositivos[1] y sensores, estas casas facilitan el trabajo doméstico de sus dueños: abren y cierran cortinas y puertas, hacen funcionar electrodomésticos (microondas, ventiladores, etc.), el aire acondicionado y la calefacción central, por ejemplo. Los sensores también controlan el movimiento de unos robots móviles que limpian las alfombras y los pisos y, en el patio, limpian la piscina y cortan el césped.

Además, la casa inteligente ofrece un uso más eficiente y múltiple de los aparatos eléctricos y electrónicos en su interior. Un microondas se puede usar para calentar comida y también para ver televisión. De la misma manera, un refrigerador puede conectarse a Internet y permitir a una persona navegar por la red o enviar mensajes electrónicos.

La casa inteligente del futuro facilita también las relaciones entre los miembros de la familia. Por ejemplo, cuando los miembros de la familia no están juntos, pueden reunirse para cenar o para pasar tiempo juntos, gracias a las tecnologías de videoconferencia en Internet. Con el video y la voz sobre IP, los miembros de la familia en todo el mundo pueden conversar, interactuar y cenar juntos de forma virtual.

La sala en la casa inteligente es el centro de entretenimiento, donde todos los dispositivos están conectados a la red inalámbrica central. Los juegos bajo demanda están disponibles[2] a través de la televisión de banda ancha[3] y satélite. Las películas de alta definición, la televisión sin anuncios y el contenido digital a petición[4] son normales. También es normal distribuir música y películas a cada habitación de la casa desde el servidor central.

En resumen, la casa del futuro es una versión técnicamente más sofisticada de la casa del presente. Es difícil predecir con exactitud cómo vamos a vivir dentro de 50 años. Sin embargo, muchos se preguntan si esta abundancia de tecnología va a afectar nuestra vida positiva o negativamente.

---

[1]*devices* [2]*available* [3]*broadband* [4]*on demand*

Después de leer

5-41 Ampliación. PRIMERA FASE. Lea la siguiente nota que el arquitecto de una casa inteligente le escribe a uno de sus colegas. Complete los espacios en blanco con la palabra adecuada.

funcionar	juegos bajo demanda	tecnológicos
funciones	películas de alta definición	urgentemente
inteligente	sensores	ventanas

Manolo,

¡Te tengo una gran sorpresa! El diseñador (*designer*) Óscar de la Renta necesita (1) ____urgentemente____ construir una casa (2) ____inteligente____ en Managua. Como sabes, de la Renta es muy rico y quiere los últimos avances (3) ____tecnológicos____ en ella. Desea una casa con dispositivos para abrir y cerrar puertas y (4) ____ventanas____ . También quiere incorporar electrodomésticos con (5) ____funciones____ múltiples. Quiere calefacción controlada por (6) ____sensores____ . Desde luego (*Of course*) quiere un centro de entretenimiento que le permita mirar (7) _películas de alta definición_ y recibir programación digital y (8) ___juegos bajo demanda___ . Tú sabes mucho de sistemas automatizados y yo de construcción, y pienso que eres la persona ideal para ayudarme en este proyecto. Vamos a darle una casa espectacular. Todo va a (9) ____funcionar____ perfectamente.

Debemos responder pronto. Llámame.

Ricardo

 SEGUNDA FASE. Ahora comparen sus propias viviendas con la casa inteligente de la lectura. Hablen de la tecnología, los electrodomésticos y los aparatos electrónicos.

A escribir

Antes de escribir

5-42 Preparación. PRIMERA FASE. El periódico *La Prensa* de Tegucigalpa, Honduras, invita al público a participar en el concurso (*contest*) *La casa automatizada del futuro*. Uno de los requisitos del concurso es escribir un panfleto, según se explica en el anuncio del periódico.

El diario *La Prensa* invita al público a participar en el concurso *La casa automatizada del futuro*.

Bases del concurso:

Los participantes deben enviar la siguiente información por correo electrónico al Comité de Selección de *La casa automatizada del futuro*:

1. información personal: nombre completo, dirección, teléfono y dirección de correo electrónico
2. un panfleto descriptivo de la casa automatizada con la siguiente información:
   a. tamaño de la casa en pies (*feet*) o metros cuadrados (*square meters*)
   b. número y nombre de las habitaciones
   c. aparatos eléctricos y electrónicos de la casa y sus funciones
   d. dispositivos y sensores y su(s) función(es)
3. si es posible, un dibujo o foto digital de la casa automatizada

Fecha límite: el 30 de marzo
Premio: Una computadora portátil de último modelo y alta resolución, con programas de alta capacidad y funcionalidad.

SEGUNDA FASE. Usted decide participar en el concurso con un proyecto excepcional. Para preparar su proyecto para el comité que selecciona a los ganadores (*winners*), tenga en cuenta las bases del concurso y tome notas de los puntos 1, 2 y 3 que aparecen en el anuncio.

Escribir

5-43 Manos a la obra. Ahora prepare su panfleto. Para hacer la descripción de *La casa automatizada del futuro*, use sus ideas de la *Segunda fase* de la actividad **5-42**. Recuerde incluir toda la información que pide el concurso. Considere la cantidad de información necesaria y el tono apropiado para sus lectores, los miembros del Comité de Selección. ¡Buena suerte!

Después de escribir

5-44 Revisión. Antes de presentar su panfleto, revise:

1. primero, la claridad de sus ideas
2. la cantidad y la sofisticación de la información dada
3. lo apropiado del tono (impersonal, serio) para un comité de periodistas
4. la precisión gramatical (el vocabulario común y corriente y el vocabulario más técnico, las estructuras que utiliza para describir, la concordancia, etc.)
5. finalmente, la ortografía y la acentuación

ESTRATEGIA

Select the appropriate content and tone for a formal description

To write a description using a formal tone, you will need to do the following:

■ Anticipate what your audience may know about the topic, including relevant details.

■ Adapt the language of your text to the level of your readership. For example, if you are writing about technology for computer experts, you do not have to explain basic terms like *servidor* or *voz sobre IP*. Focus on the amount and kind of information your readers will need.

■ Use an impersonal and formal tone. If you wish to address your reader(s) directly, use **usted/ustedes**.

Resources
■ SAM: 5-43 to 5-45

Suggestion for 5-42 Remind students that they are writing this pamphlet for a jury of experts. Depending on your students' skill, you may wish to have them do this writing task in pairs. If possible, students with artistic skills should be paired with those who may not be so artistic. As indicated in item 3 in the announcement, a drawing or digital picture of the house is optional. If some of your students are skilled in computer design, invite them to share their *Casa automatizada* with the class.

Suggestion for 5-44. If activity **5-42** has been done in pairs, you may ask that students exchange the first draft of the description with another pair. If the activity has been done individually, then have each student submit his/her project to a peer editor.

ENFOQUE CULTURAL

La geografía espectacular de Nicaragua, El Salvador y Honduras

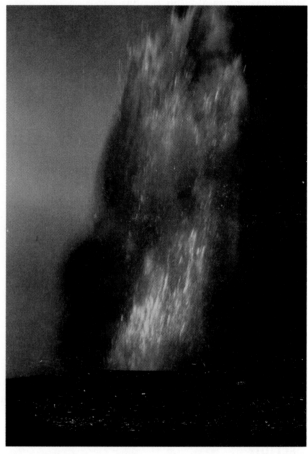

El volcán Cerro Negro de Nicaragua durante una explosión en 1995

Una característica de la geografía de Nicaragua, El Salvador y Honduras es la gran cantidad de volcanes que hay en estos países. En realidad, toda la región centroamericana del Pacífico es rica en volcanes. Algunos son grandes montañas de una belleza impresionante; algunos están activos y producen explosiones de lava o ceniza; otros, en cambio, no tienen actividad volcánica notable. Algunos son muy viejos, otros, en cambio, como el Volcán de Cerro Negro, que nació en 1850, son relativamente jóvenes.

Muchos volcanes tienen una actividad constante que consiste en pequeñas explosiones internas, expulsión de gases y temblores de tierra que los humanos no perciben, pero que se pueden medir usando instrumentos científicos. Algunas veces, esa actividad normal aumenta sin presentar un peligro inmediato. Sin embargo, los científicos y el gobierno se preocupan cuando esto ocurre. El volcán de San Cristóbal, por ejemplo, tuvo un aumento importante (pero no peligroso) de su actividad normal en mayo de 2006.

Otra característica importante de toda la región centroamericana es la propensión a producir terremotos. Managua, la capital de Nicaragua, constantemente se ve afectada por grandes terremotos. En 1931, por ejemplo, un terremoto destruyó muchos edificios y causó la muerte de más de mil personas. También en 1972, un terremoto destruyó una gran parte del centro de esta ciudad, como muestra la foto. El 13 de enero de 2001, un violento terremoto mató a más de 700 personas y dejó a más de medio millón de personas sin casa en El Salvador. Y el 13 de febrero de 2001, un terremoto de 6, 6 de intensidad destruyó en El Salvador más de 30,000 casas y dejó más de 300 muertos.

184

El terremoto de 1972 destruyó muchas casas del centro de Managua.

Finalmente, esta región también se caracteriza por ser muy montañosa y por tener selvas y playas espectaculares. El Salvador, por ejemplo, aunque es el país más densamente poblado de las Américas, tiene montañas, selvas y playas naturales de gran belleza. Las playas salvadoreñas del Pacífico son bellísimas y son un paraíso para los aficionados al surfing. Más del 80% del terreno de Honduras consiste de montañas, pero tiene también selvas. Honduras es uno de los países con mayor biodiversidad, porque tiene muchas especies diferentes de plantas y animales.

Gustavo Estrasser en una competencia en La Libertad, El Salvador

En otras palabras

Expresiones nicaragüenses

Él es **ñeque**.
He is strong/vigorous.

Ella **está jalando** con Luis.
She is Luis's girlfriend.

Ese **chavalo** es terrible.
That kid is terrible.

En otras palabras

Expresiones salvadoreñas

María **chinea** a su hijo.
María holds her child in her arms continuously.

Sólo es un **cipote**.
He is only a child.

—¿Vas a la playa mañana?
—Are you going to the beach tomorrow?

—**Primero** Dios.
—God willing.

En otras palabras

Expresiones hondureñas

Parece que José **me agarró de ojo de gallo**.
It looks like José has ill will towards me.

¿Qué está haciendo ese **güirro**?
What is that child doing?

5-45 Comprensión. PRIMERA FASE. **Reconocimiento de palabras clave.** Encuentre en el texto la palabra o expresión que mejor expresa el significado de las siguientes ideas.

1. ash — ceniza
2. increases — aumenta
3. danger — peligro
4. earthquakes — temblores de tierra/terremotos
5. mountainous — montañosa
6. jungles — selvas
7. paradise — paraíso

SEGUNDA FASE. **Oraciones importantes.** Subraye las afirmaciones que contienen ideas que se encuentran en el texto. Luego indique en qué parte del texto están.

1. Many volcanoes in this region are located near the Pacific Ocean.
2. Some volcanoes are amazingly beautiful.
3. One can find some young volcanoes in this region.
4. Volcanoes are dangerous, and people are afraid of them.
5. Most volcanoes are always active, although people may not be able to feel it.
6. Although small increments in volcano activity are not dangerous, scientists usually worry about them.
7. Central America is prone to earthquakes.
8. Earthquakes and volcanoes have destroyed the biodiversity of the surrounding area.

TERCERA FASE. **Ideas principales.** Escriba un párrafo breve en inglés resumiendo las ideas principales expresadas en el texto.

 5-46 Use la información. Usted tiene $300.000 dólares y quiere comprar una casa en Nicaragua, Honduras o El Salvador. Siguiendo los enlaces, busque la mejor casa, apartamento o propiedad rural que puede comprar con ese dinero. Prepare un afiche (*poster*) para mostrar en la clase. Debe incluir: localización, tipo de propiedad, características más importantes de la propiedad y su precio. Incluya también información adicional de interés para usted. Para preparar esta actividad, visite la página web de *Mosaicos* y siga los enlaces útiles.

VOCABULARIO

La arquitectura	Architecture
el alquiler	rent
el apartamento	apartment
el edificio	building
el estilo	style
las ruinas	ruins
la vivienda	housing

En una casa	In a home
el aire acondicionado	air conditioning
el armario	closet, armoire
el baño	bathroom
la basura	garbage, trash
la calefacción	heating
la chimenea	fireplace
la cocina	kitchen
el comedor	dining room
el cuarto	room; bedroom
la escalera	stairs
el garaje	garage
la habitación	bedroom
la lavandería	laundry room
el pasillo	corridor, hall
la piscina	swimming pool
el piso	floor; apartment
la planta baja	first floor, ground floor
la sala	living room
la terraza	terrace

Los muebles y accesorios	Furniture and accessories
la alfombra	carpet, rug
la butaca	armchair
la cama	bed
la cómoda	dresser
la cortina	curtain
el cuadro	picture, painting
el espejo	mirror
la lámpara	lamp
el sofá	sofa

Los electrodomésticos	Appliances
la aspiradora	vacuum cleaner
la lavadora	washer
el lavaplatos	dishwasher
el (horno) microondas	microwave (oven)
el/la radio	radio
el refrigerador	refrigerator
la secadora	dryer
el ventilador	fan

Para la cama	For the bed
la almohada	pillow
la manta	blanket
la sábana	sheet

En el baño	In the bathroom
la bañera	bathtub
la ducha	shower
el inodoro	toilet
el jabón	soap

el lavabo	bathroom sink
la toalla	towel

En la cocina	In the kitchen
la estufa	stove
el fregadero	kitchen sink
el plato	dish, plate

En el jardín	In the garden
la barbacoa	barbecue pit; barbecue (event)
el césped	lawn
la hoja	leaf

Los lugares	Places
las afueras	outskirts
el barrio	neighborhood
la calle	street
el centro	downtown, center
cerca (de)	near, close (to)
lejos (de)	far (from)
el pueblo	village
la zona	area

Las descripciones	Descriptions
limpio/a	clean
ordenado/a	tidy
seco/a	dry
sucio/a	dirty

Verbos	Verbs
ayudar	to help
barrer	to sweep
cocinar	to cook
cortar	to cut; to mow (lawn)
creer	to believe
doblar	to fold
limpiar	to clean
ordenar	to tidy up
pasar la aspiradora	to vacuum
planchar	to iron
preparar	to prepare
recoger (j)	to pick up
regar (ie)	to water
sacar	to take out
tender (ie)	to hang (clothes)

Palabras útiles	Useful words
la desventaja	disadvantage
el trabajo	work
la ventaja	advantage
la vista	view

See page 157 for ordinal numbers.
See *Lengua* box on page 160 for more electronic items.
See page 167 for expressions with **tener**.
See page 171 for direct object pronouns.
See pages 175–176 for demonstrative adjectives and pronouns.

187

Resources

■ IRM: Syllabi & Lesson Plans

Suggestion. This painting of Simón Bolívar by an unknown artist shows the Venezuelan hero in military uniform. Explain that Bolívar was the principal architect of South American independence movements. Born to a wealthy and aristocratic Venezuelan family, he received a first-rate education. He became the president of several South American countries while fighting against Spanish dominance on the continent.

Ask students to describe the subject of the painting by asking questions. Recycle vocabulary for colors and physical features: *¿Cómo es? ¿De qué color son sus ojos?* Introduce *llevar: Bolívar lleva un uniforme porque es militar. ¿De qué color es su uniforme?* Point out Bolívar's medal: *La medalla es de oro.* Model *llevar* and some of the vocabulary from *A primera vista* by pointing out students who are wearing jewelry: *Isabel lleva unos pendientes de oro. Elena lleva una pulsera de plata*, etc.

De compras

Simón Bolívar (1783-1830), nacido en Caracas, Venezuela, es un héroe de la independencia latinoamericana.

In this chapter you will learn how to:

- talk about clothing, prices, and shopping
- talk about past events
- express likes and dislikes

Cultural focus: Venezuela

Mar Caribe

La industria del petróleo

Islas
Los Roques

OCÉANO
ATLÁNTICO

Isla
Margarita

Maracaibo
Barquisimeto
Valencia
Caracas

Barcelona
Maturín

Lago
Maracaibo

Mérida

CORDILLERA DE MÉRIDA

Río Orinoco

Ciudad
Guayana

Ciudad
Bolívar

La moderna ciudad de Caracas

VENEZUELA

Salto Ángel

GUYANA

Las hayacas,
un plato típico venezolano

Puerto
Ayachucho

COLOMBIA

El pájaro turpial,
símbolo de Venezuela

Salto Ángel

BRASIL

A vista de pájaro. Piense en lo que sabe de Venezuela e indique si la afirmación es cierta (**C**) o falsa (**F**).

1. _C_ Venezuela es una república independiente.
2. _C_ La fauna de Venezuela es muy variada.
3. _F_ El río Amazonas pasa por Venezuela.
4. _C_ El petróleo es la industria más importante de Venezuela.
5. _F_ Caracas está cerca del océano Pacífico.
6. _F_ Panamá está al sur de Venezuela.

Suggestion. Mention the geographic diversity of Venezuela: tropical islands (*Isla Margarita* and *Los Roques*); mountains that are part of the Andes range (*Cordillera de Mérida*); one of the longest rivers in South America (*el Orinoco*); the biodiversity of the *sabana* area south of the Orinoco, where *Salto Ángel* is located. Talk about the photos. Explain that *hayacas* (also known as *hallacas*) are similar to Mexican *tamales* but are wrapped in banana leaves instead of corn husks: *Se hacen de carne, vegetales y masa de maíz. Generalmente se preparan para la Navidad.*

Standard 2.2. Students demonstrate an understanding of the relationship between the products and perspectives of the culture studied. Venezuela's status as an oil-rich nation has changed its political position in the western hemisphere in recent years. You may wish to have students look up such facts as which countries import oil from Venezuela, changes in the gross national product of Venezuela, and the retail price of gasoline in Venezuela as indicators of the impact of a product (oil) on a country and its culture.

Warm-up. Ask what students know about Venezuela. Ask about its geographic characteristics according to the map: *¿Qué países limitan con Venezuela? (Colombia, Brasil, Guyana) ¿Cuál es el río más grande de Venezuela? (el Orinoco) ¿Qué mar hay al norte de Venezuela? (el mar Caribe)* Recycle expressions of weather: *¿Cómo es el clima, frío o tropical? ¿Qué tiempo hace en el Caribe?* Personalize: *¿Conocen a alguna persona famosa de Venezuela? ¿Tienen algún amigo venezolano?*

Resources

- SAM: 6-1 to 6-10
- Supp. Activ. Book: *A primera vista*

A PRIMERA VISTA

Las compras

CD 3
Track 19

En este **centro comercial venden** de todo. Hay tiendas de **ropa** y de **zapatos**. También hay **tiendas** de muebles y accesorios para la casa, hay librerías, tiendas de **juguetes** para los niños e incluso hay un **supermercado**.

Suggestion. Provide comprehensible input to introduce new vocabulary: *Esta foto es de un centro comercial. En todas las capitales del mundo hispano hay grandes almacenes, como, por ejemplo, Macro en Venezuela y El Corte Inglés en España. Ir a estos almacenes es como ir a un centro comercial.*

Muchas personas **van de compras** a los **mercados** al aire libre. Este es un mercado de la calle en Sabana Grande, Venezuela. En los mercados tradicionales venden **telas**, objetos de **artesanía**, **joyas**, **bolsos**, etc., pero a veces también hay discos, aparatos electrónicos y otras **cosas** para la casa.

En los mercados tradicionales los turistas a veces compran **regalos** para su familia y sus amigos. A esta señora le gustan las joyas artesanales. Ella compra un **collar** de **plata** para su mejor amiga, una **pulsera** para su hermana, unos **aretes** para su hija y un **anillo** de **oro** para sí misma (*herself*).

De compras

CD 3
Track 20

José Manuel va a un **almacén** a comprar un regalo para su novia. Él necesita la ayuda de la dependienta.

DEPENDIENTA: **¿En qué puedo servirle?**

JOSÉ MANUEL: **Quisiera** comprar un regalo para mi novia. Un bolso o una **billetera**, por ejemplo.

DEPENDIENTA: Hay unos bolsos de **cuero** preciosos y no son muy **caros**. **Enseguida** le **muestro** los que tenemos.

[La dependienta trae unos bolsos.]

JOSÉ MANUEL: No sé. **Me gustaría** comprar este bolso, pero no puedo **gastar** mucho. ¿Cuánto cuesta?

DEPENDIENTA: Sólo **vale** 80 bolívares. Es bastante **barato**.

JOSÉ MANUEL: Sí, no es mucho **dinero**. Es un buen **precio**.

DEPENDIENTA: Y **están** muy **de moda**. Las chicas jóvenes los **llevan** mucho.

JOSÉ MANUEL: Bueno, lo voy a comprar.

DEPENDIENTA: Muy bien, señor. ¿Va a **pagar** con **tarjeta de crédito** o **en efectivo**?

JOSÉ MANUEL: En efectivo.

6-1 ¿Adónde van? Las siguientes personas necesitan comprar algunas cosas. Indique a qué tienda deben ir.

1. _f_ María necesita unos libros para su clase de literatura.
2. _d_ Juan quisiera cocinar comida venezolana para sus amigos.
3. _b_ Rosa piensa comprar unos regalos para sus sobrinos.
4. _a_ Felipe necesita una cómoda para su cuarto.
5. _c_ Olga necesita unos zapatos nuevos para una entrevista de trabajo.
6. _e_ Catalina va a comprar un collar elegante para ir a una fiesta.

a. mueblería
b. juguetería
c. zapatería
d. supermercado
e. joyería
f. librería

6-2 ¿Qué tienen que hacer? Ustedes tienen que hacer muchas cosas esta semana. Hablen de lo que necesitan comprar y decidan a qué tiendas van a ir.

MODELO: planear nuestro viaje a Venezuela
Necesitamos comprar un billete de avión para Caracas. Vamos a ir a una agencia de viajes.

1. preparar un postre para la fiesta de Jaime
2. hacer un regalo para mi novio/a por su cumpleaños
3. entretener a mi sobrino de cinco años
4. comprar zapatos para mi viaje
5. amueblar el comedor de mi apartamento
6. leer una novela divertida

Lengua

To soften requests, Spanish uses the forms **me gustaría** (instead of **me gusta**) and **quisiera** (instead of **quiero**). English does this with the phrase *would like*.

Me gustaría/Quisiera ir a ese almacén.
I would like to go to that department store.

Suggestion. Introduce and compare *quisiera* and *me gustaría*. Use this dialogue as a model and have students create their own interactions by looking for a different item, substituting *me gustaría* for *quisiera*, and paying with a credit card instead of cash. You may also want to do this comprehension check: *Subraye en la conversación una expresión que indica una manera de ofrecer ayuda.* (*¿En qué puedo servirle?*); *una expresión que usa el cliente para indicar que necesita algo (Quisiera..., Me gustaría...); dos formas de pagar que tiene el cliente (en efectivo o tarjeta de crédito).*

Suggestion. Explain that the *bolívar venezolano* is the official currency of Venezuela. Call students' attention to the name. Since January 2008 the *bolívar fuerte BsF* is used. The equivalent is aproximately $1.00 = BsF 2.15, but the rate varies widely. You may wish to ask students to find the current equivalent to BsF 80 in dollars.

Suggestion for 6-1. Students should have no problem guessing the meaning of *juguetería, joyería,* and *zapatería*. Call their attention to the ending. Ask what would be sold in *una carnicería, una pescadería, una papelería,* etc.

Suggestion for 6-2. Students have seen the expression *Necesito comprar* in *Capítulo 1*. You may re-enter here *tener que + infinitive* to express obligation, which they have seen in *Capítulo 4*. This is also an opportunity to recycle *ir + a + infinitive/pensar + infinitive* that appeared in *Capítulos 3* and *4*.

Note for 6-3. Argentina, Paraguay, and Uruguay are known for their leather goods. In Bolivia, Peru, Ecuador, and Guatemala, one can find beautiful Indian weavings. Chile and Argentina produce excellent wines. Some countries are famous for the high quality of their gems and silver work: Colombia (emeralds) and Peru and Mexico (silver). Isla Margarita in Venezuela is known for its miniature handicrafts.

Suggestion for 6-3. Discuss shopping at markets. Introduce the word *regatear* (haggling) or have students read the *Cultura* box and give examples. Model haggling with a student by pretending you want to buy something and bargaining for a lower price. Ask if students find haggling acceptable and in what situations in the U.S. it is most likely to occur (buying a house or car). Ask if they think it is becoming more common here, as when people try to negotiate hotel room prices to match prices online. To avoid spending too much time on this activity, you may time it and indicate when students should change roles.

Cultura

People in many cultures engage in some form of haggling (**regatear**), a business-like transaction between a customer and a salesperson/vendor that has (usually unspoken) rules as to when, where, and how it is done. In Spanish-speaking countries, haggling is not expected or acceptable in a pharmacy, supermarket, restaurant, or governmental office, for example. However, people sometimes haggle at outdoor markets.

En directo

To express discontent about a high price:

¡Qué caro/a!

To show surprise at a bargain:

¡Qué barato/a!
¡Qué ganga!
What a bargain!

6-3 En el mercado tradicional. PRIMERA FASE. Túrnense para comprar unos recuerdos (*souvenirs*) en un mercado tradicional en Caracas. Pregunten el precio de los siguientes productos. Regateen (*haggle*) para obtener un precio más barato.

cuadros de Venezuela
bolsas de cuero
platos de artesanía
aretes
collares
anillos
casas en miniatura
joyas
pulseras

MODELO: E1: *Quisiera comprar este cuadro ¿Cuánto cuesta?*
E2: *Cuesta 50 bolívares.*
E1: *¡Uy, es muy caro! Lo compro por 38.*
E2: *Pero, es muy bonito. Tiene colores muy alegres.*
E1: *Sí, es muy bonito, pero no tengo suficiente dinero.*
E2: *Bueno, está bien. Lo vendo por 40.*

SEGUNDA FASE. Ahora está con su mejor amigo/a (otro compañero/otra compañera). Muéstrele sus compras y explique:

1. qué es
2. para quién lo compra
3. cuánto cuesta

MODELO: *Esto es un collar de plata para mi prima Isabel. Cuesta 35 bolívares.*

La ropa

CD 3
Track 21

La ropa formal

el traje de chaqueta
la camisa
la corbata
el saco
el pañuelo
el cinturón
los pantalones
el impermeable
los zapatos

Roberto

la sudadera
la blusa

Marisa
el paraguas
los zapatos de tacón
la falda

La ropa informal

la camiseta

Miguel
las zapatillas
de deporte

los vaqueros/los jeans
las sandalias

Sonia

La ropa interior y de estar en casa

la bata
las pantimedias
el camisón
el/la piyama
el sostén
los calzoncillos
las medias/los calcetines
las zapatillas

6-4 ¿Cuándo se usa? Indique qué prenda(s) (*article[s]*) de vestir se usa(n) en cada situación. Answers may vary.

1. Para ir a correr o al gimnasio nos ponemos (*put on*) _____.
2. Para ir a dormir llevamos (*wear*) _____.
3. Para ir a una fiesta nos ponemos _____.
4. Después de bañarnos y antes de vestirnos nos ponemos _____.

Telas y diseño

CD 3
Track 22

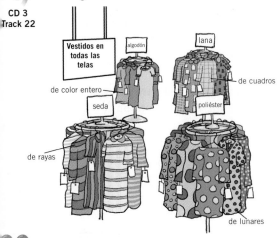

Vestidos en
todas las
telas

algodón
lana
de cuadros
de color entero
seda
poliéster
de rayas
de lunares

6-5 ¿Qué ropa llevan? PRIMERA FASE. Túrnense para describir la ropa que llevan algunas personas de la clase y adivinen (*guess*) quiénes son.

SEGUNDA FASE. Cuenten (*Count*) cuántas personas de la clase llevan los siguientes accesorios y prendas de vestir. Después comparen sus números.

1. aretes en las orejas _____
2. anillos en las manos _____
3. zapatillas de deporte _____
4. camisas de cuadros _____
5. camisas de color entero _____
6. vestidos o faldas _____

))) Las rebajas

CD 3
Track 23

Le queda **estrecha**. Le queda **ancha**.

La chaqueta y la falda están **rebajadas**.

MARTA: Las **rebajas** son **magníficas**. Mira esa falda de rayas. Está **rebajada** de 60 bolívares a 50. ¿Por qué no vemos si tienen tu **talla**?

ANA: Sí, y **me pruebo** la falda para ver si **me queda** bien. Uso la talla 38 y a veces es difícil **encontrarla**. Esta falda es de algodón y es **preciosa**.

MARTA: O te pruebas la falda en casa y si te queda mal, la **cambias**.

[**Entran en** la tienda.]

ANA: Buenos días, señorita, **quisiera** probarme la falda que está en **el escaparate** en la talla 38.

DEPENDIENTA: Lo siento, pero las únicas tallas que **nos quedan** son más grandes, la 42 y la 44.

ANA: ¡Qué lástima! Gracias.

Lengua

The word **talla** is normally used when talking about clothing size; **número** refers to shoe size. **Tamaño** means size in all other contexts: **¿Cuál es su número de zapatos?**

The word **calzado** is used to express footwear in general. The verb **calzar** is also used to ask about someone's shoe size; **¿Qué número calzas? ¿Cuánto calzas?**

6-6 La falda de rayas. Describa la experiencia de Ana, buscando la afirmación de la derecha que lógicamente se asocia con la afirmación de la izquierda.

1. _c_ Ana necesita una falda en la talla 38.
2. _e_ La falda no es de color entero.
3. _f_ Ana prefiere las telas naturales.
4. _a_ Ana entra en la tienda, pero no se prueba la falda.
5. _b_ La falda no es muy cara.
6. _d_ Marta dice que Ana debe cambiar la falda.

a. La dependienta dice que no tienen su talla.
b. Está rebajada.
c. Sabe que la talla 42 le va a quedar ancha.
d. Como no la va a comprar, no la va a cambiar.
e. Es de rayas.
f. Le gusta la falda porque es de algodón.

6-7 El cumpleaños de Nuria. Ustedes van a una tienda para comprarle un regalo a una buena amiga, pero cada artículo que ven presenta un problema. Piensen en la solución.

ARTÍCULO	PROBLEMA	SOLUCIÓN
collar	Es muy caro.	*Debemos buscar uno más barato.*
impermeable	Le queda ancho.	
vaqueros	Son de poliéster.	
sudadera	Es pequeña.	
blusa	Las rayas son muy anchas.	
bolso	No es de cuero.	

ꇗ) ¿Qué debo llevar?

CD 3
Track 24 En el **invierno** hace frío. ¿Qué ropa llevamos?

el suéter　　los guantes　la chaqueta

las botas　el abrigo
la bufanda

Cuando hace calor en el **verano,** ¿qué nos ponemos para ir a la playa?

las gafas de sol　　　la gorra
　　　　　　　　　　　　el sombrero

los pantalones cortos　las sandalias

el traje de baño

la camisa de
manga corta　　　el vestido de
　　　　　　　　verano

Y cuando llueve en la **primavera** y en el **otoño,** usamos impermeable y paraguas.

6-8 ¿Frío o calor? Indique cuándo se usa la siguiente ropa, asociando las palabras de la izquierda con la oración más lógica de la derecha.

1. _b_ los guantes
2. _d_ el traje de baño
3. _f_ las botas
4. _e_ el suéter
5. _c_ los pantalones cortos
6. _a_ el sombrero

a. Sirve para protegernos del sol.
b. Los llevamos en las manos cuando hace f...
c. Son más cómodos cuando hace buen...
d. Nos lo ponemos para ir a la pl...
e. Es de lana, para llevar cua... e frío.
f. Las llevamos en los pie... erno.

6-9 Vacaciones en Venezuela. PRIMERA FASE. U... ...u amigo/a van a pasar sus vacaciones en Venezuela. Primero escoj... ...an que más les interesa de las siguientes opciones.

1. Quince días en Isla Margarit... ...día: ir a la playa; por la noche: ir a las discotecas.
2. Tomar un curso d... ...n la Universidad Central de Venezuela en Caracas. Por l... ...a: clases de español; por las tardes: lugares de interés turístico...
3. Ex... ...auna y flora de la región de Canaima. Por el día: caminar ..., por las noches: estar en un campamento.

Note. More weather-related terms are introduced in *Capítulo 7.*

Suggestion. Use visuals to illustrate weather expressions and clothes. Tell students what you wear in winter: *En el invierno, yo llevo un suéter y pantalones largos. Cuando hace mucho frío, me pongo un abrigo y unos guantes. A veces llevo una bufanda.* Ask yes/no and either/or questions to check understanding. Personalize by asking what students wear and do in winter and in summer.

Suggestion for 6-8. Recycle vocabulary of body parts that was presented before. You may ask: *¿Dónde se pone el sombrero?* Or *Llevamos un sombrero en… ¿Qué llevamos en los pies, las botas o los guantes? En los pies nos ponemos…*

Suggestions for 6-9. Point out *Isla Margarita* on a map and explain that it is an island in the Caribbean, north of Venezuela, and that Canaima is in western Venezuela. You may also mention that the highest waterfall in the world, *Salto Ángel,* is there.

Students can expand their lists by describing the items. Have students plan a trip in another season, focusing on the different clothing they will need. Point out that there are only two seasons in Venezuela, dry (December to April) and wet (May to November).

SEGUNDA FASE. Ahora, preparen una lista de la ropa y accesorios que van a necesitar para su plan de vacaciones.

PLAN #____	YO	MI COMPAÑERO/A
por la mañana		
por la tarde		
por la noche		

TERCERA FASE. Informen a la clase sobre sus planes y la ropa y accesorios que van a necesitar.

MODELO: *Vamos a ir a la ciudad venezolana de Mérida. Yo necesito unos zapatos de tenis para caminar por la ciudad. Mi compañero/a necesita unos pantalones cortos. También necesitamos suéteres porque Mérida está en las montañas.*

6-10 Comprando ropa para todos. Cada uno/a de ustedes debe comprar ropa para hacer unos regalos a tres personas diferentes de la lista. Expliquen para quiénes son los regalos. Su compañero/a le va a dar algunas ideas de qué comprar y el lugar donde puede comprar, según la información de los anuncios.

1. su sobrinita de 6 años
2. su mamá para el Día de la Madre
3. un amigo/una amiga que necesita ropa informal
4. un hermano que va a pasar unos días en el Caribe
5. su padre para su cumpleaños
6. su novio/a para el Día de los Enamorados

6-11 Ropa para cada ocasión. You will listen to a brief conversation regarding the clothes people will wear for an event. Before you listen, list what you would wear on the following occasions.

CD 3 Track 25

fiesta elegante _____

fiesta informal _____

Now as you listen, indicate [✓] the clothes and event mentioned.

ROPA

✓ ropa elegante
___ falda y chaqueta
___ traje pantalón y blusa
___ pantalones cortos y camiseta

EVENTO

___ entrevista de trabajo
___ reunión de jóvenes
___ excursión de fin de semana
✓ fiesta formal

EN ACCIÓN

Resources
- Video
- SAM: 6-11 to 6-13

Diarios de bicicleta: Una camisa de moda

Antes de ver

6-12 En este segmento, Luciana y Gabi están preparándose para su musical. Marque (✓) los accesorios o ropa que probablemente van a llevar.

Accesorios:

- ✓ un anillo
- ✓ aretes
- ___ una bufanda
- ✓ un collar
- ___ gafas de sol
- ___ una gorra

Ropa:

- ✓ una falda y una blusa
- ___ pantalones cortos
- ___ una bata
- ✓ un vestido
- ✓ zapatos de tacón
- ___ una sudadera

Mientras ve

6-13 Indique si las siguientes afirmaciones son ciertas (**C**) o falsas (**F**) según este segmento. Si son falsas (**F**), corrija la información.

1. _F_ Luciana y Gabi se están probando ropa para ir a una fiesta de graduación. Luciana y Gabi van a ir a una presentación musical.
2. _C_ Javier va a tener una cita (*date*) con Carmen.
3. _C_ Luciana y Gabi creen que Javier debe probarse ropa distinta.
4. _F_ Javier necesita comprar una nueva camisa. Javier va a llevar la camisa azul de Marcos.
5. _F_ Marcos cree que está muy guapo con la camisa que le da Luciana. Probablemente cree que no está muy guapo en esa camisa porque no le gusta.
6. _C_ Gabi dice que es muy torpe (*clumsy*).

Después de ver

6-14 ¿Qué puede recomendar usted para resolver los siguientes problemas? Answers may vary.

1. La falda que le gusta a Gabi es muy formal.
2. La camisa que compró Javier no está de moda.
3. Los pantalones que se prueba Javier le quedan muy anchos.

Suggestion for 6-12. Like many other *Antes de ver* activities, this activity asks students to anticipate the content of the video by thinking about their own experiences. You may wish to return to this activity after students see the video segment to have them see whether their experience matches that of the characters in the video.

Suggestion for 6-13. You may wish to have students do this activity in pairs or small groups, combining what they understood to correct the false statements.

Resources

- SAM: 6-14 to 6-20
- Supp. Activ. Book: Preterit tense of regular verbs
- PPTs
- *Situaciones adicionales*

FUNCIONES Y FORMAS

1. Talking about the past: Preterit tense of regular verbs

Querido diario,

Esta mañana Álvaro y yo **gastamos** mucho dinero en ropa para vernos bien en la fiesta de boda de mi cuñada Gabriela esta tarde. Yo **compré** un hermoso vestido de fiesta y un chal de encaje (*lace shawl*). Álvaro **compró** un traje, una camisa y una corbata.

A las 7:00 de la tarde, **empezó** la ceremonia religiosa. La fiesta con familia y amigos **comenzó** a las 9:00 y **terminó** a las 4:00 de la mañana. Todos **comimos**, **bailamos** y **cantamos** mucho. Vamos a recordar este día especial por mucho tiempo. Gabriela y Gonzalo son una pareja perfecta.

Ahora voy a dormir. Estoy muy cansada.
Camila

Camila   Álvaro

Note. This chapter presents the preterit tense of regular verbs and of *ser* and *ir*. The preterit of irregular and reflexive verbs is in *Capítulo 7*.

Suggestion. Describe what you generally do each morning and mention how today differed from the routine: *Normalmente desayuno en casa, pero hoy desayuné en la cafetería. Generalmente tomo té, pero hoy tomé un café y conversé con unos estudiantes* (write preterit forms on the board or a transparency). *Después caminé a mi oficina y hablé por teléfono.* Ask questions to check understanding and then ask personal questions using the verb forms on the board: *¿Tomó usted café en el desayuno? Y usted, ¿tomó café o té? ¿Desayunó en casa o en un café?* If necessary, write the verb forms on the board. Repeat information provided by students using the *él/ella* verb form: *Pedro tomó té, pero Arturo tomó café.*

Piénselo. ¿Qué pasó el día de la boda? Ordene cronológicamente la siguiente información (1 = primer evento, etc.), según lo que Camila escribe en su diario.

__2__ La fiesta con familia y amigos **comenzó** a las 9:00.

__1__ Camila **compró** un hermoso vestido de fiesta y un chal de encaje.

__4__ La fiesta **terminó** a las 4:00 de la mañana.

__3__ Todos **comieron, bailaron** y **cantaron** mucho.

- Spanish has two simple tenses to express the past: the preterit and the imperfect (**el pretérito** y **el imperfecto**). Use the preterit to talk about past events, actions, and conditions that are viewed as completed or ended.

	HABLAR	COMER	VIVIR
yo	hablé	comí	viví
tú	hablaste	comiste	viviste
Ud., él, ella	habló	comió	vivió
nosotros/as	hablamos	comimos	vivimos
vosotros/as	hablasteis	comisteis	vivisteis
Uds., ellos/as	hablaron	comieron	vivieron

■ Note that the **nosotros/as** forms of the preterit of **-ar** and **-ir** verbs are the same as their present tense forms. Context will help you determine if a **nosotros/as** verb form is present or past.

Llegamos a la tienda a las tres.
$\left\{\begin{array}{l}\text{\textit{We arrive at the store at three.}}\\\text{\textit{We arrived at the store at three.}}\end{array}\right.$

Salí de la universidad a las dos y **llegamos** a casa a las tres.
I left the university at two and we arrived home at three.

■ Stem-changing verbs ending in **-ar** and **-er** do not have a stem change in the preterit.

pensar: pensé, pensaste, pensó, pensamos, pensasteis, pensaron

volver: volví, volviste, volvió, volvimos, volvisteis, volvieron

■ Verbs ending in **-car** and **-gar** have a spelling change in the **yo** form of the preterit that reflects how the word is pronounced. Verbs ending in **-zar** have a spelling change in the **yo** form because Spanish rarely uses a **z** before **e** or **i**.

sacar: sa**qué**, sacaste, sacó...

llegar: lle**gué**, llegaste, llegó...

empezar: empe**cé**, empezaste, empezó...

> ### Lengua
>
> The **yo** and the **usted/él/ella** preterit verb forms are stressed on the last syllable and end in a vowel. Therefore, they carry a written accent: **hablé, comí, viví; habló, comió, vivió.**

Note for _Lengua_. Remind students that they can go to the Appendix in the Student Activities Manual for additional practice with accents.

■ There are some expressions you can use with the preterit to denote past time.

anoche	*last night*	**la semana pasada**	*last week*
anteayer	*day before yesterday*	**una semana atrás**	*a week ago*
ante(a)noche	*night before last*	**hace un día/mes/año (que)**	*it has been a day/month/year since*
ayer	*yesterday*		
el año/mes pasado	*last year/month*		

6-15 Ayer yo... PRIMERA FASE. Marque (✓) sus actividades de ayer y añada una actividad en cada grupo.

POR LA MAÑANA
____ Desayuné.
____ Llegué a tiempo a mis clases.
____ Estudié varias horas.
____ Llamé por teléfono a un amigo/una amiga.

POR LA TARDE
____ Almorcé en la cafetería.
____ Saqué libros de la biblioteca.
____ Lavé la ropa.
____ Compré comida para toda la semana.

POR LA NOCHE
____ Preparé la cena.
____ Miré televisión.
____ Planché mi ropa.
____ Salí con mis amigos.

SEGUNDA FASE. Comparen sus respuestas. ¿Tienen actividades semejantes o diferentes? Expliquen.

Follow-up for 6-15 Segunda fase. After students compare their answers in pairs, they can exchange information with another pair about what they did yesterday.

Follow-up for 6-16. Assign students in pairs or small groups to write as many sentences as they can about the activities of Carmen and Rafael in one subset of the drawings. Encourage them to use as many different verbs in the preterit as possible. Then create a detailed story of the couple's day by combining the work of all. Copies of the story (with verbs removed) can be used as an activity for a future class.

 6-16 El sábado pasado. PRIMERA FASE. Miren las siguientes escenas y expliquen cómo pasaron el sábado Carmen y Rafael.

El sábado por la mañana   El sábado por la tarde

El sábado por la noche

 SEGUNDA FASE. Escriban un párrafo para compartir oralmente con la clase sobre el sábado pasado de Carmen y Rafael.

 6-17 ¿Cómo pasaron el fin de semana? PRIMERA FASE. Conversen sobre el fin de semana de ustedes.

1. ¿Cuáles fueron (*were*) las actividades de cada uno/a de ustedes?
2. ¿Dónde y con quién?
3. ¿A qué hora?
4. ¿Gastó mucho dinero? ¿Cómo lo gastó?

SEGUNDA FASE. Decidan qué persona de su grupo pasó el mejor fin de semana. Describan las actividades de esta persona en una presentación oral a la clase.

SITUACIONES

1. **Role A.** You run into a classmate whose parents visited campus the previous weekend. Ask a) what day and time his/her parents arrived; b) where they ate breakfast and lunch; c) what places on campus they visited; and d) what time his/her parents left. Express your reactions to the information.

   Role B. Your classmate wants to know about your parents' visit to campus last weekend. Answer his/her questions in as much detail as possible. Ask if your classmate's parents are going to visit soon.

2. **Role A.** Your classmate and his/her significant other (**pareja**) went on a shopping spree last weekend. Ask a) what store(s) they shopped in; b) what each of them bought; c) what time they returned home; and d) what his/her plans are for wearing or using the items he/she bought.

   Role B. Answer your classmate's questions about your shopping spree with your significant other (**pareja**) over the weekend. Then find out if your classmate went shopping over the weekend, played a sport, or watched a lot of TV.

2. Talking about the past: Preterit of *ir* and *ser*

Resources
■ SAM: 6-21 to 6-26
■ Supp. Activ. Book: Preterit of *ir* and *ser*

CLIENTA: Compré este vestido aquí el sábado pasado. Pero ahora me queda estrecho.

SUPERVISORA: ¿Quién **fue** el vendedor que le vendió el vestido, señorita?

CLIENTA: No sé su nombre, pero **fue** su compañero, un señor alto y delgado.

SUPERVISORA: ¿Qué pasó? ¿Lavó el vestido en casa?

CLIENTA: Claro que no. Hay que lavar este vestido en seco (*dry clean*). **Fui** a una lavandería (*dry cleaner*).

SUPERVISORA: Los irresponsables **fueron** los empleados de la lavandería. No limpiaron en seco su vestido. Lo lavaron.

Piénselo. Indique si las siguientes afirmaciones son ciertas (**C**) o falsas (**F**), según la conversación entre la clienta y la supervisora.

1. __C__ El vendedor **fue** el compañero de la supervisora.
2. __C__ La clienta **fue** a una tienda especializada para limpiar el vestido.
3. __C__ Lavar el vestido **fue** un error por parte de los empleados de la lavandería.
4. __C__ La supervisora **fue** amable con la clienta porque trató de comprender el problema.
5. __F__ Los vendedores de la tienda de ropa **fueron** las personas responsables del problema con el vestido.

■ The verbs **ir** and **ser** have identical forms in the preterit. They are used often in speaking and writing, and the context will help you to determine the meaning.

IR and SER			
yo	**fui**	nosotros/as	**fuimos**
tú	**fuiste**	vosotros/as	**fuisteis**
Ud., él, ella	**fue**	Uds., ellos/as	**fueron**

■ You will also be able to differentiate between **ir** and **ser** in the preterit because **ir** is often followed by the preposition **a.**

Ernesto **fue** a la tienda. — *Ernesto went to the store.*

Fue vendedor en esa tienda por dos años. — *He was a salesman at that store for two years.*

Additional practice with *ir* and *ser*. Ask: *¿Adónde fueron las siguientes personas?*
1. *Ayer fue el cumpleaños de Javier. Su novia le compró un traje de muy buena calidad. (una boutique)*
2. *Javier invitó a Paula a escoger su anillo de boda. (una joyería)*
3. *Marcela, la hermana de Javier, fue a comprar las últimas (the latest) fragancias de Óscar de la Renta y Paloma Picasso. (una perfumería)*
4. *Paula compró sus zapatos blancos. (una zapatería)*

Suggestion for 6-18. In the class before the one in which you do this activity, you may ask students to research the places mentioned so that they can contribute more in class. You may ask them to find out the following about each place: *¿En qué región de Venezuela está el lugar? ¿Cuándo se fundó el lugar? ¿Qué actividades hacen los turistas que visitan el lugar?*

Note. You may want to mention that *cataratas* (*Cataratas de Niágara*) in question #2 is another word for *salto* (*Salto Ángel*).

Follow-up for 6-18. Ask students to a) explain why they think each person chose that particular place and b) tell about three or four activities that each person probably did there.

Suggestion for 6-19. We suggest you limit the number of students per group to three. Explain in advance the format and guidelines for presenting. You may encourage students to use PowerPoint and visuals.

6-18 ¿Quién fue a este lugar? Las siguientes personas fueron a Venezuela para conocer algunos lugares, según sus intereses personales. Primero, lea cada situación y luego, relacione las fotos con cada una de ellas.

A. Salto Ángel

B. Isla Margarita

C. Maracaibo

D. El puente Angostura sobre el río Orinoco

1. _D_ Andrés visitó un lugar con agua para navegar. Le fascinan los deportes acuáticos, pero no le gusta el mar.
2. _A_ Alguien habló sobre este lugar espectacular y único en el mundo. Dice que es semejante a las cataratas de Niágara. Usted decidió ir para ver el lugar.
3. _B_ Los estudiantes del primer año de español de su universidad fueron de viaje a una playa exótica. Allí conocieron a otros turistas de muchas partes del mundo. Hablaron mucho español y un poco de inglés.
4. _C_ Los ingenieros Roberto y Angélica decidieron ir a un lugar para investigar las últimas tecnologías en el procesamiento del petróleo. Por eso, fueron a este lugar con una población de más de dos millones y medio de personas.

 6-19 ¿Quiénes fueron estas personas? Investiguen la siguiente información sobre uno de estos famosos y hagan una breve presentación en clase.

Alfonso X	Atahualpa	Roberto Clemente	Frida Kahlo
Doroteo Arango Arámbula	Simón Bolívar	Ernesto Guevara	Mario Molina
	Pablo Casals	Nicolás Guillén	Pablo Luis Picasso

1. ¿Quién fue él/ella?
2. ¿Dónde nació, vivió y murió (*died*) esta persona?
3. ¿Por qué fue famoso/a? Indiquen como mínimo dos o tres hechos (*facts*) sobre su vida.

SITUACIONES

1. **Role A.** A classmate tells you that he/she went to a concert last weekend. Ask a) where the concert was; b) what time it started; c) with whom he/she went; d) what time the concert ended; and e) where he/she went afterward. Express your reactions to the information.

   Role B. Your classmate wants to know about the concert you went to last weekend. Answer your classmates questions to find out if he/she went to a party or concert over the weekend, if he/she went out with friends, and so on. Ask for details about where, when, and with whom he/she went.

2. **Role A.** As part of your coursework in Spanish, you have been asked to interview a classmate to find out about the role some people may have had in his/her life. Ask a) who was an important authority figure (*figura de autoridad*) in his/her childhood (**infancia**); b) who was his/her best childhood friend; and c) who was his/her favorite teacher in elementary school (**escuela primera**). Express your reactions and ask additional questions.

   Role B. Your classmate will interview you to find out about some important people in your childhood (**infancia**). Answer the questions in as much detail as possible.

Resources
■ SAM: 6-27 to 6-30
■ Supp. Activ. Book: Indirect object nouns and pronouns

3. Indicating to whom or for whom an action takes place: Indirect object nouns and pronouns

> LUCY: Oye, Panchito, ¿qué **te** compran tus padres para tu cumpleaños, ropa, chocolates o qué?
>
> PANCHITO: No **me** dan ni ropa ni chocolates. Siempre **me** compran libros súper interesantes. Y tus padres, ¿qué **te** compran a ti, Lucy?
>
> LUCY: Mi mamá siempre **nos** compra ropa a mi hermano y a mí. A mí **me** gusta mucho la ropa nueva.
>
> PANCHITO: ¿Y qué **les** das tú a tus padres para su cumpleaños?
>
> LUCY: ¡A mi mamá **le** doy muchos besitos y a mi papá **le** doy muchos problemas porque no hago mi tarea!

Piénselo. Primero, identifique **quién hace** la acción: Lucy, Panchito, Lucy y su hermano, los padres de Panchito, la mamá o el papá de Lucy. Luego, en la línea de la derecha, indique **quién recibe** el beneficio de la acción.

1. <u>Los padres de Panchito</u> **le** compran libros a <u>Panchito</u> .
2. <u>La mamá de Lucy</u> **les** compra ropa a <u>Lucy y a su hermano</u> .
3. <u>Lucy</u> **le** da muchos besos a <u>su mamá</u> .
4. <u>Lucy</u> **le** causa problemas a <u>su papá</u> porque no hace la tarea.

■ Indirect object nouns and pronouns tell *to whom* or *for whom* an action is done, in other words, who is affected by an action.

INDIRECT OBJECT PRONOUNS			
me	*to/for me*	nos	*to/for us*
te	*to/for you* (familiar)	os	*to/for you* (familiar)
le	*to/for you* (formal), *him, her, it*	les	*to/for you* (formal), *them*

■ Indirect object pronouns have the same form as direct object pronouns except in the third person: **le** and **les**.

Mi madre **me** compró ropa la semana pasada.	*My mother bought me clothes last week. [My mother bought clothes for me last week.]*
Yo **te** presto mis zapatos para la fiesta.	*I will lend you my shoes for the party. [I will lend my shoes to you for the party.]*
¿El dependiente? Ella **lo** ve todas las mañanas. (*direct object*)	*The salesperson? She sees him every morning.*
¿El dependiente? Ella **le** da los recibos por la mañana. (*indirect object*)	*She gives him the receipts in the morning.*

Suggestions. Act out this and similar situations in class: *Yo le doy el bolígrafo a Mercedes. Mercedes le da el bolígrafo a Juan. ¿Qué le da Mercedes a Juan? ¿A quién le da el bolígrafo Mercedes?* (Point to Juan.) *Mercedes le da un lápiz a Lisa. ¿Qué le da Mercedes a Lisa? ¿A quién le da un lápiz Mercedes?* Write on the board one or two sentences you have used, or have them on a transparency. Circle *le* and the indirect object noun. Draw an arrow to connect *le* to the indirect object noun.

Start a chain drill by saying: *Le doy mi lápiz a X. X, ¿qué le da usted a Y?* The next student continues the chain: *Yo le doy ___ a Y. Y, ¿qué le das a Z?* etc.

Note. Point out the accent mark over the vowel directly preceding -ndo when an indirect object pronoun is attached. Remind students about the rule of accentuation for *llanas* and *esdrújulas*, which are presented in the Appendix and practiced in the Student Activities Manual.

Suggestion. Mention that the pronoun is used when the indirect object noun is stated, but the reverse is not true: The indirect object pronoun can stand alone.

Note. Double object pronouns are introduced in *Capítulo 9*.

■ Place the indirect object pronoun before a conjugated verb form. It may be attached to a present participle, in which case an accent mark is added, or to an infinitive.

Les voy a vender mi carro.⎤
Voy a vender**les** mi carro. ⎦ *I am going to sell them my car.*

Juan **nos** está preparando la cena.⎤
Juan está preparándo**nos** la cena. ⎦ *Juan is preparing dinner for us.*

■ Use indirect object pronouns even when the indirect object noun is stated explicitly.

Yo **le** presté mi libro a **Victoria.** *I lent my notes to Victoria.*

■ To eliminate ambiguity, **le** and **les** are often used with the preposition **a +** *pronoun.*

Le hablo **a usted.** *I am talking to you.* (not to *him/her*)

Siempre **les** cuento mis secretos **a ellos.** *I always tell my secrets to them.* (not to *you/ustedes*)

■ For emphasis, use **a mí, a ti, a nosotros/as,** and **a vosotros/as** with indirect object pronouns.

Pedro **te** habla a **ti.** *Pedro is talking to you.* (not to someone else)

■ **Dar** is almost always used with indirect object pronouns. Notice the difference in meaning between **dar** (*to give*) and **regalar** (*to give as a gift*). Other verbs of transmission (of things, ideas, words) that are generally used with indirect object pronouns include **decir, describir, escribir, explicar, mostrar, prestar,** and **vender.**

Ella le **da** el cinturón a Pedro. *She gives (hands) Pedro the belt.*

Ella le **regala** el cinturón a Pedro. *She gives Pedro the belt (as a gift).*

Lengua

Dar uses the same endings as **-er** and **-ir** verbs in the preterit:

di, diste, dio, dimos, disteis, dieron

Jorge le **dio** a Elena una copia de sus apuntes. *Jorge gave Elena a copy of his notes.*

Mis padres me **dieron** dinero para la matrícula. *My parents gave me money for tuition.*

6-20 La Academia de la Moda. Ustedes están tomando una clase (Elegancia con Poco Dinero) en La Academia de la Moda. Marquen (✓) las sugerencias que su profesor les da a ustedes. Answers may vary.

1. _____ Nos da nombres de tiendas de ropa buena y barata.
2. _____ A mí me recomienda artículos sobre la moda actual.
3. _____ Nos muestra telas que son elegantes y que no son muy caras.
4. _____ A mí me da ejemplos de cómo combinar ropa y accesorios.

6-21 Para estar a la última moda. Cada uno/a de ustedes desea o necesita lo que se indica en la lista a continuación. Explíquense (*to each other*) la situación. Después pidan y den una recomendación.

MODELO: E1: *Quiero llevar zapatos muy cómodos. ¿Qué me recomiendas?*
E2: *Te recomiendo unas sandalias de la marca Teva.*

1. Quiero llevar pantalones de moda (*in style*).
2. Deseo protegerme del sol.
3. Quiero ropa buena y barata.
4. Quiero verme (*look*) más delgado/a.
5. Me gustaría llevar ropa elegante y fina a la entrevista de trabajo.

Follow-up for 6-21. Have students change partners and share the recommendations they received. You may model the exchange with a student: *Mi compañero/a me recomienda sandalias de Teva porque son muy cómodas. ¿Qué te recomienda tu compañero/a?*

6-22 Afortunados. Ustedes ganaron la lotería ayer y quieren compartir su fortuna con su familia y sus compañeros de clase.

1. Hagan una lista de dos o tres miembros de su familia a quienes desean regalarles algo.
2. Indiquen el regalo que piensan hacerle a cada uno/a.

MODELO: E1: *A nuestros padres les vamos a regalar un crucero por el Caribe.*
　　　　 E2: *A Sara vamos a comprarle una mochila.*

6-23 Entrevista. PRIMERA FASE. Basándose en la siguiente lista, pregúntense sobre sus hábitos de compras y los regalos que ustedes hacen y reciben de otras personas.

1. ir de compras: ¿Qué? ¿Tienda(s) favoritas?
2. comprar regalos caros: ¿A quién(es)? ¿Cuándo?
3. le compran regalos a usted: ¿Quién(es)?

SEGUNDA FASE. Escriba una comparación entre sus hábitos y los de su compañero/a en la *Primera fase*. Use las siguientes preguntas como guía (*as a guide*). Prepárese para compatir su texto con otro compañero/otra compañera.

1. ¿Tienen ustedes hábitos de compras semejantes o diferentes?
2. ¿Compran en las mismas tiendas? ¿Compran regalos semejantes o diferentes?
3. ¿A quién(es) le(s) dan regalos? ¿Quiénes les dan regalos a ustedes? ¿Qué tipos de regalos reciben?

Follow-up for 6-22. As preparation, have students think of gifts for an elderly person, an athlete, a baby, a boyfriend/girlfriend.

Suggestion for 6-22. You may write down some gift ideas and have students decide in groups to whom in the class they will give them as awards and why: 1) *una invitación para un desfile de moda* (fashion show); 2) *una suscripción a una revista*; 3) 200 *bolívares para gastar en el Centro Sambil en Caracas*; 4) *el libro más vendido* (bestseller) *del mes.*

SITUACIONES

1. **Role A.** You are a customer at a department store. Tell the salesperson a) you are looking for a present for a friend (specify male or female); b) you are not sure what you should buy for him/her; and c) the amount that you can spend.

   Role B. You are a salesperson. A customer asks for your advice. Inquire about the friend's age, taste, size, favorite color, and any other pertinent information. Make suggestions and offer information about the quality of the products, prices, sales, and so forth.

2. **Role A.** You are shopping for clothes for your new job. Tell the salesperson that you like a garment (specify) in the window and inquire if they have your size. Answer the salesperson's questions and decide what you want to try on.

   Role B. You are a salesperson. First ask the customer for more details to identify the garment the customer is referring to. Then explain that: a) you have it in brown, blue, gray, and black; b) you also have some new items that you can show him/her (describe the styles); and c) ask if he/she would like to see them.

4. Expressing likes and dislikes: *Gustar* and similar verbs

Suggestions. You may want to recycle food vocabulary to practice with *gustar*. Using visuals, identify a few of your favorite foods. Poll students, eliciting responses as to what they like and dislike (and why).

Point out that the definite article is used with *gustar*, and that the subject usually follows the verb: *Me gustan los colores brillantes. Nos gusta la música.*

To reinforce the *gustar* construction, practice *interesar, encantar, fascinar,* and *parecer,* whose structure is parallel to English: Your story interests me. *Me interesa tu cuento.*

DEPENDIENTE:	¿**Le gustan** estas camisas?
JORGE:	No, no **me gustan,** pero **me gusta** esta chaqueta.
DEPENDIENTE:	Es una buena chaqueta para el otoño. ¿**Le interesan** los deportes, señor?
JORGE:	**Me encanta** practicar deportes, pero no **me gusta** mirar los partidos en televisión. **Me fascinan** el tenis, el béisbol y el fútbol.

Piénselo. Indique si las siguientes afirmaciones son ciertas (**C**) o falsas (**F**), según la información en esta escena. Si no hay información suficiente para contestar, indique que usted no sabe (**NS**).

1. _F_ A Jorge **le gusta** una de las camisas que le muestra el dependiente.
2. _C_ A Jorge **le interesa** comprar una chaqueta.
3. _NS_ A Jorge **le queda** poco dinero, porque la chaqueta es muy cara.
4. _C_ A Jorge **le encantan** varios deportes.
5. _F_ A Jorge **le gusta** mirar los partidos de fútbol en la televisión.
6. _NS_ A los amigos de Jorge **les interesa** jugar al fútbol con él.

■ In previous chapters you have used the verb **gustar** to express likes and dislikes. As you have seen, **gustar** is not used the same way as the English verb *to like*. **Gustar** is similar to the expression *to be pleasing (to someone)*.

Me gusta esta chaqueta. *I like this jacket.*
  (lit. This jacket is pleasing to me.)

■ The subject of **gustar** is the person or thing that is liked. The indirect object pronoun shows to whom the person or thing is pleasing.

me		*I*	
te		*you* (familiar)	
le	gusta el traje.	*you* (formal), *he/she*	*like(s) the suit.*
nos		*we*	
os		*you* (familiar)	
les		*they, you* (formal and familiar)	

■ The most frequently used forms of **gustar** in the present tense are **gusta** and **gustan** and for the preterit **gustó** and **gustaron**. If one thing is liked, use **gusta/gustó**. If two or more things are liked, use **gustan/gustaron**.

Me **gusta** ese **collar**.	*I like that necklace.*
No me **gustaron** los anillos.	*I did not like the rings.*

■ To express what people like or do not like to do, use **gusta** followed by one or more infinitives.

Nos **gusta caminar** por la mañana.	*We like to walk in the morning.*
¿No te **gusta correr** y **nadar**?	*Don't you like to run and swim?*

■ Some other Spanish verbs that follow the pattern of **gustar** are **encantar** and **fascinar** (*to like a lot, to love*), **interesar** (*to interest; to matter*), **parecer** (*to seem*), and **quedar** (*to fit; to have something left*).

No te **interesan** las humanidades.	*You are not interested in the humanities.*
Leí la novela y me **encantó**.	*I read the novel and I loved it.*
El curso me **parece** muy difícil.	*The course seems very difficult to me.*
No me **queda** mucho dinero.	*I don't have much money left.*
No le **quedan** bien los pantalones.	*His/her pants don't fit well.*
Nos **fascina** la moda europea.	*We love European fashion.*

■ To express that you like or dislike a person, use **caer bien** or **caer mal**, which follow the pattern of **gustar**.

Les cae bien Miriam.	*They like Miriam.*
Esa dependienta **me cae mal**.	*I do not like that salesclerk.*

■ To emphasize or clarify to whom something is pleasing, use **a + mí, a + ti, a + él/ella, a + usted**(es), etc. or **a + *noun***.

A mí me gustaron los zapatos, pero **a Pedro** no le gustaron.	*I liked the shoes, but Pedro did not like them.*

6-24 Mis preferencias en la ropa. **PRIMERA FASE.** Indique si le encanta(n), le gusta(n) o no le gusta(n) la ropa que sigue.

la ropa deportiva	los suéteres de lana	los vaqueros
las chaquetas de cuero	las gorras	los pantalones cortos

SEGUNDA FASE. Comparen sus preferencias, y luego, explíquenle al resto de la clase si ustedes coinciden en sus gustos.

MODELO: E1: *A dos de nosotros nos gusta la ropa deportiva.*
E2: *Y a todos nos encantan los vaqueros.*

6-25 ¿Cuánto dinero les queda? Lean estas situaciones y calculen cuánto dinero queda.

MODELO: Pilar tiene 50 bolívares. Paga 25 bolívares por un vestido y 10 por unos aretes. ¿Cuánto dinero le queda?
Le quedan 15 bolívares.

1. Ernesto tiene 75 bolívares. Le da 15 a su hermano. ¿Cuánto dinero le queda? 60 bolívares
2. Érica tiene 25 bolívares. Va al cine y a cenar con una amiga. El cine cuesta 5 y la cena 12. ¿Cuántos bolívares le quedan? 8 bolívares
3. Gilberto tiene 40 bolívares. Compra un suéter por 39. ¿Cuánto dinero le queda? 1 bolívar
4. Mis amigos tienen 30 bolívares. Van a la playa y almuerzan en un restaurante por 25 bolívares. ¿Cuántos les quedan? 5 bolívares

Note. Many Spanish speakers use *caer bien/caer mal* exclusively to talk about liking/disliking people in a general sense, reserving the use of *gustar* for talking about physical attraction.

Follow-up for 6-25. Play a game to see who can follow money transactions and answer quickly. 1. *Usted tiene $26. Compra un video por $21. ¿Cuánto dinero le queda?* 2. *Usted sale de casa con $75. Gasta $10 en el almuerzo, compra un suéter que cuesta $35 y paga $20 por unas gafas de sol. ¿Cuánto dinero le queda?* 3. *Tengo $200 y quiero salir esta noche. Gasto $40 en el restaurante, las entradas al teatro cuestan $60 y le pago $15 al taxista. ¿Cuánto dinero me queda?* 4. *Usted tiene $150 en total, $50 en la cartera y $100 en la chaqueta. Alguien le roba la chaqueta. ¿Cuánto dinero le queda?*

En directo

To state that doing something is appropriate or not:

(No) Es apropiado + *infinitivo...*

Es inapropiado + *infinitivo...*

To explain why some clothes are inappropriate:

... no es apropiado/a porque la ocasión es formal/informal.

En un/a... (*evento***) no es elegante/apropiado llevar...**

(*Ropa***)... no va bien con... (***accesorio***)**

6-26 ¿Qué les parece a ustedes? Los famosos en las siguientes fotos asisten a eventos públicos. Den su opinión sobre su ropa y accesorios.

MODELO: E1: *No me gusta el traje de... No es apropiado llevar un traje blanco en el invierno.*

E2: *Me gusta la combinación de colores del hombre, pero la corbata no va bien con la camisa.*

La jugadora de tenis Serena Williams llega a una recepción formal.

La Reina Isabel II de Inglaterra con Ricky Martin, Paul McCartney y otros cantantes

El Dalai Lama de Tibet y la actriz Penélope Cruz en una exposición de arte en Barcelona

SITUACIONES

1. **Role A.** You are shopping at an outdoor market where haggling is the norm. You select an item that you plan to give as a gift. In your interaction with the vendor a) say how much you like what the vendor is selling; b) ask the price of the item you are interested in; c) react to what you hear and offer a lower price; d) comment on the item, saying whom you plan to give it to; and e) come to an agreement on the price.

   Role B. You are a vendor at an outdoor market. A customer is interested in an item of yours. In your interaction with the customer a) respond to his/her compliments; b) give the price of the item; c) explain why you cannot accept the customer's offer of a lower price; d) respond to his/her comments on the item; and e) come to an agreement on the price.

2. **Role A.** You are at the store where you bought a pair of shorts last week. Tell the clerk that a) you tried them on at home and they didn't fit well; b) you don't like the color; and c) you want to return (**devolver**) them.

   Role B. You are the clerk at a clothing store. A customer wants to return (**devolver**) a pair of shorts. Listen to his/her case, and a) ask why the customer bought them if they didn't fit well and he/she didn't like the color; b) explain that the he/she can exchange the shorts for something else (**otra cosa**), but cannot return them; and c) show the person some other shorts and ask if he/she likes them.

5. Describing people, objects, and events: More about *ser* and *estar*

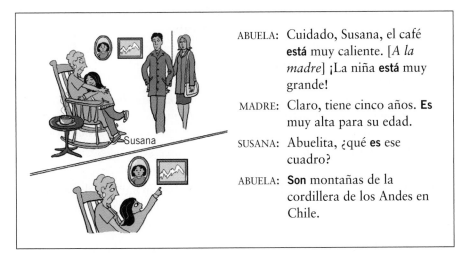

ABUELA: Cuidado, Susana, el café **está** muy caliente. [*A la madre*] ¡La niña **está** muy grande!

MADRE: Claro, tiene cinco años. **Es** muy alta para su edad.

SUSANA: Abuelita, ¿qué **es** ese cuadro?

ABUELA: **Son** montañas de la cordillera de los Andes en Chile.

Piénselo. Clasifique las frases a continuación de acuerdo con la función de **ser** o **estar**.

	CONDICIÓN	CARACTERÍSTICA
1. El café **está** caliente.	✓	——
2. ¡La niña **está** muy grande!	✓	——
3. **Es** muy alta para su edad.	——	✓
4. **Son** montañas de los Andes.	——	✓
5. La nieve (*snow*) en las montañas **es** fría.	——	✓

■ In *Capítulo 2*, you learned to use **ser** to identify, describe, and express nationality, ownership, and origin. You also learned to use **ser** to talk about dates and time and to tell where an event takes place.

Víctor **es** de Venezuela.	*Victor is from Venezuela.* (nationality)
Es un bailarín profesional.	*He is a professional dancer.* (profession)
Es alto y delgado y **es** muy fuerte.	*He is tall and thin, and he is very strong.* (distinguishing characteristics)
Estas figuras pintadas **son** de Víctor, tiene una colección grande.	*These painted figures belong to Victor; he has a big collection.* (possession)
El próximo espectáculo de su compañía de baile **es** mañana a las ocho. **Va a ser** en el Centro de Bellas Artes.	*The next performance of his dance company is tomorrow at eight o'clock. It is going to take place in the Fine Arts Center.* (time/location of event)

■ **Ser** is also used to talk about what something is made of.

El reloj **es** de oro.	*The watch is (made of) gold.*

■ You also learned in *Capítulo 2* that **estar** is used to indicate location, to talk about health and similar conditions, and to describe changes in feelings or perceptions. It is also used to express ongoing actions, presented in *Capítulo 4*.

El Centro de Bellas Artes **está** en el centro.

The Fine Arts Center is downtown. (location)

Víctor **estaba** (*was*) enfermo la semana pasada, pero ahora **está** bien.

Victor was sick last week, but now he is fine. (health)

Víctor **está** nervioso antes del espectáculo, pero siempre **está** contento después.

Victor is nervous before the performance, but he is always happy afterward. (feelings, condition)

Algunos bailarines **están** ensayando ahora.

Some dancers are rehearsing now. (ongoing action)

■ When describing people or objects, use **ser** to convey an intrinsic characteristic. Use **estar** to convey a feeling or perception. The difference in meaning is sometimes so pronounced that the adjectives have different English translations.

ADJECTIVE	WITH SER	WITH ESTAR
aburrido/a	*boring*	*bored*
bueno/a	*good* (character)	*well* (health); *physically attractive*
grave	*serious* (situation)	*seriously ill*
listo/a	*clever*	*ready*
malo/a	*bad* (character)	*ill*
muerto/a	*dead* (atmosphere)	*deceased*
rico/a	*rich, wealthy*	*delicious* (food)
verde	*green*	*unripe*
vivo/a	*lively* (personality)	*alive*

Javier **es** malo, les roba dinero a sus compañeros y dice mentiras.

Javier is bad; he steals money from his classmates and tells lies.

Roberto Tovares **es** rico. Tiene una casa en California, un rancho en México y un apartamento en París.

Roberto Tovares is wealthy. He has a house in California, a ranch in Mexico, and an apartment in Paris.

¡Esta sopa **está** riquísima! ¿Usaste una receta diferente?

This soup is delicious! Did you use a different recipe?

Follow-up for 6-27. Have students work in pairs to compare their answers and figure out the function of each use of *ser* and *estar*.

 6-27 Una familia va de compras. Observen la foto de una familia venezolana que sale de un centro comercial en Caracas. Describan a las personas que ven, e incluyan la información de las preguntas. Si es necesario, usen su imaginación.

1. ¿Quiénes son las personas?
2. ¿Cómo son?
3. ¿Dónde están?
4. ¿Cómo están?
5. ¿Qué están haciendo?

6-28 La mañana horrible de Javier. Lea el cuento sobre la mañana de Javier y complételo con la forma apropiada de **ser** o **estar**.

Javier se despierta temprano. (1) _Son_ las seis de la mañana. La casa (2) _está_ muy fría, y el agua en la ducha (3) _está_ fría también. ¡Javier no (4) _está_ nada contento! Su reunión con la profesora de historia (5) _es_ a las 10:00 y él no (6) _está_ listo. Necesita leer un artículo antes de la reunión, pero no sabe dónde (7) _está_. Tiene hambre, pero no hay pan, los plátanos (8) _están_ verdes y (9) _es_ demasiado tarde para hacer café. La situación (10) _es_ grave, piensa Javier.

Javier entra en la oficina de la profesora Guzmán a las 10:00. Ella (11) _está_ normalmente relajada, pero hoy (12) _está_ tensa. Le dice a Javier que su borrador (*draft*) no (13) _es_ bueno y que tiene que trabajar mucho más. Cuando sale de la reunión, Javier (14) _está_ muy preocupado.

6-29 ¿Quiénes son y cómo están? Mire las siguientes fotos y explique quiénes son estas personas, cómo son y cómo están en estas situaciones.

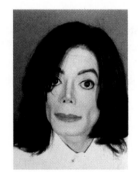

SITUACIONES

1. **Role A.** Your classmate asks about the photo of your family (or friends). Explain a) who the people are; b) where they are; c) what they are like; and d) how they are feeling in the photo.

   Role B. Ask your classmate to see the photo he/she is holding. Ask as many questions as you can about the people in the photo, their activities, and the setting.

2. **Role A.** You have lost your favorite sweater. You think you may have left it in your Spanish class, so you go to the department office, where they have a lost-and-found box (**una caja de objetos perdidos**). Explain to the secretary a) what you lost (**perder**); b) where your Spanish class is held; and c) what your sweater is made of and what it looks like. Answer the secretary's questions.

   Role B. You are the department secretary, and the lost-and-found box (**la caja de objetos perdidos**) is in your office. A student comes to ask about a lost sweater. Ask the student a) to identify himself/herself; b) what the sweater looks like; and c) where and when the student lost (**perder**) it.

Preparation for Situación 1. Have students bring a photo of family or friends to class to use for the first Situación. Have them change partners and act out the situation a second time so that everyone can take both roles.

Resources

- SAM: 6-38 to 6-41
- Supp. Activ. Book: *Mosaicos*

Audioscript for 6-31.

ANDREA: *Mamá, ustedes saben que necesito muchas cosas. Por ejemplo, para ir a mis clases ahora en invierno, necesito unas botas, guantes y una chaqueta. También necesito una bufanda y un abrigo.*

MAMÁ: *Pero, Andrea, si el año pasado te compramos ropa de invierno. Todavía la puedes usar.*

ANDREA: *No, mamá. Quiero estar a la última moda, y mi ropa ya está vieja. Quiero ir a una boutique elegante y comprarme toda mi ropa allí.*

PAPÁ: *Me parece muy bien, Andrea. Puedes comprar todo lo que quieras, pero dime, ¿de dónde vas a sacar dinero para pagar por esa ropa? Tú no trabajas.*

ANDREA: *¡Papá, por favor! Tú me puedes prestar dinero o me puedes dar tu tarjeta de crédito. Además necesito ropa para practicar deportes. Quiero comprar pantalones cortos, camisetas, una sudadera, medias y...*

MAMÁ: *Andrea, ¿estás loca? Nosotros no tenemos tanto dinero. No podemos pagar todo eso ni prestarte dinero ni mucho menos darte la tarjeta de crédito.*

ANDREA: *Mamá, escucha, para salir con mis amigos necesito pantalones vaqueros, blusas, zapatos y muchas cosas más.*

PAPÁ: *Todo me parece muy bien, Andrea. Trabaja, ahorra y gasta tu dinero, pero yo no te voy a dar ni un solo bolívar.*

ANDREA: *Pero, papá, comprende, por favor.*

PAPÁ: *Ni una palabra más.*

MOSAICOS

A escuchar

ESTRATEGIA

Take notes to recall information

When you want to remember something that you are listening to, like an academic lecture, you benefit from taking notes. Taking notes in other situations is helpful also. For example, when you ask for directions, you will remember them better if you take notes.

Antes de escuchar

6-30 Preparación. Usted va a escuchar una conversación entre Andrea, una adolescente, y sus padres. Andrea habla con ellos sobre la ropa que va a necesitar durante el año escolar. Antes de escuchar, prepare una lista de las cosas que usted tuvo que comprar para el invierno antes del comienzo de las clases este año.

accesorios de invierno: _____

ropa de invierno: _____

Escuchar

6-31 ¿Comprende usted? Now listen to the conversation between Andrea and her parents. As you listen, take notes on what she needs. Write at least three items per category that Andrea mentions.

CD 3
Track 26

1. Para ir a clases Andrea necesita... botas, guantes, una chaqueta, una bufanda y un abrigo.
2. Para practicar deportes Andrea tiene que comprar... pantalones cortos, camisetas, una sudadera, medias.
3. Para salir con sus amigos Andrea quiere... pantalones vaqueros, blusas, zapatos y muchas cosas más.

Después de escuchar

6-32 Ahora usted. Responda oralmente a las siguientes preguntas. Su compañero/a debe tomar apuntes. Luego, intercambien papeles. Finalmente, cada uno debe verificar si su compañero/a tiene la información correcta.

1. ¿Qué ropa, muebles para su cuarto y/o aparatos electrónicos compró cada uno/a de ustedes antes de comenzar sus clases en la universidad este semestre?
2. ¿Qué accesorios compró cada uno/a de ustedes? ¿Dónde los compró?
3. ¿Fueron ustedes a las rebajas? ¿Gastó cada uno/a mucho dinero?

Resources
■ SAM: 6-42
■ *Entrevistas* video

A conversar

ESTRATEGIA

Negotiate a price

In Hispanic cultures, negotiating the price of an item in an open-air market or other location in which the price is not fixed is an activity that has both linguistic and cultural rules. You should haggle over a price only if you intend to buy the item. Your initial offer, while lower than the selling price given by the vendor, should be reasonable, because an excessively low price may be insulting. In your negotiation, which may last several turns, you may include a brief comment about the desirability of the item and a reaction to the price suggested by the vendor.

En directo

To haggle:

CLIENTE/A

Me gusta este/a _____, pero no tengo tanto dinero.

Sólo puedo pagar...

¡Es muy caro/a!

¿Qué le parece(n)... bolívares/dólares (etc.)?

Le doy... bolívares/dólares (etc.).

VENDEDOR/A

¡Imposible!

Me cuesta(n) más...

El material es importado/de primera calidad.

Lo siento, pero no puedo darle... por ese precio.

Antes de conversar

6-33 Preparación. Usted quiere comprar unos regalos o algunas cosas para su cuarto/apartamento en un mercado al aire libre. Complete la tabla con la información.

¿QUÉ QUIERE COMPRAR?	¿PARA QUIÉN(ES)?	DESCRIPCIÓN DEL PRODUCTO

Conversar

6-34 Entre nosotros. Usted está en un mercado al aire libre. Pregúntele al vendedor/a la vendedora (su compañero/a) el precio de los productos que usted desea comprar. Regatee (*Haggle*) para obtener el mejor precio posible. Use las expresiones más apropiadas. Luego, cambien de papel.

Después de conversar

6-35 Un poco más. Conversen sobre su experiencia de regateo en el mercado al aire libre de la actividad **6-34**. Cuéntense lo siguiente:

1. qué productos compró y para quién los compró
2. qué precio le dio el vendedor/la vendedora por cada producto
3. cuánto dinero le ofreció usted
4. cuánto pagó finalmente

Suggestion for 6-34. Remind students about where haggling over a price is appropriate (see *Cultura* box on p. 192). Before starting the activity, you may wish to discuss with them what haggling is and review phrases used when negotiating price.

Suggestion for 6-35. Have students change partners so they can hear about each other's experiences.

Resources
■ SAM: 6-43 to 6-45

A leer

Use context to figure out the meaning of unfamiliar words

All readers encounter unknown words and phrases, even in their native language. In our native language we automatically use the surrounding context and our overall comprehension of the text to figure out the meaning of these unknown words and phrases, and we can learn to use the same strategy in the second language. As you read, think about what each sentence or paragraph means. When you come to a word you don't know, reread the last line or two, focusing on the overall meaning. In many cases, this strategy will enable you to understand the unknown word without using a dictionary.

Antes de leer

Suggestion for 6-36. Before the reading, you may wish to explain that in Spanish the doubling of some letters indicates that the letter represents a plural, such as in the double *E* and double *U* in *EE.UU.* (*Estados Unidos*), with or without the periods. You may also mention other common abbreviations, such as *FF.AA.* for *Fuerzas Armadas* (Armed Forces) and *RR.EE.* for *Relaciones Exteriores* (Foreign Affairs).

6-36 Preparación. **PRIMERA FASE.** Mire rápidamente el texto en la actividad **6-37** y use su conocimiento del tema para responder a las preguntas. Hay más de una respuesta correcta.

1. ¿Qué tipo de texto es?
   a. sugerencias para comprar en Internet
   b. publicidad (*advertising*) para una tienda virtual
   c. una lista de tiendas que venden sus productos por Internet
2. ¿Qué información lo/la ayudó a responder a la pregunta 1?
   a. el título
   b. los gráficos
   c. unas palabras clave (*key*) en el texto
3. Según su experiencia, ¿qué información sobre las compras espera encontrar en el texto?
   a. productos que están a la venta (*for sale*) y los precios
   b. formas de pago
   c. precios especiales para algunos productos

 SEGUNDA FASE. Converse con su compañero/a sobre lo siguiente:

1. ¿Les gusta comprar en Internet, o prefieren ir a las tiendas? ¿Por qué?
2. ¿Conocen algunas megatiendas en Internet? ¿Cuál(es)?
3. ¿Qué cosas compran en las megatiendas en Internet?
4. ¿Qué cosas no compran en Internet? ¿Por qué?

Leer

6-37 Primera mirada. Lea la página web de CompreenInternet.net que aparece a continuación.

Bienvenido a CompreenInternet.net

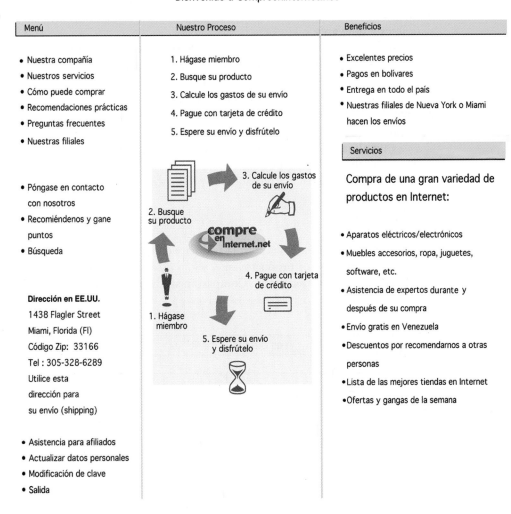

Menú	Nuestro Proceso	Beneficios
• Nuestra compañía	1. Hágase miembro	• Excelentes precios
• Nuestros servicios	2. Busque su producto	• Pagos en bolívares
• Cómo puede comprar	3. Calcule los gastos de su envío	• Entrega en todo el país
• Recomendaciones prácticas	4. Pague con tarjeta de crédito	• Nuestras filiales de Nueva York o Miami hacen los envíos
• Preguntas frecuentes	5. Espere su envío y disfrútelo	
• Nuestras filiales		**Servicios**

Compra de una gran variedad de productos en Internet:

- Aparatos eléctricos/electrónicos
- Muebles accesorios, ropa, juguetes, software, etc.
- Asistencia de expertos durante y después de su compra
- Envío gratis en Venezuela
- Descuentos por recomendarnos a otras personas
- Lista de las mejores tiendas en Internet
- Ofertas y gangas de la semana

Menú (continuación):
- Póngase en contacto con nosotros
- Recomiéndenos y gane puntos
- Búsqueda

Dirección en EE.UU.
1438 Flagler Street
Miami, Florida (Fl)
Código Zip: 33166
Tel : 305-328-6289
Utilice esta dirección para su envío (shipping)

- Asistencia para afiliados
- Actualizar datos personales
- Modificación de clave
- Salida

Ahora, indique si las siguientes afirmaciones son correctas (**C**) o incorrectas (**I**). Si son incorrectas (**I**), corrija la información.

1. __I__ Los productos y servicios que CompreenInternet.com ofrece son principalmente para personas que viven fuera de Venezuela. clientes en Venezuela
2. __C__ La sección **Nuestro proceso** de la página web les indica a los clientes las fases de una compra en Internet.
3. __I__ Las tiendas que promociona (*advertises*) CompreenInternet.com incluyen sólo tiendas que están en Venezuela. están en los EE.UU.
4. __C__ CompreenInternet.com tiene su oficina central en Venezuela.
5. __I__ Los clientes pueden comprar ropa solamente. una variedad de productos y servicios
6. __C__ Los clientes pueden ahorrar (*save*) dinero si compran en Internet.

6-38 Segunda mirada. Lea otra vez la página web de CompreenInternet.net y seleccione la alternativa correcta.

1. En el **Menú** de CompreenInternet.net, la frase **Nuestras filiales** significa...
   a. los clientes de CompreenInternet.net.
   (b.) las tiendas asociadas con CompreenInternet.net.
   c. un producto que vende CompreenInternet.net.
2. Los clientes que compran en CompreenInternet.net pagan en...
   (a.) dólares
   b. bolívares
   c. dólares y bolívares
3. La expresión **Hágase miembro** en la sección **Nuestro proceso** probablemente significa que para comprar, las personas deben...
   (a.) subscribirse a una lista de clientes de la tienda en Internet.
   b. trabajar para la compañía para comprar a precios especiales.
   c. comprar un mínimo al año.
4. La expresión **envío gratis** significa que los clientes...
   a. van a un almacén (*warehouse*) para recoger sus compras.
   (b.) no pagan por recibir los productos en su casa.
   c. pagan un precio reducido por algunos productos.

Después de leer

 6-39 Ampliación. Lean una vez más la página web de CompreenInternet.net y completen la tabla con los productos que, según ustedes, las chicas, los chicos o ambos visitan con más frecuencia. Compartan sus respuestas con las de otra pareja. Answers may vary. Accept any response that is supported.

LAS CHICAS	LOS CHICOS	AMBOS

A escribir

Resources

■ SAM: 6-46 to 6-48

ESTRATEGIA

Sequence events

In our interactions with others, we all talk about or write about experiences and events that occur over time in a sequence. That sequence can serve as the basis of the step-by-step chronological organization of the piece we are writing. Using the correct connectors to indicate the succession of events or transitions will help you make your writing clearer and easier for readers to follow.

Antes de escribir

6-40 Preparación. Usted compró un producto en Internet (ropa, un mueble, un accesorio, etc.), pero el producto resultó ser diferente de sus expectativas. Usted está muy decepcionado/a (*disapppointed*) y decide escribirle una carta a alguien de su familia para contarle su experiencia. Haga lo siguiente:

1. Escriba el nombre de la tienda donde usted compró el producto.
2. Indique qué producto compró en Internet y si compró más de uno.
3. Prepare una lista de nombres y adjetivos para describir lo que usted compró, por ejemplo, un vestido negro largo, una camisa blanca ancha, un plato decorativo de cerámica.
4. Narre lo que ocurrió en orden cronológico. ¿Cuándo hizo (*did you make*) la compra en Internet? ¿Qué ocurrió después de hacer la compra? ¿Qué hizo usted primero, después, más tarde, etc.? ¿Cuánto costó y cómo pagó usted, con una tarjeta de crédito?
5. Escriba la razón de su insatisfacción con el producto.

Escribir

6-41 Manos a la obra. Ahora escríbale la carta a alguien de su familia para contarle qué le ocurrió. Use la información que preparó en la actividad **6-40**. Incluya la fecha, el saludo, el cierre de la carta y la despedida.

Después de escribir

6-42 Revisión. Ahora lea su carta por lo menos dos veces. Piense en la persona que la va a leer. Verifique lo siguiente:

1. ¿Incluyó usted toda la información necesaria?
2. ¿Escribió en su carta la fecha, el saludo, el cierre de la carta y la despedida?
3. ¿Organizó los eventos cronológicamente para contar paso a paso lo que ocurrió? ¿Usó algunas expresiones que indican transición temporal para hacer más comprensible su narración?
4. ¿Revisó la gramática de su texto: el vocabulario correcto, la concordancia (*agreement*), el tiempo (presente, pasado)?
5. ¿Usó la puntuación y ortografía correctas?

En directo

To indicate the succession of events or temporal transitions, you may use the following connectors: **primero, luego, más tarde, antes de eso, después (de eso), finalmente**

Cultura

Although big department stores are increasingly popular in Spanish-speaking countries, people still enjoy shopping at local neighborhood stores. For example, instead of buying bread from a large supermarket, some prefer to go to the neighborhood bakery (**panadería**), where they probably have a long-standing relationship with the bakery owner and employees.

Suggestion for 6-40. We advise that the preparation phase be done either outside of class or in class in a workshop format. For this writing task, you may ask that students prepare to write about an imaginary purchase gone wrong or a real experience they had. In either case, help students with the vocabulary and structures they may need.

Note. You may want to share some background information with the class: Simón Rodríguez is one of the most important intellectuals and educators of 18th century Latin America, although he is most widely known as Bolívar's teacher. His participation in a failed revolt against Spain in 1797 sent him into exile for close to 30 years, during which he traveled to a variety of places, including Jamaica, the United States, France, Italy, Germany, Prussia, Poland, and Russia. He returned to Venezuela in 1823. Shortly thereafter he was sent to Peru and Bolivia to serve in the government of the two new republics.

Andrés Bello had a profound influence on the culture and politics of the independence movement. He was a politician, poet, linguist, philosopher, educator, and statesman. He represented the revolutionary forces to the government and business community of England, and in this capacity he helped secure British support for the rebel forces. Later he moved to Chile, where he became the Rector of the University and drafted the Civil Code of his new country. One of his most important contributions to the study of the Spanish language was his *Gramática de la lengua castellana destinada al uso de los americanos*, a work that is still often quoted by linguists.

ENFOQUE CULTURAL

El mundo fascinante de Simón Bolívar

El nombre completo de Bolívar es Simón José Antonio de la Santísima Trinidad Bolívar y Ponte Palacios y Blanco. Nace en Caracas en 1783 en una familia aristocrática y muy rica. Cuando Bolívar tiene siete años de edad, su padre muere y dos años después también muere su madre. El joven Simón vive entonces con un tío y es educado por dos de los más importantes intelectuales de la época, Simón Rodríguez y Andrés Bello. A los catorce años es un oficial en el ejército español y a los quince, viaja por primera vez a Europa. Allí se casa con una mujer española y regresa a Venezuela. Ocho meses después, su joven esposa muere, posiblemente de una enfermedad tropical, y a los 20 años, Bolívar regresa a Europa, se une a los movimientos revolucionarios de esa época y promete ganar la independencia de los países americanos.

Estatua de Simón Bolívar, el Libertador, en París

Manuela Sáenz

Su vida es muy apasionada y romántica, llena de aventuras, amor y heroísmo. Las guerras de la independencia son muy violentas y demandan mucho esfuerzo e inteligencia política. Bolívar viaja a caballo por Venezuela, Colombia, Ecuador, Perú y Bolivia en condiciones muy difíciles. Varias veces casi lo asesinan sus adversarios y sólo milagrosamente salva su vida. Durante muchos años mantiene una relación amorosa con Manuela Sáenz, una mujer de carácter fuerte y muy valiente, reconocida como una de las primeras feministas de la América hispana.

Durante más de veinte años, hasta su muerte en 1830, Bolívar es el líder político y militar más importante de la América española. Consigue la independencia de Venezuela en 1813; la de Colombia y Panamá en 1820; la de Ecuador en 1823; y la de Perú y Bolivia en 1825. Durante once años, Bolívar unifica estos cinco países, bajo el nombre de la Gran Colombia, pero después de su muerte, la Gran Colombia se divide nuevamente.

Estos países tienen mucho en común. En primer lugar, frecuentemente se llaman *países bolivarianos* porque Bolívar los liberó. Para ellos Bolívar es tan importante como George Washington para los estadounidenses. Muchos latinoamericanos recuerdan el ideal de Bolívar de hacer un país grande y fuerte de las antiguas colonias españolas. Y este ideal está presente en los Juegos Bolivarianos que se celebran cada cuatro años en distintas ciudades de estos países (en Armenia y Pereira, Colombia, en 2005 y en Sucre, Bolivia, en 2009).

Jugadoras de baloncesto en los juegos bolivarianos

Note. Remind students that *Comprensión* can be done in the text or online.

Answers for 6-43 Segunda fase. 2. *Cuando Bolívar tiene siete años de edad, su padre muere y dos años después también muere su madre. El joven Simón vive entonces con un tío.*
4. *Varias veces está cerca de ser asesinado y sólo milagrosamente salva su vida.*
5. *Durante muchos años tiene una relación amorosa con Manuela Sáenz, una mujer de carácter fuerte y muy valiente, reconocida como una de las primeras feministas de la América hispana.*
6. *Muchos latinoamericanos recuerdan el ideal de Bolívar de hacer un país grande y fuerte de las antiguas colonias españolas.*

6-43 Comprensión. PRIMERA FASE. **Reconocimiento de palabras clave.** Encuentre en el texto la palabra o expresión que mejor expresa el significado de las siguientes ideas.

1.	at age fourteen	a los catorce años
2.	officer	oficial
3.	disease	enfermedad
4.	wars	guerras
5.	travels by horse	viaja a caballo
6.	several times	varias veces
7.	feminists	feministas
8.	unifies	unifica

SEGUNDA FASE. **Oraciones importantes.** Subraye las afirmaciones que contienen ideas que se encuentran en el texto. Luego indique en qué parte del texto están.

1. There was a difference of fifteen years in the ages of Bolivar's parents.
2. After both of his parents died, Bolivar lived with an uncle.
3. Bolívar had a long and happy marriage to a Spanish woman.
4. Many times Bolívar came close to being assassinated, but managed to escape with his life.
5. He had a long love affair with a woman known as an early Latin American feminist.
6. Bolivar's ideal was to create one large, strong country out of all of the old Spanish colonies.
7. The games in honor of Bolívar are played regularly in Caracas.
8. Venezuela won the most gold medals in the most recent games.

TERCERA FASE. **Ideas principales.** Escriba un párrafo breve en inglés resumiendo las ideas principales expresadas en el texto.

6-44 Use la información. Prepare una presentación oral sobre algo relacionado con el nombre de Bolívar. Puede ser un país, una región de un país, una ciudad, dinero, una universidad, etc. Explique cuál es el objeto de su presentación, en qué país está y otras características interesantes. Para preparar esta actividad, visite la página web de *Mosaicos* y siga los enlaces útiles.

VOCABULARIO

Los accesorios / **Accessories**

el anillo	*ring*
el arete	*earring*
la billetera	*wallet*
la bolsa/el bolso	*purse*
la bufanda	*scarf*
el cinturón	*belt*
el collar	*necklace*
las gafas de sol	*sunglasses*
la gorra	*cap*
el guante	*glove*
la joya	*piece of jewelry*
el pañuelo	*handkerchief*
el paraguas	*umbrella*
la pulsera	*bracelet*
el sombrero	*hat*

Las compras / **Shopping**

el almacén	*department store; warehouse*
el centro comercial	*shopping center*
el escaparate	*store window*
el mercado	*market*
el precio	*price*
la rebaja	*sale*
el regalo	*present*
el supermercado	*supermarket*
la tarjeta de crédito	*credit card*
la tienda	*store*

La ropa / **Clothes**

el abrigo	*coat*
la bata	*robe*
la blusa	*blouse*
las botas	*boots*
los calcetíns	*socks*
los calzoncillos	*boxer shorts*
la camisa	*shirt*
la camiseta	*T-shirt*
el camisón	*nightgown*
la chaqueta	*jacket*
la corbata	*tie*
la falda	*skirt*
el impermeable	*raincoat*
las medias	*stockings, socks*
los pantalones	*pants*
los pantalones cortos	*shorts*
las pantimedias	*pantyhose*
el/la piyama	*pajamas*
la ropa interior	*underwear*
el saco	*blazer, jacket*
las sandalias	*sandals*
el sostén	*bra*
la sudadera	*sweatshirt; jogging suit*
el suéter	*sweater*
el traje	*suit*
el traje de baño	*bathing suit*
el traje de chaqueta	*suit*
el traje pantalón	*pantsuit*
los vaqueros/los jeans	*jeans*
el vestido	*dress*

las zapatillas	*slippers*
las zapatillas de deporte	*tennis shoes*
los zapatos	*shoes*
los zapatos de tacón	*high-heeled shoes*

Verbos / **Verbs**

cambiar	*to change, to exchange*
dar	*to give, to hand*
encantar	*to delight, to love*
encontrar (ue)	*to find*
entrar (en)	*to go in, to enter*
fascinar	*to fascinate, to be pleasing to*
gastar	*to spend*
gustar	*to be pleasing to, to like*
interesar	*to interest*
llevar	*to wear, to take*
mostrar (ue)	*to show*
pagar	*to pay (for)*
parecer (zc)	*to seem*
ponerse	*to put on*
probarse (ue)	*to try on*
quedar	*to fit; to be left over*
regalar	*to give (a present)*
valer	*to be worth*
vender	*to sell*

Las descripciones / **Descriptions**

ancho/a	*wide*
barato/a	*inexpensive, cheap*
caro/a	*expensive*
estrecho/a	*narrow, tight*
magnífico/a	*great*
precioso/a	*beautiful*
rebajado/a	*marked down*

Palabras y expresiones útiles / **Useful Words and Expressions**

la artesanía	*handicrafts*
la cosa	*thing*
el cuero	*leather*
el dinero	*money*
en efectivo	*in cash*
¿En qué puedo servirle(s)?	*How may I help you?*
enseguida	*immediately*
estar de moda	*to be fashionable*
ir de compras	*to go shopping*
el juguete	*toy*
Me gustaría...	*I would like . . .*
el oro	*gold*
Quisiera...	*I would like . . .*
la plata	*silver*
la talla	*size (clothes)*

See *Lengua* box on p. 193 for body parts.
See p. 193 for a list of **telas** and **diseños**.
See *Lengua* box on page 194 for expressions relating to clothing size and footwear.
See p. 195 for the seasons of the year.
See p. 199 for a list of expressions denoting past time.

221

Resources

■ IRM: Syllabi & Lesson Plans

Note. Xul Solar was born in San Fernando, Buenos Aires. He traveled to Europe in the 1920s, where he was in contact with avant-garde movements, such as cubism and surrealism. He referred to his own style as *criollismo.* A man of broad cultural knowledge, his many interests included legends and astrology.

Suggestions. Ask students to describe the painting. Recycle colors and body parts and expand on that vocabulary. You may present the following expressions: *línea; parece: parece una cara, tiene ojos y labios; esto parece un bigote; esto parece un hombre caminando; lleva un sombrero.* Ask students to guess the meaning of the title and to interpret it: *¿Por qué se llama Jefa?* Ask students: *¿Les gusta el cuadro? ¿No les gusta? ¿Por qué?*

Los deportes

***Jefa* (1923), de Xul Solar, pintor argentino (1887-1963)**
Source: The Museum of Fine Arts, Houston.

In this chapter you will learn how to:

- talk about sports and physical activities
- ask and answer questions about weather
- discuss past events

Cultural focus: **Argentina, Uruguay**

Una parrillada de carne

PARAGUAY

BRASIL

Tucumán

ARGENTINA

Córdoba

Mendoza

Distrito de La Boca

Colonia

Paysandú

URUGUAY

Punta del Este

Buenos Aires

Montevideo

LA PAMPA

Mar del Plata

Bahía Blanca

Bariloche

LA PATAGONIA

Un gaucho dirigiendo el ganado

Las playas
de Punta del Este

OCÉANO
ATLÁNTICO

Río Gallegos

Ushuaia

Glaciar Perito Moreno

OCÉANO PACÍFICO

CHILE

CORDILLERA DE LOS ANDES

Point out the photos on the map and make comments as you ask what students know: *¿Cuál es la capital de Uruguay? ¿Y la de Argentina? ¿Qué países hay al norte de Argentina? ¿Y al oeste?* Write *Cono Sur* on the board and ask what it means. Introduce weather expressions: *Cuando en el hemisferio norte es verano, ¿qué estación tienen en el hemisferio sur? ¿Qué tiempo hace ahora en el Cono Sur probablemente?* Personalize questions: *¿Conocen a alguna persona famosa de estos países? ¿Tienen algún amigo argentino o uruguayo? ¿Saben cuál es la comida típica de Argentina y Uruguay?* Introduce the word *carne* and some other foods (*pimientos, tomates*) and explain what a *parrillada* is. Ask if students like to have *parrilladas* and what they usually grill. Point to the photo of the *gaucho* and introduce *vaca* and *caballo*. Introduce some vocabulary of the chapter while pointing to Bariloche on the map. *¿Qué deportes practican los argentinos? En Argentina hay buenas pistas de esquí. ¿Les gusta esquiar a ustedes? ¿Les gusta el fútbol? ¿Conocen a algún jugador uruguayo o argentino?*

A vista de pájaro. Piense en lo que sabe de estos países y conteste las preguntas.

1. _b_ Argentina está en…   a. Centroamérica.   b. el Cono Sur de América.   c. el Caribe.
2. _a_ La capital de Uruguay es…   a. Montevideo.   b. Buenos Aires.   c. Santiago.
3. _c_ La parrillada argentina   a. pescado.   b. pollo.   c. carne de vaca o res.
     típica se hace con…
4. _b_ El deporte favorito de la   a. el esquí.   b. el fútbol.   c. la natación.
     mayoría de los uruguayos es…
5. _b_ En la Patagonia hay…   a. playas famosas.   b. glaciares.   c. pistas de esquí.

223

Resources

- SAM: 7-1 to 7-10
- Supp. Activ. Book: *A primera vista*

A PRIMERA VISTA

·)) Los deportes

El **fútbol** es el **deporte** número uno en los países hispanos.

Hay excelentes **equipos** de fútbol en Argentina, Uruguay, Colombia, México y otros países hispanos. Los mejores **jugadores** de los equipos locales forman un equipo nacional. Esta selección representa al país en los **juegos** de los **campeonatos** internacionales y participa, **cada** cuatro años, en la Copa **Mundial**.

En otras palabras

While the majority of Spanish speakers use **jugar + al + deporte**, as does *Mosaicos*, some omit **al** (**jugar tenis**, **jugar golf**, etc.).

Some speakers say **básquetbol**, with the stress on the first syllable, rather than **baloncesto**. **Vóleibol** has several variants, including **volibol**, with the stress on the last syllable.

En la zona del Caribe, el **béisbol** es el deporte más popular y muchos jugadores, como Alex Rodríguez "A-Rod" y Carlos Beltrán, son originarios de allí y juegan en los mejores equipos de Estados Unidos.

El **esquí** es un deporte que practican muchas personas en Argentina, Chile y España. Aquí vemos a unos jóvenes que van a **esquiar** en las **pistas** de Bariloche, Argentina, uno de los centros de esquí más importantes de la América del Sur.

El **ciclismo**, el **tenis** y el **golf** son otros deportes que cuentan con figuras renombradas en Hispanoamérica y España. Los españoles Miguel Indurain, Roberto Heras y Alberto Contador fueron **campeones** del Tour de France. En esta **carrera**, que **dura** más de 20 días, los **ciclistas recorren** a veces unos 200 kilómetros, el equivalente de 120 millas, en un solo día. Por otro lado, el jugador Sergio García, conocido como "El Niño", es la promesa del golf español.

En cuanto al tenis, David Nalbandian, argentino, y Fernando González, chileno, son actualmente dos de los **tenistas** más conocidos del Cono Sur. Pero la figura más importante del tenis hispano en la actualidad es el español Rafael Nadal.

7-1 Deportes: ¿Quién es? PRIMERA FASE. Asocie los deportes de la columna de la izquierda con los jugadores hispanos a la derecha.

1. _d_ ciclismo
2. _c, e_ tenis
3. _b_ béisbol
4. _a_ golf

a. Sergio García
b. Alex Rodríguez
c. Rafael Nadal
d. Alberto Contador
e. David Nalbandian

SEGUNDA FASE. Ahora hablen entre ustedes de dos de sus jugadores favoritos/jugadoras favoritas. Expliquen quiénes son y a qué deporte juegan, dónde juegan, qué campeonatos ganaron y por qué son sus jugadores favoritos/jugadoras favoritas.

Deportes y equipos deportivos

CD 3
Track 34

el béisbol
el bate
los jugadores
el guante

el golf
los palos de golf

la raqueta
la cancha
el tenis

el cesto / la cesta
el básquetbol / el baloncesto

la pelota
la red
el vóleibol

7-2 ¿Qué necesitamos para jugar? PRIMERA FASE. Escriba el equipo que se necesita para practicar cada deporte.

DEPORTE	EQUIPO
béisbol	
golf	
vóleibol	
baloncesto	
tenis	

SEGUNDA FASE. Entreviste a su compañero/a para conversar sobre el equipo que necesita para practicar deportes.

1. ¿Qué deporte(s) practicas? ¿Por qué?
2. ¿Qué equipo necesitas para practicarlo(s)?
3. ¿Dónde compras el equipo y la ropa que necesitas?

 7-3 ¿Qué deporte es? Túrnense para identificar los siguientes deportes.

1. Hay nueve jugadores en cada equipo y usan un bate y una pelota. béisbol
2. Es un juego para dos o cuatro jugadores; necesitan raquetas y una pelota. tenis
3. En este deporte los jugadores no deben usar las manos. fútbol
4. Para practicar este deporte necesitamos tener una bicicleta. ciclismo
5. En cada equipo hay cinco jugadores que lanzan (*throw*) el balón a un cesto. balonce
6. Para este deporte necesitamos una red y una pelota. Mucha gente lo juega en la playa. vóleibol

---

En otras palabras

Different words are used in Spanish for *ball*, depending on the context. The ball in basketball and volleyball is usually called a **balón**. Both **pelota** and **balón** are used for the soccer ball. **Pelota** is also used in golf and tennis. **Bola** or **bolo** is used in bowling.

 7-4 Su deporte favorito. Háganse las preguntas necesarias para averiguar lo siguiente.

1. el deporte favorito para practicar
2. el lugar donde lo practica, con quién y cuándo
3. el deporte favorito para ver
4. el lugar y las personas con quienes ve su deporte favorito
5. los nombres de sus equipos favoritos/as
6. la marca (*brand*) de ropa deportiva que más le gusta

7-5 Concurso. Ustedes van a organizar un concurso sobre deportes. En grupos de tres o cuatro, elijan a uno/a de los/las deportistas en las fotos y hagan lo siguiente en tres minutos:

1. Identifiquen al/a la atleta y su deporte. (5 pts)
2. Digan algún campeonato/torneo (*tournament*) que este/a atleta ganó. (5 pts)
3. Digan el equipo que necesita para practicar su deporte. (5 pts)
4. Cuenten algún dato personal o profesional de esta persona. (5 pts)

SEGUNDA FASE. Compartan con la clase la información sobre este/a atleta. El grupo con la información más completa es campeón.

Follow-up for 7-4. Find out how many students attend sports events and how many watch them on TV: *¿Van ustedes a los partidos de... o prefieren verlos por televisión? ¿A qué partidos van?*

Suggestion for 7-5. You may introduce the words *asistencia* and *ninguno* to facilitate students' work.

Suggestion. In this activity students will make connections with what they know. Many will be able to contribute a considerable amount of information about Tiger Woods, Lance Armstrong, and Serena Williams. To encourage competition, subtract points from teams whose members speak English. Alternatively, divide the class into groups and have them take turns answering the questions about the three athletes. If one group does not know an answer, the other group may respond. Record each group's points on the board.

El tiempo y las estaciones

CD 3
Track 35

Verano

¿Qué tiempo hace? Hace buen tiempo y hace calor. Es un día perfecto para jugar al vóleibol en la playa. El cielo **está despejado** y **hace mucho sol**.

Otoño

Hace fresco y mucho **viento**. No es fácil jugar al golf cuando hace viento. Pero el otoño es muy bonito porque muchos **árboles** cambian de color antes de **perder** las hojas.

Invierno

Hoy hace mal tiempo. Anoche **nevó** y hoy hace frío. Hay mucha **nieve** y **hielo** en las calles. Los **lagos** también **se congelaron** y algunas personas **aprovechan** para **patinar sobre el hielo**.

Primavera

Hoy **está nublado** y **está lloviendo**. Por eso, estos chicos no pueden jugar al fútbol y están **jugando a los bolos**. Pero **la lluvia** es muy buena para las plantas y las flores, y además limpia la **atmósfera contaminada**.

En otras palabras

In some Spanish-speaking countries the expressions **jugar (al) boliche** or **ir de bowling** are preferred to **jugar a los bolos**.

7-6 Condiciones meteorológicas. Asocie la situación de la columna de la izquierda con la oración más lógica de la derecha.

1. __e__ Las calles están blancas.
2. __c__ Las personas llevan impermeable y paraguas.
3. __d__ La casa es un horno y vamos a ir a la playa.
4. __b__ Los árboles se mueven (*move*) mucho.
5. __a__ Vamos a celebrar mi cumpleaños en el parque porque el clima está perfecto.
6. __f__ El cielo (*sky*) está cubierto (*overcast*) y parece que va a llover.

a. Hace muy buen tiempo.
b. Hace mucho viento.
c. Está lloviendo.
d. Hace mucho calor.
e. Está nevando.
f. Está nublado.

7-7 ¿Qué tiempo hace? Un amigo/Una amiga lo/la llama por teléfono desde otra ciudad. Pregúntele qué tiempo hace allí y averigüe cuáles son sus planes. Su amigo/a debe hacerle preguntas a usted también.

MODELO: E1: *¿Qué sorpresa! ¿Dónde estás?*
        E2: _____
        E1: *¿Qué tiempo hace allí?*
        E2: _____

En directo

To thank a friend for calling:

Mil gracias por llamar. ¡Fue un gusto escucharte!
Many thanks for calling. It was a pleasure to hear your voice!

Gracias por llamar. ¡Qué placer escucharte!
Thanks for calling. What a pleasure to hear from you!

Suggestions. Use visuals to illustrate weather expressions and to review the ones students learned in *Capítulo preliminar* and in *Capítulo 6*. Provide comprehensible input by asking when certain weather patterns are likely to occur and presenting additional weather vocabulary: *templado, cálido,* etc. Personalize: *¿Qué tiempo prefiere usted, el frío o el calor? ¿Le gusta la lluvia? ¿Y la nieve? ¿Qué deportes practica usted cuando nieva?*

Suggestions. Recycle months by asking when the following occur; for each item ask what the weather is like both in your area and in the Southern Hemisphere: 1. *Termina el año escolar.* 2. *Empieza la temporada* (season) *de béisbol.* 3. *Usted celebra su cumpleaños.* 4. *Sale de vacaciones.* 5. *Se juega al campeonato de fútbol americano "Super Bowl".* 6. *Se celebra el día de San Patricio.* 7. *Se celebra el cumpleaños de Martin Luther King.* 8. *Es el cumpleaños de su mejor amigo/a.* 9. *Este mes tiene el día más corto del año.*

Note. Some Spanish speakers use *hay* instead of *hace:* Hay *mucho sol.*

Suggestions for 7-7. Review Spanish telephone etiquette. To make the conversation more realistic, pairs can sit back to back or use their cell phones. You may wish to assign students to look up the current weather in a Hispanic city and then do the dialogue in class again using that information.

You may wish to present additional weather-related vocabulary as needed: *tornado, ciclón, humedad, huracán, granizo, nevada, llovizna, sequía, neblina, escampar, lloviznar, truenos, relámpagos.*

7-8 El tiempo y las actividades. PRIMERA FASE. Túrnense para explicar qué les gusta hacer a usted y a sus amigos en las siguientes condiciones.

1. Cuando llueve yo...
2. Cuando hace mucho calor me gusta...
3. A veces cuando nieva...
4. Mis amigos y yo... cuando hace mal tiempo.
5. En invierno...
6. Los estudiantes... cuando hace buen tiempo.
7. Cuando está nublado...
8. Hoy hace viento pero...

SEGUNDA FASE. Preparen un breve diálogo que incluya al menos (*at least*) los siguientes elementos:

1. una pregunta
2. tres expresiones de tiempo
3. un deporte

MODELO: E1: *Hola, Carmen. ¿Vamos a la playa esta tarde? Hace mucho calor.*
E2: *Sí, pero en la televisión dicen que esta tarde va a llover.*
E1: *Está nublado pero pienso que no va a llover.*
E2: *Bueno, pues vamos. Es mejor jugar al vóleibol cuando está nublado.*

 7-9 Las temperaturas. PRIMERA FASE. Escojan una ciudad de este mapa de Uruguay y túrnense para completar la siguiente conversación.

E1: *¿Qué temperatura hace en _____?*
E2: *_____ grados. Su equivalente en Fahrenheit es _____.*
E1: *¿Y qué tiempo hace allí?*
E2: *_____. ¿Y qué temperatura hace en _____?*

SEGUNDA FASE. Siguiendo el modelo de la *Primera fase*, preparen un pronóstico del tiempo (*weather report*) de su región para presentar por televisión. Indiquen:

1. la temperatura de tres ciudades
2. el tiempo que hace hoy
3. el tiempo que va a hacer mañana

Cultura

In Hispanic countries the Celsius system is used. To convert degrees Fahrenheit to the Celsius system, subtract 32, multiply by 5, and divide by 9.

$86°F - 32 = 54$

$54 \times 5 = 270$

$270/9 = 30°C$

Sol y Luna de Hoy
Sol
sale ....06:30 hs
se pone...17:29 hs
Luna
sale ....23:42 hs
se pone...11:03 hs

Fases de la luna

menguante
Jul. 24

nueva
Jul. 30

creciente
Ago. 6

llena
Ago. 15

Mapa de Uruguay:

ARTIGAS 17°c
RIVERA 18°c
SALTO 14°c
TACUAREMBÓ 15°c
PAYSANDÚ 16°c
FRAY BENTOS 12°c
DURAZNO 9°c
MONTEVIDEO 14°c

cielo claro | algo nuboso | nuboso | inestable | lluvioso | tormenta eléctrica

¿Qué pasó ayer?

CD 3
Track 36 ## Un partido importante

Ayer fue el juego decisivo del campeonato de fútbol.

Cultura

Hispanic sports fans generally do not boo opposing teams or particular players. Instead they whistle to show their displeasure. This behavior may occur at a soccer game, boxing match, or other popular sports events.

Rigoberto **se despertó** temprano.

Se levantó.

Se vistió.

Se sentó a comer un buen desayuno. Después **se fue** para el **campo** de fútbol.

Durante el partido el árbitro **pitó** un **penalti**.

Un jugador del equipo **contrario** **se enfadó** y **discutió** con el **árbitro**, pero el equipo de Rigoberto **metió un gol** y **ganó**.

Después del partido Rigoberto **se quitó** el uniforme, **se bañó** y **se puso la ropa**.

Luego fue a una fiesta para celebrar el triunfo.

Volvió a casa muy tarde, **se acostó** y **se durmió** enseguida.

Note. Students practiced reflexive verbs in *Capítulo 4* and the preterit in *Capítulo 6*. This section re-introduces reflexive verbs and adds others that may be conjugated with a pronoun. These verbs appear here in the preterit in boldface as lexical items only; students do not need to use the preterit of reflexives to answer the questions. The purpose is to offer students a contextualized preview of the forms, which are presented later in this chapter in *Funciones y formas*.

Suggestion. Introduce vocabulary here in context. Talk about the illustrations and ask: *¿Se despertó temprano Rigoberto? ¿A qué hora se levantó? ¿Desayunó mucho o poco?* etc.

Note. Point out that Spanish often borrows English sports words, giving them a Spanish pronunciation and spelling: *penalti, gol, cacher, nocaut, jonrón*. A penalty in sports is *un penal* in some parts of Latin America.

Suggestion. Videotape some segments of a baseball game, soccer match, or boxing match from a Spanish TV sports program. Have students listen for borrowed words.

Suggestion for 7-11.
Introduce the form *hizo* of the verb *hacer*, which will be used in some activities throughout the chapter. Students are not expected to conjugate the preterit of irregular or reflexive verbs here; the idea is to familiarize them with some of the forms.

Suggestions for 7-12.
Brainstorm things students did yesterday and write some sentences on the board. You may use the third person of reflexive and non-reflexive verbs: *Pablo se despertó a las 6. Leonardo comió en un restaurante argentino. Paula fue a clase de matemáticas.* Then model the first person by talking about your day: *Ayer por la mañana me levanté temprano, trabajé en mi oficina, después comí con un/a amigo/a. Por la tarde fui al gimnasio,* etc.

Explain that formulating questions is an important skill to acquire. In this activity students formulate questions in the past tense, using regular verbs only. They will learn the past tense of some irregular verbs in *Funciones y formas.*

Audioscript for 7-13.
ANUNCIADOR: *Y ahora el pronóstico del tiempo para las capitales hispanas. Montevideo: El día está muy nublado. No llueve, pero hace mucho frío. La temperatura es de 14 grados centígrados. Es un buen día para ponerse un suéter de lana y una chaqueta. Buenos Aires: Está lloviendo. La temperatura es de 10 grados centígrados. Esta noche va a hacer mucho frío. Póngase un impermeable y no olvide su paraguas. ¡Lo va a necesitar! Caracas: Hace mucho sol y no hace ni frío ni calor. La temperatura es de 20 grados centígrados y esta tarde va a ser de unos 22 grados. Un día ideal para pasear por la ciudad. Ciudad de México: El sol está muy fuerte y hace mucho calor. La temperatura es de 42 grados centígrados. Un día perfecto para quedarse en casa.*

7-10 ¿Qué significa? Busque la definición de estas palabras relacionadas con los deportes.

1. _c_ ganar
2. _f_ equipo
3. _e_ gol
4. _d_ partido
5. _b_ árbitro
6. _a_ campeón/campeona

a. jugador/a número 1 en un deporte
b. persona que mantiene el orden en un partido
c. tener más puntos al terminar un juego
d. juego entre dos equipos o individuos
e. punto en un partido de fútbol
f. un grupo de jugadores

7-11 El partido de Rigoberto. Contesten las preguntas sobre las actividades de Rigoberto el día del partido.

1. ¿Qué hizo (*did*) Rigoberto primero? Se despertó.
2. ¿Qué hizo después de levantarse? Se vistió.
3. ¿Qué desayunó Rigoberto? Un buen desayuno.
4. ¿Por qué se enfadó un jugador del equipo contrario? Porque el árbitro pitó un penalti
5. ¿Quién ganó el partido? El equipo de Rigoberto.
6. ¿Adónde fue Rigoberto después del partido? Fue a una fiesta.

7-12 ¿Las actividades de ayer? PRIMERA FASE. Háganse preguntas para obtener la siguiente información sobre las actividades de cada uno/a de ustedes ayer.

1. hora de despertarse y de levantarse ayer
2. desayuno que tomó
3. número de horas de estudio
4. deporte(s) que practicó y por cuánto tiempo
5. hora de acostarse

SEGUNDA FASE. Después, comparen sus actividades, contestando las siguientes preguntas:

1. ¿Quién de ustedes se levantó más temprano ayer?
2. ¿Quién tomó un desayuno más nutritivo?
3. ¿Quién estudió más?
4. ¿Quién practicó deportes por más tiempo?
5. ¿Quién se acostó más tarde?

7-13 El clima en Hispanoamérica. You will listen to the weather forecast for four cities in Latin America. Before you listen, write down the information that you might hear in a weather forecast in each season.

CD 3
Track 37

primavera _____
verano   _____
otoño   _____
invierno   _____

Now, focus on the general idea of what is said. As you listen, indicate (✓) whether each forecast predicts good or bad weather.

	BUEN TIEMPO	MAL TIEMPO
Montevideo		✓
Buenos Aires		✓
Caracas	✓	
Ciudad de México		✓

EN ACCIÓN

Diarios de bicicleta: Aficionados al fútbol

Antes de ver

7-14 Los deportes juegan un papel importante en el mundo hispano. Escriba los nombres de algunos atletas españoles y latinoamericanos que usted asocia con los siguientes deportes: tenis, béisbol, fútbol y boxeo. Answers may vary.

Mientras ve

7-15 Ponga en orden cronólogico las siguientes acciones de Javier, según lo que le dice a Daniel.

_5_ Me desperté.

_2_ Fui al parque.

_7_ Me invitaron a jugar al fútbol.

_3_ Me senté junto a un árbol.

_1_ Me encontré con un señor y me dijo cómo llegar al parque.

_4_ Me dormí por unos minutos.

_6_ Me encontré con Martín y Claudia.

_8_ Dejé la bicicleta junto al árbol.

_10_ Ahora necesito encontrar mi bicicleta.

_9_ No usé el candado de mi bicicleta.

Después de ver

7-16 Cuéntele a su compañero/a una experiencia en la que usted perdió algo. Incluya el mayor número de detalles posible. Answers may vary.

FUNCIONES Y FORMAS

1. Talking about the past: Preterit of reflexive verbs and pronouns

Rodolfo

REPORTERO: ¡Felicitaciones por el triunfo! ¡Jugaron como campeones!

RODOLFO: Gracias. El triunfo es de todo el equipo. Fue un partido difícil, pero **nos preparamos** bien.

REPORTERO: ¿Y cómo empezó este día de victoria para ti, Rodolfo?

RODOLFO: Bueno, anoche **me acosté** temprano. Hoy, yo **me levanté** a las 5:30, **me duché** muy rápido para el entrenamiento, **me vestí** y **me fui** a la cancha.

REPORTERO: ¿Y cómo **se prepararon** ustedes para enfrentar al equipo rival?

RODOLFO: Eh… Primero, es fundamental **sentirse** ganador y también es importante tener un buen entrenador como el nuestro.

Piénselo. Indique si las siguientes afirmaciones son probables (**P**) o improbables (**I**), según la conversación entre Rodolfo y el reportero.

1. _I_ Todos los jugadores del equipo **se acostaron** tarde la noche antes del partido.
2. _P_ Rodolfo **se levantó** temprano el día del partido.
3. _P_ Rodolfo **se duchó** rápidamente para llegar a tiempo a la cancha.
4. _I_ El equipo no **se preparó** bien para el partido, por eso, ganó.
5. _I_ Según Rodolfo, lo más importante para ganar es **sentirse** nervioso.

- In *Capítulo 4* you learned about reflexive verbs. Now you will use these verbs in the preterit. The rules that apply to reflexive verbs are the same in the past tense as in the present.

- As you have seen, reflexive verbs express what people do *to* or *for themselves.*

Los jugadores **se levantaron** a las cinco. *The players got up at five o'clock.*

Yo **me preparé** rápidamente. *I got ready quickly.*

LEVANTARSE			
yo	**me levanté**	nosotros/as	**nos levantamos**
tú	**te levantaste**	vosotros/as	**os levantasteis**
Ud., él, ella	**se levantó**	Uds., ellos/as	**se levantaron**

Note for Lengua. Remind students that they can go to the Appendix in the Student Activities Manual for additional practice with accents.

■ With a conjugated verb followed by an infinitive, place the reflexive pronoun before the conjugated verb or attach it to the infinitive.

Yo **me** empecé a preparar a las cinco.

Yo empecé a preparar**me** a las cinco.

I started to get ready at five.

Lengua

Do you know why the verb forms **duchándose** and **lavándonos** have an accent mark?

■ With the present progressive (**estar + -ndo**), place the reflexive pronoun before the conjugated form of **estar** or attach it to the present participle. When attaching a pronoun to the present participle, add a written accent mark to the stressed vowel (the vowel preceding **-ndo**).

Amelia **se** está duchando ahora.
Amelia está duch**á**ndo**se** ahora.

Amelia is taking a shower now.

Nosotros **nos** estamos lavando los dientes.
Nosotros estamos lav**á**ndo**nos** los dientes.

We are brushing our teeth.

■ Remember that when referring to parts of the body and clothing, the definite articles are used with reflexive verbs.

Me lavé **el** pelo.

I washed my hair.

Alicia se quitó **la** sudadera.

Alicia took off her sweatshirt.

■ Some verbs that use reflexive pronouns do not necessarily convey the idea of doing something to or for oneself. These verbs normally convey the idea of mental or physical states.

María **se enfermó** gravemente la semana pasada.

María got seriously sick last week.

Nos preocupamos mucho cuando fue al hospital.

We got very worried when she went to the hospital.

■ Reflexive verbs that convey the idea of mental or physical states do not take an object. The following verbs are in that category.

arrepentirse (ie)	*to regret*	**enfadarse**	*to get upset, angry*
atreverse	*to dare*	**quejarse**	*to complain*
divertirse (ie)	*to have fun*	**sentirse (ie)**	*to feel*
disculparse	*to apologize*		

La entrenadora **se disculpó** de no asistir a la práctica del viernes pasado.

The coach apologized for not attending last Friday's practice.

El público **se quejó** del pobre desempeño de los jugadores.

The public complained about the poor performance of the players.

🎎 **Standard 4.1.** Students demonstrate an understanding of the nature of language through comparisons of the language studied and their own. Here students' attention is drawn to a difference between English and Spanish: When the meaning is clear from the context, Spanish uses the definite article to refer to parts of the body and to clothing (e.g., *me lavo **el** pelo, Alicia se quitó **la** sudadera*) in contrast to English, which uses possessive adjectives (e.g., **my** hair, **her** sweatshirt).

7-17 ¿Cómo fue su día ayer? Ponga estas actividades en el orden más lógico.

<u>6</u> Me preparé para un examen. <u>1</u> Me desperté temprano.
<u>9</u> Me dormí. <u>4</u> Me senté a desayunar.
<u>2</u> Me levanté. <u>3</u> Me bañé.
<u>5</u> Me fui a la universidad. <u>7</u> Al final del día, me sentí
<u>8</u> Me acosté. cansado/a.

 7-18 ¿Cómo reaccionan? PRIMERA FASE. Cuando ustedes tienen un partido importante, ¿hacen actividades semejantes o diferentes? ¿Reaccionan bien o mal?

MODELO: E1:   *Yo me acuesto temprano la noche anterior.*
          E2:   *Yo no. Yo me acuesto a la hora de siempre.*

1. Yo me despierto…
2. A veces yo me enfado si…
3. Nuestro entrenador se queja cuando nosotros…
4. Cuando el entrenador está enfadado, yo no me atrevo a…
5. Cuando los jugadores cometen un error en la cancha, ellos…
6. Cuando esperamos el comienzo de un partido importante, nosotros siempre…
7. Cuando jugamos muy bien, nosotros…
8. Después de un partido difícil, siempre…

 SEGUNDA FASE. Comparen la información de la *Primera fase* con la de otra pareja. ¿Son semejantes o diferentes sus actividades? ¿Reaccionan igual o de una manera diferente?

MODELO: E1:   *Juan y yo nos despertamos muy temprano el día de un partido importante. ¿Y ustedes?*
          E2:   *Yo me despierto temprano también, pero Susana se levanta tarde. Dice que no está nerviosa antes de los partidos.*

7-19 Mis actividades de ayer. Haga una lista de por lo menos tres actividades físicas que usted hizo ayer para cuidar de su salud.

7-20 ¿Qué les ocurrió a estas personas? Lean las siguientes situaciones y hablen de lo que hicieron (*did*) estas personas después. Usen los verbos de la lista u otros propios. Después, comparen sus opiniones con las de otros compañeros/otras compañeras.   Answers may vary.

| afeitarse | despertarse | lavarse | mirarse | perfumarse | quitarse |
| bañarse | enfadarse | maquillarse | peinarse | probarse | secarse |

MODELO: Bernardo se despertó cuando sonó el despertador.
          E1:   *Luego se levantó lentamente. En tu opinión, ¿qué pasó después?*
          E2:   *Probablemente se afeitó.*

1. Teresa se miró en el espejo.
2. Juan y Tomás entraron en el vestuario (*locker room*) del gimnasio después del partido.
3. Marisa y Erica salieron de una tienda deportiva.
4. Ramón salió de la ducha.
5. Marta no está contenta. Habló con la capitana del equipo de unos temas personales y luego la capitana les contó todo a otras jugadoras.
6. Pablo llegó tarde a la cancha.

7-21 Nuestra preparación para el campeonato. El mes pasado ustedes representaron a su universidad en un campeonato de tenis en Montevideo. Digan lo que hicieron (*you did*)…

1. para prepararse físicamente.
2. para prepararse mentalmente.
3. para cumplir (*to fulfill*) con las responsabilidades académicas.

Suggestion for 7-21. Personalize by asking athletes in the class what they normally do to prepare for a game and what they did in their last important match or game.

7-22 Loreta se levantó con el pie izquierdo (*got up on the wrong side of the bed*). PRIMERA FASE. Observen las siguientes escenas y cuenten lo que ocurrió. Usen su imaginación y los verbos de la lista u otros, si es necesario.

acostarse	ducharse	explicar	practicar
despertarse	enfadarse	golpear (*to knock*)	sentarse
disculparse	enojarse	levantarse	sonar

¡Lo siento! Anoche me acosté tarde

SEGUNDA FASE. Cuenten lo que ocurrió entre las 8:00 y las 9:00 de la mañana.

Suggestions for 7-22. You may wish to present some of the verbs listed after the directions for this activity: *enojarse, disculparse, golpear, recriminar.* Ask students to name the characters and tell what each scene shows. You may ask them to use their imagination to explain the what, why, how of each event. Guide them through the scenes by asking questions: Scene #1: *¿A qué hora salió el sol? ¿Sonó el reloj despertador?* Scene #2: *La entrenadora, ¿se levantó antes que Loreta? ¿Cómo llegó la entrenadora al cuarto de… ? ¿Quién abrió la puerta?* Scene #3: *¿Por qué se levantó tarde… ? ¿Qué excusa le dio… a la entrenadora? ¿Por qué se acostó tarde… ?* Scene #4: *¿A qué hora llegó la tenista a la cancha?*

SITUACIONES

1. **Role A.** You are a well-known athlete who is greatly admired by young people in your country. A television reporter will interview you to prepare a special feature about your life. Answer the reporter's questions as fully as possible. Remember that you are considered a role model by young people.

   Role B. You are a television reporter. Today you are interviewing a highly respected and admired sports figure. After introducing yourself and greeting the athlete, find out a) what school he/she went to; b) when he/she started to play; c) what his/her daily routine is to keep in shape (**estar en forma**); and d) what sports he/she practiced yesterday.

2. **Role A.** You are visiting a friend who is preparing for the Olympics (**Olimpiadas**) at a training resort (**centro de entrenamiento**). Ask a) how many athletes are there; b) what time the athletes went to bed last night; c) what time they got up today; d) when they started practice today; e) what they ate for breakfast and where they ate; and d) if these activities are similar to his/her usual routine.

   Role B. A friend is visiting you today at the training resort (**centro de entrenamiento**) where you are preparing for the Olympics. Answer your friend's questions and add any information of interest.

2. Talking about the past: Preterit of -er and -ir verbs whose stem ends in a vowel

VICTOR: Federico, ¿miraste el partido entre la selección de Argentina y la de Colombia?

FEDERICO: No, Víctor. Pero **oí** las noticias por la radio, y mi hermano **leyó** la crónica del partido en el periódico. La selección colombiana ganó dos a uno. Los argentinos no jugaron bien ¿Y tú? ¿Viste el partido?

VICTOR: Desafortunadamente no, pero **leí** en Internet que los jugadores argentinos no **oyeron** las instrucciones de su entrenador y cometieron muchos errores. Por eso, el árbitro les marcó un penalti.

FEDERICO: Tienes razón, yo **oí** que el plan estratégico de defensa que **construyeron** no fue bueno. Ellos **creyeron** que ganarles a los colombianos es fácil, pero es un equipo muy bueno.

Piénselo. ¿Quién lo hizo (*Who did it*): Federico (**F**), Víctor (**V**), el hermano de Federico (**HF**), los jugadores argentinos (**JA**)?

1. _F_ **Oyó** las noticias del partido por la radio.
2. _HF_ **Leyó** la crónica en el periódico.
3. _V_ **Leyó** en Internet comentarios sobre el partido.
4. _JA_ No **oyeron** las instrucciones.
5. _JA_ **Creyeron** que ganar es fácil.
6. _JA_ **Construyeron** (*They built*) una mala estrategia de defensa.

■ You have already learned the preterit forms of regular **-er** and **-ir** verbs. For verbs whose stem ends in a vowel, the preterit ending for the **usted/él/ella** form is **-yó** and for the **ustedes/ellos/ellas** form, the ending is **-yeron**.

LEER			
yo	leí	nosotros/as	leímos
tú	leíste	vosotros/as	leísteis
Ud., él, ella	leyó	Uds., ellos/as	leyeron

OÍR			
yo	oí	nosotros/as	oímos
tú	oíste	vosotros/as	oísteis
Ud., él, ella	oyó	Uds., ellos/as	oyeron

Los jugadores **oyeron** los comentarios negativos de los reporteros deportivos.

Cuando el entrenador **oyó** el pitazo final, abrazó a los jugadores.

Los miembros del equipo **construyeron** una casa con la organización Hábitat para la Humanidad.

The players heard the negative comments of the sports commentators.

When the coach heard the final whistle, he hugged the players.

The members of the team built a house with Habitat for Humanity.

> **Lengua**
>
> Note that **-er** and **-ir** verbs whose stems end in a vowel (**creer**, **leer**, **oír**) have an accent mark on the **i** in the infinitive and in the preterit endings that begin with **i**.
>
> No la **oí** llegar anoche. *I didn't hear her arrive last night.*

Note for Lengua. Remind students that they can go to the Appendix in the Student Activities Manual for additional practice with accents.

Additional practice. In groups, have students find out how many students did the following:
1. *leyeron el periódico ayer*
2. *oyeron las noticias esta mañana*
3. *fueron a un partido de tenis o béisbol recientemente*
4. *practicaron un deporte esta semana*
5. *se levantaron antes de las ocho esta mañana*
6. *contribuyeron con por lo menos una hora a una actividad de voluntariado (volunteer) esta semana.*
Then have each group report their findings to the rest of the class

7-23 ¿Cómo se enteraron (*found out*) de los resultados? El fin de semana pasado se jugó la Copa Davis. Las siguientes personas son fanáticas del tenis. Indique cómo se enteró cada uno de ellos de los resultados de los partidos. Use los verbos creer, leer, mirar y oír.

1. Paula y su novio pasaron el fin de semana en las montañas y __oyeron__ los resultados en la radio durante su viaje de regreso a la ciudad.
2. Mercedes trabajó en la biblioteca todo el fin de semana. Cuando su hermano le contó los resultados, ella no lo __creyó__.
3. Ricardo participó en un partido de fútbol entre su universidad y una universidad rival. Él __leyó__ los resultados en el periódico.
4. Los Belmar salieron a hacer ejercicio a la hora del partido. Prefieren el aire libre a mirar televisión y __leyeron__ los resultados en el periódico al día siguiente.

7-24 La semana pasada. Miren la lista de actividades e indiquen en cuáles participaron todos ustedes la semana pasada.

concluir un proyecto importante

construir algo

contribuir con su tiempo a una organización sin fines de lucro (*non-profit*)

ir a la biblioteca

leer el periódico de la universidad

mirar una película para una clase

oír música en español

SITUACIONES

1. **Role A.** You have just written a book on Hispanics in professional sports in the United States. A reporter for your local newspaper is interviewing you. Respond to the reporter's questions about your work.

   Role B. You are a newspaper reporter interviewing the author of a new book on professional Hispanic athletes in the United States. After introducing yourself, ask a) what sports he/she wrote about; b) whether he/she read newspapers from Latin America to write the book; c) what contributions the first Hispanic players made to professional sports in the United States; and d) what he/she concluded from the research (**investigación**).

2. **Role A.** Call a friend to invite him/her to go to a sports event with you. Mention a) what the event is; b) that you read about it in the newspaper; and c) that you want to see the city's new stadium (**estadio**).

   Role B. Your friend calls to invite you to a sports event. Respond to the invitation with questions and comments. Then decide if you want to go and either accept or decline the invitation.

Suggestion for Situación 1. Before students do the first *Situación*, you may want to suggest that they do some research online about the role/history of Hispanics in professional sports in the U.S.

Resources

■ SAM: 7-24 to 7-27
■ Supp. Activ. Book: Preterit of stem-changing -ir verbs

Note. According to the *Real Academia*, monosyllabic words do not usually carry a written accent, unless their meaning or function needs to be differentiated, e.g., *el* (article) vs. *él* (pronoun). Depending on regional pronunciation, some words can be monosyllabic or bisyllabic, and in this case, a written accent is helpful to clarify pronunciation norms. As an example, the preterit of *reir*, *rió*, is pronounced as one syllable in large areas of Latin America, including Mexico and Central America. In other regions, like Spain, Argentina, Ecuador, Colombia and Venezuela, the bisyllabic pronunciation is more common. To avoid confusion about how it should be pronounced, *Mosaicos* treats it as as a bysillabic word and thus writes it with an accent. Other examples are the preterit forms of *criar*, *freír* and *guiar*.

3. Talking about the past: Preterit of stem-changing -*ir* verbs

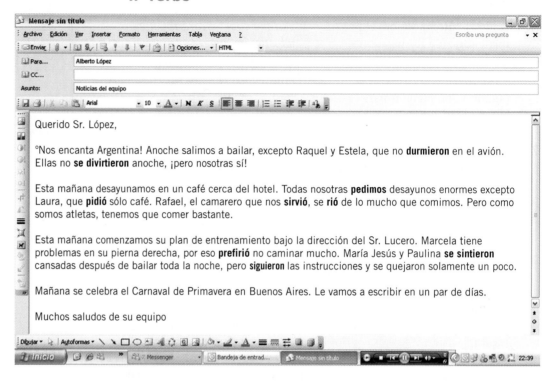

Piénselo. Después de cada oración, escriba a qué persona(s) se refiere, según la breve nota anterior.

1. No **durmieron** en el avión. ___Raquel___ y ___Estela___
2. No desayunó esta mañana; **pidió** un café solamente. ___Laura___
3. Se **rió** de lo mucho que comieron las jugadoras. ___Rafael___
4. **Prefirió** no caminar mucho. ___Marcela___
5. No **se divirtieron** anoche porque no salieron con sus amigas. ___Raquel___ y ___Estela___
6. **Se sintieron** cansadas, pero **siguieron** el plan de entrenamiento. ___María Jesús___ y ___Paulina___

■ In the preterit, stem-changing -**ir** verbs change **e → i** and **o → u** in the **usted, él, ella** and **ustedes, ellos/as** forms. The endings are the same as those of regular -**ir** verbs.

Marta **prefirió** salir temprano.   *Marta preferred to leave early.*

Las jugadoras **durmieron** tranquilamente.   *The players slept calmly.*

PREFERIR (e → i)			
yo	preferí	nosotros/as	preferimos
tú	preferiste	vosotros/as	preferisteis
Ud., él, ella	prefirió	Uds., ellos/as	prefirieron

DORMIR (o → u)			
yo	dormí	nosotros/as	dormimos
tú	dormiste	vosotros/as	dormisteis
Ud., él, ella	durmió	Uds., ellos/as	durmieron

■ The following are other stem-changing **-ir** verbs:

despedirse	*to say goodbye*	Los hinchas se despidieron de su equipo. *The fans said goodbye to their team.*
divertirse	*to have fun*	Todos se divirtieron con la presentación de las barras paralelas. *Everyone had fun with the performance of the parallel bars.*
morir	*to die*	Un hincha murió de un ataque al corazón cuando su equipo perdió. *A fan died of a heart attack when his team lost.*
pedir	*to ask for/order*	El entrenador pidió agua para los jugadores. *The coach asked for water for the players.*
reír	*to laugh*	El árbitro se rió cuando un perro cruzó la cancha. *The referee laughed when a dog crossed the field.*
repetir	*to repeat*	El reportero repitió el nombre del jugador que marcó el gol. *The reporter repeated the name of the player who scored the goal.*
seguir	*to follow*	Los jugadores siguieron las instrucciones de su entrenador. *The players followed the instructions of their coach.*
sentirse	*to feel*	Todos se sintieron felices con el triunfo. *Everyone felt happy about the victory.*
servir	*to serve*	Los hinchas le sirvieron perros calientes gratis al público. *Fans served free hot dogs to the public.*
vestirse	*to get dressed*	Los jugadores se vistieron para ir a celebrar. *The players got dressed to go out and celebrate.*

7-25 Carrera de un campeón. Un famoso deportista recibió muchas medallas durante su carrera. ¿Cómo lo logró (*accomplished*)? Marque (✓) la alternativa más apropiada, según usted. Answers may vary. Accept any logical response as long as it is supported.

1. ___ **a.** Durmió poco antes de cada partido.
   ___ **b.** Siempre durmió por lo menos ocho horas.

2. ___ **a.** Prefirió evitar el alcohol.
   ___ **b.** Prefirió beber alcohol moderadamente.

3. ___ **a.** Se preparó solo.
   ___ **b.** Prefirió prepararse con un entrenador.

4. ___ **a.** Prefirió comer poco, pero bien.
   ___ **b.** Comió mucho durante toda su vida, pero hizo mucho ejercicio físico.

5. ___ **a.** Practicó sólo antes de los partidos importantes.
   ___ **b.** Practicó constantemente.

6. ___ **a.** Repitió sus victorias con frecuencia.
   ___ **b.** Raras veces repitió sus victorias.

7. ___ **a.** Cuando no ganó un partido, se sintió deprimido y no continuó tratando.
   ___ **b.** Se sintió triste cuando no ganó un partido, pero pidió ayuda para mejorar.

Suggestion for 7-25. You may wish to return to this activity after the uses of the preterit and imperfect are presented in *Capítulo 8* and *Capítulo 9* because it provides examples of the preterit to describe activities in a period in the past (the athlete's career in sports is now over).

7-26 Momentos cruciales. Indique lo que hicieron las siguientes jugadoras del equipo femenino de básquetbol unos minutos antes del partido.

1. Marta (vestirse) __se vistió__ con la camiseta número 3.
2. Ana y Luisa Fernanda (seguir) __siguieron__ con atención los pasos del calentamiento (*warm-up*).
3. Carmen (preferir) __prefirió__ no beber agua antes del partido.
4. Las jugadoras del equipo contrario (reírse) __se rieron__ cuando su entrenador les hizo una broma (*joke*).
5. La entrenadora les (repetir) __repitió__ las instrucciones a todas las jugadoras.
6. El equipo (sentirse) __se sintió__ animado (*encouraged*) con los aplausos del público.

 7-27 Celebrando la victoria. Uno de los equipos de su universidad ganó un campeonato importante y ustedes organizaron una fiesta en su honor. Explíquenle a otra pareja los siguientes detalles de la fiesta. Usen los verbos de la lista.

despedirse	pedir	repetir	servir
divertirse	reír	sentirse	vestirse

1. hora y lugar de la fiesta
2. número de personas que asistieron y cómo se vistieron para la fiesta
3. tipo de cooperación que ustedes pidieron para los gastos de la fiesta
4. cómo se divirtieron en la fiesta
5. comida y bebida que sirvieron en la fiesta y tipo de música que escucharon
6. reconocimiento (*recognition*) que les dieron a los jugadores
7. sentimientos de los jugadores durante la fiesta
8. a qué hora los invitados se despidieron y se fueron de la fiesta

SITUACIONES

1. **Role A.** You had to work late last night and missed an important basketball game at your school. Call a friend who went to the game. After greeting your friend, a) explain why you did not go; b) ask questions about the game; c) answer your friend's questions; and d) accept your friend's invitation to go to another game next Saturday.

   Role B. A friend calls to find out about last night's basketball game. Answer your friend's questions and then a) say that there is another game on Saturday; b) find out if your friend is free that evening; and c) if free, invite him/her to go with you.

2. **Role A.** You read in today's newspaper that your favorite football (**fútbol americano**) player was interviewed on TV last night. Call your friend, who watched the interview, to find out a) on which channel (**canal**) he/she watched the interview; b) the time of the interview; c) who interviewed (**entrevistar**) the football player; and d) what they talked about.

   Role B. Your friend calls to get the details of a TV interview of his/her favorite football (**fútbol americano**) player. Answer all of your friend's questions in as much detail as possible.

4. Emphasizing or clarifying information: Pronouns after prepositions

Resources

■ SAM: 7-28 to 7-30
■ Supp. Activ. Book: Pronouns after prepositions

ROBERTO:	Estas flores son **para ti**, Cristina.
CRISTINA:	¿**Para mí**? Gracias, Roberto.
	✳ ✳ ✳
ROBERTO:	Oye, Cristina. El partido es mañana. ¿Quieres ir **conmigo**?
CRISTINA:	No puedo ir **contigo**, Roberto. Mis primos están aquí, y voy al partido **con ellos**.

Piénselo. Indique quién dice cada oración, Roberto (**R**) o Cristina (**C**).

1. _R_ ¿Quieres ir **conmigo**?
2. _R_ Estas flores son **para ti**.
3. _C_ No puedo ir **contigo**.
4. _C_ ¿**Para mí**?
5. _C_ Voy **con ellos**.

■ In *Capítulo 6* you used **a + mí**, **a + ti**, and so on, to clarify or emphasize the indirect object pronoun: **Le di el suéter a él**. These same pronouns are used after other prepositions, such as **de**, **para**, and **sin**.

a		mí
de		ti
para	+	usted, él, ella
por		nosotros/as
sin		vosotros/as
sobre		ustedes, ellos/as

Siempre habla **de ti**.	*He is always talking about you.*
Las raquetas son **para mí**.	*The racquet are for me.*
No quieren ir **sin nosotros**.	*They do not want to go without us.*

Suggestion. You may want to mention that the prepositional pronoun (*mí*) has an accent mark to distinguish it from the possessive adjective (*mi*). You may also direct students to the Appendix in the Student Activities Manual for additional practice with accents and homonyms.

■ In a few cases, Spanish does not use **mí** and **ti** after prepositions. After **con**, use **conmigo** and **contigo**. After **entre**, use **tú y yo**.

¿Vas al partido **conmigo**?	*Are you going to the game with me?*
Sí, voy **contigo**.	*Yes, I am going with you.*
Entre tú y **yo**, ella tiene unos problemas serios.	*Between you and me, she has some serious problems.*

7-28 Un amigo preguntón. Un amigo de Rosario le hace muchas preguntas. Conecte sus preguntas en la columna de la izquierda con un comentario lógico de Rosario en la columna de la derecha.

1. ¿Con quién vas a ir al partido de tenis, Rosario? c
2. ¿Por qué no vemos las finales del campeonato con Sofía? f
3. Rosario, ¿para quién es esta raqueta de tenis? a
4. ¿Pueden mis amigos ir a la cancha con nosotros? b
5. Después del partido de ayer encontramos una sudadera. ¿Es de Carlos? d
6. ¿De quién van a recibir el trofeo los ganadores? e

a. La compré para ti. ¿Te gusta?
b. Imposible. No podemos ir con ellos. Tengo sólo dos billetes.
c. Contigo, ¡por supuesto!
d. Sí, es de él.
e. De nosotros. De ti y de mí. ¡Qué emocionante!
f. Prefiero verlas sin ella. Habla mucho y no puedo concentrarme.

7-29 Haciendo planes. ¿Cuándo van a hacer las siguientes actividades? Escojan individualmente una opción en cada número y, luego pregúntense entre ustedes.

MODELO: E1: *¿Cuándo puedes ir al cine conmigo?*
E2: *Puedo ir contigo el sábado.*

1. estudiar español/historia/biología
2. ir al parque/al partido de béisbol/al concierto
3. jugar al golf/al tenis/al vóleibol

7-30 ¿Con quién va? Completen el siguiente diálogo, usando pronombres.

JULIA: Yo salgo ahora. ¿Vienes conmigo?
CELIA: No, no puedo ir __contigo__. Tengo que trabajar media hora más en la tienda.
JULIA: ¡Cuánto lo siento! Entonces, ¿vas a ir con Roberto?
CELIA: Sí, voy a ir con ___él___ más tarde.
JULIA: Seguro que él no quiere ir sin ___ti___ . Tú eres su mejor amigo/a.
CELIA: Sí, somos muy buenos amigos. ¿Y sabes dónde te vas a sentar?
JULIA: Sí, voy a sentarme entre _____ y _Answers may vary_ .

SITUACIONES

1. **Role A.** One of your friends is a basketball player. He gave you two tickets for today's game, but you have no transportation. Call a friend who has a car. After greeting him/her a) explain how you got the tickets for the game; b) invite your friend to go with you; and c) explain that you have no transportation.

   Role B. A friend calls you to invite you to today's basketball game. After exchanging greetings, a) thank your friend for the invitation; b) respond that you would be delighted to go with him/her; c) say that you can pick him/her up in your car; and d) agree on a time and place.

2. **Role A.** Your friend calls to chat and tells you that he/she went to a surprise party (*una fiesta sorpresa*) last weekend. Ask a) who gave the party; b) who it was for; c) who your friend went with; and d) what happened at the party.

   Role B. You call a friend to chat. Talk about the surprise party (*fiesta sorpresa*) you went to last weekend. Answer your friend's questions about the party in as much detail as possible.

5. Talking about the past: Some irregular preterits

Resources
■ SAM: 7-31 to 7-38
■ Supp. Activ. Book: Some irregular preterits

ABUELA: ¡Bienvenidos! Pasen, por favor. ¿No **vino** Carmencita? ¿Está enferma?

MADRE: Está trabajando. **Estuvo** en la biblioteca hasta muy tarde anoche, pero no **pudo** terminar su proyecto. Nos **dijo** que es largo y difícil.

* * *

CARMENCITA: ¿Mis padres? **Tuvieron** que ir a la casa de mi abuela, pero no **quise** ir a otra cena aburrida. Les **dije** una pequeña mentira sobre un proyecto...

Piénselo. Marque (✓) si las afirmaciones en la columna de la izquierda probablemente expresan la **verdad**, una **mentira** (*lie*) o si **no se sabe**, según la información en las conversaciones.

	VERDAD	MENTIRA	NO SE SABE
1. Carmencita **tuvo** que terminar un proyecto.	__	✓	__
2. Los padres de Carmencita **tuvieron** que ir a la casa de la abuela.	✓	__	__
3. Carmencita no **quiso** ir a la casa de su abuela.	✓	__	__
4. Carmencita **estuvo** en la biblioteca por muchas horas.	__	__	✓
5. Carmencita **hizo** un proyecto para una clase.	__	__	✓
6. Carmencita les **dijo** la verdad a sus padres.	__	✓	__

- Some verbs have irregular forms in the preterit because they use different stems than in the present tense. The preterit endings are added to those stems. Note that the **yo, usted, él,** and **ella** preterit endings of these verbs are unstressed and therefore do not have written accents.

- The verbs **hacer, querer,** and **venir** have an **i** in the preterit stem.

INFINITIVE	NEW STEM	PRETERIT FORMS
hacer	hic-	hice, hiciste, hizo, hicimos, hicisteis, hicieron
querer[1]	quis-	quise, quisiste, quiso, quisimos, quisisteis, quisieron
venir	vin-	vine, viniste, vino, vinimos, vinisteis, vinieron

[1]The verb **querer** in the preterit followed by an infinitive normally means to *try (but fail)* to do something.
  Quise hacerlo ayer.   *I tried to do it yesterday.*

Follow-up for Piénselo. After students have practiced producing irregular preterit forms in the activities in this section, you may wish to go back to *Piénselo* to have them correct the lies that Carmencita told and create an alternative account of her activities.

Suggestion. Add to the input provided by the visual presentation and *Piénselo* by relating a recent experience (real or fictional) and using visuals to introduce the preterit of these verbs and others. Example: *El año pasado estuve en Miami. Estuve en un hotel en la playa y pude hablar español en los restaurantes y en las calles, porque en Miami viven muchos hispanos. Jugué a la lotería pero no tuve suerte. No gané nada, y además gasté mucho dinero en las tiendas y los clubes. Pero me divertí mucho.* Personalize: *¿Dónde estuvo usted el verano pasado? ¿Le gustó el lugar? ¿Qué hizo allí?*

■ The verbs **estar**, **tener**, **poder**, **poner**, and **saber** have a **u** in the preterit stem.

INFINITIVE	NEW STEM	PRETERIT FORMS
estar	estuv-	estuve, estuviste, estuvo, estuvimos, estuvisteis, estuvieron
tener	tuv-	tuve, tuviste, tuvo, tuvimos, tuvisteis, tuvieron
poder[2]	pud-	pude, pudiste, pudo, pudimos, pudisteis, pudieron
poner	pus-	puse, pusiste, puso, pusimos, pusisteis, pusieron
saber[3]	sup-	supe, supiste, supo, supimos, supisteis, supieron

■ The verbs **decir**, **traer**, and all verbs ending in **-ducir** (e.g., **traducir**, *to translate*) have a **j** in the stem and use the ending **-eron** instead of **-ieron**. **Decir** also has an **i** in the stem.

INFINITIVE	NEW STEM	PRETERIT FORMS
decir	dij-	dije, dijiste, dijo, dijimos, dijisteis, dijeron
traer	traj-	traje, trajiste, trajo, trajimos, trajisteis, trajeron
traducir	traduj-	traduje, tradujiste, tradujo, tradujimos, tradujisteis, tradujeron

Follow-up for 7-31. Have students ask each other what they really did yesterday.

 7-31 ¿Qué hizo usted ayer? PRIMERA FASE. De la siguiente lista de quehaceres (*chores*), usted sólo pudo hacer dos o tres. Marque (✓) lo que hizo y lo que no pudo hacer.

	SÍ	NO
1. lavar la ropa	_____	_____
2. comprar los zapatos de tenis	_____	_____
3. probarse el uniforme nuevo	_____	_____
4. conocer al nuevo entrenador	_____	_____
5. mirar el video del último partido	_____	_____
6. comentar las estrategias del próximo partido	_____	_____

 SEGUNDA FASE. Hágale preguntas a su compañero/a para averiguar qué pudo hacer ayer.

MODELO: comprar el trofeo para el campeonato
E1: *¿Compraste el trofeo para el campeonato?*
E2: *Quise comprarlo, pero no pude.*
E1: *¿Por qué no pudiste comprarlo?*
E2: *Porque tuve que regresar al laboratorio.*

---

[2]**Poder** used in the preterit usually means *to manage to do something.*
　Pude hacerlo esta mañana.　　*I managed to do it this morning.*
[3]**Saber** in the preterit normally means *to learn* in the sense of *to find out.*
　Supe que llegó anoche.　　*I learned that he arrived last night.*

7-32 ¿Qué ocurrió? Expliquen qué le ocurrió a Javier el día de su cumpleaños. Den la mayor cantidad de información posible.

1.
2.
3.
4.
5.
6.

7-33 Unos días de descanso. Su compañero/a estuvo unos días en Argentina. Hágale preguntas sobre los siguientes puntos para saber más de su viaje.

1. lugares adonde fue
2. tiempo que estuvo en Argentina
3. cosas interesantes que hizo
4. los lugares que le gustaron más
5. si pudo hablar español y con quién(es)

SITUACIONES

1. **Role A.** Congratulations! You won a contest (**concurso**) to attend the World Cup. Tell your classmate that you won the contest and that you went to the World Cup. Answer all of his/her questions in detail.

   Role B. Your classmate won a contest and tells you about it. Ask a) how he/she found out about the contest; b) how long he/she was away; c) how many games he/she attended; d) with whom he/she went; and e) details about the last game.

2. **Role A.** Imagine that yesterday you went to a sports event and had the opportunity to meet your favorite sports star. Explain to a friend a) where you went; b) what happened and where; c) what you did when you saw this person; d) what he/she said to you; and d) what happened finally.

   Role B. Your friend tells you that he/she met a very famous sports star yesterday. Ask about what happened and what they talked about.

En directo

To express interest and to ask for details:

¡No me digas! ¿Qué pasó?
You don't say! What happened?

¿Y qué más pasó?
And what else happened?

¡Cuenta, cuenta!
Tell me more!

Lengua

Hace, meaning *ago*
■ To indicate the time that has passed since an action was completed, use **hace +** *length of time* **+ que +** *preterit verb*.

Hace dos meses **que** fui a la Copa Mundial.
*I went to the World Cup two months **ago**.*

Hace una hora **que** empezó el partido.
*The game started an hour **ago**.*

■ When **hace +** *length of time* ends the sentence, omit **que**.

Fui a la Copa Mundial **hace** dos meses.

El partido empezó **hace** una hora.

Suggestions for 7-32. You may use visual aids to teach students to construct a cohesive oral narration. Present and model the following expressions: *pero, por eso/por esa razón, primero, después,* etc. Encourage students to use a variety of verbs by brainstorming verbs they will need and writing the infinitives on the board.

Suggestion. You may wish to assign one drawing to each pair so they can develop a detailed story about it.

Suggestion for 7-33. Students can consult the *Enfoque cultural* section in this chapter for information on Argentina, or they can make up details of their trip.

Suggestions for Lengua box: *Hace* meaning *ago*. To clarify the concept, ask *¿Qué hora es?* Students reply *Es/Son la(s)...* Then ask *¿Cuándo empezó esta clase?* Then say *La clase empezó hace... minutos.* Write the formula *pretérito + hace + (minutos, horas,* etc.) on the board and give other examples. Then repeat the process with the second formulation: *hace + (minutos, horas,* etc.) *+ que + pretérito.*

You may write on the board several years and actions: 1990-llegar a San Antonio; 1992-empezar a estudiar; 1996-casarse; 2000-tener el primer hijo. Then create a story and ask questions: *¿Cuándo llegó a San Antonio? Ah, hace... años que llegó a San Antonio. ¿Y cuántos años hace que empezó a estudiar? ¿Cuántos años hace que se casó? ¿Cuántos años hace que tuvo su primer hijo?* Personalize and encourage students to tell their partners about their experiences.

Resources

- SAM: 7-39 to 7-41
- Supp. Activ. Book: *Mosaicos*

MOSAICOS

A escuchar

Differentiate fact from opinion

When you listen to a report or a newscast on the radio, television, or the Internet, you need to differentiate facts from opinions. Unlike opinions, which express personal attitudes, beliefs, or points of view, facts are provable. You may distinguish facts from opinions by identifying fact indicators, which include information that refers to data, statistics, numbers, and other verifiable evidence.

Antes de escuchar

7-34 Preparación. Usted va a escuchar una conversación entre un reportero y Nicolás, un esquiador argentino que habla sobre su viaje al centro de esquí en Bariloche, Argentina. Antes de escuchar la conversación, escriba una oración con información concreta sobre el tiempo o sobre las pendientes (*slopes*) en las canchas de esquí. Después escriba una opinión sobre la gente del lugar que, según usted, Nicolás probablemente va a conocer. Answers may vary. Accept any logical response.

Escuchar

7-35 ¿Comprende usted? Now listen to the conversation and write down in Spanish three pieces of factual information and three opinions Nicolás offered about the place and/or the people.

CD 3
Track 38

información concreta:

1. Cerro Catedral tiene 65 kilómetros de pistas para esquiar;
2. nevó unos 30 centímetros de nieve;
3. llovió dos días; Cerro Catedral está a 20 kilómetros de Bariloche.

opinión personal:

1. Me gustó mucho Cerro Catedral;
2. Cerro Catedral es un lugar maravilloso;
3. la ciudad es fantástica; la gente es muy amable.

Después de escuchar

7-36 Ahora usted. Hágale preguntas a su compañero/a para averiguar la siguiente información.

1. un deporte que practica y dónde lo practica
2. el tiempo que hace cuando lo practica
3. su atleta favorito/a en ese deporte y por qué

A conversar

Resources
■ SAM: 7-42
■ *Entrevistas* video

ESTRATEGIA

Focus on key information to report what was said

In *Capítulo 6* you practiced taking notes to comprehend and remember something you heard. In this chapter you will take the next step: turning your notes into a brief report that you will present to the class. To be successful, you should a) decide what aspects of the topic you want to report on; b) listen for and take notes on those aspects; and c) organize your notes for your presentation.

Antes de conversar

7-37 Preparación. PRIMERA FASE. Hagan una lista de los deportes que se practican en Argentina y/o Uruguay, según su conocimiento de la región.

SEGUNDA FASE. En la página web de *Mosaicos*, busquen los deportes que escribieron en la *Primera fase*. Elijan uno que se practica en Argentina o Uruguay, busquen la siguiente información sobre ese deporte y tomen apuntes.

1. el nombre del deporte
2. dos o tres datos históricos básicos sobre el deporte: a) cuándo empezó a practicarse; b) dónde empezó; c) algo interesante sobre los comienzos (*beginnings*) del deporte
3. una persona argentina o uruguaya famosa en la historia de este deporte: a) nombre, fecha y lugar de nacimiento y b) datos sobre su carrera deportiva

Conversar

7-38 Entre nosotros. Hagan una presentación de no más de un minuto sobre el deporte que investigaron, usando la información que aprendieron. Divídanse el trabajo de preparar y hacer su presentación entre ustedes. Pueden usar *PowerPoint* e imágenes de Internet para crear una presentación interesante.

Después de conversar

7-39 Un poco más. Elija un deporte y un/a atleta de las presentaciones que hicieron sus compañeros/as de clase. Usando sus apuntes, prepare dos informes breves (de no más de un minuto). Incluya la información indicada en las fichas (*note cards*) a continuación.

Deporte

Nombre:

Dónde y cuándo empezó a practicarse:

Dónde se practica ahora:

Su popularidad:

Atleta

Nombre y nacionalidad:

Fecha de nacimiento:

Campeonatos que ganó:

Su reputación nacional e internacional:

En directo

To discuss ideas while working in a group:

¿Qué te/le/les parece esto?
What do you think about this?

¿Qué te/le/les parece si decimos/organizamos... ?
How about if we say/organize . . . ?

¿Por qué no lees/hablas/miras... ?
Why don't you read/say/look at . . . ?

To propose a new idea:

¡Oigan, tengo una idea!
Listen, I have an idea.

Miren, tengo una propuesta.
Look, I have a suggestion.

En directo

To maintain the interest of listeners:

Hay hechos/datos interesantes sobre...

La información que tenemos sobre... es increíble.

¡Imagínense! Ganó el primer puesto en...

Este/a deportista juega al... como nadie.

Suggestion for 7-37 Segunda fase. Remind students of the importance of taking notes while reading. Suggest they first skim the texts to get the gist and then to do a second, focused reading to record the information they need. Once students have taken notes, it is essential that they put the information in their own words as they prepare their presentations.

Suggestions for 7-38. Guide students in dividing equitably among members of each group the tasks of preparing and presenting. Remind students that the goal is a clear, comprehensible presentation in their own words, since classmates will take notes and prepare a brief report on what they have heard. Mention that your evaluation will stress comprehensibility and speaking, rather than reading from prepared text.

To encourage classmates to participate as active listeners, have them write down at least two follow-up questions or comments for the presenters, and encourage them to ask for clarification when necessary.

Suggestion for 7-39. To enable students to give their brief reports (no more than 1 minute long), you may wish to have several simultaneous presentations to different small groups, or you may ask 2 or 3 students to give a report at the beginning or end of several future class sessions.

Suggestion for 7-39. Since sports are a popular topic for students, your students may want to expand their presentation beyond their level of proficiency. Therefore, to avoid error making, we suggest that you guide them in the preparation of their talk. Insist that students keep their presentation brief and express ideas with the help of visuals (pictures, video clips in Spanish, Internet images, etc.).

A leer

ESTRATEGIA

Predict and guess content

You may enhance your comprehension of a text by predicting and guessing its content before you start to read. Begin by brainstorming the information you are likely to find in the text and identifying the text format. Try this with a magazine article in English and think consciously about how you rely on your own knowledge and reading experiences, as well as textual information, to anticipate what you will read. When you read in Spanish, try to use the strategies that you deploy automatically when you read in your native language.

Antes de leer

7-40 Preparación. PRIMERA FASE. Mire el texto "Los deportes: Una pasión uruguaya". Lea el título y examine las fotos. Tome un minuto máximo para escanear el texto, buscando nombres de lugares y deportes conocidos. Luego responda a las preguntas.

1. Después de examinar el texto, seleccione su tema entre las posibilidades a continuación.
   a. los lugares en Uruguay dónde se practican los deportes
   b. los atletas más famosos de Uruguay
   c. el amor de los uruguayos por los deportes

2. Marque (✓) las ideas que usted anticipa encontrar en el texto.
   a. _✓_ los deportes más populares de Uruguay
   b. ___ el origen de los deportes de Uruguay
   c. _✓_ los lugares donde se practican algunos deportes en Uruguay
   d. ___ los campeonatos que ganaron los equipos de fútbol uruguayo
   e. ___ los deportes favoritos de los uruguayos en comparación con los de otros países latinoamericanos

SEGUNDA FASE. Ahora, respondan a estas preguntas.

1. ¿Les gustan los deportes individuales o prefieren los de equipo? ¿Por qué?
2. ¿Saben esquiar? ¿Esquían en la nieve o en el agua? ¿Esquían bien o regular?
3. ¿Qué tipos de surf conocen? ¿Han oído hablar (*Have you heard about*) del surf en la arena? ¿Qué saben acerca del deporte?
4. ¿Conocen el fútbol de salón? ¿Se practica en su país? ¿Dónde?

Leer

Los deportes: Una pasión uruguaya

Uruguay es un país pequeño donde los deportes forman una parte integral de la vida de la mayor parte de sus habitantes.

Entre las grandes pasiones nacionales, desde luego, está el fútbol. Desde su infancia, muchos uruguayos acompañan fielmente a sus equipos predilectos. En varias ocasiones, la selección nacional uruguaya ganó títulos y campeonatos importantes.

Pero los uruguayos son un pueblo inquieto, de una personalidad versátil que no limita su interés a un solo deporte. El básquetbol, el ciclismo, el fútbol de salón, el rugby, el boxeo y la pelota de mano son otros deportes que tienen muchos aficionados.

Las hermosas y privilegiadas playas del Uruguay también favorecen los deportes acuáticos, como el surf, que, según los expertos, cuenta hoy con un gran número de aficionados. En 1993 en Uruguay se formó la Unión de Surf del Uruguay (USU). Ese mismo año, el país envió a sus representantes a competir internacionalmente en el Primer Campeonato Panamericano de Surf en Isla Margarita, Venezuela. Hoy en día la USU promueve el surf, arbitra las competencias clasificatorias a nivel nacional, apoya a los competidores nacionales, representa a Uruguay en competencias internacionales y compite en los Juegos Olímpicos con la Selección Uruguaya de Surf.

Sin duda, uno de los lugares predilectos de los uruguayos y turistas extranjeros para practicar el surf es Punta del Este. Ubicada al sureste del Uruguay, a 140 kilometros de Montevideo, Punta Este es una hermosa península de enormes playas, con arenas finas y gruesas, rocas y un entorno de bosques y médanos[1].

Precisamente en estos médanos nació, en el siglo pasado, una variante del surf que está despertando grandes polémicas en el país: el surf en la arena o sandsurf. Los brasileños inventaron este deporte en los años ochenta para no aburrirse cuando no había olas. La agradable temperatura de las playas uruguayas, la escasez de olas que a veces impide practicar el surf en el agua y la formación arenosa de algunas playas aumentaron considerablemente el número de personas que practican el surf en la arena. Por ejemplo, los médanos de Valizas son los más grandes de Sudamérica y los terceros más grandes del mundo, algunos con 30 metros de altura y una longitud de bajada[2] de aproximadamente 125 metros. Sin embargo, las autoridades uruguayas están controlando e incluso prohibiendo la práctica de este deporte por el posible deterioro ecológico que ocasiona. No hay duda de que la prohibición del surf en la arena no va a detener el espíritu activo de los uruguayos. Su creatividad los incentivará a buscar o inventar otras opciones para entretenerse.

[1]*dunes*   [2]*slope*

7-41 Primera mirada. Diga si las siguientes citas textuales (*quotations*) representan información concreta (**C**) o una opinión (**O**) del autor.

1. _C_ Desde su infancia, muchos uruguayos acompañan fielmente a sus equipos predilectos.
2. _O_ Pero los uruguayos son un pueblo inquieto, de una personalidad versátil que no limita su interés a un solo deporte.
3. _C_ En 1993 en Uruguay se formó la Unión de Surf del Uruguay (USU).
4. _C/O_ Punta del Este es una hermosa península de enormes playas, con arenas finas y gruesas, rocas y un entorno de bosques y médanos.
5. _O_ La agradable temperatura de las playas uruguayas, la escasez de olas que a veces impide practicar el surf en el agua y la formación arenosa de algunas playas aumentaron considerablemente el número de personas que practican el surf en la arena.
6. _O_ No hay duda de que la prohibición del surf en la arena no va a detener el espíritu activo de los uruguayos.

Ahora, marque (✓) la estrategia que lo/la ayudó a predecir el contenido del texto. Answers may vary.

a. ___ Hice una lluvia de ideas (*brainstorming*) antes de leer el texto.
b. ___ Usé mi experiencia personal con los deportes.
c. ___ Analicé el formato del texto.
d. ___ Observé los elementos visuales del texto como las fotos.

7-42 Segunda mirada. Lea el artículo otra vez y, según la información que aparece en él, haga lo siguiente:

1. Indique dos razones que explican la popularidad del fútbol en Uruguay.
2. Diga por qué los uruguayos tienen un carácter inquieto.
3. Nombre tres deportes que se juegan en equipo, dos que son principalmente deportes individuales y uno que no requiere una pelota.
4. Dé dos razones para explicar por qué Punta del Este es un lugar ideal para practicar el surf acuático.
5. Explique dos hechos que provocaron el nacimiento del surf en la arena.
6. En su opinión, ¿deben prohibir el surf en la arena? ¿Por qué?

Después de leer

 7-43 Ampliación. Determinen cuál es el deporte favorito del grupo. Luego preparen una hoja descriptiva sobre ese deporte sin mencionar el nombre. Incluyan la siguiente información e intercambien su hoja con otro grupo que debe adivinar cuál es el deporte.

1. lugar donde se practica
2. deporte individual o en grupo (número de personas en el equipo)
3. clima ideal para practicarlo: Se practica en invierno… /cuando hace…
4. un jugador famoso/una jugadora famosa de este deporte
5. su opinión sobre ese jugador/esa jugadora

Answers for 7-42. 1. *Desde su infancia, muchos uruguayos acompañan fielmente a sus equipos predilectos. Los equipos uruguayos ganaron títulos y campeonatos importantes.* **2.** *Tienen interés en/Practican varios deportes.* **3.** *Deportes en equipo: fútbol, rugby, básquetbol, fútbol de salón. Deportes individuales: ciclismo, boxeo, sandsurf. No requiere una pelota: sandsurf, boxeo, ciclismo.* **4.** *Es una hermosa península de enormes playas, con arenas finas y gruesas, rocas y un entorno de bosques y médanos.* **5.** *La escasez de olas que a veces impide practicar el surf en el agua, la formación arenosa de algunas playas.* **6.** *Answers may vary.*

A escribir

Antes de escribir

7-44 Preparación. PRIMERA FASE. Los expertos afirman que el ejercicio físico beneficia a las personas. Respondan a las siguientes preguntas:

1. ¿Qué tipos de actividad física puede hacer una persona? Hagan una lista de posibles actividades físicas (ejercicio o deportes).
2. ¿Es la edad de la persona un factor importante en el tipo de actividad física que hace? ¿Por qué? Escriban una o dos razones, según los expertos.
3. ¿Son la frecuencia y la cantidad de actividad factores importantes en el ejercicio físico? ¿Por qué? Indiquen la frecuencia y la cantidad de actividad física que puede beneficiar a una persona joven y a una persona mayor, según los expertos.
4. ¿Cuáles son dos o tres beneficios del ejercicio físico, según los expertos? Escriban por lo menos una palabra (detalle) que apoye (*supports*) cada uno de los beneficios. ¿Conocen ustedes a alguna persona que se benefició con la actividad física? ¿Qué comenzó a hacer esta persona? ¿Cómo se benefició con el ejercicio?

Escribir

7-45 Manos a la obra. Como proyecto final en su clase *Ejercicio y longevidad*, usted debe escribir un artículo electrónico para los jóvenes hispanos de la escuela secundaria que no hacen actividad física. Usando la información que recogió en **7-44**, escriba su artículo. Incluya lo siguiente:

1. Los beneficios del ejercicio físico, según los expertos. Escriba detalles lógicos que apoyen cada uno de los beneficios.
2. Tipos de actividad física que pueden beneficiar a una persona joven. Escriba una o dos razones, según los expertos.
3. Indique cómo la frecuencia y la cantidad de actividad física benefician a una persona, según los expertos. Dé detalles.

Después de escribir

7-46 Revisión. Antes de presentar su proyecto, revise:

1. la organización y la cantidad de información: ¿Es lógica y clara la organización? ¿Hay suficientes detalles que apoyan la idea central de cada párrafo?
2. el vocabulario general y vocabulario especializado, las estructuras que utilizó para presentar la información, la concordancia, etc.
3. las expresiones para presentar la información factual o la opinión de los expertos
4. la división de los párrafos, la ortografía y la acentuación, etc.

Resources
■ SAM: 7-46 to 7-48

ESTRATEGIA

Add supporting details

Supporting details are sentences, facts, examples, and ideas that follow the topic sentence or main idea and make up the body of a paragraph. Details should be sequenced logically and support the main idea of the paragraph. Paragraph structure may be visualized as follows:

Main idea
  Supporting detail #1
  Supporting detail #2
  Supporting detail #3
Closing sentence

As you write, think of how you will organize the supporting details to develop the main idea of each paragraph. Anticipate and use details that your reader can expect to see after reading the topic sentence.

En directo

To express facts:

Los expertos afirman/dicen/aseguran que…

La investigación indica que…

Los estudios muestran que…

To express an opinión:

A mí me parece que…

Suggestion for 7-44. You may wish to model the activity first to guide students in giving information but without revealing the sport. To make the activity more demanding, you may wish to assign lesser-known sports to each group, such as *montañismo*, *tenis de mesa* (ping pong), *lucha libre*, *rugby*, *surf en arena*, *bungee*. Students may need to prepare their descriptions outside of class for these less familiar sports.

Suggestion for 7-45. Divide the class into groups of three or four. If time is limited, have each group answer one of the questions. Then, discuss responses with the class as a whole and ask students to take notes. For the group(s) that will answer question 1, you may organize the information they will provide as follows: 1. *Actividades al aire libre vs. actividades en un lugar cerrado.* 2. *Actividades individuales vs. actividades en parejas o grupos.*

ENFOQUE CULTURAL

El arte del asado y la tradición ganadera en Argentina y Uruguay

Si le preguntamos a una persona de Argentina o de Uruguay cuál es su comida favorita, probablemente va a responder que es la carne. En efecto, en estos dos países la carne es más que un producto para la exportación. Es, también, el núcleo de muchas tradiciones y está unida a celebraciones, fiestas familiares y, en general, a la cultura de la región. En otras palabras, la ganadería y todo lo relacionado con el ganado contribuyen no solamente a la economía de los dos países, sino también al modo de vida y a las costumbres de sus habitantes.

Un asado argentino con carne de vaca

Indiscutiblemente, en Argentina y Uruguay el asado es un verdadero arte. Algunas personas comparan el asado de Argentina y Uruguay con la parrillada o *cook-out* de Estados Unidos, pero en realidad, son muy diferentes. Aunque la parrillada tradicional en Estados Unidos se compone principalmente de hamburguesas hechas de carne molida, también incluye pollo, costillas (*ribs*) y otros cortes de carne. Inclusive, en los últimos tiempos se han empezado a usar verduras y frutas, por consideraciones de salud. Por parte, el asado de Argentina y Uruguay incluye diferentes tipos de carne, además de algunos órganos internos de la vaca. La salsa típica que acompaña el asado argentino es el *chimichurri*, una salsa de aceite y una variedad de hierbas, mientras que en Estados Unidos frecuentemente se prepara una mezcla de salsa de tomate con salsa *Worcestershire* y azúcar.

La contribución de la ganadería a la economía es impresionante. En Uruguay, por ejemplo, la ganadería constituye cerca del 20% de la economía. Este porcentaje tan alto no lo produce solamente la carne, sino también el cuero y la lana que se usan para fabricar ropa, zapatos y otros artículos de vestir. El valor de las exportaciones de carne uruguaya supera los 500 millones de dólares, pero es necesario sumar unos 150 millones que valen las exportaciones de lana de ovejas y aproximadamente 300 millones por la venta de cueros. Estos resultados son todavía más impresionantes en el caso de Argentina, donde hay unos 40 millones de vacas y aproximadamente 25 millones de ovejas, en un país que tiene unos 40 millones de personas.

Los vaqueros que trabajan en la ganadería se llaman *gauchos*. Es cierto que el modo de vida de los gauchos está unido al arte, la literatura y la cultura de estos países. En la foto se puede ver a un gaucho en su traje típico. Las imágenes de estos vaqueros y su vida romántica y aventurera pertenecen a la literatura y el arte desde el siglo XIX. Por ejemplo, *Facundo* es uno de los más famosos libros latinoamericanos del siglo XIX. En él, Domingo Sarmiento describió con detalle la vida y las costumbres de los gauchos. José Hernández inventó otro de los grandes estereotipos gauchos en un largo poema en el que cuenta la vida, las aventuras y los sufrimientos de *Martín Fierro*, un gaucho argentino. De otra parte, Ricardo Güiraldes publicó *Don Segundo Sombra*, otro ejemplo de la representación literaria del gaucho, a principios del siglo XX.

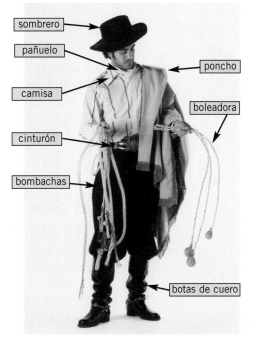

El traje típico del gaucho argentino

sombrero · pañuelo · poncho · camisa · boleadora · cinturón · bombachas · botas de cuero

Domingo Faustino Sarmiento (1811-1888), escritor, fue el primer presidente civil de República Argentina, desde 1868 a 1874.

En otras palabras

Expresiones argentinas

Che, **vos**, ¿dónde está la pelota?
Hey, you, where is the ball?

¡No te mandes la parte!
Don't brag!

En otras palabras

Expresiones uruguayas

Tengo un **gurí** y dos **gurisas**.
I have a boy and two girls.

¡Qué bárbaro!
Great!

7-47 Comprensión. PRIMERA FASE. **Reconocimiento de palabras clave.** Encuentre en el texto la palabra o expresión que mejor expresa el significado de las siguientes ideas.

1. meat or beef   carne
2. cattle ranching   ganadería
3. barbecue   asado
4. on the other hand   de otra parte
5. leather   cuero
6. sheep   oveja(s)
7. baggy trousers   bombachas

SEGUNDA FASE. **Oraciones importantes.** Subraye las afirmaciones que contienen ideas que se encuentran en el texto. Luego indique en qué parte del texto están.

1. Argentinians value meat only as a commodity for export.
2. Cattle and cattle ranching are deeply embedded in the culture of Argentina and Uruguay.
3. Besides meat, some internal organs of the cow are used in a typical Argentinian *asado*.
4. There are more cows and sheep in Uruguay than there are in Argentina.
5. About one-fifth of the economy of Uruguay depends on cattle farming.
6. The combined exports of meat, wool and leather from Uruguay are worth close to one billion dollars.
7. Argentinian cowboys love to dance the tango.
8. Many authors have portrayed the life of Argentinian cowboys in their literature since the nineteenth century.

TERCERA FASE. **Ideas principales.** Escriba un párrafo breve en inglés resumiendo las ideas principales expresadas en el texto.

 7-48 Use la información. Haga un afiche para comparar tres de las más importantes regiones ganaderas del continente americano: Texas, los Llanos de Colombia y Venezuela, y la pampa argentina. Para preparar esta actividad, visite la página web de *Mosaicos* y siga los enlaces útiles. Incluya lo siguiente:

1. una foto de cada una de las regiones y una explicación breve para cada una de ellas
2. una descripción de tres características de cada una de las regiones, por ejemplo, el clima, la naturaleza, las personas, las costumbres, la ropa, la comida, etc.

VOCABULARIO

Los deportes — *Sports*

el baloncesto/el básquetbol	*basketball*
el béisbol	*baseball*
el ciclismo	*cycling*
el esquí	*skiing, ski*
el fútbol	*soccer*
el golf	*golf*
el tenis	*tennis*
el vóleibol	*volleyball*

El equipo deportivo — *Sports equipment*

el bate	*bat*
el balón/la pelota	*ball*
el cesto/la cesta	*basket, hoop*
el gol	*goal*
los palos	*golf clubs*
la raqueta	*racquet*
la red	*net*

Los eventos — *Events*

el campeonato	*championship*
la carrera	*race*
el juego/el partido	*game*

Los lugares — *Places*

el campo	*field*
la cancha	*court, golf course*
la pista	*slope; court; track*

Las personas — *People*

el árbitro	*umpire, referee*
el campeón/la campeona	*champion*
el/la ciclista	*cyclist*
el entrenador/la entrenadora	*coach*
el equipo	*team; equipment*
el jugador/la jugadora	*player*
el/la tenista	*tennis player*

La naturaleza — *Nature*

el árbol	*tree*
la atmósfera	*atmosphere*
el lago	*lake*

El tiempo — *Weather*

está despejado	*it's clear*
está nublado	*it's cloudy*
hace fresco	*it's cool*
hace sol	*it's sunny*
el hielo	*ice*
la lluvia	*rain*
la nieve	*snow*
el viento	*wind*

Las descripciones — *Descriptions*

contaminado/a	*polluted, contaminated*
contrario/a	*opposing*
mundial	*world, worldwide*

Verbos — *Verbs*

aprovechar	*to take advantage*
congelar(se)	*to freeze*
discutir	*to argue*
durar	*to last*
enfadarse	*to get angry*
esquiar	*to ski*
ganar	*to win*
ir(se)	*to go away, to leave*
jugar (ue) a los bolos	*to bowl*
llover (ue)	*to rain*
meter un gol	*to score a goal*
nevar (ie)	*to snow*
patinar	*to skate*
perder (ie)	*to lose*
pitar	*to whistle*
recorrer	*to travel, to cover (distance)*
traducir (zc)	*to translate*

Palabras y expresiones útiles — *Useful Words and Expressions*

cada	*each*
conmigo	*with me*
contigo	*with you* (familiar)
el penalti	*penalty* (in sports)

See page 233 for other reflexive verbs.
See page 239 for other stem-changing *-ir* verbs.

Resources
- IRM: Syllabi & Lesson Plans

Note. *Autorretrato entre México y Estados Unidos* was painted by Frida Kahlo in 1932, during her stay in the U.S. With her pink dress, she is at the center of a portrait that contrasts traditional culture and modernity. Mexico—is represented in warm colors. The U.S. abounds in buildings, industries, and electric gadgets in grays and blues. The inscription on this pedestal says *Carmen (*Frida's baptismal name) *Rivera pintó su retrato en el año 1932.*

Suggestion. Ask *¿Cómo es Frida Kahlo? ¿Qué lleva? ¿De qué color es su vestido?* Recycle colors by asking students to describe the flags. Introduce foreground (*parte de delante*) and background (*parte de atrás*) to help them locate elements in the painting. Ask about the ruins and pre-Columbian figures on the Mexican side: *¿Qué edificio es este*

Nuestras tradiciones

La pintora mexicana Frida Kahlo pintó este cuadro en 1932. Su título es *Autorretrato entre México y Estados Unidos*.

In this chapter you will learn how to:

- talk about holidays, traditions, and celebrations
- express ongoing actions in the past
- narrate past events
- make comparisons

Cultural focus: **México**

Una banda de mariachis

Las ruinas prehispánicas de Teotihuacán

Las ruinas de Tulum

El mole poblano, una de las especialidades de la comida mexicana

A vista de pájaro. Complete las siguientes oraciones con sus propias palabras. Answers may vary.

1. Los mariachis son... bandas de música mexicana
2. La Catedral Metropolitana está en... el Zócalo en la Ciudad de México
3. La playa de Cancún está en... en el Golfo de México
4. Algunos platos típicos de la comida mexicana son... los tamales, los tacos, el mole poblano
5. Frida Kahlo es... una pintora mexicana
6. Los mayas y los aztecas construyeron... pirámides

A PRIMERA VISTA

Las fiestas y las tradiciones

CD 4
Track 1

Estas **carretas adornadas** y sus dueños hicieron el **camino** para llegar a El Rocío, un pequeño pueblo de la provincia de Huelva, en el suroeste de España, donde está la Ermita (*Hermitage*) de la Virgen del Rocío. En el pueblo **se reúnen** cada año cerca de un millón de personas para celebrar la fiesta de la Virgen del Rocío.

El Día de los **Muertos**, también conocido como el Día de los **Difuntos**, se conmemora el 2 de noviembre. Mucha **gente** va al **cementerio** ese día o el día anterior para **recordar** y llevarles flores a sus familiares o amigos difuntos. Especialmente en México, los **preparativos** para el Día de los Muertos **comienzan** con mucha anterioridad y hay familias que pasan la noche del primero al 2 de noviembre **acompañando** a sus muertos en el cementerio, como se ve en esta foto tomada en Pátzcuaro.

Las fiestas y los bailes que se celebran en diversas partes del mundo ayudan a **mantener** las **costumbres** de los **antepasados**. La Diablada es uno de los **festivales** folclóricos con más colorido en Hispanoamérica. Se celebra durante el **carnaval** de Oruro en Bolivia y también en el norte de Chile y en otros países, entre ellos, Perú.

La música, el baile y la **alegría** reinan en los carnavales. Hay **desfiles** de **carrozas** y **comparsas** que bailan en las calles, muchas personas **se disfrazan** y todo el mundo **se divierte**. El **último** día de Carnaval es el martes antes del **comienzo** de la Cuaresma (*Lent*).

Esta es una de las **procesiones** de Semana Santa en Antigua, Guatemala. Esta ciudad fue la antigua capital de Guatemala y es famosa por su arquitectura colonial y las **maravillosas** alfombras que se hacen con flores, **semillas** y **aserrín** para el paso de las procesiones.

258

El Día de San Fermín, el 7 de julio, se inicia la **celebración** de los sanfermines en Pamplona, España. Esta celebración, que dura del 7 al 14 de julio, es famosa mundialmente por los encierros. Los jóvenes corren por las calles seguidos de los **toros**, hasta llegar a la plaza donde **encierran** a los toros y más tarde tienen lugar las **corridas**.

8-1 Definiciones. Asocie el nombre de la festividad en la columna de la izquierda con su descripción en la columna de la derecha.

1. __e__ San Fermín
2. __a__ La Diablada
3. __f__ El Rocío
4. __b__ Carnaval
5. __c__ El Día de los Muertos
6. __d__ Semana Santa

a. Se celebra durante el carnaval de Oruro en Bolivia. personas bailan en las calles disfrazadas de demonios.
b. Muchas personas se disfrazan y bailan en comparsas por las calles.
c. Todos van al cementerio a hacer ofrendas a los seres queridos que están muertos.
d. Hay procesiones por las calles y en Antigua, Guatemala, se hacen unas alfombras de aserrín, flores y semillas.
e. Los jóvenes corren por las calles delante de los toros.
f. Es una fiesta en el sur de España. La gente va en carretas hasta una ermita.

8-2 Describir las imágenes. PRIMERA FASE. Describan las fotos anteriores detalladamente contestando las siguientes preguntas.

1. ¿Qué están haciendo las personas en las fotos?
2. ¿Qué ropa llevan las personas? ¿Qué colores hay en las fotos?
3. ¿Qué objetos hay en las fotos? ¿Para qué sirven?
4. ¿Hay animales? ¿Qué hacen estos animales?
5. ¿Piensan que la festividad de la foto es religiosa? ¿Por qué?
6. Según ustedes, ¿es la festividad divertida? ¿Por qué?

SEGUNDA FASE. Elijan una de las fotos y descríbanla en un párrafo. Incluyan las ideas sobre las que conversaron en la *Primera fase*.

8-3 Contextos. PRIMERA FASE. Hablen sobre las ideas, sentimientos o costumbres que evocan las siguientes palabras.

MODELO: el carnaval
La palabra carnaval me hace pensar en música, baile, alegría, carrozas, desfiles, calles.

1. los cementerios
2. los toros
3. las flores
4. los disfraces
5. las alfombras de aserrín
6. el baile

SEGUNDA FASE. Elijan una de las palabras de la *Primera fase* y escriban una oración en la que la palabra aparezca en un contexto familiar para ustedes. Compartan esta oración con la clase.

MODELO: *Cuando visitamos a los amigos llevamos flores.*

Cultura

El Día de Acción de Gracias (*Thanksgiving*) no se celebra en los países hispanos y tampoco es tradicional el Día de las Brujas (*Halloween*), aunque empieza a celebrarse en algunas ciudades de Hispanoamérica y de España. Por otro lado, debido a la importancia e influencia de la religión católica en los países hispanos, algunas fiestas católicas se consideran también fiestas oficiales y son días feriados. Pero lo más importante es la gran diversidad de fiestas locales. Muchas personas trabajan todo el año para garantizar el éxito de estas celebraciones en las que la gente baila y se divierte durante días enteros.

Cultura

En muchos países hispanos, los niños reciben regalos de Papá Noel o del Niño Dios el día de Navidad. Sin embargo, la Nochebuena se considera el día más importante. Muchas personas van a la **iglesia** a la medianoche para asistir a la Misa del Gallo (*Midnight Mass*). El 6 de enero, día de la Epifanía, se celebra la llegada de los Reyes Magos con sus regalos para el Niño Jesús. La noche del 5 de enero, muchos niños se acuestan esperando la visita de los tres reyes que llegan montados en sus camellos con regalos para ellos.

Otras celebraciones

CD 4 Track 2

la Nochebuena · la Navidad · la Nochevieja · el Año Nuevo

el Día de la Independencia de México · la Pascua · el Día de la Madre

el Día del Padre · el Día de Acción de Gracias · el Día de las Brujas · el Día de los Enamorados/del Amor y la Amistad

8-4 Asociaciones. PRIMERA FASE. Asocie las fechas de la izquierda con los días festivos de la derecha.

1. _h_ el 25 de diciembre
2. _g_ el 2 de noviembre
3. _f_ el 6 de enero
4. _a_ el 4 de julio
5. _c_ el 24 de diciembre
6. _d_ el 31 de diciembre
7. _e_ el 14 de febrero
8. _b_ el 31 de octubre

a. el Día de la Independencia de Estados Unidos
b. el Día de las Brujas
c. la Nochebuena
d. la Nochevieja/el Fin de Año
e. el Día de los Enamorados/del Amor y la Amistad
f. el Día de los Reyes Magos
g. el Día de los Muertos
h. la Navidad

SEGUNDA FASE. Comenten entre ustedes las respuestas a las siguientes preguntas.

1. ¿Cuál(es) de estas fiestas celebra cada uno/a de ustedes?
2. ¿Cuál es la fiesta favorita de la mayoría de las personas del grupo, y por qué?
3. ¿En cuál de estas fiestas reciben regalos? ¿Qué tipo de regalos?
4. ¿En cuál de estas fiestas hay una comida especial?

8-5 Festivales o desfiles. Piense en algunos festivales o desfiles importantes y complete el cuadro. Su compañero/a va a hacerle preguntas sobre ellos.

MODELO: E1: *¿En qué fiesta o desfile importante estás pensando?*
E2: *En el Cinco de Mayo.*
E1: *¿Dónde lo celebran?*
E2: *En México y en algunas ciudades de Estados Unidos, como Austin, Texas.*

FESTIVAL O DESFILE	FECHA	LUGAR	DESCRIPCIÓN	OPINIÓN

8-6 Unos días festivos. Hablen sobre cómo celebran ustedes estas fechas.

MODELO: E1: *¿Cómo celebras tu cumpleaños?*
E2: *Lo celebro con mi familia y mis amigos. Recibo regalos, y mi madre prepara mi comida favorita con pastel de chocolate de postre. Después escuchamos música, conversamos y a veces bailamos.*

1. la Nochevieja/el Fin de Año
2. el Día de las Brujas
3. el Día de Acción de Gracias
4. el Día de la Independencia
5. el Año Nuevo
6. el Día de la Madre

8-7 Una celebración importante. PRIMERA FASE. Escojan una celebración importante del mundo hispano (Carnaval, Semana Santa, Año Nuevo, Las Posadas, La Diablada, Día de la Independencia, etc.) y busquen información en Internet sobre:

1. el lugar donde se celebra
2. la época del año
3. las actividades
4. los vestidos o disfraces
5. la comida

SEGUNDA FASE. Imagínese que usted y su compañero/a estuvieron en un país hispano durante la celebración que investigaron en la *Primera fase*. Explíquenles a otros/as dos compañeros/as cómo celebraron y qué pasó. Ellos les van a hacer preguntas para obtener más información.

El Cinco de Mayo es una fiesta que celebra la victoria de México contra Francia en la Batalla de Puebla en 1862. Ese día hay desfiles y los mexicanos visten sus trajes típicos.

Lengua

The words **fiesta**, **festividad**, and **festival** are often used interchangeably. **Fiesta** may mean a holiday or a party or celebration. **Festividad** normally refers to a public festivity or a holiday. **Festival** often involves a series of events or celebrations of a public nature. Another term for holiday is **día festivo**. **Día feriado** is a legal holiday.

⊗ **Standard 5.2** Students show evidence of becoming life-long learners by using the language for personal enjoyment and enrichment. This chapter, with its focus on Mexico, helps students make connections between their academic experience with Spanish and the many aspects of Mexican and Mexican-American culture in their daily life. There are Mexican restaurants, supermarket shelves dedicated to Mexican food items, and activities and products related to *Cinco de mayo* are increasingly available.

·)) Las invitaciones

CD 4
Track 3 **¿Quieres salir conmigo?**

LUISA: Hola, Arturo, ¿cómo estás?

ARTURO: Bien, Luisa, ¿y tú?

LUISA: Estupendamente. Mira, me gustaría **invitarte** a cenar conmigo el sábado. Es la ocasión perfecta para hablar de tu viaje a México.

ARTURO: La verdad es que me gustaría mucho, pero mañana no puedo porque tengo un partido de fútbol.

LUISA: ¡Qué lástima! ¿Y el domingo, día 15?

ARTURO: El domingo está bien. Si quieres, podemos **quedar** antes para **dar un paseo** por la ciudad. Las calles están adornadas para las fiestas, y la ciudad está muy **animada**.

LUISA: ¡Qué buena idea! Nos vemos en la plaza a las seis.

ARTURO: Bueno, pues nos vemos allí y luego decidimos adónde vamos a cenar.

LUISA: Gracias, Arturo, hasta el domingo.

ARTURO: Hasta el domingo.

En directo

To accept an invitation:

Gracias. Me encanta la idea.

Con mucho gusto.

Encantado/a.

Será un placer.
It will be a pleasure.

To apologize:

Me gustaría ir, pero…

¡Qué lástima/pena! Ese día tengo que…

No puedo, tengo un compromiso.
I can't, I have a prior engagement.

Warm-up for 8-8. Before students invite each other to attend events, model the activity with a proficient student. Encourage students to use the expressions presented.

👥👥 **8-8 Una invitación.** PRIMERA FASE. Completen el siguiente cuadro según la conversación de Luisa y Arturo.

FECHAS DE LAS INVITACIONES	EXPRESIONES QUE USA ARTURO
primera invitación:	para disculparse por no aceptar:
segunda invitación:	para aceptar la invitación:

SEGUNDA FASE. Ahora invite a su compañero/a a cenar, o a ir al teatro o a un partido importante. Después, su compañero/a va a invitarlo/la a usted. Pueden usar las expresiones del diálogo y de *En directo*.

Celebraciones personales

CD 4
Track 4

La boda del príncipe Felipe en mayo de 2004 fue un gran acontecimiento histórico y social en España y millones de hispanos pudieron ver por televisión. En los países hispanos, el padrino de la boda es la persona que acompaña a la novia al altar y generalmente es su padre. La madrina está en el altar con el novio y normalmente es su madre.

8-9 Una invitación de boda. Lean la invitación de boda y la de la recepción, y contesten las preguntas. Luego preparen una lista con las diferencias que encuentran ustedes entre estas invitaciones y las de su país.

Agradecemos su presencia
después de la ceremonia religiosa
en el Club de Golf Chapultepec
Av. Conscripto N° 425, Lomas
Hipódromo

R.S.V.P.
529-99-43
520-16-85

Personal

Pedro Martín Salda
Juana Montoya de Martín

Eduardo Calderón Solís
Elisa Noriega de Calderón

participan el matrimonio de sus hijos

Estelita
y
Alberto

y tienen el honor de invitarle a la ceremonia religiosa que se celebrará el viernes 9 de febrero, a las diecinueve treinta horas en el Convento de San Joaquín, Santa Cruz Cocalco N° 15, Legaria, dignándose impartir la bendición nupcial el R.P. José Ortuno S.J.
Ciudad de México

1. ¿Cómo se llaman los padres de la novia? ¿Y los del novio?
2. ¿Cómo se llaman los novios?
3. ¿Qué día es la boda?
4. ¿A qué hora es?
5. ¿En qué país se celebra esta boda?
6. ¿Adónde van a ir los invitados después de la ceremonia?

Cultura

La monarquía constitucional española es una de las más antiguas de Europa. Hoy en día la familia real es muy popular en el mundo hispano. El **rey** Juan Carlos I y la **reina** Sofía tienen tres hijos: Elena, Cristina y Felipe, Príncipe de Asturias y heredero del trono. En el 2004, el príncipe Felipe se casó con la periodista Letizia Ortiz. En la actualidad tienen dos hijas, Leonor y Sofía.

Cultura

Los mariachis son grupos musicales de México que cantan y tocan violines, guitarras, guitarrones, trompetas y vihuelas[1]. Muchos creen que la palabra *mariachi* viene del francés *mariage*, que significa *boda*. En la época colonial, el novio contrataba estas bandas para festejar a la novia la noche de la boda y, aún hoy en día, los grupos de mariachis participan en muchas bodas mexicanas. Otros opinan que el término *mariachi* proviene de una palabra indígena que designa la plataforma donde se paraban los músicos para tocar.

[1] *Guitarrón* is a large guitar; *vihuela* is an early form of this instrument.

Suggestion. You may want to point out that *el padrino* and *la madrina* are generally thought of as a part of Roman Catholic weddings and baptisms.

Follow-up for 8-9. Discuss other events students have attended. You may wish to point out the abbreviations: R.P. = *reverendo padre* and S.J. = *Sociedad de Jesús*.

Suggestion for 8-10. Mention that another special event in some (not all) Hispanic countries is *la quinceañera*, the celebration of a girl's fifteenth birthday. Newspaper announcements, invitations, and video clips can help explain the custom.

Warm-up for 8-12. As a prelistening activity, have students in groups of four share in Spanish what their favorite holidays are and narrate what they usually do on those days.

Audioscript for 8-12. Conversación 1.
MUJER: *¿Por qué hay tantos niños en la calle? Y están disfrazados.*
HOMBRE: *Hoy es una fiesta muy importante para los niños de Estados Unidos.*
MUJER: *¿Y qué hacen en la calle?*
HOMBRE: *Les piden caramelos a los vecinos.*

Conversación 2.
MUJER: *Ahora salgo para la iglesia y después voy al cementerio para llevarle flores a mi padre.*
HOMBRE: *¿Cuándo murió tu padre?*
MUJER: *En el año 91.*
HOMBRE: *¿Y haces esto todos los años?*
MUJER: *Sí, todos los años, por supuesto.*

Conversación 3.
MUJER: *¿Qué le vas a regalar a tu novia mañana?*
HOMBRE: *Todavía no sé. Quizás un perfume, un collar.*
MUJER: *¿Y van a salir por la noche?*
HOMBRE: *Bueno, es un día muy especial para los novios. La voy a invitar a su restaurante favorito.*

Conversación 4.
MUJER: *¿Qué te trajeron anoche?*
NIÑO: *Me trajeron una bicicleta. Yo les pedí muchas cosas, pero sólo me trajeron la bicicleta.*
MUJER: *Es que hay muchos niños en el mundo y ellos tienen que llevarles regalos a todos.*

 8-10 Una ocasión memorable. Lean la invitación y contesten las preguntas.

Nuestro querido hijo

David

será llamado a la lectura de la Tora
con motivo de su Bar Mitzvah
el jueves 18 de noviembre
a las ocho de la mañana en la Sinagoga
Centro Hebreo, Avenida 13-15 Zona 9.

Nos sentiremos muy honrados en compartir
con ustedes tan memorable ocasión
y será un placer recibirles en el desayuno
que seguidamente ofreceremos en el
salón de fiestas de la sinagoga.

David y Ruth Bauman
Fax: (502) 238-2042
Ciudad de Guatemala, Guatemala

1. ¿Cuál es el motivo de la celebración?
2. ¿Qué día es la celebración? ¿A qué hora?
3. ¿Hay otra actividad, además de la celebración religiosa?
4. ¿Quiénes son David y Ruth Bauman?
5. ¿En qué país tiene lugar esta celebración?

8-11 Una fiesta especial. PRIMERA FASE. Piense en una celebración o fiesta en la que usted participó recientemente. Escriba algunas notas sobre lo siguiente:

1. ¿Cuál es el nombre de la fiesta?
2. ¿Dónde se celebró? ¿Cuántos invitados asistieron?
3. Describa la comida que sirvieron.
4. ¿Cómo se divirtió la gente? ¿Tocaron música?
5. ¿Gastaron mucho los anfitriones (*hosts*)?

 SEGUNDA FASE. Ahora explíquense los detalles de esta fiesta. Incluyan detalles de la *Primera fase.*

8-12 Identificar la fiesta. You will listen to four short dialogues about different holidays celebrated in the Hispanic world. Before you listen, write down the names of two holidays that you have studied or read about in this chapter.

CD 4 Track 5

Pay attention to the general idea of what is said. As you listen, identify the holiday each conversation refers to by writing the appropriate conversation number next to it.

  3   el Día del Amor y la Amistad/Día de los Enamorados
  2   el Día de los Muertos
  4   el Día de los Reyes Magos
  1   el Día de las Brujas

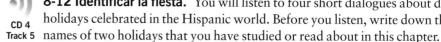

EN ACCIÓN

Resources
- Video
- SAM: 8-11 to 8-13

Diarios de bicicleta: La ponchera

Antes de ver

8-13 En este segmento, Marcos, Luciana y Javier están organizando una fiesta de cumpleaños para Gabi. Escriba cinco preguntas para averiguar si todo está listo para la fiesta. Answers may vary.

MODELO: *¿Hicieron el pastel de cumpleaños?*

Suggestion for 8-13. You may wish to have students describe what they see in the images.

Mientras ve

8-14 Indique si las siguientes afirmaciones se refieren a Marcos (**M**), a Luciana (**L**) o a Javier (**J**).

1. __L__ Quería hacer un pastel de cumpleaños.
2. __M__ Invitó a toda la gente.
3. __M, J__ Pusieron la mesa.
4. __J__ Dejó caer (*dropped*) la ponchera.

Después de ver

8-15 Responda a las siguientes preguntas.

1. ¿Cuándo recibió la ponchera la mamá de Luciana y Marcos? La recibió para su boda.
2. Según Marcos, ¿quién rompió la ponchera? Según Marcos, Luciana la rompió.
3. Según su hermana, ¿de quién fue la culpa? Según Luciana, fue la culpa de Marcos.
4. ¿Quién le dijo la verdad a la mamá? Javier le dijo la verdad a la mamá.

FUNCIONES Y FORMAS

1. Expressing ongoing actions and descriptions in the past: The imperfect

ABUELA: **Antes** la música **era** suave y romántica. **Tenía** más melodía y las orquestas **eran** magníficas. **Hoy en día** no **hay** música, sólo ruido, y a la gente **no le interesa** bailar.

NANCY: **Antes** las familias **cenaban** juntas. **Conversaban** mientras **comían**, y los hijos **se aburrían** (*got bored*) mucho. **¡Era** una tortura! **Ahora** es mucho mejor. Cuando **tengo** hambre, **preparo** algo para comer. Además, los padres no **controlan** tanto la vida de sus hijos.

Piénselo. Indique (✓) a qué función se refiere cada afirmación.

ACTIVIDAD	DESCRIPCIÓN EN EL PASADO	ACCIÓN O DESCRIPCIÓN HABITUAL EN EL PASADO	ACCIÓN EN EL PRESENTE
1. La música del pasado **tenía** más melodía.	✓		
2. Hoy en día no **hay** música.			✓
3. Antes las familias **cenaban** juntas.		✓	
4. Los hijos **se aburrían** mucho.		✓	
5. Cuando **tengo** hambre, **preparo** algo para comer.			✓
6. Los padres no **controlan** tanto la vida de sus hijos.			✓

- You have already learned to use the preterit to talk about actions in the past. In these scenes, the grandmother and granddaughter use a different past tense, the **imperfect**, because they are focusing on how things used to be and what usually took place 50 or 60 years ago. If they were talking about a specific completed action, like something they did yesterday, they would use the preterit. Generally, the imperfect is used to:

- express habitual or repeated actions in the past (without focus on the completion of the action).

Nosotros **íbamos** a casa para cenar todos los días a las seis.

We used to go home to eat dinner every day at six o'clock.

■ express an action or state that was in progress in the past (not whether the action or state was completed).

Todos los invitados **hablaban** y **bailaban**. **Estaban** muy contentos.	*All the guests were talking and dancing. They were very happy.*

■ describe characteristics and conditions in the past.

El desfile **era** muy largo y **había** muchos espectadores.	*The parade was very long and there were many spectators.*

■ tell time in the past.

Era la una de la tarde; no **eran** las dos.	*It was one in the afternoon; it was not two.*

■ express a person's age in the past.

Ella **tenía** quince años entonces.	*She was fifteen years old then.*

■ Some expressions of time and frequency that often accompany the imperfect to express ongoing or repeated actions or states in the past are **mientras, a veces, siempre, generalmente,** and **frecuentemente.**

IMPERFECT			
	HABLAR	**COMER**	**VIVIR**
yo	habl**aba**	com**ía**	viv**ía**
tú	habl**aba**s	com**ía**s	viv**ía**s
Ud., él, ella	habl**aba**	com**ía**	viv**ía**
nosotros/as	habl**ába**mos	com**ía**mos	viv**ía**mos
vosotros/as	habl**aba**is	com**ía**is	viv**ía**is
Uds., ellos/as	habl**aba**n	com**ía**n	viv**ía**n

■ Note that the endings for **-er** and **-ir** verbs are the same and have a written accent over the **í** of the ending.

■ The Spanish imperfect has several English equivalents.

Mis amigos **bailaban** mucho.

> *My friends danced a lot.*
> *My friends were dancing a lot.*
> *My friends used to dance a lot.*
> *My friends would dance a lot.*
> (implying a repeated action)

■ There are no stem changes in the imperfect.

Ella no d**ue**rme bien ahora, pero antes d**o**rmía muy bien.	*She does not sleep well now, but she used to sleep very well before.*

Note. Compare these time expressions to those related to the preterit: *ayer, una vez, la semana pasada, de repente.*

Note. Point out that the *yo, él, ella, usted* forms of the imperfect are identical. Context determines the meaning, but subject pronouns may be used for clarity.

Suggestions. Bring photos to class or assign students to bring in photos and ask: *¿Qué hacía/hacías/hacían cuando tomaron esta foto?* to preview imperfect/preterit contrast. Allow students to guess what was happening in the photos before you tell them.

Suggestion. Present the preterit form *hubo* and explain to students that it is most often used in recounting sudden events, e.g., *hubo un accidente, hubo un tornado.*

Follow-up for 8-16. Students share information in groups of four. One student reports to the class what activities they all used to do.

Suggestion for 8-17. Students should add to the chart an additional activity that they used to do very often and one they did infrequently.

Follow-up for 8-17. Find out which activities the whole class enjoyed most and least.

■ Only three verbs are irregular in the imperfect.

ir iba, ibas, iba, íbamos, ibais, iban

ser era, eras, era, éramos, erais, eran

ver veía, veías, veía, veíamos, veíais, veían

■ The imperfect form of **hay** is **había** (*there was, there were, there used to be*). It is invariable.

Había una invitación en el correo.	*There was an invitation in the mail.*
Había muchas personas en la fiesta.	*There were many people at the party.*

8-16 Cuando tenía cinco años. Marque (✓) cuáles eran sus actividades cuando usted tenía cinco años.

1. _____ Jugaba en el parque con mi perro.
2. _____ Ayudaba a mi mamá en la casa, especialmente cuando teníamos invitados.
3. _____ Salía con mis padres los fines de semana.
4. _____ Iba a la playa en el verano.
5. _____ Veía televisión hasta muy tarde.
6. _____ Celebraba el Año Nuevo con mis amigos.
7. _____ Asistía a las fiestas de la familia.
8. ...

 8-17 En mi escuela secundaria. PRIMERA FASE. Marque (✓) la frecuencia con que usted y sus amigos/as hacían estas cosas. Luego compare sus respuestas con las de su compañero/a.

MODELO: decorar los salones de clase
Frecuentemente decorábamos los salones de clase.

ACTIVIDADES	SIEMPRE	FRECUENTEMENTE	A VECES	NUNCA
hablar sobre las competencias deportivas en las clases				
organizar reuniones para aumentar el espíritu de la escuela (*pep rallies*)				
ir a los partidos de fútbol y otros deportes				
asistir a conciertos y obras de teatro				
participar en un equipo, en la banda, etc.				
otra actividad				

 SEGUNDA FASE. Hablen de los siguientes temas.

1. ¿Cuáles eran las tradiciones en su escuela para celebrar y aumentar el espíritu de equipo (*team spirit*) que realizaban con más frecuencia?
2. ¿Cuáles eran sus actividades favoritas?

8-18 El apagón (blackout). El sábado pasado los señores Herrera organizaron una fiesta en su casa. Desafortunadamente durante la fiesta hubo un apagón en su barrio. Basándose en el dibujo escriba un párrafo para explicar lo que hacían las personas cuando se fue la luz.

8-19 Mi casa. Descríbale a su compañero/a cómo era la casa o apartamento donde usted vivía cuando era niño/a. Después, su compañero/a debe hacer lo mismo.

8-20 Las fiestas infantiles. Comenten cómo eran las fiestas de cumpleaños cuando ustedes eran pequeños/as. Incluyan los siguientes puntos:

1. lugar de la celebración
2. horas (comienzo y final)
3. dos o tres actividades que hacían
4. personas que participaban
5. comida y bebida que servían
6. ropa que llevaban

8-21 Antes y ahora. Expliquen cómo era la vida antes y cómo es ahora con respecto a los siguientes temas:

1. la familia (tamaño, grado de movilidad, porcentaje de divorcios)
2. la mujer en la sociedad (participación en el mundo del trabajo/de la política, su independencia económica)
3. las ciudades (tamaño, los problemas ambientales (*environmental*) como la contaminación, la delincuencia, el crimen)

En directo

To talk about how things used to be:

Entonces…

Por aquel entonces…

En aquellos tiempos…

SITUACIONES

1. **Role A.** You are a famous public figure (a singer, professor, scientist, athlete, etc.) being interviewed by a television reporter. Offer as many details about your background as possible.

   Role B. You are interviewing a famous person for a television program. Ask a) what his/her family life and hometown were like when he/she was young; b) the type of music he/she used to listen to; c) the books he/she used to read; d) the holidays he/she celebrated most.

2. **Role A.** You are an exchange student and would like to find out about your host's weekend and summer activities when he/she was in high school. Ask a) what activites there were for high school students in his/her community, b) what he/she generally did on Saturday evenings and with whom; and c) what he/she usually did in the summer.

   Role B. You are the host of an exchange student. Answer his/her questions about your weekend and summer activities when you were in high school. Describe a summer trip to a friend's house in Guadalajara, Mexico, and say that you a) spoke Spanish every day; b) went to the outdoor markets often; c) listened to the mariachis very often; and d) used to eat excellent Mexican food every day.

Follow-up for 8-18. Have students share their descriptions with the class.

Follow-up for 8-19. Ask students to describe their childhood memories of grandparents, parents, or other relatives. Starting with a phrase like *Cuando era niño/a, mi abuelo/a vivía/era…*, etc., anchors the descriptions in the past (imperfect), rather than in the present.

Variation for 8-19. Give students names of famous people and ask for descriptions, using verbs such as *era, vivía, se dedicaba a, pintaba, and escribía* (Frida Kahlo, William Shakespeare, Simón Bolívar, George Washington).

Suggestion for 8-20. Ask students what holiday or other event was celebrated most in their families. Have them talk about that holiday with their partner.

Suggestion for 8-21. Each group may choose the era they want to compare with today (e.g., ancient/colonial times, the 1960s). After they discuss the various topics, groups should share their opinions with the class.

Suggestion for Situaciones. Encourage students to use the imperfect tense preceded by the expressions listed in *En directo* to describe what used to happen in the past.

Suggestion for Piénselo.
Explain that the events move the story forward in time, and that the background information gives interesting and important details to flesh out the story, but does not advance the action. Ask students to identify the preterit and imperfect forms in the story and help them see that the preterit recounts the events and the imperfect gives information about context and characters.

Suggestion. Create a brief narration to exemplify the use of both tenses or use the following: *Juan y su hermano Carlos fueron a Sonora, México, para pasar el verano con la familia de su padre. Sus tíos tenían una casita en la playa. El lugar era muy bonito. Las playas eran tranquilas y no había muchos turistas. Todos los días se levantaban a las ocho más o menos, desayunaban y se iban a pescar y a conversar con sus primos. Por la tarde, nadaban o hacían buceo y se reunían con sus amigos mexicanos. Pasaron las últimas dos semanas en la ciudad de Hermosillo. En Hermosillo salían por las noches y bailaban mucho en los clubes. Su último día fue muy triste para todos. Almorzaron con sus tíos y sus primos y después todos los llevaron al aeropuerto. Fue un verano maravilloso para estos chicos.*

2. Narrating in the past: The preterit and the imperfect

Había una vez una chica que **vivía** con su padre, porque su madre **estaba** muerta. La chica **se llamaba** Cenicienta. **Era** muy bella y muy buena, y todos los vecinos la **querían** mucho. Pero un día, su vida **cambió**. Su padre **se casó** con una mujer muy mala que **tenía** dos hijas. La mujer y sus hijas **vinieron** a vivir a la casa de Cenicienta. Las hijas **eran** muy crueles y **odiaban** (*hated*) a Cenicienta, su hermanastra…

Piénselo. Lea las afirmaciones y marque (✓) su función en el cuento: contar los eventos, o dar información de fondo (*background information*) sobre el contexto o los personajes.

	CONTAR LOS EVENTOS	DAR INFORMACIÓN DE FONDO
1. La chica **se llamaba** Cenicienta.		✓
2. **Era** muy bella y muy buena.		✓
3. Todos los vecinos la **querían** mucho.		✓
4. Pero un día, su vida **cambió**.	✓	
5. Su padre **se casó** con una mujer muy mala.	✓	
6. La mujer y sus hijas **vinieron** a vivir a la casa de Cenicienta.	✓	

■ The preterit and the imperfect are not interchangeable. They fulfill different functions when telling a story or talking about an event in the past.

■ Use the preterit:

1. to express a sequence of actions completed in the past (note that there is a forward movement of narrative time).

Oyeron un ruido, se **levantaron**, y **bajaron** las escaleras.	*They heard a noise, got up, and went downstairs.*

2. to talk about the beginning or end of an event, action, or condition.

Pepito **leyó** a los cinco años.	*Pepito read (began to read) at age five.*
El niño **se enfermó** el sábado.	*The child got sick (became sick) on Saturday.*
Pepito **leyó** el cuento.	*Pepito read (finished) the story.*
El niño **estuvo** enfermo ayer.	*The child was sick yesterday (and is no longer sick).*

3. to talk about an event, action, or condition that occurred over a specified period of time.

Vivieron en México por diez años.	*They lived in Mexico for ten years.*

■ Use the imperfect:

1. to talk about customary or habitual actions, events, or conditions in the past.

Todos los días **llovía** y por eso **leíamos** mucho.	*It used to rain every day, and that's why we read a lot.*

2. to express an ongoing part of an event, action, or condition.

En ese momento **llovía** mucho y los niños **estaban** muy tristes.	*At that moment it was raining a lot, and the children were very sad.*

■ In a story, the imperfect provides the background information, whereas the preterit tells what happened. Frequently an action or situation (expressed with the imperfect) is ongoing when something else (expressed with the preterit) suddenly happens.

Era Navidad. Todos **dormíamos** cuando los niños **oyeron** un ruido en el techo.	*It was Christmas. All of us were sleeping when the children heard a noise on the roof.*

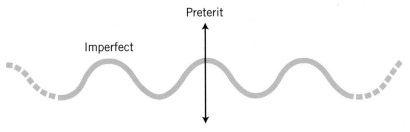

8-22 ¡Qué día más malo! Ayer iba a ser un día especial para Pedro, pero sus planes terminaron mal. Marque (✓) las tres cosas más graves que le ocurrieron a Pedro mientras trataba de realizar sus planes.

1. _____ Mientras se bañaba temprano por la mañana, se cayó en el baño.

2. _____ Mientras desayunaba tranquilamente, el teléfono sonó y no pudo terminar de comer.

3. _____ Iba a la tienda para comprarle un anillo a su novia cuando alguien le robó el dinero.

4. _____ Mientras llamaba por teléfono a un restaurante para reservar una mesa, el restaurante se incendió.

5. _____ Iba a proponerle matrimonio a su novia cuando su ex-novia lo llamó por teléfono.

6. _____ Mientras preparaba una cena deliciosa para celebrar el cumpleaños de su novia, el perro se comió el pastel.

8-23 La última vez. Túrnense para preguntarse cuándo fue la última vez que cada uno de ustedes hizo estas cosas y cómo se sentía mientras las hacía.

MODELO: ver un partido de béisbol
        E1: *¿Cuándo fue la última vez que viste un partido de béisbol?*
        E2: *Vi un partido de béisbol la semana pasada.*
        E1: *¿Y cómo te sentías mientras veías el partido?*
        E2: *Estaba aburrido/a, porque no me gusta mucho el béisbol.*

1. participar en un campeonato
2. ganar un premio
3. estar en un desfile
4. disfrazarse
5. bailar en un carnaval
6. …

Suggestion for 8-22. You may wish to have students share their responses with another pair. Alternatively, you may have the whole class compare their responses and defend their choices.

Suggestion for 8-23. Recycle *sentirse* in the context of a situation or story. Example: say how you reacted to hearing bad/good news: *Cuando escuché la noticia del accidente me sentí muy mal. Fue un accidente terrible y no pude dormir esa noche.* Then say how you were feeling later. *Por la mañana todavía me sentía mal y llamé a mi mejor amiga.*

Note. You may want to point out that *ver* uses the same preterit endings as other *-er* verbs but the *yo* and *usted/él/ella* forms do not have an accent mark.

Compradores en un mercado de Mérida.

8-24 Una visita al mercado. Imagínese que usted fue de compras a un mercado al aire libre de Mérida y ahora le cuenta a un amigo/una amiga lo que pasó. Complete las oraciones usando el imperfecto del verbo en la primera columna y el pretérito del verbo en la segunda columna.

MODELO: Ser las once cuando...
Eran las once cuando llegué al mercado.

1. Caminar al mercado cuando...	ver unas botellas bonitas
2. Mirar las botellas cuando...	hablarme la vendedora
3. Probarse un cinturón de cuero cuando...	empezar a llover
4. Ser las dos de la tarde cuando...	ver a mi amigo José
5. Tomar un café para escapar de la lluvia cuando...	(nosotros) volver al mercado para hacer nuestras compras

 8-25 Un cuento. Completen esta narración usando el pretérito o el imperfecto.

En el mes de abril del año pasado mi familia y yo (1) __fuimos__ (ir) a México de vacaciones. Primero nosotros (2) __estuvimos__ (estar) en Ciudad de México por dos días. Allí (3) __vimos__ (ver) a unos parientes y (4) __visitamos__ (visitar) lugares muy interesantes, como el Museo Nacional de Antropología, donde (5) __pudimos__ (poder) admirar una excelente colección de objetos de la cultura azteca, y a las tiendas de la Zona Rosa, donde mi mamá (6) __compró__ (comprar) unas blusas preciosas.

En la mañana del tercer día, nosotros (7) __nos fuimos__ (irse) a Iztapalapa, que está bastante cerca de la capital. (8) __Hacía__ (Hacer) un tiempo fabuloso. Como (9) __era__ (ser) primavera, muchos árboles y plantas (10) __tenían__ (tener) flores, y todo (11) __estaba__ (estar) muy verde. Nosotros (12) __salimos__ (salir) del hotel cerca de las cinco de la tarde y poco después (13) __llegamos__ (llegar) a una plaza donde (14) __había__ (haber) mucha gente. Allí (15) __vimos__ (ver) las procesiones de la Semana Santa. El ambiente (16) __era__ (ser) impresionante; las personas (17) __llevaban__ (llevar) túnicas largas y (18) __caminaban__ (caminar) lentamente por la calle. ¡Nunca vamos a olvidar esa experiencia!

 8-26 Un evento inolvidable. Cuéntele a su compañero/a algo inesperado que le ocurrió el año pasado. Indique qué pasó, dónde y cuándo. Describa la escena y los personajes.

SITUACIONES

1. **Role A.** Tell your friend about your nephew's first birthday party, which you attended recently.

   Role B. Your friend is going to tell you about his/her nephew's first birthday party. Ask a) where the party took place; b) who went to the party; c) what people did; and d) how the little boy reacted to all the attention.

2. **Role A.** You have just come back from a vacation in Mexico. Tell your classmate about a particular place you visited. Explain what it was like and what you did there.

   Role B. Your classmate has just returned from a vacation to Mexico. Ask about a particular place he/she visited while there. Find out a) what the place looked liked; b) what he/she did there; c) what special event he/she can tell you about.

3. Comparing people and things: Comparisons of inequality

Resources

■ SAM: 8-25 to 8-30
■ Supp. Activ. Book: Comparisons of inequality

Número de días del Carnaval de la Primavera	3	2
Asistencia del público	25.390	18.864
Mujeres	6.000	2.000
Hombres	4.000	5.000
Niños	25.000	27.000
puesto (Budget)	150.000.,000	180.000.,000

Para planificar el Carnaval de la Primavera debemos mirar las estadísticas de los años recientes. ¿Vamos a celebrar el carnaval **más de** dos días? En el año 2008, la asistencia fue **mayor que** la del 2009. En el 2008, había **más** mujeres **que** hombres, pero en el 2009 participaron **menos** mujeres **que** en el año anterior. Para tener un **mejor** carnaval **que** en años anteriores, vamos a necesitar **más** dinero **que** en los años pasados.

Note. The structure of comparisons in Spanish is similar to that of English. Students will find this grammar point easier than many others in *Mosaicos*. You may wish to focus on the irregular comparatives (see next page), as well as on high-frequency comparison, such as *A + verb + mejor que B* and *Me gusta más + infinitive + que + infinitive*.

Piénselo. Indique si las siguientes afirmaciones son ciertas (**C**), falsas (**F**) o posibles (**P**), según las estadísticas.

1. __C__ En el año 2009 había **menos** participación del público **que** en el 2008.
2. __F__ En el año 2009 participaron **menos** niños **que** adultos en el carnaval.
3. __C__ Los organizadores probablemente gastaron **más** dinero en el año 2009 **que** en el 2008.
4. __P__ En el futuro el carnaval va a durar **más de** dos días.
5. __P__ En el futuro, los carnavales van a ser **mejores que** los del pasado.

■ Use **más... que** or **menos... que** to express comparisons of inequality with nouns, adjectives, and adverbs.

COMPARISONS OF INEQUALITY		
Cuando Alina era joven tenía { **más** / **menos** } amigos que Pepe.	When Alina was young she had { *more* / *fewer* } friends than Pepe.	
Ella era { **más** / **menos** } activa que él.	She was { *more* / *less* } active than he.	
Salía { **más** / **menos** } frecuentemente que él.	She went out { *more* / *less* } frequently than he.	

■ Use **de** instead of **que** before numbers.

En el año 2008, había **más de** diez carrozas en el desfile.

*In 2008, there were **more than** ten floats in the parade.*

El año pasado había **menos de** diez carrozas.

*Last year there were **fewer than** ten floats.*

Suggestions for 8-27. Point to the location of Veracruz and Mérida on a map. You may mention that Mérida was chosen as *la Capital Americana de la Cultura* in 2000 by the *Organización Capital Americana de la Cultura*, an organization of Latin American nations that selects one city each year for this designation. Recycle weather expressions by asking students to guess what the weather is like in these cities. Ask them to compare the weather in Veracruz and Mérida with that of their own city: *En invierno, ¿hace más o menos frío en Mérida que en su ciudad? ¿Dónde hace menos humedad, en su ciudad o en Veracruz? ¿Dónde es peor el clima durante el período de huracanes, en Veracruz o en su ciudad?*

Suggestion for 8-27 Segunda fase. You may wish to check (or ask students to check) the exchange rate between the American dollar and the Mexican *peso* so students have a better understanding of costs per person.

Suggestion. You may wish to tell students that the coat of arms that appears on Mexican coins and bills is the national symbol that also appears on the flag. The coat of arms was inspired by the Aztec legend about the founding of Tenochtitlan. According to the legend, the war god Huitzilopochtli had commanded the Aztec people to build their capital at the spot where they found an eagle perched on a prickly pear cactus (*nopal*) growing on a rock submerged in a lake. The eagle would have a snake trapped in its mouth that it had just caught. After two hundred years of wandering, they found the promised sign on a small island in the swampy Lake Texcoco. Here they founded their new capital, Tenochtitlán, which was later known as Mexico City.

Cultura

Veracruz y Mérida son dos ciudades mexicanas importantes. Veracruz, que está a 400 kilómetros (250 millas) al sureste de la Ciudad de México, fue fundada por el conquistador Hernán Cortés en 1519. Por su puerto, que es el más importante del país, Veracruz es conocida como *la puerta al mundo*.

Mérida es la ciudad principal del estado de Yucatán, en el sureste del país. Está a más de 1.550 kilómetros (965 millas) de la capital. En 2000 Mérida fue nombrada *la Capital Americana de la Cultura* a causa de su calidad de vida y su extraordinario desarrollo en las artes.

Cultura

La moneda mexicana es el peso. Tanto en los billetes como en las monedas de metal está el escudo nacional, que tiene una águila parada sobre un nopal (un tipo de cacto) que está devorando a una serpiente. ¿Sabe usted cuál es la tasa de cambio (*exchange rate*) entre el peso mexicano y el dólar estadounidense?

■ The following adjectives have both regular and irregular comparative forms.

bueno/a	más bueno/a o mejor	*better*
malo/a	más malo/a o peor[1]	*worse*
pequeño/a	más pequeño/a o menor	*smaller*
joven	más joven o menor	*younger*
grande	más grande o mayor	*bigger*
viejo/a	más viejo/a o mayor[2]	*older*

Esta banda es $\left\{ \begin{array}{l} \textbf{mejor} \\ \textbf{peor} \end{array} \right\}$ que aquella. *This band is* $\left\{ \begin{array}{l} better \\ worse \end{array} \right\}$ *than that one.*

■ **Bien** and **mal** are adverbs. They have the same irregular comparative forms as the adjectives **bueno** and **malo**.

bien → mejor   Yo canto **mejor** que Héctor.   *I sing better than Héctor.*

mal → peor   Héctor canta **peor** que yo.   *Héctor sings worse than I.*

8-27 Comparación de dos desfiles. PRIMERA FASE. Lea la siguiente información sobre dos desfiles mexicanos, uno de Veracruz y el otro de Mérida. Complete las frases con **más que, menos que, más de** o **menos de**, según la información en la tabla.

	VERACRUZ	MÉRIDA
habitantes	444.438	649.770
promedio (*average*) de público que participa	14.000 personas	12.000 personas
número de bandas	8	6
número de policías	200	175

1. Mérida tiene ___más___ habitantes ___que___ Veracruz.
2. ___Más___ personas asisten al desfile de Veracruz ___que___ al desfile de Mérida.
3. Los dos desfiles tienen ___más___ ___de___ cinco bandas.
4. Mérida gasta ___menos___ dinero en seguridad (*security*) ___que___ Veracruz.
5. ___Menos___ ___de___ medio millón de personas viven en Veracruz.
6. Probablemente el público de Mérida es ___menos___ entusiasta ___que___ el de Veracruz.

SEGUNDA FASE. La banda de su universidad piensa participar en uno de estos desfiles, pero no puede gastar mucho dinero. Con la información de la *Primera fase* y la que aparece a continuación, decidan a qué desfile debe asistir. Expliquen por qué.

COSTO POR PERSONA	DESFILE DE VERACRUZ	DESFILE DE MERIDA
transporte	5.824,50 pesos	6.552,60 pesos
hotel por día	880,50 pesos	915,25 pesos
comidas por día	450,00 pesos	348,00 pesos

---

[1]**Más bueno/a** and **más malo/a** are not used interchangeably with **mejor** and **peor**. **Más bueno/a** and **más malo/a** refer to a person's moral qualities. **Mejor** and **peor** refer to skills and abilities.

[2]Use **mayor** to refer to a person's age. **Más viejo/a** is generally used with nouns other than people.

8-28 Las alfombras de aserrín. Los artesanos de Guatemala hacen alfombras de aserrín para celebrar la Semana Santa. Comparen las dos alfombras según los siguientes criterios. Pueden usar estas expresiones u otras.

Suggestion for 8-28. Remind students to use the appropriate form of the adjectives in doing this activity. After students do the activity, you may want to have each pair compare its reactions with that of another pair.

colores fuertes	corto	figuras	rectangular
colores suaves	diseño	imágenes	simple
colorido	elaborado	largo	sofisticado

1. el tamaño
2. los colores
3. el estilo
4. su preferencia por una de las alfombras

A.

B.

8-29 Personas famosas. Compare a las siguientes personas. Considere lo siguiente.

1. su aspecto físico
2. su edad
3. el tipo de trabajo que hacen
4. el dinero o popularidad que tienen

Brad Pitt

Salma Hayek en el papel de Frida Kahlo en la película *Frida*

SITUACIONES

1. **Role A.** You and your fiancé/fiancée disagree about wedding plans. You prefer small weddings. Try to persuade your groom/bride by comparing small and large weddings with regard to: a) expenses (**gastos**); b) stress (**estrés**); c) work involved; and d) possible problems.

   Role B. You and your fiancé/fiancée are planning your wedding. You prefer big weddings. Listen to the opinions of your fiancé/fiancée and try to come to an agreement.

2. **Role A.** You are a student government representative presenting a proposal to the dean to change the graduation ceremony. Compare the ceremony at your school with one at a rival institution. Say that the other ceremony is better because it is smaller, better organized, less expensive, and usually has better music and speeches (**discursos**).

   Role B. You are the dean. A student government representative is proposing changes in the graduation ceremony. Listen to the presentation and ask questions to compare the advantages of both types of ceremonies.

Resources
■ SAM: 8-31 to 8-34
■ Supp. Activ. Book:
  Comparison of equality

Suggestion. You may wish to use the drawing to review comparisons of inequality by asking students to make comparisons between people at the meeting, e.g., *La presidenta del comité organizador trabaja más que los otros miembros del comité.*

Follow-up for Piénselo. After students have learned to produce comparisons of equality, you may wish to return to *Piénselo* and have them correct the *Improbable* statement (#2) and then think of additional statements based on the short presentation.

4. Comparing people and things: Comparisons of equality

PRESIDENTA DEL COMITÉ ORGANIZADOR: Este año tuvimos un Carnaval de Primavera **tan** espectacular **como** el de 2008, que hasta este año era nuestro carnaval más grande. En los tres días del carnaval asistió **tanto** público **como** en el año 2008, un total de 25.400 personas. Además, los grupos musicales tocaron música **tan** buena **como** la música del carnaval de 2008. También el número de bailarines se mantuvo igual. Hubo **tantos** bailarines **como** en el 2008. Estoy muy agradecida de ustedes porque colaboraron **tanto como** en otros años. Vamos a planificar el carnaval del próximo año **tan bien como** el de este año.

Piénselo. Indique si las siguientes afirmaciones interpretan correcta (**C**) o incorrectamente (**I**) la información que dio la Presidenta del Comité Organizador.

1. _C_ En 2008 asistieron unas 25.400 personas al carnaval y este año asistió el mismo número de personas.
2. _I_ Este año los grupos musicales tocaron música que al público le gustó **menos que** en otros años.
3. _C_ Este año el Comité Organizador hizo un trabajo **tan bueno como** el trabajo de otros años.
4. _C_ La planificación del carnaval fue buena este año y la del próximo año va ser buena también.

■ In the previous section you learned to express comparisons of inequality. In this section you will learn how to indicate that two people, things, or activities are equal in some way.

COMPARISONS OF EQUALITY	
tan... como	*as ... as*
tanto/a... como	*as much ... as*
tantos/as... como	*as many ... as*
tanto como	*as much as*

■ Use **tan... como** to express comparisons of equality with adjectives and adverbs.

La boda fue **tan** elegante **como** la fiesta.	*The wedding was as elegant as the party.*
El padre bailó **tan** bien **como** su hija.	*The father danced as well as his daughter.*

■ Use **tanto/a... como** and **tantos/as... como** to express comparisons of equality with nouns.

| Había **tanta** alegría **como** en el Carnaval. | *There was as much joy as at Mardi Gras.* |
| Había **tantos** invitados **como** en mi fiesta de graduación. | *There were as many guests as at my graduation party.* |

■ Use **tanto como** to express comparisons of equality with verbs.

| Los invitados bailaron **tanto como** nosotros. | *The guests danced as much as we did.* |

8-30 Cuatro estudiantes afortunados.

Lean algunos datos personales sobre cuatro estudiantes. Luego, indiquen si las afirmaciones a continuación son ciertas (**C**) o falsas (**F**). Si son falsas (**F**), corrijan la información.

	PEDRO	VILMA	MARTA	RICARDO
hermanos	2	3	3	2
clases	5	5	4	6
dinero para gastos personales cada mes	5.000 pesos	8.500 pesos	5.000 pesos	8.500 pesos
películas en DVD	200	180	180	215
viajes a otros países	3	8	3	8

1. _F_ Pedro tiene **tantos** hermanos **como** Vilma.
2. _F_ Vilma tomó **tantas** clases este semestre **como** Ricardo.
3. _C_ La familia de Marta es **tan** grande **como** la familia de Vilma.
4. _C_ Cada mes, Ricardo recibe **tanto** dinero de sus padres **como** Vilma.
5. _F_ Marta probablemente gasta **más** dinero en películas **que** Vilma.
6. _F_ La familia de Pedro viaja **tanto como** la familia de Ricardo.

8-31 Sus opiniones. PRIMERA FASE. Haga lo siguiente.

1. Escriba los nombres de dos celebridades en su cultura.
2. Escriba los nombres de dos festividades o desfiles que se realizan en su ciudad, región o país.
3. Escriba dos programas cómicos de la televisión.

SEGUNDA FASE. Ahora, expresen su opinión y comparen los nombres que escribieron en la *Primera fase.* Usen la información dada y modifiquen los adjetivos cuando sea necesario.

MODELO: Tom Cruise y Johnny Depp: calidad de su trabajo (bueno/a, mediocre, malo/a)
E1: *Tom Cruise es tan buen actor como Johnny Depp.*
E2: *Sí, estoy de acuerdo. O: No, Johnny Depp es mejor actor que Tom Cruise.*

1. Dos celebridades: apariencia física, calidad de su trabajo (atractivo, alto, famoso, bueno...)
2. Dos desfiles o celebraciones locales o nacionales: número de personas, carrozas (divertido, colorido, numeroso, alegre)
3. Dos programas cómicos de la televisión: calidad, grado de interés para el público (bueno, malo, mediocre, cómico, loco, divertido)

SITUACIONES

1. **Role A.** You are reminiscing about Independence Day celebrations when you were a child. Tell your son/daughter (your classmate) that you think that a) in the past Americans were more patriotic (**patrióticos**); b) the celebrations were less expensive; and c) the celebrations were more family oriented (**se celebraban en familia**) than today.

   Role B. Your dad/mom (your classmate) argues that today's Independence Day celebrations are less family oriented than in the past. You disagree. State that a) today Americans are as patriotic as they were in the past; b) people used to spend less money because they made less money; and c) today families celebrate Independence Day together as much as in the past.

2. **Role A.** Your next-door neighbors are three students, two of whom are identical twins (**gemelos/as**). Even though you have lived there for a year, you cannot tell them apart. When you run into the third roommate on campus, you mention all the ways in which the twins seem absolutely alike to you. Ask your neighbor's help in telling them apart.

   Role B. You and your long-time friends, who are identical twins (**gemelos/as**), share an apartment. When your neighbor asks you for help in telling them apart, describe a) two ways in which they are exactly alike in appearance, abilities, and preferences and b) two ways in which they are different that allow you to tell them apart.

Suggestion. You may give students additional examples: *En la fiesta había tanto ruido como en el Carnaval* and *Había tantas flores como en mi fiesta de cumpleaños.*

Follow-up for 8-30. Ask questions to summarize: *¿Pedro tiene tantas clases como Vilma? ¿Tiene Pedro tanto dinero como ella? ¿Vilma tiene tantos hermanos como él?*

Ask students:
1. *¿Cuántos hermanos tiene cada uno/a de ustedes?*
2. *¿Reciben ustedes dinero de sus padres para sus gastos personales o trabajan para ganar (earn) dinero?*
3. *¿Cuándo fue la última vez que recibieron dinero de sus padres? ¿Recibieron más o menos dinero que Vilma y Pedro (aproximadamente 80 dólares)?*
4. *¿Coleccionan ustedes DVDs o CDs? ¿Son las películas tan importantes para ustedes como la música? ¿Qué otras cosas coleccionan?*
5. *¿Conocen otros países? ¿Cuáles? ¿Es la cultura de algún otro país tan interesante para ustedes como la cultura de su país?*

Additional practice with Comparisons. Have a group discussion on the impact of the media and changes students may have observed. Ask:
1. *¿Creen ustedes que hoy hay tanto sexo y violencia en las películas como en el pasado?*
2. *¿Piensan ustedes que hoy hay más violencia social porque la gente ve más televisión?*
3. *¿En su opinión, ¿influyen más los medios de comunicación en los jóvenes que sus padres y la escuela?*
4. *¿Piensan que el gobierno tenía tanto control sobre los medios de comunicación antes como ahora?*

5. Comparing people and things: The superlative

PERLA: Lupita, ¿tienes algún plan especial para el Día de los Muertos?

LUPITA: Claro que sí. En mi comunidad, visitamos a familiares y amigos muertos en el cementerio. Les llevamos **la mejor** música mexicana y su comida preferida. Es **el** día **más importante del** año para recordarlos. Creemos que ellos vuelven a su tumba el 1 y 2 de noviembre para disfrutar de **la mejor** compañía, la de su familia y amigos.

PERLA: ¡Qué interesante! Para mi familia **el** acto **más** importante es recordarlos con **las** flores **más** hermosas **de** la estación.

Piénselo. Complete las siguientes oraciones con el nombre de la persona que expresa la información.

1. __Lupita__ lleva al cementerio **la mejor** música mexicana.
2. Según __Lupita__, el Día de los Muertos es **el** día **más importante del** año para recordar a los familiares y amigos muertos.
3. __Lupita__ dice que **la** compañía **más** agradable para los muertos es la de sus familiares y amigos.
4. __Lupita__ dice que su familia lleva la comida que les gustaba **más** a sus familiares muertos.
5. __Perla__ dice que para su familia, **la** manera **más** apropiada **de** recordar a los muertos es llevarles flores.

Lengua

Spanish and English often use adjectives as nouns. Whereas English frequently uses *one* or *ones* after the adjective, Spanish simply drops the noun.

El traje rojo **es más bonito.**

El rojo **es más bonito.**
The red one is prettier.

El rojo es el más bonito.
The red one is the prettiest.

■ Use superlatives to express *most* and *least* as degrees of comparison among three or more entities. To form the superlative, use *definite article + noun +* **más/menos** *+ adjective.* To express *in* or *at* with the superlative, use **de.**

Es **el** disfraz **menos** creativo (**de la** fiesta).	*It is the least creative costume (at the party).*
México es **el** país con **más** fiestas **de** América del Norte.	*Mexico is the country with the most holidays in North America.*

■ Do not use **más** or **menos** with **mejor, peor, mayor,** or **menor.**

¿Esos desfiles? Son **los mejores** desfiles **del** país.	*Those parades? They are the best parades in the country.*
Ivonne es **la mejor** bailarina **del** grupo.	*Ivonne is the best dancer of the group.*

■ You may delete the noun when it is clear to whom or to what you refer.

Son **los mejores del** país.	*They are the best (ones) in the country.*

■ To express the idea of *extremely*, add the ending **-ísimo** (**-a, -os, -as**) to the adjective. If the adjective ends in a consonant, add **-ísimo** directly to the singular form of the adjective. If it ends in a vowel, drop the vowel before adding **-ísimo**.

fácil	Este baile es **facilísimo**.	*This dance is extremely easy.*
grande	La carroza es **grandísima**.	*The float is extremely big.*
bueno	Las orquestas son **buenísimas**.	*The orchestras are extremely good.*

> ### Lengua
> A Spanish word can have only one written accent. Therefore, an adjective with a written accent loses the accent when **-ísimo/a** is added.
>
> fácil > facilísimo/a
> rápido > rapidísimo/a

8-32 Estadísticas demográficas. Lea la información de la tabla. Luego indique a qué país de la columna B se refiere cada oración de la columna A.

	MÉXICO	GUATEMALA	ESTADOS UNIDOS
población (aprox.) del país	104.700.000 habitantes	12.728.000 habitantes	302.688.000 habitantes
población de la capital	México, DF: 19.232.000	Ciudad de Guatemala: 3.942.000	Washington, DC: 588.292
número de lenguas indígenas	62	24	aprox. 150 familias de lenguas
religión predominante	89% son católicos (aprox. 93.180.000)	49% son católicos (aprox. 6.237.000)	52% son protestantes (aprox. 157.398.000)
número de estados o departamentos	32 estados	22 departamentos	50 estados

A

1. _c_ Este país tiene **el mayor número** de habitantes.
2. _b_ Esta ciudad capital es **la más** grande.
3. _c_ Es el país donde existe **el mayor** número de lenguas indígenas.
4. _a_ Este es el país con **menos** lenguas indígenas.
5. _a_ Este país tiene **el menor** porcentaje de personas que profesan el catolicismo.
6. _c_ Este país tiene **el mayor** número de gobiernos estatales o departmentales.

B

a. Guatemala
b. México
c. Estados Unidos

8-33 ¿En qué pueblo o ciudad? Respondan a las siguientes preguntas y, luego, comparen sus respuestas con las de otra pareja. ¿Están de acuerdo o tienen opiniones diferentes?

¿En qué pueblo o ciudad de su país...

1. sirven la mejor comida étnica?
2. se come la comida más picante (*spicy*)?
3. se vende el café cubano más fuerte?
4. celebran las mejores fiestas de Año Nuevo?
5. hay el mayor número de desfiles hermosos?
6. tocan la mejor música folclórica estadounidense?

Suggestion. You may wish to point out the spelling changes in such adjectives as *rico → riquísimo* and *largo → larguísimo*. You may also remind student to go to the Appendix in the Student Activities Manual for additional practice with accents.

Additional practice with Superlatives. Have students share their answers to the following questions:
¿Cuál es...
1. *la clase más difícil en su facultad?*
2. *la fiesta universitaria más popular entre los alumnos?*
3. *el profesor/la profesora de español más interesante?*
4. *la lengua más estudiada por los alumnos?*
5. *el horario menos deseado por los estudiantes?*
6. *la facultad con más mujeres/hombres?*

SITUACIONES

1. **Role A.** You are interviewing a well-known film critic about American movies. Ask a) which is the best American film and why; b) who is the best actor/actress; c) which is the worst film of the year; and d) what he/she thinks of Hispanic films.

   Role B. You are a well-known film critic. Answer the questions according to your own opinions regarding the best/worst American films and actors. Mention that a) there are some excellent Mexican, Argentinian, and Spanish films and b) several of them won Oscars in the last ten years.

2. **Role A.** You travelled to Mexico for Spring Break and liked the country very much. Tell your classmate the five things you liked best about Mexico and if there was something you found extremely interesting. Provide examples.

   Role B. Ask questions about your classmate's trip. Then tell where you went during Spring Break. Share five of the best things you liked about the place you visited.

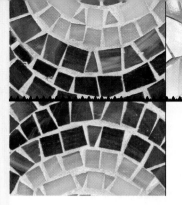

Resources
- SAM: 8-38 to 8-40
- Supp. Activ. Book: *Mosaicos*

MOSAICOS

A escuchar

ESTRATEGIA

Draw conclusions based on what you know

Understanding what someone says involves comprehending the literal meaning of the words you hear. It also may involve using the context and the information the speaker provides in order to draw conclusions that go beyond literal comprehension. This process is called inferencing, or making inferences.

When you talk to someone or overhear a conversation, you can understand what is said even when the speaker does not express the meaning explicitly. For example, if you are driving with a friend and get lost, you may say, "There is a gas station up there on the right." Your friend will probably infer that you want to stop to ask for directions.

Antes de escuchar

8-34 Preparación. Es el fin de año y dos amigos conversan sobre el feriado que se aproxima. Antes de escuchar la conversación, escriba el nombre de una festividad de la cual probablemente ellos van a hablar. Luego, escriba dos preguntas que en su opinión alguien va a hacer sobre este feriado.

Escuchar

8-35 ¿Comprende usted? First, read the statements below, and then listen as two friends talk about a Mexican holiday. After listening, mark (✓) the statements that provide information you can infer from what you heard.

CD 4
Track 6

1. ___ Daniel es mexicano.
2. ___ Sandra es una persona muy tímida.
3. _✓_ Sandra no es estadounidense.
4. ___ Daniel está triste porque no va a celebrar la Navidad con su familia.
5. ___ Pedir posada es una costumbre en que participa solamente la familia.
6. _✓_ Daniel no conoce algunas costumbres mexicanas.

Después de escuchar

8-36 Ahora usted. Comparta sus respuestas a estas preguntas con su compañero/a.

1. ¿Qué fiesta o tradición religiosa le gustaría celebrar en un país hispano? ¿Por qué?
2. ¿Celebran esa fiesta en su ciudad o país? ¿Cómo la celebran?
3. ¿Qué fiesta o tradición celebra usted solamente con sus amigos?

A conversar

Resources
■ SAM: 8-41
■ *Entrevistas* video

ESTRATEGIA

Conduct an interview

To conduct an interview, you need to ask two types of questions: (a) questions to open up a topic and (b) follow-up questions to get additional information. Open-ended questions that function as invitations to speak—such as **¿Podría hablar de los deportes que practicaba de niño/a?**—will elicit longer and more detailed responses than direct, closed-ended questions like **¿Qué deportes practicaba cuando era niño/a?** Questions that can be answered with **Sí** or **No** are not likely to elicit much information, unless you follow up with **¿Por qué?** Listen carefully to what your interviewee says so that you can ask relevant follow-up questions.

Antes de conversar

8-37 Preparación. ¿Tuvieron usted y uno/a de sus compañeros/as una infancia y adolescencia semejantes? Escriban preguntas que los/las ayuden a obtener información en las siguientes áreas, u otras áreas de interés para ustedes.

1. deportes que su compañero/a practicaba y miraba en la televisión entre los siete y los doce años de edad
2. la(s) fiesta(s) más importantes para la familia de su compañero/a y cómo la(s) celebraba
3. una o dos costumbres de la familia que a él/ella le gustaba(n) y otras que no le gustaban y por qué
4. …

Conversar

8-38 Entre nosotros. Entreviste a su compañero/a usando las preguntas de la actividad **8-37** y tome notas de sus respuestas.

Después de conversar

8-39 Un poco más. Anónimamente, escriban un breve informe comparativo de la infancia y adolescencia de ustedes. Sus compañeros van a leer su informe y van a tratar de averiguar quiénes son ustedes. Sigan los modelos y frases a continuación o combínenlos, de acuerdo con sus experiencias. Mantengan su identidad en secreto.

MODELO:

ALMAS GEMELAS	MUNDOS APARTES
Somos dos almas gemelas. Tanto mi compañero/a como yo nacimos en…	*Somos dos mundos apartes. Mi compañero/a nació en…. Yo nací en…*

1. Durante la infancia/adolescencia…
2. Con respecto a los deportes/las fiestas…
3. La persona A y la persona B tuvieron una niñez/adolescencia semejante/diferente porque…

En directo

To ask someone to talk about a topic:

¿Me podría(s) hablar sobre… ?
Can you talk to me more about . . . ?

¿Qué me puede(s) decir usted sobre/de… ?
What can you tell me about . . . ?

Me gustaría saber…
I would like to know . . .

To ask someone to expand on a topic:

¿Podría(s) hablar más sobre… ?

¿Qué más me puede(s) decir sobre… ?

En directo

To show empathy:

¡Oh! ¡Qué lástima! ¡Cuánto lo siento!
How sad! I'm so sorry.

To share someone's happiness:

¡Qué fabuloso/bueno!
How fabulous/great!

¡Cuánto me alegro!
I'm so happy to hear that!

To express interest in what someone said:

¡Qué interesante!
How interesting!

Suggestion for 8-37. Have students work in small groups helping each other prepare open-ended initial and follow-up questions for their interviews. Write examples of open-ended questions and other question types on the board as you hear students discuss them.

Suggestions for 8-39. To keep identities of the interviewees hidden, pairs can type their reports, referring to each other as *Persona A* and *Persona B*. You may wish to use your course management system to post the reports and have students try to figure out the identity of the pairs as homework and then compare notes in class.

You may wish to have students read aloud the anonymous reports (randomly handed out), and the class together guesses the identities of the pairs.

A leer

Antes de leer

ESTRATEGIA

Make inferences

Understanding a text, like listening to a speaker, involves both comprehending the words literally and using information provided to make inferences. To make inferences when you read, use your background knowledge, understanding of context, and active thinking skills, as well as your ability to understand the printed words on the page.

8-40 Preparación. Las creencias sobre la muerte varían de una cultura a otra. Indiquen si creen que las siguientes prácticas se asocian con la cultura egipcia (**E**), con alguna cultura indígena americana (**I**) o con ambas (**A**).

1. __A__ Creían que había vida después de la muerte.
2. __A__ Construían pirámides para honrar a los muertos.
3. __I__ Vestían a los muertos con ropa funeraria especial.
4. __A__ Ponían una máscara sobre la cara del muerto.
5. __A__ Enterraban (*They buried*) al muerto en las pirámides, en tumbas o sepulcros, de acuerdo al estatus social de la persona muerta.
6. __A__ La familia de la persona muerta depositaba joyas y objetos de valor en la tumba o pirámide.
7. __I__ Rociaban (*They sprayed*) el cadáver con un polvo de color rojo para simbolizar el renacimiento (*rebirth*).

Leer

Creencias y costumbres mayas sobre la muerte

El origen de los mayas es incierto. Sin embargo, se sabe que esta civilización ocupó y se desarrolló[1] en los actuales territorios de Guatemala, México, Belice, Honduras y El Salvador. Durante su período de mayor esplendor, los mayas construyeron ciudades y pirámides, donde enterraban a sus gobernantes y los veneraban después de muertos.

Los mayas compartían con otras culturas mesoamericanas algunas creencias y costumbres. Entre otras cosas, creían en la vida después de la muerte y en la interacción entre el mundo humano y el mundo espiritual. Creían que el destino de una persona después de la muerte dependía de la forma en que moría y no de su conducta mientras vivía. Las tumbas y los vestuarios funerarios confirman que los mayas creían que el espíritu se prolongaba más allá de la muerte. La mayoría de los muertos iba a Xibalbá, un lugar en el mundo de abajo.

Para llegar a Xibalbá había que superar numerosos peligros. El espíritu debía comer bien y cuidarse. Por eso, los mayas

dejaban en la tumba una vestimenta funeraria. También colocaban comida, agua y amuletos protectores, de acuerdo con el estatus social del muerto.

Los mayas rociaban el cadáver con un polvo rojo que simbolizaba el renacimiento. También lo adornaban con joyas, collares, pulseras y anillos de jade, hueso[2] o concha[3] y un cinturón ceremonial. En muchas tumbas ponían una máscara sobre la cara del muerto para ocultar su identidad. En la boca le ponían una cuenta[4] de jade, símbolo de lo precioso y lo perenne, para preservar su espíritu inmortal.

Algunas de estas creencias y costumbres todavía se conservan, con ciertas variaciones, en algunas comunidades de Guatemala, México y El Salvador.

[1]*developed* [2]*bone* [3]*shell* [4]*bead*

8-41 Primera mirada. Determine si las siguientes afirmaciones representan información explícita (**E**) en el texto o si son inferencias (**I**) basadas en el contenido. Si es una inferencia, indique la oración o las oraciones en el texto en que se basa(n).

1. __E__ Los expertos no saben de dónde vinieron los mayas.
2. __I__ Los mayas crearon una gran civilización.
3. __I__ Las comunidades mayas tenían autoridades que los gobernaban.
4. __I__ Como los egipcios, los mayas construyeron edificios magníficos para honrar la memoria de personas de alto estatus en su comunidad.
5. __E__ Los mayas, como otros grupos indígenas, pensaban que la vida continuaba después de la muerte.
6. __E__ Para los mayas, el tipo de muerte determinaba el destino de una persona.
7. __I__ No todos los mayas iban al mismo destino después de la muerte.
8. __E__ La comida, el agua y los amuletos ayudaban al espíritu del muerto a llegar a su destino final.

8-42 Segunda mirada. Complete las siguientes ideas con información explícita en el texto.

1. Los mayas, como otras culturas indígenas de Mesoamérica, creían en…
2. Dos costumbres que demuestran que los mayas tenían estas creencias son…
3. Para llegar a su destino final, el espíritu de los muertos tenía que…
4. Para indicar que el espíritu del muerto nacía otra vez, los mayas…
5. Para simbolizar la importancia y la inmortalidad del espíritu, los mayas…

Después de leer

8-43 Ampliación. Mencionen qué objetos probablemente ponían los mayas en la tumba o pirámide de un gobernante con las siguientes características: Answers may vary.

1. Era físicamente activo.
2. Le gustaba mucho el arte.
3. Estudiaba astronomía.
4. Le fascinaba la guerra.
5. Tenía ocho hijas, todas muy bellas.

Answers for 8-42.
Answers may vary, but expect variations of the following:
1. *la vida después de la muerte; la interacción entre el mundo humano y el mundo espiritual;*
2. *el espíritu se prolongaba más allá de la muerte; la mayoría de los muertos iba a Xibalbá, un lugar en el mundo de abajo;*
3. *comer bien, cuidarse, superar numerosos peligros;*
4. *rociaban el cadáver con un polvo que simbolizaba el renacimiento;*
5. *en la boca del difunto le ponían una cuenta de jade, símbolo de lo precioso y lo perenne.*

A escribir

Select and sequence details to write effective narratives

A successful narrative is characterized by a logical, clear, and believable sequence of events, and a good description of setting and characters.

Use organizational strategies such as a graphic organizer or a story map to visualize the order of events in and the time frame (present, past). Use dialogue to make your story more believable.

To describe the main characters, select feelings and traits that will make them stand out. Place the characters in the appropriate setting (rural, mysterious, etc.).

Structure your narration:

■ Introduce the character(s), describe the setting, and begin the action.
■ Present the unfolding of the action. Describe the characters and the tensions caused by their actions or by the events around them.
■ Present a closure to the actions/tensions, or leave it open for your reader to imagine the ending.

Antes de escribir

8-44 Preparación. PRIMERA FASE. Lea la siguiente narración y siga las instrucciones.

Eran alrededor de las siete de la tarde del 24 de mayo cuando ocurrió algo totalmente inesperado. Era una noche de otoño y hacía viento. Empezaba a oscurecer.

Era el cumpleaños de nuestra gran amiga Guadalupe Martínez. Aunque tenía sólo veinte años, Guadalupe era una chica excepcional. Estudiaba en la UNAM[1] y también trabajaba para ayudar a su familia de ocho hermanos. Todos sus amigos la admirábamos por su generosidad, optimismo y alegría. Guadalupe era la hermana y amiga que todos soñábamos[2] tener.

El día de su cumpleaños por la mañana, Francisco y yo rompimos nuestra rutina. Pensábamos darle una sorpresa para su cumpleaños. Después de todo, ¡sólo se cumplen veintiún años una vez en la vida! Primero, fuimos a un centro comercial y le buscamos un regalo especial. Encontramos un plato decorativo guatemalteco y un CD. Francisco también le compró un perfume, y yo agregué un libro al cesto de regalos. Más tarde, volvimos a casa y envolvimos los regalos.

A las seis de la tarde Francisco y yo caminábamos a casa de Guadalupe. Estábamos a unos 80 metros de su casa cuando la ambulancia pasó a gran velocidad. Francisco y yo intuitivamente nos miramos y empezamos a caminar con más rapidez, pero en silencio. A sólo unos metros de su casa, supimos que algo pasaba en casa de Guadalupe. Corrimos. Cuando llegamos a la puerta, un enfermero nos dijo: "La señorita Martínez tuvo un accidente. Se quebró una pierna y dos costillas. La llevamos al hospital".

Inmediatamente, Francisco y yo llamamos al resto de nuestros amigos. Esa noche, todos los amigos de Guadalupe fuimos a saludarla al hospital. Fue un cumpleaños diferente a todos los anteriores, porque lo celebramos en el hospital, al lado de la cama de nuestra gran amiga Guadalupe.

[1]Universidad Nacional Autónoma de México
[2]*dreamed*

SEGUNDA FASE. Conteste las siguientes preguntas basadas en la historia que acaba de leer.

1. ¿Cuál es el propósito de la historia? Márquelo (✓).
   a. ✓ describir un evento emocional e inesperado
   b. ___ entretener a los lectores
   c. ✓ informar a los lectores sobre una experiencia triste
   d. ___ enseñar algo
2. ¿Son efectivos la selección de los personajes y los detalles de ellos, el entorno (*setting*) y la trama (*plot*)? ✓ Sí ___No
3. ¿Cuáles son las razones posibles para su respuesta a la pregunta 2? Márquelas (✓).
   a. ✓ La protagonista se describe de una manera interesante.
   b. ✓ La historia es ágil: la acción ocurre rápidamente y hay suficiente descripción.
   c. ___ Hay demasiada descripción y la historia es lenta.
   d. ✓ Hay suficiente información sobre el entorno.
   e. ✓ La historia sigue un orden cronológico.
   f. ✓ La narración tiene una organización clara: una introducción, un desarrollo y un fin.
   g. ✓ La historia es realista para el lector.

Escribir

8-45 Manos a la obra. PRIMERA FASE. Usted va a narrar una historia personal, real o imaginaria. Primero, determine lo siguiente:

1. ¿Cuál es el objetivo de su narración, informar, relatar, entretener o enseñar?
2. ¿Cuántos protagonistas hay? ¿Qué características físicas y de personalidad tienen?
3. ¿Va a relatar usted en el pasado o en el presente? ¿Va a organizar los hechos en orden cronológico?
4. Escriba una lista de verbos que lo/la ayuden a describir el ambiente (*setting*), y otros que cuenten la acción.
5. ¿Qué información va a presentar en la introducción? ¿Cuál va a ser el conflicto? ¿Usted va a resolverlo o el lector va a imaginar el final de la historia?

> **En directo**
>
> To indicate chronological order:
>
> **Primero,...**
>
> **Después,.../Después de (un tiempo),...**
>
> **Luego,...**
>
> **Más tarde,...**
>
> **Finalmente,.../Por fin,...**

SEGUNDA FASE. Ahora, use la información de la *Primera fase* para escribir su narración, empezando del presente al pasado. Las siguientes expresiones en *En directo* pueden ser muy útiles.

Después de escribir

8-46 Revisión. Lea su narración, pensando en su lector. Verifique lo siguiente:

1. ¿Incluyó la información que su lector necesita? ¿Es la trama creíble? ¿Describió suficientemente a los personajes y el ambiente?
2. ¿Tiene su narración una introducción, un conflicto y una conclusión?
3. ¿Usó expresiones apropiadas para indicar el orden cronológico, concordancia de tiempos (presente, pasado), etc.?
4. ¿Revisó la gramática, vocabulario, puntuación y ortografía?

Ahora, comparta su narración con un/a compañero/a. Converse con él/ella sobre las áreas débiles de su narración, si los hay.

ENFOQUE CULTURAL

Cultura y tradiciones mexicanas

La cultura popular de México es una de las más ricas y variadas de toda América Latina. En México se conservan muchas tradiciones y celebraciones nacionales, regionales, religiosas, políticas y familiares. Además, existe una gran riqueza en otros aspectos de la cultura, tales como la comida, la música e inclusive el idioma. En gran parte, esta riqueza cultural se debe a la mezcla de las antiguas culturas indígenas que existían en México y la europea, en particular la española. Esta mezcla resultó en una cultura popular tradicional y original a la vez.

Aunque en México existe una separación de la iglesia y el estado, la religión es, ciertamente, uno de los aspectos más

Aunque México es hoy un país industrializado y moderno, su cultura popular es rica en tradiciones.

sobresalientes de la cultura popular. Son muchas las tradiciones y celebraciones que tienen relación con aspectos de la cultura religiosa en México. Indudablemente una de las tradiciones religiosas más

importantes es la veneración a la Virgen de Guadalupe. Según la tradición, la virgen María se le apareció a un indígena pobre llamado Juan Diego y le habló en náhuatl, el idioma de los aztecas. La virgen le pidió construir una iglesia en el Tepeyac, al norte de la actual Ciudad de México. Más tarde, una imagen de la virgen apareció milagrosamente en la camisa de Juan Diego. Esta imagen se convirtió en un símbolo de la identidad de México. Así la iglesia del Tepeyac es uno de los lugares religiosos más visitados en todo el continente americano.

La Virgen de Guadalupe es uno de los íconos más representativos de la identidad mexicana.

286

La celebración del Día de los Muertos también tiene sus orígenes en la cultura azteca. Los aztecas daban mucha importancia a la muerte y muchos de sus ritos se centraban en la muerte. La unión de esa tradición azteca con las tradiciones cristianas españolas produjo en México un culto muy especial de la muerte. Un aspecto interesante de este culto es el tratamiento a veces humorístico de la muerte, muy diferente del tratamiento solemne de la muerte en Estados Unidos o en otros países. En efecto, símbolos de la muerte como los esqueletos y las calaveras se representan en galletas, dulces y todo tipo de juguetes para niños. Las familias construyen altares en

Los Voladores de Papantla descienden girando alrededor de un poste de 30 metros de alto en una ceremonia relacionada con el calendario maya.

sus casas para ofrecer a los muertos las comidas y bebidas que disfrutaban en vida. Resulta interesante comparar la fiesta de *Halloween* en Estados Unidos y el Día de los Muertos, porque existen muchas diferencias entre ellas, a pesar de algunas semejanzas superficiales. En primer lugar, el origen celta de *Halloween* contrasta con el origen cristiano-azteca de la fiesta mexicana. En segundo lugar, mientras en Estados Unidos se trata de una fiesta principalmente para los niños que recorren las calles con disfraces macabros pidiendo dulces, la fiesta mexicana es principalmente una fiesta familiar dedicada a honrar a los muertos de cada familia.

Otra tradición muy espectacular de origen indígena es la de los Voladores de Papantla. Cuatro hombres de origen totonaca, uno de los muchos pueblos indígenas de México, se suben a un poste de 30 metros de altura que representa el árbol de la vida. Atados por la cintura, se lanzan dando círculos alrededor del poste, mientras otro hombre toca instrumentos prehispánicos y baila en lo alto del poste. Esta ceremonia se realiza en honor del Sol y tiene sus raíces en el calendario maya. Los voladores representan los cuatro elementos y los cuatro puntos cardinales.

Finalmente, la comida mexicana popular incluye muchos productos autóctonos, poco utilizados en la cocina europea, o en otras regiones americanas, tales como diferentes especies de hongos, cactus y flores. Por otra parte, la música y danza mexicanas también se unen a las tradiciones indígenas, como en el caso de la Mazoyiwua o Danza del Venado, que es una de las formas de más pura tradición prehispánica. La artesanía mexicana, con raíces en la cultura tradicional, es una de las más interesantes, coloridas y variadas de todo el mundo hispano. Y desde luego, la riqueza lingüística de México incluye más de 60 lenguas indígenas, además de innumerables variaciones del castellano.

En otras palabras

Expresiones mexicanas

¿Cómo estás, mi **cuate?**
How are you, my friend?

Pablo es **chaparro**, pero su abuelo era alto.
Pablo is short, but his grandfather was tall.

Mi amiga Stephanie es **güera** y tiene los ojos azules.
My friend Stephanie is blonde and has blue eyes.

Mi **recámara** tiene una ventana grande.
My bedroom has a large window.

Note. Although the proper word in Spanish is *cacto* (pl. *cactos*), most speakers use the Gallicism *cactus*, as in English.

8-47 Comprensión. PRIMERA FASE. **Reconocimiento de palabras clave.** Encuentre en el texto la palabra o expresión que mejor expresa el significado de las siguientes ideas.

1. at the same time ____a la vez____
2. outstanding ____sobresaliente____
3. undoubtedly ____indudablemente____
4. skulls ____calaveras____
5. cookies ____galletas____
6. pole ____poste____
7. roots ____raíces____
8. mushrooms ____hongos____

SEGUNDA FASE. **Oraciones importantes.** Subraye las afirmaciones que contienen ideas que se encuentran en el texto. Luego indique en qué parte del texto están.

1. Native cultures of Mexico mixed with Spanish traditions to produce an original culture.
2. Religion is probably not a major component of Mexican popular culture.
3. Decorations for the All Souls' Day celebration sometimes include humorous images of Death.
4. The Tree of Life is represented by a 30–meter pole in the **Flyers of Papantla** ceremony.
5. The **Flyers of Papantla** ceremony is rooted in the Mayan calendar.
6. Flowers are used as ingredients in some Mexican dishes.
7. Traditional Mexican dances are very similar to (or are modeled on) traditional Spanish dances.
8. Many native languages, as well as variations of Spanish, are regularly spoken in Mexico.

TERCERA FASE. **Ideas principales.** Escriba un párrafo breve en inglés resumiendo las ideas principales expresadas en el texto.

 8-48 Use la información. Usted fue a México y asistió a una de las siguientes celebraciones. Escríbale un correo electrónico a su profesor/a y cuéntele cuál de las siguientes celebraciones vio y dónde las vio. Incluya al menos cuatro datos sobre ella. Para preparar esta actividad, visite la página web de *Mosaicos* y siga los enlaces útiles.

a. el Cinco de Mayo
b. el Día de los Muertos
c. el Baile de los Viejitos
d. la Danza del Venado
e. el Día de la Virgen de Guadalupe

VOCABULARIO

CD 4
ks 7–13

Las fiestas y las celebraciones — *Holidays and celebrations*

la alegría	*joy*
el aserrín	*sawdust*
el carnaval	*carnival*
la carreta	*cart, wagon*
la carroza	*float (in a parade)*
la celebración	*celebration*
la comparsa	*group dressed in similar costumes*
la corrida (de toros)	*bullfight*
la costumbre	*custom*
el desfile	*parade*
el día feriado	*legal holiday*
el día festivo	*holiday*
el festival	*festival*
la festividad, la fiesta	*festivity; holiday; celebration*
la invitación	*invitation*
el preparativo	*preparation*
la procesión	*procession*
la semilla	*seed*
el toro	*bull*
la tradición	*tradition*

Las personas — *People*

el antepasado	*ancestor*
la gente	*people*
el rey/la reina	*king/queen*

La música — *Music*

la melodía	*melody*
la orquesta	*orchestra*
el ruido	*noise*

Los lugares — *Places*

el camino	*road; way*
el cementerio	*cemetery*
la iglesia	*church*
el teatro	*theater*

El tiempo — *Time*

antes	*before*
el comienzo	*beginning*
entonces	*then*
hoy en día	*nowadays*
mientras	*while*

Las descripciones — *Descriptions*

adornado/a	*decorated*
animado/a	*lively*
difunto/a, muerto/a	*dead*
maravilloso/a	*marvelous*
suave	*soft*
último/a	*last*

Verbos — *Verbs*

acompañar	*to accompany*
comenzar (ie)	*to begin*
dar un paseo	*to take a walk*
disfrazarse (c)	*to wear a costume*
divertirse (ie, i)	*to have a good time*
encerrar (ie)	*to lock up, shut in*
invitar	*to invite*
mantener (g, ie)	*to maintain*
quedar	*to arrange to meet*
recordar (ue)	*to remember*
reunirse	*to get together*

See page 260 for the names of popular celebrations.
See page 267 for expressions of time and frequency.
See pages 273, 274, and 276 for expressions to use to make comparisons.

Resources

■ IRM: Syllabi & Lesson Plans

Note. Handicrafts are an important source of income in Guatemala. Textiles, wood carvings, jewelry, baskets, ceramics, bags, worry dolls, and other forms of folk art are made by indigenous artisans all over the country. Mostly women and children are involved in the selling of these items, mainly in local markets. In recent years, however, the growth of cooperatives organized by women gives artisans greater control over the marketing and exportation of their goods.

Suggestions. Recycle vocabulary of handicrafts studied in *Capítulo 6*. Ask students to list some of the items that can be found in open air markets in Latin America and the materials they may be made of. Ask them to describe what they see in the photo: *¿Qué es esto? ¿Para qué sirve? ¿Qué formas tiene? ¿Qué colores?* Use the expressions *artesanía* and *arte popular*. Bring some handicrafts to class and ask students to describe them.

CAPÍTULO

9

Hay que trabajar

Tapices de lana en un mercado de Antigua, Guatemala. Se elaboran a mano en la región de Momostenango, que está al oeste de la capital.

In this chapter you will learn how to:

- talk about the workplace and professions
- talk about the past
- give instructions

Cultural focus: **Guatemala**

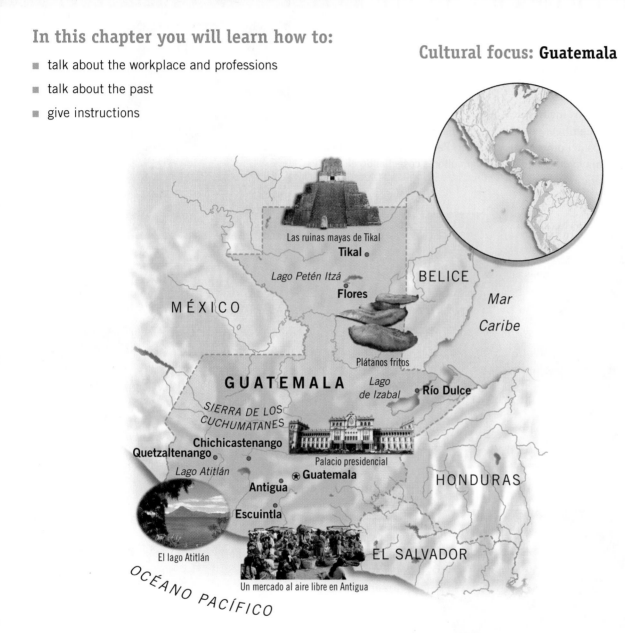

Las ruinas mayas de Tikal
Tikal

Lago Petén Itzá
Flores

MÉXICO

BELICE

Mar Caribe

Plátanos fritos

GUATEMALA

Lago de Izabal **Río Dulce**

SIERRA DE LOS CUCHUMATANES

Chichicastenango

Quetzaltenango

Palacio presidencial
⭐ **Guatemala**

Lago Atitlán

Antigua

Escuintla

HONDURAS

El lago Atitlán

Un mercado al aire libre en Antigua

EL SALVADOR

OCÉANO PACÍFICO

👁 **A vista de pájaro.** Piense en lo que sabe de Guatemala y conteste las siguientes preguntas.

1. ¿Cómo se llaman los habitantes de Guatemala? guatemaltecos
2. ¿Cuál era la antigua capital de Guatemala? Antigua
3. ¿Qué país está al este de Guatemala? Belice
4. ¿Qué civilización fue muy importante en Guatemala? maya
5. ¿Qué idiomas habla la gente (*people*)? El español es el idioma oficial, pero mucha gente habla lenguas mayas.
6. ¿Cuáles son probablemente algunos recursos económicos importantes? agricultura, artesanía

Or ask them to bring a piece of folk art or a souvenir from home and explain what it is, where it is from, what it is made of, where it was bought and by whom.

Warm-up. Brainstorm with students about what they already know about Guatemala. Ask questions to help them locate the country as they look at the map and describe its geographical features: *¿Qué países limitan con Guatemala? ¿Cómo se llama el océano que está al lado oeste del país? ¿Y el mar al este? ¿Cómo se llaman los lagos más importantes?* Call students' attention to the name of the city *Antigua*. Have them guess the meaning of the word and explain that Antigua was the old capital of Guatemala. Ask them which major civilization existed in Guatemala before the Spaniards arrived. Point out the photo of the Mayan ruins of Tikal to help them answer. You may use photos of Guatemalans from the Internet to explain that indigenous and *mestizo* people are the majority in that country and that many Guatemalans do not speak Spanish as their first language. Mention Rigoberta Menchú, who won the Nobel Peace Prize for her activism in fighting the abuses of the Guatemalan army against the indigenous population. Mention Miguel Ángel Asturias, the author of *El Señor Presidente*, who received the Nobel Prize in Literature in 1967. Ask if students know of any major natural disasters that have affected the country (Hurricane Mitch in 1998; an earthquake in 1976 that killed 23,000 people). Explain that these disasters and political instability have forced many Guatemalans to flee the country in search of better living conditions and job opportunities. Finally, you may show some photos of original crafts made in Guatemala and ask students to describe them.

291

A PRIMERA VISTA

⏴⏴ El trabajo

CD 4
Track 14

En muchos lugares de Latinoamérica la **agricultura** es un sector significativo de la economía nacional. En estos cuadros del pintor guatemalteco Pedro Rafael González Chavajay vemos a algunos **agricultores cosechando** el café y los plátanos.

Los productos del **campo** se venden después en los mercados locales junto con las telas y las joyas que **elaboran** los **artesanos.**

Este **carpintero** está trabajando la **madera** en su **taller** para hacer una silla. Otras personas que trabajan con materias primas son los **herreros,** los **peleteros,** los **ceramistas** y los **joyeros.** Desafortunadamente, para muchas personas es difícil encontrar un buen trabajo para **sobrevivir** y tienen que **emigrar** a las grandes ciudades o a otros países.

9-1 ¿A qué se dedican? Diga si las siguientes afirmaciones son ciertas (**C**) o falsas (**F**). Si la respuesta es falsa (**F**), corrija la información.

1. _C_ Los peleteros hacen zapatos, bolsas y chaquetas.
2. _F_ Los ceramistas trabajan con el hierro.
3. _C_ Los herreros trabajan los metales.
4. _F_ Los carpinteros hacen los trabajos del campo.
5. _C_ Los joyeros trabajan la plata y el oro para hacer pulseras y collares, por ejemplo.
6. _C_ Los agricultores plantan y cosechan productos naturales.

9-2 Las preparaciones. Varios estudiantes planeaban una fiesta para celebrar su graduación. Indique adónde fueron y con quiénes hablaron para conseguir lo que necesitaban para la fiesta.

MODELO: María quería comprar un kilo de carne para hacer una parrillada en el jardín.
Fue a la carnicería y habló con el carnicero/la carnicera.

1. Juan necesitaba pescado para preparar un ceviche. pescadería, pescadero/a
2. Paula tenía que comprar unos zapatos. zapatería, zapatero/a
3. Carlos y Laura querían regalarle un collar elegante a Felicia. joyería, joyero/a
4. Elisa quería encargar (*order*) una mesa de madera pequeña para poner los aperitivos. carpintería, carpintero/a
5. Sofía pensaba regalarle un libro a Diego. librería, librero/a
6. Martín y Luis necesitaban unos pantalones formales nuevos para ir a la fiesta. tienda de ropa, dependiente/a
7. Lorenzo quería comprar algo de fruta para hacer el postre. frutería, frutero/a
8. Pilar quería adornar la casa con flores. floristería, dependiente/a

9-3 Descripciones. Miren los cuadros en la p. 292 y descríbanse las escenas con el mayor detalle posible. Tengan en cuenta las siguientes ideas:

1. lugar donde están estas personas
2. rasgos físicos
3. edad aproximada
4. ropa que llevan
5. lo que están haciendo
6. lo que están pensando algunas de las personas en la escena
7. cómo se sienten

Lengua

The suffix **-ero/-era** is often used in Spanish to designate trades and professions, e.g., **camarero/a** (*server*), **plomero/a** (*plumber*), **peluquero/a** (*hairdresser*). Another common suffix is **-ista**, e.g., **electricista** (*electrician*); **contratista** (*contractor*).

Suggestion. Students have already learned how to form the names of stores by adding the ending *-ía*: *zapatería, mueblería, librería*, etc. In this activity they may recycle names of stores and figure out the terms for people who work there by adding the ending *-ero/-era* instead. You may explain that this rule does not always apply. For example, *florero* means vase, and the shop where flowers are sold is called *floristería*. In some cases students may have to use the general term *dependiente*: *El dependiente de la floristería me dijo que las rosas estaban baratas.* The use of the imperfect and the preterit in the activity previews *Funciones y formas*.

•)) Los oficios y las profesiones

CD 4
Track 15

Suggestions for Los oficios y las profesiones. Use visuals to introduce professions. Provide comprehensible input by asking questions about the photos. You may expand by having students describe the workers' job/task and the kind of preparation or education required. Personalize when possible: *¿Quién es la persona de la primera foto? ¿Dónde trabaja? Y ustedes, ¿trabajan? ¿Dónde trabaja usted? ¿Sus padres trabajan? ¿Dónde? ¿Quién no trabaja en su familia? ¿Quién trabaja mucho en su familia, pero no recibe un sueldo?*

Follow-up. Working in pairs, have students ask each other about their jobs, what they do at work, what they like or do not like about their jobs. (If students do not work, they may talk about the job of someone in their family or an imaginary job.)

Suggestions. Talk about the business card and ask questions. Mention that in most industrialized countries employees get four to seven weeks of paid vacation: *En la mayoría de los países industrializados los empleados tienen de cuatro a siete semanas de vacaciones pagadas.* Ask: *¿Piensan que en dos semanas de vacaciones hay tiempo para viajar, estar con la familia, descansar? ¿Cómo pueden los padres que tienen vacaciones cortas pasar más tiempo con sus familias y relajarse?*

Una **chef** muestra algunas de sus **especialidades**.

Dra. Alicia Gonica de Pérez
CARDIÓLOGA

Consultorio
La Concepción 81
Calle 18, 402, Ciudad de Guatemala
Teléfono: (502) 23622001
Fax: (502) 23670721

Una **médica** le inyecta antibióticos a una paciente en su **consultorio**.

Unos **bomberos apagan** un **incendio** en Ciudad de Guatemala.

Una **ejecutiva** llama por teléfono a un **cliente**.

Una **locutora espera** la **señal** para comenzar un programa de noticias en una estación de radio.

Un **técnico** revisa los controles de una **compañía** petrolera.

Cultura

Un importante cambio social en los países hispanos en las últimas décadas es el ingreso masivo de las mujeres al mercado laboral. Sin embargo, aún existen desigualdades: el desempleo entre las mujeres es mayor; su representación en las empresas de alta productividad es mucho menor; y los salarios de las mujeres son más bajos de los que reciben los hombres por el mismo tipo de trabajo.

Además, el trabajo doméstico no remunerado todavía se considera una obligación asociada con las mujeres y las niñas. No obstante, en muchos países hispanos ya se ofrecen programas educativos para combatir la discriminación. Algunos países, como Perú y Chile, tienen Ministerios de la Mujer para proteger y atender las necesidades de las mujeres.

Un **peluquero** le corta el pelo a una clienta.

Otras ocupaciones

CD 4
Track 16

la juez

el abogado

el actor

el ama de casa

el policía

la bibliotecaria

la cajera

el chofer

la científica

el contador

la electricista

la enfermera

la mujer de negocios

el ingeniero

el intérprete

el obrero

el psicólogo

la periodista

el plomero

la arquitecta

Suggestion for Otras ocupaciones. Use visual aids to introduce the various professions. Talk about them and ask questions to elicit students' opinions.

Follow-up. Add additional occupations that are cognates: *el/la astronauta, el/la mecánico/a, el/la dentista, el/la piloto, el/la recepcionista, el secretario/la secretaria, el veterinario/la veterinaria.*

Point out that both forms *la juez* and *la jueza* are accepted in Spanish.

Inform students that *el amo de casa* has come into usage in Spanish, as has *house husband* in English.

Suggestion. Recycle previously taught occupations and comparative expressions by having students compare occupations: *¿Un peluquero gana tanto dinero como un médico? ¿Es mejor ser ingeniero o actor? ¿Un profesor trabaja más o menos que un médico?*

9-4 ¿Qué profesión debe tener? Lean las siguientes descripciones y digan qué profesión u oficio de la lista deben tener las personas con estas características. **OJO:** A veces, más de una respuesta es posible. Answers may vary; however, students will likely respond as noted.

> ### En otras palabras
>
> In Spain the words for **contador**, **chofer**, and **plomero** are **contable**, **chófer**, and **fontanero**.

abogado/a	científico/a	médico/a
actor/actriz	ingeniero/a	plomero/a
artista	mecánico/a	psicólogo/a

1. A Pablo le gusta observar y analizar el comportamiento (*behavior*) de las personas. psicólogo
2. Los hermanos Pedraza siempre resuelven los problemas del auto de su padre. Lo examinan y lo reparan a la perfección. mecánicos
3. Eva y Ana tienen facilidad para resolver los problemas de otras personas. También tienen la habilidad de exponer oralmente. abogadas
4. A Jaime le fascina desarmar (*disassemble*) aparatos electrónicos para estudiar cómo funcionan. ingeniero
5. Daniela es una chica muy sensible y una gran observadora. Le fascina expresar sus sentimientos y experiencias de manera artística. actriz/artista
6. Adela siempre lee libros sobre anatomía. Ella sabe el nombre de cada parte del cuerpo humano. médica

9-5 Las profesiones y la personalidad. PRIMERA FASE. Digan cómo deben ser estos/as profesionales. Seleccionen las palabras de la lista para describir las características deseadas.

MODELO: un bombero
> *Debe ser valiente, serio y responsable. No debe ser descuidado (careless).*

autoritario	dedicado	detallista	inteligente	perezoso	serio
calculador	delgado	estudioso	irónico	responsable	simpático
cuidadoso	descuidado	guapo	paciente	romántico	valiente

1. un médico/una médica
2. un actor/una actriz
3. un hombre/una mujer de negocios
4. un peluquero/una peluquera
5. un locutor/una locutora
6. un ama de casa
7. un ejecutivo/una ejecutiva
8. un mecánico/una mecánica
9. un cocinero/una cocinera
10. un abogado/una abogada

SEGUNDA FASE. Intercambien ideas sobre lo siguiente.

1. ¿Conoce a algún/a… (*nombre de la profesión*)? ¿Cómo se llama? ¿Dónde trabaja?
2. ¿Qué características personales o especiales, en su opinión, lo/la ayudan en su profesión?

9-6 Asociaciones. Asocien una o más profesiones con los siguientes lugares de trabajo, y digan lo que hacen estas personas. Answers in last column will vary.

LUGAR	PROFESIÓN	¿QUÉ HACE?
1. el hospital	enfermero/a, médico/a	Atiende a los pacientes.
2. el restaurante	chef, camarero/a	
3. la clase	profesor/a	
4. la estación de radio	locutor/a, ingeniero/a	
5. la tienda de ropa	dependiente/a, vendedor/a	
6. el consultorio médico	médico/a	
7. la peluquería	peluquero/a	

Note for 9-6. Answers may vary but likely answers are included in column 2. Column 3 answers will depend on the students' answers to column 2.

9-7 ¿Cuál es la profesión? Primero identifiquen la ocupación o profesión, según la descripción. Luego, digan dos ventajas y una desventaja de esta ocupación o profesión.

MODELO: Trabaja en una biblioteca haciendo catálogos de libros.
E1: *Es un bibliotecario/una bibliotecaria.*
E2: *Dos ventajas de ser bibliotecario/a son estar en contacto con muchos libros y trabajar en un lugar tranquilo.*
E3: *Una desventaja es la falta de ejercicio físico.*

	PROFESIÓN	2 VENTAJAS	1 DESVENTAJA
1. Escribe artículos para el periódico.	periodista		
2. Presenta programas de televisión.	locutor/a		
3. Traduce simultáneamente.	intérprete		
4. Mantiene el orden público.	policía		
5. Apaga incendios.	bombero/a		
6. Defiende o acusa a personas delante de un/a juez.	abogado/a		

9-8 Mi ocupación ideal para el futuro. PRIMERA FASE. Piense en su ocupación o profesión ideal. Su compañero/a le va a hacer preguntas para adivinar la ocupación o profesión en que piensa.

MODELO: E1: *En tu profesión ideal, ¿las personas deben viajar mucho?*
E2: *Sí.*
E1: *¿Y deben hablar con clientes para hacer negocios?*
E2: *Sí.*
E1: *¡Ah! ¡Tú quieres ser hombre/mujer de negocios!*

SEGUNDA FASE. Haga una lista de tres requisitos de su trabajo ideal y compruebe si usted los tiene. Intercambie esta información con su compañero/a.

MODELO: *Me gustaría ser actor/actriz. Un actor/una actriz debe leer mucho; debe saber representar emociones y sentimientos y debe ser flexible para trabajar muchas horas. A mí me gusta leer y soy flexible, pero no puedo representar muy bien las emociones.*

Suggestions for 9-7. Organize students into groups of three. In preparation for the activity, have them brainstorm at least three advantages and three disadvantages of specific jobs. Model the activity: *¿Cuáles son las ventajas y desventajas de los siguientes trabajos: médico, enfermero, profesor, piloto?* Introduce the words *estrés* and *peligro* to talk about disadvantages. Have them switch roles so that all can practice identifying and describing. Alternatively, you may want to do only the identification part of the activity.

Suggestion for 9-8. Have students report their partners' plans to the class. Ask for opinions: *¿En qué trabajos... hay más estrés? ¿...se gana más dinero? ¿...dan más vacaciones?*

·)) Buscando trabajo

CD 4
Track 17 **La entrevista de trabajo**

Cultura

The **quetzal** (GQT) is the national currency of Guatemala. The exchange rate is about 7,56 GQT to $1 U.S. The word **quetzal** comes from the Náhuatl language and it refers to the strikingly colored bird that is the symbol of Guatemala.

Lengua

In Spanish, **actualmente** refers only to the present time.

> **Actualmente** yo trabajo en Antigua.
> *At the present time/Now I work in Antigua.*

Therefore, *actualmente* is a false cognate of *actually.* The equivalents of *actually* in Spanish are **realmente** or **en realidad**.

> **Realmente/En realidad** yo sólo trabajé en Ciudad de Guatemala un mes.
> *Actually I only worked in Ciudad de Guatemala for a month.*

SRA. ARCE: Buenos días, Sr. Solano. Soy Marcela Arce, presidenta de la compañía.

SR. SOLANO: Mucho gusto, señora.

SRA. ARCE: Siéntese, por favor. Usted **solicitó** el **puesto** de **gerente de ventas**, ¿verdad?

SR. SOLANO: Sí, señora. Leí en *El Diario de Centro América* que había una **vacante**. Después pedí y **llené** una **solicitud**.

SRA. ARCE: Sí, aquí la tengo, y también su **currículum**. **Por cierto**, es excelente.

SR. SOLANO: Muchas gracias.

SRA. ARCE: **Actualmente** usted trabaja en la empresa Badosa. ¿Por qué quiere **dejar** su puesto?

SR. SOLANO: Bueno, **en realidad** yo estoy muy contento allí, pero a mí me gustaría trabajar en una compañía internacional y poder usar otras lenguas. Como usted ve en mi currículum, yo hablo español, inglés y francés.

SRA. ARCE: En su solicitud, usted indica que desea un **sueldo** de 30.000 quetzales al mes. **Sin embargo**, para el puesto que tenemos, el sueldo que **se ofrece** es de 25.500 quetzales.

SR. SOLANO: Sí, lo sé, pero la diferencia no es tan importante. **Lo importante** es que aquí puedo tener la oportunidad de comunicarme con los clientes en su **propia** lengua. Yo creo que esto puede mejorar las ventas de Computel notablemente.

SRA. ARCE: Pues si le parece bien el sueldo, ¿por qué no pasamos a la oficina del director general para seguir hablando?

SR. SOLANO: ¡Cómo no!

👥 **9-9 Los datos de la entrevista.** Busquen los siguientes datos en el diálogo anterior.

1. nombre de la presidenta de la compañía   Marcela Arce
2. puesto que solicita el Sr. Solano   gerente de ventas
3. nombre de la compañía donde el Sr. Solano trabaja actualmente   Badosa
4. nombre de la compañía donde desea trabajar   Computel
5. lenguas que habla   español, inglés, francés
6. sueldo que desea el Sr. Solano   treinta mil quetzales
7. sueldo que se ofrece en el nuevo **puesto**   veinticinco mil quinientos quetzales
8. motivo para cambiar de puesto   trabajar en una compañía internacional y usar otras lenguas

9-10 ¿En qué orden? Cuando alguien busca un trabajo, normalmente ¿en qué orden ocurren las siguientes actividades? Ordénelas de 1 a 8.

_4_ Me llaman de la Compañía Rosell para una entrevista.
_7_ Les contesto que no, que se cerró el almacén.
_1_ Leo los anuncios del periódico.
_3_ Envío la solicitud a la Compañía Rosell.
_5_ Voy a la compañía para la entrevista.
_6_ Me preguntan si me despidieron (*fired*) del trabajo anterior.
_2_ Preparo mi currículum y lleno la solicitud para la Compañía Rosell.
_8_ Me ofrecen el puesto de vendedor/a.

9-11 El arte de entrevistarse. PRIMERA FASE. Escoja el anuncio más interesante del periódico *La Hora* e imagínese que solicita ese puesto. Su compañero/a, en el papel de jefe/a de personal, lo/la entrevista a usted y toma notas para obtener la siguiente información. Luego cambien de papel.

1. nombre de la persona que solicita el puesto
2. estudios que tiene
3. lenguas que habla
4. lugar donde trabaja y responsabilidades
5. experiencia anterior
6. razones para querer trabajar en esta compañía

INSTITUTO DE CIRUGÍA PLÁSTICA: CLÍNICA CÁRDENAS

Necesita enfermera

Prótesis:
implantes faciales (Botox, silicona)
liposucción papada,
abdomen,
muslos

Informes:
Clínica Centro, Zona 10
Tel: (502) 2534147

Llamar a secretaria: Marta

Hotel VILLA ANTIGUA

Necesita

RECEPCIONISTA
• Experiencia
• Bilingüe español-inglés

CAMARERA
• Mín. 2 años de experiencia
• Disponible trabajar por las mañanas y tardes

Dirigirse al Hotel VILLA ANTIGUA
Jefe de Personal
9a. Calle Poniente, Carretera a
Ciudad Vieja, Antigua, Guatemala
Teléfono: +(502) 78323956 ó +(502) 78323955

EMPRESA EXPORTADORA DE ARTESANÍAS
Requiere

CONTADOR

Requisitos:
• Experiencia mínima de 5 años
• Graduado del Colegio de Contadores Públicos
• Para cita llamar al Sr. López al (502) 2764532

EMPRESA MINERA

Requiere
3 Ingenieros de sistemas

REQUISITOS:
1. Mayor de 25 años
2. Experiencia en minas de cobre
3. Flexibilidad horaria (incluidos fines de semana)

OFRECEMOS:
1. Ingreso superior a 20.000 quetzales
2. Capacitación profesional
3. Bonos de participación

Interesados enviar currículum a: Minas de Guatemala S.A.

Oficina de Personal
Diagonal 19, 29-78, Zona 11
Ciudad de Guatemala, Guatemala
Teléfono: (502) 2762147
Fax: (502) 2763482

SEGUNDA FASE. Ahora informe al presidente de la empresa (otro compañero/otra compañera) sobre las calificaciones del candidato/de la candidata.

Follow-up for 9-12. Ask pairs to share some of their recommendations with the class. The class as a whole may choose the best ones.

Warm-up for 9-13. As a pre-listening activity, put students in groups of four to talk in Spanish about the professions they are pursuing and what they anticipate their schedules will be like.

Audioscript for 9-13. *Me llamo Julieta Odriozola y trabajo para el periódico La República. Mi trabajo es muy interesante porque escribo artículos sobre los eventos notables de la comunidad. Por ejemplo, les hago entrevistas a personalidades políticas, personas del mundo de los negocios o artistas, y esto me da la oportunidad de conocer a mucha gente fascinante. Después, estas entrevistas se publican en el periódico.*

Uno de los problemas de mi trabajo es que no tengo horario fijo, pues dependo de los horarios de los eventos o de las personas que voy a entrevistar. A veces trabajo los fines de semana o por la noche. Por ejemplo, la semana pasada, entrevisté a una mujer de negocios muy importante. Esta señora tenía varias reuniones de negocios el día que la entrevisté; por eso la tuve que entrevistar en su auto cuando íbamos de una reunión a otra. Las entrevistas a los artistas son completamente diferentes. Para la mayoría de ellos, el tiempo no es una obsesión, y es muy agradable hablar con ellos.

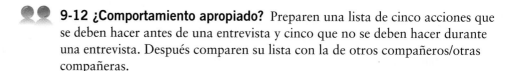

9-12 ¿Comportamiento apropiado? Preparen una lista de cinco acciones que se deben hacer antes de una entrevista y cinco que no se deben hacer durante una entrevista. Después comparen su lista con la de otros compañeros/otras compañeras.

LO QUE SE DEBE HACER ANTES DE UNA ENTREVISTA	LO QUE NO SE DEBE HACER DURANTE UNA ENTREVISTA

9-13 Mi profesión. You will listen to Julieta Odriozola talk about her profession. Before you listen, write down the names of four professions that have traditionally been associated with women.

CD 4
Track 18

Now, pay attention to the general idea of what is said. As you listen mark (✓) the appropriate ending to each statement.

1. Julieta Odriozola es…
   ____ artista.
   ____ política.
   _✓_ periodista.

2. Julieta tiene un horario…
   ____ de 9 a 5.
   _✓_ variable.
   ____ de lunes a sábado.

3. Julieta hace casi todo su trabajo en…
   ____ su auto.
   ____ su casa.
   _✓_ diferentes lugares.

4. Julieta trabaja básicamente con…
   ____ artistas jóvenes.
   _✓_ personas importantes.
   ____ empleados de la comunidad.

EN ACCIÓN

Resources
- Video
- SAM: 9-11 to 9-13

Diarios de bicicleta: ¿Qué quieres ser?

Antes de ver

9-14 Asocie cada una de las profesiones de la izquierda con una palabra relacionada en la columna derecha.

1. _e_ ingeniero/a
2. _f_ bombero/a
3. _a_ médico/a
4. _c_ chef
5. _d_ abogado/a
6. _b_ actor/actriz

a. salud
b. cine
c. comida
d. documentos legales
e. máquinas y computadoras
f. incendios

Note for 9-14. Activities like this one help students build their strategic competence, because it helps them use their lexical knowledge to enhance their self-expression, e.g., *Es una persona que trabaja con documentos legales.*

Mientras ve

9-15 Escriba todas las profesiones que se mencionan en este segmento.

ingeniero, doctor, chef, bomberos, médico, psicóloga, política, abogada, escritora, mujer policía, actriz

Suggestion for 9-15. Because the video segment features the vocabulary of professions, you may decide to use it to present some of the key vocabulary in *A primera vista.*

Después de ver

9-16 Exprese su opinión sobre los siguientes temas: Answers may vary.

- la profesión en que es posible ayudar a más gente
- la profesión más difícil
- la profesión más lucrativa
- la profesión más peligrosa (*dangerous*)

FUNCIONES Y FORMAS

1. Avoiding repetition: Review of direct and indirect object pronouns

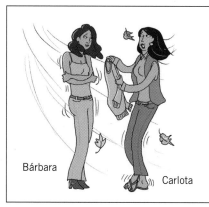

BÁRBARA:	Carlota, ¿por qué llevas chanclas (*flip-flops*)?
CARLOTA:	**Le** di mis zapatos al zapatero porque se rompieron.
BÁRBARA:	¿Y no tienes frío?
CARLOTA:	Sí, pero no tengo otra opción. El zapatero va a arreglarlos en una hora. Y tú, Bárbara, ¿por qué no tienes chaqueta? Hace frío.
BÁRBARA:	**La** dejé en casa.
CARLOTA:	Bueno, yo **te** presto mi suéter.

Bárbara

Carlota

Piénselo. Para cada oración, escriba las palabras en negrita (*boldface*) en la columna apropiada. **OJO:** En algunas oraciones hay más de un objeto directo u objeto indirecto.

	OBJETO DIRECTO	OBJETO INDIRECTO
1. **Le** di mis **zapatos** al **zapatero**.	zapatos	le, zapatero
2. El zapatero va a arreglar los **zapatos** de Carlota.	zapatos	none
3. El zapatero va a arreglar**los**.	los	none
4. ¿Por qué no tienes **chaqueta**?	chaqueta	none
5. **La** dejé en casa.	la	none
6. **Te** presto mi **suéter**.	suéter	te

- In *Capítulo 5* you learned that direct objects answer the question *what?* or *whom?* in relation to the verb. They can refer to people, animals, or objects. When a direct object noun refers to a specific person, a group of people, or a pet, the *personal* **a** precedes the direct object. To avoid repetition in speaking or writing, direct object pronouns can replace direct object nouns if the noun has already been mentioned.

¿Ves **al chef**?	*Do you see the **chef**?*
Sí, **lo** veo. Está al lado de la cocina.	*Yes, I see **him**. He is next to the kitchen.*
La Dra. Martín recibe **a sus pacientes** en la clínica.	*Dr. Martín sees **her patients** in the clinic.*
Los recibe todos los días.	*She sees **them** every day.*

■ In *Capítulo 6* you learned that indirect object nouns and pronouns tell *to whom* or *for whom* an action is done. They most often occur in the context of transferring information or objects, such as giving someone a gift, telling someone a story, or asking someone for something.

La maestra siempre **les** dice la verdad a los niños.	*The teacher always tells the children the truth.*
El camarero no **nos** trajo la sopa.	*The waiter did not bring us the soup.*

■ Direct and indirect object pronouns are placed before conjugated verbs. When a conjugated verb is followed by an infinitive or present participle, the pronouns can either precede the conjugated verb or be attached to the infinitive or present participle.

¿Las fotos de la casa?
La arquitecta está compilándo**las**.

The photos of the house?
The architect is compiling them.

¿Las fotos de la casa?
La arquitecta **las** está compilando.

Su asistente va a mandar**nos** todos los documentos.

Her assistent is going to send us all the documents.

Su asistente **nos** va a mandar todos los documentos.

■ Direct and indirect object pronouns have the same form, except in the third person. Note that **le/les** refer to either males or females.

DIRECT OBJECT PRONOUNS		INDIRECT OBJECT PRONOUNS	
me	nos	me	nos
te	os	te	os
lo	los	le	les
la	las		

9-17 Los preparativos para la evaluación. PRIMERA FASE.

Usted trabaja en la oficina de una arquitecta y mañana empieza la evaluación anual. Indique qué empleado/a está haciendo cada uno de los preparativos para la visita de los evaluadores: la arquitecta (**A**) o el asistente administrativo (**AA**). Answers may vary.

1. ____ Está terminando el último informe.
2. ____ Está examinando los materiales para ver si hay errores.
3. ____ Está sacando las fotocopias.
4. ____ Está organizando el horario.

SEGUNDA FASE. Compare sus respuestas con las de su compañero/a, siguiendo el modelo.

MODELO: E1: *¿Quién está examinando el presupuesto (budget)?*
E2: *El asistente administrativo está examinándolo.*

Suggestion. Remind students about the need for a written accent on the present participle when a pronoun is attached. You may wish to refer them to the Appendix in the Student Activities Manual for additional practice with accents.

9-18 Comunicaciones y transacciones. Mire los dibujos y explique dónde ocurre la escena y lo que pasa en cada una.

dependienta

Pancho

> **MODELO:** enviar/flores
> *Pancho está en la floristería. Le va a enviar flores a su esposa porque es el Día de los Enamorados.*

Juan

María

jefa

asistente

artesana

turistas

1. mandar/mensaje de texto **2.** dar/documentos **3.** vender/telas tradicionales

9-19 Gerentes y empleados. PRIMERA FASE. La compañía Hipertermo fabrica casas modulares que utilizan la energía solar y es famosa por la buena relación entre sus empleados. Escriban los factores que, según ustedes, contribuyen a la buena comunicación entre los gerentes y los empleados.

1. sugerir formas más eficientes de hacer el trabajo
2. dar las gracias por la alta calidad de su trabajo
3. explicar los beneficios de usar la energía solar
4. ofrecer ayuda para resolver conflictos
5. comunicar inmediatamente problemas con las máquinas
6. pedir ayuda cuando tienen dudas

LOS GERENTES...	LOS EMPLEADOS...
les explican a los empleados claramente sus responsabilidades.	les dan buenas ideas a los gerentes.

SEGUNDA FASE. Los gerentes quieren premiar (*reward*) a los empleados al final del año. ¿Qué van a hacer los gerentes para los empleados?

MODELO: escribir una carta de agradecimiento
Los gerentes van a escribirles una carta de agradecimiento.

1. subir el salario
2. dar una fiesta
3. escribir evaluaciones negativas de su trabajo
4. comprar regalos
5. decir que están muy contentos con su trabajo
6. pedir más horas de trabajo por semana

SITUACIONES

1. **Role A.** You meet with a career counselor (**consejero/a vocacional**) for tips on how to look for a job. Explain the type of job you are looking for, and answer the counselor's questions about your past experience. Ask the counselor questions of your own.

   Role B. You are a career counselor (**consejero/a vocacional**) who is meeting with a new client. After listening to the client, ask whether he/she a) prepared a résumé; b) looked for job ads (and where); c) applied for a job (which one); and d) prepared questions to ask in an interview. Be ready to answer the client's questions.

2. **Role A.** You are at an outdoor market in Antigua, Guatemala. You are at a stand that has blouses, tapestries, and jewelry. Tell the vendor that a) you want to give your sister a blouse for her birthday; b) you would like to take your parents a tapestry; and c) you want to buy a necklace for a good friend. Respond to the vendor's questions and ask an additional question about each item.

   Role B. You are a Guatemalan artisan selling your goods at a market in Antigua. An American student is interested in buying some gifts. Ask questions to help the customer make appropriate choices, and answer his/her questions about the items.

2. Avoiding repetition: Use of direct and indirect object pronouns together

CONSEJERA:	¿Ya **le** mandó su currículum al director?
CLIENTE:	Sí, **se lo** mandé la semana pasada.
CONSEJERA:	¿Recibió alguna confirmación?
CLIENTE:	Sí, ellos **me la** mandaron rápidamente. **La** recibí hoy.

Piénselo. Lea las oraciones y escriba en la columna apropiada los objetos directos y los indirectos, tanto los pronombres como los sustantivos (*nouns*).

	OBJETO INDIRECTO	OBJETO DIRECTO
MODELO: La secretaria **me** dio una cita para el lunes.	me	cita
1. ¿Ya **le** mandó su currículum al director?	le, director	currículum
2. **Se lo** mandé la semana pasada.	se	lo
3. Ellos **me la** mandaron rápidamente.	me	la
4. **La** recibí hoy.	none	la

■ You have already learned how to use indirect object pronouns or direct object pronouns in sentences. In this section you will learn how to use both types of pronouns in the same sentence.

INDIRECT OBJECT PRONOUNS		DIRECT OBJECT PRONOUNS	
me	nos	me	nos
te	os	te	os
le (se)	les (se)	lo	los
		la	las

■ When direct and indirect object pronouns are used in the same sentence, the indirect object pronoun precedes the direct object pronoun. Place double object pronouns before conjugated verbs.

Ella **me** dio **la solicitud**.
    i.o.   d.o.

She gave me the application.

Ella **me la** dio.
    i.o. d.o.

She gave it to me.

Resources

■ SAM: 9-17 to 9-22
■ Supp. Activ. Book: Use of direct and indirect object pronouns together

Warm-up. In this chapter students have reviewed direct and indirect objects as single objects in a sentence in preparation for double object pronouns. Refer students to p. 302, where they have already seen indirect object pronouns and direct object nouns used together. Although they can recognize these pronouns and some may produce them correctly in controlled situations, learners at this stage rarely use them when speaking freely. Assure students that there will be ample opportunities to practice object pronouns throughout the course.

Note. Explain that the phrase **a** + *noun* or **a** + *pronoun* may be used to clarify the meaning of *se*: *Se lo da a ella. Se lo da a Ana.*

Follow-up for Piénselo. You may wish to have students identify the referent for each object pronoun: *le = al director*; etc.

Lengua

You have learned that when the stress falls on the third syllable from the end of a word, a written accent is required. Therefore, you need to add one on the verb when double object pronouns are attached to an infinitive.

¿Va a darme la solicitud?
→ ¿Va a dármela?

When double object pronouns are attached to a present participle, the stress falls on the fourth syllable from the end, and a written accent is also required:

Se la está dando. →

Está dándosela.
   4   3 2 1

■ In compound verb constructions, you may place double object pronouns before the conjugated verb or attach them to the accompanying infinitive or present participle.

Él quiere dar**me** **el contrato**.
          i.o.   d.o.
He wants to give me the contract.

Él quiere dár**me** **lo**. ⎫
         i.o.d.o.   ⎬ He wants to give it to me.
Él **me** **lo** quiere dar. ⎭
    i.o. d.o.

Ella **te** está diciendo **la verdad**.
      i.o.   d.o.
She is telling you the truth.

Ella **te la** está diciendo. ⎫
     i.o. d.o.   ⎬ She is telling it to you.
Ella está diciéndo**te la**. ⎭
              i.o.d.o.

■ The indirect object pronouns **le** and **les** change to **se** before **lo, los, la,** or **las.**

Le dio **el puesto** a Verónica.
i.o.   d.o.
He gave the job to Veronica.

Se lo dio.
i.o. d.o.
He gave it to her.

Les va a mostrar **el anuncio**.
i.o.   d.o.
She is going to show them/you (ustedes) the ad.

Se lo va a mostrar.
i.o. d.o.
She is going to show it to them/you (ustedes).

■ When a direct object pronoun and a reflexive pronoun are used together, the reflexive pronoun precedes the direct object pronoun.

Siempre **me** envío **correos electrónicos**
        i.o.   d.o.
   para recordar lo que debo hacer.
I always send myself e-mails to remember what I have to do.

Siempre **me los** envío.
        i.o. d.o.
I always send them to myself.

 9-20 ¿Qué hizo el supervisor? Usted es el dueño/la dueña de una compañía. Habla con un empleado nuevo/una empleada nueva para saber si el supervisor hizo todo lo que tenía que hacer para explicarle cómo funciona su departamento.

MODELO: darle el manual de la compañía
        E1: *¿Le dio el manual de la compañía?*
        E2: *Sí, me lo dio.*

1. explicarle la campaña de publicidad
2. mostrarle los anuncios
3. traerle las revistas
4. pedirle un documento que faltaba
5. dejarle las fotos
6. describirle los modelos que se necesitan.

9-21 ¿Qué hace usted? PRIMERA FASE. La imparcialidad, la amabilidad y la confidencialidad son fundamentales en el trabajo. Lea las siguientes situaciones y seleccione lo que usted haría (*would do*) en cada una.

1. Un cliente le pide a usted el teléfono de la oficina del presidente de la compañía.
   a. ____ Usted se lo da.   b. ____ Usted no se lo da.
2. Alguien quiere leer un documento confidencial.
   a. ____ Usted se lo muestra.   b. ____ Usted no se lo muestra.

3. La nueva jefa de personal viene a una reunión de su departamento. Alguien tiene que presentarla a los empleados.

    a. ____ Usted se la presenta.   **b.** ____ Usted no se la presenta.

4. Una empleada nueva le dice a usted que quiere dos semanas de vacaciones después de trabajar sólo tres meses.

    a. ____ Usted se las da.   **b.** ____ Usted decide no dárselas.

SEGUNDA FASE. ¿Están de acuerdo usted y su compañero/a? Justifiquen su respuesta entre ustedes.

MODELO: Un cliente le pide a usted información personal sobre las finanzas de otro cliente. Los dos clientes son hermanos.

        E1:   *No se la doy porque no le gustaría al segundo cliente.*

        E2:   *Yo se la doy porque los dos clientes son hermanos.*

9-22 ¡El cliente siempre tiene razón! PRIMERA FASE. Ustedes se entrevistan sobre el servicio en un restaurante donde cada uno de ustedes comió recientemente. Tomen notas sobre las respuestas de su compañero/a para compartir con la clase.

1. ¿Cuándo les sirvieron el agua?

2. ¿Les trajeron pan a la mesa?

3. ¿Les dijo el camarero cuáles eran los platos especiales del día?

4. ¿Se los describió?

5. ¿Les ofreció postres y café?

6. ¿Cómo fue el servicio en general?

SEGUNDA FASE. Presenten a la clase un breve resumen del servicio en sus respectivos restaurantes.

SITUACIONES

1. Role A. You are a reporter for *El Quetzalteco*, a regional newspaper en Quetzaltenango, and you have just arrived in Guatemala City to cover a story. You were in such a rush to leave Quetzaltenango that you left your laptop and camera (**cámara**) in the taxi. Call a fellow reporter in the capital city and a) explain what happened; b) ask if he/she can lend you a laptop and camera; and c) say that you need them right away.

Role B. You are a reporter for *El Súper Canal 3* in Guatemala City. A reporter from Quetzaltenango calls to tell you about an urgent problem. Ask a) when he/she left the laptop and computer in the taxi and b) if he/she called the taxi company. When the reporter asks you for a favor, say that he/she can come to your office to pick them up right away.

2. Role A. As manager of a large bank, you asked an employee to deliver (**entregar**) an important package (**un paquete**) to another bank. When he/she returns, ask a) if he/she delivered it; b) at what time he/she delivered it; c) to whom he/she gave it.

Role B. You work at a large bank. You have just returned from delivering (**entregar**) an important package (**un paquete**) to another bank. The manager is anxious about whether the package reached its destination. Answer the manager's questions to ease his/her concerns.

Suggestion for 9-21 Segunda fase. If students have chosen the same response as their partners in the *Primera fase*, encourage them to come up with different justifications.

Suggestions for 9-22 Primera fase. Have students start the activity by explaining to their partners to which recent restaurant experience (where, when, with whom) they will be referring in the *Primera fase*. Students can alternate asking and answering the questions. You may also wish to remind students that the questions and answers refer to the group with whom they ate (*les, nos*), not just to themselves.

Suggestion for Segunda fase. You may use students' summaries as the basis for conducting a discussion on the service at restaurants that students frequent.

Resources
■ SAM: 9-23 to 9-29
■ Supp. Activ. Book: More of the imperfect and preterit

3. Talking about the past: More on the imperfect and preterit

PERIODISTA: Sr. Mario Parada, usted estaba en el Bancafé cuando entraron los ladrones (*robbers*), ¿verdad? ¿Qué **estaba haciendo**?

SR. PARADA: Yo **estaba hablando** con la cajera. **Iba a** hacer un depósito, pero claro, no **pude** realizar la transacción.

PERIODISTA: ¿Qué hicieron los empleados cuando **supieron** que había ladrones en el banco?

SR. PARADA: Todo pasó muy rápido. En el momento del robo, los cajeros **estaban respondiendo** a las preguntas de los clientes. Los oficiales de seguridad vieron a los ladrones y **quisieron** detenerlos (*stop them*) pero no **pudieron**.

Periodista   Mario Parada

Piénselo. Indique quién(es) estaba(n) haciendo las siguientes actividades cuando ocurrió el asalto: Mario Parada (**M**), los cajeros de Bancafé (**CA**), los clientes (**CL**) o los oficiales de seguridad (**O**).

1. _CA, O_ **Estaban trabajando** en Bancafé.
2. _M_ **Estaba poniendo** dinero en su cuenta de Bancafé.
3. _CL_ **Estaban haciendo** alguna transacción en Bancafé.
4. _CA_ **Estaban ayudando** a los clientes que tenían preguntas.

Suggestion for Piénselo. You may explain that statements refer to activities that serve as background to the narrative event (*el asalto*). Students can invent other background information to describe the scene in the bank (i.e., what was going on) when the robbery started. Point out to students that the imperfect is used to establish the context for an event or series of events that will be narrated.

■ You have used the imperfect to express an action or event that was in progress in the past. You may also use the imperfect progressive to emphasize the ongoing nature of the activity in the past. Form the imperfect progressive with the imperfect of **estar** and the present participle (**-ndo**).

Mario **estaba hablando** con la cajera cuando entraron los ladrones.	*Mario was talking to the teller when the robbers came in.*
Los vicepresidentes del banco **estaban trabajando** en el segundo piso cuando oyeron los gritos.	*The vice presidents of the bank were working on the second floor when they heard the shouts.*

■ To express intentions in the past, use the imperfect of **ir + a +** *infinitive*.

Iba a salir, pero era muy tarde.	*I was going to go out, but it was very late.*

Suggestion. You may wish to use the interview of the witness to the bank robbery on this page to show students additional uses of **iba a +** *infinitive* and the preterit of **poder, querer,** and **saber**.

■ In *Capítulo 7* you practiced the preterit of **saber** with the meaning of finding out about something. You also practiced the preterit of **querer** with the meaning of wanting or trying to do something, but failing to accomplish it.

Supe que Jorge consiguió trabajo. *I found out that Jorge got a job.*

Quise entrevistarme con el gerente, pero fue imposible.

I wanted (and tried) to get an interview with the manager, but it was impossible.

In the negative, the preterit of **querer** conveys the meaning of refusing to do something.

No quise ir. *I refused to go.*

■ Other verbs that convey a different meaning in English when the preterit is used are **conocer** and **poder.**

IMPERFECT		PRETERIT	
Yo **conocía** a Ana.	*I knew Ana.*	**Conocí** a Ana.	*I met Ana.*
Podía hacerlo.	*I could (was able to) do it.*	**Pude** hacerlo.	*I accomplished (managed to do) it.*
No podía hacerlo.	*I couldn't (wasn't able to) do it.*	**No pude** hacerlo.	*I couldn't do it. (I tried and failed.)*

9-23 Una oficina muy ocupada. Ustedes visitaron la oficina que aparece en la siguiente escena. Túrnense para preguntar qué estaban haciendo las personas cuando cada uno/a de ustedes llegó.

MODELO: E1: *¿Qué estaba haciendo Alicia cuando tú llegaste a la oficina?*
E2: *Estaba conversando con un cliente.*

Suggestions. Contrast the use of preterit and imperfect by giving examples: *El año pasado ustedes no estaban en mi clase de español. Yo no los conocía. Yo los conocí en septiembre cuando vinieron a mi clase. Yo no sabía entonces si eran buenos estudiantes, pero después de tener una o dos clases con ustedes supe que eran buenos.*

9-24 Una explicación lógica. Ayer ustedes tuvieron una reunión en su compañía para mostrarles unos productos nuevos a unas empresas extranjeras. Den una explicación lógica de todo lo que salió mal.

MODELO: La secretaria no contestaba el teléfono.
   E1: *Estaba buscando un intérprete para la reunión.*
   E2: *No, estaba buscando un salón más grande.*

1. Varios empleados llegaron tarde.
2. El técnico no pudo arreglar una computadora que se necesitaba para la presentación.
3. Los periodistas no podían comprender lo que decía un director extranjero.
4. No les sirvieron café ni refrescos a los invitados.
5. Uno de los vendedores no quiso mostrar los productos nuevos.
6. No se pusieron anuncios en los periódicos.

9-25 ¡A usar la imaginación! Estas descripciones indican lo que estaban haciendo varias personas ayer. Identifiquen cuál era el oficio o profesión de ellos y qué iban a hacer después.

MODELO: Esta persona llevaba un traje espacial, guantes, botas muy grandes y un plástico transparente frente a los ojos para poder ver.
   E1: *Era un astronauta.*
   E2: *Iba a caminar en la Luna.* Answers for first part of each question

1. Un señor tenía un secador en la mano y le arreglaba el pelo a una señora que estaba sentada enfrente de él. peluquero
2. Unos señores iban en un camión rojo con una sirena. El camión iba muy rápido y los autos paraban al lado derecho de la calle. bomberos
3. Una joven que llevaba un vestido similar a los que se llevaban en la época de Cleopatra hablaba frente a una cámara. Estaba muy maquillada y tenía una línea negra alrededor de los ojos. actriz
4. Un señor estudiaba los planos de un edificio y decía que ciertas cosas no estaban bien. arquitecto; answers for the second part may vary.

9-26 El diario de vida de Arturo. Lea una página del diario de Arturo, un estudiante de antropología enamorado de Guatemala. Escriba en el espacio la forma apropiada del verbo entre paréntesis, según el contexto.

En el ano 2007, yo (1) __conocí__ (conocí/conocía) a mi novia Elizabeth en mi segundo viaje a Guatemala. En ese momento, yo ya (2) __conocía__ (conocí/conocía) Antigua y un par de lugares de interés para los turistas. Después de nuestro encuentro, yo inmediatamente (3) __supe__ (supe/sabía) que mis visitas a Guatemala (4) __iban__ (fueron/iban) a ser más frecuentes. Ese año nosotros no (5) __pudimos__ (pudimos/podíamos) viajar juntos por el país, pero el año siguiente lo hicimos. Su familia, ella y yo (6) __pudimos__ (pudimos/podíamos) explorar juntos la reserva ecológica Calahuar. Caminamos todo el día por el bosque (*forest*). Después de caminar tantas horas, yo no (7) __podía__ (pude/podía) dar un paso más, pero al día siguiente (8) __pudimos__ (pudimos/podíamos) continuar el viaje a San Pedro La Laguna en Atlitán.

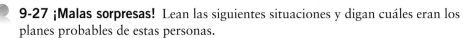

9-27 ¡Malas sorpresas! Lean las siguientes situaciones y digan cuáles eran los planes probables de estas personas.

MODELO: Martín está enfadado porque su bicicleta se descompuso (*broke*).
E1: *Martín no pudo ir al parque con sus amigos.*
E2: *Él quiso arreglar la bicicleta, pero fue imposible.*

1. Lorena está molesta porque la fotocopiadora de la oficina no funciona.
2. Usted y su pareja caminaron a su restaurante favorito, pero el restaurante estaba cerrado.
3. El jefe de producción llamó a una reunión urgente ayer. Anoche comenzó a nevar y muchos empleados no llegaron a su trabajo porque los caminos estaban en malas condiciones.
4. Al carro de Marta y Francisco se le acabó (*ran out of*) la gasolina cerca de la playa. Tuvieron que dejarlo en la carretera.
5. Esteba tenía una entrevista con el jefe de personal a las 9 pero no llegó a tiempo.

SITUACIONES

1. **Role A.** One of your employees did not come to an important meeting, so you call him/her to your office. Greet your employee and ask why he/she was not present. After listening to the explanation, say that a) this is the second time this happened and b) he/she has to attend all meetings in the future.

   Role B. You were expected to attend an important meeting at work, but you could not make it. After greeting your boss, apologize and explain the circumstances. As you were driving to work, your spouse called to say that a) there was a fire in the kitchen; b) the firefighters were there; and c) the children were fine but scared. Explain that you had to go home.

2. **Role A.** You are the caterer (**proveedor/a de comida**) hired for a large wedding party. While the party was taking place, the deck (**terraza**) of the house collapsed (**colapsar**), resulting in several injured people (**heridos**). An investigator (your classmate) interviews you about the accident.

   Role B. You are a police officer investigating the accident. Ask the caterer a) approximately how many guests and servers were on the deck (**terraza**) when it collapsed (**colapsar**); b) what the guests were doing there; and c) what the caterer was doing when the deck collapsed. Then thank the caterer for the information.

Additional practice with preterit and imperfect.
Students can complete the following account of a robbery that occurred if the offices of MayaSol using imperfect progressive, imperfect of **ir + a +** infinitive or the preterite of the verbs in parenthesis.

El lunes yo (1) (llegar) al trabajo temprano. Todo parecía normal, pero cuando entré en mi departamento, (2) (saber) que (3) (haber) un robo durante el fin de semana. Nosotros (4) (querer) hacer un inventario detallado de todo lo que había en la oficina, pero fue imposible, porque todo estaba en desorden. Mientras nosotros (5) (tratar) de preparar nuestras listas de todo lo que teníamos y de lo que faltaba, nuestra supervisora dijo que (6) (ir) a llamar a la policía. Pero primero (7) (llamar) al presidente de MayaSol, que (8) (viajar) a Chichicastenango. Al oír la noticia, el presidente le dijo a la supervisora que (9) (ir) a cancelar su viaje y volver inmediatamente. Trabajamos concentradamente, y cuando llegaron tres policías una hora más tarde, la supervisora (10) (poder) darles bastante información sobre las cosas robadas. El detective no (11) (querer) llamarnos hasta el viernes porque, según él nos dijo, él y su equipo (12) (ir) a estar muy ocupados con su investigación.

Answers: (1) *llegué;* (2) *supe;* (3) *hubo;* (4) *quisimos;* (5) *tratábamos;* (6) *iba;* (7) *llamó;* (8) *estaba viajando;* (9) *iba;* (10) *pudo;* (11) *quiso;* (12) *iban*

4. Giving instructions or suggestions: Formal commands

RICARDO: Buenos días, señorita. Me llamo Ricardo Roldán Díaz. ¿Podría darme una solicitud para el puesto de asistente de contador?

SECRETARIA: Claro que sí, Sr. Roldán. Por favor, **llene** la solicitud y **mándenosla** pronto.

RICARDO: ¿Puedo mandársela por correo electrónico?

SECRETARIA: Sí, **envíela** por correo electrónico, pero también por correo postal.

Piénselo. Ricardo llega a casa con la solicitud que le dio la secretaria. Lea las sugerencias que Ricardo leyó en un manual sobre cómo buscar puestos profesionales y marque (✓) las que le parecen apropiadas en la cultura de usted.

1. __✓__ Llene la solicitud inmediatamente.
2. __✓__ Escriba con letra clara.
3. _____ Mándele flores a la secretaria.
4. __✓__ No se olvide de incluir su currículum.
5. __✓__ Firme la solicitud.
6. __✓__ No deje ningún espacio en blanco.

Cultura

En Guatemala, los niños se dirigen normalmente a sus padres y a otras personas mayores con la forma **usted**. El uso del **tú** y del **usted** varía mucho en el mundo hispano, pero en general la forma **tú** es más común para comunicarse con los padres.

■ Commands (**los mandatos**) are the verb forms used to tell others to do something. Use formal commands with people you address as **usted** or **ustedes**. To form these commands, drop the final **-o** of the **yo** form of the present tense and add **-e(n)** for **-ar** verbs and **-a(n)** for **-er** and **-ir** verbs.

■ Verbs that are irregular in the **yo** form of the present tense maintain the same irregularity in the command form.

			USTED	USTEDES	
pensar	→	piens~~o~~	piense	piensen	*think*
dormir	→	duerm~~o~~	duerma	duerman	*sleep*
repetir	→	repit~~o~~	repita	repitan	*repeat*
poner	→	pong~~o~~	ponga	pongan	*put*

■ The use of **usted** and **ustedes** with command forms is optional. When used, they normally follow the command.

Pase/Pase **usted.**   *Come in.*

■ To make a formal command negative, place **no** before the affirmative command.

No salga ahora.   *Do not leave now.*

■ Object pronouns and reflexive pronouns are attached to the end of affirmative commands. (Note the written accent over the stressed vowel). Object pronouns and reflexive pronouns precede negative commands and are not attached.

Cómprela.	*Buy it.*
No la **compre.**	*Do not buy it.*
Háblenle.	*Talk to him/her.*
No le **hablen.**	*Do not talk to him/her.*
Siéntese.	*Sit down.*
No se **siente.**	*Do not sit down.*

Suggestion. Remind students that they saw some of these orthographic changes while practicing the preterit in *Capítulo 6*.

■ The verbs **dar, ir, ser,** and **saber** have irregular command forms.

dar: **dé, den** ir: **vaya, vayan** ser: **sea, sean** saber: **sepa, sepan**

■ Verbs ending in **-car, -gar, -zar, -ger,** and **-guir** have spelling changes in command forms.

sacar	sac~~o~~	→	sa**que**, sa**quen**
jugar	jue~~go~~	→	jue**gue**, jue**guen**
almorzar	almuer~~zo~~	→	almuer**ce**, almuer**cen**
recoger	reco~~jo~~	→	reco**ja**, reco**jan**
seguir	si~~go~~	→	si**ga**, si**gan**

9-28 Preguntas de un/a estudiante. Usted no asistió a clase durante la semana dedicada a Guatemala y quiere saber qué tiene que hacer para ponerse al día. Su compañero/a, en el papel de profesor/a, va a contestar afirmativamente a sus preguntas. Después, cambien de papel.

MODELO: estudiar el Capítulo 9
    E1: *¿Estudio el Capítulo 9?*
    E2: *Sí, estúdielo.*

1. contestar las preguntas sobre los lugares turísticos en Guatemala
2. mirar los DVDs de bailes folklóricos de Guatemala
3. escribir algunas expresiones populares entre los jóvenes guatemaltecos
4. leer el *Enfoque cultural* sobre Guatemala
5. hacer la tarea sobre las culturas indígenas de Guatemala

9-29 En el hospital. Un enfermero/Una enfermera entra en la habitación y le hace las siguientes preguntas al/a la paciente. Túrnense para hacer los papeles de enfermero/a y paciente.

MODELO: E1: *¿Le abro las cortinas?*
E2: *Sí, ábramelas, por favor. Quisiera leer.*

1. ¿Le pongo la televisión?
2. ¿Le traigo un jugo?
3. ¿Le pongo otra almohada?
4. ¿Me llevo estas flores?
5. ¿Le traigo el teléfono?
6. ...

 9-30 Mandatos del entrenador de un equipo. Preparen una lista de sugerencias que el entrenador/la entrenadora puede darles a los miembros de su equipo para lograr los objetivos siguientes. Comparen su lista con la de otra pareja.

MODELO: para mantenerse en buen estado físico
Practiquen todos los días. No se acuesten tarde.

1. para tener mejor rendimiento (*performance*)
2. para prepararse mentalmente para un partido difícil
3. para evitar problemas con el árbitro
4. para dormir bien cuando tienen mucho estrés
5. para ser buenos alumnos y buenos deportistas también

Cultura

En la ciudad de Cobán, en el centro de Guatemala, se celebra anualmente un festival de personas nativas de Guatemala, La Fiesta Nacional Indígena de Guatemala (Festival Folclórico). Incluye un certamen (*contest*) de belleza para mujeres indígenas de Guatemala. Participan aproximadamente 100 señoritas que expresan sus ideales en su idioma materno y en español. La ganadora es coronada con el título de *Rabin Ajau*, que significa Hija del Rey en Q'eqchi', un idioma maya.

 9-31 ¿Qué deben hacer estas personas? Busquen una solución a los siguientes problemas y díganle a cada persona lo que debe hacer.

MODELO: El Sr. Álvarez dice: "No estoy contento en mi trabajo".
E1: *Sr. Álvarez, busque otro trabajo inmediatamente.*
E2: *Hable con su jefe y explíquele la situación.*

1. La Sra. Jiménez dice: "Necesito más vendedores en mi compañía".
2. El Sr. Jiménez se queja (*complains*): "Tengo que terminar un informe económico mensual pero mi computadora no funciona".
3. Unos hombres de negocios van a ir a Ciudad de Guatemala, pero no saben hablar español.
4. La Sra. Peña tuvo un accidente serio con su auto; el chofer que provocó el accidente no quiere darle la información que ella necesita para informar a su seguro.
5. La Sra. Hurtado entra en su apartamento y ve que hay agua en el piso de la cocina.
6. Su esposa quiere ir al Festival Folclórico Nacional de Cobán, pero el Sr. Fernández no se siente bien.

Note for Situación 2. You may want to explain that *Banco de Café* is the official name of the financial institution, but it is commonly referred to as *Bancafé*.

SITUACIONES

1. **Role A.** Tell your neighbor that you are leaving for three days for job interviews. Ask if your neighbor can do a few things for you. After he/she agrees, tell him/her to a) feed (**dar de comer a**) the cat and play with her every day; b) water the plants; c) pick up the mail (**correspondencia**); and d) any other things that you may need. Thank him/her for helping out.

   Role B. Your neighbor tells you that he/she is going to be away. Agree to help him/her out. After you find out what you will have to do, ask: a) whom should you call if there is an emergency (**emergencia**) and b) get the telephone number of the vet (**veterinario/a**).

2. **Role A.** You have moved to Quetzaltenango, Guatemala, and want to open a checking account (**cuenta corriente**) at Bancafé. Since you are not familiar with their system, ask an employee for help. After the employee gives you all the details, thank him/her, and say that you are very happy with the service the bank provides the customers.

   Role B. You are an employee at Bancafé in Quetzaltenango, Guatemala. Explain to a new customer a) how to write a check in Spanish (see example below); b) how to write the date in Spanish; c) where to put the name of the person to whom he/she is writing the check; d) how to write the amount (**cantidad**) in numbers; e) how to write the amount in words; and f) where to sign the check (**firmar el cheque**).

Serie AD   6703690 $ _____

12 Av. 5-50   012-0587
Zona 1   446

_____ · _____ DE _____ AÑO _ _ _ _ _

PÁGUESE A
LA ORDEN DE _____
                                                    O AL PORTADOR
LA CANTIDAD DE _____

_____ PESOS M/L

BANCO DE CAFÉ, S.A. _____

06703690   01905874460042102   01

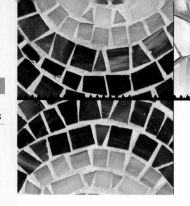

Resources
- SAM: 9-38 to 9-40
- Supp. Activ. Book: *Mosaicos*

Warm-up for 9-33. As a pre-listening activity, have students talk in groups of four in Spanish about the professions of four different people they know (one person each), what they do, and what their personal characteristics are.

Audioscript for 9-33.
ESTELA: *Susana, te digo que me encanta ser mujer de negocios. El sueldo es excelente y los beneficios son estupendos. Imagínate, tengo un seguro médico maravilloso y cuatro semanas de vacaciones al año. Lo que no me gusta mucho es que tengo que viajar por lo menos treinta semanas al año y que no tengo tiempo para estar mucho con mi familia.*
SUSANA: *Me alegro de que te guste tu trabajo, Estela. A mí también me encanta el mío, pero es diferente, por supuesto.*
ESTELA: *Sí, como neuróloga ayudas a muchas personas. Eso debe ser maravilloso. Es horrible tener neuralgias o dolores de cabeza. ¡Tener un buen médico especialista si uno está mal de los nervios es primordial!*
SUSANA: *Sí, me encanta ayudar a la gente. El único problema que tengo es que el horario es muy variable. Si alguien se enferma de noche, me tengo que levantar para ir a verlo al hospital si es necesario. También tengo guardias una vez a la semana cuando me tengo que quedar 24 horas en el hospital.*
ESTELA: *Comprendo. No hay nada perfecto.*
SUSANA: *Pero, no me quejo. Me gusta mi trabajo y gano un buen sueldo.*

MOSAICOS

A escuchar

ESTRATEGIA

Use contextual guessing

When you have a conversation in a second language, it is very possible that you may not understand everything the other person says. You can figure out the overall message by using contextual cues; that is, by paying attention to the topic or to the words that precede or follow what you did not understand.

Antes de escuchar

9-32 Preparación. En la siguiente conversación, dos amigas hablan sobre las ventajas y desventajas de su trabajo. Antes de escuchar, escriba el nombre de una profesión relacionada con los negocios y otra con la salud. Luego, escriba una ventaja y una desventaja para cada una de las profesiones.

PROFESIÓN	VENTAJA	DESVENTAJA
_____	_____	_____
_____	_____	_____

Escuchar

9-33 ¿Comprende usted? First, read the words in the left column and listen to the conversation between Estela and Susana. Then state the probable meaning of each word in English based on the contextual cues you heard in the conversation. Finally, write down the cue words that helped you understand.

CD 4 Track 19

Answers for last column may vary; possible responses are given.

ESCUCHÉ...	POSIBLE SIGNIFICADO	ADIVINÉ EL SIGNIFICADO PORQUE...
1. neuróloga	neurologist	neuralgias, nervios (cognados), dolores de cabeza.
2. primordial	prime, fundamental	médico especialista cuando uno está mal
3. guardias	to be on duty	una vez a la semana, quedarse en el hospital 24 horas

Después de escuchar

 9-34 Ahora usted. Compartan las respuestas a las siguientes preguntas.

1. ¿Cuáles son las ventajas y desventajas de la profesión que le gusta a usted?
2. En general, ¿qué profesión u ocupación le parece a usted que es menos estresante?
3. ¿Qué profesión u ocupación, según usted, da más satisfacciones personales? ¿Por qué?

A conversar

Resources
■ SAM: 9-41
■ *Entrevistas* video

ESTRATEGIA

Gather information strategically to express a decision

When you speak to communicate a decision, you need to present your decision and the reasons behind it in an organized and convincing way. To do so, it helps to lay out your facts and arguments logically in your mind, or in notes that you make before you begin to speak.

Antes de conversar

9-35 Preparación. Lea los siguientes anuncios con ofertas de trabajo, escoja un anuncio para un puesto que a usted le interese y prepare una lista de requisitos que, en su opinión, usted cumple (*meet*). Comparta su lista con su compañero/a.

JEFE DE SERVICIO
necesita importante empresa
MANUFACTURERA DE PLÁSTICOS

Nos urge un buen diseñador gráfico
Requisitos: Conocer al 100% PhotoShop y Freehand. Manejar ambiente Mac y PC. De preferencia estudiante de diseño en la U, con ideas frescas. Dispuesto a trabajar bajo presión.
Ofrecemos: Salario a convenir. Capacitación constante. Desarrollo dentro de la organización. Horario flexible. Seguro de vida y médico.
Interesados, enviar currículum y fotografía reciente, especificando pretensiones de sueldo, a Casilla 2568, Correo Guatemala, zona 1, Guatemala

INSTITUTO PRIVADO
necesita
DIRECTOR/A
Lugar de residencia, Región de los Lagos

Empresa de Hotelería necesita
Director/a

Requisitos: Estudios universitarios avanzados. Experiencia mínima de 1 a 2 años en ventas directas, preferiblemente en el área de servicios. Edad 26 a 32 años. Excelente presentación. Poseer vehículo propio. Buenas relaciones interpersonales.

Ofrecemos: Salario a convenir según experiencia, gasolina, comisiones sobre ventas. Excelente ambiente de trabajo. Oportunidades de crecimiento.

Sueldo compatible con calificaciones

Interesados, enviar currículum a
gruporecursoshumanos@hotmail.com

EMPRESA DE EXPORTACIONES
necesita para Chile y el extranjero
VENDEDORES/AS REPRESENTANTES

Sueldo inicial 1,000.000
Comisión de ventas

Casa Tadeo necesita
Asistente de Ventas y Mercadeo
Requisitos: Estudios universitarios de administración de empresas o mercadeo. De preferencia con experiencia en puesto similar de 1 año, no indispensable. Proactivo, extrovertido, dinámico, con autoridad, con iniciativa, organizado, colaborador. Habilidad para trabajar independientemente. Excelente manejo de equipos de cómputo. Buen dominio del inglés. Filosofía de servicio al cliente.
Ofrecemos: Salario competitivo. Oportunidades de capacitación. Excelente oportunidad de desarrollo en una empresa de alto crecimiento. Ambiente agradable de trabajo.

Interesados, llamar al teléfono
2533-2459
Lunes a viernes de 8:30 a 15:00 hrs.

BANCO AZTECA
necesita
10 CONTADORES AUDITORES
Lugar de trabajo ideal: Viña del Mar

- Título universitario
- Mínimo dos años de experiencia
- Flexibilidad horaria
- Deseo de viajar a otras regiones del país
- Capacidad de organización y trabajo

Sueldo atractivo

Interesados, enviar currículum, con fotografía a:
Bco. Azteca, 7 Av. 19-28, zona 5

Cultura

La manera de expresar la dirección de un negocio o un domicilio en Guatemala puede confundir a los extranjeros. Por ejemplo, "7 Av. 11-38, zona 9" significa que la casa está en la avenida 7, entre las calles 11 y 12 en la zona 9, y el número de la casa es 38. Las zonas tienen la misma función que los códigos postales (*zip codes*) en Estados Unidos.

Decir la zona es importante, porque los números de las avenidas (que van del norte al sur) y de las calles (que van del este al oeste) se repiten en cada zona.

En directo

To welcome someone to your office:

Pase/Adelante, por favor./Tenga la amabilidad de pasar. *Please come in.*

Por favor, tome asiento. *Please have a seat.*

Siéntese aquí, por favor. *Sit here, please.*

To put someone at ease:

Por favor, póngase cómodo/a. *Please, make yourself comfortable.*

To say good-bye at the end of an interview:

Fue un placer conocerlo/la. *It was a pleasure to meet you.*

Conversar

9-36 Entre nosotros. Ahora escojan un papel. Uno/a de ustedes es el jefe/la jefa de personal de una compañía representada en los anuncios y dos son personas que solicitan el mismo trabajo en esa compañía. Sigan las siguientes instrucciones para cada papel.

Jefe/a de personal: Entreviste separadamente a dos personas que están interesadas en el mismo puesto. Pregúnteles sobre su experiencia, sus estudios, sus preferencias de sueldo, etc. y decida cuál es la persona indicada para el puesto.

Personas que buscan trabajo: Escojan el anuncio con el trabajo que los dos necesitan. Respondan a las preguntas del jefe/de la jefa de personal y háganle preguntas para saber más acerca del puesto.

Después de conversar

9-37 Un poco más. PRIMERA FASE. Los jefes de personal y las personas que buscaban trabajo deben informar a la clase sobre lo siguiente:

Informe de las personas que buscaban trabajo:

1. ¿Qué puesto buscaba usted? ¿Qué requisitos para el puesto cumple usted?
2. ¿Qué aspecto de la oferta de trabajo le pareció más atractivo?
3. ¿Cree usted que va a recibir la oferta de trabajo? ¿Por qué?

Informe de los jefes de personal:

1. ¿Qué puesto ofrecía su compañía en el anuncio?
2. ¿Qué requisitos debía tener el candidato/la candidata que buscaba su compañía?
3. ¿A qué candidato/a(s) va a contratar usted? ¿Por qué?

SEGUNDA FASE. Presenten la entrevista ideal entre el jefe de personal y el candidato más apropiado para cada anuncio de trabajo.

A leer

Resources
■ SAM: 9-42 to 9-44

Organize textual information into categories

To understand what you are reading, you need to focus on what is being conveyed by the text. By *focus* we mean organizing the information into meaningful categories, which helps you connect the information to what you already know. As you read, focus on the main points in each of the three sections. Use the subtitles to help you anticipate the content.

Antes de leer

9-38 Preparación. Lea el título y los subtítulos del texto y mire la foto. Basándose en esta información y en lo que usted sabe sobre la inmigración, marque (✓) las ideas que piensa encontrar en el texto.

1. ____ Muchas mujeres guatemaltecas en Estados Unidos se casan con hombres mexicanos.
2. ✓ El término "guatemexicoestadounidense" se refiere a familias cuyos (*whose*) miembros pertenecen a estas tres culturas.
3. ✓ La concentración más grande de guatemaltecos en Estados Unidos está en Los Ángeles.
4. ✓ La inmigración de guatemaltecos a Estados Unidos tiene un impacto económico positivo en Guatemala.

Leer

Los guatemaltecos en Estados Unidos

Matrimonios entre guatemaltecos y mexicanos

Gustavo Rivera conoció a Marta Rodríguez en un club hispano de Los Ángeles y la invitó a bailar.

"¿De dónde eres?", preguntó Marta. "De México", respondió Gustavo.

Después de esa noche, los dos empezaron a conversar por teléfono y a salir juntos. Marta, que era de Ciudad de México, se dio cuenta que Gustavo hablaba español con un acento diferente y usaba unas palabras diferentes también. Después de un tiempo, ella le preguntó: "¿De dónde eres realmente, Gustavo?" Esta vez, Gustavo le dijo la verdad: "Soy de Guatemala". Pasaron dos años y Gustavo y Marta se casaron. Ahora tienen tres hijos: Martita, de tres años, Gustavo, de dos y la bebé Rosita, de seis meses. Esta familia representa una tendencia demográfica que está aumentando en Los Ángeles y en otras ciudades del suroeste: más inmigrantes guatemaltecos y mexicanos se casan entre sí y tienen hijos, creando familias hispanas mixtas que tienen conexiones con tres países al mismo tiempo. Esa mezcla es ahora tan común que dio lugar al nombre de "guatemexicoestadounidenses" para describir a esas familias.

Nuevas tendencias demográficas

Hay varias razones que explican esta nueva tendencia demográfica. Primero, el número de personas de ascendencia guatemalteca en Estados Unidos está creciendo. Según la Organización Internacional para las Migraciones (OIM), en 2006 había 1.178.000 guatemaltecos en Estados Unidos. La mayoría de ellos son jóvenes, entre 15 y 44 años, y hay muchos más hombres que mujeres. Se estima que el 72% son hombres y el 28% mujeres. Es evidente que, por esta razón, cuando los guatemaltecos en Estados Unidos se casan, muchos se casan con mujeres no guatemaltecas.

Segundo, cuando llegan a Estados Unidos, los inmigrantes guatemaltecos buscan vivienda en comunidades hispanas establecidas, donde viven principalmente inmigrantes mexicanos, el grupo hispano más grande del país. La constante interacción de hombres guatemaltecos y mujeres mexicanas inevitablemente resulta en más matrimonios entre los dos grupos.

Esta mezcla de culturas hispanas no se limita a guatemaltecos y mexicanos. Los hispanos son, como los estadounidenses, de diversas nacionalidades. Una persona puede decir, por ejemplo, "la madre de mi madre es de Irlanda, y los padres de mi padre eran alemanes". Lo mismo está ocurriendo con los hispanos.

Impacto económico en Guatemala

En muchos sentidos, Gustavo Rivera es un inmigrante guatemalteco típico. Como el 88% de los guatemaltecos que viven en Estados Unidos, Gustavo se mantiene activo económicamente, trabaja en una fábrica que manufactura materiales para tejados (*roofs*). Como el 33% de los guatemaltecos en Estados Unidos, vive en Los Ángeles. Y como el 93% de los emigrantes guatemaltecos, mantiene contacto con su familia en Guatemala. Llama a sus padres todas las semanas y les envía remesas todos los meses. Según la OIM, más de 600.000 familias en Guatemala reciben remesas de familiares que viven en el extranjero.

El impacto económico de las remesas en Guatemala es considerable. Se estima que las remesas estimulan la economía de Guatemala, igual que la de otros países centroamericanos. También ayudan a estos países a evitar la recesión.

Ⓢ **Standard 5.1** Students use the language both within and beyond the school setting. Mexicans and Guatemalans are only two groups of the growing Hispanic population of the U.S. You may wish to encourage students to talk about and perhaps do some research on how their future career plans could be expanded and enhanced by having sufficient proficiency in Spanish to use it in their chosen professions.

Note. Other cities with a high concentration of Guatemalans include Phoenix, Houston, Chicago, Miami, Washington, D.C. and New York.

Note. Families in Guatemala use 50% of the money they receive from family members in the United States for basic needs such as food and clothing. The other 50% goes for living and health expenses, products for the home and for savings.

9-39 Primera mirada. Indique a qué categoría pertenecen las siguientes afirmaciones, según el contenido del artículo: información personal sobre una familia (**P**), información general sobre los inmigrantes guatemaltecos en Estados Unidos (**EU**) o información sobre Guatemala (**G**).

1. _EU_ Viven en comunidades donde el grupo predominante son los mexicanos.
2. _P_ Se conocieron en un club de baile.
3. _G_ Reciben dinero de sus familiares que viven en el extranjero.
4. _EU_ Se casan con personas de otras culturas.
5. _G_ El dinero que viene del exterior estimula la economía.
6. _P_ No dijo la verdad sobre su país de origen.
7. _EU_ Hay más hombres que mujeres.
8. ____ Muchas veces sus hijos nacen en un país diferente de donde nacieron los padres.

9-40 Segunda mirada. El artículo explica algunos fenómenos de causa y efecto. Conecte cada fenómeno en la columna de la izquierda con su resultado lógico en la columna de la derecha.

1. _c_ La mayoría de los inmigrantes son jóvenes.
2. _d_ Hay más hombres que mujeres entre los inmigrantes guatemaltecos.
3. _a_ Los mexicanos son el grupo hispano más numeroso en Estados Unidos.
4. _b_ La gran mayoría de los inmigrantes guatemaltecos tienen trabajo.
5. _e_ Hay una tendencia en Estados Unidos a casarse con personas de diferentes ascendencias culturales.

a. Hay muchas parejas en las que una persona es mexicana y la otra es de otra cultura hispana.
b. Mandan remesas a sus familiares en Guatemala.
c. Se casan en su nuevo país.
d. Se casan con mujeres no guatemaltecas.
e. Hay cada vez más familias hispanas compuestas de (*composed of*) personas de diferentes países.

Después de leer

 9-41 Ampliación. Con su compañero/a, escriban una lista de la información nueva que aprendieron del artículo. Luego, indiquen qué información les parece más interesante.

Follow-up for 9-41. Have pairs of students share their lists with another group, or create a master list of new information on the board. You may wish to take a poll to see which points were new information for most members of the class.

A escribir

Resources
■ SAM: 9-45 to 9-47

ESTRATEGIA

Focus on purpose, content, and audience

Getting the job you want may be a challenge in today's competitive labor market. Responding effectively to an employment ad is an important first step. Answering an ad takes as much skill as being interviewed.

To get the job that is right for you, whether during college or after graduation, consider the following when responding to an ad in any language:

■ Your purpose: What kind of job do you want (management or entry level; full- or part-time; permanent or temporary, etc.)?
■ Your response: What academic degree do you need for the job (high school, college, other)? What general abilities and job-specific skills should you possess?
■ Your audience: What experience does the employer require? What personality characteristics will you need to be considered a serious candidate?

Antes de escribir

9-42 Preparación. Usted ve un anuncio de trabajo en Internet de la señora Álvarez de Colón de Guatemala. La familia va a mudarse a Estados Unidos y quiere contratar a dos estudiantes en Estados Unidos para el verano, uno/a para cuidar a sus dos hijos (de 4 y 6 años) y enseñarles inglés y el otro/la otra para preparar comidas típicamente americanas. Planee un correo electrónico para solicitar uno de los trabajos. Haga una lista de las categorías de información sobre su experiencia y sus talentos que piensa mencionar.

Escribir

9-43 Manos a la obra. Ahora escríbale un correo electrónico a la señora Álvarez de Colón. En un mensaje breve, organizado y convincente, preséntese y explique cómo su experiencia, su conocimiento y sus talentos lo/la preparan para el puesto.

Después de escribir

9-44 Revisión. Lea lo que escribió, pensando en su lectora. Verifique lo siguiente:

1. ¿Qué categorías de información incluyó? ¿Falta alguna categoría importante?
2. Como usted no conoce a esta persona, ¿se dirigió a ella usando la forma *usted*?
3. ¿Tiene su correo electrónico una organización clara, es decir, una introducción, un cuerpo y un cierre?
4. ¿Revisó el vocabulario, expresiones de cortesía y de despedida, la concordancia, el tiempo (presente, pasado), el uso de los mandatos, etc.?

Comparta su mensaje electrónico con un compañero/una compañera. Esto puede darle la perspectiva de un lector/una lectora sobre la claridad de su texto y sobre la cantidad de información que usted incluyó.

ENFOQUE CULTURAL

Historia y trabajo en Guatemala

Los restos de la gran civilización maya sobreviven hoy día en sitios como Tikal, Yaxha y Naachtun en Guatemala. Las ruinas que se conservan nos permiten imaginar cómo fueron esas ciudades en sus momentos de esplendor. Cuando las visitamos, frecuentemente pensamos en la complejidad y el simbolismo religioso de muchas de esas construcciones, o en el lujo de los palacios, o en la avanzada técnica de construcción. Y sin embargo, un aspecto muy importante que con

Gran Plaza de Tikal

frecuencia olvidamos es la diversidad de profesiones, trabajos y artes que tuvieron que desarrollar los mayas para construir dichas ciudades. En efecto, fue necesario especializar a los trabajadores, de manera que surgieron profesiones independientes para realizar actividades específicas. Pintores, escultores, cortadores de piedra, carpinteros, ceramistas, astrónomos, todos contribuyeron con su trabajo especializado.

Mientras estas personas trabajaban en la construcción de las ciudades, los agricultores tenían que cultivar la comida para alimentar a todos estos trabajadores urbanos que no tenían tiempo para producir su propia alimentación. Y como es lógico, cuando el centro de producción es diferente del centro de consumo, los comerciantes se ocupan de llevar los productos del campo y venderlos en los mercados de la ciudad. Pero los comerciantes mayas hicieron más que eso, pues desarrollaron unas rutas comerciales que los llevaron más allá de las fronteras locales. Efectivamente, la red de caminos de los comerciantes mayas cubría una inmensa parte de México y Centroamérica.

Xaman-ek, considerado el dios de los comerciantes, según está representado en el Códice Dresden

322

El mercado indígena de Antigua, un ejemplo del llamado "capitalismo del centavo"

Cultura

La economía guatemalteca
El 50% de la fuerza laboral de Guatemala trabaja en la agricultura. Los productos principales son el café, la caña de azúcar y los plátanos, que constituyen dos tercios (*thirds*) de las exportaciones del país. Guatemala exporta también madera y níquel. El turismo también es un motor importante de la economía guatemalteca. Guatemala recibe aproximadamente 1.800.000 turistas cada año.

Cuando vemos la sofisticación y la complejidad de la antigua civilización maya, nos preguntamos por qué es hoy Guatemala uno de los países más pobres del continente. Aunque la respuesta a esta pregunta es demasiado compleja para contestarla en pocas palabras, sí podemos decir que la sociedad creada a partir de la colonia española marginó a la población indígena y limitó su posibilidad de participar en la economía. Y, puesto que más del 60% de la población guatemalteca hoy día se considera indígena, un porcentaje muy elevado de la población tiene que encontrar su subsistencia en una economía limitada, a la que Sol Tax, un famoso antropólogo de la Universidad de Chicago, llamó "capitalismo del centavo". Lo más interesante, sin embargo, es que a pesar de tantos años de marginalización, el espíritu comerciante de los indígenas no ha desaparecido y continúa muy visible hoy día en los mercados indígenas.

Desafortunadamente, en la actualidad, los más emprendedores entre los marginados de Guatemala buscan en la emigración mejores condiciones de trabajo y formas para participar en la economía. Esta necesidad de buscar oportunidades económicas fuera de Guatemala se ve reforzada por las periódicas catástrofes naturales que ocurren en la región, tales como terremotos y huracanes. Otro factor que afecta a la ola migratoria son los acontecimientos de carácter político, tales como las guerras civiles o las dictaduras militares que persiguen a los indígenas. En la actualidad, más de una cuarta parte de los inmigrantes centroamericanos en Estados Unidos son de Guatemala, y se calculan en cerca del millón.

En otras palabras

Expresiones guatemaltecas

Me gusta Luis, pero es muy **codo**.
I like Luis, but he is very stingy.

¡Me muero de hambre! Necesito **una refacción**.
I am starving! I need a snack.

¡Anda rápido que ya viene **la camioneta**!
Hurry up! The bus is coming!

9-45 Comprensión. PRIMERA FASE. Reconocimiento de palabras clave. Encuentre en el texto la palabra o expresión que mejor expresa el significado de las siguientes ideas.

1. remnants — restos/ruinas
2. stonecutters — cortadores de piedra
3. to feed — alimentar
4. merchants — comerciantes
5. trade routes — rutas comerciales
6. complexity — complejidad
7. civil wars — guerras civiles

SEGUNDA FASE. Oraciones importantes. Subraye las afirmaciones que contienen ideas que se encuentran en el texto. Luego indique en qué parte del texto están.

1. For all their complexity, Mayan cities lacked religious symbolism.
2. We often fail to see the variety of trades that were required to build a Mayan city.
3. Mayan farmers were forced to stop growing food crops to work on the construction of the great Mayan cities.
4. Mayan merchants traded their products well beyond the borders of the Maya Empire.
5. Guatemala is one of the poorest countries in the continent today.
6. Well over half of the population of Guatemala is considered to be indigenous.
7. Military dictatorships have been successful in curbing emigration.
8. Natural disasters are one of the factors that motivate Guatemalans to emigrate.

TERCERA FASE. Ideas principales. Escriba un párrafo breve en inglés resumiendo las ideas principales expresadas en el texto.

 9-46 Use la información. Escriba una carta contestando a un anuncio de trabajo en Guatemala. Su carta debe incluir lo siguiente:

1. qué trabajo solicita usted
2. dónde trabaja actualmente y por cuánto tiempo
3. qué experiencia tiene usted en ese tipo de trabajo
4. cuándo puede empezar a trabajar

Para preparar esta actividad, visite la página web de *Mosaicos* y siga los enlaces útiles.

VOCABULARIO

Las profesiones, oficios y ocupaciones — *Professions, trades, and occupations*

el/la abogado/a	*lawyer*
el actor/la actriz	*actor/actress*
el/la agricultor/a	*farmer*
el ama/o de casa	*housewife, homemaker*
el/la arquitecto/a	*architect*
el/la artesano/a	*craftsman/woman, craftsperson*
el/la bibliotecario/a	*librarian*
el/la bombero/a	*firefighter*
el/la cajero/a	*cashier*
el/la carpintero/a	*carpenter*
el/la ceramista	*potter*
el/la chef	*chef*
el/la chofer	*driver*
el/la científico/a	*scientist*
el/la contador/a	*accountant*
el/la contratista	*contractor*
el/la ejecutivo/a	*executive*
el/la electricista	*electrician*
el/la empleado/a	*employee*
el/la enfermero/a	*nurse*
el/la gerente (de ventas)	*(sales) manager*
el herrero	*blacksmith; ironworker*
el hombre/la mujer de negocios	*businessman/woman*
el/la ingeniero/a	*engineer*
el/la intérprete	*interpreter*
el jefe/la jefa	*boss*
el/la joyero/a	*jeweller*
el/la juez	*judge*
el/la locutor/a	*radio announcer*
el/la médico/a	*medical doctor*
el/la obrero/a	*worker*
el/la peletero/a	*furrier*
el/la peluquero/a	*hairdresser*
el/la periodista	*journalist*
el/la plomero/a	*plumber*
el/la policía	*policeman/woman*
el/la (p)sicólogo/a	*psychologist*
el/la técnico/a	*technician*
el/la vendedor/a	*salesman, saleswoman*

Los lugares — *Places*

el banco	*bank*
el campo	*countryside*
la compañía/la empresa	*company*
el consultorio	*office (of doctor, dentist, etc.)*
la peluquería	*beauty salon, barbershop*
el taller	*workshop*

El trabajo — *Work*

la agricultura	*farming*
el anuncio	*ad, advertisement*
el cliente/la clienta	*client*
el currículum	*résumé*
la entrevista	*interview*
la especialidad	*specialty*
la experiencia	*experience*
el incendio	*fire*
la madera	*wood*
el puesto	*position*
la solicitud	*application*
el sueldo	*salary*
la vacante	*opening*
las ventas	*sales*

Verbos — *Verbs*

apagar	*to extinguish, to turn off*
cosechar	*to harvest*
dejar	*to leave*
elaborar	*to produce*
emigrar	*to emigrate*
enviar	*to send*
esperar	*to wait for*
llenar	*to fill (out)*
mandar	*to send*
ofrecer (zc)	*to offer*
sobrevivir	*to survive*
solicitar	*to apply (for)*

Palabras y expresiones útiles — *Useful words and expressions*

actualmente	*at the present time*
¡Cómo no!	*Of course!*
en realidad/realmente	*in fact, really*
lo importante	*the important thing*
por cierto	*by the way*
propio/a	*own*
la señal	*signal*
sin embargo	*nevertheless*

Note. This painting is attributed to 18th-century painter Vicente Albán and can be found in the Museo de América in Madrid. The Yumbo people, who lived in the northern and northwestern valleys around Quito, are known to have emigrated there from the Amazon after a volcanic eruption around 1500 B.C.

Suggestion. Ask students to describe the painting by asking: *¿Qué hay en este cuadro? ¿De qué etnia es esta persona? ¿Cómo va vestido? ¿Hay personas que todavía se visten así? ¿Dónde? ¿En qué ocasiones se visten así?* You may introduce *lanza* (spear) and *cazar* (to hunt). *¿Qué tiene en la mano derecha y en la mano izquierda? ¿Por qué llevaban los indígenas estas armas probablemente?*

CAPÍTULO

10

¡A comer!

Este cuadro del siglo XVIII presenta a un indígena yumbo cerca de Quito, Ecuador. Junto a él hay árboles y frutas típicas de su país.

In this chapter you will learn how to:

- discuss food, menus, diets, and shopping for food
- state impersonal information
- give instructions
- talk about the recent past and the future

Cultural focus: **Ecuador**

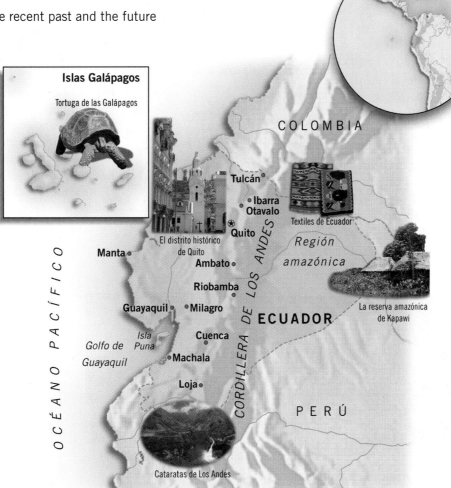

Islas Galápagos

Tortuga de las Galápagos

COLOMBIA

Tulcán

Ibarra
Otavalo

El distrito histórico
de Quito

Quito

Textiles de Ecuador

Manta

Ambato

Región amazónica

Riobamba

Guayaquil • Milagro

ECUADOR

Isla Puna

Cuenca

La reserva amazónica
de Kapawi

Golfo de Guayaquil

Machala

Loja

PERÚ

O C É A N O   P A C Í F I C O

C O R D I L L E R A   D E   L O S   A N D E S

Cataratas de Los Andes

A vista de pájaro. Mire los siguientes grupos de palabras y ponga un círculo alrededor de la palabra que no corresponde.

1. pescado, comida, lima, tomate, papaya, volcán
2. tela, diseño, artesanía, bombero, mercado, joyas
3. catedral, toro, casa, calle, iglesia, ciudad
4. selva, río, plato, planta, árbol, calor
5. montaña, tortilla, catarata, agua, nube, verde
6. tortuga, isla, naturaleza, textil, animal, roca

327

¿Para la guerra? ¿Para cazar?
Make connections: *¿Se puede cazar en Estados Unidos? ¿Qué animales se pueden cazar?* (ciervo, pavo, pato, oso, alce, etc.) *¿Qué otros animales comemos, vacas, cerdos, pollos, ovejas? ¿Hay vegetarianos en esta clase?* Introduce the subject of fruit in the painting. *¿Qué fruta comían estos indígenas probablemente?* Name the fruits as you point them out in the painting: *piña, papaya, plátano.* Ask about students' preferences: *¿Qué fruta prefieren? ¿Les gustan las frutas tropicales?*

Suggestion. Explain the photos. Call students' attention to the different regions of Ecuador. Ask them to associate the location of the country with its name. Have them describe its geographical features: *¿Qué mar u océano está al oeste de Ecuador? ¿Tiene montañas este país? ¿Cómo se llaman?* Point out that the Galápagos Islands lie approximately 600 miles (965 kilometers) west of Ecuador. Discuss the photos and ask students to compare: *¿Qué diferencias hay entre la región del Amazonas y la de los Andes? ¿Dónde hace más calor probablemente? ¿Qué tipo de animales hay en Galápagos?* Explain that the Galápagos are a very important natural reserve and that Darwin based his theory of evolution in part on studies he did during his travels in that region. Mention that Otavalo, with its markets of textiles and crafts, is a popular tourist destination. You may ask students to do some research on food from Ecuador as an introduction to the topic of the chapter. Point out that fish is the basis for many of the dishes on the coast, e.g., *ceviche* is a typical dish in Ecuador, as well as in Peru and Chile.

A PRIMERA VISTA

Los productos y las recetas

En Ecuador se cultiva mucha fruta, sobre todo **piña, limón, melón, papaya, maracuyá** y **plátano**. Mucha de esta fruta se exporta a Estados Unidos y otros países. Aquí vemos a unas personas trabajando en una compañía de exportación de plátanos cerca de Guayaquil.

En los mercados ecuatorianos, como en los de otros países hispanoamericanos, hay buenos puestos de **pasteles** donde se venden los **dulces** típicos de la región.

El pescado y los **mariscos** son muy importantes en la dieta de algunos países hispanoamericanos como Chile, Perú y Ecuador. En la provincia de Esmeraldas, en Ecuador, uno de los platos típicos es el encocado, pescado que se cocina con **leche de coco**.

En otras palabras

The words for some vegetables and spices vary from region to region. **Aguacate** is known as **palta** in some South American countries; **maíz** is known as **elote** in Mexico and in some Central American countries and as **choclo** in parts of South America. Other examples are **cilantro/culantro**, **achiote/pimentón** (paprika), and **frijoles/porotos**. Names of fruits also vary: **plátano** in Spain becomes **cambur** in Venezuela; in other places, like Colombia, **banano** is used, and elsewhere (in Uruguay, for example) it is **banana**. Other examples include **melocotón** (Spain)/**durazno** (Latin America); **fruto de la pasión** (Spain)/**maracuyá** (Colombia)/**parchita** (Venezuela, Mexico).

Esta mujer ecuatoriana vende frutos secos mientras cuida las **ovejas**. De las ovejas se aprovechan la carne en comida y la lana en suéteres, mantas, etc. Además, los **campesinos** usan la leche para hacer queso y yogur. Junto a la carne de **cordero**, la de **res** y la de cerdo son las que más se usan en la comida de Ecuador y se venden en los mercados y en las carnicerías.

En el mercado de Zumbahua se encuentran los productos que se usan en las muchas **recetas** de la comida de Ecuador. La forma de combinar estos productos con el cilantro y otras **hierbas** y **especias** dan fama a la gastronomía ecuatoriana.

10-1 Definiciones. Asocie las definiciones a continuación con las palabras que aparecen en los textos y fotos anteriores.

1. una lista de ingredientes y de instrucciones para elaborar una comida   receta
2. un animal del que se aprovecha la lana, la leche y la carne   oveja
3. una fruta alargada que se pela y que les gusta mucho a los monos   plátano
4. un plato ecuatoriano que se cocina con pescado y leche de coco   encocado
5. una tienda donde se vende pescado   pescadería
6. las personas que cultivan productos del campo   campesinos
7. dulces que se venden en las pastelerías y en los mercados   pasteles
8. la carne de una oveja pequeña   cordero

10-2 Una receta ecuatoriana. Lea la siguiente receta y clasifique sus ingredientes según las siguientes categorías.

a. carnes o pescados: pescado crudo, camarones, almejas
b. vegetales: cebolla, tomate, pimiento
c. condimentos: culantro, perejil, ajo, aceite, achiote, sal, pimienta, comino
d. frutas: coco

Pescado encocado

Ingredientes:
1 coco
1 libra de camarones
2 libras de pescado crudo

1 un tomate grande rojo, pelado y picado
un poquito de achiote
sal, pimienta, comino al gusto

Refrito:
1 cebolla paiteña finamente picada
¼ taza de cebolla blanca finamente picada
1 pimiento picado
4 cucharadas de cilantro picado
4 cucharadas de perejil picado
2 dientes de ajo machacados
4 cucharadas de aceite

Elaboración:
Haga un refrito con los ingredientes. Agréguele una libra de camarones crudos, pelados y limpios y dos libras de pescado crudo, cortado en trozos. Refríalos durante un rato y luego agregue la mitad de la leche del coco. Tape la olla y deje cocinar durante 20 ó 30 minutos. Después, añada la otra mitad de la leche del coco. Sirva inmediatamente, acompañado de arroz blanco y plátano verde asado.

10-3 Mi receta favorita. Escojan una receta simple. Escriban los ingredientes y después explíquenle a otra pareja cómo se prepara el plato. Las siguientes palabras pueden facilitarles la explicación:

batir (*to beat*)   **cortar** (*to cut*)   **freír** (**i**) (*to fry*)   **hervir** (**ie**) (*to boil*)

Lengua

These are some useful words that appear in the recipe: **almejas** (*clams*), **perejil** (*parsley*), **paiteña** (*a type of onion*), **diente de ajo** (*clove of garlic*), **picado** (*chopped*), and **comino** (*cumin*). Other cooking expressions include **picar** (*chop*), **pelar** (*peel*), **machacar** (*crush*), **tapar** (*cover*), **agregar/añadir** (*add*), **taza** (*cup*), and **cucharada** (*spoonful*).

Lengua

To give instructions on how to prepare a recipe, the following grammatical constructions may be used: 1. commands (**cocine el arroz, añada la sal**); 2. se + verb (**se cocina el arroz, se añade la sal**); 3. the infinitive (**cocinar el arroz, añadir la sal**).

Note. Explain that *refrito* refers to the fried or sautéed ingredients of the dish to which the other ingredients will be added.

Note. The conjunction o (equivalent to *or*) carries a written accent when used between numbers: 20 ó 30.

Suggestion for 10-3. The structure *se + verb* may be used to write a recipe and will be studied in *Funciones y formas* in this chapter. For the moment they may use the present tense of the verbs, or some formal commands.

Follow-up for 10-3. Have students present a few of their own recipes.

))) En el supermercado

CD 4
Tracks 26–30
or CD 5
Tracks 2–6

Las frutas y las verduras

Los productos lácteos

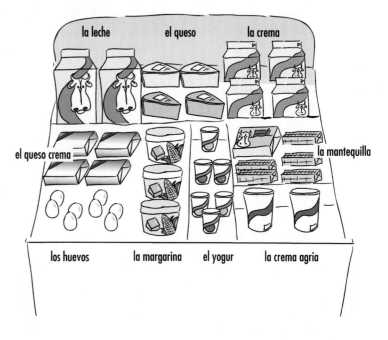

El pescado y la carne

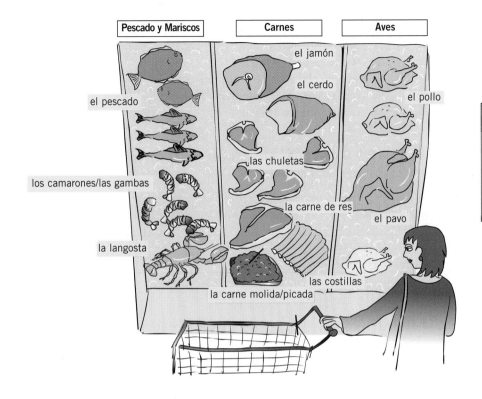

| Pescado y Mariscos | Carnes | Aves |

- el jamón
- el cerdo
- el pollo
- el pescado
- las chuletas
- los camarones/las gambas
- la carne de res
- el pavo
- la langosta
- las costillas
- la carne molida/picada

En otras palabras

Other names of foods that vary by country are **pavo**, which is **guajolote** in Mexico, and **camarones**, which are **gambas** in Spain.

Suggestion. Using visual aids, introduce other foods. After you have introduced a number of items, re-describe some and have students identify them. Then have students in pairs or groups a) describe items; b) categorize them in groups; or c) put together balanced meals.

Los condimentos y las legumbres

- la sal
- la pimienta
- la vainilla
- la mostaza
- la harina
- el aderezo
- el/la azúcar
- el vinagre
- el aceite
- la manteca
- la salsa de tomate
- la mayonesa
- los frijoles
- las lentejas
- los garbanzos

El pan y las bebidas

- el pan
- los churros
- las galletas
- el pan dulce
- los refrescos
- el vino tinto
- el vino blanco

Note. The noun *azúcar* may take the masculine or feminine modifier. Therefore, *el/la azucar moreno/a*.

Cultura

Muchos hispanohablantes que viven en Estados Unidos mantienen las tradiciones y costumbres de su país natal (*native*) con respecto a las comidas. Estas tradiciones y costumbres, que varían mucho de un país a otro, se reflejan en las recetas, maneras de cocinar y aun en las horas diferentes de comer. Hay productos como los frijoles, el arroz, los chiles, los plátanos y el maíz, que constituyen la base de la dieta de muchos países de Hispanoamérica y que se encuentran en casi todos los supermercados de Estados Unidos.

En directo

To give some general advice:

Deben + *infinitive* **(comer/beber/etc...)**

Para bajar de peso, recomendamos + *noun* **(las verduras, el agua, etc.)**

Para obtener calcio/proteínas/fibra es bueno + *infinitive* **(comer/beber/etc.)**

10-4 Asociaciones. Después de asociar cada explicación con la palabra adecuada, comenten si les gustan o no estos alimentos.

1. __d__ Se toma mucho en el verano, cuando hace calor.
2. __e__ Se pone en la ensalada.
3. __b__ Se usan para hacer vino.
4. __a__ Se come en el desayuno con huevos fritos.
5. __f__ Se prepara para el Día de Acción de Gracias.
6. __c__ Se usa para preparar la ensalada de atún o de pollo.

a. el jamón
b. las uvas
c. la mayonesa
d. el helado
e. el aderezo
f. el pavo

10-5 Dietas diferentes. PRIMERA FASE. Completen la tabla con comidas adecuadas para estas dietas.

DIETA	SE DEBE COMER	NO SE DEBE COMER
vegetariana		
para diabéticos		
para desarrollar músculos		
para bajar de peso (*lose weight*)		

SEGUNDA FASE. Completen las siguientes ideas con sus recomendaciones para cada una de estas personas. Digan por qué.

1. Laura, que es vegetariana, debe comer...
2. Mi padre, que es diabético,...
3. Luis, que levanta pesas (*weights*),...
4. Joaquín y Amalia quieren bajar de peso. Por lo tanto...

10-6 ¿Qué necesitamos? PRIMERA FASE. Ustedes son estudiantes de intercambio en Ecuador. Le quieren preparar una cena a su familia ecuatoriana. Hagan lo siguiente.

1. Describan el menú: ¿Qué plato principal van a servir? ¿Van a hacer ensaladas? ¿Van a servir bebidas? ¿Qué bebidas?
2. Hagan una lista de los ingredientes que necesitarán. ¿Van a necesitar verduras, vegetales, legumbres, especias, frutas?

SEGUNDA FASE. Ahora compartan sus planes con otra pareja.

10-7 Los estudiantes y la comida. PRIMERA FASE. Hablen de las comidas típicas de los estudiantes de su universidad. Respondan a las siguientes preguntas.

1. ¿Qué comieron hoy?
2. ¿Cuándo y dónde comieron?
3. ¿Cuánto gastaron en comida?

SEGUNDA FASE. Hagan una lista de recomendaciones para una dieta estudiantil más saludable (*healthy*) y compártanla con el resto de la clase. Piensen en el desayuno, el almuerzo, la cena y las meriendas (*snacks*).

))) La mesa

) 4
k 31
D 5
ck 7

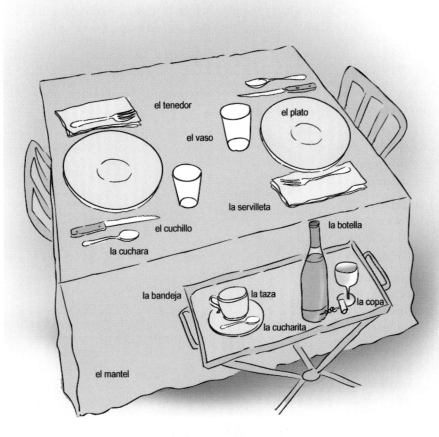

el tenedor
el plato
el vaso
la servilleta
el cuchillo
la cuchara
la bandeja   la taza
la botella
la cucharita
la copa
el mantel

10-8 Entrenamiento de un camarero/una camarera. Ustedes son camareros en un restaurante pero uno/a de ustedes es nuevo/a en el puesto. Dígale a al camarero nuevo/a la camarera nueva dónde debe poner cada cosa de acuerdo con el dibujo. Después cambien de papel.

MODELO: E1: *Ponga el cuchillo a la derecha del plato.*
E2: *Muy bien. ¿Y dónde pongo la copa?*
E1: _____

10-9 Los preparativos de un banquete. Ustedes trabajan en el servicio de comidas de la universidad y tienen que organizar un banquete para sus profesores. Primero preparen un menú, una lista de lo que tienen que comprar para el banquete y un presupuesto (*budget*). Luego deben dividirse el trabajo. Cada uno/a de ustedes es responsable de dar instrucciones a los otros/las otras sobre lo siguiente:

1. cómo elaborar el menú
2. cómo preparar la mesa
3. cómo decorar la sala

Follow-up for 10-8. This is another opportunity to recycle formal commands. Ask what students need in order to eat/drink certain foods/beverages. You may introduce *cubiertos*: *¿Qué (cubiertos) necesita usted para comer un bistec? ¿Y para tomar sopa? ¿Y para comer una ensalada? ¿Necesita usted un plato o una copa para beber vino? Y para beber café, ¿qué necesita?*

Notes for 10-9. Spanish uses the definite article to express "per": *20 centavos la libra, 44 centavos el kilo.* Practice conversion from kilos to pounds and vice versa (1 kilo = 2.2 pounds). Tell students that you also give body weight in kilos, as in *¡Después de mi dieta, peso sólo 50 kilos!*

Beginning in 2000, Ecuador started using the U.S. dollar as its national currency. Use this exercise as an opportunity to mention exchange rates of currencies of several Spanish-speaking countries that they have already studied: *¿Qué otras monedas conoce usted? ¿Cuál es la moneda oficial de México? ¿Y de Perú?* Students can look up exchange rates on the Internet.

Suggestions for 10-9. Have students list foods to buy to prepare meals for a picnic and a Sunday brunch. Have them prepare the menu, the shopping list with approximate prices of each item, and the quantities. Encourage them to look up additional vocabulary.

10-10 Una cena. Usted estuvo muy ocupado/a ayer porque tuvo invitados a cenar. Dígale a su compañero/a todas las cosas que hizo. Él/Ella le va a preguntar dónde hizo las compras, a quién invitó, qué sirvió, y si lo pasaron bien. Después cambien de papel.

CD 4
Track 32
or CD 5
Track 8

10-11 Una cena perfecta. You will listen to a married couple talk about their plans for their dinner party tonight. Before you listen, make a list of four ingredients you would need to prepare a salad and an entrée.

ensalada _____

plato principal _____

Now, pay attention to the general idea of what is said. As you listen, mark (✓) the appropriate ending to each statement.

1. Rodolfo es...
   ✓ un buen cocinero.
   ___ muy perezoso.
   ___ vegetariano.

2. Manuela va a...
   ___ cocinar ceviche.
   ✓ poner la mesa.
   ___ llamar a los invitados.

3. Rodolfo va a comprar...
   ✓ pescado y maíz.
   ___ limón y camarones.
   ___ espinacas y aguacates.

4. Manuela tiene...
   ___ todos los ingredientes.
   ___ muchos vegetales y frutas.
   ✓ casi todos los ingredientes.

Cultura

La comida de los países hispanoamericanos es muy variada. En Ecuador, al igual que en Perú, el ceviche de pescado o de camarón es muy popular. Otro plato muy popular es la fritada, un combinado de diversas carnes con plátano (*plantain*) maduro, plátano tostado y maíz. Y entre los postres, además de la pastelería, es muy sabroso el dulce de higos (*candied figs*).

EN ACCIÓN

Resources
- Video
- SAM: 10-11 to 10-13

Diarios de bicicleta: Lección de cocina

Antes de ver

10-12 Prepare una lista de algunos problemas inesperados que pueden ocurrir antes de una fiesta o de una cena importante. Answers may vary.

Note for 10-12. Students draw on their general knowledge and experiences to anticipate the content of the video segment.

Mientras ve

10-13 Muchas recetas para pozole incluyen los siguientes ingredientes. Marque (✓) los que menciona Luciana.

1. _✓_ carne de cerdo
2. _✓_ chiles
3. _✓_ ajos
4. _✓_ cebollas

5. ___ tomates
6. ___ cilantro
7. _✓_ maíz
8. _✓_ aceite

Note for 10-13. Explain to students that *pozole* is a traditional soup or stew (the word comes from the Nahuatl *potzolli*) that contains hominy (a kind of corn), meat, garbanzos, tomatoes, and chiles.

Después de ver

10-14 Ponga en el orden apropiado los siguientes pasos para hacer pozole.

_3_ Se quitan las semillas de los chiles y se cocinan con el tomate.

_4_ Se licuan los chiles, los tomates y el cilantro.

_1_ Se pone a cocinar la carne con las cebollas y ajos.

_5_ Se unen la carne, los chiles y tomates y el maíz.

_2_ Se corta la carne ya cocinada en trocitos muy pequeños.

_7_ Se sirve en platos hondos y se adorna con tostadas.

_6_ Se agrega sal y se deja sazonar unos minutos.

Suggestion for 10-14. Point out to students the use of *se + verb*, which they see here and have seen earlier in the chapter. They will learn how to use the structure in the *Funciones y formas* section of this chapter.

FUNCIONES Y FORMAS

1. Stating impersonal information: *Se* + verb constructions

PROFESOR: **Se consumen** muchos carbohidratos y mucha grasa. ¿Sabían ustedes que en Estados Unidos **se comen** 23 libras de pizza por persona al año?

RICARDO: [piensa] ¿Cuánta cerveza **se bebe** con 23 pizzas?

PROFESOR: **Se comen** sólo 16 libras de manzanas, bla bla bla…

RICARDO: [piensa] En esta clase **se duerme** mucho.

Piénselo. ¿Cuánto más sabe usted sobre la dieta estadounidense? Indique si las siguientes afirmaciones son ciertas (**C**) o falsas (**F**), según la información del profesor y lo que usted sabe.

1. __C__ **Se consumen** muchas grasas (*fats*).
2. __F__ **Se compra** más fruta en el supermercado ahora que en el pasado.
3. __C__ **Se dice** que los niños comen más y hacen menos actividad física.
4. __C__ **Se bebe** mucho café, especialmente en las universidades.
5. __C__ **Se consume** más pizza que manzanas.
6. __C__ **Se recomienda** desayunar todos los días.

- Spanish uses the **se +** *verb* construction to emphasize the occurrence of an action rather than the person(s) responsible for that action. The noun (what is bought, sold, offered, etc.) usually follows the verb. The person(s) who buy(s), sell(s), offer(s), and so on, is not mentioned. This is normally expressed in English with the passive voice (is/are + *past participle*).

  Se habla español en este restaurante.   *Spanish is spoken in this restaurant.*

- Use a singular verb with singular nouns and a plural verb with plural nouns.

  Se necesita un horno para hacer galletas.   *An oven is needed to make cookies.*

  Se venden vegetales allí.   *Vegetables are sold there.*

■ Use a singular verb when the **se** + *verb* construction is followed not by a noun, but rather by an adverb, an infinitive, or a clause. This is expressed in English with indefinite subjects such as *they*, *you*, *one*, and *people*.

Se trabaja mucho en ese manzanal.	*They work a lot in that apple orchard.*
Se puede encontrar muchos tipos de manzanas allí.	*You can find many different types of apples there.*
Se dice que venden sidra excelente también.	*People say they sell excellent cider too.*

10-15 Asociaciones. PRIMERA FASE. Asocie las actividades con los lugares donde ocurren.

1. _c_ Se cambian cheques en…   a. un almacén.
2. _a_ Se vende ropa en…   b. un restaurante.
3. _d_ Se toma el sol y se nada en… c. un banco.
4. _b_ Se sirven comidas en…   d. una playa.

SEGUNDA FASE. Piense en un edificio o lugar público que le gusta mucho. Luego dígale a su compañero/a qué se hace allí.

MODELO: *Me gusta mucho la zona peatonal* (pedestrian area) *de mi ciudad. Allí se camina mucho y en el verano se escucha la música de conjuntos locales.*

10-16 El supermercado y las tiendas de conveniencia. Indique (✓) los productos y/o servicios que se encuentran en los supermercados solamente y los que se encuentran comúnmente en las tiendas de conveniencia también. Compare sus respuestas con las de su compañero/a. Expected responses as shown. Students should justify their responses.

PRODUCTOS/SERVICIOS	SUPERMERCADO SOLAMENTE	SUPERMERCADO Y TIENDA DE CONVENIENCIA
productos lácteos		✓
carnes orgánicas	✓	
frutas de América del Sur	✓	
detergente para lavadoras		✓
alimentos enlatados (*canned*)		✓
pescado fresco	✓	
DVDs para alquilar		✓

En otras palabras

The concept of *convenience stores* is expressed differently according to the country. In Mexico they are **tiendas de conveniencia**, translated directly from English. In Costa Rica the term **tiendas de gasolinera** is used because of where such stores are usually located. In Spain they are **tiendas de 24h** to convey the convenience of being always open.

10-17 Recetas creativas. PRIMERA FASE. Lean estas recetas originales. Luego, intercambien opiniones sobre cuáles les gustaría probar y cuáles no.

1. Plátano derretido (*melted*): Se corta un plátano en rebanadas (*slices*) no muy finas. Se echa azúcar. Se calienta en el microondas por uno o dos minutos.
2. Batido de tarta de manzana (*apple pie smoothie*): Se ponen en la licuadora (*blender*): media taza de jugo de manzana, tres cucharadas de helado de vainilla y media cucharadita de canela (*cinnamon*). Se bate por un minuto.
3. Hamburguesa y salsa con queso (*nacho cheese sauce*): Se calienta la parrilla. Se pone la hamburguesa en la parrilla. Se pone la salsa con queso en el panecillo y se calienta. Se pone la hamburguesa en el panecillo.
4. Ensalada de pollo: Se abre una bolsa de lechuga prelavada. Se cortan en rebanadas dos pechugas de pollo (*chicken breasts*) cocidas, y se corta media libra de queso en cubos pequeños. Se combinan los ingredientes en una fuente (*bowl*). Se agrega un aliño de vinagre balsámico.

SEGUNDA FASE. Preparen juntos una receta para compartir con la clase.

Follow-up for 10-15. Primera fase. Have students answer these questions: *En casa, ¿qué se hace en la cocina? ¿en el dormitorio? ¿en el comedor?* Ask students to mention typical activities in certain places using the impersonal *se* construction. Have the rest of the class try to guess the place.

Follow-up for 10-16. If you wish, expand this activity as follows: *Marque las cuatro cosas y/o servicios que considera más esenciales en los supermercados hoy en día y compare sus resultados con los de su compañero/a. Después, en grupos pequeños, escojan las cuatro cosas y/o servicios que obtuvieron más votos y comenten entre todos por qué se necesitan. Comparen sus resultados con los de otros grupos.*

10-18 ¿Cómo se prepara este plato? PRIMERA FASE. Usted y su compañero/a quieren darle una sorpresa a otra persona. Por eso, deciden prepararle su plato favorito. Primero, seleccionen uno de estos platos:

Luego, escriban en la caja una lista de los ingredientes que se necesitan para hacer el plato.

CARNES	VERDURAS/VEGETALES	ESPECIAS	OTROS

SEGUNDA FASE. Usted sabe cocinar, pero su amigo/a no. Responda a sus preguntas mientras ustedes preparan el plato. Los siguientes verbos pueden ser útiles.

asar	dorar (*brown*)	rallar (*grate*)
cocinar	hervir	(so)freír
cortar	hornear	tostar

MODELO: E1: *Vamos a preparar pollo asado. ¿Qué se hace con el pollo?*
E2: *Primero se lava bien el pollo. Luego se ponen sal y pimienta.*
E1: *¿Y después?*
E2: *Se asa en el horno por dos horas y se dora.*

SITUACIONES

1. **Role A.** You are an international student who has just arrived in town. A student has offered to help with your orientation. You are not familiar with shopping in the United States, so you ask a) where one buys personal items like vitamins and toothpaste (**pasta de dientes**); b) where on campus one can find a decent meal; c) where one goes to buy fresh fruit; and d) where one can get good American pizza. Ask follow-up questions to be sure you understand the answers.

   Role B. You have offered to show a new international student around campus. Answer his/her questions about where one goes to buy different things. Offer several options, and be prepared to answer your new friend's questions.

2. **Role A.** You have just moved into your own apartment, and you are living away from home for the first time. You have never done your own food shopping and are not sure how to go about it. Ask a friend for help and ask questions so he/she will expand on the explanation.

   Role B. A friend has just told you that he/she does not know how to go food shopping. Explain the process step by step, starting with the shopping list (**se hace una lista...**). Provide additional explanation or clarification in response to your friend's questions.

2. Talking about the recent past: Present perfect and participles used as adjectives

ALICIA: Hola, César, ¿qué tal?

CÉSAR: Hola, Alicia. ¿**Has visto** a Javier? ¡Estoy muy molesto!

ALICIA: ¿Por qué? ¿Qué te pasa?

CÉSAR: Como sabes, el examen de historia es pasado mañana y yo no **he leído** el libro todavía. ¿Lo **has leído** tú? ¿Lo **ha leído** Javier? ¿Javier te **ha dado** sus notas? No sé qué voy a hacer sin sus notas. ¡Las necesito para estudiar!

ALICIA: Cálmate, César. Yo **he leído** el libro y **he escrito** unas notas. **He hablado** con Javi. No **ha terminado** el libro todavía, pero va a llamarte esta tarde.

Piénselo. Lea las afirmaciones e indique a quién(es) se aplica cada una: a Alicia (**A**), a César (**C**) y/o a Javier (**J**).

1. __A__ **Ha hablado** con Javier.
2. __A__ **Ha escrito** unas notas.
3. __J__ **Ha leído** una parte del libro.
4. __C__ No **ha hecho** mucho en su curso de historia.
5. __A, C__ No **han visto** a Javier.
6. __C__ No **ha abierto** el libro.

■ Both Spanish and English have perfect tenses that are used to refer to past actions, events, and conditions. Both languages use an auxiliary verb (**haber** in Spanish, *to have* in English) followed by a past participle.

■ Use the present perfect to refer to a past event, action, or condition that has some relation to the present.

Lucho, ¿ya **has leído** la receta de paella?

Lucho, have you read the recipe for paella yet?

No, no **he leído** la receta todavía.

No, I have not read the recipe yet.

PRESENT TENSE OF HABER	+	PAST PARTICIPLE
yo	he	
tú	has	
Ud., él, ella	ha	hablado
nosotros/as	hemos	comido
vosotros/as	habéis	vivido
Uds., ellos/as	han	

Resources

■ SAM: 10-20 to 10-26
■ Supp. Activ. Book: Present perfect and participles used as adjectives

Suggestion. Talk to students about a trip you have taken: *Yo he visitado Florida muchas veces. He nadado en el mar y he corrido en la playa. He ido a México y a Venezuela, pero no he ido a Ecuador.* Write the verb forms *visitar → he visitado, nadar → he nadado, comer → he comido, correr → he corrido, ir → he ido* on the board as you say them. Ask: *Y usted, ¿ha ido a ciudades en Estados Unidos donde hay muchos hispanos, como Miami o San Antonio? ¿A qué ciudades ha ido? ¿Cuántas veces? ¿Ha comido fajitas/comida mexicana en San Antonio? ¿Ha comido comida hispana? ¿Ha visitado un país hispano? ¿Qué país ha visitado? ¿Cuántas veces?* Then have students work in pairs to find out what countries or cities they have visited and how many times.

Alternate. Give commands: *Escoja/Piense en el plato que va a pedir. Corte el pan. Pague la cuenta.* Students answer: *Ya he...*

Suggestion. Review *tener que + infinitive.* Give examples contrasting its use with that of *haber + past participle*: *Eduardo no ha terminado el proyecto porque está muy ocupado. Tiene que terminar el proyecto esta noche.*

Suggestion. Introduce *romper, cubrir,* and *morir* through comprehensible input. Use visuals if possible. You may explain that compounds of verbs whose past participles are irregular have the same irregularity: *escribir → escrito; describir → descrito; volver → vuelto; devolver → devuelto.*

Suggestion. Remind students that they can go to the Appendix in the Student Activities Manual for additional practice with accents.

■ Form the present perfect by using the present tense of **haber** as an auxiliary verb with the past participle of the main verb. **Tener** is never used as the auxiliary verb to form the perfect tense.

Los cocineros **han trabajado** mucho en el banquete.	*The cooks have worked a lot on the banquet.*
Unos miembros de la organización ya **han traído** los manteles.	*Some members of the organization have already brought the tablecloths.*

■ All past participles of **-ar** verbs end in **-ado**, whereas past participles of **-er** and **-ir** verbs generally end in **-ido**. If the stem of an **-er** verb ends in a vowel, use a written accent on the **i** of **-ido** (leer → leído). In English, past participles are often formed with the endings *-ed* and *-en*, as in *finished* and *eaten*.

■ Some **-er** and **-ir** verbs have irregular past participles. Here are some of the more common ones:

IRREGULAR PAST PARTICIPLES			
hacer	**hecho**	abrir	**abierto**
poner	**puesto**	escribir	**escrito**
romper	**roto**	cubrir	**cubierto**
ver	**visto**	decir	**dicho**
volver	**vuelto**	morir	**muerto**

■ Place object and reflexive pronouns before the auxiliary **haber**. Do not place any word between **haber** and the past participle.

¿**Le** has dado las servilletas a César?	*Have you given César the napkins?*
No, todavía no **se las** he dado.	*No, I have not given them to him yet.*

■ The present perfect of **hay** is **ha habido** with both singular and plural nouns.

Ha habido más trabajo últimamente.	*There has been more work lately.*
Ha habido varios banquetes y otros eventos.	*There have been several banquets and other events.*

■ **OJO:** To state that something has just happened use the present tense of **acabar + de +** *infinitive*, not the present perfect.

Acabamos de volver del supermercado.	*We have just returned from the supermarket.*
Acabo de probar la sopa y está deliciosa.	*I have just tasted the soup, and it is delicious.*

■ Spanish uses **estar +** *past participle* to express a state or condition resulting from a prior action.

ACTION	RESULT
Ella preparó la sopa.	La sopa **está preparada**.
Luego cerró las ventanas.	Las ventanas **están cerradas**.

■ When a past participle is used as an adjective, it agrees with the noun it modifies.

una puerta **cerrada**	*a closed door*
los restaurantes **abiertos**	*the open restaurants*
unas botellas **lavadas**	*some washed bottles*

10-19 Lo que no he hecho. Usted y su compañero/a deben decir las cosas de cada lista que no han hecho. Después, comparen sus respuestas con las de otros estudiantes.

1. Yo nunca he estado en...
   a. Paraguay.
   b. Guatemala.
   c. Ecuador.
2. Yo nunca he visto...
   a. las Islas Galápagos.
   b. un volcán activo.
   c. un huracán.
3. Yo nunca he comido...
   a. aguacate.
   b. un postre con leche de coco.
   c. langosta.
4. Yo nunca he escrito...
   a. una receta.
   b. una lista de compras (*shopping list*) en español.
   c. el menú para una cena formal.
5. Yo nunca he roto...
   a. una taza.
   b. un vaso.
   c. un plato.
6. Yo nunca he dicho...
   a. "no" a una invitación a cenar.
   b. una broma (*joke*) de mal gusto durante una comida formal.
   c. una palabra en español en un resturante hispano en este país.

10-20 Hispanos famosos/Hispanas famosas. PRIMERA FASE. Piensen en un hispano famoso/una hispana famosa y preparen una lista de cinco cosas que ustedes creen que ha hecho para tener éxito (*to be successful*). Después compartan su lista con la de otra pareja y háganse preguntas.

MODELO: *Cameron Díaz es una actriz famosa.*
Ha actuado en más de treinta películas.

HISPANO FAMOSO/HISPANA FAMOSA	LO QUE HA HECHO PARA TENER ÉXITO
_____	_____
	_____
	_____
	_____

SEGUNDA FASE. Digan tres cosas que ustedes han hecho que los/las ha ayudado a tener éxito en su vida personal, académica o profesional.

Follow-up for 10-19. Have students share information with the class: *Mi compañero/a nunca ha estado en... Nunca ha hecho...* Then take a poll to find out what students have never done.

Preparation for 10-20. One class before doing activity 10-20, prepare students by brainstorming with them the names of famous Hispanics in various fields: film, music, fiction, sports, science, journalism, etc. Assign pairs to gather information about a person of their choice ahead of time.

10-21 Para hacer una cena importante. Usted y su compañero/a van a preparar una cena para la visita de una persona importante a su universidad. Háganse preguntas para ver qué preparativos ha hecho cada uno/a para la cena.

MODELO: comprar la carne
   E1: *¿Has comprado la carne?*
   E2: *No, no la he comprado todavía.*

1. determinar el número de invitados
2. leer las recetas
3. cortar los vegetales
4. hacer el postre
5. decidir qué música se va a tocar
6. poner la mesa
7. asignar los asientos
8. decorar el lugar de la cena

10-22 Justo ahora. Con su compañero/a, digan qué acaban de hacer estas personas. Den la mayor información posible.

MODELO: Juan y Ramiro salen del estadio.
   E1: *Acaban de ver un partido de béisbol muy importante.*
   E2: *Fueron a ver a los Calcetines Rojos porque es su equipo favorito.*

1. Maricarmen y sus amigos ya no tienen hambre.
2. Pedro y Alina salen de una tienda donde se alquilan películas.
3. Mercedes y Paula traen palomitas de maíz (*popcorn*) para todo el grupo.
4. Un hombre sale corriendo de un banco.
5. Jorge y Rubén salen de un supermercado.
6. Frente a todos sus amigos, Rubén le da una sorpresa a su novia.

10-23 Robo (*Robbery*) en un restaurante. El siguiente párrafo cuenta algo que ocurrió en el restaurante del chef Marco Tovares. Para saber lo que pasó, llene los espacios en blanco con la forma correcta del participio pasado de los verbos entre paréntesis.

El chef Marco Tovares salió de la cocina de su restaurante en Nueva York para asegurarse de que todo iba bien en el comedor esa noche. Vio que el locutor de televisión Jorge Ramos y otras tres personas estaban (1) __sentados__ (sentar) en una mesa. De repente Marco vio que la bolsa de una de las mujeres estaba (2) __abierta__ (abrir) y que un hombre en otra mesa la estaba mirando. Como la mujer estaba (3) __distraída__ (distraer), el ladrón aprovechó el momento (4) __esperado__ (esperar). Sacó la billetera de la bolsa de ella. La mujer no se dio cuenta, pero Marco lo vio todo. Se acercó a la mesa y le dijo al hombre: —¿Cómo está la comida esta noche? ¿Todo bien? El hombre parecía muy nervioso, y curiosamente tenía las manos (5) __cerradas__ (cerrar). Marco le dijo: —¿Podría acompañarme un momento, por favor? El hombre fue con Marco al fondo del restaurante, le dio la billetera (6) __robada__ (robar) y salió. Marco se acercó a la mesa de Jorge Ramos y les explicó lo ocurrido. Todos estaban muy (7) __sorprendidos__ (sorprender). La mujer víctima del robo dijo: —Hace diez años que vivo en Nueva York, y ¡nunca he (8) __sido__ (ser) víctima de un robo hasta esta noche! Muchísimas gracias por su ayuda.

10-24 ¿Qué ha pasado? PRIMERA FASE. Su compañero/a y usted han ordenado su apartamento esta mañana. Pero acaban de entrar por la tarde, y ven que todo está muy desordenado. Túrnense para describirle al/a la policía lo que han hecho para ordenar el apartamento y lo que ven ahora, usando las palabras entre paréntesis. Añadan más información donde sea posible.

MODELO: las ventanas (cerrar, abrir)
         POLICÍA: *¿Qué ha pasado con las ventanas?*
             E1: *Las he cerrado esta mañana...*
             E2: *pero ahora están abiertas.*

1. el espejo del baño (usar, romper)
2. la cama (tender, desordenar)
3. el televisor (apagar, encender)
4. las camisas (colgar, tirar al piso)
5. la puerta del apartamento (cerrar, abrir)
6. la comida en el refrigerador (cubrir, descubrir [*to uncover*])

SEGUNDA FASE. Después de escuchar el relato de ustedes, el/la policía hace lo siguiente:

1. Les hace preguntas para conseguir más información.
2. Les dice tres cosas que hay que hacer ahora.

Suggestion for 10-24.
Organize students in groups of three: one police officer and two victims.

SITUACIONES

1. **Role A.** You are a reporter who has been assigned to interview the new chef of a restaurant in your community. Ask about a) other restaurants where he/she has worked; b) prizes (*premios*) he/she has won; c) some examples of dishes he/she has developed; and d) changes he/she has already made in the restaurant.

   Role B. You are the new chef of one of the nicest restaurants in town, and a reporter is interviewing you for the local newspaper. Answer the reporter's questions, adding as many details possible.

2. **Role A.** You are in charge of discipline at a strict boarding school. Call one of the students to your office to ask about his/her activities. Explain that the teachers have just told you that a) he/she has not attended classes for four days; b) he/she has not done homework for two weeks; and c) he/she has not eaten in the cafeteria all week. Say that the teachers are worried. You want to track his/her every movement to determine the problem. Start with **¿A qué hora te has levantado hoy?** and continue from there.

   Role B. You are a student at a strict boarding school. You have been acting strangely, and you don't want to explain why. The teacher in charge of discipline has asked to speak to you. Answer the teacher's questions with enough detail to fool him/her into thinking you are telling the truth.

Note. *Féculas* (starches) includes grains, bread, and starchy vegetables like corn and peas.

3. Giving instructions in informal settings: Informal commands

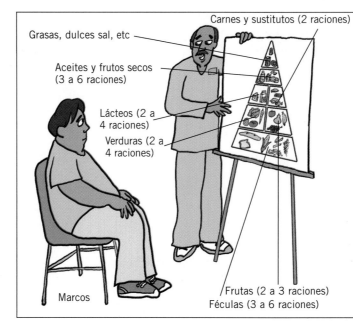

Carnes y sustitutos (2 raciones)

Grasas, dulces sal, etc

Aceites y frutos secos (3 a 6 raciones)

Lácteos (2 a 4 raciones)

Verduras (2 a 4 raciones)

Frutas (2 a 3 raciones)
Féculas (3 a 6 raciones)

Marcos

Marcos, la buena alimentación es fundamental para la buena salud. **Toma** desayuno siempre. Es la comida más importante del día. Para tener energía, **consume** carbohidratos y proteínas en las tres comidas. **Come** carbohidratos complejos, como pasta y pan, pero siempre integrales (*made from whole grains*). **No olvides** las frutas, las verduras y la leche, son muy buenas para la salud. **Evita** comer grasas y azúcares, excepto en cantidades moderadas.

Piénselo. Según las sugerencias del enfermero, escoja los alimentos o bebidas que Marcos debe consumir o evitar para alimentarse bien.

1. __c, e__ Come...
2. __a, b, g__ Evita...
3. ___d___ Bebe...

a. helado todos los días.
b. pan blanco.
c. manzanas, peras, plátanos, uvas.

d. suficiente leche.
e. pollo y pescado.
f. refrescos.

Suggestions. Write the *tú* form of some verbs (*cocinas, bebes, escribes*) on the board and erase the final *-s*. Do TPR using informal commands. Model several *tú* commands, going from the negative to the affirmative (*no leas/lee; no llames/llama*). Then give the negative and have students supply the affirmative, and vice versa.

◼ To ask a friend to do or not to do something, use an informal command. Use that form with anyone else you address as **tú,** such as someone your own age or someone with whom you have a close relationship.

◼ To form the affirmative **tú** command, use the present indicative **tú** form without the final **-s.**

	PRESENT INDICATIVE	AFFIRMATIVE *TÚ* COMMAND
cocinar	cocinas	**cocina**
beber	bebes	**bebe**
consumir	consumes	**consume**

◼ For the negative **tú** command, use the negative **usted** command form and add the final **-s.**

	NEGATIVE *USTED* COMMAND	NEGATIVE *TÚ* COMMAND
preparar	no prepar**e**	no prepar**es**
comer	no com**a**	no com**as**
subir	no sub**a**	no sub**as**

■ Placement of object and reflexive pronouns with **tú** commands is the same as with **usted** commands.

AFFIRMATIVE COMMAND	NEGATIVE COMMAND
Prepárelo (usted).	No **lo** prepare (usted).
Bébela (tú).	No **la** bebas (tú).

■ The plural of **tú** commands in Spanish-speaking America is the **ustedes** command.

Cocina (tú).	**Cocinen (ustedes).**
Bebe (tú).	**Beban (ustedes).**
Sube (tú).	**Suban (ustedes).**

Note. See presentation of the *vosotros/as* commands in the *Expansión gramatical* in the Appendix.

■ Some **-er** and **-ir** verbs have shortened affirmative **tú** commands, but their negative command is regular.

	AFFIRMATIVE	NEGATIVE
poner	**pon**	**no pongas**
salir	**sal**	**no salgas**
tener	**ten**	**no tengas**
venir	**ven**	**no vengas**
hacer	**haz**	**no hagas**
decir	**di**	**no digas**
ir	**ve**	**no vayas**
ser	**sé**	**no seas**

Sal a las tres si quieres llegar a las cuatro.	*Leave at 3:00 if you want to arrive at 4:00.*
No salgas sin paraguas; va a llover.	*Don't leave without an umbrella; it is going to rain.*
Sé generoso con tus amigos.	*Be generous with your friends.*
No **seas** impaciente.	*Don't be impatient.*
Dime la verdad.	*Tell me the truth.*
No nos digas mentiras.	*Don't tell us any lies.*

Follow-up for 10-25. Have students write down five questions they would ask if they needed advice regarding a healthy diet: *¿Cuánto líquido debo beber todos los días? ¿Debo tomar desayuno o comer algo rápido antes de almorzar?* Then have them exchange roles asking and giving advice using a *tú* command. Ask if classmates agree with the advice given; if not, they should provide their own advice.

10-25 Consejos. Escoja los consejos más adecuados, según cada situación.

1. Su compañero/a comió demasiado en una fiesta de cumpleaños y ahora le duele mucho el estómago.
   a. Come más para recuperarte.
   ⓑ Llama al médico.
   ⓒ Ve a la farmacia y compra medicamentos.
   d. Camina una hora esta tarde.
   e. Practica deportes para olvidarte del dolor de estómago.
   f. No te acuestes.

2. Su hermana está enferma. Está congestionada y tiene fiebre.
   ⓐ Toma sopa de pollo.
   b. Come una hamburguesa.
   c. No duermas mucho.
   ⓓ Bebe jugos y agua.
   ⓔ No bebas vino ni cerveza.
   ⓕ No consumas mucha cafeína.

3. A su hijo le fascina la comida chatarra (*junk food*), por eso, subió diez libras en un mes.
   a. Ve a los restaurantes de comida rápida.
   b. Bebe muchas gaseosas.
   ⓒ Come en casa, no en restaurantes.
   ⓓ No tomes alcohol.
   ⓔ Evita los batidos de McDonald's.
   f. No pidas ensaladas.

4. Su mamá quiere alimentarse mejor para tener más energía y bajar de peso.
   ⓐ Evita la grasa.
   b. Toma muchos helados.
   ⓒ Come huevos moderadamente.
   d. Compra papas fritas.
   e. Acuéstate y descansa.
   f. Si no tienes energía, consume mucha cafeína.

5. Su mejor amigo quiere preparar una cena espectacular para su novia.
   a. Compra pizza.
   ⓑ Haz un plato sofisticado.
   ⓒ No olvides de comprar un buen vino.
   ⓓ Prepara la mesa el día anterior.
   ⓔ No le pongas chile picante al plato. Ella detesta la comida picante.
   f. Ponle mucha sal a la comida.

10-26 Una cura de reposo. Su amigo/a estuvo muy enfermo/a y su médico le recomendó pasar dos semanas de descanso en las Termas de Papallacta o en la reserva natural Playa de Oro en Ecuador. Como usted ha visitado los dos lugares, dígale a su amigo/a qué debe hacer allí. Después cambien de papel.

MODELO: visitar la reserva/no pensar en los negocios
Visita la reserva Playa de Oro./No pienses en los negocios.

1. disfrutar del sol
2. respirar aire puro y descansar
3. no hacer tarea
4. tomar fotos y hacer videos
5. probar un plato típico ecuatoriano
6. salir por las noches y conversar con las personas del lugar
7. tomar baños termales a diario
8. asistir a un concierto de música andina

10-27 Buenos hábitos alimenticios. PRIMERA FASE. Ustedes están preocupados por los hábitos de comida de uno/a de sus amigos/as. Lean lo que esta persona come y bebe en un día típico e identifiquen los problemas que tiene.

Se levanta al mediodía todos los días. Tan pronto se levanta, toma varias tazas de café. Una hora más tarde, come tres huevos fritos con tocino y tostadas. Toma dos tazas de café cubano con bastante azúcar. Luego lee el periódico en su dormitorio, mira televisión y come chocolate mientras habla por teléfono con sus amigos. Por la tarde, llama por teléfono al restaurante de la esquina y pide una hamburguesa con papas fritas y toma unas cervezas. Después, duerme una siesta larga. Por la noche, tiene problemas para dormir, por eso, toma un batido.

SEGUNDA FASE. Hagan una lista con cinco recomendaciones o instrucciones que su amigo/a debe seguir. Comparen su lista con las de otros grupos.

10-28 Cocina paso a paso (*step by step*). PRIMERA FASE. Busquen una receta para el sancocho, una sopa que se come en Ecuador. Escriban la lista de los ingredientes y estén listos/as para describirlos.

SEGUNDA FASE. En el papel de dos chefs de televisión, presenten la preparación del sancocho. Sigan los siguientes pasos: a) describan el plato; b) presenten sus ingredientes; y c) expliquen cómo se prepara el plato.

SITUACIONES

1. **Role A.** You are not feeling well, so you call your friend to ask for the recipe to make chicken soup. Take notes as your friend gives you the recipe. Ask questions as necessary.

   Role B. Your friend is not feeling well and calls to ask for the recipe for chicken soup. Tell him/her to a) buy skinless chicken (**pollo sin piel**); b) wash and cut garlic, onions, carrots, and celery (**apio**); c) sauté (**saltear**) the chicken and vegetables with a little olive oil; and d) add water, salt, and pepper and cook for 30 minutes.

2. **Role A.** To improve your health, you visit a nutritionist. Explain what you generally eat for breakfast, lunch, and dinner. Ask questions and answer the nutritionist's questions.

   Role B. A client comes to you for help with eating habits. Ask what he/she eats for breakfast, lunch, and dinner. Advise your client a) to eat fruits, vegetables, fish, and chicken; b) not to drink soft drinks or alcohol; c) to consume foods with lots of fiber; and d) to do physical activity daily. Answer your client's questions.

Resources

■ SAM: 10-33 to 10-38
■ Supp. Activ. Book: The
 future tense

4. Talking about the future: The future tense

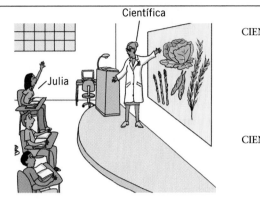

CIENTÍFICA: Según los expertos, para el año 2030 la población geriátrica **se duplicará** en comparación con la del presente. La gente **comerá** mejor y **vivirá** más años porque **tendrá** buena salud.

JULIA: ¿Y nuestra dieta **será** semejante a la de hoy? ¿Qué **comeremos**?

CIENTÍFICA: Se piensa que **consumiremos** más alimentos naturales, porque más gente **comprenderá** sus beneficios. Al mismo tiempo, muchos alimentos **serán** modificados genéticamente. Los individuos **tratarán** de protegerse de ciertas condiciones y enfermedades, como la diabetes y el cáncer.

Piénselo. Indique si las siguientes afirmaciones son ciertas (**C**) o falsas (**F**), según la científica. Si la respuesta es falsa (**F**), corrija la información.

1. __F__ **Habrá** menos personas mayores en el futuro.   habrá más
2. __C__ Las personas **tendrán** una vida más larga.
3. __C__ Más personas **comprenderán** el beneficio de los alimentos naturales.
4. __F__ La gente **podrá** comer grasas y dulces porque la ciencia los protegerá contra las enfermedades.   La gente tratará de protegerse de ciertas condiciones y enfermedades.

Suggestion. Show and narrate visuals in context. For example: *La semana próxima Rafael va a ir en viaje de negocios a Ecuador. Estará dos días en Quito, donde tendrá varias reuniones de negocios. Su secretaria le hará una reservación en un hotel que le recomendaron. Visitará algunas plantaciones de banano en la costa del Pacífico. Después de regresar a Estados Unidos, se pondrá en contacto con algunas compañías que quieran importar bananas de Ecuador.* Ask yes/no questions using the future to check comprehension. Follow up with information questions, using the visuals.

Note. The *ir a + infinitive* construction is commonly used to express future action; allow students to answer using either construction.

■ You have been using the present tense and **ir a** + *infinitive* to express future plans. Spanish also has a future tense. Although you have these other ways to express a future action, event, or state, it is important to be able to recognize the future tense in reading and in listening.

■ The future tense is formed by adding the endings **-é, -ás, -á, -emos, -éis,** and **-án** to the infinitive. All verbs, **-ar, -er, -ir,** regular or irregular, use these endings.

	HABLAR	**COMER**	**VIVIR**
yo	hablar**é**	comer**é**	vivir**é**
tú	hablar**ás**	comer**ás**	vivir**ás**
Ud., él, ella	hablar**á**	comer**á**	vivir**á**
nosotros/as	hablar**emos**	comer**emos**	vivir**emos**
vosotros/as	hablar**éis**	comer**éis**	vivir**éis**
Uds., ellos/as	hablar**án**	comer**án**	vivir**án**

FUTURE TENSE

Rafael **visitará** Ecuador el mes próximo.	*Rafael will visit Ecuador next month.*
Él y sus colegas **volverán** después de dos semanas.	*He and his colleagues will return after two weeks.*
Se reunirán con los dueños de unas haciendas de café.	*They will meet with the owners of some coffee plantations.*

■ Some verbs have irregular stems in the future tense and can be grouped into three categories according to the irregularity. The first group drops the **-e** from the infinitive ending.

IRREGULAR FUTURE—GROUP 1		
INFINITIVE	**NEW STEM**	**FUTURE FORMS**
poder	**podr-**	podré, podrás, podrá, podremos, podréis, podrán
querer	**querr-**	querré, querrás, querrá, querremos, querréis, querrán
saber	**sabr-**	sabré, sabrás, sabrá, sabremos, sabréis, sabrán

■ The second group replaces the **e** or **i** of the infinitive ending with a **-d**.

IRREGULAR FUTURE—GROUP 2		
poner	**pondr-**	pondré, pondrás, pondrá, pondremos, pondréis, pondrán
salir	**saldr-**	saldré, saldrás, saldrá, saldremos, saldréis, saldrán
tener	**tendr-**	tendré, tendrás, tendrá, tendremos, tendréis, tendrán
venir	**vendr-**	vendré, vendrás, vendrá, vendremos, vendréis, vendrán

■ The third group consists of two verbs that have completely different stems in the future tense.

IRREGULAR FUTURE—GROUP 3		
decir	**dir-**	diré, dirás, dirá, diremos, diréis, dirán
hacer	**har-**	haré, harás, hará, haremos, haréis, harán

Los estudiantes **sabrán** más sobre la nutrición después de tomar el curso.	*The students will know more about nutrition after taking the course.*
Tendrán que leer mucho.	*They will have to read a lot.*
También **harán** un proyecto de investigación.	*They will also do a research project.*
¿A qué hora vendrán a cenar?	*What time will they be coming for dinner?*
Querrán probar un poco de todo.	*They will want to try a little of everything.*

Suggestion. You may divide the class into small groups and have students think of a dish they will cook together, whose step-by-step preparation they will describe to the class. Their classmates will guess the name of the dish.

Model the activity with two of your better students as follows:

Nosotros prepararemos un plato cubano. Necesitaremos arroz, carne, aceite, sal y especias. Yo comenzaré. Pondré aceite en una olla/cazuela. Jorge lavará el arroz, Mary pondrá el arroz en la olla y lo dorará. Yo freiré la carne, pero antes Jorge pondrá especias y después, and so on and so forth. Students will finally guess the name of the dish: *arrroz con carne deshilachada.*

Suggestion. To give students further practice with irregular verbs, have them finish the idea using the verb tener, hacer, o poder.

1. *Es la ultima semana de clase. Los estudiantes...(tener)*
2. *Roberto dará una fiesta de graduación formal el próximo fin de semana. En la fiesta, Jorge... (tener)*

3. *Mario y Ernesto irán de vacaciones juntos. Ellos... (poder)*

Cultura

Ecuador tiene muchos parques nacionales y reservas ecológicas cuyo propósito es conservar la riqueza natural de las cuatro regiones del país: las Islas Galápagos, la costa, la sierra y la selva amazónica. En las reservas se encuentran muchas especies de flora y fauna. Para los visitantes, hay muchas maneras de explorar las reservas y gozar de la naturaleza.

10-29 ¿Qué lugares de Ecuador visitarán estas personas? Complete las oraciones de la izquierda con la forma correcta del verbo en la columna de la derecha.

1. A Carlos y Eugenia les gusta comer bien. Ellos __c__ al restaurante especializado en la cocina de Guayaquil.
2. A doña Lourdes y a su hija les fascinan la zoología y la botánica. Ellas __e__ un viaje a las Islas Galápagos para ver la gran variedad de especies animales.
3. Don Jorge y yo __d__ el mercado indígena de Cuenca para comprar artesanía ecuatoriana.
4. A ti te gusta disfrutar del aire libre, ver la arquitectura colonial y las montañas. Tú __b__ por la Plaza San Blas en Quito.
5. A mí me interesa la protección de los animales y la flora. Yo __a__ a la Reserva Cuyabeno que está a 500 kilómetros de Quito.

a. viajaré
b. caminarás
c. irán
d. visitaremos
e. harán

 10-30 Intercambio: Un viaje a Guayaquil. PRIMERA FASE. Ramiro va a Guayaquil a visitar a su familia. Háganse preguntas y contesten de acuerdo con la agenda que Ramiro preparó.

MODELO: E1: *¿Qué hará Ramiro el miércoles por la noche?*
E2: *Cenará con unos amigos.*
E1: *¿Cuándo irá al cine con los primos?*
E2: *Irán al cine el martes.*

LUNES	MARTES	MIÉRCOLES	JUEVES	VIERNES
salir para Guayaquil	visitar el Parque de las Iguanas	salir de compras al Mercado Artesanal	viajar al Parque Nacional El Cajas	empacar las maletas
cenar con los tíos	conocer a otros familiares	ir a un museo	caminar en la reserva, sacar fotos	almorzar con toda la familia
acostarse temprano	ir al cine con los primos	cenar con unos amigos	dormir en el parque	regresar a Estados Unidos

SEGUNDA FASE. Hagan una lista de cinco actividades que Ramiro probablemente hará al regresar a Estados Unidos. Expliquen por qué.

 10-31 Planes para una fiesta para celebrar un matrimonio. PRIMERA FASE. Sus amigos José y Silvia se casaron durante sus vacaciones en Ecuador. Regresarán a Estados Unidos en dos semanas y ustedes van a organizar una fiesta para celebrar su matrimonio. Planifiquen la fiesta considerando lo siguiente: número de invitados, lugar de la fiesta, menú que ofrecerán (comida y bebida), música, baile y otras actividades en la fiesta.

 SEGUNDA FASE. Compartan sus planes con otra pareja. Hagan una lista de tres semejanzas y tres diferencias entre las fiestas que las dos parejas organizarán.

10-32 ¿Qué recomendaciones seguirá? Maricela sufre de estrés, insomnio y anemia. Por eso les pide sugerencias a su mejor amiga y a su nutricionista. A continuación aparecen sus recomendaciones. Discutan qué recomendaciones probablemente seguirá Maricela y expliquen por qué. Answers will vary. Encourage students to support their responses logically.

RECOMENDACIONES DE LA NUTRICIONISTA	RECOMENDACIONES DE SU MEJOR AMIGA
1. Coma en pequeñas cantidades por lo menos cuatro veces al día.	1. Come cuando quieras. Si subes de peso puedes seguir una dieta.
2. No consuma cafeína para tener energía. Consuma proteínas para obtener energía.	2. Para tener energía, come mucho chocolate y, luego, haz ejercicio.
3. Consuma calcio. Beba leche y coma frutas.	3. Toma helado todos los días porque la leche tiene mucho calcio.
4. Para eliminar la tensión y relajarse, haga yoga.	4. Escucha música suave y no contestes el teléfono de la oficina.
5. Compre verduras y carnes orgánicas en supermercados especializados en productos naturales.	5. Pide ensalada con pollo en los restaurantes de comida rápida y un refresco de dieta.

Follow-up for 10-32. You may wish to have students discuss what Maricela will do and what she probably won't do, and why.

SITUACIONES

1. **Role A.** You are organizing a picnic and some of the guests are vegetarians. Call your nutritionist friend (your classmate) to discuss what food to serve. Say that a) you will prepare vegetarian and non-vegetarian food; b) for the vegetarians, you will make salads and a Spanish tortilla; c) for the meat eaters, you will serve a chicken salad and want to have hamburgers; and d) you will serve beer, soft drinks, and juice. Ask your friend for advice.

   Role B. A friend is calling to ask for advice regarding the menu for a picnic that will include both vegetarian and non-vegetarian guests. Give your friend feedback on the proposed menu and offer additional advice.

2. **Role A.** You and a friend are concerned about people's quality of life and the food they eat. Tell your friend that you think in ten years from now people will eat a) more healthful foods; b) fewer fats and sugars; and c) less junk food (**comida chatarra**). Add that you think food will be more expensive but of better quality and that people will live longer because they will be healthier.

   Role B. You don't agree with your friend's opinions about what people will eat ten years from now. In your view, a) people will continue to eat unhealthful food; b) people will continue to eat fats and sugar; c) children will have more opportunities to eat junk food (**comida chatarra**) because parents will be very busy; d) food will cost less, so people will eat more; and e) people will die younger but happier.

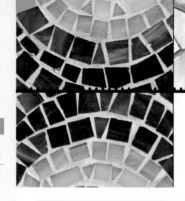

MOSAICOS

Resources

■ SAM: 10-39 to 10-41
■ Supp. Activ. Book: *Mosaicos*

Audioscript for 10-34.
Andrea decidió cocinar dos platos esta vez, paella y una ensalada de papas. Como tenía pescado para la paella en casa, decidió comprar pollo y camarones. Para la ensalada de papas compró zanahorias y papas. También compró aguacates para decorar la ensalada.

Carolina iba a comprar aguacates y tomates para preparar guacamole, pero decidió comprar ajos, cebollas, espinacas, maíz y pollo para hacer una tortilla de verduras y pollo asado.

Roberto pensó que era una buena idea llevar uno de los platos favoritos de Óscar. Por eso compró langosta, sal, pimienta y aguacates.

Darío estaba enfermo y no pudo ir al supermercado. Su hermana hizo las compras para él. Ella compró jamón, papas, aderezo y pimientos verdes.

Todos compraron carne molida.

ESTRATEGIA

Record relevant detail

Note-taking is a useful strategy for recording what you hear. To take useful notes, you need to sort out and prioritize the information as you listen, writing down what is relevant to your purpose. For example, you may want to write down the directions for making a new dish that you hear on a cooking show. As you listen, you need to jot down important details to prepare the dish yourself. The details the chef chats about may be fun to listen to but may not be essential to the recipe.

Lengua

Pimienta refers to the spice (*ground pepper*) and **pimiento** refers to the vegetable. Therefore, **pimienta roja** is the red (*cayenne*) pepper that one sprinkles on pizza, and **pimiento rojo** is a red bell pepper. Chili pepper has its own word—**un chile** or **ají**, as in **chile habanero, chile jalapeño**, and so forth.

A escuchar

Antes de escuchar

10-33 Preparación. Usted escuchará una lista de productos que compraron Andrea, Carolina, Roberto y Darío. Antes de escuchar, prepare una lista de productos que usted compra regularmente y otra de aquellos que usted compra en ocasiones especiales.

Escuchar

10-34 ¿Comprende usted? Andrea, Carolina, Roberto, and Darío have each offered to contribute a dish for their friend Óscar's birthday party. Each has bought some kind of vegetable and meat or seafood to prepare his/her dish. As you listen, mark (✓) the foods that each of them bought.

CD 4
Track 33
or CD 5
Track 9

ANDREA	CAROLINA	ROBERTO	DARÍO
___ sal	✓ ajos	___ mermelada	___ huevos
✓ pollo	___ cerdo	___ pepinos	___ ajos
✓ carne molida	✓ espinacas	✓ pimienta	___ fruta
___ azúcar	___ jamón	___ aceite	✓ jamón
✓ zanahorias	___ langosta	___ pavo	✓ aderezo
✓ aguacates	✓ maíz	✓ aguacates	✓ pimientos verdes
✓ camarones	✓ pollo	___ zanahorias	___ pasta

Después de escuchar

10-35 Ahora usted. Compartan las respuestas a las siguientes preguntas.

1. ¿Cuál es su plato favorito?
2. ¿Qué productos o ingredientes compra usted para prepararlo?
3. ¿Con quién comparte generalmente su plato favorito? ¿Por qué?
4. ¿Qué dice esta persona cuando usted prepara este plato?

A conversar

Antes de conversar

10-36 Preparación. PRIMERA FASE. Marque cuáles de los siguientes alimentos son más saludables (**+**) o menos saludables (**–**). Answers may vary, but the following may be expected.

_+_ los camarones	_+_ las espinacas	_–_ el jamón	_+_ el pollo
_+_ la carne de res	_+_ la fruta	_+_ las legumbres	_–_ el queso
_–_ la cerveza	_–_ las galletas	_–_ el pan blanco	_–_ los refrescos
_–_ los dulces	_–_ el helado	_+_ las papas	_+_ el vino

SEGUNDA FASE. Escriban en la tabla los productos o alimentos de la *Primera fase* que en general producen los siguientes efectos. Prepárense para explicar por qué. **OJO:** Algunos se pueden poner en más de una categoría.

ENGORDAN	ADELGAZAN (*ARE SLIMMING*)	DAN ENERGÍA	AUMENTAN EL COLESTEROL

Conversar

10-37 Entre nosotros. Averigüen las preferencias de comida de los miembros del grupo en las siguientes categorías. Después, sumen los números en las columnas para saber qué comida les gusta más y cuál les gusta menos.

MODELO: los mariscos
   E1:   *¿Te gustan los mariscos?*
   E2:   *Me encantan. ¿Y a ti?*
   E1:   *A mí no me gustan.*

ALIMENTO	ENCANTAR	GUSTAR MUCHO	GUSTAR	NO GUSTAR
la fruta				
las verduras				
la carne				
los mariscos				
los productos lácteos				
los dulces				

Después de conversar

10-38 Un poco más. Comparen los resultados de **10-37** para determinar las categorías de alimentos que se consumen más en la clase. Luego, respondan a estas preguntas.

1. ¿Qué tipos de comida se comen más en la clase?
2. En general, ¿ustedes se alimentan bien o mal? ¿Por qué?
3. ¿Deben ustedes mejorar su dieta? ¿Qué deben hacer?

ESTRATEGIA

Give and defend reasons for a decision

When you make a decision that you wish to communicate effectively to others, it is important to a) state your decision clearly; b) present and explain your reasons logically; and c) urge your listeners to consider your point of view.

En directo

To influence someone's decision:

Es mejor/menos dañino (*harmful*) + *infinitive*.

¿No te/le(s) parece más saludable + *infinitive*?

¿Qué te/le(s) parece si + *indicative*… ?

Suggestion for 10-36 Primera fase. Answers will vary. Model for students ways to state and defend their classifications and their points of view.

Suggestion for 10-36 Segunda fase. Answers will vary according to students' beliefs about food and health, so once again encourage them to present and support their points of view, and to persuade their group mates.

Suggestion for 10-37. Put students in groups of 4 or 6. Ask them to interview each other in pairs and then record their combined results in the group table.

Suggestion for 10-38. Once groups have compared their results, they can share their conclusions with the whole class.

Resources

■ SAM: 10-43 to 10-45

A leer

ESTRATEGIA	**Learn new words by analyzing their connections with known words**

All readers of a second language encounter words that are unfamiliar to them. In some cases it is possible to skip over the word and still understand the overall meaning of the sentence or paragraph. In other cases, it is better to focus on the unfamiliar word and guess its meaning. You may find you can guess the meaning of the unfamiliar word by mentally linking it to words you know that are related to it in meaning or in grammatical form. Figuring out word meanings in this way can help you expand your vocabulary.

Antes de leer

10-39 Preparación. Lea el título y los subtítulos de la lectura en la p. 355, mire las fotos y lea sus leyendas. Luego, conteste las preguntas, usando esos elementos y también su conocimiento general. *Answers may vary, but the following can be expected.*

1. ¿Qué información espera encontrar en el artículo?
   a. una definición del término *fusión culinaria*
      (Sí) No
   b. una dieta para bajar de peso
      Sí (No)
   c. recetas para platos de cocina fusión
      Sí (No)
   d. información sobre la influencia china en la cocina de un país
      (Sí) No
   e. información sobre la cocina Tex-Mex
      (Sí) No

2. Marque (✓) los elementos que lo/la ayudaron a responder a la pregunta 1.
   a. ____ el título y los subtítulos
   b. ____ las fotos junto con sus leyendas
   c. ____ mi conocimiento de cocina

3. ¿Qué es la fusión culinaria? Marque (✓) la definición más lógica, según su conocimiento general.
   a. ____ La combinación de la cocina con otras artes, como la decoración de interiores
   b. _✓_ Una cocina que combina la influencia de dos tradiciones culinarias
   c. ____ Una manera tradicional de preparar la comida que la gente conserva por muchas generaciones

4. Prepare una lista de comidas Tex-Mex que usted conoce. ¿Cuáles le gustan más? Luego, indique si aparecieron en el artículo.

Suggestion for 10-39.
Encourage students to draw on their general knowledge about food to guess what *fusión culinaria* means. You may draw their attention to the italicized food items in the first paragraph (*California roll, taco pizza*) as examples of *fusión culinaria*, and ask them to figure out what these two items have in common.

Leer

La fusión culinaria: una tendencia nueva con una historia larga

Tortilla española envuelta en una tortilla mexicana

La fusión en la cocina contemporánea

Todos hemos comido platos que combinan la cocina de dos países o culturas. El llamado *California roll*—el sushi japonés con un relleno[1] de cangrejo[2], queso crema y aguacate—es un ejemplo; la *taco pizza*, que se hace con la masa de una pizza cubierta de los ingredientes típicos del taco—carne molida, frijoles refritos, salsa, queso amarillo y especias picantes—es otro. La fusión culinaria, o cocina fusión, es un concepto que señala la mezcla de ingredientes y estilos culinarios de diferentes culturas en el menú de un restaurante o aun en un mismo plato. El término *cocina fusión* fue inventado en California en la década de los 1960s por unos chefs que combinaban los estilos de las cocinas de Asia (china, japonesa, tailandesa) con las legumbres frescas y naturales de California y las salsas hechas de frutas cítricas y tropicales. Hoy en día es común encontrar restaurantes en Estados Unidos con nombres como *Roy's Hawaiian Fusion Cuisine* o *Fusion Restaurant and Lounge*. Hay muchas posibles combinaciones, limitadas solamente por la creatividad del chef y los gustos de los clientes.

La fusión en la historia culinaria

A pesar de la creciente popularidad de estas combinaciones gastronómicas, sería un error pensar que la cocina fusión es un fenómeno nuevo. Siempre donde conviven grupos de personas de dos culturas nace una fusión de sus tradiciones culinarias. Dos ejemplos de este antiguo fenómeno en las Américas son la cocina chino-peruana y la cocina mexicano-norteamericana, o Tex-Mex.

El Chifa: La cocina fusión de Perú

La cocina peruana es una mezcla de muchas influencias: indígena, española, africana, china y japonesa. El Chifa, o cocina chino-peruana, es el resultado de la mezcla de la comida criolla de Lima con la cocina traída por los inmigrantes chinos desde mediados del siglo XIX. El término *el Chifa* se refiere tanto a la comida como a los restaurantes donde se sirve.

Los chinos que fueron a Perú se adaptaron a la sociedad y sus costumbres, pero siempre mantuvieron sus tradiciones culinarias. Con el progreso económico, luego pudieron importar de China unas especias y otros productos esenciales para su comida, pero por lo general tenían que cultivar las verduras que necesitaban o sustituirlas por ingredientes locales.

No es una exageración decir que la cultura chino-peruana de los inmigrantes chinos asimilados a la sociedad peruana revolucionó la gastronomía. Algunos platos considerados típicamente peruanos, como el arroz chaufa (preparado con carne picada, cebollitas, pimentón, huevos y salsa de soja) y el tacu-tacu (una tortilla hecha de un puré de frijoles, arroz, ajo, ají y cebolla) reflejan la influencia de la cocina china.

La comida Tex-Mex: La cocina mexicana en Estados Unidos

Un ejemplo de la cocina fusión que se conoce en todas partes de Estados Unidos es la cocina Tex-Mex. Se trata de una fusión de dos estilos, el de México y el de Texas. La cocina que conocemos hoy en día como Tex-Mex se originó en una mezcla de la comida del pueblo nativo de Texas y la cocina española. Los indígenas contribuyeron con ingredientes como los frijoles pintos, los nopales (las hojas de un cacto), las cebollas silvestres[3] y el mesquite. La influencia española empezó con la llegada del ganado[4] a la región, traído por los colonizadores al final del siglo XVI. También hay influencias del norte de África en la comida Tex-Mex. Un grupo de colonizadores de las Islas Canarias y de Marruecos inmigraron a lo que es ahora San Antonio, Texas en el siglo XVIII. De ellos vinieron combinaciones nuevas de especias (sobre todo el comino), cilantro y chiles en la comida Tex-Mex. El chili con carne de San Antonio todavía retiene los sabores de la cocina marroquí.

Nachos, un plato popular de la cocina Tex-Mex

En los últimos treinta años ha habido esfuerzos de separar lo que se considera *la cocina mexicana* de lo que conocemos como *la cocina mexicana americanizada*, o Tex-Mex. En comparación con la cocina mexicana, la Tex-Mex utiliza más carne y usa las tortillas para envolver una mayor variedad de rellenos. Los nachos, los tacos fritos, las chalupas, el chile con queso y el chile con carne son invenciones Tex-Mex que no se encuentran en la cocina mexicana tradicional. La costumbre universal en los restaurantes Tex-Mex de servir las *tortilla chips* con salsa picante como aperitivo tampoco existe en la cocina mexicana tradicional.

[1]*filling*   [2]*crab*   [3]*wild*   [4]*cattle*

10-40 Primera mirada. Según el contenido del artículo, ¿son las siguientes afirmaciones ciertas (**C**) o falsas (**F**)? Si la afirmación es falsa, corrija la información.

1. _C_ El término *cocina fusión* fue inventado por unos chefs en Estados Unidos.
2. _F_ El artículo afirma que la cocina fusión se limita a la combinación de influencias asiáticas en la cocina del Oeste. Hay muchas combinaciones posibles.
3. _C_ La cocina peruana incorpora influencias culinarias de muchos países.
4. _F_ Llegaron inmigrantes chinos a Perú en el siglo XVIII. Llegaron en el siglo XIX.
5. _F_ Los chinos en el Perú han mantenido su tradición culinaria sin cambios. Ha cambiado.
6. _C_ El Chifa es un término que se refiere a la cocina chino-peruana.
7. _F_ La cocina Tex-Mex es igual a la cocina mexicana. Hay diferencias.
8. _F_ Se usa menos carne y menos queso en la cocina Tex-Mex que en la cocina mexicana tradicional. Usa más carne y más queso que la cocina mexicana.
9. _C_ Los nachos y las fajitas son invenciones de la cocina Tex-Mex.
10. _C_ El chile con carne que se come en San Antonio, Texas usa especias similares a las que se usan en Marruecos, en el norte de África.

10-41 Segunda mirada. Busque en el artículo palabras que se asocien con lo siguiente.

1. dos sinónimos de *fusión culinaria*: la cocina fusión, las combinaciones gastronómicas

2. carnes: carne molida, chili con carne

3. Asia: sushi japonés, cocinas de Asia (china, japonesa, tailandesa), influencia china y japonesa en la cocina peruana, inmigrantes chinos a Perú

4. platos de la cocina Chifa: arroz chaufa, tacu-tacu

5. platos de la cocina Tex-Mex: chili con carne, nachos, tacos fritos, chalupas, chili con queso, tortillas con salsa

6. referencias a países: Estados Unidos, Japón, Perú, China, México, España, Marruecos

Después de leer

10-42 Ampliación. PRIMERA FASE. Preparen una lista de platos que ustedes comen o que han visto en restaurantes que, en la opinión del grupo, son ejemplos de la cocina fusión. Luego, seleccionen uno de estos platos.

SEGUNDA FASE. Preparen una presentación sobre el plato y sus antecedentes culinarios y preséntenla a la clase. Recuerden de dirigirse a su público cuando hacen la presentación.

Suggestion for 10-42. You may wish to remind students that dishes that are Americanized versions of other national cuisines are examples of fusion cuisine. You may also ask students to think about when a dish ceases to be considered "fusion" and is seen as native to a particular cuisine. For example, pasta with tomato sauce, considered an Italian dish, actually represents a fusion of influences from China (noodles) and the New World (tomatoes).

A escribir

Resources
■ SAM: 10-46 to 10-48

Summarize information

We often face the need to report or summarize what we have heard or read. A good summary maintains the structure of the original text and synthesizes its principal ideas and information. It concisely and accurately captures the central meaning of the original. Keep the following strategies in mind when you write a summary:
- Read the text carefully for the main ideas. Read it more than once.
- Write one or two sentences that summarize the main idea of each section you identify in the text.
- Try to use your own words.
- Do not inject your own opinion or add anything not in the original text.

10-43 Preparación. Lea una vez más el artículo "La fusión culinaria: una tendencia nueva con una historia larga" en la p. 355. Haga lo siguiente:

1. Identifique las secciones del artículo.
2. Pase su marcador (*highlighter*) por las ideas centrales de cada sección.

Suggestion for 10-43. You may wish to have students do this activity in pairs. In preparation for 10-44, you may also suggest students identify concepts they will need to express in their own words in the summary.

Escribir

10-44 Manos a la obra. Escriba en sus propias palabras un resumen del artículo, usando las ideas principales que marcó en *Preparación*.

Después de escribir

10-45 Revisión. Antes de compartir el resumen con un compañero editor/una compañera editora, léalo y verifique lo siguiente:

1. ¿Representa su resumen una síntesis del texto original? ¿El resumen refleja con precisión las ideas expresadas en el texto? ¿Hay detalles innecesarios?
2. ¿Sigue el resumen la estructura del texto original?
3. ¿Escribió transiciones claras que muestran las diversas secciones del texto original?
4. ¿Fluyen (*flow*) las ideas de una manera clara y natural? ¿Hay que aclarar algunos puntos?
5. ¿Usó el vocabulario y las estructuras correctas?
6. ¿Revisó la ortografía y la acentuación?

Resources

- SAM: 10-49 to 10-50
- Supp. Activ. Book: *Enfoque cultural*
- *Vistas culturales* video

ENFOQUE CULTURAL

Ecuador: alimentación y salud pública

La diversidad geográfica del Ecuador le permite producir una gran variedad de alimentos. Y como es un país tropical, produce una cantidad suficiente de alimentos para satisfacer sus necesidades internas y para la exportación. En la región de la costa, se cultivan soya, café y aceite de palma, además de frutas tales como mango, cacao, banano, maracuyá y limón, entre otras. Por su parte, en la sierra, con sus diferentes niveles de clima, los campesinos producen una gran cantidad de comida, por ejemplo, papas, verduras (tomate, brócoli, cebolla) y frutas como manzanas y naranjas.

Una plantación de banano en Ecuador

La región amazónica produce principalmente carne de res, y algunos otros productos vegetales, como la yuca, que forman parte de la dieta ecuatoriana. Sin embargo, esta región tiene un déficit alimentario, porque sólo un porcentaje pequeño de su territorio está dedicado a la agricultura.

Note. Canned tuna and frozen shrimp are related productions to the fish industry in Ecuador. Over 120,000 people work in the plants that process the fish, the majority being women. The United States is the main importer of this production.

La industria del pescado en el Océano Pacífico

No hay que olvidar que la costa ecuatoriana es rica en pescado. Las aguas del Pacífico cercanas a las costas de Ecuador, Perú y Chile son rutas migratorias de grandes peces, y tradicionalmente los pescadores han aprovechado esas rutas para pescar. El puerto de Manta, por ejemplo, es conocido como la capital atunera del mundo. Además, en los últimos treinta años, se ha desarrollado en Ecuador una gran industria de cultivo de pescado o acuicultura. Uno de los productos más importantes de la acuicultura de Ecuador es el camarón. Gracias al camarón ecuatoriano, un producto que antes era de lujo, actualmente está al alcance de la clase media en Estados Unidos y Europa.

Los niños son las principales víctimas de la malnutrición, no sólo en Ecuador, sino en muchos países.

A pesar de que Ecuador es un país capaz de producir suficiente comida para su mercado interior y para la exportación, la salud de sus habitantes presenta varios problemas relacionados con la nutrición. En la actualidad aproximadamente una cuarta parte de la población ecuatoriana tiene problemas de desnutrición crónica. El sobrepeso y la obesidad afectan aproximadamente a un 10% de la población, mientras que la anemia es otra condición que afecta a amplios sectores, especialmente a los adolescentes, a las mujeres y a los infantes. Desafortunadamente, al igual que en otros países latinoamericanos, muchos de estos problemas son la consecuencia de la excesiva pobreza de muchos de sus habitantes. En efecto, más del 70% de los ecuatorianos viven en la pobreza.

Algunos datos sobre el consumo de alimentos en Ecuador son verdaderamente preocupantes. A causa de las crisis económicas, muchos ecuatorianos, principalmente de las clases más pobres, han perdido la capacidad de comprar alimentos básicos en los últimos diez años. Esas reducciones tienen un efecto desastroso sobre la alimentación y, por lo tanto, sobre la salud de los ecuatorianos. Según estadísticas del propio gobierno de Ecuador, en el año 2001 las tres comidas diarias se habían reducido a dos, especialmente en los sectores sociales más pobres. Desgraciadamente, los esfuerzos del gobierno de Ecuador y de muchas organizaciones internacionales de ayuda, no han tenido mucho éxito. Hoy día la pobreza parece relacionarse con los mayores problemas sanitarios del país: la malnutrición y el VIH/SIDA. Según un informe del gobierno ecuatoriano de 2004, se registraron más de mil casos nuevos de esta enfermedad en ese año.

En otras palabras

Expresiones ecuatorianas

Mi **ñaña** se fue para Guayaquil.
My sister left for Guayaquil.

Tengo mucha sed, voy a tomar una **colita**.
I am very thirsty; I'm going to drink a soda.

Sí, sí, **te creo ocho veces**.
Yeah, sure, I believe you. (said with disbelief)

10-46 Comprensión. PRIMERA FACE. **Reconocimiento de palabras clave.** Encuentre en el texto la palabra o expresión que mejor expresa el significado de las siguientes ideas.

1. enough .... suficiente
2. beef .... carne de res
3. close to/near .... cercanas
4. aquaculture ...... industria de cultivo de pescado/acuicultura
5. shrimp .... camarón (camarones)
6. overweight .... sobrepeso
7. poverty .... pobreza

SEGUNDA FASE. **Oraciones importantes.** Subraye las afirmaciones que contienen ideas que se encuentran en el texto. Luego indique en qué parte del texto están.

1. All three of the geographical regions of Ecuador produce food in excess of their needs.
2. Many fisheries in Europe and the United States have gone out of business because of the industrial production of shrimp in Ecuador.
3. Manta, a port on the Pacific, was prohibited by the government of Ecuador from investing in the tuna fishing industry.
4. As a rule, Ecuador produces enough food to satisfy the needs of its internal markets, and even to export some of its crops.
5. Malnutrition is the cause of a number of health problems among Ecuadorians.
6. Women, infants, and adolescents are among the most common victims of health problems related to malnutrition.
7. Excessive poverty is at the root of malnutrition in Ecuador, as well as in other countries.
8. AIDS is still a problem in Ecuador, where over a thousand new cases were reported in 2004.

TERCERA FASE. **Ideas principales.** Escriba un párrafo breve en español resumiendo las ideas principales expresadas en el texto.

 10-47 Use la información. Prepare un afiche sobre el tema de la pobreza y la malnutrición. Estas son algunas preguntas que usted puede tratar de responder en su afiche: ¿Cómo se comparan entre sí algunos países de América Latina en cuanto a la malnutrición? ¿Qué progresos o retrocesos han ocurrido recientemente en cuanto a la malnutrición en América Latina y otras regiones del mundo? ¿Qué papel juega la malnutrición en el desarrollo económico de los países? ¿Por qué es importante la buena nutrición materno-infantil? ¿Qué organizaciones están luchando contra la malnutrición a nivel global? Para preparar esta actividad, visite la página web de *Mosaicos* y siga los enlaces útiles.

VOCABULARIO

Las especias y los condimentos — *Spices and seasonings*

el aceite	*oil*
el aderezo	*salad dressing*
el azúcar	*sugar*
las especias	*spices*
las hierbas	*herbs*
la mayonesa	*mayonnaise*
la mostaza	*mustard*
la pimienta	*pepper*
la sal	*salt*
la salsa de tomate	*tomato sauce*
la vainilla	*vanilla*
el vinagre	*vinegar*

Las frutas y las verduras — *Fruits and vegetables*

el aguacate	*avocado*
el ajo	*garlic*
la cebolla	*onion*
la cereza	*cherry*
las espinacas	*spinach*
la fresa	*strawberry*
el limón	*lemon*
el maíz	*corn*
la manzana	*apple*
el maracuyá	*passion fruit*
el melón	*melon*
la papaya	*papaya*
el pepino	*cucumber*
la pera	*pear*
el pimiento verde	*green pepper*
la piña	*pineapple*
el plátano/la banana	*banana, plantain*
la toronja/el pomelo	*grapefruit*
la uva	*grape*
la zanahoria	*carrot*

El pescado y la carne — *Fish and meat*

las aves	*poultry, fowl*
el camarón/la gamba	*shrimp*
la carne	*meat*
molida/picada	*ground meat*
de res	*beef/steak*
el cerdo	*pork*
la chuleta	*chop*
el cordero	*lamb*
la costilla	*rib*
la langosta	*lobster*
los mariscos	*shellfish*
la oveja	*sheep*
el pavo	*turkey*

Otros productos — *Other products*

los churros	*fried dough*
la crema	*cream*
el dulce	*candy/sweets*
la galleta	*cookie*
la harina	*flour*
la leche de coco	*coconut milk*
las legumbres	*legumes*
las lentejas	*lentils*
la manteca/la mantequilla	*butter*
la margarina	*margarine*
el pan dulce	*bun, small cake*
el pastel	*pastry*
el queso crema	*cream cheese*
el yogur	*yogurt*

En la mesa — *On the table*

la bandeja	*tray*
la botella	*bottle*
la copa	*(stemmed) glass*
la cuchara	*spoon*
la cucharita	*teaspoon*
el cuchillo	*knife*
el mantel	*tablecloth*
el plato	*plate, dish*
la servilleta	*napkin*
la taza	*cup*
el tenedor	*fork*
el vaso	*glass*

Verbos — *Verbs*

agregar/añadir	*to add*
batir	*to beat*
disfrutar	*to enjoy*
freír (i)	*to fry*
hervir (ie, i)	*to boil*
probar (ue)	*to try, to taste*
recomendar (ie)	*to recommend*

Las descripciones — *Descriptions*

agrio/a	*sour*
lácteo/a	*dairy (product)*

Palabras y expresiones útiles — *Useful words and expressions*

el campesino/la campesina	*peasant*
la receta	*recipe*
todavía	*still, yet*
ya	*already*

See *Lengua* boxes on p. 329 and on p. 352 for additional food vocabulary.

Note. Wilfredo Lam (1902–1982) was one of the most renowned painters of the 20th century. Born in Cuba to a Chinese immigrant father and a mother who was the daughter of a former Congolese slave, Lam was surrounded by people of African descent and was exposed to African rituals and healing methods from an early age. He studied art in Spain and later lived in Paris, where he was influenced by Surrealism and developed a close friendship with Pablo Picasso, whose work deeply impressed him. He lived in Cuba and Haiti in the 1940s, where he produced his most important painting, *La Jungla* (1943).

Suggestions. Recycle vocabulary of the body studied in previous chapters. Have students describe the painting: *¿Hay personas en el cuadro? ¿Hay animales?* Recycle *parece: ¿Parece un animal? ¿Qué formas tiene?* Introduce *redondo, cuadrado, triangular, rectangular. ¿Qué colores hay en este cuadro?*

La salud es lo primero

Sin título, del pintor cubano Wilfredo Lam (1902-1982)

In this chapter you will learn how to:

- discuss health and medical treatments
- talk about the body
- express emotions, opinions, expectations, and wishes

Cultural focus: Cuba, República Dominicana

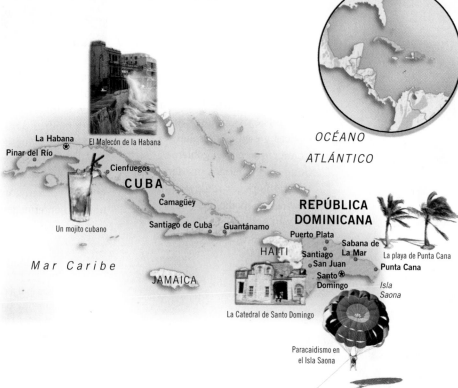

La Habana
Pinar del Río
El Malecón de la Habana
Cienfuegos
CUBA
Camagüey
Un mojito cubano
Santiago de Cuba Guantánamo
Mar Caribe
JAMAICA

OCÉANO
ATLÁNTICO

REPÚBLICA DOMINICANA
Puerto Plata
Sabana de
La Mar
La playa de Punta Cana
HAITÍ
Santiago
San Juan
Santo
Domingo
Punta Cana
Isla Saona
La Catedral de Santo Domingo
Paracaidismo en el Isla Saona

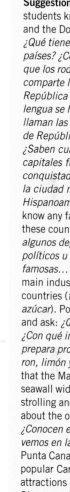

 A vista de pájaro. Compruebe lo que sabe sobre Cuba y República Dominicana contestando las siguientes preguntas.

1. ¿Cuál es la capital de Cuba? La Habana
2. ¿Qué país limita por tierra (*land*) con República Dominicana? Haití
3. ¿Qué lugar de República Dominicana es muy popular entre los turistas? Punta Cana
4. ¿Con qué tres ingredientes se prepara el mojito cubano? ron, limón y menta
5. ¿Cuáles son algunas de las industrias más importantes de esta región? ron, azúcar, tabaco
6. ¿Cuál es el deporte favorito en estos países? el béisbol

Ask if students are familiar with *el cubismo, el surrealismo. ¿Quién era un pintor cubista?* (Picasso, Braque). *¿Conocen a algún pintor surrealista?* (Dalí). Ask *¿Les gusta este tipo de arte? ¿Por qué?*

Suggestions. Ask what students know about Cuba and the Dominican Republic. *¿Qué tienen en común estos países? ¿Cómo se llama el mar que los rodea? ¿Qué otro país comparte la isla con República Dominicana? ¿Qué lengua se habla allí? ¿Cómo se llaman las capitales de Cuba y de República Dominicana? ¿Saben cuál de estas capitales fundada por los conquistadores europeos es la ciudad más antigua de Hispanoamérica?* Ask if they know any famous people from these countries: *¿Conocen algunos deportistas, líderes políticos u otras personas famosas...?* Ask about the main industries of these countries (*tabaco, ron, azúcar*). Point to the photos and ask: *¿Qué es un mojito? ¿Con qué ingredientes se prepara probablemente?* (*con ron, limón y menta*). Explain that the Malecón is a paved seawall wide enough for strolling and driving. Talk about the other photos: *¿Conocen este deporte que vemos en la foto?* Explain that Punta Cana is one of the most popular Caribbean tourist attractions for Americans. Give some background about the history of these two countries. The island of *La Hispaniola* (*La Española*), homeland for Haiti and the Dominican Republic, was the first Spanish colony in the New World. Columbus landed there on December 5, 1492. It served as the base of operations for further discoveries. Cuba was the last Spanish colony to fight for its independence, which it did in the Spanish-American War of 1898, with the help of the U.S.

A PRIMERA VISTA

Médicos, farmacias y hospitales

CD 5
Track 18

En la mayor parte de los países hispanos existen **hospitales, clínicas** y **centros de salud** financiados por el **gobierno** donde los **enfermos** pueden ir sin tener que pagar nada por los servicios o **medicinas** que reciben.

En las **farmacias** se venden todo tipo de **remedios** y **artículos de belleza**. Al igual que en Estados Unidos, en muchos lugares se necesita tener **receta** médica para comprar **antibióticos**. Muchas veces los clientes de la farmacia le preguntan **al farmacéutico/a la farmacéutica** qué remedio deben comprar para **curar** o **tratar** su **enfermedad**.

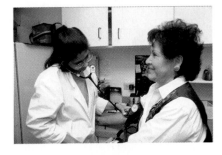

Esta enfermera le toma la **tensión/presión arterial** a una **paciente** en un **sanatorio**.

Algunas personas prefieren curarse con hierbas medicinales. Por ejemplo, para el **dolor de estómago** se recomienda tomar un té de manzanilla (*chamomile*) o un té de ruda (*rue*). Otra hierba medicinal muy conocida es la uña de gato (*cat's claw*), que se considera buena para el **tratamiento** del **cáncer**.

Cultura

Los indígenas del continente americano nos han transmitido muchos conocimientos de medicina natural. Gracias al conocimiento que tenían de hierbas, animales y minerales, los indígenas elaboraban remedios que utilizaban contra las fiebres o como antídotos para otros males. Conocían los efectos positivos de los baños e infusiones de hierbas y tenían fórmulas para cerrar las heridas (*wounds*) y curar las úlceras. También trataban fracturas de huesos, aplicando una pasta de semillas, polvo de ciertas plantas y resina. Acompañaban muchas de estas prácticas con ceremonias en las que invocaban a sus dioses, pidiéndoles protección y ayuda.

11-1 Definiciones. Complete las siguientes oraciones con las palabras apropiadas.

1. En las ____farmacias____ se venden medicinas y productos de belleza.
2. El té de manzanilla se recomienda para el ____dolor____ de estómago.
3. Los/Las ____enfermeros/as____ ayudan a los médicos en los hospitales y cuidan de los enfermos.
4. Según la creencia popular las ____hierbas____ medicinales pueden curar las enfermedades.
5. Los/Las ____farmacéuticos/as____ les venden a sus clientes los remedios que necesitan.
6. El ____gobierno____ financia muchos hospitales y centros de salud en los países hispanos.
7. Los/Las ____pacientes____ son las personas que sufren enfermedades.
8. Algunas personas piensan que la uña de gato es un buen tratamiento contra el ____cáncer____.

11-2 Conversación. PRIMERA FASE. Háganse las siguientes preguntas para intercambiar información.

1. Cuando necesitas una operación o tienes un accidente, ¿adónde vas? ¿Tienes que pagar o no?
2. ¿Hay muchos hospitales en tu ciudad? ¿Cómo se llaman?
3. Cuando estás enfermo/a y necesitas medicinas, ¿adónde vas a comprarlas? ¿Qué necesitas del médico/de la médica para poder comprarlas?
4. ¿Qué venden en las farmacias de tu país? ¿En qué farmacia compras normalmente?
5. ¿Usas hierbas medicinales? ¿Para qué las usas? ¿Alguien en tu familia las usa?
6. ¿Te interesa la medicina alternativa? ¿Alguna vez usaste la acupuntura, la homeopatía o alguna otra? ¿Cómo fue tu experiencia?

> **En otras palabras**
>
> In some Spanish-speaking countries, the word **sanatorio** is used instead of **hospital**; in others, **sanatorio** connotes a hospital that specializes in pulmonary and respiratory diseases. In some countries **clínica** refers to a private hospital. **Hospital** may refer to a government- or church-run facility that may provide free medical care.

SEGUNDA FASE. En Cuba y en otros países hispanoamericanos, hay una Academia de Ciencias que protege la investigación y organiza numerosas actividades relacionadas con la salud, la botánica, la física y otras áreas. Busquen en Internet la siguiente información sobre la Academia de Ciencias de Cuba y preparen un breve informe:

1. cuándo se fundó
2. los nombres de tres instituciones que se relacionan con ella
3. alguna de las actividades que organiza

11-3 Una emergencia. PRIMERA FASE. Usted y su amigo/a están de viaje en República Dominicana, y su amigo/a tiene un problema de salud. En un cibercafé de Santo Domingo, han encontrado este anuncio con información sobre médicos y farmacias de turno. Decidan cuál es el número más apropiado para llamar, basándose en el problema médico de su amigo/a.

SEGUNDA FASE. Haga la llamada para pedir la dirección del consultorio o de la farmacia. El/La recepcionista le debe explicar cómo llegar allí.

CYBER CENTRO AGUITA
CYBER CENTRO AGUITA
✚ — *Servicios Médicos* —
10-2-2001 | Santo Domingo
■ Badosa Farmacéutica. 563-4230 ········· ➤ Medicina Natural
■ Centro de Cirugía Plástica Santo Domingo. 686-7863 ·➤ Cirugía
■ Clínica Dental. 685-3752 ···················· ➤ Odontología
■ Clínica Dental Dra. Carmen Gómez. 587-3576 ···· ➤ Odontología
■ Consultores en Psicología y Sexualidad. 548-3690 ··➤ Psicología
■ Dr. Rubén Suárez, MD. 538- 2943 ··········➤ Medicina General
■ Dr. Eliseo Alonso, DDS. 672-3928 ··········➤ Medicina General
■ Farmacia Estrella. 688-4799 ···················· ➤ Farmacia
■ Óptica Central, CxA. 682-9505; 689-1308 ··········➤ Óptica
■ Productos Naturales. 686-1576 ··➤ Farmacéuticos - productos
■ Sándalo, 672-3287 ···················· ➤ Medicina Aromática

Suggestions for 11-3. Explain that pharmacies take turns staying open at times when businesses are normally closed (nights, holidays). The schedule for *farmacias de guardia/de turno* appears in local newspapers. Recycle the vocabulary for giving directions and phone numbers. Have pairs of students perform this activity as a role-play in class.

ᐧᗴ) Las partes del cuerpo

CD 5
Track 19

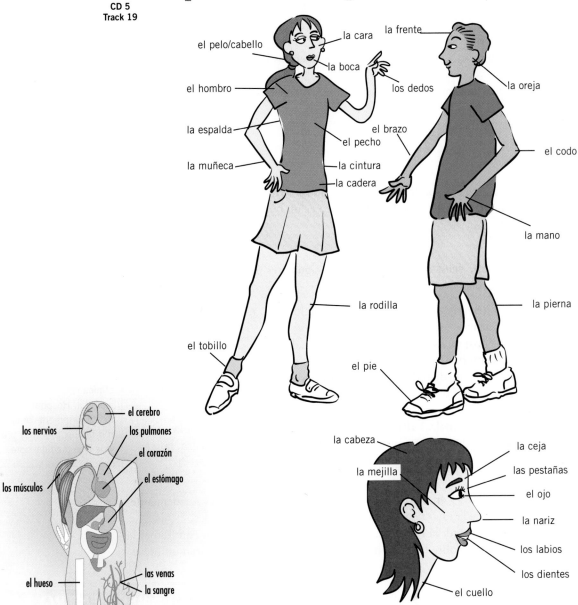

11-4 Asociación. PRIMERA FASE. Indique en qué parte del cuerpo se ponen estos accesorios y esta ropa.

1. __e__ los calcetines
2. __f__ los guantes
3. __b__ el cinturón
4. __d__ el collar
5. __c__ los aretes
6. __a__ el reloj

a. la muñeca
b. la cintura
c. las orejas
d. el cuello
e. los pies
f. las manos

 SEGUNDA FASE. Digan qué accesorios de la lista en la *Primera fase* no tienen ustedes y mencionen tres que consideren indispensables. Comparen sus respuestas.

11-5 ¿Para qué sirve(n)? Lean las siguientes definiciones y asócienlas con la parte del cuerpo correspondiente.

los brazos	la nariz
el cerebro	los ojos
el corazón	las piernas
los dientes	los pulmones
las manos	la sangre

1. ___Los brazos___ unen las manos con el cuerpo.
2. ___Los ojos___ permiten que las personas vean.
3. ___Los pulmones___ toman el oxígeno del aire y lo pasan a la sangre.
4. ___La sangre___ es un líquido rojo que circula por el cuerpo.
5. ___Las piernas___ unen el cuerpo con los pies.
6. ___Los dientes___ se deben lavar después de comer.
7. ___Las manos___ están al final de los brazos.
8. ___El cerebro___ le da órdenes al cuerpo.
9. ___El corazón___ impulsa la sangre por las venas del cuerpo.
10. ___La nariz___ está entre la frente y la boca.

Suggestion for 11-5. You may wish to turn this activity into a contest similar to Jeopardy, in which you ask *Unen las manos con el cuerpo* and teams of students compete to come up with the question *¿Qué son los brazos?*

11-6 Partes del cuerpo. PRIMERA FASE. Indiquen qué parte(s) del cuerpo probablemente se relaciona(n) con cada una de las siguientes situaciones.

SITUACIÓN	PARTE DEL CUERPO
1. A Felipe le gusta escuchar música muy fuerte.	los oídos
2. María se maquilla todos los días.	la cara
3. Necesito ponerme gafas porque veo mal.	los ojos
4. Un futbolista le pasa la pelota a un compañero de su equipo.	las manos/los pies
5. Se necesita mucha agilidad para tocar el piano.	los dedos
6. Esta paciente ha perdido 30 libras. Los pantalones le quedan anchos.	la cintura/las piernas
7. Daniela lleva siempre muchas pulseras.	los brazos, las muñecas
8. El té de hierbas es muy bueno para la digestión.	el estómago

SEGUNDA FASE. Ahora inventen ustedes dos adivinanzas cada uno/a para hacer asociaciones con partes del cuerpo.

MODELO: E1: *sirven para besar (to kiss)*
   E2: *los labios*

·)) La salud

Jorgito está enfermo

SRA. VILLA: Jorgito, **tienes muy mala cara.** ¿Estás **enfermo?**

JORGITO: **Me siento** muy mal y **tengo dolor de garganta.** Anoche tosí mucho.

SRA. VILLA: (Le pone el **termómetro.**) Tienes 39 grados de **fiebre.** Enseguida voy a llamar a la Dra. Bosque.

[En la clínica...]

DOCTORA: Vamos a ver, Jorgito. Cuéntame cómo te sientes.

JORGITO: Ahora **me duele** la cabeza y también me duelen los **oídos.** Además **estornudo** mucho.

DOCTORA: Vamos a **examinarte** los oídos y la garganta. Abre bien la boca y di "Ah". Tienes una **infección.** No es **grave,** pero es necesario que **te cuides.**

JORGITO: Doctora, no quiero que me ponga una **inyección.**

DOCTORA: ¡No, qué va! Te voy a **recetar** unas **pastillas.** Debes tomarlas **cada cuatro horas.**

JORGITO: Está bien, doctora.

DOCTORA: Además, tienes **gripe.** Debes descansar y beber mucho líquido. Aquí está la receta, señora.

SRA. VILLA: Gracias, doctora.

Lengua

Most words that refer to medical specialists derive from Latin and thus are similar to English: **pediatra** (*pediatrician*), **psiquiatra** (*psychiatrist*), **cirujano/a** (*surgeon*), **radiólogo/a** (*radiologist*), etc. A construction with **de** may also be used: **especialista** or **médico/a del corazón, del estómago,** etc. The primary care doctor is called **médico/a de familia,** or **médico/a de cabecera.**

11-7 La enfermedad de Jorgito. Complete la tabla con la información correcta.

SÍNTOMAS	RECOMENDACIONES	NOMBRE Y ESPECIALIDAD DE LA MÉDICA
Jorgito tiene mala cara; se siente mal; tiene dolor de cabeza; tosió anoche; tiene fiebre, etc.	Jorgito tiene que cuidarse, tomar una pastilla cada cuatro horas, descansar y beber líquidos.	La Dra. Bosque es pediatra.

¿Qué les pasa a estas personas?

CD 5
Track 21

Juan **se torció** el tobillo. Joaquín **se cayó** y **se fracturó** el brazo.

11-8 Remedios y consejos. Usted es médico/a y va a aconsejar remedios a sus pacientes. Primero, escoja la mejor recomendación. Luego compare sus respuestas con las de su compañero/a, y piensen en otras dos sugerencias.

1. Su paciente tiene una infección en los ojos. Le recomiendo…
   a. nadar en la piscina.   (b.) tomar antibióticos.   c. leer mucho.

2. Su paciente tiene fiebre y le duele el cuerpo. Le aconsejo…
   (a.) descansar y tomar aspirinas.   b. comer mucho y caminar.   c. ir a su trabajo.

3. Su paciente se torció un tobillo. Le sugiero…
   a. correr todos los días.   b. tomar clases de baile.   (c.) descansar y no caminar.

4. Su paciente se fracturó un brazo. Le recomiendo…
   a. jugar al tenis.   (b.) no usar el ordenador por una semana.   c. hacer ejercicio.

Follow-up for 11-8. Set up other situations, asking pairs to come up with recommendations. Have each pair share its suggestions with the class.

11-9 ¿A quién debo llamar? Lea los anuncios a continuación. Luego, explíquele a su compañero/a sus síntomas o lo que usted necesita. Él/Ella le va a decir a quién debe llamar de acuerdo con la información de los anuncios.

MODELO: necesitar un examen médico para el trabajo.
   E1:   *Necesito un examen médico para el trabajo.*
   E2:   *Debes llamar a la Dra. Corona López.*

Dr. Fco. Javier Amador Cumplido
Cirugía y enfermedades de los ojos
86-43-57
Consultorio 204

Dra. Silvia Corona López
Medicina Interna
86-51-49

Clínica de Asma y Alergias
Dr. Rubén Shturman
Amsterdam 219-A
2º piso
294-3866
584-0153

Dr. Raúl Elguezábal R.
Medicina Familiar y Cirugía
86-34-73 EU.
428-4846
Consultorio 309

Dr. Héctor Molina Oviedo
Psiquiatra
86-51-49
Consultorio 402

Dr. Jaime A. Rodríguez Peláez
Pediatra
Niños y Adolescentes
86-17-15

Dra. Gabriela Jacobo de Alcaraz
Cirujano Dentista
86-48-44
Consultorio 314

1. dolerle la cabeza cuando lee o mira televisión Dr. Amador Cumplido
2. sentirse triste y deprimido/a Dr. Molina Oviedo
3. estar enfermo/a y tener fiebre Dra. Corona López/Dr. Elguezábal
4. no poder dormir Dra. Corona López/Dr. Elguezábal/Dr. Molina Oviedo
5. no poder respirar bien y tener la piel (*skin*) irritada Dr. Shturman
6. dolerle los dientes cuando come Jacobo de Alcaraz
7. buscar un médico/una médica para un sobrino de cinco años Dr. Rodriguez peláez
8. …

Suggestions for 11-9. You may review informal commands: *Llama a la Dra. Corona López.* Encourage students to list other symptoms for themselves or family members. You may also assume the role of a doctor, asking students how they feel. Prescribe accordingly; then have students in pairs play the roles of doctor and patient: —*Todavía me duelen mucho los ojos. No sé qué tengo.* —*Pues, tiene una infección. Le voy a recetar unos antibióticos.* Review proper salutations and how a doctor and patient address each other. Make sure students use *usted*.

Suggestions for 11-10. Before this activity, brainstorm with students the most common symptoms of a bad cold. You may also write down a list with recommendations that they may get from the doctor: *tomar vitaminas, especialmente vitamina C, beber ocho vasos de agua todos los días, no salir de casa, descansar y dormir más, tomar un analgésico para el dolor de cabeza,* etc.

Warm-up for 11-11. As a pre-listening activity, have students form groups of four to discuss if they or someone they know has ever had an injury or accident and what he/she did to take care of himself/herself.

Audioscript for 11-11.
ESTEBAN: *Papá, tú sabes, esta mañana cuando jugaba al fútbol, me torcí el pie. Mira qué hinchado está. Me duele mucho.*
PADRE: *Esteban, parece que te has fracturado el dedo del pie. Creo que lo mejor será llevarte al médico para que te saquen una radiografía.*
ESTEBAN: *¿Crees que sea necesario? ¿No sería mejor acostarme y descansar? Quizás si tomo una aspirina y me pongo una bolsa de hielo en el pie, me sentiré mejor.*
PADRE: *¿Por qué no quieres ir al hospital? Allí te pueden examinar con cuidado.*
ESTEBAN: *Es que... es que quiero jugar al fútbol mañana y no quiero que el médico me diga que no puedo hacerlo.*
PADRE: *Es necesario que el médico te diga qué tienes y qué puedes hacer. Ven, te llevo al hospital.*
ESTEBAN: *Bueno, si tú lo dices... ¡Ay! Me duele mucho; no puedo caminar.*
PADRE: *Pronto te vas a sentir mejor. Vas a ver. Vamos, déjame ayudarte a caminar, así, poco a poco.*
ESTEBAN: *Gracias, Papá.*

Lengua

Traditionally, law and medicine were professions dominated by men. Therefore, only the masculine form was used in Spanish: **el médico, el abogado.** Now that more women practice these professions, the feminine forms have entered the language. The feminine article is sometimes used before a masculine noun (**la médico, la abogado, la juez**), but it is increasingly common to use the feminine forms of the nouns: **la médica, la abogada, la jueza.**

11-10 En el consultorio. Usted tiene un catarro terrible y va a ver a su médico/a. Dígale cómo se siente y pregúntele qué debe hacer. El médico/La médica debe hacerle alguna recomendación y contestar sus preguntas.

MODELO: E1: *Me siento... /Tengo...*
E2: *Creo que...*
E1: *¿Es bueno comer muchas frutas y verduras?*
E2: *Es excelente comer frutas y verduras porque tienen muchas vitaminas.*

11-11 Me duele mucho. You will listen to a young man talk to his father about how he feels after hurting his toe. Before you listen, list two symptoms you think he probably has.

CD 5 Track 22

Now, pay attention to the general idea of what is said. As you listen, circle the letter that indicates the appropriate ending to each statement.

1. Esteban tiene...
   a. una infección en el dedo.
   (b.) mucho dolor.
   c. fiebre.

2. El padre de Esteban cree que...
   (a.) su hijo se ha fracturado el dedo del pie.
   b. Esteban debe acostarse.
   c. es necesario que Esteban ponga hielo en el pie.

3. El padre de Esteban quiere...
   a. que Esteban descanse y se cuide.
   (b.) llevar a Esteban al hospital.
   c. que Esteban tome una aspirina.

4. El padre de Esteban le dice que...
   (a.) lo ayuda a caminar para llevarlo al hospital.
   b. decida si prefiere descansar o ir al hospital.
   c. el médico puede verlo esa tarde.

5. Esteban decide...
   a. no escuchar a su padre.
   b. jugar al fútbol al día siguiente.
   (c.) ir al hospital con su padre.

EN ACCIÓN

Resources
- Video
- SAM: 11-11 to 11-13

Diarios de bicicleta: El "accidente"

Antes de ver

11-12 Empareje los síntomas de la izquierda con las sugerencias de la derecha.

1. _d_ Me duele el estómago.
2. _c_ Me torcí el tobillo.
3. _b_ Me duele una muela.
4. _a_ Tengo fiebre.

a. Tome mucho líquido.
b. Vaya al dentista.
c. Póngase hielo.
d. No coma nada.

Note for 11-12. Point out again to students that *doler* has the same structure as gustar: *Me duele el estómago; le duelen los oídos.*

Mientras ve

11-13 Indique si Javier (**J**) o Gabi (**G**) menciona los siguientes problemas de salud.

1. _G_ Tengo catarro.
2. _J_ Tengo gripe.
3. _J_ Estoy tosiendo.
4. _G_ Me torcí el tobillo.

Suggestions for 11-13. You may wish to use the photos to have students invent or reproduce the phone conversation, or to imagine the reaction of the friend in each photo after hearing only one side of the conversation.

Después de ver

11-14 Al final del segmento, Gabi y Javier se dan cuenta de que se han mentido (*they have lied to each other*). Con un compañero/una compañera, haga un diálogo que ilustre qué pasa ahora entre los dos. Answers may vary.

FUNCIONES Y FORMAS

1. Expressing expectations and hopes: Introduction to the present subjunctive

PABLO: ¿Qué me recomienda, doctor?

MÉDICO: Le **recomiendo** que **tome** agua y caldo de pollo. **Quiero** que **duerma** mucho y que no **vaya** a clase.

Mas tarde...

ALICIA: ¿Qué dice el médico?

PABLO: **Dice** que **me quede** en cama. También **quiere** que tú me **prepares** un caldo de pollo, que **limpies** mi apartamento, que me **traigas** helado…

Piénselo. Para cada oración, marque (✓) quién recomienda (**R**) la acción y quién va a hacer (**H**) la acción.

	MÉDICO	PABLO	ALICIA
1. Le **recomiendo** que **tome** agua y caldo de pollo.	R	H	—
2. **Quiere** que tú me **prepares** un caldo de pollo.	R	—	H
3. **Deseo** que **duerma** mucho.	R	H	
4. **Dice** que **me quede** en cama.	R	H	
5. **Quiere** que **limpies** mi apartamento.	R	—	H
6. **Quiere** que me **traigas** helado.	R	—	H

- To form the present subjunctive, use the **yo** form of the present indicative, drop the final **-o** and add the subjunctive ending. Notice that as with the endings of the **usted/ustedes** commands, **-ar** verbs change the **-a** to **-e**, while **-er** and **-ir** verbs change the **e** and the **i** to **a**.

	HABLAR	COMER	VIVIR
yo	hab**le**	com**a**	viv**a**
tú	hab**les**	com**as**	viv**as**
Ud., él, ella	hab**le**	com**a**	viv**a**
nosotros/as	hab**lemos**	com**amos**	viv**amos**
vosotros/as	hab**léis**	com**áis**	viv**áis**
Uds., ellos/as	hab**len**	com**an**	viv**an**

- The present subjunctive of the following verbs with irregular indicative **yo** forms is as follows:

conocer: cono**zca**, cono**zcas**...	salir: sal**ga**, sal**gas**...
decir: di**ga**, di**gas**...	tener: ten**ga**, ten**gas**...
hacer: ha**ga**, ha**gas**...	traer: tra**iga**, tra**igas**...
oír: o**iga**, o**igas**...	venir: ven**ga**, ven**gas**...
poner: pon**ga**, pon**gas**...	ver: **vea**, **veas**...

- The present subjunctive of **hay** is **haya**. The following verbs also have irregular subjunctive forms:

dar: **dé, des**...	saber: **sepa, sepas**...
estar: **esté, estés**...	ser: **sea, seas**...
ir: **vaya, vayas**...	

- Stem-changing **-ar** and **-er** verbs follow the same pattern as the present indicative.

  pensar: p**ie**nse, p**ie**nses, p**ie**nse, pensemos, penséis, p**ie**nsen

  volver: v**ue**lva, v**ue**lvas, v**ue**lva, volvamos, volváis, v**ue**lvan

- Stem-changing **-ir** verbs follow the same pattern as the present indicative but have an additional change in the **nosotros/as** and **vosotros/as** forms.

  preferir: pref**ie**ra, pref**ie**ras, pref**ie**ra, pref**i**ramos, pref**i**ráis, pref**ie**ran

  dormir: d**ue**rma, d**ue**rmas, d**ue**rma, d**u**rmamos, d**u**rmáis, d**ue**rman

- Verbs ending in **-car, -gar, -ger, -zar**, and **-guir** have spelling changes.

  sacar: sa**que**, sa**ques**, sa**que**, sa**que**mos, sa**qué**is, sa**quen**

  jugar: jue**gue**, jue**gues**, jue**gue**, jue**gue**mos, jue**gué**is, jue**guen**

  recoger: reco**ja**, reco**jas**, reco**ja**, reco**ja**mos, reco**já**is, reco**jan**

  almorzar: almuer**ce**, almuer**ces**, almuer**ce**, almor**ce**mos, almor**cé**is, almuer**cen**

  seguir: si**ga**, si**gas**, si**ga**, si**ga**mos, si**gá**is, si**gan**

- Notice in the examples below that there are two clauses, each with a different subject. When the verb of the main clause expresses a wish or hope, use a subjunctive verb form in the dependent clause (the clause that begins with **que**).

MAIN CLAUSE	DEPENDENT CLAUSE
La doctora **quiere**	que Alfredo **respire** profundamente.
The doctor wants	*Alfredo to breathe deeply.*
Yo **espero**	que Alfredo no **tenga** asma.
I hope	*Alfredo doesn't have asthma.*

Lengua

Remember that you have seen these same orthographic changes in the formal commands:

Saque los platos.

No jueguen ahora.

Suggestion. You may wish to explain that the connector *que* is required in Spanish but that the connector *that* is not required in similar sentences in English. For example, *Espero que el examen sea fácil.*

🐚 **Standard 4.1** Students demonstrate understanding of the nature of language through comparisons of the language studied and their own. Students are aware that many words in English come from Spanish and Mexican influence in the American Southwest: *adobe, canyon, hacienda, lasso, vigilante,* and many others. The lexical influence of Arabic on Spanish is similarly pervasive: Common words like *aceite, álgebra, azúcar, café, máscara, ojalá, olé,* and *tarea* come from Arabic. Explain to students that Arabic-speaking Moors from northern Africa ruled the Iberian peninsula from 711 until 1492, and that their culture is still alive in present-day Spain in architectural style, monuments, place names, and language.

Note. This *Funciones y formas* section is divided into two parts to facilitate learning the new concepts and forms presented here. The first part contains the preceding explanation and activities 11-15, 11-16, and 11-17. Additional explanation and activities 11-18, 11-19, and 11-20 follow.

■ When there is only one subject, use the infinitive instead of the subjunctive.

Lola **necesita llamar** a la farmacia para pedir una medicina.	*Lola has to call the pharmacy to order some medicine.*
Ella **quiere recogerla** esta tarde.	*She wants to pick it up this afternoon.*
Desea recogerla antes de las tres.	*She wants to pick it up before 3:00.*

■ Some common verbs that express expectations, wants and hopes are **desear, esperar, necesitar, preferir,** and **querer.**

Los residentes del barrio prefieren que la clínica no **cierre** antes de las siete.	*The residents of the neighborhood prefer that the clinic not close before seven o'clock.*
La niña espera que el enfermero no le **ponga** una inyección.	*The girl hopes that the nurse will not give her a shot.*

■ The expression **ojalá (que)** (*I/we hope [that]*), which comes from Arabic, originally meaning *May Allah grant that . . .* , is always followed by the subjunctive.

Ojalá (que) ellos **vengan** temprano.	*I hope (that) they will come early.*
Ojalá (que) **puedas** llevarme a la cita con la médica.	*I hope (that) you can take me to the doctor's appointment.*

11-15 Comentarios y deseos. Los miembros del Club de Estudiantes de Pre-Medicina están hablando de la fiesta que van a dar mañana. ¿Cuáles de las afirmaciones siguientes probablemente son comentarios de ellos? Márquelas (✓). Answers may vary.

1. ____ Queremos que la fiesta empiece puntualmente.
2. ____ Ojalá que no sirvan comida.
3. ____ Preferimos que pongan música caribeña, porque queremos bailar salsa y merengue.
4. ____ Esperamos que también asistan estudiantes de odontología (*dentistry*) y de enfermería.
5. ____ Necesitamos que la fiesta termine temprano.
6. ____ Deseamos que nuestros profesores vayan a la fiesta.
7. ____ Queremos que todos recojan la basura después de la fiesta.
8. ____ Ojalá que nos divirtamos.

11-16 Trabajo voluntario en el hospital. PRIMERA FASE. Unos estudiantes trabajan de voluntarios en el hospital. ¿Qué espera la directora del programa de voluntarios que hagan estas personas? Túrnense para hablar sobre cada escena.

MODELO: Elena: llevar flores/conversar con los pacientes
  E1: *La directora espera que Elena les lleve flores a los pacientes.*
  E2: *También espera que Elena converse con los pacientes. Algunos pacientes se sienten muy solos.*

1.

José y Camila: jugar con los niños/hablar con los padres de los niños/leerles libros infantiles a los niños

2.

Marisa: trabajar en la tienda de regalos/hacerles recomendaciones a los clientes/poner flores frescas en el mostrador de la tienda

3.

Sofía y Eduardo: conversar con los familiares de los pacientes/ofrecerles café/darles almohadas si quieren dormir mientras esperan

SEGUNDA FASE. ¿Qué más esperan los pacientes que hagan los voluntarios en el hospital? Escriban una lista de cuatro cosas más como mínimo.

MODELO: *Los pacientes esperan que los voluntarios les traigan su comida.*

11-17 Se abre la Clínica de la Familia. Se abre una nueva clínica en una semana y usted está ayudando con los preparativos. Haga una lista de las cosas que usted necesita hacer y otra lista de lo que espera que hagan los empleados indicados en la tabla. Después, compare su lista con la de su compañero/a.

MODELO: E1: *Necesito pintar la sala de espera.*
  E2: *Y yo necesito limpiar los pisos.*
  E1: *Espero que los carpinteros terminen su trabajo esta semana.*
  E2: *Y yo espero que los empleados lleguen a tiempo.*

LO QUE YO NECESITO HACER	LO QUE ESPERO QUE HAGAN
_____	los médicos: _____
_____	los enfermeros: _____
_____	el/la recepcionista: _____
_____	el/la chofer de la ambulancia: _____

Suggestion for 11-16. Explain to students that object pronouns are placed immediately before the subjunctive verb form.

Follow-up. After each student compares his/her list with a partner, they can compare their lists with another pair of students.

Lengua

You have seen that a stressed **i** or **u** requires a written accent when preceded or followed by another vowel (**oír, frío, reúno**). This is because no diphthong results, and the vowels are pronounced as two separate syllables. The same rule applies to an **h** between the two vowels (**prohíbo, prohíbe**), since the **h** has no sound. When **i** or **u** is not stressed, the vowel combination is pronounced as one syllable, and no accent is required (**prohibir**).

More about the present subjunctive

■ Verbs that express an intention to influence the actions of others (**aconsejar, pedir, permitir, prohibir, recomendar**) also require the subjunctive in the dependent clause. With these verbs, Spanish speakers often use an indirect object.

El médico **le** recomienda que no **salga** por unos días.	*The doctor recommends that he not go out for a few days.*
La enfermera **me** aconseja que no **coma** por una hora.	*The nurse advises me not to eat for an hour.*

■ You may also try to impose your will or express your influence, wishes, and hopes through some impersonal expressions such as **es necesario, es importante, es bueno,** and **es mejor.**

Es necesario que los atletas **duerman** un mínimo de siete horas por noche.	*It is necessary that the athletes sleep a minimum of seven hours a night.*
Es mejor que **coman** pescado y pollo, porque tienen menos grasa que la carne de res.	*It is better that they eat fish or chicken, because they have less fat than beef.*

■ If you are not addressing or speaking about someone in particular, use the infinitive.

Es mejor **comer** pescado y pollo.	*It is better to eat fish and chicken.*

■ With the verb **decir**, use the subjunctive in the dependent clause when expressing a wish or an order. Use the indicative when reporting information.

Dice que los atletas **consumen** mucha proteína. (*report information*)	*She says (that) the athletes consume a lot of protein.*
Dice que los atletas **consuman** mucha proteína. (*express an order*)	*She tells the athletes to eat a lot of protein.*

 11-18 Normas de conducta en el trabajo. PRIMERA FASE. Su amiga Rebeca tiene un trabajo nuevo como recepcionista y le pide a usted consejos sobre las normas de conducta. Indique (✓) sus recomendaciones y luego, compárelas con las recomendaciones de su compañero/a.

	SE PROHÍBE	SE PERMITE	SE RECOMIENDA
1. fumar			
2. comer chocolates			
3. hablar por teléfono con amigos			
4. almorzar en la oficina			
5. conversar con los pacientes			
6. llevar vaqueros			

SEGUNDA FASE. Piensen en un trabajo que tienen ahora o que tiene un miembro de su familia. Hagan una lista de las actividades que se prohíben, las que se permiten y las que se recomiendan. ¿Son semejantes o diferentes las normas en sus respectivos lugares de trabajo?

11-19 Consejos y sugerencias. Usted está organizando un nuevo programa en República Dominicana para estudiantes que quieren trabajar en las profesiones de salud. Explíqueles a dos compañeros los aspectos del programa que aún no están resueltos. Ellos le recomendarán qué hacer.

MODELO: viajar a República Dominicana
> E1: *Hay varias opciones: podemos viajar en grupo, o cada estudiante puede hacer su propia reservación.*
> E2: *Es mejor que viajen en grupo, así se consigue mejor precio.*
> E3: *Y también es importante que todos los estudiantes lleguen juntos.*

1. empezar clases de español
2. establecer conexiones con las clínicas en la capital
3. buscar alojamiento (*lodging*)
4. escoger actividades de ocio (*free time*)

11-20 Excursión a República Dominicana. **PRIMERA FASE.** Su clase está planeando una excursión a la playa Boca Chica en República Dominicana. Primero, busquen en Internet la siguiente información y coméntenla entre ustedes.

1. localización
2. clima
3. lugares de interés
4. tipo de alojamiento
5. tipo de transporte para llegar allí
6. costo del viaje

SEGUNDA FASE. Ahora escriban una lista de todas las cosas que hay que hacer para preparar la excursión.

MODELO: E1: *Es importante reservar los pasajes.*
          E2: *Sí, y necesitamos comprar unas mochilas.*

TERCERA FASE. Por último, decidan qué quieren ustedes que haga cada persona de su grupo. Compartan la información con la clase.

MODELO: reservar los pasajes
Queremos que Juan reserve los pasajes.

Warm-up for 11-19.
Encourage students to use their imagination. Give details: The program is for students in the health professions (*las profesiones de la salud, como medicina, odontología, enfermería, terapia física, etc.*). Ask for ideas about setting up the program, such as publicity to recruit students, location, programming, living arrangements, etc. Write *Es importante/bueno/mejor que...* on the board and ask for students' suggestions.

Suggestion for 11-19. Put students in groups of three for this activity. They can change groups, redoing parts of the activity as needed, in order to play different roles.

Follow-up for 11-20. You may create groups of six and assign one research item to each student. Once they exchange the information they have obtained, encourage them to brainstorm what they will need or have to do to prepare for the trip. Recycle vocabulary for clothes and weather expressions. Example: *¿Qué necesitas llevar para protegerte del sol? ¿Qué ropa es más cómoda para caminar mucho?*

SITUACIONES

1. **Role A.** You are sick today so you will miss the review session for the Spanish midterm. Call a classmate and a) say that you need him/her to take notes for you; b) give him/her advice about what you think is most important to write down; c) say when you want your friend to bring you the notes; and d) thank your friend.

   Role B. When a friend from your Spanish class calls to ask a favor, say that you will be happy to take notes for him/her. Ask a) when your friend wants you to bring over the notes; b) how your friend is feeling; and c) what the doctor's recommendations are. Say that it is important that your friend rest and that you hope he/she feels better soon.

2. **Role A.** You are allergic to (**ser alérgico/a a**) cats, and you have just come back from spending the weekend with your friend who has two cats. Now you have a headache, your eyes itch (**me pican los ojos**), your lungs hurt, and it is hard to breathe. Call the clinic to a) explain your situation; b) describe your symptoms; and c) ask what the nurse recommends that you do. Ask questions to be sure you understand the recommendations.

   Role B. You work as a nurse at the clinic, and someone calls for advice about an allergic reaction. Ask about the person's symptoms and offer advice about what he/she should do.

Resources

■ SAM: 11-21 to 11-26
■ Supp. Activ. Book: The subjunctive with expressions of emotion

2. Expressing emotions, opinions, and attitudes: The subjunctive with expressions of emotion

ERNESTO: **Me molesta** que **fumen.** Y no me gusta que **hablen** tan alto.

SARA: **Estoy contenta de** que **se vayan** pronto. Ya han terminado de comer.

Ernesto   Sara

Piénselo. Indique (✓) si cada verbo expresa un sentimiento o una acción.

	VERBO/FRASE DE SENTIMIENTO	VERBO DE ACCIÓN
1. **Les molesta** que **fumen.**	molesta	fumen
2. No **les gusta** que **hablen** tan alto.	gusta	hablen
3. **Están contentos de** que **se vayan** pronto.	están contentos	se vayan
4. **Es triste** que **permitan** fumar en su restaurante.	es triste	permitan
5. **Es una lástima** que **fumen** en la mesa, tan cerca de otra gente.	es lástima	fumen

■ When the verb of the main clause expresses emotion (e.g., fear, happiness, sorrow), use a subjunctive verb form in the dependent clause. Note that the subjects of the two clauses must be different.

Sentimos mucho que el niño **tenga** fiebre.	*We are very sorry (that) the child has a fever.*
Me alegro de que **estés** con él.	*I am glad (that) you are with him.*

■ Some common verbs that express emotion are **alegrarse (de), estar contento/a (de), sentir, gustar, encantar, molestar,** and **temer** (*to fear*).

■ Impersonal expressions and other expressions that show emotion are also followed by *que* + subjunctive.

Es triste que el niño **esté** enfermo.	*It is sad that the child is sick.*
¡Qué lástima que no **pueda** ir a la fiesta!	*What a shame that he cannot go to the party!*

11-21 Un amigo enfermo. Asocie cada comentario sobre la enfermedad de su amigo con la reacción adecuada.

1. __b__ Pedro está muy enfermo.
2. __a__ Sus padres llegan hoy para estar con él.
3. __c__ Creo que el doctor Pérez lo va a operar.
4. __e__ Dicen que es una operación seria.
5. __d__ No va a poder participar en el campeonato.

a. Me alegro de que vengan.
b. Siento mucho que esté tan mal.
c. ¡Qué bueno que sea ese el médico!
d. Es una lástima que no pueda jugar.
e. Ojalá que no tenga complicaciones.

Suggestions for Piénselo. Since the subjunctive is a new concept for most students, you may wish to provide guidance by doing the first sentence with the whole class. As a follow-up, lead students in discovering that the verb that expresses the emotion is in the indicative, and the verb that conveys the action related to the emotion is in the subjunctive.

Suggestions. Introduce the verb *molestar*, give examples, and clarify meaning, i.e., that it does not have any sexual connotations. Give examples using expressions of emotion: *Me alegro de que estén todos aquí. A mí me gusta que todos lleguen temprano y practiquen español con sus compañeros. Siento que no tengamos películas en español para hoy.* Ask students to finish the following introductory clauses: *Me alegro de que tú... Siento que tú... No me gusta que tú...*

11-22 Una visita. Usted está en la clínica, visitando a su compañero/a, a quien han operado de la rodilla. Él/Ella le cuenta sobre su experiencia en la clínica y cómo se siente. Escoja entre las expresiones de *En directo* para responderle. Intercambien papeles.

MODELO: E1: *No me gusta la comida del hospital.*
E2: *Siento que la comida no sea buena. ¿Qué te sirven?*
E1: …

1. Me duele bastante la rodilla.
2. Tengo fiebre y dolor de cabeza.
3. Tengo dolor de estómago porque las medicinas son muy fuertes.
4. Tengo náuseas por los efectos de la anestesia.
5. Detesto estar en cama tanto tiempo.
6. La comida del hospital es malísima.
7. Las enfermeras vienen a verme cada media hora.
8. La cirujana que me operó es muy simpática.

11-23 Reacciones. Luisa y Rafael llegan temprano a su trabajo en el hospital. Su compañero/a le va a decir lo que ellos piensan hacer la semana próxima. Reaccione usando las expresiones de *En directo*. Después cambien de papel.

MODELO: Luisa / no desayunar
E1: *Luisa no va a desayunar.*
E2: *No me gusta que Luisa no desayune. Temo que no tenga energía.*

PERSONAS	LUNES	MIÉRCOLES	VIERNES	DOMINGO
Luisa	empezar una dieta	ir al gimnasio	hacer ejercicio en su casa	caminar 2 kms
Rafael	trabajar en el hospital todo el día	salir del hospital temprano para ir al cine	quedarse en su casa	reunirse con sus amigos

11-24 ¿Qué me molesta? PRIMERA FASE. Haga una lista de los hábitos de otras personas que le molestan. Compare su lista con la de su compañero/a.

MODELO: *Me molesta que mis amigos lleguen tarde.*

SEGUNDA FASE. En pequeños grupos, comparen sus listas y escojan los seis hábitos que les molestan más a todos en el grupo. Digan por qué. Compartan sus resultados con el resto de la clase.

En directo

To express empathy:
Siento que…
Me alegro de que…
Temo que…
Espero que…
No me gusta que…
¡Qué agradable que…

SITUACIONES

1. **Role A.** Recently you decided to join an aerobics class (**clase de ejercicios aeróbicos**). You are also following a healthful diet and you feel great. When you run into a friend whom you have not seen for some time, you try to convince him/her to join you in your exercise class.

   Role B. You run into a friend whom you have not seen for some time. Say that he/she looks (**verse**) great, and ask what he/she is doing. Inquire a) how many times a week he/she goes to aerobics class (**clase de ejercicios aeróbicos**); b) how she feels about the class; and c) what he/she likes and doesn't like about his/her new plan for eating better. He/She will try to persuade you to join the program.

2. **Role A.** You have gone to your doctor for a physical examination. Describe your symptoms and your lifestyle (**vida activa**, **vida sedentaria**). Respond to the doctor's reactions and recommendations with questions and comments.

   Role B. You are a doctor doing a routine physical examination. As the patient talks, you a) ask pertinent questions; b) express approval or disapproval of the patient's lifestyle; and c) give advice or prescribe medication. Respond to the patient's comments about your recommendations.

Follow-up for 11-24.
Students list what they like others to do, and then share their lists with partners.

3. Expressing goals, purposes, and means: Uses of *por* and *para*

Vive más **por** unos pasos más **por** día

- **Para** vivir más no necesitas más dinero. No pagues miles de pesos **por** aparatos de ejercicio. ¡Muévete!

- Sube a tu clase u oficina **por** las escaleras; no tomes el ascensor.

- Camina **para** tu tienda favorita.

- Si caminas 30 minutos **por** día vivirás más. Pasea **por** el parque con tus amigos o tu familia y guarda tu dinero **para** cosas necesarias.

- Relájate mientras caminas al aire libre y vive con menos estrés **por** ti y **para** ti.

Piénselo. Indique si las afirmaciones son ciertas (**C**) o falsas (**F**), según la información en el panfleto. Luego escoja el significado de **por** o **para** que corresponde a cada afirmación y escríbalo en el espacio indicado.

a causa de algo o alguien

en beneficio de alguien

duración

en dirección a un lugar

medio de transporte

objetivo

	CIERTO/FALSO	SIGNIFICADO DE POR/PARA
1. **Para** tener una vida larga es importante mantenernos activos.	C	objetivo
2. Caminar **por** 30 minutos al día ayuda a vivir más años.	C	duración
3. Es mejor ir en automóvil cuando vamos **para** el supermercado y otras tiendas.	F	en dirección a un lugar
4. Debemos relajarnos y vivir con menos estrés **por** nosotros mismos.	C	en beneficio de alguien

- As you learned in *Capítulo 3*, the prepositions **por** and **para** have several meanings and uses. You have used them easily in some contexts in which they are similar to "for" in English, as in **Compré estas vitaminas *para* Anita** (*I bought these vitamins for Anita*).

▪ Other uses of **por** and **para** that are not similar to English can be learned by grouping them into functional categories: expressions of movement, time, purpose, and means.

POR	PARA
MOVEMENT	
▪ through or by a place Caminaron **por** el hospital. *They walked through the hospital.*	▪ toward a destination Caminaron **para** el hospital. *They walked toward the hospital.*
TIME	
▪ duration of an event Estuvo con la médica **por** una hora. *He was with the doctor for an hour.*	▪ deadline Necesita el antibiótico **para** el martes. *He needs the antibiotic by Tuesday.*
PURPOSE	
▪ reason or motive Ana fue al consultorio **por** el dolor de garganta. *Ana went to the doctor's office because of a sore throat.*	▪ for whom something is intended or done Compró el antibiótico **para** Ana. *He bought the antibiotic for Ana.*

Por is also used to express the following:

▪ means of transportation

Mandaron los órganos para el trasplante **por** avión.

They sent the organs for the transplant by plane.

▪ exchange or substitution

Irma pagó $120 **por** las pastillas.

Irma paid $120 for the pills.

Cambió esas pastillas rojas **por** las amarillas.

She exchanged those red pills for the yellow ones.

▪ unit or rate

Yo camino 5 kilómetros **por** hora.

I walk 5 kilometers per hour.

El seguro de salud cubre el sesenta **por** ciento de las cuentas.

The health insurance covers 60 percent of the bills.

▪ object of an errand

Sara fue a la farmacia **por** jarabe para la tos.

Sara went to the drugstore for the cough syrup.

Pasamos **por** ti a las 5:00.

We'll come by for you at 5:00.

Para is also used to express the following:

▪ judgment or point of view

Para nosotros, es la mejor farmacia.

For us, this is the best drugstore.

Es un caso difícil **para** un médico joven.

It is a difficult case for a young doctor.

▪ intention or purpose, when followed by an infinitive

Fueron a la farmacia **para** comprar jarabe para la tos.

They went to the drugstore to buy cough syrup.

Come bien **para** vivir más.

Eat well to live longer.

11-25 ¿Quieren decir *por* o *para*? Trace un círculo alrededor de la preposición que debe usarse, según el significado entre paréntesis.

1. Salimos **por/para** el consultorio del médico a las nueve de la mañana. (*toward a destination*)
2. Fuimos **por/para** el túnel para llegar más rápido. (*through*)
3. Ana fue a ver al médico **por/para** su dolor de garganta y tos. (*reason or motive*)
4. El médico escribió la receta de un antibiótico **por/para** Ana. (*for whom it is intended*)
5. Yo fui a la farmacia **por/para** el antibiótico. (*object of an errand*)
6. ¿Cuánto pagaste **por/para** el antibiótico? (*exchange or substitution*)

 11-26 En el laboratorio. Túrnense para averiguar cuándo estarán listos los resultados del análisis (*test*) de unos pacientes. Consulten la tabla para obtener la información correcta.

MODELO: Alfredo Benítez 2:00 de la tarde
E1: *¿Cuándo va a estar listo el análisis del Sr. Benítez?*
E2: *Va a estar listo para las dos de la tarde.*

PACIENTE	RESULTADOS DEL ANÁLISIS
Hilda Corvalán	11:00 de la mañana
Alfonso González	esta tarde
Jorge Pérez Robles	3:15 de la tarde
Aleida Miranda	mañana por la mañana
César Gómez Villegas	martes
Irene Santa Cruz	…

 11-27 Una cura del estrés. Para curarse del estrés, el médico le recomienda a su amiga que pase quince días de descanso y relajación. Usted le aconseja que vaya a República Dominicana. Indíquele algunas actividades que ella puede hacer allí y el propósito de cada actividad. Use las actividades de la lista. Después cambien de papel.

comer mariscos y pescado

bailar en las calles

disfrutar del paisaje, la flora y la fauna

tomar clases de baile caribeño

ver los espectáculos con delfines y leones marinos

ver la puesta del sol

MODELO: visitar el Museo Bacardí/aprender cómo se hace el ron cubano
Visita el Museo Bacardí en Santiago de Cuba para aprender cómo se hace el ron cubano.

1. participar en el Carnaval de Santiago
2. ir al Acuario Nacional en La Habana
3. ir a la Escuela Danza y Movimiento de la Habana
4. caminar por el Malecón en la Habana
5. visitar el Valle de Viñales en Pinar del Río
6. salir a cenar en El Pescador en la playa de Santa Lucía

Suggestions for 11-27. Encourage students to give additional advice, using affirmative and negative commands.

Follow up for 11-27. Ask students to present a brief report on one of the places mentioned in the activity.

11-28 La graduación de un nuevo médico. Complete estos párrafos sobre la graduación de Fernando con **por** o **para**, según el contexto. Luego escoja la razón de su elección en la columna de la derecha.

El 14 de junio es la graduación de Fernando en la Facultad de Medicina de la Universidad Católica Madre y Maestra de Santiago de los Caballeros en República Dominicana. Sus padres, los señores Rovira, viven en Puerto Plata, pero van a Santiago (1. a) _para_ asistir a la graduación y quieren llevarle un regalo. El lunes pasado fueron a una tienda y pagaron $100 (2. d) _por_ un regalo muy bonito (3. g) _para_ Fernando. Graciela, su hermana gemela, vive en Miami y no puede ir (4. h) _por_ su trabajo. Ella también le compró un regalo y se lo envió (5. c) _por_ avión porque quiere que llegue (6. f) _para_ el día de la graduación.

El día 14, los padres de Fernando salieron (7. e) _para_ la universidad. Estaba lloviendo, y (8. h) _por_ eso salieron temprano. Normalmente, ellos pueden estar en la universidad en una hora más o menos, pero (9. h) _por_ la lluvia, el viaje duró casi dos horas. (10. b) _Para_ ellos, que son mayores, el viaje fue un poco largo, pero al final pudieron pasar ese día con su hijo.

To express or indicate...

a. intention or purpose (with infinitive).
b. judgment or point of view.
c. means of transportation.
d. exchange or substitution.
e. toward a destination.
f. deadline.
g. for whom something is intended or done.
h. reason or motive.

SITUACIONES

1. **Role A.** You hurt your ankle while playing soccer, so you go to the health center at your college or university. Tell the doctor that a) you fell while running to make a goal (**marcar un gol**); b) your ankle is swollen (**hinchado**); and c) you cannot walk. Ask questions and answer your doctor's questions.

   Role B. A patient comes see you with a sports injury. After you hear how the injury happened, ask a) what the coach did for him/her and b) how he/she got to the health center. After determining that the ankle is not broken, recommend that the patient a) rest for three or four days; b) take aspirin for the pain; and c) put ice on his/her ankle to reduce the swelling (**reducir la hinchazón**). Add that because of the injury, he/she should not play soccer for a month.

2. **Role A.** You want to rent a furnished apartment at the beach. You see a promising ad and call the landlord. Explain when you will need the apartment and for how long. Inquire about the rent, furnishings and the number of rooms.

   Role B. You are a landlord who is renting an apartment at the beach. A prospective renter calls you. Answer his/her questions and ask how many people will be staying at the apartment. Mention that the rent must be paid by the first of the month. Agree on a date and time to show the property.

Resources

■ SAM: 11-33 to 11-37
■ Supp. Activ. Book: Relative pronouns

4. Referring to people and things: Relative pronouns

El perro, ¿el mejor amigo de los diabéticos?

Científicos irlandeses, **quienes** investigan la habilidad del perro para detectar los niveles de azúcar de los diabéticos, esperan probar que los caninos pueden ayudar a los **pacientes que** sufren de esta enfermedad a vigilar (*watch*) sus niveles de azúcar en la sangre.

Según los investigadores, los **perros, que** poseen un agudo sentido de olfato, pueden recibir entrenamiento para anticipar la hipoglucemia por su excelente olfato. Si los expertos prueban su hipótesis, los millones de **diabéticos que** existen alrededor del mundo se beneficiarán con este descubrimiento, especialmente los **diabéticos que** además son ciegos, sordos o **que** sufren de otras discapacidades.

Piénselo. Primero, compruebe si las siguientes afirmaciones son ciertas (**C**) o falsas (**F**) según el texto anterior. Luego indique a qué palabra se refiere el pronombre en negrita.

1. <u>F: los científicos</u> Los científicos, **quienes** quieren probar su hipótesis sobre la capacidad de los perros para cuidar diabéticos, son franceses.
2. <u>F: una persona</u> Una persona diabética **que** no puede oír ni ver no podrá vivir independientemente sin la ayuda de estos perros.
3. <u>C: los perros</u> Los perros **que** vigilan el azúcar de los diabéticos son entrenados.
4. <u>F: la habilidad</u> La habilidad **que** tienen los perros para anticipar la baja de azúcar de los pacientes es maravillosa.
5. <u>C: la persona</u> La persona a **quien** ayuda el canino puede sufrir de una hipoglucemia, pero el canino la detectará con su olfato.

Suggestions. Point out that the use of relative pronouns makes conversation more interesting, concise, and adult and that it is a sign of the speech of a more advanced speaker.

Model the use of relative pronouns with visuals, pretending you are related to the people portrayed in them. *La chica que está jugando al vóleibol es mi hermana.*

You may wish to review with students the difference between dependent and independent clauses.

■ The relative pronouns **que** and **quien(es)** combine two clauses into one sentence.

Los médicos trabajan en ese hospital.	*The doctors work at that hospital.*
Los médicos son excelentes.	*The doctors are excellent.*
Los médicos **que** trabajan en ese hospital son excelentes.	*The doctors who work at that hospital are excellent.*

■ **Que** is the most commonly used relative pronoun. It introduces a dependent clause, and it may refer to persons or things.

Las pastillas **que** tomo son muy caras.	*The pills that I take are very expensive.*
Ese es el médico **que** me receta las pastillas.	*That is the doctor who prescribes the pills for me.*

■ **Quien(es)** refers only to persons and may replace **que** in a clause set off by commas.

Los García, quienes/que viven en la ciudad, prefieren el campo	*The Garcías, who live in the city, prefer the country.*

■ Use **quien(es)** after a preposition (**a, con, de, por, para,** etc.) when referring to people.

Allí está el enfermero **con quien** hablé esta mañana.	*There is the nurse with whom I spoke this morning.*
Esos son los pacientes **a quienes** les debes dar la medicina.	*Those are the patients to whom you should give the medicine.*

11-29 Una telenovela dominicana. Joaquín está enfermo hoy. Por eso, empezó a mirar una telenovela en la televisión. Le mandó un correo electrónico a su amigo Ramiro para contarle detalles de la telenovela. Complete el correo electrónico de Joaquín con **que** o **quien** para averiguar qué opina sobre la telenovela.

> Hola Ramiro,
>
> ¡No me vas a creer! He mirado un episodio de la sensacional telenovela que están pasando en el canal 13. Te cuento lo que pasó por si te interesa.
>
> *Mi corazón* es una telenovela dominicana (1) ___que___ tiene mucho público. El actor principal es Agustín Montalvo. Él es el actor de (2) __quien__ todos hablan. La crítica cree que este año va a ganar el premio Talía, (3) __que__ es el equivalente del Óscar norteamericano. Muchas chicas dicen que Agustín es el actor con (4) __quien__ les gustaría salir. Agustín hace el papel del médico (5) __que__ quiere salvar la vida de Silvina del Bosque, la actriz principal, (6) _quien/que_ tuvo un accidente terrible y está inconsciente. Agustín es el hombre al (7) __que__ ella quiere, pero Agustín está enamorado de Esmeralda del Valle, una mujer a (8) __quien__ sólo le interesa el dinero de Agustín. La telenovela es muy melodramática y siempre hay problemas (9) __que__ mantienen el interés del público.
>
> Mírala y mañana y me cuentas qué piensas.
>
> Chao,
>
> Joaquín

11-30 Mi dentista. PRIMERA FASE. Dígale a su compañero/a cómo es su dentista. Mencione por lo menos tres características.

MODELO: *Mi dentista es… Es un dentista/una dentista que…*

SEGUNDA FASE. Conversen sobre su experiencia médica más reciente. Usen las preguntas como guía.

1. ¿Cuándo fue la última vez que usted visitó al/a la dentista?
2. ¿Le dio algunas recomendaciones que no le gustaron a usted? ¿Le recetó alguna medicina?
3. ¿Le gusta su dentista? ¿Por qué?

11-31 El médico lo sabe todo. Describan las siguientes escenas, pensando en las preguntas a continuación.

1. ¿Qué está haciendo el médico que está en la foto de la izquierda? ¿Y la médica en la foto de la derecha?
2. ¿Qué problema de salud tiene cada una de las niñas que están en las fotos?
3. ¿Qué diferencias hay entre las situaciones en las dos fotos?

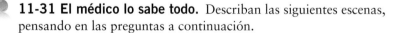

SITUACIONES

1. **Role A.** A relative of yours has recently had surgery (**una operación**), and you need some information to fill out an insurance form. Call the hospital and ask a) the name of the doctor who performed surgery; b) the amount of time that the surgery took; c) the prescriptions that the doctor gave your relative; and d) the number of days that he/she will have to stay at the hospital.

   Role B. You work at a hospital. A relative of one of the patients calls to find out some information for an insurance form. Identify yourself and answer the caller's questions.

2. **Role A.** You want a second opinion about your back pain. Tell the second doctor that a) the pain that you have is in your back; b) it is an acute pain (**un dolor agudo**) that starts every time you go to bed; and c) the pills that you are taking do not alleviate (**calmar**) your pain. Ask if the health problem that you have is serious.

   Role B. A new patient comes to your office for a consultation. Ask the patient a) to describe his/her pain; b) to tell you what he/she does to keep the pain under control; and c) when the pain started. Finally, make some recommendations.

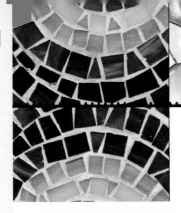

Audioscript for 11-33.

NUTRICIONISTA: *Como ustedes saben, es necesario mantener una dieta sana y balanceada para evitar enfermedades y mantener un peso ideal. En primer lugar, es necesario hacerse un examen médico anual, alimentarse bien, mantenerse activo, no fumar ni consumir mucho alcohol.*

FABIÁN: *Pero aquí en la universidad muchos estudiantes toman cerveza para relajarse y divertirse. ¿Qué tiene eso de malo?*

NUTRICIONISTA: *En realidad tomar cerveza o alcohol no es malo. Lo importante es la moderación. La sal, por ejemplo, es buena, pero en altas cantidades puede ser dañina.*

FABIOLA: *¿Y la carne roja?*

NUTRICIONISTA: *Un factor importante es limitar el consumo de grasas animales para evitar el aumento del colesterol en la sangre; el pescado y el pollo tienen menos grasa. Consuman estos últimos con más frecuencia.*

FABIÁN: *En mi casa mis padres comen muchas frutas y verduras, pero a mí no me gustan mucho.*

NUTRICIONISTA: *Es una lástima, porque las frutas y verduras tienen muchos minerales y vitaminas. Además, tienen fibra, y la fibra es buena para la salud.*

FABIOLA: *Yo quiero bajar de peso. ¿Qué debo hacer?*

NUTRICIONISTA: *Mantén una dieta balanceada y haz ejercicios regularmente, por lo menos veinte minutos, tres veces a la semana. Es preferible bajar de peso poco a poco y cambiar los hábitos de comida y ejercicios. Así se puede mantener el peso ideal, mejorar la salud y la apariencia física.*

FABIOLA: *Suena fácil, pero debo tener mucha disciplina.*

FABIÁN: *Sí, sobre todo los fines de semana cuando se socializa con amigos.*

NUTRICIONISTA: *Recuerden, todo con moderación. Buena suerte, y si necesitan más información pueden venir a verme en el hospital.*

MOSAICOS

A escuchar

Antes de escuchar

11-32 Preparación. Usted escuchará una conversación entre un nutricionista y un grupo de estudiantes universitarios hispanos. Antes de escuchar, escriba dos preguntas que los alumnos probablemente le harán al nutricionista y dos sugerencias que les dará el nutricionista.

posibles preguntas:
posibles consejos:

Escuchar

CD 5 Track 23

11-33 ¿Comprende usted? First read the following statements and then listen to the exchange between the nutritionist and a group of college students. Mark (✓) the statements that best identify the main ideas of what you have heard.

1. __✓__ Consultar al médico una vez por año es importante para evitar enfermedades.
2. ____ El consumo de tomates, lechugas, uvas, naranjas, cerveza y carne de res es recomendable para tener energía.
3. __✓__ La buena alimentación y el ejercicio tienen un efecto positivo en la salud.
4. ____ Se recomienda comer bastante y hacer muchísimo ejercicio para mantener una vida saludable.
5. ____ Bajar de peso afecta positivamente a la salud y a la apariencia de las personas.
6. __✓__ La buena salud requiere de disciplina.

Después de escuchar

11-34 Ahora usted. Compartan sus respuestas a las siguientes preguntas.

1. ¿Qué hábitos de comida y actividad física tiene usted? ¿Son sus hábitos buenos o malos?
2. ¿Cree usted que usted es lo que come?
3. ¿Qué aspecto de su vida piensa usted que puede cambiar para mejorar su estado físico?

A conversar

> **ESTRATEGIA**
>
> **Select appropriate phrases to offer opinions**
> When you are talking with someone, it is natural to offer opinions and evaluations of what the other person has said and to express agreement or disagreement. An effective way to do this is to acknowledge the value of what the other person has said and then express your reaction to it.

Antes de conversar

11-35 Preparación. PRIMERA FASE. Marque (✓) los hábitos o condiciones que, según usted, ayudan a prolongar la vida de las personas.

1. ___ hacer ejercicio físico regularmente
2. ___ trabajar poco
3. ___ poner el cuerpo bajo mucho estrés
4. ___ ser vegetariano/a
5. ___ beber vino con el almuerzo o la cena
6. ___ llevar una vida sedentaria
7. ___ tomar remedios de casa para curar el catarro
8. ___ evitar fracturarse los huesos

SEGUNDA FASE. Comparen sus respuestas a las preguntas de la *Primera fase*. Luego, escriban un cuestionario para determinar si las personas hacen lo necesario para vivir más años. Consideren las siguientes áreas en su cuestionario.

TEMAS	EJEMPLOS
1. actividades/hábitos	¿Se mantiene usted activo/a?
2. comida	¿Come verduras regularmente?
3. bebidas	¿Bebe alcohol? ¿Con qué frecuencia?

Conversar

11-36 Entre nosotros. Usen el cuestionario de la actividad **11-35** *Segunda fase*, para entrevistarse entre ustedes. Tomen notas de la información adicional importante que mencione su compañero/a durante la conversación. Esto los/las puede ayudar a determinar si cada uno/a de ustedes realmente se cuida para vivir más.

Después de conversar

11-37 Un poco más. Use la información que le dio su compañero/a en **11-36** y converse con él/ella sobre lo siguiente:

1. Mencione a) las actividades y b) los buenos hábitos de alimentación (comida, bebida) de su compañero/a que, según usted, van a contribuir a una vida más larga. Felicítelo/la. (*Congratulate him/her.*)
2. También indique las áreas en las que usted y su compañero/a tienen opiniones diferentes.
3. Si es necesario, déle consejos o recomendaciones para mejorar sus hábitos.

> **En directo**
>
> To congratulate or praise someone:
>
> **Felicitaciones por +** *verb, noun.*
>
> **Te felicito. Te cuidas muy bien.**
>
> **¡Qué bien! Vas a vivir muchos años.**
>
> To express happiness at someone's success:
>
> **Me alegro de que +** *subjunctive.*
>
> **¡Qué fabuloso que +** *subjunctive*!
>
> To introduce a differing opinion:
>
> **Lo que dices es interesante, pero mi perspectiva es diferente./ Yo lo veo diferente.**
>
> **Entiendo tu punto de vista, pero no estoy de acuerdo contigo.**

> **En directo**
>
> To make a general recommendation:
>
> **Es importante/bueno/ conveniente/aconsejable +** *infinitive.*
>
> To make a recommendation to someone specific:
>
> **Es importante que +** *name*(s) + *subjunctive.*

Resources
▪ SAM: 11-42 to 11-44

ESTRATEGIA

Focus on relevant information

Identifying the relevant information in a text and disregarding the irrelevant helps you read faster and understand more. Techniques that help you identify what is important include a) reading the titles and subtitles; b) looking at the visuals and reading the captions; c) brainstorming the possible content by using your knowledge of the topic; and d) comparing those ideas with what you find as you read.

A leer

Antes de leer

11-38 Preparación. PRIMERA FASE. Lea el título y los subtítulos del texto, mire las fotos y lea la nota debajo de la foto. Use esta información y su conocimiento sobre el tema para escoger la mejor respuesta a la pregunta: ¿Qué ideas e información importantes espera encontrar en el artículo?

1. A causa de la globalización, hay cada vez más enfermedades nuevas.
2. Las enfermedades conocidas en una región del mundo pasan a otras regiones, gracias al movimiento de la gente.
3. Unas enfermedades que se consideraban desaparecidas empiezan a reaparecer en el mundo a causa de cambios en el medio ambiente.

 SEGUNDA FASE. Marque (✓) las enfermedades tropicales de la lista que usted conoce. Busque más información sobre la(s) enfermedad(es) en la página web de *Mosaicos*. Answers will vary.

1. ___ la viruela (*smallpox*)
2. ___ la tuberculosis
3. ___ el dengue
4. ___ el virus del Nilo
5. ___ la malaria
6. ___ la enfermedad del sueño

Leer

Las enfermedades y la globalización

La malaria aumenta a causa de las inundaciones del río Amazonas.

Enfermedades tropicales como el dengue, la viruela, la malaria, la tuberculosis y el virus del Nilo que, según muchos expertos, ya no existían, ahora reaparecen y se extienden por todo el mundo. Las causas de su reaparición son evidentes: cambios en el medio ambiente[1] y el constante movimiento de personas entre los continentes. Los turistas, los trabajadores migratorios y los inmigrantes transportan estos virus e infecciones. De la misma manera, los cambios climáticos facilitan la adaptación de los virus a nuevos ambientes y los hacen resistentes.

Bacterias, parásitos y virus viajeros y resistentes

Un claro ejemplo de la adaptabilidad de estas enfermedades infecciosas es la tuberculosis. Los científicos pensaban que estaba controlada en los países desarrollados. Sin embargo, los hechos nos muestran que esta enfermedad ha evolucionado y ha retornado. En varios países de Europa, hay pacientes con tuberculosis porque las bacterias no reaccionan a los medicamentos tradicionales. Se piensa que alrededor de un 32% de la población del mundo sufre y morirá de esta enfermedad. La Organización Mundial de la Salud (OMS) expresa gran preocupación por la malaria. El mosquito que la provoca puede sobrevivir largos viajes interoceánicos. Por eso, hay personas enfermas de malaria en muchas partes del mundo. La malaria es peligrosa si no se detecta a tiempo. Los médicos sin experiencia en este tipo de enfermedades la pueden confundir con la gripe y tratarla con medicamentos inadecuados.

El virus del Nilo constituye otra enfermedad que afecta a los turistas. Se reportaron 3.500 casos de la enfermedad en Estados Unidos en el 2007, de los que murieron más de cien personas.

Las enfermedades migratorias

A fines del siglo XX, gracias a una campaña mundial contra la viruela, casi toda la población mundial fue inmunizada contra esta enfermedad. Sin embargo, en la actualidad, la viruela de los monos, una variedad típica de la selva de algunos países africanos, ya se reproduce en otros lugares, como Estados Unidos. En este país es necesario fabricar vacunas contra la viruela que no se producían desde hacía años.

El dengue es indudablemente la enfermedad más extendida del mundo en los últimos años. Los expertos afirman que es posible que el 40% de la población del mundo contraiga[2] esta mortal fiebre. Geográficamente, el dengue nació en el suroeste de Asia, pero rápidamente pasó al Caribe y Centro y Sudamérica. En los últimos años se han descubierto casos incluso en España.

La lista de enfermedades que surgen de nuevo por la movilidad de la población del mundo actual es larga, pero los fondos mundiales para realizar investigaciones sobre las enfermedades que causan el 90% de las muertes en el mundo son mínimos y limitados. Sin duda, la globalización ha resuelto algunos problemas, pero ha creado otros.

[1]*environment*   [2]*contracts*

11-39 Primera mirada. De las siguientes afirmaciones, indique cuáles representan ideas principales (**P**) del artículo y cuáles son ideas secundarias (**S**).

1. _P_ La reaparición de algunas enfermedades es causada por la interconexión de los mercados del mundo.

2. _P_ La gran movilidad de las personas por razones económicas causa la reaparición de enfermedades tropicales que en algún momento desaparecieron.

3. _P_ Los cambios de clima, provocados por los cambios en el medio ambiente, ayudan a que algunos virus sean más resistentes.

4. _S_ Las enfermedades migratorias mataron a norteamericanos y europeos.

5. _P_ Algunas enfermedades que nacieron en un punto específico del mundo se expanden a otros continentes.

6. _S_ Los países desarrollados como Estados Unidos están fabricando vacunas para combatir algunas enfermedades contagiosas.

11-40 Segunda mirada. Según el contenido del artículo, subraye las expresiones que se relacionan con estos temas.

1. enfermedades tropicales: las infecciones, la viruela, la tuberculosis, el virus del Nilo

2. desafíos de las enfermedades para los expertos: la infección, la adaptabilidad, el desarrollo, la evolución, la resistencia

3. medidas que los gobiernos toman para enfrentar estas enfermedades: campañas, inmunización, reproducción, vacunas, prevención

Después de leer

11-41 Ampliación. En el artículo usted encontró palabras asociadas con los verbos de la siguiente lista. Primero, seleccione la palabra apropiada, y luego use la forma adecuada (sustantivo o forma verbal) de la palabra para completar el texto a continuación.

adaptar	globalizar	migrar	reaparecer
enfermarse	investigar	mover	retornar

La interconexión del mundo actual

Muchos piensan que los efectos de la (1) _globalización_ siempre son positivos. Sin embargo, hay un gran número de personas en todo el mundo que cree lo contrario. Según ellos, es triste ver que muchas de las (2) _enfermedades_ que ya se creían eliminadas (3) _reaparecen_ con mucha fuerza y pueden matar a millones de víctimas inocentes en todos los continentes. Piensan que los científicos de los países desarrollados y más ricos deben hacer (4) _investigaciones_ para descubrir medidas para eliminarlas o controlarlas. No obstante, la realidad indica que el (5) _movimiento_ masivo de inmigrantes entre los continentes inevitablemente facilita el (6) _retorno_ de estas.

Suggestion for 11-39. Have students find additional *ideas principales* and *ideas secundarias* in the text. Have them explain the difference.

Resources

■ SAM: 11-45 to 11-47

A escribir

ESTRATEGIA	**Persuade through suggestions and advice**

Persuasion is a social, communicative task that we pursue to gain something we want or to provoke a behavior change in someone else. One method of persuasion is to offer suggestions or advice. Here are some points to remember when offering advice in Spanish.

■ Pay special attention to your degree of familiarity with the person you are trying to persuade. Is he/she a friend, an acquaintance, or someone you don't know personally? Is the person younger or older than you? Your superior at work or someone under your supervision?

■ Use expressions that signal your degree of familiarity. In Spanish this is indicated, among other ways, with the personal pronouns **tú** or **usted**.

Antes de escribir

11-42 Preparación. PRIMERA FASE. Usted acaba de recibir esta carta de uno de sus buenos amigos, quien ha permanecido en silencio por algún tiempo. Léala.

Hola amigo/a,

Perdón por no escribirte antes, pero tengo algunas razones válidas. Desde hace un mes, no me siento bien. Aunque estoy trabajando sólo cuatro horas por día, a las 3:00 de la tarde ya quiero irme a casa a descansar. No tengo apetito, así es que generalmente preparo una sopa enlatada o huevos fritos con tocino. De vez en cuando cocino una hamburguesa y, a veces, cuando me canso de la carne, tomo una buena porción de helados con galletas. ¡Ah, claro, mis amigos siempre me encuentran en los cafés de la universidad bebiendo un expreso o un capuchino! Necesito la cafeína para tener energía y hacer mi trabajo. El único problema es que por la cafeína no puedo dormir de noche. Las mañanas son una verdadera tortura. Generalmente me levanto tarde, falto a clases a veces y no me alcanza el tiempo para hacer mi trabajo.

Creo que debo buscar ayuda. Quisiera ver un médico, pero no tengo dinero ahora. ¿Qué te parece? Estoy pobre y enfermo.

Bueno, escríbeme para saber de ti. Te contestaré tan pronto pueda. Cuídate mucho.

Un fuerte abrazo,

Tomás

Suggestion for 11-42. In preparation for the upcoming writing task, you may wish to have students write (type) an anonymous letter—outside of class—to *Querida Lola* (an equivalent to Dear Abby). The content of the letter should be related to ailments and health issues.

Ask students to bring a printed copy of the letter to class. Collect the letters and, depending on the time you have, you may distribute one to each student or to pairs of students.

Students read the letter and discuss the problem(s) stated or implied in it and write at least two or three specific recommendations.

Point out that recommendations should be given with the intent to modify certain behaviors of the individual who wrote the letter. Also, make students aware of the issue of register.

Alternate. Ask students to email you their letter so you can choose one of them and have the whole class work on only one letter. This will give students the chance to compare analysis of the letter and strength of their persuasiveness.

SEGUNDA FASE. En la actividad **11-43**, usted va a responder a la carta de Tomás. Pero antes, escriba tres problemas de Tomás en la primera columna y en la otra, algunas ideas para ayudarlo a resolver cada problema.

PROBLEMAS DE TOMÁS	ALGUNAS POSIBLES SOLUCIONES
1.	1.
2.	2.
3.	3.

Escribir

11-43 Manos a la obra. Respóndale a la carta a su amigo. Use la información que preparó en la actividad **11-42**. No se olvide de expresarle sus sentimientos o preocupación por los problemas e indicarle algunas sugerencias para que los resuelva.

Después de escribir

11-44 Revisión. Lea su carta de respuesta y verifique lo siguiente, pensando en Tomás.

1. ¿Le demostró a Tomás interés por su situación? ¿Le indicó los problemas más serios, en su opinión? ¿Le dio algunas posibles soluciones? ¿Usó las formas apropiadas para hacerle recomendaciones?
2. ¿Tiene la carta una introducción, un cuerpo, un párrafo de cierre y una despedida?
3. ¿Corrigió la concordancia, la puntuación y la ortografía? ¿Usó comas, puntos, etc. donde eran necesarios?
4. ¿Usó vocabulario apropiado al tema y expresiones de cohesión? ¿Revisó el tiempo (presente, pasado, futuro) y los modos (indicativo, subjuntivo)?

Finalmente, comparta su carta con su compañero editor/compañera editora.

En directo

To express concern or sympathy:

Me preocupa (mucho) que...

Siento/Lamento que...

Qué lástima que...

To persuade a friend through suggestions:

Te recomiendo/sugiero/ aconsejo que...

Es importante/necesario/ urgente/mejor que...

Ojalá (que)...

En directo

To put ideas together cohesively:

Por un lado...
On one hand . . .

Por otro (lado)...
On the other (hand) . . .

En primer/segundo lugar...
In the first/second place . . .

Además...
Besides/Furthermore . . .

To contrast ideas:

No obstante
However

Sin embargo
Nevertheless

Suggestion for 11-42, Segunda fase. Depending on your group, you may wish to turn this into a paired activity. Weak students may profit from the skills of stronger ones.

ENFOQUE CULTURAL

Cuba y República Dominicana: la música y el baile

¿Usted cree que la única manera de hacer ejercicio es correr muchas millas cada semana? ¿Piensa que el ejercicio es siempre una cosa aburrida que se hace por obligación y no por diversión? Pues en el Caribe hispano, sobre todo en Cuba, República Dominicana y Puerto Rico, han descubierto el mejor método de ejercitar el cuerpo y el espíritu, mientras uno se divierte y socializa con sus amigos y amigas. No se trata de un descubrimiento nuevo, sino de una de las prácticas más antiguas de la humanidad: el baile. Lo especial

Una mujer baila la rumba en las calles de La Habana.

en este caso es que bailan al ritmo de una música que reúne características europeas, africanas e indígenas. Pero si esto es lo que usted quiere hacer, prepárese porque en una sesión de baile caribeño usted tendrá que mover la cabeza, el pecho, la cintura, las caderas, los brazos y las manos y, naturalmente, ¡los pies!

La música caribeña es muy rica y variada, aunque la mayoría de nosotros pensamos principalmente en la salsa, el merengue, la bachata o el reguetón. Sin embargo, bailes muy populares en los años 50, tales como el son y el bolero, la rumba y el mambo, por ejemplo, forman parte de la misma tradición musical. Esos bailes, algunos de ritmo lento y sensual, exigen una coordinación en los movimientos de las diferentes partes del cuerpo, pero especialmente de los hombros, las caderas, las rodillas y los pies. En realidad, un componente muy importante es el movimiento

Tito Puente y Celia Cruz, dos de los grandes mitos de la música caribeña

392

sincronizado de las extremidades inferiores del cuerpo, algo que le da al baile de esta región características eróticas.

La verdad es que el cuerpo humano está presente en la música no sólo a través del movimiento sino también en la letra de las canciones. En las canciones caribeñas frecuentemente se hace referencia a la boca, los labios, los ojos, los hombros, la cintura y las piernas. Algunas canciones populares explican cómo bailar ciertos ritmos y cómo mover los pies a la derecha, a la izquierda, adelante, atrás. Otras canciones, como es el caso de una famosa canción caribeña de Colombia, nos invitan a "mover la colita". Esos movimientos rítmicos del cuerpo hicieron famosos los bailes cubanos y a muchas estrellas del cine latinoamericano en los años 50 y 60. Las actrices del cine cubano y mexicano de esa época cantaban y bailaban con trajes muy pequeños, ceñidos al cuerpo y adornados con plumas y sombreros locos y espectaculares. Los músicos de las orquestas llevaban camisas de seda con grandes mangas de colores brillantes.

El cine europeo adoptó muchos de los ritmos del Caribe. Por ejemplo, La dolce vita, una película del director italiano Federico Fellini, incluyó la música de "Patricia", un mambo de Pérez Prado, uno de los más famosos compositores de música popular cubana. Igualmente, el cine latinoamericano de los años 50 y 60 está lleno de imágenes de cantantes, bailarines y bailarinas, tales como Resortes y Tin Tan, dos cómicos mexicanos, o divas como María Antonieta Pons, Amalia Aguilar o Yolanda Montes "Tongolele", una hispana de Spokane, Washington.

En los años 50, la fascinación de Estados Unidos por la música caribeña era evidente en el concurso semanal de mambo del famosísimo Savoy Ballroom en Harlem.

11-45 Comprensión. PRIMERA FASE. **Reconocimiento de palabras clave.** Encuentre en el texto la palabra o expresión que mejor expresa el significado de las siguientes ideas.

1. boring   aburrido
2. feathers   plumas
3. shirts   camisas
4. sleeves   mangas
5. stars   estrellas
6. composers   compositores
7. singers   cantantes

SEGUNDA FASE. **Oraciones importantes.** Subraye las afirmaciones que contienen ideas que se encuentran en el texto. Luego indique en qué parte del texto están.

1. Music is important in the culture of Puerto Rico, but not in the cultures of Cuba and the Dominican Republic.
2. People in the Caribbean have invented a way to exercise while also socializing and having a good time.
3. Parts of the body such as shoulders, arms, and legs are seldom mentioned in Caribbean songs.
4. The tradition of Caribbean music includes the bolero, son, rumba, and mambo.
5. The erotic qualities of Caribbean dance are due to the rhythmic movements of the lower body.
6. The most famous Latin American movie stars of the 1950s and 1960s wore crazy hats and revealing clothes adorned with feathers.
7. European films were quick to integrate Caribbean music and dance.
8. The United States only recently became interested in Caribbean rhythms.

TERCERA FASE. **Ideas principales.** Escriba un párrafo breve en español resumiendo las ideas principales expresadas en el texto.

 11-46 Use la información. Durante los años 50 y 60 muchas estrellas y orquestas de música caribeña se hicieron muy famosas en todo el mundo. Mire o escuche algunos fragmentos de cine latinoamericano de la época y escoja a una de las estrellas que aparece en un fragmento. Luego, prepare cinco preguntas que usted le haría (*would ask*) si este/a artista estuviera vivo/a (*were alive*). Para preparar esta actividad, visite la página web de Mosaicos y siga los enlaces útiles.

VOCABULARIO

El cuerpo humano	The human body
la boca	mouth
el brazo	arm
el cabello	hair
la cabeza	head
la cadera	hip
la cara	face
la ceja	eyebrow
el cerebro	brain
la cintura	waist
el codo	elbow
el corazón	heart
el cuello	neck
el dedo	finger
el diente	tooth
la espalda	back
el estómago	stomach
la frente	forehead
la garganta	throat
el hombro	shoulder
el hueso	bone
el labio	lip
la mano	hand
la mejilla	cheek
la muñeca	wrist
el músculo	muscle
la nariz	nose
el nervio	nerve
el oído	(inner) ear
la oreja	(outer) ear
el pecho	chest
la pestaña	eyelash
el pie	foot
la pierna	leg
el pulmón	lung
la rodilla	knee
la sangre	blood
el tobillo	ankle
la vena	vein

La salud	Health
el cáncer	cancer
el catarro	cold
el dolor	pain
la enfermedad	illness
el enfermo/la enferma	ill person
la fiebre	fever
la gripe	flu
la infección	infection
el/la paciente	patient
el síntoma	symptom
la tensión/la presión (arterial)	(blood) pressure
la tos	cough

Los proveedores de salud	Health care providers
la clínica/el centro de salud/el sanatorio	clinic
el farmacéutico/ la farmacéutica	pharmacist
la farmacia	pharmacy
el gobierno	government
el hospital	hospital

Los tratamientos médicos	Medical treatments
el antibiótico	antibiotic
la inyección	injection
la medicina	medicine
la pastilla	pill
la receta	prescription
el remedio	remedy, medicine
el termómetro	thermometer

Verbos	Verbs
alegrarse (de)	to be glad (about)
caer(se)	to fall
cuidar(se) (de)	to take care of
curar	to cure
doler (ue)	to hurt, ache
enfermarse	to become sick
estornudar	to sneeze
examinar	to examine
fracturar(se)	to fracture, to break
fumar	to smoke
molestar(le)	to bother, be bothered by
recetar	to prescribe
respirar	to breathe
sentir (ie, i)	to feel
temer	to fear
torcer(se) (ue)	to twist
toser	to cough
tratar	to treat

Las descripciones	Descriptions
deprimido/a	depressed
enfermo/a	sick
grave	serious
serio/a	serious

Palabras y expresiones útiles	Useful words and expressions
el artículo de belleza	beauty item
cada... horas	every . . . hours
¿Qué te/le(s) pasa?	What's wrong (with you/them)?
tener dolor de...	to have a(n) . . . ache
tener mala cara	to look terrible

See *Lengua* box on page 368 for words that refer to medical specialists.

Resources

■ IRM: Syllabi & Lesson Plans

Note. The *mola* is part of the traditional clothing of the Kuna, an indigenous people of Panama and Colombia. In Dulegaya, the Kuna language, the word *mola* means "clothing." The design of the *mola* comes from geometrical drawings that the Kuna used in the past to adorn their bodies. Later they started sewing these patterns on cotton or other fabrics brought by European settlers. Typical *molas* are made in layers of different colors. They are sewn by hand, and some require a great deal of work. Today, the production of *molas* includes dresses, T–shirts, wall hangings, quilts, and blouses.

Suggestions. Ask students to describe the shapes and colors of the *mola*. Explain that the traditional garment is a blouse made of two *molas*, one in front and the other in back. Use this opportunity to recycle vocabulary for clothing. You may wish to

CAPÍTULO

12

¡Buen viaje!

Una mola tradicional de los Kuna, indígenas de Isla San Blas en Panamá

In this chapter you will learn how to:

- discuss travel arrangements, hotel reservations, and correspondence
- talk about things that may not exist
- express possession
- talk about the past

Cultural focus: Panamá, Costa Rica

show other examples of *molas* found online. Point to Panama's Island of San Blas on the map and explain that the Kuna now live on a large reservation there. Online you will find photos of the Kuna in their traditional dress. You may introduce the topic of travel by explaining that San Blas is a tourist destination for many cruises (*cruceros*). Producing and selling *molas* is an important source of income for the natives. Ask questions about *molas*: *¿Cuánto cuestan las molas, probablemente? ¿De qué depende el precio? ¿Del trabajo? ¿Del tamaño?* You may assign students to research price, size, color, and patterns of the *molas*. Help students make connections with the art of quilting in the U.S.

Suggestion. Ask what students know about Costa Rica and Panama. Point to the photos on the map and introduce vocabulary as you ask: *¿Dónde está el Canal de Panamá? ¿Qué océanos conecta? ¿Cuándo se construyó?* (early 1900s) *¿Por dónde pasaban antes los barcos?* Using the maps in the book, show the old route around Cape Horn (*Cabo de Hornos, Chile*) to go from the Atlantic Ocean to the Pacific. Recycle expressions to compare: *¿Qué viaje es más largo?* Explain that going from New York to San Francisco using the Panama Canal is only 6,000 miles (9,500 km), compared to 14,000 miles (20,500 km) going around Cape Horn. You may write these figures on the board to recycle numbers. Ask if students know any tourist destinations in Costa Rica. Personalize to introduce the chapter topic: *¿Adónde les gusta ir de vacaciones, a la playa, a la montaña?* Explain that tourism is very important in Costa Rica: *En Costa Rica hay playas muy buenas donde se puede hacer surf. ¿Les gusta el surf? ¿Les gusta visitar lugares exóticos? En las playas de Costa Rica venden cocos. ¿Probaron el agua de coco alguna vez?*

 A vista de pájaro. Piense en lo que sabe de Panamá y Costa Rica y complete las afirmaciones.

1. _c_ El Canal de Panamá se construyó en…
   a. el siglo XVI.
   b. el siglo XXI.
   c. el siglo XX.

2. _b_ La capital de Costa Rica es…
   a. San Juan.
   b. San José.
   c. Santo Domingo.

3. _a_ Panamá limita al oeste con Costa Rica y al este con…
   a. Colombia.
   b. Nicaragua.
   c. República Dominicana.

4. _c_ Una industria muy importante de Costa Rica es…
   a. la carne de res.
   b. el tabaco.
   c. el turismo.

397

Resources

- SAM: 12-1 to 12-10
- Supp. Activ. Book: *A primera vista*

Suggestions. Talk about the photos and ask questions to practice vocabulary: *¿Viene usted a la universidad en autobús? ¿Prefiere venir en autobús o en auto? ¿Le gusta viajar en tren? ¿Qué es el AVE?* You may wish to introduce *moto(cicleta)*.

Use the photos in the book or other visuals to talk about modes of transportation.

Ask: *¿Viajó usted el año pasado? ¿Adónde fue? ¿Cómo viajó? ¿Cuánto tiempo estuvo allí?* Have students give a quick impression of the trip. Recycle the subjunctive: *¿Qué recomiendan ustedes que hagan los turistas cuando viajan a un país extranjero?* Ask students to search the Internet and bring in maps of Spanish-speaking countries to talk about places of interest. Begin with Costa Rica or Panama and move on to other locations. You may talk about the tours that cross the Andes from Puerto Montt, Chile to Bariloche in Argentina, the mountains, the southern lakes, the wine industry, etc. If possible, show pictures of these regions. Point out that many Spanish-speaking destinations are popular getaways for long weekends; for example: Cancún; Acapulco; México, D.F.; San Juan; Santo Domingo. Introduce the expression *un puente* or *feriado largo* (long weekend) and ask about students' activities during holidays.

Standard 3.2 Students acquire information and recognize the distinctive viewpoints that are only available through the foreign language and its cultures. With the exception of a few large cities, public transportation is utilized much less in the U.S. than in Latin America and Spain. Learning about the various modes of public transportion and how heavily they are used will give students

A PRIMERA VISTA

◀)) Los medios de transporte

CD 5
Track 31

Mucha gente usa el transporte público. Los **autobuses** son populares en las ciudades y también para **viajar** largas distancias. Son la solución para las personas que no tienen carro, o a quienes simplemente no les gusta **manejar** en las **carreteras** y **autopistas**. El **metro** es otra forma de transporte eficiente en los centros urbanos, como Madrid, Barcelona, Santiago, Buenos Aires, Caracas y Ciudad de México.

El AVE, el **tren** español de alta **velocidad** entre Madrid y otras grandes ciudades españolas, viaja a unos 300 kilómetros por hora. La RENFE (Red Nacional de Ferrocarriles Españoles) es tan importante en España como las **líneas aéreas** en Estados Unidos. Gracias al turismo se ha recuperado en Costa Rica la antigua tradición de **recorrer** el país en tren. Algunas agencias organizan **trayectos** desde San José a la costa este.

El **crucero** es otra forma de viajar. En **barcos** modernos con una capacidad de 400 hasta más de 2.000 **pasajeros**, se puede hacer de todo. En las **escalas** en los diferentes puertos hay excursiones organizadas y oportunidades para ir de compras. De noche, la diversión continúa en la discoteca, el casino y el teatro. El barco es un medio de transporte y también puede servir para pasar las vacaciones.

En un avión

CD 5
Track 32 El **avión** es la manera, aunque más cara, de viajar rápidamente de un lugar a otro, especialmente en zonas como las selvas y en las montañas, donde es difícil construir carreteras por la geografía o el clima.

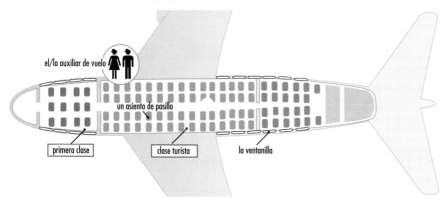

En el aeropuerto

CD 5
Track 33 Los pasajeros **hacen cola** frente al **mostrador** de la **aerolínea** para **facturar** el **equipaje**, pedir un **asiento** y conseguir la **tarjeta de embarque** para su **vuelo**.

> ### En otras palabras
>
> Other words for **auxiliar de vuelo** are **azafata**, used especially in Spain, and **aeromozo/a**, used mostly in Latin America. Depending on the region, the word **billete** (Spain), **pasaje**, or **boleto** is preferred.

En el mostrador de la línea aérea

CD 5
Track 34

EMPLEADA: Buenos días. Su **pasaporte** y su **boleto**, por favor.

VIAJERO: Aquí están. Y si es posible, prefiero un asiento cerca de una **salida de emergencia**.

EMPLEADA: Muy bien. ¿Ventanilla o pasillo?

VIAJERO: Pasillo, por favor. Señorita, ¿usted sabe si hay un **cajero automático** aquí en el **aeropuerto**?

EMPLEADA: Sí, hay una oficina del Banco Popular enfrente a la derecha.

VIAJERO: Gracias. ¿Me acreditó los kilómetros a mi programa de viajero frecuente?

EMPLEADA: Sí, y su **pasaje** es **de ida y vuelta**, así que va a tener bastantes kilómetros. Su asiento a San José es el 10F. Aquí tiene su tarjeta de embarque. La puerta de salida es la C20. ¡Que tenga un buen viaje!

insight into the cultural perspectives and economic factors that affect social mobility in the Spanish-speaking world.

Suggestions. Use visuals to talk about a plane and recycle comparisons by asking students to compare first class and tourist class. In groups, students decide which is their favorite means of transportation and why. Have them share their conclusions with the class.

Suggestions. Introduce the phrases *pasaje/boleto de ida y vuelta* and *pasaje/boleto de ida*. Use visuals to introduce vocabulary by talking about the illustration. Ask where the people are, what they are doing, what luggage they have, and so on. Have students plan a one-year trip. Where would they go? How much would such a trip cost? Ask them to make a list of items they would take on the trip. What arrangements would be necessary in advance?

Suggestions. As a warm-up, talk about the dialogue to practice vocabulary. You may have students listen to it first and then ask: *¿Qué prefiere el pasajero, ventanilla o pasillo? ¿Qué necesita? ¿Cuál es su puerta de salida?*

12-1 Asociaciones. Asocie cada palabra con su descripción. Luego, compare sus respuestas con las de un compañero/una compañera.

1. _d_ tren de alta velocidad
2. _h_ viaje en un barco grande de pasajeros
3. _a_ persona que sirve la comida en un vuelo
4. _e_ transporte subterráneo
5. _f_ inspección al llegar a otro país
6. _b_ documento de identificación necesario para viajar al extranjero
7. _g_ pasaje para ir de Panamá a Costa Rica y volver a Panamá
8. _c_ se viaja en un asiento cómodo y se come bien

a. el/la auxiliar de vuelo
b. pasaporte
c. primera clase
d. AVE
e. metro
f. aduana
g. boleto de ida y vuelta
h. crucero

 12-2 Salidas y llegadas. Miren los horarios y la puerta de salida de los siguientes vuelos y háganse preguntas.

SALIDA DEPARTURE	ABORDAR BOARDING	PUERTA GATE	DESTINO DESTINATION
3:30	3:00	1A	SAN JOSÉ
3:50	3:20	4	MANAGUA
4:10	3:40	6	GUATEMALA
4:25	3:55	10	PANAMÁ
4:45	4:15	8	LIMÓN
5:10	4:40	5	MÉXICO D.F.
6:00	5:30	5	KINGSTON

MODELO: E1: *¿A qué hora sale el vuelo para San José?*
E2: *El avión para San José sale a las tres y media por la puerta 1A.*

 12-3 Haciendo turismo. Usted es un/a agente de viajes y su compañero/a es su cliente/a. Hágale preguntas para averiguar la siguiente información. Usen los enlaces a la actividad en la página web de *Mosaicos* para obtener itinerarios posibles. Intercambien roles.

1. destino al que quiere llegar
2. fechas de viaje
3. medio de transporte que desea utilizar
4. tipo de boleto (primera clase, turista,) y asiento (ventanilla, pasillo, etc.)
5. datos del cliente (nombre, tarjeta de crédito, número de viajero frecuente, etc.)

SEGUNDA FASE. Hablen entre ustedes de fechas, precios y otras opciones. Después hágale a su compañero/a algunas recomendaciones para el viaje: necesidad de pasaporte, recomendaciones para pasar por la aduana, etc.

Viajando en coche

CD 5
Track 35

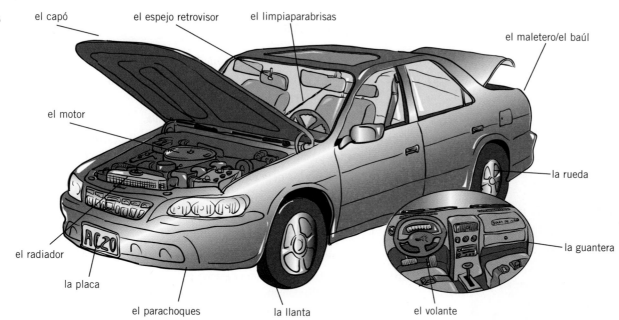

el capó   el espejo retrovisor   el limpiaparabrisas

el maletero/el baúl

el motor

la rueda

el radiador

la guantera

la placa

el parachoques   la llanta   el volante

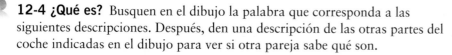

12-4 ¿Qué es? Busquen en el dibujo la palabra que corresponda a las siguientes descripciones. Después, den una descripción de las otras partes del coche indicadas en el dibujo para ver si otra pareja sabe qué son.

1. Es para poner el equipaje. _____el maletero_____
2. Permite ver bien cuando llueve. __el limpiaparabrisas__
3. Son negras y llevan aire por dentro. _____las llantas_____
4. Controla la dirección del coche. _____el volante_____
5. Tiene letras y números y sirve para identificar el coche._____la placa_____
6. Hay que ponerle agua si no queremos que se caliente el motor.
   _____el radiador_____

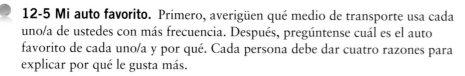

12-5 Mi auto favorito. Primero, averigüen qué medio de transporte usa cada uno/a de ustedes con más frecuencia. Después, pregúntense cuál es el auto favorito de cada uno/a y por qué. Cada persona debe dar cuatro razones para explicar por qué le gusta más.

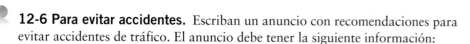

12-6 Para evitar accidentes. Escriban un anuncio con recomendaciones para evitar accidentes de tráfico. El anuncio debe tener la siguiente información:

1. un título o eslogan (*motto*)
2. el nombre de la compañía o grupo que patrocina (*sponsors*) el anuncio
3. tres recomendaciones para evitar accidentes

Cultura

Aunque en los países hispanoamericanos se usa mucho el transporte público, el tráfico y la contaminación son problemas serios en las ciudades grandes. Además, cada vez es más difícil encontrar estacionamiento. Por eso se usan mucho las motos y los carros pequeños.

Follow-up for 12-4. Expand the car vocabulary by using newspaper or magazine ads. Ask yes/no and either/or questions to review and reinforce vocabulary. Discuss cars with students by talking about *carros/coches pequeños/grandes*, *consumo de gasolina*, *contaminación*, etc. After students have studied car vocabulary, give half the class the picture of a car without the parts identified. The other students say the part of the car, and the first group must label it correctly.

Suggestion for 12-5. Have students ask each other what their favorite car is and why. Encourage them to use the vocabulary in this section to justify their answers.

Suggestion for 12-6. This is a good opportunity to review the use of the subjunctive when giving advice (*Capítulo 11*). You may wish to do a quick review of the forms.

·)) El alojamiento y las reservaciones

CD 5
Track 36 ## Buscando alojamiento

EMPLEADA: Buenas tardes. ¿En qué les puedo servir?

SRA. CANO: Buenas tardes. Tenemos dos **habitaciones** reservadas a nuestro nombre, señores Cano.

EMPLEADA: Sí, señora. Tengo una **doble** y una **sencilla**.

SRA. CANO: Muy bien. Una es para nosotros y otra para nuestro hijo. Quisiera dejar los pasaportes en un lugar seguro. ¿Podría usted... ?

EMPLEADA: ¿Por qué no los deja en la **caja fuerte** de su habitación?

SRA. CANO: Muy bien.

EMPLEADA: Bueno, aquí tiene dos **tarjetas magnéticas**. Ya no usamos **llaves**. Sus habitaciones están en el segundo piso.

SR. CANO: Y..., ¿nos puede indicar cómo llegar a la Plaza 5 de Mayo?

EMPLEADA: Sí, cómo no. Mire, **sigan derecho** por esta calle hasta la próxima **esquina**. Allí, **doblen** a la izquierda y caminen una **cuadra** hasta la plaza que está a la derecha. No **se** pueden **perder**.

SR. CANO: Muchísimas gracias.

 12-7 Estoy perdido/a. Usted está en la Ciudad de Panamá y está perdido. Use el plano siguiente y pregúntele a un ciudadano/una ciudadana (su compañero/a) cómo ir a ciertos lugares. Su compañero/a le debe explicar cómo llegar.

USTED ESTÁ EN	USTED DESEA IR
la Plaza 5 de Mayo	al Palacio Presidencial
la Avenida Ancón y la Avenida A	al Casco Viejo
el Museo de Historia del Canal de Panamá	al Centro Turístico Mi Pueblito

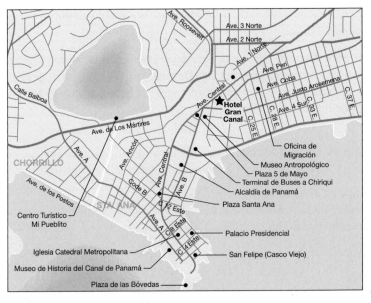

Ciudad de Panamá

El correo y la correspondencia

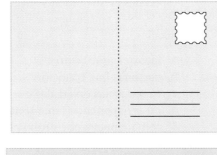

una carta

una postal

un sello

un sobre

Sra. Teresa Silva de Granados
504 Edificio Los Pinos
Panamá 3, Rep. de Panamá

el cartero

el paquete

el buzón

12-8 La correspondencia. PRIMERA FASE. Complete las oraciones con la palabra adecuada y escriba la letra correspondiente al lado del número.

1. __b__ El lugar donde a veces se recoge la correspondencia y se compran sellos es el…
2. __a__ La persona que reparte cartas y postales es el/la…
3. __f__ El depósito donde ponemos las cartas que queremos enviar es el…
4. __d__ Para mandar una carta la ponemos dentro de un…
5. __e__ Si queremos mandar un regalo de una ciudad a otra, tenemos que preparar un…
6. __c__ No se puede mandar una carta sin escribir la dirección y ponerle un…

a. cartero/a.
b. correo.
c. sello.
d. sobre.
e. paquete.
f. buzón.

SEGUNDA FASE. Respondan a las siguientes preguntas.

1. ¿Cuándo fue la última vez que usted fue al correo?
2. ¿Para qué fue? ¿Para comprar sellos o un sobre o para enviar un paquete?
3. ¿Es el correo electrónico un medio de comunicación más eficaz (*efficient*) que el correo postal? ¿Por qué?

Cultura

Hoy en día las personas prefieren comunicarse mediante los *chats* o el correo electrónico. En todas las ciudades del mundo hay cibercafés desde donde podemos comunicarnos instantáneamente con los familiares y amigos. Sin embargo, en los lugares turísticos venden postales muy lindas para enviar por correo normal. Los sellos para enviar postales y cartas se compran en las tiendas de tabaco y en las oficinas de correos. En algunas épocas del año, estas oficinas están llenas de gente que quieren enviar paquetes a sus conocidos.

Note for 12-9. You may explain that in some countries the words *correo* or *e-mail* are used when referring to an e-mail message.

Warm-up for 12-10. As a pre-listening activity, have students in groups of four discuss if they have traveled abroad and where, what documents they had to get before they traveled, and what inconveniences they had to deal with.

Audioscript for 12-10.
AGENTE: *Buenas tardes, señor. Su pasaje y pasaporte, por favor.*
VIAJERO: *Buenas tardes. Aquí están.*
AGENTE: *Muy bien. ¿Cuántas maletas va a facturar?*
VIAJERO: *Dos. Llevo también un maletín de mano, pero no lo voy a facturar.*
AGENTE: *Muy bien. Ponga las maletas aquí, por favor. Ahora dígame, ¿prefiere ventanilla, pasillo o en el centro?*
VIAJERO: *En el pasillo, por favor. Y quisiera uno de los primeros asientos.*
AGENTE: *Lo siento, pero sólo quedan asientos después de la fila 27. Le puedo dar el 28 C.*
VIAJERO: *Bueno, está bien.*
AGENTE: *La puerta de salida es la número 8. Aquí tiene su pasaporte y tarjeta de embarque. Ahora, pase por seguridad y luego diríjase a la puerta de salida.*
VIAJERO: *Gracias, señor. ¿Tengo tiempo para hacer una llamada?*
AGENTE: *Sí, el avión sale en 45 minutos. No se preocupe. Que tenga un buen viaje.*

 12-9 Un correo electrónico nostálgico. Envíele un mensaje electrónico o una postal a su compañero favorito/compañera favorita. Cuéntele algunos aspectos especiales de sus últimas vacaciones. Después, su compañero/a le responderá por escrito, reaccionará a sus comentarios y le hará preguntas para obtener más detalles.

1. lugar(es) que visitó
2. personas que conoció
3. experiencias divertidas que vivió
4. otras experiencias que recuerda con nostalgia
5. comida nueva que probó
6. regalos que compró

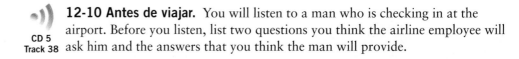

CD 5
Track 38

12-10 Antes de viajar. You will listen to a man who is checking in at the airport. Before you listen, list two questions you think the airline employee will ask him and the answers that you think the man will provide.

Now listen to the exchange, and choose the appropriate ending to each statement.

1. El empleado le pide al viajero...
   a. su boleto de ida y vuelta.
   b. su tarjeta de embarque.
   c. su pasaporte y su pasaje.

2. El viajero va a facturar...
   a. tres maletas.
   b. un maletín de mano.
   c. dos maletas.

3. El viajero prefiere un asiento...
   a. al lado de la ventanilla.
   b. en el pasillo.
   c. en la parte posterior del avión.

4. El empleado le puede conseguir un asiento...
   a. de pasillo, el 28C.
   b. en el centro, entre la ventanilla y el pasillo.
   c. en la ventanilla en primera clase.

5. El empleado le dice al pasajero que...
   a. tiene tiempo para llamar por teléfono.
   b. puede llamar desde el avión.
   c. no tiene que pasar por seguridad.

EN ACCIÓN

Resources
■ Video
■ SAM: 12-11 to 12-13

Diarios de bicicleta: El premio

Antes de ver

12-11 Usted está ayudando a un amigo a planear un viaje. ¿Cuáles son, según usted, las cinco cosas que él/ella debería hacer primero? Answers may vary.

___ Es necesario que obtenga un pasaporte.
___ Recomiendo que haga reservaciones de hotel.
___ Es importante que compre un boleto de avión.
___ Sugiero que hable con un agente de viajes.
___ Es importante que compre una guía turística del país.
___ Es necesario que haga las maletas.
___ Recomiendo que compre una cámara de fotos.
___ Es importante que cargue la batería del iPod.

Suggestion for 12-11. Ask students additional questions about their experiences with travel arrangements. *¿Es mejor comprar el boleto de avión en Internet o en una agencia de viajes? ¿Hay problemas con los dispositivos electrónicos cuando se viaja a otro país?* etc.

Mientras ve

12-12 Escoja la oración que es equivalente a cada cita (*quote*).

1. Javier: "¿Quién se cree estos engaños?"
   a. No puede ser verdad.
   b. No soy religioso.
2. Gabi: "Me tocó la lotería…"
   a. Voy a cancelar mis planes.
   b. Tengo mucha suerte.
3. Gabi: "…puedo elegir cualquier destino."
   a. Puedo escoger cualquier lugar.
   b. Puedo viajar durante cualquier época del año.
4. Javier: "¿Nos vemos al rato?"
   a. Nos vemos en otro lugar.
   b. Nos vemos más tarde.

Suggestion for 12-12. Suggestions for additional comprehension activities:
1. Have the class describe and recount everything they remember about the scene in the still photograph from the video segment.
2. Have pairs or small groups of students write one sentence about something they remember from the video segment. A representative from each pair/group writes the sentence on the board, and the class works together to put the sentences in chronological order.

Después de ver

12-13 En este segmento, tres personajes han recibido un correo electrónico que dice que han ganado un viaje a Centroamérica. Escriba el mensaje que han recibido. Incluya tres instrucciones de cómo reclamar (*reclaim*) este premio.
Answers may vary.

405

FUNCIONES Y FORMAS

Resources

- SAM: 12-14 to 12-20
- Supp. Activ. Book: Subjunctive in adjective clauses
- PPTs
- *Situaciones adicionales*

1. Talking about things that may not exist: Subjunctive in adjective clauses

MUJER: Por favor, ¿dónde está el tren que **sale** a las 9:00?

AGENTE: No hay trenes que **salgan** por la noche, señorita. El último tren sale a las 6:00 de la tarde.

MUJER: ¡Ay, Dios mío! ¿Hay un tren que **salga** temprano por la mañana?

AGENTE: Sí, señorita. El primer tren sale a las 7:00.

MUJER: Bueno, tendré que esperar hasta mañana, entonces. ¿Me puede recomendar un hotel que **esté** cerca? Necesito uno que no **sea** caro.

AGENTE: Sí, cómo no. Le recomiendo el Hotel Colonial. Es un buen hotel que **tiene** precios módicos.

Suggestion for Piénselo.
Guide students to make the connection between situations that exist + the indicative vs. situations that do not exist or that possibly exist + the subjunctive.

Suggestions. Use visuals to illustrate existent versus nonexistent antecedents versus antecedents whose existence is unknown. For example, a beach scene: *Hay personas que juegan al voleibol. Hay personas que están tomando helados, pero no hay nadie que escuche la radio. No hay nadie que esté nadando.* Present comparisons: *Sí, hay personas que toman helado.* (Existent) *No, no hay nadie que beba café, porque hace mucho calor.* (Nonexistent) *Los niños buscan una tienda que venda refrescos.* (Existence unknown)

Piénselo. Para cada oración, indique si la persona habla de algo que existe (**E**), de algo que no existe (**NE**) o de algo que posiblemente exista (**PE**).

1. __E__ ¿Dónde está el tren que **sale** a las 9:00?
2. __NE__ No hay trenes que **salgan** por la noche.
3. __PE__ ¿Hay un tren que **salga** temprano por la mañana?
4. __PE__ ¿Me puede recomendar un hotel que **esté** cerca?
5. __PE__ Necesito un hotel que no **sea** caro.
6. __E__ Es un buen hotel que **tiene** precios módicos (*moderate*).

- As you have learned, the subjunctive in Spanish is used primarily in sentences that have two clauses. In this section, you will learn about using the subjunctive in adjective clauses.

- Both adjectives and adjective clauses provide descriptive information about a noun in the independent clause.

Vamos a ir a un hotel muy <u>ADJECTIVE</u>
moderno.

Vamos a ir a un hotel <u>ADJECTIVE CLAUSE</u>
que es muy moderno.

■ Use the indicative in an adjective clause that refers to a person, place, or thing (antecedent) that exists or is known.

Hay un buen hotel que **queda** cerca de la playa.
There is a good hotel that is close to the beach.
(You are familiar with the hotel.)
Quiero visitar el museo que **tiene** la exposición de molas.
I want to visit the museum that has the exhibit of molas.
(You know there is such a museum.)

■ Use the subjunctive in an adjective clause that refers to a person, place, or thing that does not exist or whose existence is unknown or in question.

No hay hoteles en esta zona que **tengan** precios módicos.
There are no hotels in this area that have moderate prices.

Quiero comer en un restaurante que **sirva** comida vegetariana.
I want to eat in a restaurant that serves vegetarian food.
(Any restaurant, as long as it serves vegetarian food.)

■ When the antecedent is a specific person and functions as a direct object, use the indicative and the personal **a**. If the antecedent is not a specific person, use the subjunctive and do not use the personal **a**.

Busco **a** la auxiliar que **trabaja** en ese vuelo.
I am looking for the flight attendant who is working on that flight.
(A specific flight attendant, who is among those working on that flight.)

Busco una auxiliar que **trabaje** en ese vuelo.
I am looking for a flight attendant who is working on that flight.
(Any flight attendant, as long as she is working on that flight.)

■ In questions, you may use the indicative or the subjunctive according to the degree of certainty you have about the matter.

¿Hay viajeros aquí que **salen** en el vuelo 420?
Are there any travelers here who are leaving on flight 420?
(I do not know, but I assume there are.)

¿Hay viajeros aquí que **salgan** en el vuelo 420?
Are there any travelers here who are leaving on flight 420?
(I do not know, but I doubt it.)

12-14 ¿Cuál es la respuesta correcta? Escriba la letra de la forma verbal (indicativo o subjuntivo) para completar cada grupo de oraciones.

1. No hay ningún vuelo que _b_ por la noche.
2. Pero hay un vuelo que _a_ a las 7:00 de la mañana.

  a. sale
  b. salga

3. Me interesa encontrar un hotel (*any hotel*) que _b_ cerca del centro.
4. Hay un hotel que no es muy caro y que _a_ en el centro.

  a. queda
  b. quede

5. Busco al empleado que _a_ inglés.
6. Hay algún empleado (*any employee*) en este departamento que _b_ inglés?

  a. habla
  b. hable

Affirmative and negative expressions are presented in the next chapter. Those relevant to the use of the subjunctive in adjective clauses appear in this chapter. Presenting those words in meaningful contexts will help students use them in the next chapter. You may wish to write *alguien, nadie,* and *ninguno/alguno* (and their variants) on the board as you present the words and their meanings.

Suggestion. The concept of known versus unknown antecedent may be difficult for students to grasp, especially because sentences of both types may have identical English translations. You may wish to provide additional examples in which the personal **a** signals the difference between the two kinds of antecedents: *busco un profesor que enseñe español* vs. *busco al profesor que enseña español.*

Suggestion. Ask questions with *hay,* using the indicative and the subjunctive: *¿Hay una clase que termina/termine a las cuatro?* Point out that when the speaker is not sure or has no knowledge of the existence of the antecedent, he/she uses the subjunctive.

12-15 Por curiosidad. Usted tiene curiosidad por saber algo sobre la familia y los amigos de su compañero/a. Túrnense para hacerse preguntas. Si la respuesta es afirmativa, diga quién es la persona y dé información adicional.

MODELO: dormir mucho durante los viajes largos por auto/tu familia

E1: *¿Hay alguien en tu familia que duerma mucho durante los viajes largos por auto?*

E2: *Sí, mi hermano siempre duerme mucho en el auto. El año pasado fuimos a la casa de mis abuelos y él durmió durante todo el viaje.*

1. viajar mucho/tu famila
2. trabajar en vez de viajar durante las vacaciones de la primavera/tus amigos
3. conocer los parques nacionales de Costa Rica/tus amigos
4. saber pilotear un avión/tu familia
5. ir a esquiar en sus vacaciones/tus amigos
6. viajar a Panamá este año/tu familia

12-16 Emergencia en el aeropuerto. Varios empleados de la aerolínea costarricense Travelair están enfermos, y otras personas tienen que hacer su trabajo. Túrnense para hacer los papeles de dos empleados de Travelair que buscan otros empleados que puedan hacer ciertos trabajos. Sigan el modelo.

MODELO: programar la computadora (alguien)

E1: *Necesito a alguien que programe la computadora para los itinerarios.*

E2: *No hay nadie en el aeropuerto que pueda programarla.*

E1: *Bueno, es necesario buscar a alguien que lo haga.*

1. hablar inglés, japonés y español para el vuelo a Tamarindo (auxiliar)
2. recibir el vuelo que viene de Puerto Jiménez (agente)
3. darles esta información a los pasajeros del vuelo 562 (empleado/a)
4. llevar a los pasajeros a inmigración (empleado/a)
5. poder trabajar este fin de semana (dos auxiliares)
6. …

12-17 Un lugar para ir de vacaciones. PRIMERA FASE. Túrnense para hacerse preguntas sobre un lugar para ir de vacaciones. Contesten según la información de la tabla.

MODELO: hotel/tener piscina

E1: *¿Hay un hotel que tenga piscina?*

E2: *Sí, hay un hotel que tiene piscina. O No, no hay ningún hotel que tenga piscina.*

HAY	NO HAY
tiendas/vender ropa para esquiar	autobús/llegar por la mañana
cines/dar películas en español	cafetería/servir comida vegetariana
restaurantes/tener cajero automático	restaurantes/aceptar cheques personales

SEGUNDA FASE. Ahora ustedes deben describir cómo es su lugar ideal de vacaciones, explicando su localización, ambiente y atracciones. Después, intercambien ideas con otra pareja.

MODELO: E1: *Quiero ir de vacaciones a una isla que tenga playas blancas y un ambiente tranquilo. ¿Y tú?*

E2: *Mi lugar de vacaciones ideal es diferente. Quiero ir a una ciudad que tenga muchos conciertos y obras de teatro.*

12-18 Agencia *Viaje ahora*. Usted piensa viajar al extranjero, pero no conoce ninguna buena agencia de viajes. Dígale a su compañero/a adónde quiere ir y pídale información sobre una agencia. Su compañero/a le va a dar información basándose en el anuncio de la agencia *Viaje ahora*. Hágale por lo menos tres preguntas adicionales.

TURISMO
Viaje ahora
Servicio de viajes
Le planeamos su viaje a cualquier parte
de Panamá y del extranjero.
Boletos de avión, de barco; alquiler de autos;
reservaciones de hoteles; excursiones
20 años sirviendo al público
TELÉFONOS: (507) 2702040   (507) 2703230
Calle 50 #134
Panamá 5, República de Panamá

SITUACIONES

1. **Role A.** You want to visit Panama. Call your travel agent to find out a) the cost of the flight; b) the flight schedule; and c) if you need a visa. Then explain the type of hotel you want in Panama City and where you will spend the first week of your trip.

   Role B. You are a travel agent. A customer calls to discuss a possible trip to Panama. Provide all the necessary information.

2. **Role A.** You own a small inn near the college that houses international faculty who visit the campus. You need to hire two people for your staff, so you call an employment agency. Explain that you are looking for a) a receptionist who speaks French, German, or Spanish (preferably two of those languages) and who has experience as a secretary, and b) a chef who is familiar with European cuisines and who is able to work nights and weekends.

   Role B. You work at an employment agency, and you receive a call from an innkeeper who is looking for a receptionist and a chef. Listen to the innkeeper's requirements and ask about any other qualifications that may be desired. Tell the innkeeper you will start looking right away.

Resources
■ SAM: 12-21 to 12-25
■ Supp. Activ. Book:
Possessive pronouns

2. Expressing possession: Possessive pronouns

MADRE: Ramiro, mi maleta casi está lista. ¿Y **la tuya**?

RAMIRO: **¡La mía** no! Después del programa la empaco. ¿Ya empacaste tus libros, mamá?

MADRE: **Los míos** ya están en mi maletín. ¿Y los juguetes de Panchito?

RAMIRO: **Los suyos** están en su mochila, pero **los de** Laurita no sé dónde están.

Piénselo. Lea las siguientes afirmaciones tomadas de la conversación anterior e indique si las dijo la madre (**M**) o Ramiro (**R**). Luego, indique (✓) a qué se refiere la palabra en negrita.

1. _R_ **¡La mía** no!
   La mía se refiere ___ al programa. ✓ a la maleta.

2. _M_ **Los míos** ya están en mi bolso de mano.
   Los míos se refiere a ✓ los libros. ___ los juguetes.

3. _R_ **Los suyos** están en su mochila.
   Los suyos se refiere a ___ los maletines de mano. ✓ los juguetes de Panchito.

4. _R_ **Los de Laurita** están en su cuarto.
   Los de Laurita se refiere a ___ los libros. ✓ los juguetes.

■ Possessive pronouns express ownership or possession. They are used to avoid repetition of the noun to which they refer.

SINGULAR		PLURAL	
MASCULINE	FEMININE	MASCULINE	FEMININE
mío	mía	míos	mías
tuyo	tuya	tuyos	tuyas
el { suyo	la { suya	los { suyos	las { suyas
nuestro	nuestra	nuestros	nuestras
vuestro	vuestra	vuestros	vuestras

■ The definite article precedes the possessive pronoun, and both article and pronoun agree in gender and number with the noun to which they refer.

¿Tienes la mochila de Mario?   *Do you have Mario's backpack?*

Sí, tengo **la suya** y **la mía** también.   *Yes, I have his and mine too.*

Suggestions. Remind students that pronouns are used to avoid repetition of the noun. Provide examples: *¿Tienes tu mochila? ¿Dónde está la mía? Mi lugar favorito de vacaciones es la playa. Yo siempre hago mis reservaciones para viajar en Internet. Y tú, ¿cómo haces las tuyas? Las maletas que llevo durante mis viajes son viejas. Y las tuyas, ¿son viejas también?*

Practice possessive pronoun forms by holding up items that belong to various students and saying: *¿Es mi mochila? No, es la suya,* etc.

■ After the verb **ser**, the article is usually omitted.

Esa maleta es **mía**.   *That suitcase is mine.*

■ To be clearer and more specific, the following structures may be used to replace any corresponding form of **el suyo/la suya**.

la mochila suya → **la suya** *or*

$$\begin{cases} \text{la de usted} & \textit{yours (singular)} \\ \text{la de él} & \textit{his} \\ \text{la de ella} & \textit{hers} \\ \\ \text{la de ustedes} & \textit{yours (plural)} \\ \text{la de ellos} & \textit{theirs (masculine, plural)} \\ \text{la de ellas} & \textit{theirs (feminine, plural)} \end{cases}$$

12-19 ¿De quién(es) son estas cosas? En su clase de español ustedes decidieron hacer un viaje de estudios a Costa Rica. En este momento van a tomar el bus para ir al aeropuerto. Escoja la repuesta correcta para cada una de las preguntas.

1. Miguel, ¿es tuya esta mochila?   (**a.**) Sí, es mía.   **b.** Sí, es tuya.
2. ¿Son estas maletas de Pedro?   (**a.**) Sí, son suyas.   **b.** Sí, son mías.
3. ¿El maletín color café es de Alicia?   **a.** No, es tuya.   (**b.**) No, no es suyo.
4. Este mapa de San José, ¿es tuyo?   **a.** Sí, es mía.   (**b.**) Sí, es mío.
5. ¿Son nuestros estos boletos?   (**a.**) Sí, son suyos.   **b.** Sí, son suyas.

En otras palabras

Depending on the region, different words for **autobús** are used: **camión** (Mexico), **ómnibus** (Peru), **bus**, **guagua** (Puerto Rico, Cuba), **colectivo** (Argentina), **micro** (Chile), **chivita** (Colombia).

12-20 ¿Quién tiene carro? PRIMERA FASE. Entrevístense para saber quién(es) tiene(n) carro. Hablen de sus carros: marca, modelo, año y color. Tomen apuntes sobre la información.

MODELO: E1: *Mi carro es un Toyota Corolla de 2005. ¿Y los suyos?*
           E2: *El mío es un Ford Taurus de 2003.*
           E3: *Yo no tengo carro, pero uso el de mi hermana.*

SEGUNDA FASE. Combinen la información de todos los grupos y preparen un informe sobre los rasgos (*features*) más comunes de los carros de los miembros de la clase.

12-21 Preparándose para un viaje. Ustedes van a hacer un viaje en auto y deben tomar varias decisiones antes de salir. Háganse preguntas para decidir lo que van a hacer, y den una razón. Al conversar, usen un pronombre posesivo para evitar la repetición.

MODELO: usar mi coche o tu coche
           E1: *¿Vamos a usar mi coche o el tuyo?*
           E2: *Prefiero usar el tuyo porque es más nuevo.*

1. hablar con mi agente o tu agente
2. llevar tus maletas o las de mi hermano
3. usar mis mapas o tus mapas
4. llevar tu cámara o mi cámara
5. llevar tu celular o el de mi madre
6. usar tu GPS o el de mis hermanos

Suggestion for 12-20
Primera fase. You may create a category of family cars so that students who do not have their own vehicles may talk about a car owned by a member of the family.

Note for 12-21. GPS in Spanish is *Sistema de Posicionamiento Global.* However, people commonly call it GPS [ge-pe-ese].

12-22 Recuerdo de vacaciones. PRIMERA FASE. Túrnense para hablar de sus vacaciones favoritas. En su conversación, incluyan los siguientes aspectos de sus respectivas vacaciones. Busquen aspectos similares y diferentes entre sus experiencias.

1. adónde fueron y con quiénes
2. cómo viajaron al lugar
3. el alojamiento
4. la comida
5. sus diversiones
6. sus actividades culturales

SEGUNDA FASE. Ahora, comparen sus vacaciones favoritas con las de otra pareja.

MODELO: adónde fueron

E1: *Nuestras vacaciones favoritas fueron en Estados Unidos, las mías en Florida y las de Carlos en Colorado.*

E2: *Las nuestras fueron en otros países, las mías en Costa Rica y las de Isabel en Chile.*

12-23 Objetos perdidos. Durante un viaje por avión usted perdió algunas pertenencias. Converse con el empleado/la empleada (su compañero/a) de la Oficina de Objetos Perdidos de la aerolínea y descríbale detalladamente cada objeto.

MODELO: E1: *Perdón. Anoche perdí mis llaves en el vuelo 1239.*

E2: *Aquí tengo algunas llaves. ¿Puede describirme las suyas?*

E1: *Las mías son negras y están en un llavero (keyholder) con otras llaves. El llavero tiene un juguete plástico amarillo.*

E2: *¿Son estas?*

E1: *Sí. Muchas gracias.*

SITUACIONES

1. **Role A.** Yesterday, you lost your wallet (color, size, contents) at a hotel in Panama City. Answer the questions of the employee at the Lost and Found desk. Then show him/her an identification document and thank him/her.

   Role B. You are a hotel employee who is helping a guest who has lost a wallet. Find out a) the person's name; b) a description of the wallet and its contents; and c) when he/she lost it. Ask for identification to verify ownership, and then return the wallet.

2. **Role A.** On the plane home from an ecotourism trip to Costa Rica, you sit next to a student returning from a similar trip. Ask your seatmate a) why he/she went on an ecotourism trip; b) what national park he/she liked best, and why; c) one thing he/she learned from the trip; and d) whether he/she has plans to return to Costa Rica. Answer your seatmate's questions about your trip.

   Role B. On the plane home from an ecotourism trip to Costa Rica, you sit next to a student returning from a similar trip. After answering your seatmate's questions, ask him/her similar questions about his/her trip. Comment on how your experience was similar to that of your seatmate.

Suggestions for 12-23. Before the activity, review the names of the items in the drawings. You may wish to have students describe each object in detail. Have students change roles during the activity.

Suggestion. For the second *Situación*, students may need to prepare ahead of time so they can talk about their ecotourism activities in Costa Rica.

3. Expressing possession: Stressed possessive adjectives

Resources
■ SAM: 12-26 to 12-30
■ Supp. Activ. Book: Stressed possessive adjectives

MANOLO: ¡Ay, Dios mío! Se me perdió la llave. No está en mi bolsillo. Adelita, ¿tienes la tuya?

ADELITA: Por supuesto, mi amor. **La llave mía** está aquí. Dejaste **la llave tuya** en la recepción, ¿no te acuerdas?

MANOLO: Ah, tienes razón. ¿Y los teléfonos celulares?

ADELITA: Sí, tengo **el celular tuyo** y **el celular mío** también. No te preocupes.

Suggestion. Before introducing stressed possessive adjectives, review short-form possessives: *mi, mis, tu, tus,* etc. Then compare *mis llaves* with *las llaves mías.* Have students practice using a few nouns with possessives.

Piénselo. Mire el dibujo e indique a quién pertenece cada objeto en la lista a continuación.

1. _b_ la llave que tiene la mujer
2. _a_ la llave que está en la recepción
3. _c_ los teléfonos celulares

a. a Manolo
b. a Adelita
c. a los dos

■ In the previous section, you learned to use possessive pronouns to avoid repetition in speaking and writing. Stressed possessive adjectives, whose forms are the same, emphasize to whom a particular object belongs. Because they are adjectives, they always immediately follow the noun to which they refer.

Suggestion. To reinforce the distinction between possessive adjectives and possessive pronouns, explain that adjectives are used with the nouns to which they refer, whereas pronouns are used instead of the nouns to which they refer.

SINGULAR		PLURAL		
MASCULINE	**FEMININE**	**MASCULINE**	**FEMININE**	
mío	mía	míos	mías	*my, (of) mine*
tuyo	tuya	tuyos	tuyas	*your (familiar), (of) yours*
suyo	suya	suyos	suyas	*your (formal), his, her, its, their, (of) yours his, hers, theirs*
nuestro	nuestra	nuestros	nuestras	*our, (of) ours*
vuestro	vuestra	vuestros	vuestras	*your (familiar), (of) yours*

■ Stressed possessive adjectives agree in gender and number with the noun they modify. An article or demonstrative adjective usually precedes the noun. Use stressed possessives for emphasis.

El cuarto **mío** es grandísimo.	*My room is very big.*
La maleta **tuya** está en la recepción.	*Your suitcase is at the front desk.*
Esos primos **míos** llegan hoy.	*Those cousins of mine arrive today.*
Las llaves **nuestras** están encima del escritorio.	*Our keys are on the desk.*

■ The third-person possessive adjectives **suyo**, **suya**, **suyos**, and **suyas** have more than one meaning. You can avoid confusion by using **de** + *subject pronoun/name* instead of the possessive adjective.

la maleta **suya**	la maleta **de él/ella**	*his/her suitcase*
	la maleta **de usted/ustedes**	*your (sing./pl.) suitcase*
	la maleta **de ellos/ellas**	*their suitcase*

los billetes **suyos**	los billetes **de él/ella**	*his/her tickets*
	los billetes **de usted/ustedes**	*your (sing./pl.) tickets*
	los billetes **de ellos/ellas**	*their tickets*

Suggestion for 12-24 Segunda fase. Students should talk about objects that they have misplaced or lost recently. If none come to mind, they should think of small objects that are frequently lost, such as iPods, cell phones, and appointment books (*agendas*).

12-24 En la sala de embarque (*departure*). PRIMERA FASE. La familia Suárez está esperando su vuelo. Complete la conversación entre los padres y sus hijos con la forma apropiada del adjetivo posesivo entre paréntesis.

SR. SUÁREZ: ¡Lalo y Lucy, no se vayan, vengan acá y siéntense! ¿Dónde están sus mochilas?

LALO: La mochila (1) __mía__ (mío) está aquí.

LUCY: No, Lalo, no es la mochila (2) __tuya__ (tuyo), tú no tienes una mochila rosada. Mamá, Lalo quiere todas las cosas (3) __mías__ (mío).

SRA. SUÁREZ: Niños, no discutan. ¿Dónde están los bolsos (4) __nuestros__ (nuestro)? En uno de ellos están los sándwiches que preparé.

LALO: Sí, tengo hambre. Mamá, ¿cuál es el sándwich (5) __mío__ (mío)? Quiero un sándwich de jamón.

SRA. SUÁREZ: Tranquilo, Lalo, hay sándwiches para todos. (*Le da un bolso.*) Dale un sándwich a tu hermana. Los almuerzos (6) __suyos__ (suyo) están en este bolso.

SEGUNDA FASE. Cada uno de ustedes no encuentra dos objetos personales de la siguiente lista. Usen los adjetivos posesivos y otras formas que sean necesarias para hablar de sus objetos perdidos.

carnet de estudiante	libro de español
gafas de sol	tarjeta magnética para entrar a la residencia
iPod	teléfono celular

Preparation for 12-25. Ask students, either the whole class or in groups of 6–8, to put a small, identifiable personal item (e.g., cell phone, notebook, calculator, mug) in a bag that you bring to class for this purpose. Explain to them that they will reclaim their object during the activity. If the activity is done in groups, appoint the *agente de la Oficina de Objetos Perdidos* for each group. You may wish to draw students' attention to the model, and point out that they should use at least one stressed possessive adjective and one possessive pronoun per reclaimed object.

12-25 Identificar los objetos perdidos. Todas las personas de su grupo han perdido una de sus pertenencias. Un/a agente de la Oficina de Objetos Perdidos les muestra los objetos. Identifique y reclame (*reclaim*) su objeto. Siga el modelo.

MODELO: AGENTE: *Aquí tengo un libro de biología.*
E1: *¡Qué bueno! Es el libro mío.*
AGENTE: *X dice que el libro es suyo. ¿Es cierto? ¿Es de él/ella?*
E2: *Sí, es el libro suyo.*

12-26 Inventos del futuro. PRIMERA FASE. Lea la descripción de un invento fantástico. Luego diseñe su propio invento. Escriba una lista de sus rasgos, usando adjetivos y pronombres posesivos.

Suggestions for 12-26.
Explain *desplegable* by referring to the drawing. After students complete the *Segunda fase*, you may wish to have a display of the ads for the futuristic inventions of the whole class.

Este DVD es mucho mejor que el tuyo porque:

- El DVD nuestro es pequeño. Lo puedes llevar en tu bolsillo o cartera.
- El DVD nuestro es desplegable.
- El DVD nuestro te permite ver tus películas favoritas en una pantalla grande.

Para más información, visita nuestro sitio web www.mp3origami.com.

 SEGUNDA FASE. Describan sus inventos a su grupo. Decidan entre todos cuál es el más creativo y el más útil. En su opinión, ¿cuáles serán inventados en el futuro?

SITUACIONES

1. **Role A:** You represent a company that offers a beach-and-sun spring break trip on a Caribbean island. The price includes transportation, hotel, one meal per day, and snorkeling (*buceo*) lessons. Describe your trip to a group of students, contrasting it with the trip being offered by a rival company (your partner's).

   Role B. You represent a company that offers a service-oriented spring break trip to a rural area of Panama. Participants will help build a children's community center. The price includes lodging with a local family and all meals. Participants pay $200 toward their airfare. Describe your trip to a group of students, contrasting it with the one being offered by a rival company (your partner's).

2. **Role A.** A friend of yours has been accepted to your college/university and is trying to decide between it and another school. Mention several positive points about your college/university, and respond to your friend's comments about the other school.

   Role B. You have been accepted to two colleges/universities and are trying to decide which one to attend. Ask your friend about his/her school. You already know quite a lot about the other school, so explain some of the differences between it and your friend's school.

Resources

■ SAM: 12-31 to 12-35
■ Supp. Activ. Book: Review of the preterit and imperfect

Note. Information on the history of the Panama Canal can be found in several places in this chapter, including the chapter opener, a *Cultura* note, and the *Enfoque cultural*.

Suggestion. After students have done some of the activities in this section, you may wish to have them come back to this short text to identify the communicative functions represented by each verb in boldface type.

4. Talking about the past: Review of the preterit and imperfect

(José le explica a Alejandra un poco sobre la historia del Canal de Panamá).

JOSÉ: Mira, esta es una foto del Canal de Panamá.

ALEJANDRA: ¡Qué grande! ¿Y cuándo lo **construyeron**?

JOSÉ: **Abrieron** el tránsito por el Canal en 1914, pero sólo en 1999 Panamá **asumió** la responsabilidad total de él. Antes, **estaba** bajo el control de Estados Unidos. Hay datos muy interesantes sobre el Canal.

ALEJANDRA: ¿Cómo cuáles?

JOSÉ: Antes de 1914, los barcos **viajaban** 22.500 km (14.000 millas) para ir de Nueva York a San Francisco. Después de 1914, pasar del Atlántico al Pacífico por el Canal, **resultó** ser un viaje más corto, de 9.5000 km (6.000 millas). **¿Sabías** que en 1928, Richard Halliburton, un aventurero y escritor norteamericano, **transitó** el Canal nadando? **Estuvo** en el agua por diez días y **pagó** el peaje más bajo en la historia del Canal, de sólo treinta y seis centavos.

Cultura

La construcción del Canal de Panamá, que une el Océano Atlántico con el Océano Pacífico, hizo realidad un sueño de más de tres siglos. Requirió la participación de varios países y es una de las iniciativas internacionales que más positivamente ha influido en la economía mundial. El Canal de Panamá se inauguró en 1914 y tiene 71 kms de largo. Ver *Enfoque cultural* para más información.

Piénselo. Identifique los verbos en el diálogo que narran los eventos (**E**) que ocurrieron y los que ofrecen una descripción (**D**) del Canal de Panamá en el pasado.

1. _E_ **Abrieron** el tránsito por el Canal en 1914.
2. _E_ En 1999 Panamá **asumió** la responsabilidad total de él.
3. _D_ Antes, **estaba** bajo el control de Estados Unidos.
4. _D_ Antes de 1914, los barcos **viajaban** 22.500 km (14.000 millas) para ir de Nueva York a San Francisco.
5. _E_ **Pagó** el peaje (*toll*) más bajo en la historia del Canal.

Suggestion. The preterit is presented in *Capítulos 6* and 7, the imperfect in *Capítulo 8*, and the preterit and imperfect together in *Capítulos 8* and 9. You may wish to go back to some of the activities that have students use preterit and imperfect together, and have students self-assess their understanding of the differences in their meaning and communicative function in the context of story-telling.

■ In previous chapters you learned two tenses that Spanish uses to express the past: the preterit (**el pretérito**) and the imperfect (**el imperfecto**). You used the preterit to talk about past events, actions, and conditions that are viewed as completed or ended. You used the imperfect to describe characteristics and conditions in the past, to express habitual or repeated actions, or states in progress at a particular time in the past, and to tell the time and someone's age in the past. In this section you will gain further experience using both tenses to narrate in the past.

Refer to *Capítulos 6* through 8 for a review of verb endings of regular and irregular verbs.

12-27 Un viaje accidentado. Unos turistas hicieron un viaje de turismo al Volcán Arenal en Costa Rica. Mientras viajaban al lugar, el volcán comenzó a erupcionar. Un turista cuenta la historia. Indique si las siguientes afirmaciones narran los eventos (**E**) que ocurrieron o si describen (**D**) el lugar y los personajes.

Una erupción del Volcán Arenal, uno de los volcanes más activos del mundo

Al acercarnos al área del Volcán Arenal, **nos dimos cuenta**[1] _E_ de que todos **miraban**[2] _D_ desde la distancia el humo y la lava que **salían**[3] _D_ del volcán. Algunos **sacaron**[4] _E_ sus cámaras de video y **comenzaron**[5] _E_ a grabar. El guía turístico nos **indicó**[6] _E_ qué hacer. Todos **sabíamos**[7] _D_ que acercarnos al volcán no **era**[8] _D_ prudente. Después de treinta minutos **llegaron**[9] _E_ dos helicópteros y nos **llevaron**[10] _E_ a un lugar seguro. Todos **estábamos**[11] _D_ aliviados (*relieved*) de estar fuera de peligro. Esa noche, les **contamos**[12] _E_ la historia de nuestro escape del volcán a los otros huéspedes del hotel. Nos **hicieron**[13] _E_ muchas preguntas y **hablamos**[14] _E_ por varias horas. Después, yo no **podía**[15] _D_ dormir. **Pensaba**[16] _D_ en los eventos del día, y **sentía**[17] _D_ la tensión y la incertidumbre otra vez. Finalmente **me dormí**[18] _E_ , y **me desperté**[19] _E_ al día siguiente con ganas de continuar la excursión.

Note for 12-27. The Arenal Volcano, one of the world's ten most active volcanos, erupted in 1968 after being dormant for more than 400 years, killing 78 people. Since then it has remained constantly active, emitting columns of ash and steam almost every day, as well as occasional explosions and lava flows.

12-28 Un viaje inolvidable. **PRIMERA FASE.** Ustedes viajaron a Panamá durante sus vacaciones. Tomen apuntes sobre lo siguiente.

1. las fechas del viaje
2. dos o tres actividades relacionadas con estas fotografías que ustedes hicieron en varios lugares
3. el tiempo, las personas que conocieron, la ropa de las personas, la comida
4. algún aspecto de la cultura local que les interesó

Una guacamaya de Panamá

Playa Boca del Toro

Cestos tejidos por los indios emberá de Panamá

Palacio Presidencial Ciudad de Panama

 SEGUNDA FASE. Cuéntenles a sus compañeros/as los diversos aspectos de su viaje. Sus compañeros van a hacerles preguntas sobre sus experiencias.

12-29 La flora y fauna de Costa Rica. PRIMERA FASE. Ustedes hicieron una excursión a los Canales de Tortuguero en Costa Rica para informarse y luego preparar un panfleto sobre la flora y fauna de esa región para los alumnos de su universidad. Sigan las instrucciones a continuación para preparar su panfleto con estas fotos que tomaron. Visiten la página web de *Mosaicos* y sigan los enlaces para encontrar más fotos e información útil sobre los Canales de Tortuguero.

Tomen apuntes sobre...

1. una descripción del Parque Nacional del Tortuguero: ¿Dónde está? ¿Cómo es?
2. las características de las especies de animales y vegetación que hay allí

Iguana en la jungla costarricense

Flor silvestre en Costa Rica

Madre y crío de monos ardilla (*squirrel monkey*)

SEGUNDA FASE. Ahora escriban el panfleto publicitario para atraer la atención de los alumnos de su universidad. Pueden preparar una presentación visual del panfleto, usando las fotos de la *Primera fase* u otras apropiadas.

SITUACIONES

1. **Role A.** You and a friend just started your trip to the San Blas island in Panama, the home of the Kuna people. Call home to say that a) your plane left your city on time; b) the weather between your city and the city where you will take the connecting flight (**vuelo de conexión**) was very bad, so the airline cancelled your flight; and c) you and your friend are at the airport waiting. Finally, d) promise that you will call again soon.

   Role B. Your son/daughter and a friend just left for a trip to Panama. After a few hours, he/she calls you with some bad news. React appropriately and ask pertinent questions. Ask him/her to call you again soon. Wish them a good trip.

2. **Role A.** You just won a trip to the Spanish-speaking country of your choice. Call a friend who has traveled a lot and a) tell him/her the news; b) ask for suggestions about where to go; c) mention how much money you received to spend in the country (**dinero para llevar**); and d) invite her/him to go with you.

   Role B. Your friend calls with some good news. React appropriately and: a) answer his/her questions; b) offer ideas about where to go; and c) accept his/her invitation.

⚙ **Standard 5.2** Students show evidence of becoming life-long learners by using the language for personal enjoyment and enrichment. Costa Rica is famous for its national parks and the preservation of its flora and fauna. Activities like **12-29** help students combine their interest in ecology and nature with their emerging knowledge of Spanish, which may expand their professional horizons and present new options for leisure travel.

Alternate for 12-29. Depending on the size of your class and your students' interests, this may be turned into a small-group activity. To challenge students, you may encourage them to be creative, though accurate in terms of content, in their presentation of the information. Students experienced with computers and the Internet may create a webpage-based activity to share with the class. Those less technology-oriented may write the pamphlet— including visuals—share it in PowerPoint format with their classmates, and request comments or suggestions.

Suggestion for 12-29. Whichever orientation you give the activity, have students make brief presentations to the class. Students in the audience should be expected to react to the content and quality of the information presented by asking questions, offering opinions and suggestions, etc.

Preparation for Situación 1. You may wish to have students do some research on San Blas and the Kuna people.

Resources

- SAM: 12-36 to 12-38
- Supp. Activ. Book: *Mosaicos*

MOSAICOS

A escuchar

Antes de escuchar

12-30 Preparación. Usted escuchará una conversación telefónica entre una agente de viajes y el señor Hernández, quien busca un hotel para él y su familia en San José. Antes de escuchar, escriba tres características que el Sr. Hernández probablemente desea que tenga el hotel y tres preguntas que él probablemente hará.

Escuchar

12-31 ¿Comprende usted? Read the statements below. Then, as you listen to the conversation between Mr. Hernández and the travel agent, check (✓) the statements that best report what was said.

CD 5
Track 39

1. _____ El Sr. Hernández dice que quiere un hotel económico que esté cerca del centro de la ciudad.
2. ✓ La agente tiene varias posibilidades y le describe tres hoteles para que él escoja.
3. ✓ El Sr. Hernández afirma que él prefiere que sus hijos y esposa estén cómodos aunque (*even though*) él tenga que tomar un taxi o manejar mucho.
4. _____ La agente le dice al cliente que su elección no es buena porque el hotel es muy caro y está muy lejos del centro de la ciudad.

Después de escuchar

12-32 Ahora usted. Compartan sus respuestas a las siguientes preguntas.

1. Cuando usted busca un hotel, ¿es más importante que sea económico o que sea de lujo (*luxurious*)?
2. ¿Qué servicios o comodidades prefiere usted que ofrezca un hotel?
3. ¿Cuál es el hotel más cómodo en el que usted se ha alojado? Explique.

A conversar

Antes de conversar

12-33 Preparación. PRIMERA FASE. Cuando alguien vuelve a casa después de un viaje, sus amigos y familiares siempre le dicen: "Cuéntanos de tu viaje. ¿Te pasó algo interesante?" Piense en sus viajes y elija una experiencia durante uno de ellos que podría (*you could*) contarles a sus amigos. Puede usar uno de los temas de la lista.

- perderse en un lugar desconocido
- un artículo perdido
- un error lingüístico o cultural
- un robo
- una situación embarazosa o peligrosa (*dangerous*)

SEGUNDA FASE. Ahora, usando la tabla a continuación, organice sus ideas sobre la experiencia que escogió en la *Primera fase*. Después, marque (✓) los elementos que ha escrito que considera más importantes para su cuento.

EVENTOS	DESCRIPCIÓN (dónde, cuándo, con quiénes y otros detalles)	PARTES IMPORTANTES
1.		
2.		
3.		

Conversar

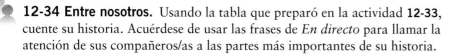

12-34 Entre nosotros. Usando la tabla que preparó en la actividad **12-33**, cuente su historia. Acuérdese de usar las frases de *En directo* para llamar la atención de sus compañeros/as a las partes más importantes de su historia.

Después de conversar

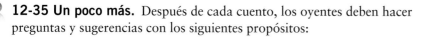

12-35 Un poco más. Después de cada cuento, los oyentes deben hacer preguntas y sugerencias con los siguientes propósitos:

1. aclarar lo que pasó
2. aclarar información sobre dónde y cuándo pasaron los eventos
3. saber más sobre los sentimientos del narrador/de la narradora durante los eventos
4. sugerir maneras de fortalecer (*strengthen*) el impacto del cuento en los oyentes

En directo

To draw a listener's attention to the next part of your story:

¿Sabes lo que pasó después?

¡No lo vas a creer!

No puedes imaginar lo que me pasó.

To express emotions about moments in your story:

¡Y esto me sorprendió mucho!
And this surprised me very much!

¡Estaba tan asustado/a!
I was so scared!

Por poco me muero de la risa/del susto.
I almost died laughing./I almost died, it was so scary.

Resources
■ SAM: 12-39
■ *Entrevistas* video

Suggestion for Estrategia. You may wish to explain that stories about personal experiences are made up of three elements: facts about what happened (usually recounted using the preterit), descriptive background information about the setting, the people, etc. (usually told using the imperfect), and evaluation, which consists of comments on the parts of the story that the narrator wants listeners to pay attention to.

Suggestion for 12-34. Have students work in groups of three so that each person will have enough time to tell his/her story. To maximize the oral storytelling focus of the activity, you may wish to limit students to the notes they wrote in *Preparación*.

Follow-up for 12-35. You may wish to have students write their stories after telling them orally and receiving feedback from the members of their group.

Note about Estrategia.
Previous *Estrategias* for reading have highlighted the visual aspects of texts that help readers anticipate the content and the sequence of topics. This *Estrategia* deals with the rhetorical structure of expository texts, which include advantages and disadvantages, problems and solutions, comparisons, and advice/recommendations.

Suggestion for 12-36. You may wish to have students read the title of the text and, in conjunction with activity 12-36, try to guess what the text will be about.

A leer

ESTRATEGIA

Focus on logical relationships

Magazine articles often address current issues, such as identity theft, sedentary lifestyles, or travel comfort and convenience. When you read an article of this type, you can take advantage of its structure to maximize your comprehension. As you read, look for the issues or problems that the author introduces, and then focus on the logical relationships that the author establishes, such as between problems and their causes, or problems and their solutions. An individual case often appears at the beginning of the article as an example of the problem, and then returns at the end to illustrate a possible solution.

Antes de leer

12-36 Preparación. PRIMERA FASE. Marque (✓) las oraciones que reflejan su opinión y sus experiencias con respecto a los viajes. Answers may vary.

1. _____ Prefiero viajar por tierra porque los autobuses y los carros son más seguros que los aviones.
2. _____ Me encantan los viajes por avión porque son más rápidos.
3. _____ Cuando viajo por avión, no facturo mi maleta porque no quiero que la aerolínea la pierda.
4. _____ Me molestan mucho las medidas (*measures*) de seguridad en los aeropuertos, como quitarme los zapatos y limitar la cantidad de líquidos.
5. _____ Prefiero organizar mi propio viaje que comprar un paquete de hotel, comida, excursiones, etc., por medio de una agencia de viajes.
6. _____ Me gusta alquilar un auto cuando viajo para explorar los lugares nuevos.
7. _____ Cuando viajo, siempre llevo el dinero y las tarjetas de crédito en un cinturón especial o en una bolsa debajo de mi ropa, no en la billetera.
8. _____ He tenido problemas alguna vez para cruzar una frontera internacional.

SEGUNDA FASE. Ahora comparen sus respuestas y respondan a las siguientes preguntas.

1. ¿Qué preferencias de viaje tienen ustedes en común?
2. ¿Qué experiencias de viaje tienen ustedes en común?
3. ¿Qué problema serio ha tenido cada uno/a de ustedes en un viaje?
4. ¿Han tenido problemas semejantes o diferentes?

Leer

Vacaciones o pesadilla[1]: Cómo reducir los problemas en los viajes

Isabel y Mario, una pareja de nacionalidad norteamericana y origen uruguayo, decidieron celebrar su aniversario de boda en Costa Rica. Para preparar el viaje se pusieron en contacto por Internet con una agencia de nombre algo pomposo, y desgraciadamente irónico, como comprobarían[2] después: Viajes Reales. La agencia ofrecía paquetes de excursiones que incluían billete de avión, hotel y coche de alquiler por precios bastante módicos. Las fotos prometían una estancia relajada en un hotel de ambiente exótico al noroeste del país. La variedad de piscinas, la cercanía del mar, la apetecible gastronomía local y los cócteles refrescantes que se veían en lujosas mesitas junto a las hamacas de los afortunados clientes confirmaban que se trataba de un verdadero paraíso.

Isabel y Mario pagaron la cantidad requerida y no dudaron ni un momento de lo acertado[3] de su decisión, a pesar de no haber recibido garantías razonables de que sus expectativas se iban a cumplir. Al llegar a su destino comprobaron que las fotos no correspondían a la realidad. El hotel no tenía ni vista al mar ni jardines exóticos. Las habitaciones eran pequeñísimas e incómodas y la comida dejaba mucho que desear.

Lamentablemente, esta no es una anécdota aislada entre los viajeros. ¿Quién no ha sufrido alguna vez la pérdida de su equipaje, las incomodidades de un vuelo cancelado, el robo de su pasaporte o sus tarjetas de crédito, los problemas en la aduana por comprar un producto comestible que no se permite pasar?

Sin embargo, algunos de estos problemas se pueden prevenir. La experiencia de los viajes nos enseña a ser prudentes y prever los riesgos. La facilidad que proporciona Internet es conveniente, pero cuando se viaja por primera vez es preferible dirigirse a una agencia local para que los especialistas de viajes nos ayuden a elegir las mejores opciones. Frecuentemente es más caro hacerlo así, pero se puede ahorrar tiempo y evitar sorpresas desagradables. Por otra parte, a veces resulta más barato comprar un seguro de cancelación que arriesgarse a perder, por una razón u otra, el costo de un billete de avión.

Algunos incidentes ligados a los viajes son naturalmente inevitables, pero otros se pueden prevenir. Por ejemplo, es posible minimizar el riesgo de un robo llevando los pasaportes y papeles importantes en una bolsita colgada del cuello que se oculta debajo de la ropa, o en un bolsillo doble del pantalón. En cuanto a los impedimentos en la aduana, hay que tener en cuenta que las medidas de seguridad son cada vez más estrictas. Ya no se puede subir al avión con productos líquidos de más de tres onzas y sólo se permite viajar con las bebidas y comestibles comprados en las tiendas interiores del aeropuerto. Recuerdo el disgusto de un amigo mío cuando los agentes de aduana le confiscaron el jamón que le habían regalado unos amigos españoles.

Por suerte, las vacaciones de Mario e Isabel no fueron un desastre total. La pareja pudo disfrutar del maravilloso país en sus excursiones a Puntarenas, Puerto Limón y los parques naturales cercanos a Orosí. También pudieron celebrar su aniversario en un magnífico restaurante de primera clase. ¡Qué lástima que la experiencia completa no fuera tan agradable! Como dice el sabio refrán[4]: Más vale prevenir... que curar.

[1]nightmare [2]would find out [3]the wisdom [4]proverb

12-37 Primera mirada. Marque (✓) los problemas que enfrentan los viajeros, según el artículo.

1. ✓ agencias de viajes deshonestas
2. ✓ maletas perdidas
3. ✓ vuelos cancelados
4. ___ choques de avión
5. ✓ robo de las tarjetas de crédito
6. ___ autos aquilados que no funcionan
7. ✓ problemas para entrar en otro país
8. ___ enfermedades causadas por la comida

12-38 Segunda mirada. Busque en el artículo la siguiente información.

1. Tres problemas que tuvieron Isabel y Mario en sus vacaciones
2. Causa principal de la situación desagradable de Isabel y Mario
3. Recomendaciones para evitar o minimizar los siguientes problemas

Después de leer

12-39 Ampliación. ¿Qué palabras y frases del artículo están asociadas con las siguientes funciones retóricas?

1. Una agencia quiere hacer publicidad para atraer clientes.
2. Los problemas que tienen algunas personas durante un viaje:
   a. la pérdida de su equipaje
   b. un vuelo cancelado
   c. encuentros con los oficiales en los aeropuertos (aduana, seguridad)
3. Presentar el tema del artículo por medio de un refrán.

A escribir

<table>
<tr><td>ESTRATEGIA</td><td>

Use facts to support a point of view

In academic life, you are often faced with tasks that require presenting factual information. Facts are considered objective, neutral, or impartial representations of reality. Therefore, to maintain objectivity, you should provide reliable data, such as statistics, opinions, and statements made by experts, and so on.

Facts also serve as the basis to support a personal point of view on an issue. For example, a person may be against drinking and driving (personal point of view) because statistics show that drunk driving causes accidents (facts).

Therefore, to support your point of view on a particular issue in an objective manner…

■ inform yourself by consulting reliable sources.
■ base your statements on the information you gathered.
■ acknowledge your sources of information.
</td></tr>
</table>

Antes de escribir

 12-40 Preparación. En un concurso, su amigo/a ganó diez mil dólares para viajar a San José, Costa Rica. Puesto que él/ella nunca ha hecho un viaje largo, siente mucha ansiedad (*anxiety*). Por eso, le pidió a usted ayuda con la planificación de su viaje. Para escribirle una carta objetiva y ayudarlo/la, haga lo siguiente:

1. En la página web de *Mosaicos*, lea uno o dos artículo(s) sobre el tema o sobre temas relacionados.
2. Subraye las ideas y los datos concretos.
3. Tome nota de los datos objetivos más relevantes que puedan ayudar a su amigo/a.
4. Seleccione la información y las ideas que lo/la ayudarán a sustentar (*support*) su posición personal sobre la planificación de los viajes.
5. Organice la información y las ideas en orden de importancia.
6. Seleccione las palabras adecuadas para lograr (*achieve*) el tono adecuado.

Escribir

12-41 Manos a la obra. Escríbale una carta a su amigo/a. Incluya la información que preparó en la actividad **12-40**. Además, dele buenos consejos para disminuir su ansiedad.

> *Querido/a amigo/a:*

Después de escribir

12-42 Revisión. Ahora lea su carta y verifique lo siguiente, pensando en su lector/a.

1. ¿Es evidente en la carta la posición de usted sobre la planificación de los viajes? ¿Sustenta usted su posición con información objetiva basada en estadísticas, en evidencia o en la opinión de los expertos? ¿Le da algunas sugerencias a su amigo/a?
2. ¿Sigue la carta un orden claro? ¿Hay transiciones claras entre las diferentes ideas?
3. ¿Usó vocabulario relevante al tema? ¿Usó el tiempo (presente, pasado, futuro) y los modos (indicativo, subjuntivo, etc.) apropiados?
4. ¿Utilizó la puntuación necesaria y la ortografía correcta?

San José, Costa Rica

Resources

■ SAM: 12-46 to 12-47
■ Supp. Activ. Book:
  Enfoque cultural
■ *Vistas culturales* video

Note. Ernesto Cardenal (born 1925) is one of the best known contemporary Nicaraguan poets. A Roman Catholic priest, he was active in the fight against the Somoza dictatorship in his country, and served as minister of culture in the Sandinista government (1979–1987). His poetry covers many different topics: love, history, politics and, of course, religion. *El estrecho dudoso* contains some of his best known historical writing. It deals with the internal struggles among the several Spanish conquistadors in what today are the countries of Panama and Costa Rica. He dedicates some of his most caustic language to Pedrarias Dávila, the man who had Balboa imprisoned, accused of treason, and executed.

ENFOQUE CULTURAL

Centroamérica: un puente entre dos océanos

El poeta nicaragüense Ernesto Cardenal escribió en 1966 un libro de poemas titulado *El estrecho dudoso*[1]. En ese libro, Cardenal reflexiona sobre los viajes de los primeros españoles que llegaron a explorar Centroamérica. Estos conquistadores, entre los que figuran Balboa y Pedrarias Dávila, pronto oyeron hablar de una zona estrecha de tierra que comunicaba el Caribe con otro océano en el sur. Ellos tenían muchas dudas de si verdaderamente existía ese otro océano porque las noticias que tenían eran confusas y contradictorias. Y esta es la razón del título del libro de Cardenal. Sin

El viaje de Balboa entre los dos océanos

embargo, Balboa hizo amistad con Comogre, un jefe indígena, y este lo guió en un difícil viaje a través de las selvas de la región hasta que el 25 de septiembre de 1513, Balboa pudo ver por primera vez las aguas del mar del sur desde una montaña, de manera que él fue el primer europeo en ver el Océano Pacífico.

El Canal de Nicaragua fue una propuesta alternativa a la del Canal de Panamá, pero nunca se construyó.

Después del "descubrimiento" del Océano Pacífico, la importancia estratégica de Panamá y América Central fue evidente. Esta región se convirtió en un verdadero puente entre los dos océanos, de manera que la distancia entre España y sus colonias en América del Sur se reducía mucho. En los años siguientes, todos los viajes hacia Perú, y más tarde hacia las islas Filipinas en el Pacífico, usaron este puente para el transporte. Es imposible saber con seguridad cuántas personas hicieron el viaje entre los dos océanos siguiendo una ruta semejante a la de Balboa, pero lo que sí podemos asegurar es que una gran cantidad de oro, plata, perlas, seda y otros productos de gran valor hicieron este viaje.

---
[1]*The Doubtful Strait*

Era un viaje muy difícil, lento y costoso. El clima extremo de esta región, con fuertes calores y lluvias intensas, dificultaba el transporte, además de que en esa época los viajes se hacían a pie o a caballo y el terreno era selvático y pantanoso. Por estas razones, desde muy pronto los españoles empezaron a pensar en construir un canal para facilitar el viaje entre los dos océanos.

Los primeros estudios recomendaron la construcción de un canal en un lugar diferente de donde hoy está el Canal de Panamá. Desde muy pronto se hicieron proyectos para construir un canal en territorio que hoy pertenece a Nicaragua, aprovechando ríos

El presidente Theodore Roosevelt maneja una de las modernas máquinas usadas para la construcción del Canal de Panamá.

y lagos que existen en ese país. Durante el siglo XIX, Estados Unidos se interesó muchísimo en este proyecto, pero la oposición de Inglaterra impidió la construcción del canal. Sin embargo, Cornelius Vanderbilt, un empresario de Nueva York, construyó una ruta terrestre, paralela al proyectado canal, que se convirtió en la principal vía de comercio entre Nueva York y San Francisco durante muchos años. Y aunque Vanderbilt tenía planes para construir el canal, ese proyecto nunca se realizó. A pesar de eso, los planes para construir un canal alternativo al de Panamá en Nicaragua vuelven a aparecer periódicamente y esa es una idea que no ha desaparecido completamente.

En la década de 1880, La Compañía del Canal de Panamá, una empresa francesa, inició los trabajos de construcción del actual Canal de Panamá. Ferdinand de Lesseps, el ingeniero que construyó el Canal de Suez, fue nombrado presidente de la compañía, pero el mal diseño del proyecto, la tecnología inadecuada, la corrupción, la mala administración y las malas condiciones de salud de esta región paralizaron la construcción. Muchas personas murieron víctimas de la malaria y otras enfermedades tropicales durante la construcción del canal. Entonces, una compañía de Estados Unidos compró los derechos de construcción y empezó a trabajar en el canal en 1904, cuando Panamá se independizó de Colombia. Esta empresa cambió el diseño del proyecto, introdujo nuevas máquinas y finalmente un viejo barco francés, el "Alexander La Valley", fue el primero en hacer el viaje completo a través del canal el 7 de enero de 1914, casi exactamente 400 años después de que Comogre guiara a Balboa hasta el mar del sur.

12-43 Comprensión. PRIMERA FASE. Reconocimiento De Palabras Clave.

Encuentre en el texto la palabra o expresión que mejor expresa el significado de las siguientes ideas.

1. bridge   puente
2. jungle   selva
3. silk   seda
4. swampy   pantanoso
5. enterprise   empresa
6. health   salud
7. machines   máquinas

SEGUNDA FASE. Oraciones importantes. Subraye las afirmaciones que contienen ideas que se encuentran en el texto. Luego indique en qué parte del texto están.

1. A contemporary poet from Nicaragua wrote a book about the first men who explored the region of Panama and Costa Rica.
2. Although the natives gave the Spaniards confusing information, Balboa and his friends clearly understood that there was another ocean nearby, and they were quick to discover it on their own.
3. Balboa was the first European to see the Pacific Ocean.
4. Many people and products were transported across Panama from Peru and other Spanish colonies to Spain.
5. Among the difficulties travelers had to face were extreme weather, travel by foot or on horseback, tropical forests, and swampy terrain.
6. The present location of the Panama Canal was favored by the earliest studies and recommendations.
7. The American company that finally built the Panama Canal had to make major changes to the original design of the project.
8. If Balboa had lived 400 years, he would have been proud to see the "Alexander La Valley" sail the canal.

TERCERA FASE. Ideas principales. Escriba un párrafo breve en español resumiendo las ideas principales expresadas en el texto.

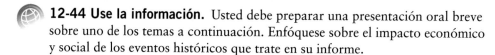 **12-44 Use la información.** Usted debe preparar una presentación oral breve sobre uno de los temas a continuación. Enfóquese sobre el impacto económico y social de los eventos históricos que trate en su informe.

- Cornelius Vanderbilt
- el Canal de Nicaragua
- el Canal de Panamá
- la ampliación del Canal de Panamá
- la ecología del Canal de Panamá

Para preparar esta actividad, visite la página web de *Mosaicos* y siga los enlaces útiles.

VOCABULARIO

Los medios de transporte — *Means of transportation*

el autobús/bus	*bus*
el avión	*plane*
el barco	*ship/boat*
el metro	*subway*
el tren	*train*

En el aeropuerto — *At the airport*

la aduana	*customs*
la aerolínea/línea aérea	*airline*
el asiento	*seat*
de pasillo/ventanilla	*aisle/window seat*
la clase turista	*tourist class*
el mostrador	*counter*
la primera clase	*first class*
la puerta (de salida)	*gate*
la salida de emergencia	*emergency exit*
el vuelo	*flight*

Las personas — *People*

el/la agente de viajes	*travel agent*
el/la auxiliar de vuelo	*flight attendant*
el cartero/la cartera	*mail carrier*
el pasajero/la pasajera	*passenger*

Las partes de un coche — *Parts of a car*

el capó	*hood*
el espejo retrovisor	*rearview mirror*
la guantera	*glove compartment*
el limpiaparabrisas	*windshield wiper*
la llanta	*tire*
el maletero/el baúl	*trunk*
el motor	*motor*
el parachoques	*bumper*
la placa	*license plate*
el radiador	*radiator*
la rueda	*wheel*
el volante	*steering wheel*

Los viajes — *Trips*

la agencia de viajes	*travel agency*
la autopista	*freeway*
el boleto/el pasaje	*ticket*
la carretera	*highway*
el crucero	*cruise*
el equipaje	*luggage*
la escala	*stopover*
la maleta	*suitcase*
el maletín	*briefcase*
el pasaporte	*passport*
la tarjeta de embarque	*boarding pass*
el trayecto	*route*
la velocidad	*speed*

En el hotel — *In the hotel*

el alojamiento	*lodging*
la caja fuerte	*safe*
la habitación doble/sencilla	*double/single room*
la llave	*key*
la recepción	*front desk*
la tarjeta magnética	*key card*

Los lugares — *Places*

la cuadra	*city block*
la esquina	*corner*

El correo — *Mail*

el buzón	*mailbox*
el correo electrónico	*email*
la carta	*letter*
el paquete	*package*
la postal	*postcard*
el sello	*stamp*
el sobre	*envelope*

Las descripciones — *Descriptions*

lleno/a	*full*
vacío/a	*empty*

Verbos — *Verbs*

cancelar	*to cancel*
doblar	*to turn*
facturar	*to check in (luggage)*
manejar	*to drive*
perderse (ie)	*to get lost*
recorrer	*to cover, to travel*
reservar	*to make a reservation*
revisar	*to inspect*
viajar	*to travel*
volar (ue)	*to fly*

Palabras y expresiones útiles — *Useful words and expressions*

el cajero automático	*ATM*
de ida y vuelta	*round trip*
hacer cola	*to stand in line*
seguir (i) derecho	*to go straight*
una vez	*once*

> See pages 410 and 413 for a list of stressed possessive adjectives and pronouns.

Resources

■ IRM: Syllabi & Lesson Plans

Chapter contents. *A primera vista* (p. 432): *La literatura y el cine*; *La pintura y el arte*; *La música y la cultura popular*; ***En acción*** (p. 439): *Diarios de bicicleta: Una novela curiosa*; ***Funciones y formas*** (p. 440): 1. Expressing affirmation and negation: Affirmative and negative expressions; 2. Expressing doubt and uncertainty: Subjunctive with expressions of doubt; 3. Hypothesizing: The conditional; 4. Expressing reciprocity: Reciprocal verbs and pronouns; ***Mosaicos*** (p. 454): *A escuchar:* Identify the speaker's intentions; *A conversar:* Make your presentations comprehensible and interesting. *A leer:* Use your knowledge of narrative structure to support comprehension; *A escribir:* Write to spark interest. ***Enfoque cultural*** (p. 460): *La maravillosa música de los Andes*; ***Vocabulario*** (p. 463).

Note. This painting on wood dates from just after the Spanish arrival in Bolivia. It combines both native and Spanish motifs, representing the cultural encounter of two continents. In this detail we see representations of indigenous people in colorful clothes and surrounded by birds and lush vegetation.

Suggestions. Discuss the painting and describe the figures and the motifs. You may show photos of the indigenous people of Bolivia, who were the source of inspiration for this anonymous artist, and have students describe their features and clothes. Mention colors and shapes. On the *Mosaicos* webpage you will find other examples of Bolivian art. Talk about Hispanic art by reviewing some of the painters presented in previous chapters, such as Pablo

CAPÍTULO

13

Las artes y las letras

Detalle de tabla de madera pintada, siglo XVI. Museo Casa de Murillo. La Paz, Bolivia

In this chapter you will learn how to:

- talk about art and culture
- express doubt and uncertainty
- hypothesize about the future
- describe states and conditions

Cultural focus: Bolivia, Paraguay

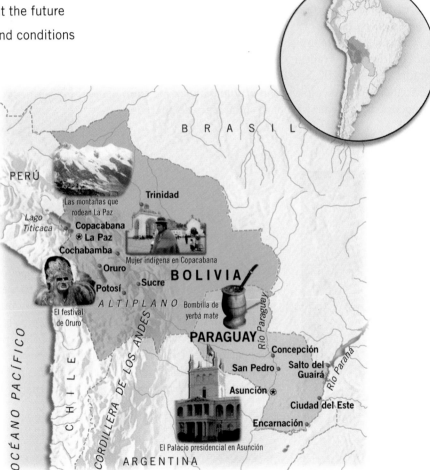

Las montañas que rodean La Paz

Mujer indígena en Copacabana

Bombilla de yerbá mate

El festival de Oruro

El Palacio presidencial en Asunción

 A vista de pájaro. Piense en lo que sabe de Bolivia y Paraguay e indique si las siguientes afirmaciones son ciertas (**C**) o falsas (**F**).

1. _F_ La capital más alta del mundo es Asunción.
2. _F_ El río Paraná está en la frontera entre Paraguay y Argentina.
3. _C_ Bolivia es más grande que Paraguay.
4. _C_ El Altiplano está en la cordillera de los Andes.
5. _C_ El lago Titicaca está entre Perú y Bolivia.
6. _C_ El guaraní es una de las lenguas oficiales de Paraguay.

431

A PRIMERA VISTA

◄)) La literatura y el cine

CD 6
Track 1

Uno de los **novelistas** más importantes de Hispanoamérica es el paraguayo Augusto Roa Bastos (1917-2005). Su novela *Yo, el supremo* (1974) **trata** el **tema** de las dictaduras. Su **personaje principal** se basa en la figura de José Rodríguez de Francia, dictador de Paraguay en las primeras décadas del siglo XIX. Este **escritor** fue uno de los iniciadores del movimiento literario conocido como *realismo mágico* que combina elementos mágicos o irracionales con unas situaciones de aparente normalidad.

Gabriel García Márquez (1928-), colombiano, es otro escritor que se asocia con el realismo mágico. **A través de** sus **novelas** y **cuentos** ha sabido recrear un mundo mítico de gran riqueza humana. En su novela *Cien años de soledad* (1967) narra en tono épico la historia de una familia y la **fundación** y **desarrollo** de Macondo, un pueblo creado en su imaginación. En 1982 este autor recibió el **Premio** Nobel de Literatura. Algunas de sus obras han sido llevadas al cine, por ejemplo, *El amor en los tiempos del cólera* (2007), con el actor español Javier Bardem.

La **poesía** tiene nombres **destacados** en las letras hispanas. Gabriela Mistral (1889-1957), chilena, fue la primera persona de Hispanoamérica en recibir el Premio Nobel de Literatura, en 1945. Algunos de sus temas son el **amor** y la **amistad**. En otros de sus **poemas** habla de la identidad latinoamericana, con su mezcla de sangre mestiza y europea. Otros **poetas** universalmente conocidos son Pablo Neruda, también chileno, y César Vallejo, peruano.

432

El cine hispano ha dado numerosos ejemplos de **calidad** en películas de todos los países. Entre las que han sido **nominadas** o han ganado algún Óscar se encuentran las españolas *Mar adentro* (2004), de Alejandro Amenábar, y *Volver* (2006), de Pedro Almodóvar. La cubana *Fresa y chocolate* (1994), de Tomás Gutiérrez Alea, ganó el Oso de plata en el festival de Berlín, y la colombiana *La estrategia del caracol* (1993), de Sergio Cabrera, fue premiada en el festival de Valladolid. Entre los directores jóvenes más **prometedores** está la española Iciar Bollaín, autora de *Mataharis* (2007) y de *Te doy mis ojos* (2003), que **denuncia** el tema de la violencia doméstica.

Iciar Bollaín

13-1 Cineastas (*Filmmakers*) y escritores. PRIMERA FASE. Llenen la tabla con la información que obtuvieron sobre ciertos hispanos prominentes.

NOMBRE	PROFESIÓN	LUGAR DE ORIGEN	DATOS INTERESANTES	OTRO DATO
Sergio Cabrera	director de cine	Colombia	Ganó un premio en el festival de Valladolid.	
Gabriela Mistral	poeta	Chile	Answers may vary.	
Pedro Almodóvar	director de cine	España	Es el director de la película *Volver*.	
Iciar Bollaín	directora de cine	España	Una película suya denuncia el tema de la violencia doméstica.	
Gabriel García Márquez	escritor	Colombia	Ganó el Premio Nobel.	

SEGUNDA FASE. Comparen su tabla con la de otra pareja, y entre todos hagan una lista de otros artistas o escritores hispanos famosos. Pueden incluir a gente del cine, la música, la pintura, el periodismo, la arquitectura, el diseño de ropa, etc. Incluyan el nombre y cubran los siguientes puntos:

1. profesión   **2.** lugar de origen   **3.** algunos datos interesantes de su carrera

13-2 ¿De qué trata? PRIMERA FASE. Intercambien información sobre un libro que han leído o una película que han visto últimamente. Utilicen las siguientes preguntas como guía.

1. ¿Quién es el autor/la autora del libro o el director/la directora de la película?
2. ¿Cuál es el tema?
3. ¿Quién es su personaje principal? ¿Cómo es?
4. ¿Le gustó la película/el libro? ¿Por qué?

SEGUNDA FASE. Comparta con la clase la información que ha obtenido de su compañero/a.

13-3 Un poema. PRIMERA FASE. Lean el siguiente poema de Gabriela Mistral y digan si las siguientes afirmaciones son ciertas (**C**) o falsas (**F**). Si son falsas, den la respuesta correcta.

Dame la mano

Dame la mano y danzaremos;
dame la mano y me amarás.
Como una sola flor seremos,
como una flor, y nada más...

5 El mismo verso cantaremos,
al mismo paso bailarás.
Como una espiga ondularemos,
como una espiga, y nada más.

Te llamas Rosa y yo Esperanza;
10 pero tu nombre olvidarás,
porque seremos una danza
en la colina y nada más...

1. _C_ Es un poema de amor.
2. _F_ El poema habla de tres personas.
3. _F_ El tiempo del poema es el pasado.
4. _C_ Es un poema alegre.

SEGUNDA FASE. Hablen entre ustedes de la importancia de los siguientes temas en el poema y luego escriban un resumen breve del poema.

1. el amor
2. la naturaleza
3. la danza

 TERCERA FASE. Busquen información en Internet sobre los siguientes poetas hispanos y preparen una breve presentación incluyendo los siguientes datos:

César Vallejo
Alejandra Pizárnik
Pablo Neruda
Federico García Lorca
Blanca Andreu
Adela Zamudio

1. Lugar de origen
2. Época en que viven/vivieron
3. Explicación de uno de sus poemas (tema y características de estilo)

La pintura y el arte

CD 6
Track 2

El Museo del Prado tiene una excelente colección de cuadros de **pintores** españoles, como Diego Velázquez, del siglo XVII, y Francisco de Goya, del siglo XVIII. Uno de los cuadros más importantes de Velázquez es *Las Meninas*, donde **retrata** una **escena** en el palacio real. En esta escena vemos a una hija del rey Felipe IV **rodeada** de sus sirvientas. En el cuadro hay un espejo donde **se reflejan** los reyes. También hay un **autorretrato** del pintor.

Algunos de los mejores pintores del siglo XX, como Pablo Picasso y Salvador Dalí, también son españoles. En este cuadro vemos el estilo **surrealista** de Dalí, con sus relojes **blandos** y su obsesión por los insectos. Este **paisaje**, con el mar **al fondo**, es un **recuerdo** del pueblo del Mediterráneo donde él vivió, y se repite en muchos de sus cuadros. Picasso desarrolló el estilo **cubista** y fue muy original en el uso de los colores y las **formas**.

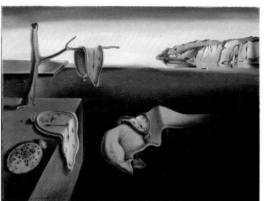

Source: Salvador Dali. "The Persistence of Memory."
© The Museum of Modern Art/Licensed by SCALA/Art Resource, NY. (162.1934). © 2005 Kingdom of spain.
© 2005 Salvador Dali, Gala-Salvador Dali Foundation/ Artists Rights Society (ARS), New York.

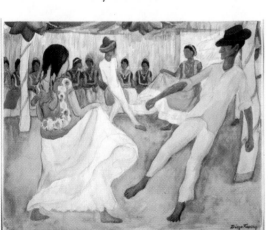

Los mexicanos Frida Kahlo y Diego Rivera muestran en sus **obras** las costumbres y las condiciones sociales de su país. Este cuadro **se titula** "Danza en Tehuantepec" y en él se ve a una pareja haciendo una danza tradicional. Rivera es muy famoso por sus grandes **murales**. Algunos de ellos se pueden visitar en Ciudad de México.

El **escultor** y pintor colombiano Fernando Botero es conocido por sus voluminosas figuras humanas que **se exponen** en todos los museos del mundo. Botero reconoce la influencia artística de los grandes pintores españoles Velázquez y Goya, así como la de los **muralistas** mexicanos. En su obra, Botero critica con humor una sociedad infantilizada o inmadura en la que **abundan** los **símbolos** de la autoridad y del poder, como clérigos, presidentes y burgueses (*members of the middle class*).

13-4 Descripciones. Relacione las siguientes afirmaciones con los pintores correspondientes que se mencionan en las presentaciones anteriores.

1. Pinta con humor retratos de figuras poderosas. Fernando Botero
2. Sus cuadros son de estilo surrealista. Salvador Dalí
3. Es muy famoso por sus murales. Diego Rivera
4. Fue un pintor español del siglo XVIII. Francisco de Goya
5. Es el pintor de *Las Meninas*. Diego Velázquez
6. Es una pintora mexicana que retrata las costumbres de su país. Frida Kahlo
7. Hizo retratos de la familia real. Diego Velázquez
8. Sus formas de estilo cubista son muy originales. Pablo Picasso

 13-5 Biografías. Escojan uno de los pintores anteriores y busquen información sobre él/ella en la página web de *Mosaicos*. Preparen una presentación visual para la clase que incluya lo siguiente.

1. lugar y fecha de nacimiento
2. título y descripción de una de sus obras más famosas
3. algún acontecimiento (*event*) notable de su vida

 13-6 Comparación. Comparen *Las Meninas* de Picasso con *Las Meninas* de Velázquez en la página anterior. Analicen los siguientes aspectos y expliquen cuál les gusta más y por qué.

Source: Pablo Picasso, "Las Meninas, after Velazquez, No. 1." Museu Picasso, Barcelona.
© 2004 Estate of Pablo Picasso/Artists Rights Society (ARS), New York. Bridgeman-Giraudon/ Art Resource, NY.

1. el color
2. la localización de los personajes
3. las formas
4. el estilo

La música y la cultura popular

CD 6
Track 3

El español Paco de Lucía es uno de los **guitarristas** más famosos de la actualidad. Ha sabido **popularizar** la música del flamenco al combinarla con otros tipos de música, como el jazz y la música latina, abriendo grandes posibilidades para las nuevas generaciones de músicos flamencos. Sus conciertos son **inolvidables** por su indiscutible arte flamenco, su destreza (*skill*) y su profesionalidad.

La variedad de la música hispanoamericana, que cubre **desde** la música afrocaribeña **hasta** las melodías de los Andes, es impresionante. Entre todas estas formas musicales, el tango siempre **se ha distinguido** por la riqueza de las **voces** de sus más notables **intérpretes**, como Carlos Gardel. El tango **surgió** entre los europeos que emigraron a Argentina a comienzos del siglo XX en busca de una vida mejor.

La danza latinoamericana tiene una larga tradición, tanto en su manifestación clásica como contemporánea. Alicia Alonso, de Cuba, Julio Bocca, de Argentina, y la **bailarina** mexicana Laura Rocha, quien **dirige** su propia **compañía**, Barro Rojo, se han presentado en muchos países de América Latina, en Estados Unidos y en Europa.

Los actores son a menudo los protagonistas de las **revistas del corazón**. Los medios de comunicación hablan de sus **éxitos** y de sus **fracasos**, de sus relaciones y de la ropa que llevan. Considerada una **estrella** en Argentina, su país natal, Cecilia Roth vivió como exiliada política en España durante los años 70 y principios de los 80. Allí **actuó** en algunas películas conocidas y se hizo muy famosa al protagonizar *Todo sobre mi madre*, dirigida por Pedro Almodóvar.

13-7 Información. Asocie la descripción de la columna de la izquierda con la expresión apropiada de la columna de la derecha.

1. _e_ lo contrario del éxito
2. _f_ un/a artista muy famoso/a
3. _a_ una persona cuya profesión es la danza
4. _b_ un grupo de artistas que hace un espectáculo
5. _c_ un espectáculo de música
6. _d_ una publicación sobre la vida de los artistas

a. un bailarín/una bailarina
b. una compañía
c. un concierto
d. una revista del corazón
e. el fracaso
f. una estrella

Cultura

El flamenco es un tipo de música que se originó en Andalucía, en el sur de España, hacia el siglo XV. Inicialmente eran canciones breves, sin acompañamiento instrumental, que los gitanos (*gypsies*) cantaban para lamentarse de sus malas condiciones de vida. A través de los siglos, el flamenco ha continuado su desarrollo y ha añadido instrumentos musicales, principalmente la guitarra. A partir del siglo XVIII adquirió gran popularidad el baile flamenco, que es uno de los más emocionantes y variados del mundo.

Cultura

La música de Hispanoamérica incluye una gran variedad de instrumentos, desde los tambores y trompetas, de la música del Caribe, hasta las quenas y los charangos característicos de los Andes. La quena es una flauta tradicional, generalmente de bambú, y el charango es parecido a una guitarra pero más pequeño. El instrumento típico del tango argentino es el bandoneón, que es como un acordeón con botones a los lados. La música típica de Paraguay incluye en ocasiones el arpa (*harp*).

Suggestion. Bring samples of music to class from different regions of Latin American and Spain. Have students recognize the styles (salsa, tango, Andean music, Cuban jazz, flamenco, etc.) and some of the instruments. Refer students to the *Enfoque cultural* for more information about the music of Bolivia and Paraguay.

13-8 Personajes célebres. PRIMERA FASE. Usted va a escribir un breve artículo sobre uno de los personajes mencionados en *A primera vista*. Escriba al menos ocho preguntas relacionadas con los siguientes aspectos de su vida que usted investigará para su artículo.

1. su lugar de origen
2. su familia
3. algún recuerdo o anécdota de su vida
4. los inicios de su carrera artística
5. sus mayores éxitos y sus fracasos
6. sus planes para el futuro

 SEGUNDA FASE. Busque en Internet información sobre este personaje y escriba un breve artículo sobre él/ella incluyendo esta información. Comparta el contenido de este artículo con la clase.

 13-9 La cultura en los medios de comunicación. PRIMERA FASE. En una revista o un periódico en español escoja un artículo sobre algún concierto o película que le interese, léalo y resúmalo.

SEGUNDA FASE. Comparta con la clase el contenido del artículo que leyó en la *Primera fase*. Puede incluir la siguiente información en su presentación:

1. ¿Cómo se llama la revista o el periódico de donde obtuvo el artículo?
2. ¿Quién lo escribió?
3. ¿Cuál es el tema del artículo?
4. ¿Cuáles son las ideas centrales que se presentan?
5. ¿Por qué escogió usted este artículo?
6. ¿Cuál es su opinión sobre el contenido del artículo?

CD 6
Track 4
13-10 ¿Adónde vamos? You will listen to a young couple trying to decide where to go on a Friday evening. Before you listen, list three places where you think they might want to go.

Now, pay attention to the general idea of what is said. As you listen, circle the appropriate ending for each statement.

1. Entre los eventos culturales a los que Alberto y Josefina consideran ir están...
   a. una exposición de arte precolombino.
   b. una lectura de poemas.
   c. un concierto de música popular.
2. Josefina prefiere ir al...
   a. concierto de la orquesta sinfónica.
   b. museo de arte latinoamericano.
   c. lugar que sea más barato.
3. Para averiguar si hay entradas, Josefina va a...
   a. usar Internet.
   b. llamar por teléfono a todos los lugares.
   c. ir personalmente al centro.
4. Según esta conversación podemos ver que...
   a. Alberto siempre decide a qué lugar van a ir y no escucha a nadie.
   b. Josefina no acepta ninguna sugerencia e impone su voluntad.
   c. Alberto y Josefina discuten las posibilidades y deciden juntos.

Cultura

El boliviano es la moneda oficial de Bolivia. $1 es equivalente a 7.5 BOB.

EN ACCIÓN

Diarios de bicicleta: Una novela curiosa

Antes de ver

13-11 En este segmento, Javier escribe una descripción de sus amigos. ¿Qué cree usted que dice sobre ellos? Escriba dos adjetivos que usted usaría para describir a cada persona: Luciana, Daniel y Gabi. Answers may vary.

Mientras ve

13-12 En la novela de Javier, ¿a quién se refiere cada afirmación?

__G__ No tiene talento ni para ver una película, mucho menos para actuar en una.

__L__ La gracia que tiene está sólo en las letras de su nombre.

__D__ Es una lástima que... sea un alcornoque de primera clase.

¿Puede adivinar lo que significa *alcornoque* en este contexto?

a. tonto   **b.** tacaño   **c.** antipático

Después de ver

13-13 Ahora Luciana, Gabi y Daniel quieren escribir una descripción de Javier. ¿Qué cree usted que van a escribir? Escriba cinco oraciones que tal vez formen parte de la descripción de Javier. Answers may vary.

Resources
- Video
- SAM: 13-11 to 13-13

Suggestion. Following the theme of the chapter, Javier is engaging in creative writing. Ask students if they have written creative prose or poetry: *¿Escriben poemas? ¿Intentaron alguna vez escribir una novela? ¿Qué es más fácil, describir o narrar?*

Suggestion. You may wish to ask students to expand on these one-line descriptions. *¿Qué más dice Javier sobre sus amigos? ¿Qué otras descripciones comprendieron ustedes?*

Standard 1.2 Students understand and interpret written and spoken language on a variety of topics. The video segment and activities in each chapter provide students with opportunities to expand their comprehension skills by applying the strategy of anticipating what they are going to hear.

In this chapter, students base their predictions about what Javier has written about his friends on their understanding of earlier video segments, which includes their comprehension of the language as well as their grasp of the relationships among the characters and the humorous tone, which have been created by the writers of the script and through the performance of the actors.

FUNCIONES Y FORMAS

1. Expressing affirmation and negation: Affirmative and negative expressions

Josefina   Alberto

JOSEFINA: Alberto, ¿sabes una cosa? **Siempre** trato de comprender el arte abstracto, pero no me gusta **ningún** cuadro en esta sala. **Todos** son feísimos. Estoy segura que **nunca** me va a gustar el arte abstracto.

ALBERTO: A mí **tampoco** me gusta el arte abstracto. No hay **nada** aquí que me interese. ¿Quieres ver la sala de escultura?

JOSEFINA: Buena idea. Vamos. Espero encontrar **algunas** esculturas que me gusten.

Piénselo. Para cada oración, indique quién lo dice: Josefina (**J**) o Alberto (**A**).

1. __J__ **Siempre** trato de comprender el arte abstracto.
2. __J__ No me gusta **ningún** cuadro en esta sala.
3. __J__ **Nunca** me va a gustar el arte abstracto.
4. __A__ A mí **tampoco** me gusta el arte abstracto.
5. __A__ No hay **nada** aquí que me interese.
6. __J__ Espero encontrar **algunas** esculturas que me gusten.

- You have already seen and used some affirmative and negative expressions in previous chapters. In this section you will study the most frequently used expressions.

AFFIRMATIVE		NEGATIVE	
algo	*something, anything*	nada	*nothing*
todo	*everything*		
alguien	*someone, anyone*	nadie	*no one, nobody*
todos/as	*everybody, all*		
algún, alguno/a (-os, -as)	*some, any, several*	ningún, ninguno/a	*no, not any, none*
o... o	*either . . . or*	ni... ni	*neither . . . nor*
siempre	*always*	nunca	*never, (not) ever*
una vez	*once*		
alguna vez	*sometime, ever*	jamás	*never, (not) ever*
algunas veces	*sometimes*		
a veces	*at times*		
también	*also, too*	tampoco	*neither, not*

■ Negative words may precede or follow the verb. If they follow the verb, use the word **no** before the verb.

Nadie va a ese museo.
No va **nadie** a ese museo.
} *No one/Nobody goes to that museum.*

■ **Alguno** and **ninguno** shorten to **algún** and **ningún** before masculine singular nouns.

¿Ves **algún** cuadro interesante?   *Do you see any interesting paintings?*

No veo **ningún** cuadro interesante.   *I do not see any interesting paintings.*

■ Use the personal **a** when **alguno/a/os/as** and **ninguno/a** refer to persons and are the direct object of the verb. Use it also with **alguien** and **nadie** since they always refer to people. Note that **ninguno/a** is normally used only in the singular.

¿Conoces a **alguno** de los artistas?   *Do you know any of the artists?*

No, no conozco **a ninguno**.   *No, I do not know any (of them).*

¿Conoces **alguna** de sus novelas?   *Do you know any of his/her novels?*

No, no conozco **ninguna**.   *No, I do not know any (of them).*

> ### Lengua
>
> **Ningunos/as** is used only with plural nouns that do not have a singular form, like **gafas**, for example. **No tenemos ningunas gafas de seguridad.** (*We don't have any safety glasses.*)

13-14 Nada de nada. Asocie cada pregunta con su probable respuesta.

1. __e__ ¿Visitó usted Paraguay alguna vez?   **a.** No, ninguna.
2. __d__ ¿Conoce a alguien en Bolivia?   **b.** No, ninguno.
3. __b__ ¿Baila alguno de los bailes típicos de la región?   **c.** Nadie lo sabe.
4. __c__ ¿Alguien sabe quién escribió la novela *Pasiones griegas*?   **d.** No, a nadie.
5. __f__ ¿Hay muchos estudiantes que viajaron a Bolivia?   **e.** No, nunca.
6. __a__ ¿Conoce alguna canción de Rubén Blades?   **f.** Sólo fueron algunos.

Note for 3-14. The author of *Pasiones griegas* is Roberto Ampuero, a Chilean writer who lives in the U.S.

13-15 ¿Con qué frecuencia? Indique la frecuencia con que usted participa en cada una de las actividades y diga por qué las hace. Después pregúntele a su compañero/a y anote la información obtenida.

MODELO: ver una película en español
       E1: *Veo una película en español todas las semanas porque me gusta escuchar la lengua. ¿Y tú?*
       E2: *Yo nunca veo películas en español porque no tengo un DVD en casa.*

Follow-up for 13-15. Have students change partners and share the information they have just gathered with the new partner.

ACTIVIDAD	YO	RAZÓN	MI COMPAÑERO/A	RAZÓN
ver obras de teatro				
escribir poesía				
aprender bailes nuevos				
asistir a conciertos				
leer novelas como diversión				
ir a museos de arte				
ver películas extranjeras				

Warm-up for 13-16. In this activity, since the partner's visit to the museum already took place, students should use the preterit in their questions and responses. Call attention to the verb forms in the *modelo* and ask some additional questions before students do the activity in pairs. Point out that some questions ask about the partner's experience and others inquire about museum policies.

Suggestion for 13-16. You may wish to have students change roles (asker or responder) midway through the activity or to do it with two different partners, each time taking a different role.

Warm-up for 13-18. Have students tell you what they want to do: *Quiero aprender unas frases en guaraní.* You agree: *Yo también.* Then have students tell you what they do not want to do: *No quiero ir a la ópera...* You agree: *Yo tampoco.*

Suggestion for 13-18. You may wish to highlight the cultural information in this activity by referring students to the photos in the chapter opener and the *Enfoque cultural* section of this chapter. You may want to explain that *tereré*, mentioned in item #6 of this activity, is a popular drink in Bolivia and Paraguay. It is similar to the herbal infusion *mate*, but it is served ice cold as a refreshment in hot weather. It is sometimes flavored with lime juice or lemongrass.

Suggestion for 13-18 Segunda fase. Have students brainstorm ways to respond negatively to others' plans: *Nunca voy a los parques nacionales. No me gusta caminar mucho. No he ido jamás a ningún partido de fútbol.*

SITUACIONES

1. **Role A.** You are a flight attendant on a flight to Asuncion. Ask a passenger if he/she would like to watch the film. Then respond to his/her complaints and requests by saying that a) there are no blankets but you can bring a pillow; b) there are no magazines in Spanish; and c) they do not have iced coffee because nobody ever asks for it.

   Role B. You are a passenger on a flight to Asuncion. Tell the flight attendant that you can never sleep on planes. Ask if you can have a magazine in Spanish and some iced coffee. It's a long flight, and you are in a bad mood, so respond negatively to whatever the flight attendant says.

2. **Role A.** You call the box office of a theater to purchase tickets for a children's play. When the clerk answers, ask a) if sometimes they offer free tickets for children under three; b) if they have any tickets for Friday or Saturday; and c) whether there are any family restaurants close to the theater. You may express your annoyance at all the negative answers you receive when you thank the clerk for his/her help.

   Role B. You are the clerk in a theater box office. A customer calls to ask about tickets for a children's play. Reply that a) they never give free tickets to young children; b) there aren't any tickets for the first day the customer inquires about, but there are some for the second day (but the seats are not good); and c) there are no suitable restaurants near the theater. You are in a bad mood and you let it show during the conversation.

13-16 Una exposición de arte mala. Usted piensa ir a una exposición de arte. Su compañero/a, que vio la exposición y piensa que fue un desastre, va a contestar sus preguntas negativamente.

MODELO: ofrecer excursiones guiadas
E1: *¿Ofrecieron excursiones guiadas de la exposición?*
E2: *No, no ofrecieron ninguna excursión guiada.*

1. ver esculturas antiguas
2. gustar algunos cuadros
3. comer un buen plato en el restaurante del museo
4. dejar entrar gratis a los estudiantes universitarios
5. aceptar tarjetas de crédito
6. ...

13-17 ¡La negatividad es contagiosa! Después de pasar el día con un amigo negativo/una amiga negativa, usted se siente influenciado/a y contesta a todo negativamente.

MODELO: llamar a un amigo
E1: *¿Vas a llamar a un amigo?*
E2: *No, no voy a llamar a nadie.*

1. visitar La Paz alguna vez en el futuro
2. ver alguna película argentina esta noche
3. leer una novela o escuchar música
4. salir con algún amigo a un restaurante peruano
5. invitar a alguien a un concierto
6. ...

13-18 Planeando un viaje. **PRIMERA FASE.** Ustedes quieren hacer un viaje a Paraguay para conocer su cultura. Comenten qué van a hacer allí.

MODELO: pasar una semana en la capital
E1: *Quiero pasar una semana en la capital.*
E2: *Yo también. Es una ciudad bonita.*

1. hacer una excursión al parque nacional en el Chaco
2. visitar el Museo del Barro, un museo de los artes visuales en Asunción
3. conocer las comunidades menonitas (*Mennonite*)
4. comprar unos textiles bordados en ñandutí, el encaje (*lace*) típico de Paraguay
5. asistir a un partido de fútbol
6. probar el tereré, una bebida paraguaya refrescante

SEGUNDA FASE. Conversen sobre dos o tres actividades que quieren hacer en Paraguay. Después, reúnanse con otra pareja, explíquenle sus planes y escuchen los planes de sus compañeros/as. Respondan negativamente a los planes de la otra pareja.

2. Expressing doubt and uncertainty: Subjunctive with expressions of doubt

Resources

■ SAM: 13-20 to 13-26
■ Supp. Activ. Book: Subjunctive with expressions of doubt

ANA MARÍA: ¡Qué buenos son! Es seguro que **ganan** el premio.

JULIO: No creo que **sean** tan buenos, y dudo que **salgan** bien en el concurso.

ANA MARÍA: Es posible que **tengan** éxito, ¿no?

JULIO: Creo que no. No tienen ni melodía ni ritmo. Es dudoso que **ganen**.

Piénselo. Indique (✓) si las siguientes oraciones expresan **certeza** o **duda**.

	CERTEZA	DUDA
1. Es seguro que **ganan** el premio.	✓	
2. No creo que **sean** tan buenos.		✓
3. Dudo que **salgan** bien en el concurso.		✓
4. Es posible que **tengan** éxito.		✓
5. Es dudoso que **ganen**.		✓

Suggestion for Piénselo. To help students anticipate the grammatical explanation that follows, you may help them make the connection between certainty and the indicative vs. doubt/uncertainty and the subjunctive.

■ You learned in *Capítulo 12* to use the subjunctive in sentences that refer to a person, place, or thing that may not exist, for example, **¿Hay algún cantante en este concurso que sea muy bueno?** In this chapter you will learn to use the subjunctive for a related communicative function: to express doubt and uncertainty.

■ When the verb in the main clause expresses doubt or uncertainty, use a subjunctive verb form in the dependent clause (the clause that begins with **que**).

Dudo que **vendan** libros en español.   *I doubt (that) they sell books in Spanish.*

Es dudoso que el actor **llegue** tarde al teatro.   *It's doubtful (that) the actor will arrive late to the theater.*

■ Use the subjunctive with impersonal expressions that denote doubt or uncertainty, such as **es dudoso que**, **es difícil que**, **es probable que**, and **es posible que**.

Es dudoso que **encontremos** artesanía paraguaya en ese mercado.	*It is doubtful that we will find Paraguayan handicrafts in that market.*
Es posible que **tengan** textiles guatemaltecos.	*It is possible that they have Guatemalan textiles.*

■ Use the indicative with impersonal expressions that denote certainty: **es cierto/verdad que**, **es seguro que**, and **es obvio que**. When these expressions are negative, the following verb is in the subjunctive.

Es verdad que el arpa y la guitarra **son** instrumentos muy populares en Paraguay.	*It is true that the harp and the guitar are very popular instruments in Paraguay.*
No es cierto que la música paraguaya se **conozca** mucho en Estados Unidos.	*It is not true that Paraguayan music is well known in the United States.*

■ When the verbs **creer** and **pensar** are used in the negative, the subjunctive is used in the dependent clause. In questions with these verbs, the subjunctive may be used to express uncertainty or to anticipate a negative response. If the question simply seeks information, use the indicative.

SUBJUNCTIVE	
Hace sol. No creo que **llueva**.	*It is sunny out. I don't think it will rain.*
¿Crees que **haga** frío en La Paz?	*Do you think it is/ will be cold in La Paz? (I am not sure.)*

INDICATIVE	
¿Crees que **hace** frío en La Paz?	*Do you think it is/will be cold in La Paz? (I think so, and I am seeking confirmation.)*

■ Since the expressions **tal vez** and **quizá(s)** convey uncertainty, the subjunctive is normally used.

Tal vez el conjunto **toque** una polca paraguaya.	*Perhaps the group will play a Paraguayan polka.*
Quizá(s) todos **empiecen** a bailar.	*Perhaps everyone will start to dance.*

13-19 ¿Están de acuerdo? PRIMERA FASE. Lea las siguientes opiniones y marque (✔) si está de acuerdo o no con ellas.

	SÍ	NO
1. Yo creo que la poesía es fácil de comprender e interpretar.	_____	_____
2. Yo dudo que el fútbol sea más popular en Estados Unidos que en América Latina.	_____	_____
3. Creo que las películas que se hacen en Hollywood en general son muy buenas.	_____	_____
4. Es posible que el cine mexicano sea más artísticamente arriesgado (*risky*) que el cine americano.	_____	_____
5. Es obvio que el rock es más popular entre la gente joven que la música clásica.	_____	_____
6. No creo que los niños del siglo XXI lean tanto como leían sus padres cuando eran niños.	_____	_____

SEGUNDA FASE. Ahora complete el párrafo sobre los temas de la *Primera fase* con la forma apropiada del verbo.

Algunas personas creen que la poesía es fácil de comprender e interpretar, pero otras personas no creen que la poesía (1) ___sea___ (ser) fácil. No piensan que la música rock (2) ___tenga___ (tener) ninguna relación con la poesía. Sin embargo, es posible que las canciones (3) ___sean___ (ser) poemas, ya que muchos profesores las usan en sus clases para enseñar varios aspectos de la poesía, como la rima y las metáforas.

Hay mucho debate sobre el cine hoy en día. Muchas personas dudan que Hollywood (4) ___produzca___ (producir) buenas películas, y es cierto que la popularidad del cine de otros países, como México, España e India, (5) ___está___ (estar) creciendo rápidamente. Es dudoso que las compañías cinematográficas de otros países (6) ___puedan___ (poder) gastar tanto dinero en sus películas como las de Estados Unidos. En consecuencia, es verdad que en el cine de Hollywood siempre se (7) ___encuentran___ (encontrar) más efectos especiales y otros elementos costosos de los que se (8) ___ven___ (ver) en las películas hechas en otros países.

13-20 Opiniones. Intercambien opiniones sobre los siguientes temas. Después, comparen sus opiniones con las de otros compañeros/otras compañeras y compartan el resultado con la clase. Usen expresiones de certeza y duda (*creo/no creo*; *dudo/no dudo*; *tal vez/quizás*) en su conversación.

MODELO: el cine de Hollywood
E1: *Creo que el cine de Hollywood es malo. Prefiero ver películas extranjeras. Y tú, ¿qué opinas?*
E2: *Dudo que todas las películas de Hollywood sean malas. Hay unas que me gustan mucho.*

1. las películas de acción
2. leer novelas como diversión
3. la música country
4. ver exposiciones de arte

Follow-up for 13-19 Primera fase. Check how many students agreed or disagreed with the statements. Have them explain.

En directo

To report agreement:
Todos creemos/pensamos que…
Nosotros estamos de acuerdo con que…

To report different opinions:
No hay consenso entre nosotros/ellos. Unos piensan que… , otros creen que…

Note: Gael García Bernal is a Mexican actor who has appeared in *The Motorcycle Diaries, Babel,* and *Blindness,* among others.

 13-21 Una cena con un/a artista famoso/a. PRIMERA FASE. Ustedes ganaron un concurso, y su premio es cenar con un/una cantante, pintor/a, autor/a, etc., que ustedes admiran mucho. Escojan a la persona y hagan una lista de tres cosas que esperan que pasen en la cena y tres cosas que dudan que pasen. Expliquen por qué.

Gabriel García Bernal en *Diarios de motocicleta*

MODELO: *Gael García Bernal*

E1: *Esperamos que Gael García Bernal nos hable acerca de sus películas, que nos permita sacarle una foto y que se quede por mucho tiempo en la cena.*

E2: *Dudamos que Gael García Bernal revele información de su vida personal porque él es muy reservado. Dudamos que nos invite a su casa y dudamos que nos cuente los detalles de su próxima película.*

 SEGUNDA FASE. Reúnanse con otra pareja y explíquenle a quién escogieron ustedes y por qué. Infórmenle sobre sus esperanzas y dudas con respecto a la situación. Comenten si están de acuerdo con lo que dicen sus compañeros.

SITUACIONES

1. **Role A.** You are showing a friend how to play the game "Two Truths and a Lie" (**"Dos verdades y una mentira"**). State three pieces of information about yourself, two of which are true and one that is not. Comment on your friend's responses. Then change roles and play the game again.

   Role B. A friend is showing you how to play the game "Two Truths and a Lie" (**"Dos verdades y una mentira"**). Your friend will tell you three pieces of personal information, two of which are true and one that is not. Say which statement you think is true, which is possibly true, and which you doubt is true. Then change roles and play the game again.

2. **Role A.** You are the parent of a high school student who went out last night and got home three hours late. Ask your child to explain the late arrival. Express doubt about at least three things your child says. To avoid ongoing conflict with your child, make sure the situation is resolved.

   Role B. You are in high school, and you can't wait to be free of your parents and their restrictive rules. Last night you went out with some friends and got home three hours late. Now you have to explain yourself. You know better than to say that you just didn't feel like coming home, so you make up a detailed story about what happened. Your parent is skeptical, so you try to convince him/her to believe you. To avoid ongoing conflict with your parent, make sure the situation is resolved.

3. Hypothesizing: The conditional

GLORIA: Aquí veo sólo dos de los instrumentos para el concierto de esta noche. ¿Dónde están los otros?

AMARU: Siempre grabamos digitalmente la música de los otros instrumentos. Yo los **traería** todos, pero **sería** carísimo. **Gastaríamos** demasiado para traer los tambores, las guitarras y las quijadas (*jawbone*), por ejemplo.

GLORIA: ¿Cuánto **costaría** traer los otros instrumentos?

AMARU: Bueno, yo **tendría** que pagar 200 dólares sólo para traer mi guitarra. Para traer todos los instrumentos, **pagaríamos** una fortuna.

Piénselo. Indique (✓) en la columna correspondiente si cada una de las siguientes afirmaciones se refiere a la **realidad** o a una **hipótesis**.

	REALIDAD	HIPÓTESIS
1. Aquí **veo** sólo dos de los instrumentos para el concierto.	✓	—
2. Siempre **grabamos** digitalmente la música de los otros instrumentos.	✓	—
3. ¿Cuánto **costaría** traer los otros instrumentos?	—	✓
4. **Sería** carísimo.	—	✓
5. **Tendría** que pagar $200 sólo para traer mi guitarra.	—	✓
6. **Pagaríamos** una fortuna.	—	✓

■ You have used the expression **me gustaría...** to express what you would like. **Gustaría** is a form of the conditional.

■ The conditional in Spanish is similar to the English construction *would + verb*. It is used to hypothesize about a situation that is not part of the speaker's present reality.

Yo **saldría** temprano para el concierto, pero trabajo hasta tarde.

I would leave early for the concert, but I work late.

■ When English *would* implies *used to*, the imperfect is used in Spanish.

Cuando era chica, mi papá me **llevaba** a los conciertos al aire libre en el parque.

When I was little, my father would (used to) take me to open-air concerts in the park.

Resources
■ SAM: 13-27 to 13-31
■ Supp. Activ. Book: The conditional

Note. The instruments in the photo are *la zampoña* (also called *el siku*), a traditional flute of the Andean region, and *el bombo*, a type of drum (*tambor*). Other instruments mentioned in *Piénselo* are *la quijada* (lit. *jawbone*), a percussion instrument made from the jawbone of a donkey or similar animal, and *la guitarra*. The traditional Bolivian guitar is *el charango*, with 5 double strings, which was adapted from a guitar brought to the Andean region by the Spaniards.

Suggestions. Review the future tense before introducing the conditional and model it in a few sentences: *Este fin de semana pasarán una película española. ¿Irán algunos de ustedes a ver la película? También habrá una presentación de música andina. ¿Asistirá usted al concierto?* Use conditional forms in questions: *De tener tiempo, ¿le gustaría aprender a tocar la guitarra? ¿Qué instrumento le gustaría tocar? Y usted, ¿tomaría clases de alguna lengua indígena?*

You may remind students that the conditional is also used to soften requests and statements: *Me gustaría visitar el museo. ¿Podría darme la dirección?*

Suggestion. Point out that the endings of the conditional are the same as the endings for the imperfect of **-er** and **-ir** verbs.

Suggestions. You may wish to remind students that *haber* is the infinitive of *hay, había,* etc. The verbs are ordered according to the categories of the irregularity of their stems.

■ The conditional is easy to recognize. It is formed by adding the endings **-ía, -ías, -ía, -íamos, -íais, -ían** to the infinitive.

CONDITIONAL			
	HABLAR	**COMER**	**VIVIR**
yo	hablaría	comería	viviría
tú	hablarías	comerías	vivirías
Ud., él, ella	hablaría	comería	viviría
nosotros/as	hablaríamos	comeríamos	viviríamos
vosotros/as	hablaríais	comeríais	viviríais
Uds., ellos/as	hablarían	comerían	vivirían

■ Verbs that have an irregular stem in the future have that same stem in the conditional.

IRREGULAR CONDITIONAL VERBS		
INFINITIVE	**NEW STEM**	**CONDITIONAL FORMS**
haber	**habr-**	habría, habrías, habría...
poder	**podr-**	podría, podrías, podría...
querer	**querr-**	querría, querrías, querría...
saber	**sabr-**	sabría, sabrías, sabría...
poner	**pondr-**	pondría, pondrías, pondría...
salir	**saldr-**	saldría, saldrías, saldría...
tener	**tendr-**	tendría, tendrías, tendría...
venir	**vendr-**	vendría, vendrías, vendría...
decir	**dir-**	diría, dirías, diría...
hacer	**har-**	haría, harías, haría...

Yo **pondría** la pintura sobre la chimenea.	*I would put the painting over the fireplace.*
¿**Podrías** escribir un poema de amor en español?	*Would you be able to write a love poem in Spanish?*

13-22 ¿Qué haría usted? PRIMERA FASE. Lea las siguientes situaciones y marque con un círculo lo que usted probablemente haría.

1. Es el cumpleaños de su mejor amigo, quien sigue cursos avanzados de español, y usted le quiere regalar algo útil.
   a. Le compraría una novela de Roa Bastos traducida al inglés.
   b. Le regalaría *El Quijote* de Cervantes.
   c. Le daría un buen diccionario.
2. El dúo boliviano Tupay va a dar un concierto en su ciudad este fin de semana.
   a. Invitaría a mi novio/a al concierto.
   b. Llamaría a mis amigos para ir al concierto.
   c. Compraría un charango para tocar con ellos durante el concierto.
3. Van a estrenar (pasar por primera vez) una nueva película de Cecilia Roth.
   a. La iría a ver la noche del estreno.
   b. No vería la película porque no me interesa la actriz.
   c. Leería las reseñas (*reviews*) antes de ir a verla.
4. Usted va a pasar unos días en Madrid. ¿Qué haría de tener tiempo para visitar el Museo del Prado?
   a. Pasaría unos minutos en el museo para conocerlo.
   b. Me informaría sobre lo que se puede ver en el museo.
   c. Visitaría las salas donde están las pinturas de Velázquez.

SEGUNDA FASE. Comparen sus respuestas y después digan qué harían ustedes realmente en esas situaciones.

13-23 Fantasías de lotería. PRIMERA FASE. Imagínese que ganó quinientos mil dólares en la lotería. Diga qué haría usted con el dinero y por qué. Considere lo siguiente:

1. lo que haría por un miembro de su familia o un amigo/una amiga
2. lo que haría para alguna organización caritativa (*charitable*)
3. lo que haría para fomentar (*encourage*) las artes en la educación pública

SEGUNDA FASE. Comenten sus planes hipotéticos. Luego, seleccionen el mejor plan, expliquen por qué lo escogieron y compartan esta información con la clase.

13-24 Buscar soluciones. Primero digan qué harían ustedes en las siguientes situaciones. Después comparen sus respuestas con las de otros estudiantes.

1. Ustedes entran en un museo donde se muestran obras de pintores famosos y ven que en una de las salas, que está vacía, alguien está tratando de robar un cuadro.
2. Ustedes consiguieron las tres últimas entradas para un concierto de la cantante boliviana Emma Junaro, e invitaron a una persona importante, pero ahora no pueden encontrar las entradas.
3. Ustedes acaban de descubrir que alguien de la Oficina de Estudiantes Extranjeros está vendiendo entradas falsas y muy baratas para un concierto de música folclórica de Paraguay.

Suggestion for 13-22. Review the cultural material presented in *A primera vista* by talking about it and asking some questions. For example, *Augusto Roa Bastos es un novelista latinoamericano importante. ¿Sabe usted de dónde es? ¿Cuál es su novela más conocida? ¿En qué figura histórica está basada? ¿Quién es Cecilia Roth? ¿De dónde es?*

Note for 13-22. All answers are possible. You may wish to have students explain why they chose their answers.

Suggestion for 13-23 Segunda fase. Maximize the use of the conditional by having students react and comment on their classmates' plans as follows: *Y ustedes, ¿harían lo mismo que proponen sus compañeros/as o harían algo diferente? ¿Por qué harían algo diferente? ¿Sería una buena idea hacer... ? ¿o sería aconsejable + infinitive?*

Suggestion for 13-24. You may wish to have pairs compare answers in groups or with the whole class together.

13-25 Mis planes hipotéticos. PRIMERA FASE. Su nombre aparece en la nómina de posibles Ministros de Cultura de su país. El presidente le ha pedido a cada uno/a de los ministros potenciales un plan hipotético de lo que haría si es elegido/a. Indique por lo menos una medida que usted tomaría con los siguientes propósitos:

1. para educar al ciudadano promedio (*average*) a apreciar las bellas artes (*fine arts*)
2. para identificar y coleccionar algunas formas de arte popular casi extintas
3. para promover la expresión artística entre los niños y los jóvenes
4. para subvencionar (*subsidize*) a artistas jóvenes
5. para exponer obras de arte de manera que lleguen a más personas

 SEGUNDA FASE. Compartan sus planes y escojan uno en cada área para compartir con la clase.

SITUACIONES

1. **Role A.** You decide to speak to a friend who is majoring in literature because you would like some advice. Explain that a) you have written some short stories and your literature teacher thinks they are of excellent quality and b) you would like to send them to a publishing house (**casa editorial**). Ask whether your friend would be able to read them and would help with any necessary revisions.

   Role B. You would like to give your friend good advice, but you need more information. Ask a) what the short stories are about; b) when he/she wrote them; and c) how many he/she has written. Say that you would be glad to read the stories and that it would be a good idea for your friend to ask his/her literature teacher for advice also. Tell your friend that you would have time to help him/her tomorrow.

2. **Role A.** You are considering visiting Paraguay next summer so you call a friend who has been to Paraguay. Include the following in your conversation: a) ask how much money you would need for food and lodging for a month in Paraguay; b) tell your friend that you would like to see a lot of Paraguayan handicrafts; c) ask your friend to recommend some Paraguayan folk music; and d) find out how long it would take to learn Guaraní, the indigenous language of Paraguay.

   Role B. Your friend is thinking of visiting Paraguay, a country you love and know a lot about. Tell your friend the following a) he/she would probably need around U.S.$1,500 for food and lodging for a month if he/she stays at youth hostels (**albergues juveniles**); b) he/she can usually find Paraguayan handicrafts in every city square (**plaza**); c) you would recommend the Teatro Nacional in Asuncion for concerts of Paraguayan folk music; and d) he/she would probably be able to learn some basic expressions in Guaraní during the trip, but it's totally different from Spanish.

Resources
■ SAM: 13-32 to 13-35
■ Supp. Activ. Book:
  Reciprocal verbs and
  pronouns

4. Expressing reciprocity: Reciprocal verbs and pronouns

En general, los artesanos hispanos forman comunidades donde abundan las relaciones de solidaridad. **Se conocen** entre ellos y, puesto que generalmente viven modestamente, **se ayudan** mutuamente. Así lo indican las afirmaciones de Camilo, uno de los artesanos de este taller. "Mario y yo somos amigos y compartimos casi todo. Cuando uno de los dos no tiene dinero, **nos prestamos** dinero. Pero aun más importante, **nos respetamos** el uno al otro porque **nos necesitamos**."

Piénselo. Busque el significado de las afirmaciones de la columna izquierda en la columna de la derecha.

1. __c__ **Se conocen** entre ellos.
2. __d__ **Se ayudan** mutuamente.
3. __e__ **Nos prestamos** dinero.
4. __a__ **Nos respetamos** el uno al otro.
5. __b__ **Nos necesitamos**.

a. Yo respeto a Mario y él me respeta a mí.
b. Mario me necesita a mí y yo lo necesito a él.
c. Mario conoce a Camilo y Camilo conoce a Mario.
d. Camilo ayuda a Mario y viceversa.
e. Yo le presto dinero a Mario y él hace lo mismo para mí.

■ Use plural reflexive pronouns (**nos, os, se**) to express reciprocal actions. In English, reciprocal actions are usually expressed with *each other* or *one another*.

Muchos hispanos **se abrazan** cuando **se saludan**.	*Many Hispanics embrace when they greet each other.*
Los artesanos de este taller **se ven** todos los días.	*The artisans in this workshop see each other every day.*
En este centro de arte **nos ayudamos** mucho.	*In this art center, we help each other a lot.*
Nos llamamos cuando hay una nueva exposición de arte para ir juntos.	*We call each other when there is a new art exhibit so that we can go together.*

Suggestions. Introduce reciprocal verbs and pronouns by talking about visuals you bring to class and/or members of your class. For example, look at a student and say: *Yo miro a Pedro. Pedro me mira a mí.* [use hand gesture] *Pedro y yo nos miramos. Él y yo nos respetamos. Nos hablamos en la clase y a veces nos vemos en la cafetería o en un pasillo y nos saludamos.* Practice *llevarse bien/mal.* You may introduce additional vocabulary and expressions such as *darse la mano, extrañarse/echarse de menos.*

13-26 Indicaciones de reciprocidad. Escoja las ideas de la columna de la derecha que mejor completen las oraciones de la izquierda.

1. Cuando Mario y Camilo no se ven durante el día, ellos __b__
2. El perro y el gato de Mario se pelean todo el tiempo. Ellos __d__
3. Alberto y yo somos muy buenos amigos, pero vivimos en ciudades diferentes. No hablamos mucho por teléfono, pero __a__
4. Mario y Alicia son novios y se quieren mucho. Cuando se despiden por la noche, ellos __e__
5. Mario y Camilo dicen que el secreto de su larga amistad es que ellos __c__

a. nos mandamos correos electrónicos.
b. se llaman por teléfono.
c. se aprecian y se respetan.
d. se detestan.
e. se abrazan y se besan.

 13-27 ¿Qué hacen los buenos colegas? PRIMERA FASE. Determinen si los buenos colegas deben hacer lo siguiente, y bajo qué circunstancias.

MODELO: respetarse
  E1: *Yo creo que los buenos colegas se respetan, a pesar de sus diferencias.*
  E2: *Estoy de acuerdo. En las reuniones se escuchan mucho y se tratan con respeto siempre.*

1. ___ llamarse todos los días
2. ___ comprenderse
3. ___ ayudarse cuando tienen jefes problemáticos
4. ___ insultarse y pelearse
5. ___ regalarse cosas
6. ___ darse consejos cuando los necesitan
7. ___ comunicarse constantemente
8. ___ criticarse continuamente
9. ___ pedirse disculpas (*apologize*) después de una discusión
10. ___ demostrarse empatía

 SEGUNDA FASE. Compartan sus ideas con otra pareja. Luego, hagan lo siguiente:

1. Preparen una lista de las actitudes que ustedes consideran importantes para mantener una buena relación con los colegas en el trabajo.
2. Escojan las cuatro actitudes más importantes y justifiquen su selección.
3. Escojan las dos actitudes que consideran las más problemáticas. Den ejemplos de los problemas que podrían causar entre colegas.
4. Compartan su lista con la clase.

Suggestion for 13-27. You may give examples of what students could say when comparing their lists: *Para nosotros, la generosidad es importante en una buena amistad.* You may also wish to do item #1 with the whole class by brainstorming the desirable/undesirable attitudes and values that benefit or hurt work relations, such as: *el respeto, la consideración, la generosidad, la empatía, la sinceridad, la envidia, el chisme, la mentira, la hipocresía.* It may be helpful for students if you write the two lists in columns on the board/transparency.

13-28 Consejos. Identifiquen los problemas de las siguientes personas. Luego, recomiéndenles una solución.

1. Rafael y Magdalena son novios, pero no se ven con mucha frecuencia. Él es un pintor que vive en Monterrey, México, y ella trabaja en Los Ángeles. Mantienen una relación a distancia.
2. Catalina y Raquel trabajan en un taller de arte. Cuando Catalina quiere pintar un cuadro, necesita absoluto silencio para inspirarse. Pero cuando ella llega al taller, siempre encuentra a Raquel hablando por teléfono con su novio.
3. Los empleados de Pablo tienen miedo de expresar sus opiniones sobre las piezas de cerámica que él crea porque Pablo siempre toma los comentarios de sus empleados como un ataque personal o parece no escucharlos. Sus colegas evitan hablar con él de este tema.

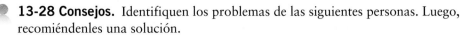

En directo
To complain about something or someone:
Tengo una queja.
I have a complaint.
Quisiera quejarme de…
I would like to complain about . . .
Quisiera hablar con usted sobre un problema que tengo con…
I would like to discuss with you a problem that I have with . . .

13-29 Mis relaciones con… Piense en una persona importante en su vida (padre/madre, novio/a, pariente, amigo/a, etc.) y dígale a su compañero/a cómo son las relaciones entre ustedes. Dé ejemplos concretos. Las preguntas siguientes pueden serle útiles.

MODELO: *Mis relaciones con mi hermano son muy buenas. Nosotros nos queremos. A veces…*

1. ¿Se respetan?
2. ¿Se quieren?
3. ¿Se detestan?
4. ¿Se comunican?
5. ¿Se pelean?
6. …

SITUACIONES

1. **Role A.** You have problems with a colleague at the museum where you work, so you talk to your boss (your classmate). Explain that you and your colleague do not get along (**llevarse bien**) well. Then say that the two of you a) argue with each other a lot at meetings; b) never listen to each other because you are always angry; and c) have to communicate a lot at work, but you never talk in person. Ask your boss for some suggestions to improve your relationship.

   Role B. You are the curator of a museum in La Paz. Listen to the complaints of an employee about a colleague. Ask questions to find out a) what they argue about; b) how often they have to see each other at meetings; and c) how they communicate with each other. Suggest that the two meet (**reunirse**) with a mediator (**mediador**) for several sessions of work therapy (**terapia laboral**) to understand and respect each other better.

2. **Role A.** You are talking with the owner of a popular art studio in your community where you are taking a pottery class. You are new in town and think this will be a good place to meet people. You trust this person enough to ask the following personal questions: a) if he/she has many good friends; b) when he/she met his/her best friend (**conocerse**); and c) what the key (**la clave**) to a long friendship (**amistad**) is.

   Role B. You own an art studio that is very popular in your community. You are talking with a new student who is eager to make friends with people in the class. Share with him/her some of your own experiences. Explain a) when you and your best friend met (**conocerse**); b) how your friendship (**amistad**) started; c) that you do not see each other every day but you stay in touch (**mantenerse en contacto**); and d) that you respect each other, although you do not always agree on everything.

Resources

- SAM: 13-36 to 13-38
- Supp. Activ. Book: *Mosaicos*

Audioscript for 13-31. 1. *A mí me encantan las comedias y los dramas. Aunque por lo general sólo tengo que leer algunas escenas de las obras para mis clases de literatura, yo busco el tiempo para leer toda la obra. Este año vamos a tener otro festival de teatro latinoamericano, donde se presentarán dramas y comedias clásicas y algunas obras de algunos autores bolivianos. El año pasado no pude ir y lo sentí muchísimo, pero este año va a ser diferente.* 2. *Voy a graduarme de la escuela de artes en algunos meses, pero para enseñar necesito estudios de posgrado. Ya he investigado sobre el arte moderno y, en particular, algunos escultores contemporáneos de varios países hispanoamericanos. Afortunadamente habrá una exposición de escultores bolivianos en el salón de exposiciones de la universidad este mes. Esto me ayudará muchísimo para aclarar mis ideas.* 3. *El piano es un instrumento fascinante. Si quieres aprender a tocarlo profesionalmente debes practicar desde pequeño. Si lo haces con dedicación y arte, tendrás muchas satisfacciones. Yo empecé mis clases de piano en la escuela primaria y las seguí durante la escuela secundaria. Ahora voy a casa de mi maestra dos veces al mes para escuchar sus críticas y perfeccionar mis técnicas. Hago esto porque me gusta, y no pienso en el sacrificio ni en las horas que paso haciéndolo. Vale la pena. Nunca lo he lamentado.* 4. *Pinto desde hace varios años. Mi profesor cree que puedo llegar a ser un buen pintor. A mí me gustan las pinturas de Velázquez, Goya y el Greco, pero en realidad, hay algo especial en las obras de los pintores mexicanos con las cuales me identifico más. De hecho, hoy quiero ir a una exposición de arte mexicano. Sé que exhiben las obras de Kamilo Almanza y José Baray. No me la puedo perder.*

MOSAICOS

A escuchar

Antes de escuchar

13-30 Preparación. Usted va a escuchar a cuatro estudiantes universitarios que hablan sobre actividades culturales. Antes de escuchar, haga una lista de tres actividades culturales que tal vez les interesen.

Escuchar

CD 6
Track 5 **13-31 ¿Comprende usted?** Now read the following statements, and then listen to the students. As you listen, next to each statement write the number of the passage associated with the student who probably uttered it.

___2___ Miguel probablemente quiere escuchar o conversar con los artistas latinoamericanos para decidir sus estudios de posgrado.

___4___ Joaquín es el pintor a quien le gusta más la pintura mexicana.

___1___ Rosa María piensa ir a ver las obras de teatro este año.

___3___ Eugenia es pianista y quiere convencer a otra persona de las ventajas de aprender a tocar el piano.

Después de escuchar

13-32 Ahora usted. Comparta sus respuestas con un compañero/una compañera.

1. ¿Es importante que los jóvenes aprendan a apreciar las diversas expresiones artísticas (la pintura, la música clásica, el teatro, o la escultura)? ¿Por qué?
2. ¿Qué aspecto prefieren ustedes, la música o la pintura?
3. ¿Cuál es su pintor o músico favorito? ¿Por qué le gusta?

A conversar

Resources
■ SAM: 13-39
■ *Entrevistas* video

ESTRATEGIA

Make your presentations comprehensible and interesting

When you give a presentation in your Spanish class, your two challenges are a) to make it understandable to your classmates; and b) to make it interesting so they will listen. The following guidelines will help you achieve these goals:

■ Keep it simple. If you use Internet and print sources to prepare your presentation, it should be in your own words. If you copy sentences or paragraphs from your sources or look up a lot of words in the dictionary, your audience will probably not understand what you are saying.

■ Practice your presentation, so you can talk, not read, to your audience. When you read, you tend to go too fast for people to understand you. Use brief notes as a guide, but do not read your notes aloud.

■ Use PowerPoint, photos, and props to make your presentation more lively and interesting. If you have written information on your PowerPoint slides, be sure to talk about the slides. Do not read the text aloud.

■ Involve your audience. Make eye contact, ask questions, check that they understand you, and invite them to ask questions.

Antes de conversar

13-33 Preparación. Escojan a una de las personas de la lista. Luego, busquen la información indicada en la tabla sobre la persona que escogieron. También pueden buscar otra información que les interese a ustedes.

Pablo Casals
Carlos Colombino
Plácido Domingo
Carlos Gardel

Alfonso Gumucio Dagrón
Jaime Laredo
Marina Núñez del Prado
Violeta Parra

NOMBRE	DATOS PERSONALES	PROFESIÓN	LOGROS
_____	fecha de nacimiento: _____ lugar de nacimiento/ muerte: _____	_____ contribución a su profesión:	premios: _____ reconocimientos: _____

Conversar

13-34 Entre nosotros. Hagan una breve presentación sobre la persona escogida en **13-33**. Incluyan la mayor cantidad de información posible.

Después de conversar

13-35 ¡Nos quitamos el sombrero (*We take our hats off*)! Decidan a cuál de las figuras famosas de la actividad **13-34** elegirían ustedes como la persona más admirable. Expliquen por qué, usando las expresiones de *En directo*.

En directo

To support a decision:

Hemos elegido a... porque...
We have chosen . . . because . . .

Lo que más influyó en nuestra decisión fue/fueron...
What most influenced our decision was/were . . .

Nuestra decisión está basada en lo siguiente...
Our decision is based on the following . . .

Alternatives for 13-33.
Depending on the time you have available for class presentations, you may wish to have students do their presentations individually, in pairs, or in small groups.

Suggestions for 13-33.
Students will be able to find information on their famous person in the arts on the Internet or print sources. Encourage them to find out about individuals whose names may not be as well known: Carlos Colombino (Paraguayan painter), Alfonso Gumucio Dagrón (Bolivian writer, filmmaker, and photographer), Jaime Laredo (Bolivian-American violinist and conductor), Marina Núñez del Prado (Bolivian sculptor), Augusto Roa Bastos (Paraguayan writer).

Remind students to follow the guidelines in the *Estrategia* box when preparing their presentations.

Suggestions for 13-34.
Before students begin their presentations, you may wish to remind them to engage with their audience and to speak, rather than read from their notes. Students in the audience should take notes, ask questions, and be ready to answer questions from the speaker and from you.

Suggestions for 13-35. Give students other expressions to use when answering classmates' questions. To acknowledge not having some information:
Lamentablemente, no tengo/tenemos esa información.
Lo siento/sentimos, pero no sé/sabemos...
To acknowledge you didn't think of something, but will look into it:
La verdad es que no pensé/pensamos en eso, pero lo averiguaré/averiguaremos.

ESTRATEGIA

Use your knowledge of narrative structure to support comprehension

All of us have read short stories and novels in our native language, and we are familiar with their structure: a sequence of events involves a conflict or problem that builds throughout the narrative and is resolved at the end. The skillful author weaves the outcome of the narrative by carefully threading together the conflicts created by characters and circumstance.

When you read a narrative in your second language, you can increase your comprehension by trying to anticipate what the characters will do, and how the story will turn out in the end.

A leer

Antes de leer

13-36 Preparación. PRIMERA FASE. Lea el título de la narrativa y examine la foto. Luego responda a las preguntas, basándose en su conocimiento general y su conocimiento del tema.

1. ¿Cuál puede ser el tema principal de la narrativa? Indique (✓) los temas posibles.
   - ✓ **a.** la vida de un etnógrafo/una etnógrafa mientras estudia una comunidad
   - ✓ **b.** una relación romántica que tiene un etnógrafo/una etnógrafa mientras hace su trabajo de campo (*fieldwork*)
   - ___ **c.** una descripción de los miembros de un grupo indígena y de sus viviendas

2. ¿Cómo está organizada la narrativa? Indique (✓) las descripciones probables.
   - ✓ **a.** Puede empezar con una escena retrospectiva (*flashback*) en la que el narrador/la narradora presenta el problema.
   - ✓ **b.** Se presenta a los personajes principales al comienzo de la narrativa.
   - ✓ **c.** Los personajes revelan sus sentimientos y su personalidad por medio de sus acciones.
   - ✓ **d.** El conflicto llega a un punto culminante (*climax*).
   - ✓ **e.** La narrativa no tiene una conclusión definitiva; los lectores tienen que hacer su propia interpretación.

SEGUNDA FASE. Indique si es probable (**P**) o improbable (**I**) que un etnógrafo/una etnógrafa haga las siguientes afirmaciones sobre las costumbres de una comunidad indígena después de vivir en la comunidad.

	PROBABLE	IMPROBABLE
1. Existen brujos (*sorcerers*) que revelan sus secretos sólo a los iniciados (*apprentices*) que quieren aprender.	✓	
2. Los indígenas hablan mi lengua mejor que yo.		✓
3. Me levantaba al alba, es decir, antes de la salida del sol.	✓	
4. Me cubría el cuerpo con ropas extrañas.	✓	
5. Me encantaba comer sus comidas ásperas y desagradables.		✓
6. Cuando recién llegué, tomaba notas sigilosamente (*discreetly*) para evitar las sospechas de los indígenas.	✓	
7. Al clarear el día (*dawn*), siempre tenía sueños extraños.	✓	
8. Viví tanto tiempo entre los indígenas que comencé a pensar como ellos.	✓	

Leer

El etnógrafo de Jorge Luis Borges

El caso me lo refirieron en Texas, pero había acontecido en otro estado. Cuenta con un solo protagonista, salvo que en toda historia los protagonistas son miles, visibles e invisibles, vivos y muertos. Se llamaba, creo, Fred Murdock. Era alto a la manera americana, ni rubio ni moreno, de perfil de hacha,[1] de muy pocas palabras. Nada singular había en él, ni siquiera esa fingida singularidad que es propia de los jóvenes. Naturalmente respetuoso, no descreía de los libros ni de quienes escriben los libros. Era suya esa edad en que el hombre no sabe aún quién es y está listo para entregarse a lo que le propone el azar,[2] la mística del persa o el desconocido origen del húngaro, las aventuras de la guerra o del álgebra, el puritanismo o la orgía. En la universidad le aconsejaron el estudio de las lenguas indígenas. Hay ritos esotéricos que perduran en ciertas tribus del oeste; su profesor, un hombre entrado en años, le propuso que hiciera su habitación en una toldería,[3] que observara los ritos y que descubriera el secreto que los brujos revelan al iniciado. A su vuelta, redactaría una tesis que las autoridades del instituto darían a la imprenta.[4] Murdock aceptó con alacridad.[5] Uno de sus mayores había muerto en guerras de la frontera; esa antigua discordia de sus estirpes era un vínculo ahora.

Previó,[6] sin duda, las dificultades que lo aguardaban; tenía que lograr que los hombres rojos lo aceptaran como uno de los suyos. Emprendió la larga aventura. Más de dos años habitó en la pradera, bajo toldos de cuero o a la intemperie. Se levantaba antes del alba, se acostaba al anochecer, llegó a soñar en un idioma que no era el de sus padres. Acostumbró su paladar[7] a sabores ásperos, se cubrió con ropas extrañas, olvidó los amigos y la ciudad, llegó a pensar de una manera que su lógica rechazaba. Durante los primeros meses de aprendizaje tomaba notas sigilosas, que rompería después, acaso para no despertar la suspicacia de los otros, acaso porque ya no las precisaba. Al término de un plazo prefijado por ciertos ejercicios, de índole moral y de índole física, el sacerdote le ordenó que fuera recordando sus sueños y que se los confiara al clarear el día. Comprobó que en las noches de luna llena soñaba con bisontes.[8] Confió estos sueños repetidos a su maestro; éste acabó por revelarle su doctrina secreta. Una mañana, sin haberse despedido de nadie, Murdock se fue.

En la ciudad, sintió la nostalgia de aquellas tardes iniciales de la pradera en que había sentido, hace tiempo, la nostalgia de la ciudad. Se encaminó al despacho del profesor y le dijo que sabía el secreto y que había resuelto no publicarlo. —¿Lo ata su juramento?[9]—preguntó el otro. —No es ésa mi razón —dijo Murdock—. En esas lejanías aprendí algo que no puedo decir. —¿Acaso el idioma inglés es insuficiente? —observaría el otro. —Nada de eso, señor. Ahora que poseo el secreto, podría enunciarlo de cien modos distintos y aun contradictorios. No sé muy bien cómo decirle que el secreto es precioso y que ahora la ciencia, nuestra ciencia, me parece una mera frivolidad. Agregó al cabo de una pausa:—El secreto, por lo demás, no vale lo que valen los caminos que me condujeron a él. Esos caminos hay que andarlos. El profesor le dijo con frialdad:—Comunicaré su decisión al Concejo.[10] ¿Usted piensa vivir entre los indios? Murdock le contestó:—No. Tal vez no vuelva a la pradera. Lo que me enseñaron sus hombres vale para cualquier lugar y para cualquier circunstancia. Tal fue, en esencia, el diálogo. Fred se casó, se divorció y es ahora uno de los bibliotecarios de Yale.

[1]*hatchet-faced*   [2]*chance*   [3]*awning-like dwelling consisting of animal hides supported by poles*   [4]*would have it published*   [5]*quickly, gladly*
[6]*foresaw, predicted*   [7]*palate*   [8]*bison*   [9]*bound by your oath*   [10]*council*

13-37 Primera mirada. Indique si las siguientes oraciones relacionadas con el cuento son ciertas (**C**) o falsas (**F**).

1. __F__ El narrador del cuento es Fred Murdock.
2. __C__ No sabemos cómo se llama el narrador.
3. __F__ El protagonista es una persona que físicamente llama la atención porque es muy distinto de los demás.
4. __C__ Por su edad, el protagonista no había decidido qué quería hacer profesionalmente.
5. __F__ Las experiencias que el protagonista vivió no lo afectaron para nada.
6. __C__ Al hablar con una persona importante de la comunidad donde vivía, el protagonista experimentó un cambio significativo en su vida.
7. __C__ El descubrimiento de un secreto cambió la vida del protagonista.
8. __F__ Después de volver a la ciudad, el protagonista publicó un libro sobre sus experiencias.

Suggestion for 13-37. You may wish to have students locate in the text the evidence for their *Cierto* responses and correct the sentences they label as *Falso*.

Alternative for 13-38. If you think that your students will have difficulty putting so many events in chronological order, you can label the first five for them. Another option is to separate the sentences into two groups (1–6; 7–12) so that the task is reduced in scope.

13-38 Segunda mirada. Reconstruya el cuento en el orden cronológico apropiado. La primera situación ya está marcada.

_1_ Alguien en la universidad le sugirió a Murdock que estudiara una lengua indígena.

_7_ Entre los indios, se acostumbró a comer su comida, a hablar la lengua de ellos, a vestirse y a pensar como ellos.

_4_ Fred aceptó la oferta.

_13_ Murdock se casó y ahora trabaja en la biblioteca de la universidad de Yale.

_2_ Su profesor le propuso que viviera entre los indígenas para aprender sobre sus ritos y descubrir un secreto.

_11_ El joven etnógrafo salió de la comunidad indígena sin decirle adiós a nadie.

_5_ Antes de llegar a la comunidad indígena, pensó en los problemas que tendría al vivir en una cultura diferente a la suya.

_8_ Al principio, tomaba notas secretamente, las cuales probablemente rompería más tarde.

_10_ El gran maestro espiritual le contó el gran secreto.

_3_ El profesor le dijo que probablemente, a su regreso, se publicaría su tesis.

_6_ Empezó su aventura y se fue a vivir entre los indios por un periodo de dos años.

_9_ Después de algunos ejercicios morales y físicos, Murdock tuvo que recordar sus sueños y contárselos a su guía espiritual.

_12_ El protagonista fue a la oficina de su profesor y le dijo que había aprendido el secreto, pero que no podía compartirlo con nadie.

Después de leer

Suggestions for 13-39. Encourage students to be responsible for the group discussion by asking that each member of the group take notes on the comments about each question. When the class gets together to share responses, each student should be able to report the views of his/her group.

 13-39 Ampliación. Comenten las siguientes preguntas y prepárense para compartir las respuestas con la clase.

Sobre la vida de Murdock en la comunidad indígena:

1. ¿Qué cambios en su vida diaria tuvo que hacer Murdock para adaptarse a la comunidad indígena?
2. ¿Qué hacían los indígenas para aceptar a Murdock en su comunidad?
3. ¿Qué decían las notas que tomaba Fred Murdock?

Sobre el secreto que Murdock descubrió:

4. ¿Qué secreto descubrió el etnógrafo? ¿Por qué no podía compartirlo con nadie?
5. ¿Por qué decidió el protagonista trabajar de bibliotecario en la universidad de Yale?

A escribir

Antes de escribir

13-40 Preparación. PRIMERA FASE. En la página web de *Mosaicos*, busque información biográfica sobre una persona hispana que a usted le interese en uno de estos campos: los deportes, las artes, la ciencia o la política. Obtenga la siguiente información y tome notas.

1. nombre, fecha y lugar de nacimiento: ¿Cuándo y dónde nació?
2. información personal: ¿Es soltero/a, casado/a, divorciado/a? ¿Tiene hijos? ¿Cuántos?
3. estudios y formación profesional: ¿Cuáles son los mayores logros personales y/o profesionales de esta persona? ¿Cómo lo hizo?
4. su comunidad: ¿En qué área se destaca (*stands out*): religiosa, étnica, profesional, científica, artística, etc.? Sus éxitos, ¿han beneficiado a la comunidad? ¿Cómo?

SEGUNDA FASE. Ahora seleccione la información que va a ayudarlo/la a escribir su informe biográfico. Haga lo siguiente:

1. Seleccione los datos personales y/o profesionales más interesantes sobre la vida de la persona escogida en la *Primera fase*.
2. Escriba algunas formas lingüísticas que lo/la ayudarán a expresar información concreta (hechos) y destacar la figura de esta persona.

Escribir

13-41 Manos a la obra. Su comunidad ha decidido empezar una campaña para incentivar a los jóvenes a encauzar (*channel*) mejor sus vidas en un mundo en crisis. Usted es uno/a de los responsables de presentarles a una personalidad del mundo hispano que, en su opinión, representa un excelente ejemplo. Escriba un informe biográfico para una revista electrónica, usando la información obtenida en la actividad **13-40** *Segunda fase*. Su propósito es despertar la curiosidad de los jóvenes por conocer qué sacrificios han hecho los famosos para tener éxito.

Después de escribir

13-42 Revisión. Su compañero editor/compañera editora va a ayudarlo/la a expresar mejor sus ideas para que sus lectores jóvenes se beneficien de las experiencias reales de otros. No se olvide de verificar que...

1. el informe biográfico tenga información interesante para su lector/a, como alguna anécdota o experiencia personal.
2. las ideas estén bien organizadas y el texto se enfoque en la vida y logros de esta persona.
3. su texto tenga un título que capte la atención de su público.
4. haya conexión dentro de los párrafos y entre ellos (use conectores para hacer transiciones).
5. el vocabulario sea variado y dinámico.
6. la ortografía, puntuación, acentuación, etc., sean apropiadas.

Resources
■ SAM: 13-43 to 13-45

ESTRATEGIA

Write to spark interest

To hold the interest of your reader, these tips may prove useful.

1. Be sure you are knowledgeable about the topic before you start to write. Do some research if necessary.
2. Organize the information to keep the text focused on the topic.
3. Vary your vocabulary.
4. When appropriate, add a hint of controversy by including provocative statements or questions.
5. When appropriate, incorporate the element of fun with a personal story or anecdote.
6. Choose a title that will grab the attention of your readers.

Resources

■ SAM: 13-46 to 13-47
■ Supp. Activ. Book: *Enfoque cultural*
■ *Vistas culturales* video

Note. Every two years since 1996 the *Festival de Música Renacentista y Barroca* is celebrated in Chiquitos, Bolivia. More than 18 communities from eastern Bolivia host concerts in their magnificent temples, performing sacred music written by both natives and Europeans during the sixteenth and seventeenth centuries. The festival is organized by the Asociación Pro Arte y Cultura (APAC), whose goal is to share with the world the richness of Bolivian culture.

ENFOQUE CULTURAL

La maravillosa música de los Andes

Normalmente, cuando pensamos en la música andina, nos vienen a la mente las canciones y bailes tradicionales, principalmente de Perú y Bolivia. Sin embargo, la música de los Andes ofrece una gran variedad de otros estilos musicales, muchos de los cuales están relacionados con los ritmos, melodías y cadencias de la música tradicional de esta región. También hay géneros musicales que tienen otras raíces, tanto europeas como propiamente latinoamericanas. En efecto, encontramos en Bolivia documentos que muestran la

Ruinas de la misión jesuita de Trinidad en Paraguay

La quena es uno de los instrumentos más distintivos de la música andina.

existencia de una notable corriente de música barroca que empezó en las misiones jesuitas de los siglos XVI y XVII y que todavía perdura. Y en el otro extremo, hay una variedad de géneros de música popular que tiene muchos seguidores entre la gente joven.

Durante la época colonial los jesuitas construyeron misiones en Paraguay, en Bolivia y en otras regiones del imperio español. En varias de estas misiones utilizaron la música como uno de los medios para conseguir la conversión al cristianismo de los indígenas. Esta historia está en el trasfondo de la película *The Mission*, dirigida por Roland Joffé y con música de Ennio Morricone, que trascurre en las misiones de Paraguay. Recientemente se ha descubierto en las misiones de Bolivia, Santa Ana, San Javier y Chiquitos, una gran riqueza de partituras de música barroca en la que se incluyen varios instrumentos típicos de la región andina. Esta tradición de música culta realizada por la población indígena se continúa hoy en Bolivia gracias al trabajo de algunas organizaciones, como por ejemplo la organización no gubernamental SICOR (Sistema de Coros y Orquestas), que se dedican a enseñar y a diseminar este tipo de música entre los jóvenes del Amazonas.

460

Además de este importante género culto, la música popular andina se distingue por las peculiares melodías y ritmos de sus instrumentos tradicionales. Esta música se reconoce fácilmente por la interesantísima combinación de varios instrumentos autóctonos de

El charango es un instrumento original de los Andes que une las raíces europeas e indígenas de la región.

viento, instrumentos de cuerda adaptados de la música europea, tales como la guitarra, y otras variaciones locales como el charango, y una percusión basada en grandes tambores de madera y cuero. Entre los instrumentos de viento más característicos de la música andina sobresalen la quena, una flauta dulce hecha de bambú, y la zampoña, o siku, una colección de tubos de caña de diferente tamaño, originaria de la región del Lago Titicaca. El charango, el instrumento de cuerda más característico de la música tradicional popular de los Andes, es un curioso instrumento construido con la concha de un armadillo. Muchas de las canciones populares andinas están compuestas en una clave menor, por lo cual transmiten con frecuencia un sentimiento de tristeza que algunos asocian con la pobreza y la dureza de la vida de los habitantes de esta región después de la caída del imperio inca.

A pesar de la riqueza y popularidad de la música tradicional, los jóvenes de la región han adoptado otras formas musicales más modernas. Mucha de la música que escuchan los jóvenes se basa en la de otros países latinoamericanos, por ejemplo, la cumbia, o en la música rock, de la cual hacen adaptaciones locales. Hay una gran variedad de grupos, cantantes y estrellas de la canción andina que mezclan géneros y utilizan algunas de las marcas de identidad de la música andina para componer piezas de ritmos modernos con influencia de la música internacional. En sus composiciones introducen instrumentos eléctricos y los combinan con otros más tradicionales, lo cual produce un sonido muy característico. Con frecuencia también buscan presentar esta fusión mediante los trajes que usan, ya que los diseños unen lo tradicional y lo moderno. Estos grupos son seguidos con gran pasión por sus admiradores jóvenes.

Un capítulo especial en la música de los Andes se debe a una mujer indígena, nacida en Perú, supuestamente descendiente de Atahualpa, el último rey inca. Desde su infancia, empezó a cantar canciones tradicionales de Perú, y a los trece años ya cantaba en la radio de Argentina. Más tarde viajó a Hollywood, donde se convirtió en una verdadera diva, apareció en muchas películas y finalmente se hizo ciudadana de Estados Unidos. La característica más sorprendente de la voz de Yma Sumac era su amplio espectro, que cubría cerca de cinco escalas. Se dice que sólo algunas pocas mujeres alcanzan las notas más altas que ella producía, pero que no hay otra cantante que tenga un registro tan amplio como ella.

En otras palabras

Expresiones bolivianas

Es tan desconfiado/a como **gallo tuerto**.
He/She mistrusts everyone.

Te voy a dar una **samba canuta**.
I am going to spank you.

Expresiones paraguayas

No seas **caigue**.
Don't be lazy.

Suggestion. You may wish to access the official website of Yma Sumac and provide students with some samples of her songs. You will also find photos, interviews, and a biography.

13-43 PRIMERA FASE. Reconocimiento de palabras clave. Encuentre en el texto la palabra o expresión que mejor expresa el significado de las siguientes ideas.

1. roots   raíces
2. followers   seguidores
3. background   trasfondo
4. musical scores   partituras
5. string instruments   instrumentos de cuerda
6. sound   sonido
7. wide range   amplio espectro o registro amplio

SEGUNDA FASE. Oraciones importantes. Subraye las afirmaciones que contienen ideas que se encuentran en el texto. Luego indique en qué parte del texto están.

1. The music of the Andean region is richer than its better known traditional forms. It includes other genres that originated elsewhere.
2. Young people from the Andes have developed a more visual culture than their ancestors, and they are less inclined to listen to music.
3. As part of their missionary work in several parts of the Spanish empire, the Jesuits resorted to the musical education of the Indians as a means to convert them to Christianity.
4. The indigenous peoples of the Andes were not interested in adapting the musical forms and instruments brought by the Jesuits.
5. Today, some non-governmental organizations continue to teach indigenous boys and girls how to play classical music.
6. Traditional folk music of the Andes can be easily recognized by its peculiar combination of several kinds of flutes, different string instruments, and large drums made of wood and leather.
7. The most valued trait of Yma Sumac's voice was her wide range, which covered about five scales.
8. Yma Sumac was an American citizen born in Hollywood, but she claimed to be a direct descendant of the last Inca king.

TERCERA FASE. Ideas principales. Escriba un párrafo breve en español resumiendo las ideas principales expresadas en el texto.

 13-44 Use la información. Escuche alguna grabación o vea un video de la actuación de un grupo o cantante boliviano/a o paraguayo/a y escriba un informe breve. Incluya lo siguiente:

1. Mencione y describa algunos de los instrumentos musicales que usted reconozca.
2. Describa el género de la canción (popular tradicional, popular moderno o clásico).
3. Explique si las canciones están cantadas en español, en otro idioma de la región, o en ambos.
4. Describa los vestidos que usan los artistas y otros detalles que le parezcan más notables.

Para preparar su informe, visite la página web de *Mosaicos* en y siga los enlaces útiles.

VOCABULARIO

Las personas — *People*

el bailarín/la bailarina — *dancer*
la compañía (de danza, de teatro) — *(dance, theater) company*
el escritor/la escritora — *writer*
el escultor/la escultora — *sculptor*
la estrella — *star*
el/la guitarrista — *guitar player*
el/la intérprete — *performer, artist*
el/la muralista — *muralist*
el/la novelista — *novelist*
el pintor/la pintora — *painter*
el/la poeta — *poet*

Las obras de arte — *Works of art*

el autorretrato — *self-portrait*
el cuento — *story*
la escena — *scene*
la forma — *shape, form*
el mural — *mural*
la novela — *novel*
la obra — *work*
el paisaje — *landscape*
el personaje principal — *main character*
la pintura — *painting*
el poema — *poem*
la poesía — *poetry*
el símbolo — *symbol*
el tema — *theme*
la voz — *voice*

Verbos — *Verbs*

abrazar(se) (c) — *to embrace*
abundar — *to abound*
actuar — *to act*
denunciar — *to denounce*
dirigir (j) — *to direct*
distinguir — *to distinguish*
exponer (g) — *to exhibit*

nominar — *to nominate*
popularizar (c) — *to popularize*
reflejar — *to reflect*
retratar — *to portray*
rodear — *to surround*
surgir (j) — *to emerge*
titular(se) — *to be called*
tratar — *to treat, to be about*

Las descripciones — *Descriptions*

blando/a — *soft*
destacado/a — *outstanding*
inolvidable — *unforgettable*
prometedor/a — *promising*

Useful words and expressions — *Palabras y expresiones útiles*

al fondo — *at the back, in the rear*
la amistad — *friendship*
el amor — *love*
a través de — *through*
la calidad — *quality*
cubista — *cubist*
el desarrollo — *development*
desde — *since*
en la actualidad — *at the present time*
el éxito — *success*
el fracaso — *failure*
la fundación — *founding (noun)*
hasta — *including*
el premio — *award, prize*
el recuerdo — *memory*
la revista de corazón — *gossip magazine*
surrealista — *surrealist*
tener éxito — *to be successful*

See page 440 for a list of affirmative and negative expressions.

Resources
▪ Testing Program

Resources

■ IRM: Syllabi & Lesson Plans

Note. *Grafiti* (in Spanish, from the Italian word *graffiti*, and the English *graph*) refers to painting or lettering which is usually done in public places, such as on walls, benches, or trains. It can be found all over the world. Some consider it an art form. Others consider it vandalism. It is often used to communicate social or political messages, although it can also have a purely aesthetic purpose. The graffiti image on this page was photographed in Santiago de Chile.

Suggestions. Point out that this graffiti image was painted on a wall. Ask students to describe it. You may recycle some vocabulary: *cara, frente, cejas, nariz, ojos, calle.* Ask if they have seen graffiti and where: *¿Vieron grafiti en algún lugar? ¿Dónde? ¿Expresaban algún mensaje?*

Los cambios sociales

Grafiti cultural, Santiago de Chile

In this chapter you will learn how to:

- discuss demographics and social conditions
- indicate conditions, goals, and purposes
- express conjecture
- talk about the past from a past perspective

Cultural focus: **Chile**

Arica
Iquique
El desierto de Atacama
Antofagasta
Desierto de Atacama
CORDILLERA DE LOS ANDES
BOLIVIA
PARAGUAY
ARGENTINA
URUGUAY
Isla de Pascua
CHILE
Viña del Mar
Valparaíso
Santiago
Concepción
Valdivia
Puerto Montt
Punta Arenas
Santiago de Chile
Viñas en otoño
Punta Arenas
OCÉANO PACÍFICO
OCÉANO ATLÁNTICO
Estrecho de Magallanes

A vista de pájaro. Complete las siguientes oraciones con información que usted conoce de Chile.

1. El desierto de ___Atacama___, uno de los desiertos más áridos del mundo, está en el norte de Chile.
2. En ___Santiago___, la capital de Chile, viven más de cinco millones de habitantes.
3. Chile exporta ___fruta___ y vino a Estados Unidos. Answers may vary.
4. Punta Arenas es la ciudad más al sur del mundo. Está junto al Estrecho de ___Magallanes___.

¿Prefieren las imágenes o las letras en los grafiti? Ask for reactions to this image: *¿Qué expresa esta imagen, en su opinión? ¿Es triste o alegre? ¿Por qué?*

Suggestion. Ask what students know about Chile. Point out the photos on the map and make comments to introduce some vocabulary as you ask: *¿Cuál es la capital de Chile? ¿Qué países limitan con Chile? ¿Cuáles son las características geográficas del país? ¿Dónde está el desierto de Atacama? ¿Dónde está el Estrecho de Magallanes? ¿Y la Isla de Pascua? ¿Por qué es famosa esta isla?* Explain that Isla de Pascua (Easter Island), also known as Rapa Nui, belongs to Chile. Located in Polynesia, 3,600 km (2,237 mi.) west of Chile, it is a volcanic island known for its large stone statues (Moai). Show the photo of the vineyards and remind students that Chile is a major producer of fruit and wine, much of which is exported to the U.S. The country is also rich in minerals, especially copper (*cobre*), mainly produced in the Atacama desert. Explain that although Spanish is the official language of Chile, some indigenous languages are spoken there, such as Mapuche, which has more than half a million speakers, Aymara, and Quechua. Remind students that they read a poem by Gabriela Mistral in the previous chapter. Ask if they know of other famous authors from Chile. Nobel Prize winner Pablo Neruda (1904–1973) is perhaps Chile's most outstanding literary figure.

A PRIMERA VISTA

◄)) Cambios en la sociedad

CD 6
Track 11 En las últimas décadas ha habido **cambios** muy importantes en el mundo hispano. Varios países, como Chile, Uruguay, Argentina y España, pasaron de tener **regímenes dictatoriales** a ser **democracias** modernas. Michelle Bachelet ganó la presidencia en las elecciones democráticas de Chile en 2006. Esta mujer **políglota** (habla español, francés, inglés, alemán y portugués), médica de profesión y madre de tres hijos, fue la primera mujer en llegar a la presidencia de su país.

En Argentina, Cristina Fernández de Kirchner fue **elegida** en 2007 por una **amplia mayoría**. Su esposo, Néstor Kirchner, la **precedió** en la presidencia. Aunque es la segunda mujer **presidenta** de su país (en los años 70 **gobernó** Isabel Perón), es la primera en ser elegida en un proceso democrático.

Evo Morales, de origen aymara, ganó las elecciones presidenciales de Bolivia en 2005. Es el primer presidente indígena de su país desde la conquista española hace 470 años. Morales se **destacó** muy pronto por su capacidad de organizar a los campesinos en la **lucha** por sus **derechos**. Es un defensor del cultivo de la coca en la región andina como producto natural de gran tradición que se usa para hacer té y con fines medicinales. Sin embargo, se opone a la comercialización de la coca por las bandas internacionales del **tráfico de drogas**.

Las condiciones de vida aún son difíciles en algunos países de Hispanoamérica donde la **pobreza** y el **analfabetismo** todavía son problemas importantes entre sus **habitantes**. Sin embargo, la economía de Chile y de otros países **ha mejorado** considerablemente en las últimas décadas gracias a la **diversificación** de los cultivos y a la intensificación de las **exportaciones**. Hoy en día Chile exporta vino y fruta a todo el mundo.

2002–2008	CHILE	BOLIVIA	COLOMBIA	GUATEMALA
POBLACIÓN	16.454.143	9.247.816	45.013.674	13.002.206
TASA DE CRECIMIENTO ANUAL	0,91%	1,38%	1,41%	2,11%
ESPERANZA DE VIDA ENTRE LAS MUJERES	80,59	69,33	76,5	71,86
ESPERANZA DE VIDA ENTRE LOS HOMBRES	73,88	63,86	68,71	68,22
TASA DE FERTILIDAD	1,9 HIJOS POR MUJER	2,7 HIJOS POR MUJER	2,5 HIJOS POR MUJER	3,6 HIJOS POR MUJER
ANALFABETISMO ENTRE LOS HOMBRES	4,2%	6,9%	7,1%	24,6%
ANALFABETISMO ENTRE LAS MUJERES	4,4%	19,3%	7,3%	36,7%
LA TASA DE DESEMPLEO	7%	7,5%	11,2%	3,2%
MORTALIDAD INFANTIL	7,9 POR CADA MIL NACIMIENTOS	49 POR CADA MIL NACIMIENTOS	19 POR CADA MIL NACIMIENTOS	29 POR CADA MIL NACIMIENTOS

Fuente: CIA World Fact Book

Estos **datos** muestran y comparan algunos de los problemas sociales de Hispanoamérica. Por ejemplo, el **desempleo** es muy alto en Colombia. El **porcentaje** de mujeres analfabetas es más alto que el de los hombres en casi todos los países. Las mujeres guatemaltecas tienen el **promedio** más alto de hijos. La **esperanza de vida** es en general más alta para las mujeres que para los hombres, y Bolivia tiene la **tasa** más alta de **mortalidad infantil**.

14-1 ¿Cómo es la sociedad en Hispanoamérica? Determinen si las siguientes afirmaciones son ciertas (**C**) o falsas (**F**) de acuerdo con lo que leyeron. En caso de que sean falsas, corrijan la información.

1. _F_ Cristina Kirchner es la primera mujer presidenta de su país.
2. _F_ Evo Morales fue elegido presidente de Chile.
3. _C_ Michelle Bachelet habla varias lenguas.
4. _C_ El presidente de Bolivia defiende el cultivo tradicional de la coca.
5. _F_ El analfabetismo en estos países ya no es un problema grande.
6. _C_ La economía de Chile es ahora mejor que antes.
7. _F_ En Bolivia hay menos analfabetismo entre las mujeres que entre los hombres.
8. _C_ Bolivia tiene menos habitantes que Guatemala.
9. _F_ Las chilenas tienen más hijos que las guatemaltecas.
10. _F_ En Colombia se mueren más niños que en Bolivia por cada mil nacimientos.

Cultura

El índice de natalidad en los países hispanos ha descendido de manera espectacular en los últimos treinta años. A pesar de las circunstancias particulares de cada país, esta parece ser la tendencia general. En Perú y Bolivia, por ejemplo, los gobiernos han apoyado campañas para mostrar las ventajas de los planes familiares y el control de la natalidad. En Venezuela, sin embargo, el promedio de hijos ha bajado en treinta años de 6,7 a 2,7 sin campañas por parte del gobierno. Esto se debe a varios factores, como la crisis económica, la escasez de vivienda y el mayor acceso de las mujeres al trabajo y a la educación. Pero tal vez el caso más extremo de esta tendencia es el de España, que ha pasado de ser el país de Europa con más hijos por pareja en los años 1960, a ser, junto con Italia, el país con el índice de natalidad más bajo.

Expansion for 14-1. You may wish to bring to class copies of other tables of data and have students work in groups to create statements like those in **14-1**.

14-2 Los datos demográficos. PRIMERA FASE. Busquen en los textos y en la tabla en la página anterior la información necesaria para contestar las siguientes preguntas. Después comparen sus respuestas con las de otros compañeros/otras compañeras.

1. ¿Cuál de los países en la tabla está más poblado? Colombia
2. ¿Cuál tiene menos habitantes? Bolivia
3. ¿En qué país viven más años los hombres y las mujeres? Chile
4. ¿En qué país crece con más rapidez la población? Guatemala
5. ¿De dónde son las mujeres que tienen más hijos? Guatemala
6. ¿Dónde hay más analfabetos probablemente, en el campo o en las ciudades? en el campo
7. ¿En qué país hay menos desempleo? Chile
8. ¿En qué país se mueren más niños cuando son bebés? Bolivia
9. ¿En qué país mueren antes los hombres? Bolivia
10. ¿Qué país parece que les ofrece más oportunidades educativas a las mujeres? Chile

SEGUNDA FASE. Compare los siguientes temas con datos sobre su propio país:

1. analfabetismo
2. desempleo
3. promedio de hijos
4. mortalidad infantil
5. esperanza de vida para los hombres
6. esperanza de vida para las mujeres

 14-3 Una encuesta sobre las familias. PRIMERA FASE. Háganse preguntas para obtener los siguientes datos sobre sus respectivas familias.

1. número de personas que forman la familia nuclear
2. número de hombres y de mujeres
3. edad promedio de los miembros de la familia
4. número de personas que estudian
5. número de personas que trabajan

 SEGUNDA FASE. Recopilen (*Compile*) la información obtenida. Con esta información, preparen una tabla que indique el porcentaje de familias que hay en su clase...

1. con menos de tres miembros o más de tres.
2. con mayoría de mujeres o de hombres.
3. con edad promedio de 40 años más o menos.
4. con más o menos de dos personas con estudios universitarios.
5. donde trabajan más o menos de dos miembros.

El papel de la mujer

CD 6
Track 12

■ (FEMPRESS) En un reciente estudio realizado en 553 empresas colombianas, Luz Gabriela Arango encontró que sólo el 23,7% de las directivas están constituidas por mujeres. Con todo, el estudio muestra que en este terreno, así como en otros, ha habido enormes cambios. En los años 1950, por ejemplo, todas las sucursales bancarias tenían un varón como gerente. En los años 1990, una alta proporción era dirigida por mujeres.

La encuesta "clase empresarial", realizada a ejecutivos, señala que la confianza en el desempeño profesional de la mujer es mayor que en el del hombre. De hecho, el 96,8% de los entrevistados le dio la más alta calificación a su honestidad; el 80% a la calidad de su trabajo; el 81,6% en materia de confiabilidad; el 79,2% lo dio a su cumplimiento.

En cuanto al manejo de la autoridad, las ejecutivas entrevistadas por *Dinero* consideran que mientras se valora a un hombre por ser enérgico, cuando una mujer asume posiciones fuertes puede causar rechazo. En cuanto al poder, se sienten menos ambiciosas y le dan menor prioridad que los hombres.

Las gerencias administrativas y de recursos industriales en manos de mujeres están aumentando. En algunas entrevistas de *Dinero,* se destaca y se apoya la participación de las mujeres en la empresa pues las consideran más responsables, más comprometidas, más honestas, se ausentan menos del trabajo que los hombres, demuestran mayor eficiencia en el manejo del tiempo y son más transparentes en el trabajo.

Es interesante ver, dice CIDER (Centro Interdisciplinario de Estudios Regionales), las áreas en las cuales se ha concentrado la presencia femenina. Estas son, en sectores financieros y de servicios en el caso de la empresa privada, y en instituciones de servicio y manejo de relaciones públicas en el sector público, como son los ministerios de salud, educación, trabajo y relaciones exteriores. La mayor concentración de fuerza laboral femenina en un alto nivel se ubica en las labores ejecutivas, mientras que sólo el 8,2% de los funcionarios hombres está en ese nivel no directivo.

Estos fragmentos de información reflejan cómo el papel de la mujer ha cambiado y sigue cambiando desde los años 1950 en Hispanoamérica.

14-4 La mujer de hoy. Prepare un informe sobre la situación de la mujer en el mundo hispanohablante, utilizando la información que leyó en las estadísticas (p. 467) y las citas (*quotations*) (p. 469). Compare su informe con el de su compañero/a.

 14-5 Mujeres ejecutivas. PRIMERA FASE. Cada uno/a de ustedes debe hacer una lista de cinco mujeres que ocupan puestos importantes en países hispanos o en su país. Hablen sobre estas mujeres, basándose en los siguientes puntos:

1. puesto que ocupan y responsabilidades que tienen
2. su personalidad y rasgos (*traits*) de carácter
3. obstáculos que cada una ha tenido que superar en su área de trabajo

SEGUNDA FASE. Ahora, comenten lo siguiente.

1. ¿Qué tipo de personalidad y rasgos de carácter tienen en común estas mujeres?
2. ¿Hacen estas mujeres trabajos tradicionalmente femeninos, o han incursionado en el mundo laboral típicamente masculino?
3. ¿Hay semejanzas entre los obstáculos que estas mujeres han tenido que superar? ¿Cuáles son? ¿Cómo han logrado superarlos?

 14-6 Los tiempos cambian. Conversen sobre los logros de la mujer en este siglo y el pasado. Hagan una lista de los cambios que han afectado a la mujer en las siguientes áreas en los últimos 50 años.

1. la familia
2. el trabajo
3. la casa
4. el gobierno/la política
5. la educación

CD 6
Track 13

Temas de hoy: los jóvenes y la emigración

El **desplazamiento** de personas de un país a otro es algo muy común en los últimos tiempos. En general, los jóvenes que emigran de sus países lo hacen por motivos económicos o políticos. Muchos tienen la esperanza de mejorar sus condiciones de vida. Entre los países hispanos, Chile y España son los que más **emigrantes** reciben.

> ### Lengua
> **La emigración** refers to the act of *leaving* one's country to settle somewhere else.
> **La inmigración** refers to *entering* another country for the purpose of setting up permanent residence there.

En Chile, los argentinos y los peruanos son los dos grupos de extranjeros más numerosos. En España también las comunidades peruana y argentina son muy numerosas, sólo superadas por los inmigrantes de origen ecuatoriano. La ventaja de estas **migraciones** inter-hispanas es que todos hablan la misma lengua y esto hace que las dificultades de **adaptación** sean menores.

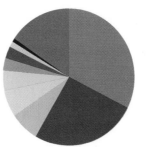

- Argentina
- Perú
- Ecuador
- Bolivia
- Brasil
- Venezuela
- Colombia
- Uruguay
- Paraguay
- Otros

Muchos hispanoamericanos, especialmente mexicanos y caribeños, prefieren emigrar a Estados Unidos **en vez de** a Europa en busca de oportunidades económicas y una mayor **proximidad** con sus países. Los jóvenes por lo general se adaptan más fácilmente que sus padres porque aprenden inglés rápidamente. Además, hoy en día las ventajas de ser bilingüe en EE.UU. son evidentes.

14-7 Los emigrantes. Complete las siguientes ideas con la forma correcta de las palabras de la lista.

bilingüismo	emigración	habitante
condición	emigrante	proximidad

1. En España hay muchos _habitantes, emigrantes_ de nacionalidad ecuatoriana.
2. Una ventaja para los caribeños que emigran a Estados Unidos es la _proximidad_ a los países del Caribe.
3. El _bilingüismo_ es útil para los jóvenes hispanos que buscan trabajo.
4. Frecuentemente las personas se desplazan para mejorar sus _condiciones_ de vida.
5. La _emigración_ es un fenómeno de nuestros días que está relacionada con la globalización.
6. Chile es uno de los países de Hispanoamérica que más _emigrantes_ recibe.

Warm-up. Introduce the theme of immigration by asking students what they know. *¿Cuál es el país o continente de origen de gran parte de la población norteamericana? ¿De dónde eran sus abuelos? ¿Cuántos de ustedes tienen orígenes europeos, asiáticos, africanos, hispanos? ¿Qué comunidades de emigrantes hay en su estado o en su ciudad? ¿Qué productos de otros países se pueden comprar? ¿Qué restaurantes internacionales conocen?*

Suggestion. Remind students that the reasons for emigration vary. Many Cubans in the U.S. left their country for ideological reasons. On the other hand, Puerto Ricans are American citizens and their choice to move to the mainland is often motivated by economic reasons.

Audioscript for 14-9.

REPORTERO: *Buenas tardes, Dra. Gómez. Muchas gracias por acceder a esta entrevista.*

DRA. GÓMEZ: *Gracias por invitarme.*

REPORTERO: *Dígame, Dra. Gómez, ¿cuál es la situación de la mujer en los países hispanos en la actualidad?*

DRA. GÓMEZ: *Bueno, la situación de la mujer ha cambiado mucho en los últimos años, sobre todo en el aspecto legal.*

REPORTERO: *¿Qué quiere decir?*

DRA. GÓMEZ: *Bueno, las nuevas leyes protegen a la mujer, pero así y todo es más difícil para la mujer conseguir trabajo que para el hombre.*

REPORTERO: *Sí, pero hoy muchas mujeres trabajan.*

DRA. GÓMEZ: *Es verdad. Sin embargo, a las mujeres se les exige más preparación. Además, no se les paga lo mismo que a los hombres.*

REPORTERO: *¿Y ha mejorado la situación de la mujer en el hogar?*

DRA. GÓMEZ: *Muy poco. Algunos hombres colaboran con las labores domésticas y en la crianza de los niños, pero es la mujer la encargada de la casa. La mujer tiene dos trabajos, uno fuera de casa por el que le pagan muy poco, y otro en la casa donde no se le paga absolutamente nada.*

REPORTERO: *¿Usted cree que hay alguna esperanza de que esto cambie?*

DRA. GÓMEZ: *Poco a poco las cosas van cambiando. Hay más mujeres que estudian y no forman una familia tan pronto como antes. Las mujeres ahora quieren ser independientes económicamente. Cada vez habrá más mujeres como jefas de empresas, ministras, médicas, abogadas, economistas.*

REPORTERO: *Bueno, Dra. Gómez, muchas gracias por compartir su opinión con nosotros.*

DRA. GÓMEZ: *Gracias a usted.*

14-8 Los habitantes de su comunidad. Preparen preguntas para entrevistar a un compañero/una compañera sobre sus orígenes y las costumbres de su comunidad o grupo étnico. Usen los puntos a continuación como guía para elaborar su cuestionario.

MODELO: E1: *¿Cuál es el origen de tu familia?*
E2: *Mis abuelos eran italianos.*
E1: *¿Cuándo emigraron a este país?*
E2: *Emigraron cuando mi padre tenía cinco años.*

1. origen de tu apellido
2. grupo(s) étnico(s) que asocias con tu familia
3. número de habitantes de ese grupo étnico o comunidad
4. área de concentración en Estados Unidos
5. costumbres e idioma
6. fiestas o celebraciones
7. productos que consumen
8. comida típica

14-9 La mujer en los países hispanos. You will listen to a conversation between a reporter and a Professor of Sociology at the University of Santiago de Chile about the status of women in the Hispanic world. Before you listen, write two questions the reporter may ask the professor and the answers that you think she may provide.

CD 6
Track 14

As you listen, focus on the main ideas of what is said. Circle the appropriate ending to each statement.

1. La doctora Gómez dice que la situación de la mujer ha mejorado porque...
   a. más mujeres son jefas de empresas.
   b. ahora hay más leyes que las protegen.
   c. hay muchas mujeres que no tienen hijos.
2. Según la doctora Gómez, en comparación con los hombres, las mujeres...
   a. no tienen que trabajar tanto.
   b. tienen que estar mejor preparadas.
   c. no estudian tanto.
3. Las mujeres hispanas ganan...
   a. más dinero que los hombres.
   b. tanto dinero como los hombres.
   c. menos dinero que los hombres.
4. En los hogares hispanos, el trabajo de la casa y la crianza de los hijos...
   a. están principalmente en manos de las mujeres.
   b. son compartidos por todos los miembros de la familia.
   c. son la responsabilidad de los empleados domésticos.

EN ACCIÓN

Resources
- Video
- SAM: 14-11 to 14-13

Diarios de bicicleta: Elecciones "presidenciales"

Antes de ver

14-10 Marque (✓) las características que usted considera más importantes en un líder y añada una más. Answers may vary.

___ activo/a	___ culto/a	___ popular
___ atractivo/a	___ decidido/a	___ progresista
___ autoritario/a	___ diplomático/a	___ razonable
___ compasivo/a	___ egoista	___ responsable
___ conservador/a	___ generoso/a	___ solidario/a

Mientras ve

14-11 Escriba los temas que Luciana dice que va a tratar como presidenta. Honestidad, la igualdad para todos, soluciones a los problemas financieros y programas para que todas las personas aprendan a leer

Suggestion for 14-10. You may wish to ask students to qualify their responses depending on the type of leadership position, e.g., *presidente del gobierno estudiantil*, *capitán de un equipo deportivo*, etc.

Suggestion for 14-11. You may wish to have students describe the people in the photo, using different adjectives from the ones above.

Después de ver

14-12 Al final de este segmento, nos damos cuenta de que Luciana es candidata a la presidencia del equipo de natación. ¿Cree usted que Luciana ganará las elecciones? ¿Tiene ella las características necesarias para ocupar este puesto? ¿Cree usted que Gabi ganará las elecciones? ¿Por qué? ¿Alguna vez ha sido nominado/a usted para un puesto en alguna elección? Explique. Answers may vary.

FUNCIONES Y FORMAS

1. Expressing conjecture: Adverbial conjunctions that require the subjunctive

Estos inmigrantes cosechan cebollas en Texas. Según la ley, pueden trabajar en Estados Unidos **con tal de que** tengan estatus legal en el país. Muchos inmigrantes mandan dinero a su familia **para que** sus hijos vivan mejor. Muchos vuelven a su país, **a menos que** su familia pueda venir a Estados Unidos también.

Piénselo. Escoja en la columna de la derecha el significado de las palabras en negrita.

1. __a__ Pueden trabajar en Estados Unidos **con tal de que** tengan estatus.
2. __d__ Mandan dinero a su familia **para que** sus hijos vivan mejor.
3. __c__ Volverán a su país **a menos que** su familia pueda venir a Estados Unidos.
4. __c__ Para muchos inmigrantes es difícil conseguir trabajo **sin que** sus amigos los ayuden.
5. __b__ Los hijos de algunos inmigrantes pasan muchos años con sólo su madre **antes de que** su padre vuelva a casa.

a. si
b. anterioridad de tiempo
c. si... no
d. con la intención

■ Conjunctions are words or phrases that function as connectors in sentences. Some conjunctions introduce dependent clauses known as adverbial clauses, which communicate how, why, when, and where an action takes place.

■ Some conjunctions always require the subjunctive when followed by a dependent clause.

a menos que	*unless*	**para que**	*so that*
antes (de) que	*before*	**sin que**	*without*
con tal (de) que	*provided that*		

Las mujeres tendrán una reunión **antes de que** sus representantes **hablen** con los oficiales.

The women are having a meeting before their representatives speak with the officials.

Las mujeres votarán por los oficiales **con tal de que** ellos **implementen** los cambios mencionados en la petición.	*The women will vote for the officials provided that they implement the changes mentioned in the petition.*
Las representantes negocian con los oficiales **para que** todos los niños **tengan** acceso a servicios médicos.	*The representatives negotiate with the officials so that all children have access to medical services.*

■ Use an infinitive after the prepositions **antes de, para,** and **sin** when there is no change of subject.

Las comunidades ofrecen clases **para que** los inmigrantes **aprendan** inglés.	*Communities offer classes so that immigrants can learn English.*
Los inmigrantes estudian inglés **para aprender** la lengua rápidamente.	*Immigrants study English to learn the language quickly.*

14-13 En el futuro. PRIMERA FASE. Túrnense para leer la primera parte de cada oración y después busquen el final apropiado a la derecha. Deben fijarse (*take note*) en el contexto y también en la forma verbal correcta.

1. _c_ Muchos empleados trabajarán en casa sin...

2. _f_ Las compañías de limpieza programarán los robots para que...

3. _h_ Podremos jubilarnos (*retire*) antes de...

4. _a_ Casi todos los cursos universitarios se ofrecerán en Internet sin que...

5. _g_ Los jóvenes no tendrán que trabajar a menos que...

6. _d_ Habrá computadoras de uso gratis en muchos lugares públicos para...

7. _b_ Los empleados de las compañías multinacionales podrán comunicarse fácilmente con tal de que...

8. _e_ Después de nacer sus hijos, los padres no volverán a trabajar antes de que los niños...

a. los profesores ni los alumnos tengan que ir a la universidad.

b. tengan aparatos de interpretación simultánea.

c. tener que comunicarse con los clientes o colegas en persona.

d. facilitar la comunicación entre las personas.

e. cumplan 5 años de edad.

f. limpien los edificios sin intervención de los seres humanos.

g. les interese hacer trabajo de voluntariado.

h. los 50 años.

SEGUNDA FASE. Ahora escojan dos de las oraciones de la izquierda y complétenlas de acuerdo con sus propias ideas. Después comparen sus respuestas con las de otra pareja.

Suggestion for 14-14.
This activity requires that students choose between the infinitive and a present subjunctive form. To avoid having students respond without understanding the sentences, you may wish to have them focus on the meaning of the conjunctions.

Alternate for 14-15. You may need to have students brainstorm possible responses for E2, as well as various ways for E1 and E2 to start their sentences. You may decide to do one or two mini-conversations as a group before putting students in pairs to continue on their own.

14-14 Una ingeniera se entrevista. La ingeniera industrial María Victoria Martín se entrevista hoy con Sanofi Aventis, una compañía que fabrica medicinas. Para saber qué pasó en la entrevista, llene los espacios en blanco con la forma correcta del verbo apropiado: **decir, hacer, ofrecer, pasar,** o **saber.**

María Victoria llega temprano a la cita con la directora, y la secretaria le pide que espere unos minutos antes de (1) _pasar_ a su oficina. María Victoria trata de tranquilizarse para que nadie (2) _sepa_ que está muy nerviosa. Piensa que podrá dar una buena impresión con tal de que la directora le (3) _haga_ preguntas relevantes a su experiencia. Finalmente la directora se presenta y la invita a entrar en su oficina sin que María Victoria (4) _diga_ una palabra. Al final de la entrevista la directora le ofrece el puesto. María Victoria dice que no puede aceptar la oferta a menos que la compañía le (5) _ofrezca_ seguro médico. La directora acepta esta condición.

 14-15 ¿Estudio en Chile o no? Usted está considerando la posibilidad de estudiar en Chile el próximo semestre. Indique lo que piensa sobre esta posibilidad, usando las expresiones adverbiales de la lista. Su compañero/a va a responder de forma lógica. Answers may vary.

a menos que   antes (de) que   con tal (de) que   para que   sin que

MODELO: el programa sea muy caro
       E1: *Voy a estudiar en Chile, a menos que el programa sea muy caro.*
       E2: *No participes en el programa a menos que te den una beca.*

1. el semestre termine para el 1 de junio
2. mis amigos y yo aprendamos mucho español
3. viva con una familia amable
4. mi familia me visite durante el semestre
5. haya oportunidades de viajar o otros países
6. mi amigo/a también participe en el programa
7. conozca la cultura mapuche
8. pasemos las vacaciones esquiando en los Andes

SITUACIONES

1. **Role A.** You are a Chilean exchange student who recently arrived in the United States. Ask a friend a) what his/her family does to help him/her attend college; b) if in big lecture classes students can use their cell phones and read e-mail without their professors' knowledge; and c) what your friend hopes to accomplish before graduating.

   Role B. Your Chilean friend is new to the United States. Answer his/her questions about university life here and ask about university life there.

2. **Role A.** You are a lawyer informing a client that he/she is going to inherit (**heredar**) a million dollars from a distant relative (**pariente lejano/a**), provided that he/she a) give one third (**la tercera parte**) to four low-income families so that they can send their children to college; and b) wait five years before spending another third. He/She can spend the remaining third now.

   Role B. Your lawyer calls with some surprising news about an inheritance (**herencia**). Ask about the conditions of the will (**testamento**).

2. Expressing conjecture or certainty: Adverbial conjunctions that take the subjunctive or indicative

Resources
- SAM: 14-19 to 14-23
- Supp. Activ. Book: Adverbial conjunctions that take the subjunctive or indicative

SRA. LÓPEZ: ¿Qué le interesa hacer **cuando se gradúe?**

VICENTE: **Después de terminar** mis estudios, me gustaría trabajar en otro país para una organización sin fines de lucro (*non-profit*).

SRA. LÓPEZ: Muy bien. **Tan pronto como terminemos** de hablar, le mandaré una lista de organizaciones. No espere **hasta que se gradúe** para empezar a buscar trabajo. Familiarícese con las posiblidades ahora, **mientras es** estudiante.

Sra. López   Vicente

Piénselo. Indique si la persona que habla se refiere al presente (**P**) o al futuro (**F**).

1. _F_ ¿Qué le interesa hacer **cuando se gradúe?**
2. _F_ **Tan pronto como terminemos** de hablar, le mandaré una lista de organizaciones.
3. _F_ No espere **hasta que se gradúe** para empezar a buscar trabajo.
4. _P_ Familiarícese con las posiblidades ahora, **mientras es** estudiante.
5. _F_ Vicente va a buscar trabajo en una organización sin fines de lucro, **aunque gane** poco dinero.
6. _P_ Estas organizaciones siempre apoyan a las comunidades aun (*even*) **después de que** las comunidades **terminan** el proyecto.

Suggestion for Piénselo. Help students make the proper association between the time frame of the dependent clause (present or future) and the mood of the verb (indicative or subjunctive). Bring to their attention sentence #6, in which the event in the adverbial clause refers to an activity that always takes place, not to the future. This understanding will be good preparation for the explanation that follows.

■ Earlier in this chapter you learned about conjunctions that are always followed by the subjunctive. Here you will practice using conjunctions that are followed by a verb in either the subjunctive or indicative, depending on whether the event in the adverbial clause has occurred or not, or whether it is factual or unknown.

aunque	*although, even though, even if*	**en cuanto**	*as soon as*
cuando	*when*	**hasta que**	*until*
después (de) que	*after*	**mientras**	*while*
donde	*where, wherever*	**según**	*according to, as*
		tan pronto (como)	*as soon as*

Suggestion. A mnemonic device to remember the conjunctions that can take either the subjunctive or the indicative is MATCHED CDS, which stands for:

m	ientras
a	unque
t	an pronto como
c	uando
h	asta que
e	n cuanto
d	espués de que
c	omo
d	onde
s	egún

■ These conjunctions require the subjunctive when the event in the adverbial clause has not yet taken place. Note that the main clause expresses future time.

Va a luchar **hasta que** la comunidad **ofrezca** clases gratis para los inmigrantes nuevos.
She is going to fight until the community offers free classes for new immigrants.

Suggestion. Guide students to notice the sequence of tenses in these examples. A preterit verb in the independent clause usually signals indicative in the dependent clause. A future verb (or *ir a* + *infinitive*) in the independent clause usually signals subjunctive in the dependent clause.

Suggestion. The distinction in meaning between definite/known vs. indefinite/unknown in the dependent clause may be difficult for students to grasp. You may wish to provide additional examples.

Suggestions for 14-16. The activities in this section include the conjunctions presented in the previous section, as well as those presented in this section, to help students internalize the concept of whether the action in the dependent clause has or has not already taken place. You may wish to highlight that concept, especially by pointing out the importance of the temporal information conveyed by the verb in the main clause.

Lengua

You learned that in Spanish, the subject is normally placed after the verb when asking a question: **¿Les dio instrucciones el alcalde?** (*Did the mayor give them instructions?*) You may also place the subject after the verb in statements, especially when you wish to emphasize the subject: **Les habló el alcalde.** (*The mayor talked to them.*) To avoid misinterpreting statements with this structure, you should locate the subject first, and not assume that the first noun or pronoun in the sentence is the subject.

Nos reuniremos **después de que comiencen** las clases.
We will meet after classes start.

Me llamará **tan pronto reciba** la aprobación del alcalde.
She will call me as soon as she receives approval from the mayor.

■ These conjunctions require the indicative when the event in the adverbial clause has already taken place, is taking place, or usually takes place.

Nos reunimos **después de que comenzaron** las clases.
We met after classes started.

Me llamó **tan pronto recibió** la aprobación del alcalde.
She called me as soon as she received approval from the mayor.

La organización apoya a los inmigrantes **hasta que se establecen** en la comunidad.
The organization supports the immigrants until they become established in the community.

■ **Donde** and **según** require the indicative when they refer to something definite or known, and the subjunctive when they refer to something indefinite or unknown.

Vamos a reunirnos **donde** ella **dice**.
We are going to meet where she says. (She has already announced the place.)

Vamos a reunirnos **donde** ella **diga**.
We are going to meet wherever she says. (She has not yet announced the place.)

Llena el formulario **según dice** el consejero.
Fill out the form according to what the adviser says. (Instructions have already been given.)

Vamos a seguir el procedimiento **según diga** el alcalde.
We will follow the procedure in accordance with whatever the mayor says. (Instructions have not yet been given.)

■ **Aunque** also requires the subjunctive when it introduces a condition not regarded as fact.

Lo compro **aunque es** caro.   *I will buy it, although it is expensive.*
Lo compro **aunque sea** caro.   *I will buy it, although it may (turn out to) be expensive.*

14-16 ¿Cuáles serán los cambios? Escoja la forma verbal correcta para completar las siguientes afirmaciones.

1. No se permite que un inmigrante sea presidente de este país a menos de que cambia/cambie la Constitución. cambie
2. Las leyes de los impuestos cambiaron según lo que pidieron/pidan los miembros de la comisión. pidieron
3. Las familias que tenían pocos hijos protestaron cuando se aprobaron/se aprueben las nuevas leyes. se aprobaron
4. Como resultado, el gobierno quiere disminuirles los impuestos a las familias numerosas para que las mujeres tienen/tengan más hijos. tengan
5. Muchas personas dicen que no creerán en esta disminución de los impuestos hasta que la ven/vean. vean

14-17 La educación a distancia. Ustedes toman un curso en Internet sobre la historia de Chile por medio del programa VirtualU de la Universidad de Chile. Todo lo hacen en la computadora y se comunican por mensajes de texto y correo electrónico. Digan lo que van a hacer, terminando las oraciones abajo con una frase apropiada de la lista a continuación. Answers may vary.

ser las 12:00
tener tiempo
ser muy tarde
tener sus horas de consulta
llegar el día del examen final
escribirme mi compañero virtual
leer unos mensajes electrónicos de la profesora
terminar de leer sobre los regímenes dictatoriales

MODELO: Voy a trabajar en la computadora hasta que... empezar las
            noticias/ser la hora de cenar
   E1:   *Voy a trabajar en la computadora hasta que empiecen las noticias.*
   E2:   *Y yo voy a trabajar hasta que sea la hora de cenar.*

1. Voy a hablar con la profesora en cuanto...
2. Comeré después de que...
3. Voy a comprobar los datos tan pronto como...
4. Haré la mayoría del trabajo en nuestro ensayo hasta que...
5. Voy a estudiar el tema de la inmigración chilena esta noche aunque...
6. Le mandaré mi informe sobre las últimas lecturas a la profesora antes de que...

14-18 Después de que termine el año escolar. PRIMERA FASE. Usted quiere descansar y divertirse después de que terminen las clases, pero también quiere hacer algo por su comunidad. Complete dos de las opciones que más le interesen en cada columna y añada una más para expresar sus propias ideas. Después comparta sus planes con su compañero/a.

DIVERSIÓN	AYUDA COMUNITARIA
1. Quiero dormir hasta que...	1. Trabajaré de voluntario donde...
2. No voy a abrir los libros aunque...	2. Ayudaré en la biblioteca después de que...
3. Haré un crucero por... tan pronto como...	3. Les serviré comida a los desamparados (*homeless*) mientras...
4. Iré a la playa todos los días a menos que...	4. Organizaré juegos infantiles en el parque para que...
5. ...	5. ...

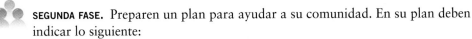

SEGUNDA FASE. Preparen un plan para ayudar a su comunidad. En su plan deben indicar lo siguiente:

1. sector de la comunidad
2. tipo de ayuda
3. frecuencia de su participación
4. medios que van a usar
5. resultados que esperan obtener

Suggestion for 14-17. You may wish to remind students that when there is no change of subject, they should use *antes de* + infinitive or *después de* + infinitive rather than *antes de que/después de que* + conjugated verb.

Note for 14-18. Note that this activity has three parts. In the *Primera fase*, students first work individually and then compare results with a partner. In the *Segunda fase*, small groups pool their results to create a plan for their community. You may find it helpful to give students instructions for one step at a time, so that the activity can proceed with input from all students in the class.

14-19 El hombre y la mujer en la sociedad. PRIMERA FASE. Indique (✓) si, según usted, las situaciones presentadas en las siguientes afirmaciones existen o no existen hoy en día.

LOS HOMBRES Y LAS MUJERES...	SÍ	NO
1. reciben la misma educación		
2. son tratados de la misma forma en el trabajo.		
3. ganan el mismo sueldo por el mismo trabajo.		
4. tienen las mismas oportunidades.		
5. hacen las mismas tareas domésticas.		
6. tienen los mismos derechos en un divorcio.		
7. sufren las mismas consecuencias cuando violan una norma moral, por ejemplo, si son infieles.		

SEGUNDA FASE. Ahora compare sus respuestas con las de su compañero/a. Defienda sus opiniones negativas y diga cuándo o bajo qué condiciones usted cree que los cambios necesarios ocurrirán.

MODELO: E1: *Los hombres y las mujeres ocupan más o menos el mismo número de puestos importantes.*

E2: *No estoy de acuerdo. Los hombres ocupan la mayoría de los puestos importantes en las compañías y en el gobierno. Esto va a cambiar cuando las generaciones jóvenes puedan tomar más decisiones.*

> ### En directo
>
> To make a polite request or a proposal:
>
> **Quiero/Queremos proponer (que)...**
>
> **Sugiero/Sugerimos (que)...**

SITUACIONES

1. **Role A.** As the employee representative for your company, you meet with the president to ask that a yoga class be held for employees who are experiencing neck and back pain from working at their computers. Explain their needs and the advantages of yoga. Stress that the employees are willing to take the class wherever and whenever the president wishes.

   Role B. As president of a large company, you meet with an employee representative who wants the company to offer a yoga class during the work day. Ask a) how many employees would be interested; b) who would teach the class; and c) when and where it would take place. Say that you have no problem with the idea, provided that the board of directors (**junta directiva**) is in favor of it.

2. **Role A.** You make a presentation to the city council (**concejo municipal**) about starting an adult literacy program. Explain how the lives of participants will improve when they know how to read and write well. In response to questions, say that you will a) organize the program; b) hold classes wherever the council says; and c) decide on class schedules according to the needs of the participants.

   Role B. You are the president of the city council (**concejo municipal**). After listening to a presentation by a specialist in adult literacy who wants to start a program in the community, ask a) where and when the classes will be held; and b) who will pay for the program.

3. Talking about the past from a past perspective: The past perfect

Resources
- SAM: 14-24 to 14-28
- Supp. Activ. Book: The past perfect

VIOLETA: Oye, mamá, mi profesora habló un poco de Gabriela Mistral. ¿Tú sabes algo de ella?

MADRE: ¡Uf! Gabriela Mistral fue una gran poeta chilena que ganó el Premio Nobel de literatura en 1945. Pero antes de recibir el premio, Gabriela ya **había hecho** muchas cosas importantes.

VIOLETA: ¿Qué **había hecho**? Yo no sé nada de ella.

MADRE: Antes de ser famosa, Gabriela **había tenido** una vida muy dura. Su padre **había abandonado** a la familia cuando ella tenía tres años.

VIOLETA: ¡Qué triste la vida de Gabriela, mamá!

MADRE: Sí y no. Ella utilizó su sufrimiento positivamente para lograr mucho. Por ejemplo, a los 15 años, ya **había escrito** sus primeras poesías y **se había graduado** de profesora. Además, antes de ella, ningún escritor latinoamericano **había ganado** el Premio Nobel.

Note. Point out that the events of Gabriela Mistral's life resonate in the central themes of her poetry, which include betrayal, love, a mother's love, sorrow and recovery, travel, and Latin American identity as seen as a mixture of Indian and European influences.

Piénselo. Indique si las siguientes experiencias de Gabriela Mistral y su madre se refieren a un momento cronológicamente anterior (**A**) al momento cuando Gabriela se hizo internacionalmente famosa.

1. _A_ Gabriela ya **había hecho** muchas cosas importantes.
2. _A_ Su madre y ella **habían tenido** una vida muy dura.
3. ___ **Ganó** el Premio Nobel en 1945.
4. _A_ Su padre **había abandonado** a Gabriela y a su madre.
5. _A_ **Había escrito** poesías antes de cumplir los 15 años.
6. _A_ Ningún escritor latinoamericano **había ganado** el Premio Nobel.

Suggestion for Piénselo. Draw students' attention to how different verb forms (preterit vs. past perfect) effect a change in meaning (past vs. anterior past). You may also wish to come back to the statements in *Piénselo* after students have done some of the activities in this section.

■ Use the past perfect to refer to a past event, action or condition that occurred prior to another past event, action or state.

Ningún escritor latinoamericano **había ganado** el Premio Nobel de Literatura antes de Mistral.

No Latin American writer had won the Nobel Prize for Literature before Mistral.

Otros escritores **habían sido** nominados para el premio, pero ella lo recibió.

Other writers had been nominated for the award, but she received it.

■ Form the past perfect with the imperfect tense of **haber** and the past participle of the main verb.

Suggestions. Present the past perfect in the same manner as the present perfect in *Capítulo 10* (pp. 339–341). You may wish to contrast the use of the two tenses: *Gracias por invitarme, pero ya he comido. Cuando Luis me invitó a cenar, ya había comido.*

IMPERFECT OF *HABER*		PAST PARTICIPLE
yo	había	
tú	habías	
Ud., él, ella	había	hablado
nosotros/as	habíamos	comido
vosotros/as	habíais	vivido
Uds., ellos/as	habían	

14-20 ¡Recuerdos! PRIMERA FASE. Para cada afirmación, ponga un círculo alrededor de la acción que ocurrió primero.

MODELO: Cuando yo cumplí diez años, ya había escuchado discusiones políticas.

1. Cuando cumplimos diecisiete años, mis amigos y yo ya nos habíamos inscrito en un partido político.
2. Cuando terminé la escuela secundaria, mis padres ya me habían comprado un carro.
3. Yo ya había trabajado y había ahorrado (*saved*) algún dinero cuando empecé la universidad.
4. Cuando pasó el primer mes de clases en la universidad, yo ya me había acostumbrado a todo el trabajo que tenía que hacer.
5. Mis padres ya sospechaban que yo me había hecho más independiente cuando los visité después de algunos meses.

 SEGUNDA FASE. ¿Cuáles de las acciones de la *Primera fase* concuerdan (*agree*) con su experiencia personal? Comparta sus respuestas con las de su compañero/a.

 14-21 Una investigación. PRIMERA FASE. Marque (✓) sus respuestas en la columna correspondiente y dígale a su compañero/a si usted o miembros de su familia ya habían hecho estas cosas antes del año 2005.

MODELO: buscar trabajo en Internet antes del año 2005

	SÍ	NO	¿QUIÉNES?
E1: *Mi hermano y yo ya habíamos buscado trabajo en Internet. En 2004 los dos conseguimos trabajo por Internet.*	✓		*Mi hermano y yo*
E2: *Pues, yo nunca había usado Internet para buscar trabajo. En 2004 yo era muy joven.*			

	SÍ	NO	¿QUIÉNES?
1. manejar un carro híbrido			
2. hacer trabajo voluntario			
3. votar en las elecciones presidenciales			
4. leer el periódico			
5. comunicarse con los amigos por correo electrónico			
6. comprar un iPod			
7. diseñar una página web			
8. dejar comentarios sobre una foto en Facebook de un amigo/una amiga			

 SEGUNDA FASE. Hagan una encuesta para averiguar qué tres actividades de la *Primera fase* marcaron más personas del grupo. Determinen si más hombres o más mujeres hicieron cada una de las tres actividades.

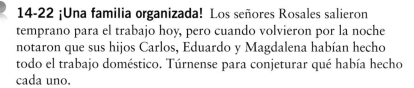

14-22 ¡Una familia organizada! Los señores Rosales salieron temprano para el trabajo hoy, pero cuando volvieron por la noche notaron que sus hijos Carlos, Eduardo y Magdalena habían hecho todo el trabajo doméstico. Túrnense para conjeturar qué había hecho cada uno.

MODELO: Al salir, les dijeron a sus hijos que iban a llegar un poco tarde y que no tendrían tiempo para cocinar. *Al volver, vieron que Eduardo había cocinado unos espaguetis para toda la familia.*

1. Después del desayuno dejaron los platos sucios en el lavaplatos.
2. Antes de irse a la oficina, la señora Rosales vio que había un montón de libros de la biblioteca en la mesa del comedor.
3. Cuando salía de casa el señor Rosales notó que el garaje estaba sucio.
4. Los dormitorios de sus hijos estaban desordenados; había ropa y libros en el piso.
5. Como tenía prisa, la señora Rosales olvidó mandar por correo unas cuentas importantes.
6. No llevaron a la tintorería (*dry cleaner*) una ropa que querían lavar en seco (*dry clean*).

Additional practice. You may wish to have students describe the experiences of the *arpilleras* of Chile using the past perfect tense. They may research this topic on the Internet for more information. Explain that: *Durante la dictadura en Chile entre 1973 y 1991, las arpilleras chilenas hicieron tapices en los cuales protestaban la desaparición o muerte de un familiar. Usen su intuición o conocimiento de la historia para hacer una lista de posibles experiencias que las arpilleras habían tenido durante esa dictadura.*

MODELO: *Antes de la democracia, las mujeres probablemente habían mostrado sus tapices en secreto.*

You may wish to give students the following verbs to help them with their descriptions: *escribir, participar, protestar, llorar, pedir ayuda, relatar, luchar, perder, sufrir*

SITUACIONES

1. **Role A.** You are the founder of a company that conducts opinion polls (**encuestas de opinión**). Answer the questions that a reporter asks. Give detailed information on how you think polls will be conducted in the future.

   Role B. You are a reporter interviewing the founder of a company that conducts opinion polls (**encuestas de opinión**). Ask a) the date he/she started the company; b) what he/she had done before starting the company (studies, positions held, places of residence); and c) his/her ideas on how opinion polls will be conducted in the future.

2. **Role A.** You are interviewing a Chilean student for your campus newspaper. Ask a) what he/she had studied in Chile before deciding to study here; b) what U.S. schools he/she had considered before choosing this one; and c) how his/her experience has been different from what he/she had expected.

   Role B. You are an exchange student from Chile who is being interviewed for the campus newspaper. Provide as much information to the reporter as possible, including your expectations (**lo que había pensado**) while still in Chile and the reality you found when you started to live in the United States and study at this school.

Resources
■ SAM: 14-29 to 14-33
■ Supp. Activ. Book: The
   infinitive as subject or object

4. Expressing actions: The infinitive as subject or object

LAURA: Mamá, ¿viste la marcha en la tele? Yo también estaba allí con todos mis compañeros de la clase de sociología.

MAMÁ: **Luchar** por la igualdad entre los sexos es tiempo perdido, hija. No hemos avanzado mucho. Mira, yo continúo trabajando en casa, pero no me importa.

LAURA: Pero **quedarse** de brazos cruzados tampoco es una opción para mí, mamá.

MAMÁ: **Trabajar** duro es lo que debemos hacer. Ninguna protesta nos ayudará.

LAURA: Mamá, ¿cómo puedes pensar así? **Guardar** silencio es **hacerse** cómplice de la injusticia. **Exigir** igualdad y respeto por nuestra dignidad es nuestro derecho.

Piénselo. Indique si usted cree que las siguientes acciones representan las opiniones de Laura (**L**) o las de su madre (**M**).

1. _M_ **Trabajar** en casa no es un problema para la mujer.
2. _L_ **Protestar** nos ayudará a cambiar la sociedad.
3. _L_ No **resignarse** al trato desigual es fundamental para conseguir el cambio.
4. _L_ **Mantenerse** de brazos cruzados significa aceptar la desigualdad y la injusticia.

■ The infinitive is the only verb form that may be used as the subject of a sentence. As the subject, it corresponds to the English *-ing* form.

Dialogar es necesario para lograr cambios.	*Talking is necessary for changes to occur.*
Hacer comentarios negativos no es bueno para nuestras negociaciones.	*Making negative pronouncements is not good for our negotiations.*

■ Use an infinitive after a preposition.

Llama **antes de ir**.	*Call before going.*
No trates de argumentar **sin prepararte**.	*Do not try to argue without preparing yourself.*

■ **Al** + *infinitive* is the equivalent of **cuando** + *verb*.

Al recibir su carta de despido, llamó al director.	*Upon receiving his pink slip, he called the director.*
Cuando recibió su carta de despido, llamó al director.	*When he received his pink slip, he called the director.*

■ When used in signs and instructions, the infinitive functions as a command.

No **comer** en clase.	*No eating in class.* (Lit. *Don't eat in class*)
Hablar en voz baja.	*Speak softly.*

Suggestion. Bring international signs (e.g., a lighted cigarette crossed by a diagonal line) and have students give the Spanish equivalents.

14-23 Ciudadanos (*Citizens*) responsables. Asocie lógicamente las opciones de la columna de la izquierda con las ideas de la columna de la derecha. Answers may vary.

1. _b_ Educarse…
2. _c_ Estudiar idiomas…
3. _a_ Votar en las elecciones…
4. _d_ Aceptar a los inmigrantes…

a. es importante para mantener la democracia.
b. es vital para conseguir un buen trabajo.
c. es la mejor manera de aprender sobre otras culturas.
d. es indispensable para una convivencia sana dentro de una comunidad.

14-24 Opiniones. PRIMERA FASE. Indique si las siguientes actividades son necesarias, opcionales o inaceptables. Después, compare sus respuestas con las de su compañero/a y explíquele las razones de sus respuestas.

ACTIVIDAD	OPINIÓN
1. ofrecer seguro de salud para todos	
2. informarse sobre lo que pasa en el mundo	
3. prohibir la proliferación de armas nucleares	
4. hacer investigación sobre células troncales (*stem cell*)	
5. discriminar a algunas personas por su etnia (*ethnicity*)	

SEGUNDA FASE. Escojan el tema más importante para ustedes en la *Primera fase*. Expliquen por qué es importante y qué es necesario hacer para captar la atención de la gente.

14-25 Interpretar los mensajes. PRIMERA FASE. Observen los siguientes letreros y escriban una nota bajo cada uno de ellos.

1. _No beber alcohol_
2. _No fumar_
3. _No entrar/pasar_
4. _No sacar fotos_

SEGUNDA FASE. Preparen su propio letrero. Otra pareja tiene que decir dónde sería bueno ponerlo y por qué.

SITUACIONES

1. **Role A.** As president of the Student Association, you are designing a campaign to promote cross-cultural understanding in your area. Discuss with a friend who is an anthropology major a) what students can do to better understand people from other cultures; b) how students can reach out to (**comunicarse con**) people from other cultures who live in the community.

   Role B. A friend wants to discuss a project to promote cross-cultural understanding in your area. Explain your views about a) what students can do to learn about cultural diversity; b) how students can reach out to (**comunicarse con**) people from other cultures who live in the community.

2. **Role A.** You are a relationship counselor. A client comes to see you for help with a problem. Provide some sound advice.

   Role B. You go to see a relationship counselor for help. Explain that a) your partner becomes (**ponerse**) aggressive after she/he drinks alcohol; b) you have tried to discuss this when she/he is sober (**sobrio/a**); and c) you always have to keep quiet (**callarse**) so that he/she doesn't get angry. Ask how you can help your partner.

Expansion for 14-25 Segunda fase. After groups have finished *Segunda fase*, have them share their signs with the class.

Additional practice. Have students ask a partner what he/she typically does (*¿Qué haces…?*) in the following situations:
1. *antes de votar en las elecciones presidenciales de su país*
2. *antes de darle una mala noticia a alguien*
3. *después de descubrir que su jefe/a es sexista*
4. *después de asistir a un concierto de música rock*
5. *después de discutir acaloradamente con alguien*
6. *para ofrecerse de voluntario en una organización caritativa*

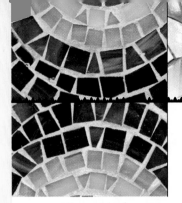

Resources

■ SAM: 14-34 to 14-36
■ Supp. Activ. Book: *Mosaicos*

Warm-up for 14-27. As a prelistening activity, have students in small groups discuss the advantages and disadvantages of having both parents work outside the home.

Audioscript for 14-27.

VILMA: *¿Qué te parece la sociedad en que vivimos, Sonia? Todo lo que ha ocurrido en los últimos años ha tenido repercusiones en la familia.*

SONIA: *Sí, es verdad, pero los cambios han sido positivos, ¿no crees?*

VILMA: *No sé qué decirte, Sonia. Antes las labores estaban bien definidas y cada uno sabía lo que tenía que hacer. La responsabilidad del padre era mantener económicamente a la familia, mientras que la madre se ocupaba de las labores domésticas y de la educación de los niños. Ahora, parece que nadie se ocupa de la casa.*

SONIA: *Bueno, pero acuérdate que siempre la última palabra la tenía el padre y él era el rey del hogar. La mujer tenía un papel secundario. Yo prefiero la vida de las mujeres hoy. Ellas juegan un papel más importante tanto en la familia como en la sociedad.*

VILMA: *Pero, ¿cuál es el costo? Antes toda la familia colaboraba en la crianza de los hijos. Los abuelos ayudaban a cuidarlos y todos los miembros de la familia les mostraban cariño. Ahora, los niños están en las guarderías infantiles y los abuelos en las residencias de ancianos.*

SONIA: *Sí, eso sí es triste. Aunque el papel de la mujer en la sociedad sea mejor ahora, no me gusta que los niños pasen tantas horas del día separados de sus padres y abuelos. Debería haber más equilibrio para que la mujer no se sacrifique y deje de crecer intelectual y profesionalmente.*

VILMA: *Tú eres más moderna que yo, Sonia. Yo prefiero el pasado cuando todo era más sencillo.*

SONIA: *Yo no. Yo prefiero ver a la mujer desarrollarse igual que el hombre.*

MOSAICOS

A escuchar

Antes de escuchar

14-26 Preparación. Dos mujeres mayores conversan sobre los cambios que han ocurrido en las sociedades hispanas. Antes de escuchar, escriba un cambio que cree que mencionarán en cada una de estas áreas: los quehaceres de casa y la crianza de los hijos.

Escuchar

14-27 ¿Comprende usted? First read the statements below and then listen to Sonia and Vilma talk about the changes in the Hispanic family that have occurred during their lifetime. As you listen, indicate if each statement reflects Sonia's (**S**) point of view or Vilma's (**V**). Finally, check (✓) the clues that helped you identify Vilma's point of view and that of Sonia.

CD 6
Track 15

	WORD CHOICE	ORGANIZATION OF IDEAS
1. _S_ Los cambios que han ocurrido en la sociedad han sido positivos.		
2. _V_ Ahora nadie se ocupa de los quehaceres de casa.		
3. _S_ No era bueno el papel secundario que tenía la mujer en la casa.		
4. _V_ Los abuelos han perdido la importancia que tenían en la familia.		
5. _S_ La mujer debe desarrollarse profesional e intelectualmente.		

Después de escuchar

14-28 Ahora usted. Expliquen su punto de vista sobre los siguientes asuntos.

1. ¿Es necesario que uno de los padres se quede en casa mientras los hijos son pequeños?
2. Si ambos padres trabajan fuera de casa, ¿cómo se podría resolver la cuestión de la educación de los hijos?

A conversar

Antes de conversar

14-29 Preparación. Indiquen y expliquen por lo menos un problema (local, nacional o mundial) en cada una de las siguientes áreas.

MODELO: **Área:** seguridad

Problema: *terrorismo*

Explicación del problema: *Hoy existen grupos terroristas que atacan y crean caos en el mundo. Nadie se siente seguro.*

ÁREA

1. economía
2. igualdad
3. educación
4. salud

Conversar

14-30 Entre nosotros. Conversen sobre los problemas que ustedes identificaron en **14-29**. Hagan lo siguiente:

1. Digan cuál de los problemas que identificaron en **14-29** es más serio. Expliquen por qué.
2. Luego, háganse preguntas relacionadas con ese problema. Utilicen en sus respuestas las expresiones indicadas en *En directo* y tomen notas de las respuestas del grupo.

MODELO: la falta de seguridad en las escuelas
   E1: *¿Creen que haya solución al problema de la falta de seguridad en las escuelas?*
   E2: *Sí, la solución es tener/establecer más comunicación con los padres, para que controlen mejor a sus hijos.*
   E3: *A mí me parece que la solución es instalar máquinas en las entradas de las escuelas que registren a todas las personas que quieran entrar en la escuela.*

3. Lleguen a una conclusión entre todos sobre cuándo y cómo se solucionará el problema. Usen las siguientes expresiones: *después de que, tan pronto como, en cuanto, cuando.*

Después de conversar

14-31 Un poco más. Preséntenle a la clase la información y conclusión a la que llegaron en la actividad **14-30**. Prepárense para defender su posición.

ESTRATEGIA

Organize ideas to present solutions to problems

When you present your ideas about how to solve a problem, organize your presentation so that you can communicate clearly to your listeners a) what the problem is, to whom it is important, and why; b) how your proposal is to be implemented and how it addresses the problem; and c) the likely consequences of your solution. Your underlying goal is to convince your listeners of the wisdom of your approach.

En directo

To present a group's conclusion:

Después de hablar sobre el tema, hemos llegado a la siguiente conclusión. Nuestro grupo cree/piensa que…

A nuestro grupo le parece que…

Para nosotros, el problema más serio es…

To support a group's view or position:

No tenemos duda de que sea… el problema más serio porque…

Si miramos/observamos… nos damos cuenta de que…

Las estadísticas/La opinión de los expertos apoya(n) nuestra conclusión.

Resources
■ SAM: 14-37
■ *Entrevistas* video

Note. Translation of expressions in the *En directo* box has not been provided because by now learners should be familiar with these expressions.

Standard 1.3 Students present information, concepts, and ideas to an audience of listeners or readers on a variety of topics. The strategies and *En directo* boxes offer students useful information on how to organize and present facts and opinions orally. Such skills can help students not only in their language classes, but in any course where they give oral presentations.

Suggestion for 14-30. You may wish to point out that the *Modelo* represents opinions at opposite extremes of the spectrum. Whatever the range of the opinions of the group, members should ask each other to explain their opinions in as much detail as possible. It may not be possible to arrive at the consensus suggested in part 3 of the instructions.

Suggestion for 14-31. Before students present their reports, you may wish to model how to present and defend a personal or a group position on a controversial issue.

ESTRATEGIA

Identify the tone of a text

Identifying the tone of a text is a task usually associated with works of literature. But expository and argumentative texts also use tone to present a point of view. Even a text that appears to be objective owes that tone to the choices in vocabulary and phrasing made by the author.

A leer

Antes de leer

14-32 Preparación. Lea el título del artículo y examine la foto. Luego responda a las preguntas.

1. ¿Cuál puede ser el tema principal de la narrativa? Seleccione los temas posibles.
   a. la deserción escolar de los jóvenes hispanos
   b. por qué muchos estudiantes hispanos no asisten a la universidad
   c. programas en las universidades para ayudar a estudiantes minoritarios
2. ¿Cuáles cree que son los temas secundarios?
   a. Se incluye información demográfica.
   b. Se presentan los casos de estudiantes específicos.
   c. Se cita (*quote*) la opinión de unos expertos.

Leer

Alumnos hispanos preparados que no pueden acceder a la universidad

Cada vez son más los jóvenes hispanos con la preparación académica adecuada para entrar a la universidad, pero por falta de recursos económicos no pueden hacerlo, de acuerdo con un informe reciente. El informe preparado por la Junta de Regentes del Sistema de Universidades de Colorado indica que hay más alumnos de grupos minoritarios en la universidad hoy que en el pasado, pero todavía queda mucho por hacer.

Los administradores de estas universidades dicen que el aumento en el número de estudiantes minoritarios probablemente se debe al crecimiento del número de hispanos en el estado, sobre todo en el sur. Es decir, el aumento del número de alumnos hispanos que se gradúan de la escuela secundaria se debe simplemente a cambios demográficos, no al éxito de los programas de promoción universitarios.

Cada vez más hispanos se gradúan de las escuelas secundarias y aspiran a asistir a la universidad.

Según un comentario del canciller de la Universidad de Colorado en Denver, el número de latinos y de otras minorías que estudian en su universidad ahora llega al 22 por ciento y pronto subirá al 38 por ciento. Parte del aumento se debe a un acuerdo entre la universidad en Denver y el Departamento de Educación de EE.UU. para promover los estudios universitarios en las escuelas secundarias locales.

A pesar de estos proyectos, aún es pequeño el número de estudiantes hispanos y de otras minorías que llega a la universidad.

El reporte de los regentes indica que sólo el 40 por ciento de los estudiantes minoritarios de las escuelas públicas de Colorado que pueden ir a la universidad lo hacen, debido al costo. Por ejemplo, según la organización CollegeInColorado, durante el año 2006-2007, el costo promedio para un estudiante de tiempo completo en la Universidad de Colorado o en la Escuela de Minería era de $9.000 dólares por año, sin incluir otros gastos como alojamiento, libros, transporte y seguro médico. En comparación, durante ese mismo período el costo de la matrícula para estudiantes de tiempo completo en instituciones de educación de nivel terciario[1] fue de $3.800 dólares al año.

Por ley, los alumnos que se gradúan de las escuelas secundarias de Colorado reciben un subsidio de hasta $2.670 dólares al año, sin importar la situación financiera de la familia del estudiante. Pero aun con esa ayuda, el costo promedio de seguir estudiando después de la educación secundaria oscila entre los $1.800 y los $7.800 dólares, para instituciones de educación de nivel terciario o grandes universidades, respectivamente.

Para muchos latinos, de acuerdo con CollegeInColorado, el costo se incrementa porque al llegar a la universidad, descubren que necesitan clases de recuperación, especialmente en matemáticas, lectura y escritura. Esas clases no se cuentan entre los cursos necesarios para obtener un título, pero cuestan como promedio $77 dólares por hora de crédito, y retrasan el inicio de los estudios universitarios.

[1]*community* colleges

14-33 Primera mirada. Indique si las siguientes afirmaciones relacionadas con el artículo son ciertas (**C**) o falsas (**F**). Si son falsas, corríjalas.

1. _C_ El artículo trata de la educación de los hispanos en el estado de Colorado.
2. _F_ Menos estudiantes hispanos se gradúan de las escuelas secundarias ahora que en el pasado.
3. _C_ La población hispana en el estado está creciendo.
4. _F_ Los programas para atraer a más estudiantes minoritarios a la universidad han tenido éxito.
5. _C_ El número de hispanos en la Universidad de Colorado en Denver está creciendo.
6. _C_ Muchos estudiantes hispanos muy calificados para hacer estudios universitarios asisten a universidades en otros estados.
7. _C_ Hay diferencias grandes en el costo de los estudios universitarios, dependiendo del tipo de universidad.
8. _F_ Las clases de recuperación son gratis para los estudiantes que las toman por obligación.

14-34 Segunda mirada. Indique si las oraciones representan un problema (**PB**) o progreso (**PG**) para la educación de los hispanos en Colorado.

1. _PB_ Cada vez son más los jóvenes hispanos con la preparación académica para entrar a la universidad, pero por falta de recursos económicos no pueden hacerlo.
2. _PG_ Según un comentario del canciller de la Universidad de Colorado en Denver, el número de latinos y de otras minorías que estudian en su universidad ahora llega al 22 por ciento y pronto subirá al 38 por ciento.
3. _PB_ Para muchos latinos, el costo se incrementa debido a que, una vez que llegan a la universidad, descubren que necesitan clases de recuperación, especialmente en matemáticas, lectura y escritura.
4. _PB_ Esas clases no se cuentan entre los cursos necesarios para obtener un título.

Después de leer

14-35 Ampliación. Comenten en parejas el siguiente tema y prepárense para compartir las respuestas con la clase.

1. Según el artículo, el costo de asistir a la Universidad de Colorado es mucho mayor que el costo de asistir a una institución de educación de nivel terciario.

   ■ ¿Es justo que existan estas diferencias en el costo de la matrícula?

   ■ ¿Debería costar lo mismo la matrícula en todas las universidades públicas del estado?

Suggestion for 14-34. You may wish to point out that the predominance of statements in the article that are associated with the problem rather than progress toward a solution is part of its tone. You may also wish to have students identify words and phrases that intensify the tone of the article; e.g., *queda mucho por hacer, a pesar de estos proyectos, es pequeño el número.*

Suggestions for 14-35. Encourage students to be responsible for the group discussion by asking that each member of the group take notes on the discussion about each question. You can then organize a whole-class discussion in which each student should be able to report the views of his/her group.

Resources

■ SAM: 14-41 to 14-43

A escribir

| ESTRATEGIA | **Use language to express emotions** |

Emotions have a psychological and social function in communication. We express emotions for various reasons and with different purposes. For example, we may express anger to complain about a computer malfunction or appreciation to thank someone for a gift.

Poetry is a genre well suited to the expression of emotions. Writing a poem may enable us to describe artistically feelings of heroism, beauty, love, sadness, loss, or injustice, or to celebrate a special event. To compose an effective poem, it is important to think carefully about the feelings we want to convey and our purpose in writing it.

Remember that poetry is a reflection of human experience, and in that sense, anyone can write poetry!

Antes de escribir

Suggestions for 14-36. We suggest you assign this activity as homework and concentrate on the next activity in preparation for writing.

Note. You may wish to provide students with the following background on Alfonsina Storni. She was born in Switzerland in 1892, and then her parents moved to Argentina, where she lived until her death in 1938. Storni was an actress, a cashier, a playwright, a teacher, and a poet. Her book *Languidez* received first prize in the Municipal Poetry Prize competition and second place in the National Literary Prize.

14-36 Preparación. PRIMERA FASE. Lea el siguiente poema que alude a las emociones de una persona en una relación tradicional en la sociedad.

> ### *Hombre pequeñito*
>
> de Alfonsina Storni
>
> Hombre pequeñito, hombre pequeñito,
> Suelta a tu canario, que quiere volar...
> Yo soy el canario, hombre pequeñito,
> Déjame saltar.
> Estuve en tu jaula, hombre pequeñito,
> Hombre pequeñito que jaula me das,
> Digo pequeñito porque no me entiendes,
> Ni me entenderás.
> Tampoco te entiendo, pero mientras tanto
> Ábreme la jaula que quiero escapar;
> Hombre pequeñito, te amé media hora.
> No me pidas más.

SEGUNDA FASE. Indique si las siguientes afirmaciones interpretan el poema correcta (**C**) o incorrectamente (**I**).

1. __I__ El poema tiene un tono alegre.
2. __I__ La persona que habla en este poema es un hombre.
3. __C__ La voz del poema expresa su sentimiento de disgusto por la opresión en la que ha vivido.
4. __I__ La persona expresa la esperanza de que su pareja lo/la comprenda en el futuro.
5. __C__ Al usar la palabra *pequeñito* la voz del poema expresa irónicamente su desprecio por su pareja.
6. __I__ La voz del poema quiere continuar viviendo con su compañero/a.
7. __I__ La voz del poema desea expresarle amor a su pareja.

A escribir

14-37 Manos a la obra. PRIMERA FASE. Prepárese para expresar sus sentimientos y emociones en su propio poema, siguiendo el modelo del poema de la actividad **14-36**. Haga lo siguiente:

1. Determine el tono (alegre, triste, nostálgico, etc.) y el propósito de su poema:
2. Decida a quién le va a escribir el poema: ¿a una mujer o a un hombre?
3. Escriba una o dos palabras que describan a esta persona:
4. Escoja un objeto, un animal, u otro elemento que simbolice sus sentimientos sobre la relación que usted tiene con esa persona:
5. Escriba tres o cuatro cosas que usted le pediría a esta persona hacer por usted:
6. Indique un lugar que usted asocia con esta relación:
7. Mencione una o dos cosas que usted le pediría a la persona no hacer.

SEGUNDA FASE. Ahora, complete su poema, siguiendo el poema en **14-36**. No se olvide de darle un título que exprese sus sentimientos.

Título: _____ Autor: _____
_____, _____,
_____ a tu _____, que quiere _____...
Yo soy _____, _____,
_____.
_____, _____,
_____ que _____ me das.
Digo _____ porque no _____,
Ni _____.
Tampoco te _____, pero mientras tanto
_____ que quiero _____;
_____, te _____ media hora.
No me _____ más.

Después de escribir

14-38 Revisión. PRIMERA FASE. Lea su poema una vez más y responda a estas preguntas.

1. ¿Está usted satisfecho/a con el mensaje de su poema?
2. ¿Son comprensibles y coherentes las ideas?
3. ¿Tendrá el efecto que usted quiere?

SEGUNDA FASE. Ahora, revise si...

1. el vocabulario es apropiado para describir a esta persona y los sentimientos que usted tiene por él/ella.
2. la ortografía, puntuación, acentuación, etc. son apropiadas.

Finalmente, déle el poema a un compañero/una compañera para que lo lea y lo disfrute.

ENFOQUE CULTURAL

La compleja vida política de América Latina

Una de las actividades que más apasiona a muchos latinoamericanos es la política. Desde la independencia, la política ha despertado intensas pasiones en el continente, y muchos países han sufrido guerras civiles o conflictos de fronteras con países vecinos. El interés por la política y el deseo de solucionar los problemas sociales se entienden fácilmente en una región donde hay muchas diferencias entre la ciudad y el campo, entre las clases educadas y las que no tienen acceso a la educación, o entre las clases más ricas y las más pobres.

Dentro de este contexto, la vida política de Chile ofrece ejemplos de grandes triunfos democráticos, al igual que ejemplos de algunos de los grandes problemas que

caracterizan la política en América Latina. A finales del siglo XIX, por ejemplo, Chile vivió un conflicto de fronteras con Bolivia y Perú. Esta guerra, que ocurrió entre 1879 y 1884 y que se conoce como La Guerra del Pacífico, enfrentó a estos países por los derechos sobre el desierto de Atacama. Este desierto es rico en minerales, especialmente en salitre, que es un mineral usado como fertilizante y también en la fabricación de explosivos. Como resultado de esta guerra, Perú y Bolivia perdieron parte de su territorio, que hoy pertenece a Chile.

Durante la década de 1930, varios países latinoamericanos tuvieron guerras con países vecinos y así, por ejemplo, entre 1932 y 1935, Bolivia y Paraguay se vieron envueltos en la Guerra del Chaco. Este conflicto se considera el más violento del siglo XX en América Latina. También en 1933, Colombia y Perú lucharon por problemas de fronteras.

Todos los países latinoamericanos han buscado un camino para conseguir la democracia, aunque en algunos momentos ese ideal ha sido difícil de alcanzar. Las dictaduras militares que se han instalado en varios países han ocasionado episodios muy problemáticos en la región. Una de las dictaduras más violentas de los últimos tiempos fue la de Augusto Pinochet en Chile, que duró desde 1973 hasta 1990. El 11 de septiembre de 1973, Pinochet dirigió un golpe militar contra el gobierno del Presidente Salvador

Allende. Durante los diecisiete años de la dictadura de Pinochet, miles de personas fueron detenidas, torturadas y miles de ellas desaparecieron. Esas escenas de violencia y violaciones de los derechos humanos fueron representadas en la película *Missing*, del director Constantín Costa-Gavras. Una de las víctimas más simbólicas de esta dictadura fue el cantautor Víctor Jara, asesinado en un estadio de Santiago.

Esta arpillera representa a las madres de detenidos desaparecidos durante la dictadura de Pinochet.

Por la misma época, Argentina también se encontraba gobernada por una dictadura militar. Se dice que la dictadura argentina hizo desparecer a 30.000 personas durante esos años. Las madres de los desaparecidos formaron un grupo llamado Las Madres de Plaza de Mayo para protestar ante la Casa Rosada, la oficina del presidente en Buenos Aires, por la desaparición de sus hijos e hijas. El problema de los desaparecidos en Argentina también fue motivo de una película muy famosa, *La historia oficial*, del director Luis Puenzo.

Los esfuerzos de muchas personas en América Latina por construir una democracia sólida y estable han dado muy buenos resultados en Chile, ya que este país acaba de terminar una transición de la dictadura militar de Pinochet a un sistema de gobierno civil. Durante casi veinte años el pueblo chileno ha luchado para acercarse cada vez más al ideal político de la democracia. En 2006, Michelle Bachelet fue elegida como la primera presidenta de Chile, y la octava mujer en ocupar un cargo semejante en América Latina, después de Isabel Martínez de Perón en Argentina, Lidia Gueiler Tejada en Bolivia, Violeta Chamorro en Nicaragua, Ertha Pascal Troullot en Haití, Mireya Moscoso en Panamá, Janet Jagan en Guyana y Rosalía Arteaga en Ecuador. Para los chilenos, desde la década de los 90 en adelante, cuando empezó la transición, han sido años difíciles, y muchas de esas dificultades han sido retratadas en otra película, *Fiesta patria*, del director Luis Vera. Esta película presenta una reflexión sobre el estado social del Chile de hoy.

493

14-39 PRIMERA FASE. **Reconocimiento de palabras clave.** Encuentre en el texto la palabra o expresión que mejor expresa el significado de las siguientes ideas.

1. border conflicts — conflictos de fronteras
2. neighboring countries — países vecinos
3. fertilizer — fertilizante
4. human rights — derechos humanos
5. good results — buenos resultados
6. portrayed — retratadas

SEGUNDA FASE. **Oraciones importantes.** Subraye las afirmaciones que contienen ideas que se encuentran en el texto. Luego indique en qué parte del texto están.

1. Politics has caused many Latin Americans to fall in love.
2. Many Latin American countries have suffered through civil wars and border conflicts.
3. Latin American societies are divided in many different ways. Among these divisions are the division between urban and rural areas and between the rich and the poor.
4. Chile fought Bolivia and Peru over the Atacama Desert.
5. Peru and Colombia went to war over their common border with Chile.
6. Michelle Bachelet is the first woman to become president of a Latin American country.
7. Military dictatorships are the cause of some of the most difficult times in Latin American political history.
8. Argentina was under military rule while Chile was under the Pinochet dictatorship.

TERCERA FASE. **Ideas principales.** Escriba un párrafo breve en español resumiendo las ideas principales expresadas en el texto.

14-40 Use la información. Prepare un afiche sobre un desaparecido/una desaparecida. Presente la información sobre esta persona, incluyendo su nombre, el país y la fecha de su desaparición y otra información que usted crea importante. Para ayudarse en esta actividad, visite la página web de *Mosaicos* y use los enlaces útiles para preparar su presentación.

CD 6
ks 16–21

VOCABULARIO

La sociedad — *Society*

la adaptación	*adjustment, adaptation*
al analfabetismo	*illiteracy*
el cambio	*change*
la confianza	*trust*
la democracia	*democracy*
el derecho	*right*
el desempleo	*unemployment*
el desplazamiento	*movement, displacement*
la diversificación	*diversification*
la eficiencia	*efficiency*
la elección	*election*
la emigración	*emigration*
la esperanza de vida	*life expectancy*
la exportación	*export*
la honestidad	*honesty*
la igualdad	*equality*
la inmigración	*immigration*
la lucha	*fight*
la migración	*migration*
la mortalidad	*mortality*
la pobreza	*poverty*
la proximidad	*proximity*
el régimen	*regime*
el tráfico de drogas	*drug trafficking*

Las encuestas — *Surveys/Polls*

los datos	*data*
la mayoría	*majority*
el porcentaje	*percentage*
el promedio	*average*
la tasa	*rate*

Las personas — *People*

el/la emigrante	*emigrant*
el/la habitante	*inhabitant*
la población	*population*
el presidente/la presidenta	*president*

Las descripciones — *Descriptions*

actual	*present, current*
amplio/a	*ample*
analfabeto/a	*illiterate*
dictatorial	*dictatorial*
enérgico/a	*energetic*
infantil	*children's*
políglota	*polyglot, multilingual*

Verbos — *Verbs*

destacarse	*to stand out*
elegir (i, i)	*to choose, to elect*
gobernar (ie)	*to govern*
mejorar	*to improve*
preceder	*to precede*
realizar (c)	*to carry out*

Palabras y expresiones útiles — *Useful words and expressions*

el nivel	*level*
en vez de	*instead of*
la sucursal	*branch (business)*

See pages 474 and 477 for a list of adverbial conjunctions.

Resources

■ IRM: Syllabi & Lesson Plans

Chapter contents. *A primera vista* (p. 498): *La ciencia y la tecnología en el mundo de hoy*; *La conservación del medio ambiente*; *Otros retos del futuro*; **En acción** (p. 505): *Diarios de bicicleta: La despedida*; **Funciones y formas** (p. 506): 1. Expressing wishes and recommendations in the past: The imperfect subjunctive; 2. Hypothesizing about the present and the future: *If*-clauses; 3. Expressing the unexpected: *Se* for unplanned occurrences; **Mosaicos** (p. 516): *A escuchar:* Identify the speaker's intention through the main idea and specific information; *A conversar:* Use drama and humor in telling a personal anecdote; *A leer:* Identify the narrator's perspective; *A escribir:* Use imagination and humor in writing a narrative; **Enfoque cultural** (p. 522): *La ciencia y la tecnología*; **Vocabulario** (p. 525).

Note. Zulia Gotay de Anderson is a Puerto Rican painter who specializes in female subjects and Hispanic themes. She uses mainly oils and watercolors in her paintings.

Suggestions. Introduce the words *óleo* (oil painting) and *acuarela* (watercolor) when talking about this artist. Use questions to help students describe the painting: *¿Dónde están estas mujeres? ¿Están felices? ¿Tienen miedo?* Introduce other words that refer to emotions: *Las mujeres están preocupadas. Están aterradas probablemente.* Ask students to explain those emotions: *¿Por qué? ¿Qué pasa en el mar?* Recycle climate and weather vocabulary: *¿Qué pasa cuando hay una tormenta en el mar?* Help students describe the ongoing actions in the painting.

Ask students about their artistic talents: *¿Les gusta pintar? ¿Prefiere usted pintar*

CAPÍTULO

15

Hacia el futuro

La tormenta (2000), de Zulia Gotay de Anderson, pintora puertorriqueña

In this chapter you will learn how to:

- talk about advances in science and technology
- express wishes and recommendations in the past
- hypothesize about the present and the future
- express unexpected occurrences

Cultural focus: **Puerto Rico**

OCÉANO ATLÁNTICO

Calles de El Viejo San Juan

Parque Nacional de El Yunque

Arecibo
Observatorio astronómico de Arecibo

San Juan
Bayamón
Manatí **Guaynabo** **Carolina**

Trujillo Alto
Caguas

PUERTO RICO
Mayagüez
Cerro de Punta ▲

CORDILLERA CENTRAL

Humacao

La cascada La Coca

Isla de Culebra

El coquí, la rana nativa de Puerto Rico

Isla de Vieques

San Germán **Ponce** **Guayama**
Arroyo

Cabo Rojo

Mar Caribe

El Carnaval de Ponce

al óleo o con acuarela? Ask: ¿Alguien en esta clase usa la computadora para dibujar? ¿Qué programas para pintar conocen?

Note. The Arecibo observatory, which provides technical support to scientists worldwide, has a sensitive radio telescope with a surface of 305 meters (1,000 feet) in diameter. Situated in a natural crater in the mountains of Puerto Rico, its dual reflector antenna system sends and receives signals to study planets and asteroids.

Note. Remind students that since 1952, Puerto Rico has been a commonwealth (*Estado Libre Asociado*) of the U.S., which controls all areas of Puerto Rico's government except its internal affairs. The differences between Puerto Rico and the 50 states are its exemption from some aspects of the Internal Revenue Code, and its lack of representation in both houses of the U.S. Congress. Puerto Ricans cannot vote in U.S. presidential elections unless they are residents of one of the 50 states. The political status of the island has been the object of controversy over the years.

Suggestions. Ask students about Puerto Rico: *¿Cómo es el clima? ¿Cuál es la capital? ¿Qué relación tiene con Estados Unidos? ¿En qué ciudades continentales de Estados Unidos viven muchos puertorriqueños? ¿Conocen alguna comida típica de Puerto Rico?* Talk about *mofongo,* a typical dish made from fried plantains or yucca, served with chicken or meat. *¿Conocen alguna costumbre de Puerto Rico? ¿Alguna persona famosa de Puerto Rico?* Ask if students have heard of the *coquí* and point to the photo. You may refer students to the *Enfoque cultural* for more information about Arecibo.

 A vista de pájaro. Complete las siguientes oraciones con información de Puerto Rico que usted sabe. Answers may vary.

1. Una comida típica de Puerto Rico es _____el mofongo_____.
2. Un animal típico de Puerto Rico es _____el coquí_____.
3. Muchos puertorriqueños hablan dos idiomas, el _____inglés_____ y el _____español_____.
4. El deporte más popular en Puerto Rico es _____el béisbol_____.
5. El clima de Puerto Rico es _____tropical_____.
6. El Yunque es _un parque nacional_.

497

Resources

- SAM: 15-1 to 15-10
- Supp. Activ. Book: *A primera vista*

A PRIMERA VISTA

La ciencia y la tecnología en el mundo de hoy

CD 6
Track 22

Antes de salir para la universidad Ángel, un joven puertorriqueño, **enciende** su computadora, abre Internet y **se conecta** con sus amigos. Entra en Facebook, le da un *poke* a Laura y le manda un *hug* a Carmen. Luego mira su correo electrónico por si tiene algún *podcast* para su clase *online* y le envía a su profesor de ciencias naturales un **mensaje** con un **documento adjunto.**

Entonces, Lorena, la hermana de Ángel, le pide que le **baje** una canción de Internet para **meterla** en su *mp3*. Por último, entra en el *blog* de su amigo Juanjo para leer las últimas novedades sobre sus **videojuegos** preferidos. Allí encuentra un **enlace** que le interesa.

Actualmente, la ciencia y la tecnología **contribuyen** a **unificar** algunas de las diferencias culturales que existen entre los pueblos. Los jóvenes de Europa e Hispanoamérica tienen muchas cosas en común con los de Asia, África o Estados Unidos. El **acceso** a Internet y a los teléfonos celulares hacen más fluida la comunicación y el **intercambio** de información.

Hace unos años se creó en Puerto Rico el Instituto de la Ciencia y la Tecnología para **difundir** noticias relacionadas con estas materias en América Latina. Pero el ICLT no es un instituto tradicional, sino una **biblioteca virtual.** Hoy en día las bibliotecas virtuales y los **buscadores** son una importante **fuente** de **recursos** y **diseminación** de **conocimientos.**

15-1 ¿Para qué lo usamos? En las siguientes afirmaciones relacionadas con diversos usos de tecnología, marque (✓) el uso que *no* corresponde.

1. Internet sirve para…
   a. acceder a información sobre muchas disciplinas.
   b. ver películas.
   c. enviar felicitaciones.
   d. calentar el café del desayuno.

2. El correo electrónico se usa para…
   a. comunicarse con los amigos.
   b. hacer fotografías.
   c. enviar un documento adjunto.
   d. recibir mensajes.

3. La biblioteca virtual se utiliza para…
   a. saludar a los profesores de la universidad.
   b. encontrar enlaces.
   c. bajar artículos.
   d. identificar documentación.

4. Los videojuegos sirven para…
   a. divertirse con los amigos.
   b. practicar deportes al aire libre.
   c. diseminar ciertos conocimientos.
   d. intercambiar información.

Suggestion for 15-1. To prepare for this activity have students brainstorm the uses of the Internet: *¿Para qué sirve Internet?* Write down their answers.

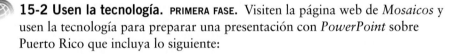

15-2 Usen la tecnología. **PRIMERA FASE.** Visiten la página web de *Mosaicos* y usen la tecnología para preparar una presentación con *PowerPoint* sobre Puerto Rico que incluya lo siguiente:

1. localización de un lugar en un mapa
2. descripción y tres datos que se refieran a las características físicas del lugar, la gente del lugar y una costumbre del lugar
3. fotos

SEGUNDA FASE. Compartan la información con la clase, incluyendo una descripción de los recursos tecnológicos que utilizaron.

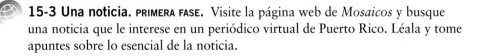

15-3 Una noticia. **PRIMERA FASE.** Visite la página web de *Mosaicos* y busque una noticia que le interese en un periódico virtual de Puerto Rico. Léala y tome apuntes sobre lo esencial de la noticia.

SEGUNDA FASE. Mande un correo electrónico a tres personas de la clase, incluyendo un resumen de la noticia y su opinión sobre la noticia.

Suggestion for 15-3 Segunda fase. As an alternative for the *Segunda fase*, if some students agree to use their cell phones, you may ask them to leave the class and call those still in the class to comment on the piece of news that they read.

Suggestion. Ask students to mention some ecological problems in the world, such as the damage of the ozone layer, pollution, acid rain, overpopulation, or the destruction of the rain forest. Provide any needed vocabulary. Move the discussion into speculation about the future. For example, in the field of medicine, will there be a cure for cancer, heart disease, AIDS?

La conservación del medio ambiente

CD 6
Track 23

La contribución de América Latina a la ciencia **se ha enfocado** principalmente en la biología, **debido a** la riqueza de la flora y la fauna, la **conservación** de la **naturaleza**, la agricultura y la medicina. Aunque a veces las **infraestructuras** y los recursos son insuficientes, algunos científicos de esta región han hecho **descubrimientos** importantes. Esta es una foto de El Yunque, en Puerto Rico, una de las muchas **reservas naturales** de Hispanoamérica.

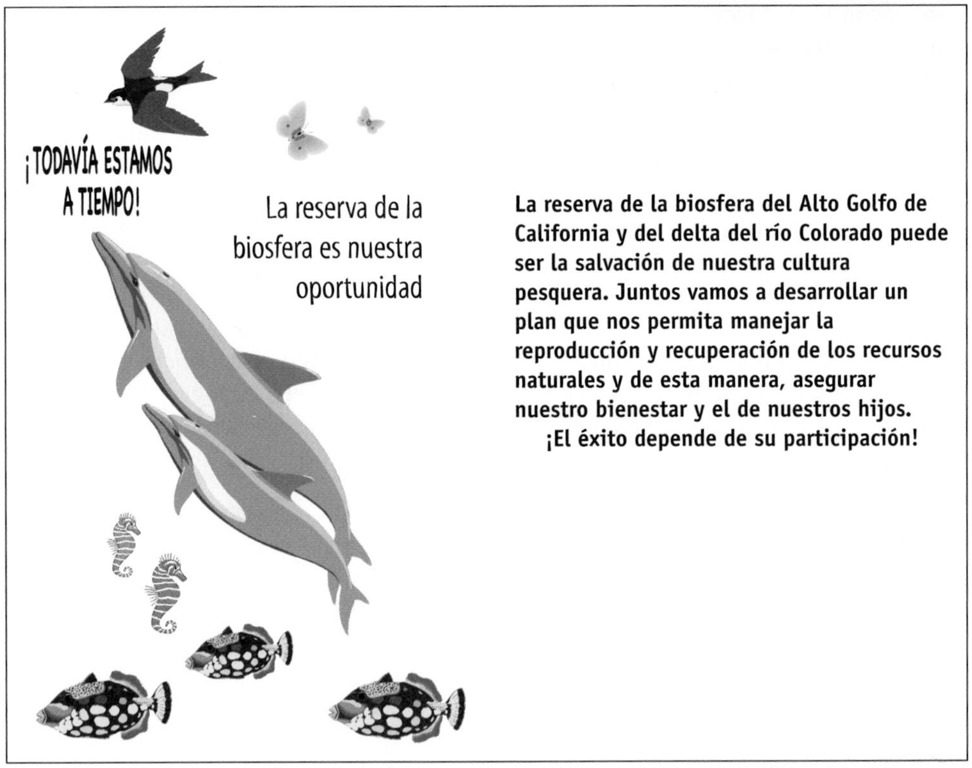
¡TODAVÍA ESTAMOS A TIEMPO!
La reserva de la biosfera es nuestra oportunidad
La reserva de la biosfera del Alto Golfo de California y del delta del río Colorado puede ser la salvación de nuestra cultura pesquera. Juntos vamos a desarrollar un plan que nos permita manejar la reproducción y recuperación de los recursos naturales y de esta manera, asegurar nuestro bienestar y el de nuestros hijos.
¡El éxito depende de su participación!

Suggestion. Some students may find it helpful for you to explain the metaphor *pulmón del planeta*.

La **cuenca** del río Amazonas cubre un área de más de siete millones de kilómetros cuadrados, región comparable en extensión a dos terceras partes del territorio continental de Estados Unidos. Debido a su densa vegetación selvática, esta área es conocida como el "pulmón" del **planeta**. Hoy en día, miles de campesinos llegan a la selva **en busca de tierra** para cultivar. La **deforestación** de nuestros **bosques** se considera una **pérdida** irreparable para el **medio ambiente**.

15-4 Amigos de la tierra. PRIMERA FASE. Indiquen cuáles de los siguientes problemas se asocian con la industria pesquera (**IP**), con los bosques tropicales (**BT**) o con los dos.

1. ___BT___ la construcción de carreteras
2. ___BT___ la desertización
3. ___BT___ la erosión
4. ___BT, IP___ la exterminación de especies animales
5. ___BT___ la tala (*felling*) de árboles
6. ___IP___ la contaminación provocada por aguas residuales (*sewage*) y substancias químicas
7. ___BT___ la disminución de la capa de ozono
8. ___IP___ la pesca indiscriminada

SEGUNDA FASE. Den ideas para resolver cada problema.

15-5 Los adelantos (*Advances*) científicos. PRIMERA FASE. Haga una lista de tres adelantos científicos y tres cambios sociales que usted espera que se realicen en las próximas décadas.

ADELANTOS CIENTÍFICOS	CAMBIOS SOCIALES

SEGUNDA FASE. Comparen sus listas y justifiquen la razón de los cambios que indicaron en la *Primera fase*. ¿Por qué ocurrirán? ¿Son cambios necesarios?

15-6 Organizaciones ecologistas. Busquen información en Internet sobre organizaciones como Greenpeace o el Club Sierra, cuyo propósito es la protección del medio ambiente. Escojan una de esas organizaciones y preparen un breve informe oral con la siguiente información:

1. ¿Qué objetivos tiene la organización?
2. ¿Cómo se financia?
3. ¿Quiénes trabajan o hacen voluntariado en ella?
4. ¿Cuál fue una de sus campañas recientes?
5. ¿Qué objetivos tenía la campaña?
6. ¿Cómo la realizaron?
7. ¿Cuál fue el resultado de la campaña?
8. ¿En qué capacidad cree usted que podría ayudar?

Follow-up for 15-4. Compare the proposals of various pairs of students, emphasizing the variety of ideas presented to solve current ecological problems.

Suggestion for 15-5. Have one student write on the board the advances and changes that students include in their lists. The class can try to reach a consensus on the feasibility of achieving such progress.

ɾ)) Otros retos del futuro

CD 6
Track 24

LAS CIUDADES

■ Se **construirán** ciudades verticales con edificios **climatizados** por medio de **energía solar.** Algunas se construirán sobre el mar.

■ El 90% de la población vivirá en las ciudades.

■ Todas las basuras urbanas serán **recicladas.**

EL MAR

■ El nivel del mar subirá por los **deshielos** debido al **calentamiento** de la atmósfera y causará **inundaciones** y **la desaparición** de algunas costas.

■ La contaminación de los mares provocará la **extinción** de los **bancos de peces.**

LA ATMÓSFERA

■ El agujero de la **capa de ozono** hará aumentar el número de enfermos de cáncer de piel.

■ Se cultivarán plantas que mejoren la calidad del aire.

LAS VIVIENDAS

■ Todos los hogares estarán conectados a Internet. Las compras se harán siempre **virtualmente.**

■ Las puertas y los aparatos electrónicos serán activados por la voz o con sensores que reconocerán a cada individuo.

■ Habrá **robots** que se ocuparán de hacer la limpieza.

EL TRANSPORTE

■ Los trenes de alta velocidad conectarán las grandes ciudades y circularán por **rieles** suspendidos a la altura de los edificios.

■ Los coches combinarán la energía eléctrica y la energía solar. Serán pequeñas **cápsulas voladoras** que podrán **despegar** y **aterrizar** verticalmente como los helicópteros.

■ El tráfico aéreo será controlado por satélite.

LA CIENCIA Y LA TECNOLOGÍA

■ Habrá **clonaciones** de animales **extinguidos**.

■ Los embriones humanos se seleccionarán **genéticamente**.

■ Todos los teléfonos móviles tendrán una computadora incorporada.

■ Se explorarán energías alternativas.

■ Se **repoblarán** los bosques con técnicas avanzadas para eliminar la desertización.

15-7 Un futuro mejor. PRIMERA FASE. Comparen el mundo de hoy con el del futuro basándose en las fotos anteriores. Consideren por lo menos dos de los siguientes temas: uso de ciencia-tecnología, medio ambiente, transporte, calidad de vida, criminalidad, delincuencia, consumismo, salud.

SEGUNDA FASE. Ahora hablen sobre dos problemas específicos que existen en la ciudad contemporánea. Hagan una lista de dos aspectos de cada problema que les gustaría mejorar. Luego, compartan sus ideas con el resto de la clase.

MODELO: *En la ciudad del presente hay poca seguridad física. Cualquier persona puede tener un arma y matar a quien quiera. Nos gustaría proponer una ley para limitar el uso de las armas de fuego (firearms).*

15-8 El reto más serio de hoy. Preparen un informe oral sobre el reto más serio que enfrentan el mundo y el ser humano hoy, según su opinión. Describan detalladamente el problema y ofrezcan algunas soluciones.

15-9 ¡El futuro es hoy! Primero, individualmente hagan una lista de cinco cosas (aparatos, sistemas de comunicación, transporte, etc.) que existen hoy y que no existían cuando sus padres tenían la edad de usted. Luego, comparen su lista entre ustedes y expliquen el impacto y las consecuencias de estas nuevas cosas en sus vidas.

15-10 Los OVNIS (Objetos Voladores No Identificados). Lean la tira cómica de Mafalda. Imagínense que han visto una nave espacial de otro planeta. Describan todo lo que vieron, comentando las semejanzas y las diferencias entre ustedes y los visitantes desconocidos.

 15-11 ¿Vamos al planeta Marte? ¿Creen ustedes que, durante su vida, será posible viajar al planeta Marte? Planeen el viaje y expliquen con quiénes irán, qué llevarán, cuánto tiempo tardarán en llegar, qué verán allí y cómo se sentirán física y emocionalmente en este nuevo ambiente. Compartan su plan con otros astronautas (sus compañeros/as) para formular el mejor plan posible.

15-12 El problema de la alimentación. You will listen to a short talk about the problem of feeding the world's population. Before you listen, list two problems you think the speaker may mention and two solutions you think she may provide.

CD 6
Track 25

First, read the following incomplete ideas. Then, as you listen, pay attention to the general idea of what is said and mark (✓) the appropriate ending to each statement.

1. Los gobiernos tienen que solucionar el problema de…
   ___ la agricultura tradicional.
   _✓_ la falta de alimentos para la población.
   ___ las pocas variedades de productos.
2. La tecnología y los científicos…
   _✓_ pueden ayudar a solucionar este problema.
   ___ trabajan en las Islas Filipinas.
   ___ desarrollan computadoras de mucha utilidad.
3. Si se aumenta la producción del arroz, los gobiernos pueden…
   ___ exportarlo y ganar más dinero.
   _✓_ alimentar a más personas.
   ___ obtener variedades más nutritivas.
4. Hay que aprovechar los avances de la tecnología, pero también es necesario…
   ___ aumentar la productividad en un 70%.
   ___ conseguir alimentos básicos.
   _✓_ preservar el medio ambiente.

EN ACCIÓN

Resources
- Video
- SAM: 15-11 to 15-13

Diarios de bicicleta: La despedida

Antes de ver

15-13 En el siguiente segmento, Javier graba (*tapes*) a sus amigos hablando de sí mismos. ¿De qué cree usted que podrían hablar? Answers may vary.

Mientras ve

15-14 Indique si las siguientes afirmaciones son ciertas (**C**) o falsas (**F**), según lo que dicen los personajes.

Luciana
1. _F_ Conocí a Javier en un concierto.
2. _C_ Si no fuera por Javier, no sabría nada de Colombia, Panamá ni Costa Rica.
3. _C_ El Distrito Federal es una de las ciudades más grandes del planeta.

Gabi
4. _C_ Estudio teatro y danza en la universidad.
5. _F_ No soy de México sino de Medellín.

Daniel
6. _C_ Vengo de Oaxaca y estudio computación.
7. _F_ Espero ir a España algún día.

Después de ver

15-15 PRIMERA FASE. Mire sus respuestas en *Antes de ver* y subraye los temas de los que los personajes hablaron.

SEGUNDA FASE. Complete las siguientes frases: Answers may vary.
1. Si Gabi viajara en bicicleta por Centroamérica _____.
2. Si Daniel fuera a Colombia _____.
3. Si (yo) conociera a Javier, _____.

Suggestion for 15-13. Have students base some of their hypotheses on the title of this segment, *La despedida,* in conjunction with the still photos at the bottom of this page.

Suggestion for 15-14. You may wish to have students correct the statements that are false.

FUNCIONES Y FORMAS

1. Expressing wishes and recommendations in the past: The imperfect subjunctive

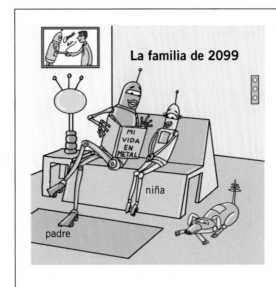

La familia de 2099

padre

niña

PADRE: ¿Qué quieres que **hagamos** ahora?

NIÑA: Papá, quiero que me **cuentes** un cuento.

PADRE: Muy bien, hija. Cuando mi abuelo era niño, los seres humanos querían que los robots **hicieran** todo su trabajo. Mis abuelos limpiaban la casa, preparaban las comidas, hacían las tareas de los niños...

NIÑA: ¡Qué terrible, papá! Pero luego, ¿qué pasó?

PADRE: Los políticos recomendaron que los científicos **produjeran** robots más complejos. Querían que los robots **tuvieran** computadoras muy potentes (*powerful*). Los científicos temían que los robots **fueran** más inteligentes que ellos, pero los políticos insistieron en que los científicos los **construyeran** con más capacidad intelectual. Entonces...

Piénselo. Indique (✓) si las siguientes oraciones se refieren al presente/al futuro o al pasado.

	PRESENT/FUTURO	PASADO
1. ¿Qué quieres que **hagamos** ahora?	✓	
2. Quiero que me **cuentes** un cuento.	✓	
3. Los seres humanos querían que los robots **hicieran** todo su trabajo.		✓
4. Los políticos recomendaron que los científicos **produjeran** robots más complejos.		✓
5. Querían que los robots **tuvieran** computadoras muy potentes.		✓
6. Los científicos temían que los robots **fueran** más inteligentes que ellos.		✓
7. Los políticos insistieron en que los **construyeran** con más capacidad intelectual.		✓

■ In previous chapters, you studied the forms and uses of the present subjunctive. Now you will study the past subjunctive, also called the imperfect subjunctive. All regular and irregular past subjunctive verb forms are based on the **ustedes/ellos/ellas** form of the preterit. Drop the **-on** preterit ending and substitute the past subjunctive endings. Note the written accent on the **nosotros/as** forms.

PAST OR IMPERFECT SUBJUNCTIVE				
	HABLAR	**COMER**	**VIVIR**	**ESTAR**
	(hablar~~on~~)	(comier~~on~~)	(vivier~~on~~)	(estuvier~~on~~)
yo	habl**ara**	com**iera**	viv**iera**	estuv**iera**
tú	habl**aras**	com**ieras**	viv**ieras**	estuv**ieras**
Ud., él, ella	habl**ara**	com**iera**	viv**iera**	estuv**iera**
nosotros/as	habl**áramos**	com**iéramos**	viv**iéramos**	estuv**iéramos**
vosotros/as	habl**arais**	com**ierais**	viv**ierais**	estuv**ierais**
Uds., ellos/as	habl**aran**	com**ieran**	viv**ieran**	estuv**ieran**

■ The present subjunctive is oriented to the present or future, whereas the past subjunctive focuses on the past. In general, the same rules that determine the use of the present subjunctive also apply to the past subjunctive.

HOY O MAÑANA → PRESENT SUBJUNCTIVE

Sandra quiere comprar una computadora portátil que **sea** ligera.
Sandra wants to buy a laptop that is lightweight.

Hablará con sus amigos para que le **den** unas recomendaciones.
She will talk to her friends so that they will give her some recommendations.

AYER → PAST SUBJUNCTIVE

Sandra quería una computadora portátil que **fuera** ligera.
Sandra wanted a laptop that was lightweight.

Habló con sus amigos para que le **dieran** unas recomendaciones.
She talked to her friends so that they would give her some recommendations.

■ Always use the past subjunctive after **como si** (*as if, as though*).

Gastan dinero en aparatos electrónicos **como si fueran** millonarios.
They spend money on electronic gadgets as though they were millionaires.

Hablaba con la científica **como si entendiera** el problema.
He talked with the scientist as if he understood the problem.

Suggestions. You may wish to review the *Uds./ellos/ellas* forms of the preterit before introducing the past subjunctive. Do a quick question/answer activity: *¿Salieron ustedes anoche? ¿Adónde fueron? ¿Y qué hicieron allí?* Use related questions to simulate natural conversation and spontaneity. Remind students that they have used the imperfect subjunctive of *querer* for polite requests: *Quisiera comprar un regalo para un amigo.*

Suggestion. You may wish to review (or have students review at home) the functions and forms of the present subjunctive, starting with *Capítulo 11.*

15-16 Cuando era niño/a. PRIMERA FASE. Marque (✓) lo que sus padres querían o no querían que usted hiciera cuando era niño/a. Después compare sus respuestas con las de su compañero/a.

____ **1.** Querían que yo comiera muchos vegetales y frutas.

____ **2.** Querían que yo estudiara ciencias.

____ **3.** No querían que yo viera programas violentos en la televisión.

____ **4.** Querían que yo cuidara el medio ambiente.

____ **5.** Querían que yo leyera sobre el programa espacial y los astronautas.

____ **6.** No querían que yo estuviera sin hacer nada.

SEGUNDA FASE. Ahora, marque con un círculo lo que usted quería que sus padres hicieran cuando era niño/a. Luego, compare sus respuestas con las de su compañero/a. Añada otra opción, si es necesario.

1. Para divertirme con la tecnología…
 a. yo quería que mis padres me llevaran a ver una nave espacial.
 b. deseaba que mis padres me permitieran jugar a videojuegos muchas horas.
2. Para estar con mis amigos…
 a. yo quería que mis padres me llevaran al parque los fines de semana.
 b. les pedía a mis padres que me permitieran jugar en las casas de ellos.
3. Para pasarlo bien los fines de semana…
 a. yo quería que mis padres me dieran más dinero.
 b. insistía en que mis padres me permitieran tener fiestas en casa.
4. Para celebrar mi cumpleaños…
 a. siempre quería que mis padres me regalaran juguetes electrónicos.
 b. prefería que mis padres me compraran ropa.

 15-17 En el laboratorio. Miguel es un estudiante muy inteligente, pero muy distraído. Hoy hizo unos experimentos con su profesor de química en el laboratorio. ¿Qué le dijo el profesor en estas situaciones? Túrnense para dar respuestas lógicas.

MODELO: Miguel no se puso los guantes para hacer el experimento.
 El profesor le dijo que se pusiera los guantes.

1. Llegó tarde al laboratorio.
2. Escuchaba música mientras hacía un experimento.
3. Dejó una botella de alcohol cerca de una estufa.
4. No esterilizó unos instrumentos.
5. Recibió una llamada en su celular.
6. La mesa donde Miguel trabajaba estaba muy desordenada.
7. No comparó sus resultados con los del estudiante graduado del profesor.
8. Salió del laboratorio durante un experimento para conversar con su novia.

Answers for 15-17. 1. *El profesor le dijo que no llegara tarde.* 2. *Le dijo que no escuchara música mientras hacía un experimento.* 3. *Le sugirió que no dejara el alcohol cerca de una estufa.* 4. *Le dijo que esterilizara los instrumentos.* 5. *Le pidió que no recibiera llamadas.* 6. *Le aconsejó que ordenara la mesa.* 7. *Le dijo que comparara sus resultados con los del estudiante graduado.* 8. *Le dijo que no saliera para hablar con su novia durante un experimento.*

En otras palabras

For cell phones both **teléfonos móviles** and **teléfonos celulares** are used. The phrases are usually shortened to **móvil** and **celular**.

15-18 Alguien que no nos cae bien. PRIMERA FASE. Imagínense que ustedes conocen a una persona arrogante que se cree mejor que nadie. Digan cómo se comporta esta persona en los siguientes aspectos de su vida. Pueden usar los verbos que aparecen más abajo u otros.

MODELO: cuando va de un lugar a otro a pie
Camina como si fuera la única persona en la calle.

cambiar	manejar
caminar	usar
discutir	vestirse
gastar	vivir

1. cuando quiere comprar algo
2. cuando se prepara para salir con un grupo de amigos
3. cuando habla con otras personas
4. cuando sube a (*gets into*) su automóvil

SEGUNDA FASE. Ahora respondan a las siguientes preguntas.

1. ¿Conoce usted a alguna persona que sea arrogante?
2. ¿Qué hábito o comportamiento de esa persona le molesta a usted? ¿Por qué?
3. ¿Le gustaría a usted que esta persona cambiara? Si es así, ¿qué costumbre o comportamiento le gustaría que cambiara?

Alternate for 15-18. Have students finish the following ideas in a chain: 1. *Mi carro traga (gulps) gasolina como si...* 2. *Los programadores de computadoras trabajan como si...* 3. *Los pilotos manejan los aviones como si...* 4. *La gente consume gasolina como si...* 5. *Todas las compañías se modernizan con nueva tecnología como si...*

SITUACIONES

1. **Role A.** You belong to an organization that wants to reduce pollution and the deterioration of the environment. You are disappointed that the organization has not accomplished more. Tell your partner a) what activities you hoped the group would organize; b) what impact you wanted those activities to have on the community; and c) what the group has accomplished up to now. Explain how you feel as a member of the group.

   Role B. Your partner tells you about an ecological organization to which he/she belongs. After listening to a description of the group and its activities, ask about members' duties, meetings, and so on. Say that you have some ideas to make the group more effective, and find out the date and time of the next meeting.

2. **Role A.** You are unhappy with your new laptop. You go back to the store where you bought it and tell the manager that a) you hoped the laptop would be lightweight, but it isn't; b) you were looking for a computer that had graphics applications (**aplicaciones gráficas**), but this one doesn't; and c) you would like to return (**devolver**) it.

   Role B. You are the manager of the computer department of an electronics store. A customer is unhappy with a recent laptop purchase and tells you why. Explain that a) the store does not give refunds (**devolver el dinero**); b) you would be glad to exchange the laptop for a different one; and c) you hope that the customer will like the new laptop.

Resources

■ SAM: 15-21 to 15-27
■ Supp. Activ. Book:
    If-clauses

2. Hypothesizing about the present and the future: *If*-clauses

MATEO: Oye, Lucía. ¿Has visto el nuevo teléfono celular cámara? ¡Es increíble! **Si** la tecnología **continúa** avanzando así, pronto **producirán** un automóvil-tanque.

LUCÍA: **Si** lo **hicieran**, no me **sorprendería**. Pero **si** la ciencia **avanza** tan rápidamente, ¿por qué no **podemos** conseguir la paz? Yo no quiero que se perfeccione la tecnología para matar a la gente.

MATEO: Buen punto, Lucía. **Si** los jóvenes no **hacemos** nada para controlar los usos de la tecnología, no **tendremos** un mañana.

Suggestion for Piénselo. You may wish to draw students' attention to the sequence of tenses in the P/F vs. I statements. Help students understand the logical relationships between the actions in the two clauses in each type of sentence.

Piénselo. Indique si las siguientes afirmaciones hechas por Mateo y Lucía indican una condición relacionada con el presente (**P**), con el futuro (**F**) o si indican una condición que es improbable (**I**) que se cumpla (*fulfill*).

1. __F__ **Si** la tecnología **continúa** avanzando así, pronto **producirán** un automóvil-tanque.
2. __I__ **Si** lo **hicieran**, no me **sorprendería**.
3. __P__ Pero **si** la ciencia **avanza** tan rápidamente, ¿por qué no **podemos** conseguir la paz?
4. __F__ **Si** los jóvenes no **hacemos** nada para controlar los usos de la tecnología, no **tendremos** un mañana.

Suggestion. Students may grasp the temporal and logical relationships in the statements if they identify whether the action in the dependent clause (the *if*-clause) refers to the present or the future, with respect to the time frame established in the dependent clause.

■ To express what happens or will happen *if* certain conditions are met, use the present or future indicative in the main clause and the present indicative in the *if*-clause.

Si **continuamos** cortando árboles, los bosques **van a** desaparecer.
If we continue cutting down trees, forests will disappear.

Si **creamos** tecnología para cuidar los recursos naturales, las generaciones futuras **tendrán** una vida mejor.
If we create technology to protect the natural resources, future generations will have a better life.

Puedes obtener información sobre las últimas novedades tecnológicas si la **buscas** en Internet.
You can get information on the latest technology if you look for it on the Internet.

■ To express a condition that is unlikely or contrary to fact, use the imperfect subjunctive in the *if*-clause. Use the conditional in the main clause.

Si le **dieran** más dinero al aeropuerto, el tráfico aéreo **podría** mejorar.
If they gave more money to the airport, air traffic could improve.

Si **usáramos** la energía solar en las casas, **ahorraríamos** mucho petróleo.
If we used solar energy in our homes, we would save a lot of oil.

15-19 El mundo que todos queremos. Complete cada idea de la izquierda con una de las conclusiones de la derecha. En algunos casos, puede haber más de una respuesta lógica. Luego compare sus respuestas con las de su compañero/a.

1. __b__ Si tuviéramos más dinero en las escuelas,…
2. __e__ Si hubiera menos armas de fuego en manos de la gente,…
3. __a__ Si cuidáramos más nuestro planeta,…
4. __c__ Tendríamos un mundo mejor,…
5. __d__ Si hubiera trenes de alta velocidad,…
6. __f__ Gastaríamos menos gasolina,…

a. no contaminaríamos tanto el medio ambiente.
b. todos los alumnos tendrían acceso a los laboratorios para hacer investigación.
c. si todos nos respetáramos y dialogáramos en vez de pelear.
d. las personas manejarían menos en las carreteras.
e. habría menos homicidios en la sociedad.
f. si usáramos el transporte público.

15-20 ¿Qué pasa si… ? Túrnense para decir qué resultados se pueden obtener si se hacen ciertas cosas.

MODELO: leer los periódicos
Si todos leen los periódicos regularmente, sabrán qué está pasando en el mundo.

1. usar solamente tecnología para aprender otra lengua
2. inventar aparatos electrónicos desechables (*disposable*)
3. proteger los recursos naturales
4. legalizar las drogas
5. comunicarse solamente por correo electrónico
6. construir más estaciones espaciales

15-21 ¿Cómo sería el mundo? Den sus razones para explicar cómo sería el mundo si se dieran las siguientes circunstancias. Después, compartan sus ideas con otros/as estudiantes.

1. si no hubiera televisión
2. si los seres humanos viviéramos más de 150 años
3. si la clonación fuera legal
4. si no existieran fronteras entre los países
5. si pudiéramos viajar en autos supersónicos a todas partes
6. si toda la educación se hiciera por Internet

En directo

To ask that people request the floor before speaking:

Por favor, no interrumpa(n) sin pedir la palabra.
Please don't interrupt without requesting the floor.

Pida(n) la palabra.
Request the floor.

To request the floor:

Yo quisiera decir/añadir/ explicar algo.
I would like to say/add/explain something.

¿Podría añadir/agregar algo?
Could I add something?

To give the floor to someone:

X tiene la palabra.
X has the floor.

Dinos lo que tú piensas.
Tell us what you think.

15-22 Cambios. PRIMERA FASE. Identifique un problema serio en cada una de las siguientes áreas en la vida de su comunidad, de su país o del mundo. Tome notas de por qué lo considera un problema serio.

1. la seguridad personal y/o colectiva
2. el consumo excesivo de alcohol por los jóvenes
3. el transporte público
4. el costo de las necesidades básicas, como la comida y la gasolina

SEGUNDA FASE. Ahora compartan el problema más serio en cada área, según ustedes. Explíquenles a sus compañeros por qué lo consideran serio. ¿Qué harían para eliminar cada problema si pudieran?

MODELO: **Área:** el medio ambiente

Problema serio: *la contaminación del aire y el agua*

Razón: *El mal uso y el descuido (neglect) de los recursos naturales como el petróleo han causado el calentamiento del planeta. Todos usamos carros que contaminan el aire. Además, las industrias ponen sus desperdicios (waste) en los ríos. Contaminan el agua que todos bebemos.*

Plan hipotético: *Crearíamos incentivos para usar el transporte público y pondríamos multas (fines) muy altas a las compañías que tiran desperdicios en los ríos.*

SITUACIONES

1. **Role A.** You are the coordinator of your university's new and very strict recycling program. At a meeting with the Student Council, you explain that a) if the publicity campaign (**campaña de publicidad**) starts soon, students and faculty can volunteer to help; b) there will be fines if people don't cooperate; and c) if everyone collaborates, the program will be successful.

   Role B. You are at a meeting of the Student Council at which a new and very strict recycling program is being discussed. Listen to the presentation of the coordinator of the program (your classmate) and ask a) when it will go into effect (**ponerse en marcha**) and b) what will happen if people don't want to cooperate with such a strict program.

2. **Role A.** You are a multi-millionaire who believes that higher education should be radically different in the future. Offer the president of your local college twenty million dollars to implement these innovations: a) there would be no required courses; students could choose all their own courses; b) there would be no exams, only projects and papers; and c) students would tell the faculty what courses should be taught. Respond to the reaction of the college president.

   Role B. You are a college president. A multi-millionaire (your classmate) wants to donate twenty million dollars to your institution to realize his/her vision of an ideal education. Listen and respond with your hypotheses of what would happen if there were no requirements or final exams, and if professors had to create new courses every semester according to students' interests.

Resources

■ SAM: 15-28 to 15-33
■ Supp. Activ. Book: *Se* for unplanned occurrences

3. Expressing the unexpected: *Se* for unplanned occurrences

Piénselo. Indique si en las siguientes afirmaciones se pone énfasis en el evento (**E**) o en la persona responsable del evento (**PR**).

1. __E__ **Se me rompió** la computadora.
2. __PR__ **Rompí** la computadora.
3. __PR__ **Olvidé** las llaves del carro en el café.
4. __E__ **Se me olvidaron** las llaves del carro en el café.
5. __E__ **Se nos perdieron** temporalmente dos planos.
6. __PR__ **Perdimos** temporalmente dos planos.

■ Use **se** + *indirect object* + *verb* to express unplanned or accidental events. This construction puts the focus on the unexpected nature of the event rather than on personal responsibility for its occurrence. Some verbs often used with this construction include **olvidar** (*to forget*), **apagar** (*to turn off*), **acabar** (*to run out of something*), **romper** (*to break, to tear*), and **quedar** (*to leave something behind*).

Se les apagaron las luces del carro.	*The headlights of their car went out.*
A él **se le acabó** el dinero.	*He ran out of money.*
Se nos olvidó el código.	*We forgot the code.*
Se te rompió la chaqueta.	*Your jacket got torn.*

Suggestions. Pretend to accidentally drop your keys, then deliberately drop them: *Se me cayeron las llaves./Dejé caer las llaves.* Have one individual and a group drop, break, or tear one object, then several objects in order to demonstrate the difference between *Se le(s)* and *cayó/cayeron.* Ask *¿Qué le(s) pasó?*

Follow-up for 15-23. Show visuals and ask *¿Qué le(s) pasó?* Visuals may show someone with a broken leg, a baseball catcher missing the ball, a groom who forgot the ring. Be imaginative!

■ Use an indirect object pronoun (**me, te, le, nos, os, les**) to indicate whom the unplanned event affects. Place the pronoun between **se** and the verb. If what is lost, forgotten, and so on, is plural, the verb also must be plural.

Se me quedó el DVD en la computadora. *I left the DVD in the computer.*

Se me quedaron los cables en casa. *I left the cables at home.*

15-23 ¿Qué les pasó? Termine lógicamente las ideas de la columna de la izquierda, usando las ideas de la columna de la derecha.

1. _e_ Hablaron con el plomero porque...
2. _a_ Tuve que usar la tarjeta de crédito porque...
3. _c_ No pude llamarte por el celular porque...
4. _f_ Tuvieron que llamar al electricista porque...
5. _b_ Tuvimos que llamar al técnico porque...
6. _d_ Llegué tarde a casa de mi novia porque...

a. se me quedó el dinero en casa.
b. se nos rompió la computadora.
c. se me olvidó tu nuevo número de teléfono.
d. se me perdió la llave del coche.
e. se les inundó el baño.
f. se les apagaron las luces en la casa.

15-24 Problemas. Usted trabaja en un laboratorio de ingeniería genética. Ayer hubo muchos problemas técnicos. Explique qué pasó. Seleccione su respuesta entre las opciones de la lista u otras propias.

MODELO: El investigador no pudo completar el experimento.
Se le olvidó la fórmula.

perder las llaves	romper la computadora
acabarse la gasolina	escapar el perro en el parque
enfermarse un hijo	perder unos datos importantes
romper el microscopio	quedar documentos confidenciales en un café

1. Los técnicos estaban preocupados después de empezar a observar algunas bacterias. Se les rompió el microscopio.
2. El director nunca falta al trabajo, pero ayer no fue a trabajar. Se le enfermó el hijo.
3. Los ayudantes llegaron tarde de un viaje a un laboratorio en otra ciudad. Se les acabó la gasolina.
4. La doctora Milán no pudo entrar en el laboratorio durante el fin de semana. Se le perdieron las llaves.
5. El subdirector no recibió un correo electrónico importante. Se le rompió la computadora.
6. El presidente de la compañía estaba histérico cuando llegó a la oficina y se dio cuenta de lo que le había ocurrido. Se le habían quedado documentos confidenciales en un café.

15-25 Momentos difíciles. Miren los dibujos y túrnense para contestar las preguntas que siguen.

a. b.

1. ¿Qué les pasó a las personas en los dos dibujos? Inventen un cuento para cada situación: ¿Cuándo y dónde pasó, cómo se sintieron las personas y qué hicieron después?
2. ¿Les ha pasado a ustedes una situación semejante? Cuéntense la historia de su problema y cómo lo resolvió cada uno de ustedes.
3. Si usted viviera una experiencia semejante otra vez, ¿haría algo diferente esta vez? ¿Su respuesta es similar o diferente a la de su compañero/a?

SITUACIONES

1. **Role A.** You are driving too fast in a school zone. A police officer stops you. Explain that you left your license at home. Try to politely talk your way out of the situation.

   Role B. You are a police officer who is looking for speeders in a school zone. You stop a driver who is going too fast and ask a) what speed must be maintained in a school zone; b) at what speed he/she was driving; and c) if you can see his/her driver's license. Finally, say that if he/she is driving without a license, you will have to give him/her a fine.

2. **Role A.** You have had a bad day and you call your friend to vent. Say that a) you forgot to set your alarm clock so you got up late and missed your first class; b) you ran out of gas on the highway; c) you left your homework for your Spanish class at home; and d) in the cafeteria you accidentally dropped your soup and salad on your friend's backpack.

   Role B. Your friend calls to complain about his/her day. Commiserate with him/her and describe what happened to you last night: a) there was a big storm in your city and the lights went out so you could not watch your favorite TV show; b) you decided to drive to your parents' house, but when were leaving your apartment, both of your cats accidentally escaped; and c) when you were walking in the dark (**oscuridad**), you accidentally dropped your wallet and could not find it.

Suggestions for 15-25. Encourage students to use their imagination to describe and narrate what they see in each drawing. You may wish to have students tell the stories of their similar experiences to the class, or turn them into a writing activity.

En directo

To talk about traffic violations:

¿Podría ver su permiso/carnet de conducir?
May I see your driver's license?

Tengo que ponerle/darle una multa.
I have to give you a fine/ticket.

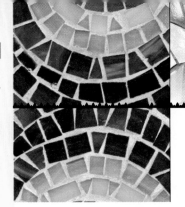

Resources

■ SAM: 15-34 to 15-36
■ Supp. Activ. Book: *Mosaicos*

Warm-up for 15-27. As a prelistening activity, have students work in small groups and discuss what they know about the use of computers and technology in medicine for such purposes as the prevention and treatment of diseases.

Audioscript for 15-27. *La tecnología se usa cada día más para tratar a los enfermos y a las personas que han sufrido accidentes.*

El médico norteamericano Paul Soll implantó el primer marcapasos, un pequeño generador electrónico que regula los latidos del corazón, en 1952. Desde entonces, el marcapasos ha salvado de la muerte a infinidad de enfermos del corazón y los adelantos en los implantes continúan multiplicándose.

Otro adelanto es un implante, mejor dicho una microcomputadora, que se coloca en el oído interno. Con este implante, los sordos pueden oír, pero los sonidos que reciben son diferentes, como si se tratara de una lengua extranjera. Pronto los sordos podrán escuchar los sonidos exactamente como se producen.

En la actualidad se están haciendo investigaciones en diferentes áreas; por ejemplo, se están haciendo grandes esfuerzos para crear un implante que funcione como un ojo artificial para que los ciegos puedan ver. También se está trabajando en la posibilidad de diseñar implantes que envíen corrientes eléctricas a los músculos para que los parapléjicos puedan caminar.

Sin duda, el futuro de la tecnología y su uso en la medicina es impredecible. Lo que sí es cierto es que probablemente en el futuro dependeremos más de la tecnología en la prevención y el tratamiento de las enfermedades.

MOSAICOS

A escuchar

Antes de escuchar

15-26 Preparación. Usted escuchará una breve presentación sobre el futuro de la tecnología en la medicina. Antes de escuchar, escriba dos avances tecnológicos o médicos que, según usted, ayudarán a los pacientes del futuro.

Escuchar

15-27 ¿Comprende usted? PRIMERA FASE. Read the statements below and then listen to the presentation. As you listen, circle the statement(s) that reflect the main idea and the supporting details.

CD 6
Track 26

	IDEA PRINCIPAL	DETALLES
1. El marcapasos…	**a.** se usa para ayudar a los corredores. **b.** les ha salvado la vida a muchas personas. (circled) **c.** es un tipo de tecnología obsoleta.	**a.** regula los latidos del corazón. (circled) **b.** se inventó hace diez años. **c.** es una microcomputadora.
2. Con el implante en el oído…	**a.** los sonidos suenan como una lengua extranjera. (circled) **b.** los sordos pueden oír muy pocos sonidos. **c.** los sordos no sufren de dolor de oídos.	**a.** el aparato se pone en la parte externa del oído. **b.** el aparato aumenta el volumen. **c.** el aparato se coloca en el oído interno. (circled)

SEGUNDA FASE. What is the speaker's intention in sharing this information?

a. aliviar a los pacientes
b. informar al público (circled)
c. entretener a la familia de los pacientes

Después de escuchar

 15-28 Ahora usted. Compartan sus respuestas a las siguientes preguntas.

1. Según ustedes, ¿de qué otra forma la tecnología puede ayudar a la medicina?
2. ¿En qué otras áreas, puede ayudar la tecnología? Expliquen.

A conversar

Resources
■ SAM: 15-37
■ *Entrevistas* video

ESTRATEGIA

Use drama and humor in telling a personal anecdote

You learned in *Capítulo 12* to keep your listeners interested in your story by inserting remarks to draw their attention to moments that are particularly funny, frightening, or surprising. You can use these remarks, called *evaluations*, to make your story humorous or to heighten the drama. You can also increase the drama by strategically using descriptive details to slow down the pace and thus create suspense.

Note for Estrategia. You may want to remind students to use preterit when recounting a particular moment and imperfect when providing descriptive details surrounding the moment.

Antes de conversar

15-29 Preparación. PRIMERA FASE. Lea las siguientes anécdotas que les ocurrieron a dos celebridades.

Suggestion for 15-29 Primera fase. Have students identify the dramatic and humorous elements of the sample narratives. They should note the narrators' use of exclamations to express strong emotions, the incorporation of descriptive detail to heighten the dramatic tone, and the humorous comments by the narrator of the second story. You may want to practice with expressions in *Lengua* box by having students select a logical place for the narrator to insert one of these comments.

> "Hace dos años, una amiga mía vino a San Francisco para visitarme. Como era su cumpleaños, el sábado por la noche fuimos a un restaurante francés muy elegante y caro para celebrarlo. Después de comer muy bien y beber el mejor champán que tenían, me trajeron la cuenta. La cantidad era enorme, pero no había problema, porque mis películas siempre tenían mucho éxito y me pagaban bien. Llevé la mano al bolsillo de mi chaqueta y me di cuenta de que la billetera estaba en mi casa, no en mi chaqueta. Llamé al camarero y le expliqué la situación. Incluso le dije quién era. Con una mirada irónica y un tono más frío que la Antártida en invierno, el camarero me dijo: Si usted es... , yo soy Brad Pitt. Por favor, no me cuente historias."

> "Una tarde de verano mi esposo y yo decidimos ir de incógnito a Manhattan. Íbamos a pasar unas horas comprando, y luego íbamos a ver una película. Después de viajar como veinte minutos por la carretera, se nos descompuso el Jag. ¡Qué feo! Había mucho tráfico y hacía un calor insoportable. Bajamos del carro y mi esposo, que tiene talento para eso, levantó el capó y revisó lo que había allí dentro. Como aparentemente no había ningún problema mecánico, volvimos al carro. De repente, mi esposo se acordó de que el marcador de gasolina no funcionaba, y que ¡se le había olvidado llenar el tanque! En ese momento llegaron dos policías y nos preguntaron cuál era el problema. Les contamos la historia, pero no nos creyeron y nos pusieron una multa altísima. ¡Claro, estábamos en Nueva York, donde todo es carísimo!"

Lengua

Spanish has several expressions with **se** that speakers use daily. Read the following and think of possible situations in which they may be used.

Se me puso la piel de gallina.
I got goosebumps.

Se me fue el alma a los pies.
My heart sank.

Se me fue la lengua.
I gave myself away.

Se me congeló la pantalla.
The screen froze up on me.

En directo

To make your story dramatic:

¿Y qué crees/creen que pasó después?
And what do you think happened then?

¡No vas/van a creerlo!
You're not going to believe it!

Espera/Esperen, que todavía no has/han escuchado la mejor parte.
Wait, you still haven't heard the best part.

To incorporate humor:

Hacía más frío/calor que...
It was colder/warmer than . . .

Me/Nos miró con cara de...
You/He/She looked at me/us with an expression of . . .

Me/Nos respondió como si...
You/He/She answered me/us as if . . .

En directo

To express sympathy:

¡Qué lástima!/¡Cuánto lo siento!
I am (so) sorry.

¡Qué triste/horrible!
How sad/horrible!

To express happiness:

¡Qué bueno/bien!
Great!

¡Cuánto me alegro!
I am really happy!

To express relief after a tense situation:

¡Qué alivio!
What a relief!

¡Por fin!
Finally!

¡Gracias a Dios!
Thank goodness!

SEGUNDA FASE. Ahora piense en una experiencia real suya semejante (trágica, cómica, tragicómica) a la de los relatos de la *Primera fase*. Tome nota de los siguientes detalles para compartir con su compañero/a.

1. Quién(es) estaba(n) presente(s).
2. Cuándo y dónde ocurrió. Escriba algunas palabras (adjetivos, verbos, adverbios) que describan el escenario.
3. Qué ocurrió, qué hicieron y cómo reaccionaron usted y la(s) otra(s) persona(s).
4. Cómo terminó la situación.
5. Qué haría usted si esto ocurriera otra vez.

En el recuadro hay algunas ideas que lo/la pueden ayudar.

> Se le quedó algo importante en un lugar que ya estaba cerrado.
>
> Se le rompió algo de mucho valor: una joya, un jarrón de cristal, un espejo fino...
>
> Al regresar de un viaje, se da cuenta de que se le quedó algo indispensable en el hotel.

Conversar

15-30 Entre nosotros. Comparta su experiencia con el grupo. Use las expresiones de *En directo* para que su anécdota tenga humor y un tono dramático. Cada miembro del grupo debe hacerle preguntas y consultar el segundo recuadro de *En directo* para expresar sus reacciones efectivamente. Finalmente, el grupo debe señalar los aspectos de cada anécdota que la hicieron graciosa (*funny*) o dramática.

Después de conversar

15-31 Un poco más. Un miembro de cada grupo de la actividad anterior debe compartir con la clase la anécdota más dramática o graciosa de su grupo. Al final, todos deben votar por la anécdota favorita de la clase. Finalmente, la persona que tuvo esta experiencia responderá a las preguntas o reaccionará a los comentarios de sus compañeros/as.

A leer

Resources
■ SAM: 15-38 to 15-40

Identify the narrator's perspective

A narrative can be told by a narrator from one of several perspectives. Two important points of view are the perspective of a protagonist (someone who tells his/her own experiences: I, we) and that of a witness (someone who tells what he/she sees or witnesses: he, she, they). Therefore, to identify the perspective of the narrator, the following questions will help you: Who witnesses the event? Who is speaking? Who is responding?

Antes de leer

15-32 Preparación. PRIMERA FASE. De la siguiente lista, marquen (✔) las máquinas, aparatos o servicios que ustedes esperarían encontrar en una sociedad donde se usa una tecnología avanzada.

___ **1.** automóviles voladores
___ **2.** electricidad generada por la energía eólica (energía del viento)
___ **3.** servicio postal automatizado
___ **4.** computadoras nanomecánicas
___ **5.** impresoras que escanean, faxean y fotocopian
___ **6.** aviones de pasajeros sin pilotos

SEGUNDA FASE. Lea el título del cuento a continuación y luego ponga en un círculo la respuesta a cada pregunta, basándose en su conocimiento de la tecnología.

1. ¿Qué ideas o conceptos asocia usted con la palabra *apocalipsis*? Hay más de una respuesta lógica.
   a. el nacimiento
   (**b.**) la muerte
   (**c.**) la destrucción
   d. la vida

2. Pensando en el título, ¿cuál de las frases podría ser el tema del cuento?
   a. Un científico usa la tecnología para destruirse a sí mismo.
   b. Los seres humanos usan la tecnología para hacer la vida más fácil.
   (**c.**) La tecnología tiene dos caras, una constructiva y la otra destructiva.

3. Ahora, lea por encima (*skim*) el cuento. Anote por lo menos dos palabras que apoyen sus respuestas a las preguntas 1 y 2. extinción, desapareciendo, reducido, se extinguieron.

Suggestion for 15-32. The theme of the conversation between the father and daughter robots and accompanying drawing on page 506 is related to the theme of the *microcuento* in this section. You may wish to reintroduce it here and have students hypothesize about how it might relate to the story they are about to read.

Cultura

Marco Denevi (1922-1998), escritor argentino, escribió novelas, obras de teatro y cuentos cortos (entre ellos, cuentos muy cortos o *microcuentos*). También fue abogado y periodista. Tanto en su ficción como en sus escritos periodísticos expresó su preocupación por los problemas políticos y sociales de su tiempo.

Leer

15-33 Primera mirada. Lea el siguiente microcuento escrito por Marco Denevi, un conocido escritor argentino, y luego siga las instrucciones.

Apocalipsis I

La extinción de la raza de los hombres se sitúa aproximadamente a fines del siglo XXXI. La cosa sucedió así: las máquinas habían alcanzado tal perfección que los hombres no necesitaban comer, ni dormir, ni leer, ni escribir, ni siquiera pensar. Les bastaba apretar botones y las máquinas lo hacían todo por ellos.

Gradualmente fueron desapareciendo las mesas, los teléfonos, los Leonardo da Vinci, las rosas de té, las tiendas de antigüedades, los discos con las nueve sinfonías de Beethoven, el vino de Burdeos[1], las golondrinas, los cuadros de Salvador Dalí[2], los relojes, los sellos postales, los alfileres[3], el Museo del Prado, la sopa de cebolla, los transatlánticos, las pirámides de Egipto, las Obras Completas de don Benito Pérez Galdós.[4] Sólo había máquinas.

Después los hombres empezaron a notar que ellos mismos iban desapareciendo paulatinamente[5] y que en cambio las máquinas se multiplicaban. Bastó poco tiempo para que el número de los hombres quedase reducido a la mitad y el de las máquinas aumentase al doble y luego al décuplo.[6] Las máquinas terminaron por ocupar todo el espacio disponible. Nadie podía dar un paso, hacer un simple ademán[7] sin tropezarse[8] con una de ellas. Finalmente los hombres se extinguieron.

Como el último se olvidó de desconectar las máquinas, desde entonces seguimos funcionando.

[1]región de Francia famosa por sus vinos   [2]famoso pintor y diseñador español conocido por su estilo surrealista y su excentricidad
[3]*pins*   [4]famoso novelista español (1843–1920)   [5]*gradualmente*   [6]*tenfold*   [7]*gesture*   [8]*stumble*

Marque (✔) la información relacionada con la perspectiva del narrador.

1. ___ El narrador habla de una experiencia que le contaron.
2. _✓_ El narrador habla de una experiencia que ha vivido.

Marque (✔) la información relacionada con el narrador.
3. _✓_ Al final del cuento descubrimos quién es el narrador.
4. _✓_ El narrador habla desde la perspectiva del tiempo futuro.
5. _✓_ El narrador es una máquina.

Marque (✔) la información relacionada con la trama de esta historia.
6. ___ El ser humano, según el narrador, se dio cuenta de que las máquinas lo estaban controlando, y las destruyó.
7. _✓_ Al final del cuento, ya no había seres humanos, sino solamente máquinas.

Después de leer

 15-34 Segunda mirada y ampliación. Respondan a las preguntas y apunten las ideas que salgan en su discusión. Estén listos para presentar sus respuestas y justificaciones a la clase.

1. ¿Cuál es el significado del título de este cuento? Explíquenlo.
2. ¿Hace un comentario social este cuento? ¿Cuál es el mensaje?
3. ¿Están ustedes de acuerdo con el mensaje? Expliquen sus ideas.

A escribir

Resources
■ SAM: 15-41 to 15-43

ESTRATEGIA

Use imagination and humor in writing a narrative

In creative writing you can use your imagination to invent events and characters that would be impossible in real life. You can use fantasy and humor to exaggerate events and characters' behaviors in order to entertain your readers. To write an imaginative and humorous story, consider the following tips:
■ Create situations or behaviors that differ from people's expectations.
■ Use contradictions within a character to create humor. The humor will be apparent when you poke fun at the contradictions.
■ Base your humor on situations and characterizations that will be familiar to your audience.

Antes de escribir

15-35 Preparación. Imagínese que usted es una de las máquinas que quedaron funcionando después de la desaparición de los seres humanos.

1. Escriba algunas ideas que describan la existencia de las máquinas después de la desaparición del ser humano: ¿Es su existencia semejante o diferente a la del pasado? ¿Es más o menos divertida? ¿Qué hacía usted antes que ya no hace hoy o viceversa?
2. Mencione tres errores cometidos por el ser humano que, según usted, tuvieron relación directa con su desaparición y explique por qué.

Escribir

15-36 Manos a la obra. Ahora, en el papel de una de las máquinas que sobrevivió la desaparición del ser humano, escriba una narración. Use la información que preparó en **15-35**.

1. Describa su existencia antes y después de la desaparición de los seres humanos. Use humor para captar la atención de su lector.
2. Indique con humor algunos aspectos de su interacción y trabajo cotidianos con los humanos que usted extraña con nostalgia.
3. Especule sobre algunos errores que, según usted, provocaron la extinción de la raza humana.

Después de escribir

15-37 Revisión. Recuerde que su texto va a ser leído por otras máquinas de inteligencia superior a la humana que disfrutan del humor, pero que no toleran errores ni imprecisiones de ningún tipo.

1. ¿Usó ideas y situaciones originales y absurdas para captar la atención del lector? ¿Exageró las situaciones o los comportamientos?
2. ¿Hay un orden lógico y claro?
3. ¿Usó vocabulario apropiado? ¿Revisó la concordancia, el tiempo y los modos? ¿Utilizó la puntuación y ortografía correctas?

Suggestion for 15-35. Divide the class in small groups to brainstorm possible humorous situations that involve humans and machines, computers in this case.

Remind students that accentuating the negative, exaggerating, and emphasizing the absurd will provoke laughter.

ENFOQUE CULTURAL

La ciencia y la tecnología

Muchos científicos latinoamericanos y españoles se han distinguido por sus descubrimientos e inventos, como se verá en una actividad posterior en esta sección. Un gran número de investigadores hispanos forma parte de equipos científicos en universidades de Estados Unidos y Europa. Sin embargo, la mayoría de los países latinoamericanos no son productores de ciencia y tecnología. La razón de esto es que los inventos y descubrimientos modernos por lo general son el resultado del trabajo de equipos humanos especializados y de laboratorios muy costosos y estos países tienen que dedicar sus recursos a otras necesidades urgentes, como por ejemplo, desarrollar la infraestructura de

El Observatorio Interamericano de Cerro Tololo en Chile es un ejemplo de la cooperación internacional para el desarrollo de la ciencia en América Latina.

comunicaciones o mejorar la salud de sus ciudadanos. En la actualidad los cambios tecnológicos se producen más rápidamente que nunca. Y la distancia entre los países que usan más tecnología y los que usan menos aumenta más rápidamente que nunca.

Algunos países hispanos se han asociado con universidades o con instituciones científicas de Estados Unidos o de Europa para construir centros de investigación científica dentro de su territorio. Un ejemplo sobresaliente de esta cooperación es el observatorio astronómico de Cerro Tololo en Chile. Este centro de investigación es administrado por un consorcio de universidades de varios países llamado AURA (Asociación de Universidades para la Investigación en Astronomía). El observatorio está situado a más de 2.000 metros sobre el nivel del mar, en un lugar que tiene excelentes condiciones de clima para la observación de las estrellas. Cerro Tololo es utilizado por un gran número de astrónomos de todo el mundo durante un promedio de unos 300 días al año para la observación y el estudio de las estrellas del hemisferio sur.

El Radiotelescopio de Arecibo, Puerto Rico, es uno de los centros científicos más importantes de América Latina.

La antena esférica de Arecibo fue hasta hace muy pocos años la más grande del mundo.

Otro ejemplo de la cooperación internacional para el desarrollo de la ciencia y la tecnología en los países hispanos es el Radiotelescopio de Arecibo, situado en la ciudad puertorriqueña de ese mismo nombre. Este telescopio tiene la segunda antena esférica más grande del mundo y fue construido entre 1960 y 1963. A diferencia del observatorio de Cerro Tololo, Arecibo funciona mediante un receptor de ondas de radio. En Arecibo se han realizado importantes observaciones astronómicas, como por ejemplo, la de los primeros planetas descubiertos fuera de nuestro sistema solar.

A pesar de su importancia científica, muchas personas conocen este observatorio porque ha aparecido en varias películas de ciencia ficción y en alguna de las series de James Bond. Otras personas asocian Arecibo principalmente con el famoso "Mensaje de Arecibo", un texto codificado que se envió desde este radiotelescopio a una zona muy lejana del universo con una descripción del sistema solar, la Tierra y el ADN de los seres humanos. La idea de enviar un mensaje de radio con la esperanza de que los habitantes de una región lejana del universo puedan entenderlo ha fascinado a la imaginación de los humanos, pero a pesar de ello, nadie está esperando una respuesta, ya que el mensaje tardará más de 20.000 años en llegar a su destino.

En otras palabras

Expresiones puertorriqueñas

Tengo la **monga**.
I have the flu.

Después del trabajo, nos fuimos de **juerga**.
After work, we went partying.

No me gustó la fiesta. Había tremendo **revolú**.
I didn't like the party. Things were very chaotic.

¡Esa película es **brutal**!
That film is awesome!

15-38 Comprensión. PRIMERA FASE. **Reconocimiento de palabras clave.** Encuentre en el texto la palabra o expresión que mejor expresa el significado de las siguientes ideas.

1. teams   _equipos_
2. to develop   _desarrollar_
3. outstanding   _sobresaliente_
4. sea level   _nivel del mar_
5. average   _promedio_
6. radio waves   _ondas de radio_
7. hope   _esperanza_

SEGUNDA FASE. **Oraciones importantes.** Subraye las afirmaciones que contienen ideas que se encuentran en el texto. Luego indique en qué parte del texto están.

1. Modern science requires expensive human teams and laboratories.
2. Partnerships with foreign universities and institutions have helped some Hispanic countries develop important research centers.
3. Although Cerro Tololo is located very high up in the mountains, the humidity of the region produces heavy clouds that often cover the sky.
4. Because of adverse weather conditions, Cerro Tololo is open only five months a year.
5. Scientists at the observatory in Arecibo were the first to view planets from outside our solar system.
6. The telescope in Arecibo works with a combination of laser and gamma rays.
7. The Arecibo Message contains an English text that describes the most important achievements of the human race.

TERCERA FASE. **Ideas principales.** Escriba un párrafo breve en español resumiendo las ideas principales expresadas en el texto.

 15-39 Use la información. Escriba una breve biografía de un científico/una científica o inventor/inventora del mundo hispano. Explique de qué país proviene y en qué época vivió, donde estudió, cuál fue su contribución más importante a la ciencia o la tecnología, qué premios importantes recibió, y otros datos de interés que usted encuentre. Para preparar esta actividad, visite la página web de *Mosaicos* y siga los enlaces útiles.

VOCABULARIO

CD 6
ks 27–31

La ciencia y la tecnología / *Science and technology*

el acceso	*access*
el adelanto	*advance*
la biblioteca virtual	*virtual library*
el buscador	*search engine*
la cápsula	*capsule*
la clonación	*cloning*
el conocimiento	*knowledge*
el descubrimiento	*discovery*
la diseminación	*dispersal, dissemination*
el documento adjunto	*attachment, attached document*
la energía solar	*solar energy*
el enlace	*link*
la fuente	*source*
la infraestructura	*infrastructure*
el intercambio	*exchange*
el mensaje	*message*
el reto	*challenge*
el riel	*rail*
el robot	*robot*
el videojuego	*video game*

El medio ambiente / *Environment*

el banco de peces	*shoal; school of fish*
el bosque	*forest*
el bosque tropical	*rain forest*
el calentamiento	*warming*
la capa de ozono	*ozone layer*
la conservación	*preservation*
la cuenca	*(river) basin*
la deforestación	*deforestation*
la desaparición	*disappearance*
el deshielo	*thaw, thawing*

la extinción	*extinction*
la inundación	*flood*
la naturaleza	*nature*
la pérdida	*loss*
el planeta	*planet*
los recursos	*resources*
la reserva natural	*nature preserve*
la tierra	*land, soil*

Las descripciones / *Descriptions*

climatizado/a	*air-conditioned*
extinguido/a	*extinguished*
reciclado/a	*recycled*
volador/a	*flying*

Verbos / *Verbs*

aterrizar (c)	*to land*
bajar	*to download*
conectarse	*to connect*
construir (y)	*to build*
contribuir (y)	*to contribute*
despegar (u)	*to take off (airplane)*
difundir	*to spread, to disseminate*
encender (ie)	*to turn on*
enfocarse (qu)	*to focus*
meter	*to insert*
repoblar	*to reforest*
unificar (qu)	*to unify*

Palabras y expresiones útiles / *Useful words and expressions*

debido a	*due to*
en busca de	*in search of*
genéticamente	*genetically*
virtualmente	*virtually*

525

Expansión gramatical

This grammatical supplement includes structures often considered optional for the introductory level, because the functions and forms presented here are far beyond the performance level of most first-year students. Many instructors choose to present them for recognition only, if at all. The *vosotros* command forms are included in this section for the instructors who use them to address their students.

The explanation and activities in this section use the same format as the grammatical material throughout *Mosaicos* in order to facilitate their incorporation into the core lessons of the program or their addition as another chapter in the book.

Funciones y formas

1. Giving informal orders or commands to two or more people (in Spain): *Vosotros* commands
2. Expressing an indirect wish that a third party do something: Indirect commands
3. Suggesting that someone and the speaker do something: The Spanish equivalents of English *let's*
4. Reacting to a past occurrence or event: The present perfect subjunctive
5. Hypothesizing about an occurrence or event in the past: The conditional perfect and the pluperfect subjunctive
6. Expressing contrary-to-fact conditions in the past: *If*-clauses (using the perfect tense)
7. Emphasizing a fact resulting from an action by someone or something: The passive voice

1. Giving informal orders or commands to two or more people (in Spain): *Vosotros* commands

	AFFIRMATIVE	NEGATIVE
hablar	habla**d**	no **habléis**
comer	come**d**	no **comáis**
escribir	escribi**d**	no **escribáis**

- To use the affirmative **vosotros** command, change the final **-r** of the infinitive to **-d.**

- Use the **vosotros** form of the present subjunctive for the **vosotros** negative command.

- For the affirmative **vosotros** command of reflexive verbs, drop the final **-d** and add the pronoun **os: levantad + os = levantaos.** The verb **irse** is an exception: **idos.**

EG-1 Buenos consejos. Usted quiere que sus mejores amigos cambien sus hábitos y vivan una vida más sana. Dígales qué deben hacer.

MODELO: caminar dos kilómetros todos los días
        Caminad dos kilómetros todos los días.

1. comer muchas frutas y vegetales
2. empezar un programa de ejercicios
3. no respirar por la boca
4. no cansarse mucho los primeros días
5. relajarse para evitar el estrés
6. dormir no menos de ocho horas

EG-2 Órdenes en grupo. Cada uno/a de ustedes va a hacer el papel de profesor/a de educación física y le va a dar una orden a los otros estudiantes del grupo. Los estudiantes deben hacer lo que el/la profesor/a les indica.

MODELO: *Levantad los brazos y las piernas.*

SITUACIONES

You and your partner have rented a cabin in the mountains for a month. Some of your friends are going to use the cabin part of the time and you would like to give them some rules to make sure they leave everything in order. Write the rules and then compare them with those of another couple.

Suggestions. Write some infinitives on the board or a transparency, crossing out the final **-r** and writing a **d** instead. Give some affirmative *vosotros* commands *(levantad la mano, leed, escribid)* for students to follow.

For negative commands, first say what you hope or expect they will not do: *Espero que no habléis en inglés en esta clase. ...no llevéis refrescos al laboratorio.* You may display one or two sentences; then cross out the first part of the sentence, leaving only the command.

Use visuals showing people doing various activities: writing, skating, swimming, dancing, etc. Students should give affirmative and negative *vosotros* commands: *Haced la tarea. No patinéis ahora.* In addition to the activities below, you may also do activity 9-30, p. 314, using *vosotros* instead of *ustedes.*

Suggestion for Situaciones. Students should use the *vosotros* commands when writing the rules. You may wish to specify the kinds of rules students should set, for example: those related to cleaning, use of appliances, care of the lawn, consumption of electricity, gas, water, etc.

2. Expressing an indirect wish that a third party do something: Indirect commands

You have used commands directly to tell others to do something: **Salga/Salgan ahora.** Now you are going to use indirect commands to say what someone else should do: **Que salga Berta.** Note that this indirect command is equivalent to saying **Quiero que Berta salga,** but without expressing the main verb **quiero.**

■ The word **que** introduces the indirect command. The subject, if stated, normally follows the verb.

Que cocine Roberto.	*Let Roberto cook.*
Que descanse María.	*Let María rest.*

■ Reflexive and object pronouns always precede the verb.

Que **se siente** a la mesa.	*Let him sit at the table.*
Que **le sirvan** la cena.	*Let them serve him dinner.*
Que **se la sirvan** ahora.	*Let them serve it to him now.*

 EG-3 Una clase de cocina. Un chef muy conocido ha accedido a dar una clase de cocina con el fin de recaudar (*raise*) dinero para una obra social. Usted y su compañero/a forman parte del comité que organiza la clase. Su compañero/a tiene la lista de las personas que desean ayudar y usted tiene la lista de las tareas pendientes. Háganse preguntas y contéstense con la información que cada uno/a tiene.

MODELO: *Eduardo, Alicia y Pedro preparar los anuncios, comprar los refrescos*
   E1: *¿Quién va a preparar los anuncios?*
   E2: *Que los preparen Alicia y Pedro. ¿Y qué va a hacer Eduardo?*
   E1: *Que compre los refrescos.*

Personas

Beatriz

Alberto y Rubén

Miguel

Elena y Amanda

Ana María

Emilio

Un camarero

Tareas

traer los platos

tener los ingredientes listos

buscar las sillas

copiar las recetas

servir el vino

recibir a las personas

ayudar al chef

EG-4 Una fiesta hispana. PRIMERA FASE. Para celebrar el final de curso ustedes han decidido organizar una fiesta en el departamento de español. Hagan una lista de todo lo que necesitan y otra lista de todas las personas que van a invitar, además de sus compañeros/as de clase.

SEGUNDA FASE. Decidan qué otras personas de la clase pueden encargarse de cada sección y por qué. Su compañero/a, que está de acuerdo con usted, le dará algunas ideas.

MODELO: E1: *Que se encargue Juan de comprar las invitaciones porque tiene que ir al supermercado esta tarde.*

E2: *Sí, pero que las escriban María y Pedro que escriben mejor.*

Suggestion for EG-4. Encourage students to use indirect commands when assigning responsibilities to the various members of the group.

En directo

To negotiate politely:

Esperamos que...

Es mejor que...

Proponemos que...

To show agreement:

¡Claro!

¡Por supuesto!

¡Cómo no!

¡Desde luego!

SITUACIONES

Role A. You are a new manager for the Student Union who wants to improve the food and the service at the cafeteria. In a meeting with the cafeteria manager, say a) that it is important that students receive a better service, b) inform the manager of the type of food you would like to find in the cafeteria and of the ways in which the service could be improved, and c) say that you hope the prices will not increase (**subir**) this semester.

Role B. You are the cafeteria manager. Agree with the Student Union manager and tell him/her a) that you have a good team and you want everyone to do a good job, b) that you will be happy to meet with a student committee and have students suggest (**sugerir**) menus, and c) that you will do your best (**hacer lo posible**) to convince your team to incorporate your suggestions.

3. Suggesting that someone and the speaker do something: The Spanish equivalents of English *let's*

In Spanish, you may suggest that two or more people, including yourself, do something together in the following ways.

■ **Vamos + a +** *infinitive* is commonly used in Spanish to express English *let's +* *verb*.

Vamos a llamar al doctor.	*Let's call the doctor.*

■ Use **vamos** by itself to mean *let's go*. The negative *let's not go* is **no vayamos**.

Vamos al hospital.	*Let's go to the hospital.*
No vayamos al hospital.	*Let's not go to the hospital.*

■ Another equivalent for *let's + verb* is the **nosotros** form of the present subjunctive.

Hablemos con el médico.	*Let's talk to the doctor.*
No hablemos con la enfermera.	*Let's not talk to the nurse.*

■ The final **-s** of reflexive affirmative commands is dropped when the pronoun **nos** is attached. Note the additional written accent.

Levantemos + nos	→	**Levantémonos.**
Sirvamos + nos	→	**Sirvámonos.**

■ Placement of object and reflexive pronouns is the same as with **usted(es)** commands.

Comprémosla.	*Let's buy it.*
No la compremos.	*Let's not buy it.*

 EG-5 ¿Qué debemos hacer? Usted y un/a compañero/a están estudiando y cuidando a su hermanito al mismo tiempo. El niño les dice que se siente mal. Cada uno/a de ustedes debe escoger tres de las siguientes opciones y decirle a su compañero/a lo que deben o no deben hacer.

MODELO:	llevarlo a su cuarto	llamar a tus padres
	E1: *Llevémoslo a su cuarto.*	E2: *Llamemos a tus padres.*

1. darle agua
2. llevarlo al parque
3. comprarle juguetes
4. ponerle el termómetro
5. llamar al médico
6. preguntarle qué le duele
7. prepararle una hamburguesa
8. explicarle los síntomas al doctor
9. ponerle la televisión
10. acostarlo

EG-6 Resoluciones. Usted y su compañero/a deciden llevar una vida más sana. Túrnense para decir lo que piensan hacer. Su compañero/a va a decirle si está de acuerdo o no con su sugerencia.

MODELO: comer más verduras
E1: *Vamos a comer más verduras.*
E2: *Sí, comamos más verduras./No, (no comamos más verduras,) comamos más frutas.*

1. tomar vitaminas y minerales
2. caminar tres kilómetros diariamente
3. beber ocho vasos de agua todos los días
4. acostarse más temprano
5. dormir ocho horas todas las noches
6. ...

EG-7 Los preparativos para un beneficio. En pequeños grupos, decidan qué actividades van a hacer para recaudar (*collect*) fondos a beneficio de un hospital. Deben mencionar cinco actividades.

MODELO: *Organicemos un partido del equipo de basquetbol.*

SITUACIONES

You and your partner are planning to visit a classmate who is in the hospital. Decide a) when you will visit him/her, b) what you are going to take him/her, and c) what you can do for your classmate after he/she leaves the hospital. Then, exchange this information with another pair of students.

4. Reacting to a past occurrence or event: The present perfect subjunctive

Use the present perfect subjunctive to react to a past occurrence, event or condition. The present perfect subjunctive is formed with the present subjunctive of the verb **haber** + *past participle*.

PRESENT SUBJUNCTIVE OF *HABER* + *PAST PARTICIPLE*		
yo	**haya**	
yú	**hayas**	
Ud., él/ella	**haya**	**hablado**
nosotros/as	**hayamos**	**comido**
vosotros/as	**hayáis**	**vivido**
Uds., ellos/as	**hayan**	

Note that the dependent clause using the present perfect subjunctive describes what has happened before the time expressed or implied in the main clause, which is the present. Its English equivalent is normally *has/have* + *past participle*, but it may vary according to the context.

Your friend tells you:	Your reaction to this past event:
Mis hijos volvieron de sus vacaciones. →	Me alegro de que **hayan llegado**. *I'm glad they arrived early.*

Your secretary informs you:	Your reaction to this past news:
El gerente de ventas no vino a trabajar ayer. } →	Es posible que **haya estado** enfermo. *It's possible that he may have been sick.*

 EG-8 ¿Qué espera usted? Escoja la oración que complete lógicamente las siguientes situaciones. Compare sus respuestas con las de su compañero/a.

1. Su computadora no estaba funcionando bien y usted se la dio a un técnico para que la reparara. Usted espera que...
   a. la haya vendido.
   b. haya destruido sus programas.
   c. haya encontrado el problema.
2. Su amigo acaba de regresar de Puerto Rico, donde fue a pasar sus vacaciones. Usted le dice: "Espero que...
   a. hayas visitado el Viejo San Juan".
   b. te hayas aburrido mucho".
   c. hayas perdido todo tu dinero".
3. Uno de sus compañeros ha estado muy grave en el hospital, pero ya está en la casa. Usted le habla y le dice: "Siento mucho que...
   a. hayas vendido la casa".
   b. hayas estado tan mal".
   c. hayas salido del hospital".

4. Usted llama por teléfono a un amigo para invitarlo a cenar, pero nadie contesta el teléfono. Es probable que su amigo...
   a. haya cenado ya.
   b. haya salido de su casa.
   c. haya cambiado su teléfono.
5. Uno de sus parientes dijo una mentira (*lie*). Como es natural, a usted le molesta mucho que no...
   a. haya dicho la verdad.
   b. haya dicho nada.
   c. haya hablado con sus parientes.

EG-9 Un viaje. Uno de sus amigos pasó un semestre en Los Ángeles. Túrnese con su compañero/a para decirle lo que esperan que haya hecho en su visita.

MODELO: ir a Beverly Hills / visitar la Biblioteca Huntington
      E1: *Espero que hayas ido a Beverly Hills.*
      E2: *Y yo espero que hayas visitado la Biblioteca Huntington.*

1. ver las Torres de Watts
2. ir a los Estudios Universal
3. caminar por la calle Olvera
4. comer comida mexicana
5. manejar hasta el observatorio del Monte Wilson
6. asistir al Desfile de las Rosas

Note for EG-9. The Huntington Library, built in a 200–acre garden, houses a Guttenberg Bible and original Shakespearean works.

EG-10 Los adelantos científicos. Usted y su compañero/a trabajan con otros científicos en un laboratorio de ingeniería genética. Háganse preguntas para saber qué han logrado o no en sus investigaciones.

MODELO: aislar el nuevo virus / es posible que
      E1: *¿Han aislado el nuevo virus?*
      E2: *Es posible que lo hayamos / hayan aislado.*

1. cambiar la estructura de la célula / dudar
2. no hacer implantes nuevos / es una lástima
3. duplicar órganos / no creer que
4. regular el ritmo del corazón / esperar
5. reactivar los músculos atrofiados / es probable que
6. modificar los genes / es importante que

En directo

To express that you remember or recognize someone in a photo:

Mira, mira, este/esta es...
Look, this is . . .

Te equivocas
You are wrong.

Pero, ¿no ves que es.../ Tiene/lleva...
But, don't you see it is . . .
(a person's name)

¿Has visto a...?

SITUACIONES

You and your classmate graduated years ago and are remembering the times when you were at the university. You have found a group photo of your Spanish class. Talk about each of your classmates saying a) what you know they have done in their lives, b) what you hope they have done, and c) what you doubt they have done. Use your imagination and the expressions in the box to sound more natural.

Suggestion. Contrast present perfect subjunctive and pluperfect subjunctive. Write *Hoy* and *Ayer* on the board. Under *Hoy*, write *Espero* and under *Ayer*, *que hayan estudiado*. Ask questions so students can say what they wish happened yesterday. Then write *La semana pasada* to the right of *Ayer*. Write *Esperaba* under *Ayer* and *que hubieran estudiado* under *La semana pasada*. Say what you wished had happened last week.

Note. The verb forms presented in this sections are rather complex; an average first-year student may be able to recognize them in reading, but will definitely have difficulty producing them orally and/or in writing.

5. Hypothesizing about an occurrence or event in the past: The conditional perfect and the pluperfect subjunctive

In this section you will study two new verb tenses: the conditional perfect and the pluperfect subjunctive. Use this tense to hypothesize about an occurrence or event in the past.

■ Use the conditional of **haber** + *past participle* to form the conditional perfect.

CONDITIONAL PERFECT		
yo	habría	
tú	habrías	
Ud., él, ella	habría	hablado
nosotros/as	habríamos	comido
vosotros/as	habríais	vivido
Uds., ellos/as	habrían	

■ The conditional perfect usually corresponds to English *would have + past participle*.

Sé que le **habría gustado** esta casa.   *I know you/he/she would have liked this house.*

■ Use the past subjunctive of **haber** + *past participle* to form the pluperfect subjunctive.

PLUPERFECT SUBJUNCTIVE		
yo	hubiera	
tú	hubieras	
Ud., él, ella	hubiera	hablado
nosotros/as	hubiéramos	comido
vosotros/as	hubierais	vivido
Uds., ellos/as	hubieran	

■ The pluperfect subjunctive corresponds to English *might have, would have, or had + past participle*. It is used in constructions where the subjunctive is normally required.

Dudaba que **hubiera venido** temprano.   *I doubted that he had/would have come early.*

Esperaba que **hubieran comido** en casa.   *I was hoping that they would have eaten at home.*

Ojalá que **hubieran visto** ese letrero.   *I wish they had seen that sign.*

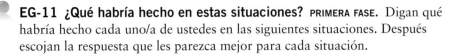 **EG-11 ¿Qué habría hecho en estas situaciones?** PRIMERA FASE. Digan qué habría hecho cada uno/a de ustedes en las siguientes situaciones. Después escojan la respuesta que les parezca mejor para cada situación.

MODELO: Usted recibió una invitación para una recepción en la Casa Blanca.
    E1: *Se lo habría dicho a todos mis compañeros.*
    E2: *Habría leído la invitación varias veces porque habría pensado que era una broma.*

1. En el aeropuerto le dijeron que podía viajar en primera clase todo el año sin pagar.
2. Le pidieron sugerencias para mejorar la situación de los vuelos y los aeropuertos.
3. La NASA lo/la llamó para ver si le interesaba vivir tres meses en una estación espacial.
4. Le dijeron que organizara la fiesta de fin de curso de su clase.
5. Le pidieron que revisara los programas en su universidad y sugiriera los cambios necesarios.

SEGUNDA FASE. Comparen las respuestas que escogieron con las de otra pareja y decidan cuál es la mejor. Después compartan sus respuestas con el resto de la clase.

EG-12 Nuestras esperanzas. Usted y su compañero/a esperaban que el nuevo gobierno hiciera muchas cosas en beneficio de la sociedad. Se lograron algunas cosas, pero otras no. Túrnense para decir qué esperaban que el nuevo gobierno y su gabinete hubieran hecho y si lo han hecho o no.

MODELO: subir el sueldo mínimo / mejorar el sistema de educación
    E1: *Esperaba que hubieran subido el sueldo mínimo y (no) lo han hecho.*
    E2: *Y yo esperaba que hubieran mejorado el sistema de educación y (no) lo han hecho.*

1. bajar los impuestos (*taxes*)
2. mejorar el transporte público
3. terminar con la corrupción
4. construir viviendas (*housing*) para familias pobres
5. ofrecer mejores planes de salud
6. proteger el medio ambiente
7. …

SITUACIONES

Role A. You had an argument (**pelea**) with your significant other. Explain to your best friend what happened and ask him/her what he/she would have done in your place. Then tell him/her what you intend to do.

Role B. Your best friend explains to you that he/she had an argument (**pelea**) with his/her significant other. Ask questions to obtain some details. Then a) tell him/her what you would have done in the same situation, b) ask him/her what he/she intends to do and c) give him/her your advice.

Note. Hypothesizing about the past is a more appropriate function for students with a higher degree of proficiency. You may wish to present this section for recognition only or to satisfy the needs and/or curiosity of more motivated students.

6. Expressing contrary-to-fact conditions in the past: *If*-clauses (using the perfect tenses)

The conditional perfect and pluperfect subjunctive are used in contrary-to-fact if-statements which refer to actions, events, experiences related to the past.

Si **hubieras venido**, te **habría gustado** la conferencia.	*If you had come (which you did not), you would have liked the lecture.*

 EG-13 La vida sería diferente. Con su compañero/a, diga cuáles habrían sido las consecuencias si…

MODELO: no se hubieran inventado los aviones
     E1: *Habríamos viajado en barco, en tren o en autobús.*
     E2: *Habríamos contaminado menos la atmósfera.*

1. no se hubiera inventado la bomba atómica
2. no se hubieran deforestado los bosques
3. los ingleses hubieran descubierto América
4. las mujeres hubieran tenido siempre las mismas oportunidades que los hombres
5. no se hubieran creado las vacunas (*vaccination*)
6. los jóvenes hubieran gobernado el mundo

 EG-14 Unas excusas. ¿Qué excusas darían ustedes en las siguientes situaciones?

MODELO: Un amigo le pidió que participara en un experimento.
     E1: *Si mis padres me lo hubieran permitido, habría participado.*
     E2: *Si hubiera tenido tiempo, habría participado.*

1. Una organización quería que usted donara botellas y papeles para reciclar.
2. Le pidieron su coche para llevar unas ratas al laboratorio.
3. Lo/La necesitaban de voluntario/a para probar una vacuna contra el catarro.
4. Un/a compañero/a quería venderle su computadora portátil.
5. Una compañía necesitaba probar unos paracaídas (*parachutes*) y buscaba personas interesadas en las pruebas.
6. Alquilaban un robot para que hiciera las tareas domésticas.

 EG-15 Volver a vivir. Piense en una experiencia negativa que usted haya tenido. Cuéntele a su compañero/a qué le pasó y dígale qué habría hecho si hubiera sabido en ese momento lo que sabe hoy. Después, su compañero/a debe hacer lo mismo.

SITUACIONES

Role A. You attended a conference/lecture about the city of the future. Tell your classmate a) where and when the conference/lecture took place, b) that he/she would have found it very interesting, and c) the things that he/she would have learned if he/she had attended.

Role B. Your classmate has attended a conference/lecture about the city of the future. Ask him/her questions to find out more about the things he/she learned.

7. Emphasizing a fact resulting from an action by someone or something: The passive voice

The passive voice emphasizes a fact resulting from the action by someone or something.

■ The passive voice in Spanish is formed with the verb **ser** + *past participle*; the passive voice is most commonly used in the preterit, though at times you may see it used in other tenses.

La planta nuclear **fue construida** en 1980.	*The nuclear plant was built in 1980.*

■ Use the preposition **por** when indicating who or what performs the action.

El bosque **fue destruido**. (Who or what did it is not expressed.)	*The forest was destroyed.*
El bosque **fue destruido por** el fuego. (The fire did it.)	*The forest was destroyed by the fire.*

■ The past participle functions as an adjective and therefore agrees in gender and number with the subject.

Los árboles fueron **destruidos** por la lluvia ácida.	*The trees were destroyed by acid rain.*
La cura fue **descubierta** el año pasado.	*The cure was discovered last year.*

■ You'll most often find the passive voice in written Spanish, especially in newspapers and formal writing. However, in conversation, Spanish speakers normally use two different constructions that you have already studied—a third person plural verb or a **se** construction.

Vendieron el laboratorio.	*They sold the laboratory.*
Se vendió el edificio.	*The building was sold.*

EG-16 La comunicación oral. Túrnense para decir lo que pasó en una reunión del presidente y los ministros. ¿Cómo lo dirían los periódicos? ¿Cómo lo dirían ustedes en una conversación?

MODELO: ministros / recibir / el presidente
      E1: *Los ministros fueron recibidos por el presidente.*
      E2: *El presidente recibió a los ministros.*

1. la agenda / preparar / el secretario fue preparada/preparó
2. la agenda / aprobar / todos fue aprobada/aprobaron
3. el proyecto para disminuir la contaminación / escribir / el Sr. Sosa fue escrito/escribió
4. el proyecto / presentar / la Ministra de Salud fue presentado/presentó
5. unos comentarios / leer / el presidente fueron leídos/leyó
6. las preguntas / contestar / el ministro fueron contestados/contestó

EG-17 Dos reporteros. Túrnense para decir cómo escribirían las siguientes noticias para un periódico.

MODELO: la lluvia ácida dañó las cosechas
          Las cosechas fueron dañadas por la lluvia ácida.

1. La zona del Amazonas se conoce como el "pulmón" del planeta. es conocida
2. Los campesinos deforestaron la selva. fue deforestada
3. Los campesinos cultivaron la tierra. fue cultivada
4. Estos grupos cortaron muchos árboles. fueron cortados
5. La invasión de los seres humanos exterminó muchas especies de animales. fueron exterminadas
6. El gobierno plantará mil árboles para mejorar la situación. serán plantados

SITUACIONES

You and your classmate are TV newscasters. You must write and give a piece of news to your viewers on a great discovery. Inform them that a) some very secret plans have been discovered by the CIA, b) that important security measures have been taken, c) that politicians are now deliberating on how to respond to a possible threat (**peligro**) to the population, d) that public transport has been interrupted in major cities, e) that the situation is under control and f) that nobody should be afraid.

Appendix 1

Stress and Written Accents in Spanish

Rules for Written Accents

The following rules are based on pronunciation.

1. If a word ends in *n*, *s*, or a vowel, the penultimate (second-to-last) syllable is usually stressed.

    Examples: cami**nan**
                muchos
                silla

2. If a word ends in a consonant other than *n* or *s*, the last syllable is stressed.

    Example: fa**tal**

3. Words that are exceptions to the preceding rules have an accent mark on the stressed vowel.

    Examples: sar**tén**
                lápices
                ma**má**
                fácil

4. **Separation of diphthongs.** When *i* or *u* are combined with another vowel, they are pronounced as one sound (a diphthong). When each vowel sound is pronounced separately, a written accent mark is placed over the stressed vowel (either the *i* or the *u*).

    Example: gracias día

Because the written accents in the following examples are not determined by pronunciation, the accent mark must be memorized as part of the spelling of the words as they are learned.

5. **Homonyms.** When two words are spelled the same, but have different meanings, a written accent is used to distinguish and differentiate meaning.

Examples:				
de	*of*	dé	*give* (formal command)
el	*the*	él	*he*
mas	*but*	más	*more*
mi	*my*	mí	me
se	*him/herself,*	sé	*I know, be* (formal
	(to) him/her/them		command)
si	*if*	sí	*yes*
te	*(to) you*	té	*tea*
tu	*your*	tú	*you*

6. **Interrogatives and exclamations.** In questions (direct and indirect) and exclamations, a written accent is placed over the following words: **dónde, cómo, cuándo, cuál(es), quién(es), cuánto(s)/cuánta(s),** and **qué.**

Word Formation in Spanish

Recognizing certain patterns in Spanish word formation can be a big help in deciphering meaning. Use the following information about word formation to help you as you read.

■ **Prefixes.** Spanish and English share a number of prefixes that shade the meaning of the word to which they are attached: **inter-** (between, among); **intro/a-** (within); **ex-** (former, toward the outside); **en-/em-** (the state of becoming); **in-/a-** (not, without), among others.

inter-	interdisciplinario, interacción
intro/a-	introvertido, introspección
ex-	exponer (*expose*)
en-/em-	enrojecer (*to turn red*), empobrecer (*to become poor*)
in-/a-	inmoral, incompleto, amoral, asexual

■ **Suffixes.** Suffixes and, in general, word endings will help you identify various aspects of words such as part of speech, gender, meaning, degree, etc. Common Spanish suffixes are **-ría, -za, -miento, -dad/tad, -ura, -oso/a, -izo/a, -(c)ito/a,** and **-mente.**

-ría	place where something is made and/or bought: **panadería, zapatería** (*shoe store*), **librería.**
-za	feminine, abstract noun: **pobreza** (*poverty*), **riqueza** (*wealth, richness*).
-miento	masculine, abstract noun: **empobrecimiento** (*impoverishment*), **entrenamiento** (*training*).
-dad/tad	feminine noun: **ciudad** (*city*), **libertad** (*liberty, freedom*)
-ura	feminine noun: **verdura, locura** (*craziness*).
-oso/a	adjective meaning having the characteristics of the noun to which it's attached: **montañoso, lluvioso** (*rainy*).
-izo/a	adjective meaning having the characteristics of the noun to which it's attached: **rojizo** (*reddish*), **enfermizo** (*sickly*).
-(c)ito/a	diminutive form of noun or adjective: **Juanito, mesita** (*little table*), **Carmencita.**
-mente	attached to the feminine form of adjective to form an adverb: **rápidamente, felizmente** (*happily*).

■ **Compounds.** Compounds are made up of two words (e.g., *mailman*), each of which has meaning in and of itself: **altavoz** (*loudspeaker*) from **alto/a** and **voz**; **sacacorchos** (*corkscrew*) from **sacar** and **corcho**. Your knowledge of the root words will help you recognize the compound; and likewise, learning compounds can help you to learn the root words. What do you think **sacar** means?

■ **Spanish-English associations.** Learning to associate aspects of word formation in Spanish with aspects of word formation in English can be very helpful. Look at the associations below.

SPANISH	ENGLISH
es/ex + consonant	*s +* consonant
esclerosis, extraño	*sclerosis, strange*
gu-	*w-*
guerra, Guillermo	*war, William*
-tad/dad	*-ty*
libertad, calidad	*liberty, quality*
-sión/-ción	*-sion/-tion*
tensión, emoción	*tension, emotion*

Verb Charts

Regular Verbs: Simple Tenses

Infinitive Present Participle Past Participle	Indicative					Subjunctive		Imperative
	Present	Imperfect	Preterit	Future	Conditional	Present	Imperfect	Commands
hablar hablando hablado	hablo hablas habla hablamos habláis hablan	hablaba hablabas hablaba hablábamos hablabais hablaban	hablé hablaste habló hablamos hablasteis hablaron	hablaré hablarás hablará hablaremos hablaréis hablarán	hablaría hablarías hablaría hablaríamos hablaríais hablarían	hable hables hable hablemos habléis hablen	hablara hablaras hablara habláramos hablarais hablaran	habla (tú), no hables hable (usted) hablemos hablad (vosotros), no habléis hablen (Uds.)
comer comiendo comido	como comes come comemos coméis comen	comía comías comía comíamos comíais comían	comí comiste comió comimos comisteis comieron	comeré comerás comerá comeremos comeréis comerán	comería comerías comería comeríamos comeríais comerían	coma comas coma comamos comáis coman	comiera comieras comiera comiéramos comierais comieran	come (tú), no comas coma (usted) comamos comed (vosotros), no comáis coman (Uds.)
vivir viviendo vivido	vivo vives vive vivimos vivís viven	vivía vivías vivía vivíamos vivíais vivían	viví viviste vivió vivimos vivisteis vivieron	viviré vivirás vivirá viviremos viviréis vivirán	viviría vivirías viviría viviríamos viviríais vivirían	viva vivas viva vivamos viváis vivan	viviera vivieras viviera viviéramos vivierais vivieran	vive (tú), no vivas viva (usted) vivamos vivid (vosotros), no viváis vivan (Uds.)

Regular Verbs: Perfect Tenses

	Indicative										Subjunctive			
Present Perfect		**Past Perfect**		**Preterit Perfect**		**Future Perfect**		**Conditional Perfect**		**Present Perfect**		**Past Perfect**	
he	hablado	había	hablado	hube	hablado	habré	hablado	habría	hablado	haya	hablado	hubiera	hablado
has	comido	habías	comido	hubiste	comido	habrás	comido	habrías	comido	hayas	comido	hubieras	comido
ha	vivido	había	vivido	hubo	vivido	habrá	vivido	habría	vivido	haya	vivido	hubiera	vivido
hemos		habíamos		hubimos		habremos		habríamos		hayamos		hubiéramos	
habéis		habíais		hubisteis		habréis		habríais		hayáis		hubierais	
han		habían		hubieron		habrán		habrían		hayan		hubieran	

Irregular Verbs

Infinitive / Present Participle / Past Participle	Indicative					Subjunctive		Imperative
	Present	**Imperfect**	**Preterit**	**Future**	**Conditional**	**Present**	**Imperfect**	**Commands**
andar andando andado	ando andas anda andamos andáis andan	andaba andabas andaba andábamos andabais andaban	anduve anduviste anduvo anduvimos anduvisteis anduvieron	andaré andarás andará andaremos andaréis andarán	andaría andarías andaría andaríamos andaríais andarían	ande andes ande andemos andéis anden	anduviera anduvieras anduviera anduviéramos anduvierais anduvieran	anda (tú), no andes ande (usted) andemos andad (vosotros), no andéis anden (Uds.)
caer cayendo caído	caigo caes cae caemos caéis caen	caía caías caía caíamos caíais caían	caí caíste cayó caímos caísteis cayeron	caeré caerás caerá caeremos caeréis caerán	caería caerías caería caeríamos caeríais caerían	caiga caigas caiga caigamos caigáis caigan	cayera cayeras cayera cayéramos cayerais cayeran	cae (tú), no caigas caiga (usted) caigamos caed (vosotros), no caigáis caigan (Uds.)
dar dando dado	doy das da damos dais dan	daba dabas daba dábamos dabais daban	di diste dio dimos disteis dieron	daré darás dará daremos daréis darán	daría darías daría daríamos daríais darían	dé des dé demos deis den	diera dieras diera diéramos dierais dieran	da (tú), no des dé (usted) demos dad (vosotros), no deis den (Uds.)
decir diciendo dicho	digo dices dice decimos decís dicen	decía decías decía decíamos decíais decían	dije dijiste dijo dijimos dijisteis dijeron	diré dirás dirá diremos diréis dirán	diría dirías diría diríamos diríais dirían	diga digas diga digamos digáis digan	dijera dijeras dijera dijéramos dijerais dijeran	di (tú), no digas diga (usted) digamos decid (vosotros), no digáis digan (Uds.)

Irregular Verbs (continued)

Infinitive / Present Participle / Past Participle	Indicative Present	Indicative Imperfect	Indicative Preterit	Indicative Future	Indicative Conditional	Subjunctive Present	Subjunctive Imperfect	Imperative Commands
estar estando estado	estoy estás está estamos estáis están	estaba estabas estaba estábamos estabais estaban	estuve estuviste estuvo estuvimos estuvisteis estuvieron	estaré estarás estará estaremos estaréis estarán	estaría estarías estaría estaríamos estaríais estarían	esté estés esté estemos estéis estén	estuviera estuvieras estuviera estuviéramos estuvierais estuvieran	está (tú), no estés esté (usted) estemos estad (vosotros), no estéis estén (Uds.)
haber habiendo habido	he has ha hemos habéis han	había habías había habíamos habíais habían	hube hubiste hubo hubimos hubisteis hubieron	habré habrás habrá habremos habréis habrán	habría habrías habría habríamos habríais habrían	haya hayas haya hayamos hayáis hayan	hubiera hubieras hubiera hubiéramos hubierais hubieran	
hacer haciendo hecho	hago haces hace hacemos hacéis hacen	hacía hacías hacía hacíamos hacíais hacían	hice hiciste hizo hicimos hicisteis hicieron	haré harás hará haremos haréis harán	haría harías haría haríamos haríais harían	haga hagas haga hagamos hagáis hagan	hiciera hicieras hiciera hiciéramos hicierais hicieran	haz (tú), no hagas haga (usted) hagamos haced (vosotros), no hagáis hagan (Uds.)
ir yendo ido	voy vas va vamos vais van	iba ibas iba íbamos ibais iban	fui fuiste fue fuimos fuisteis fueron	iré irás irá iremos iréis irán	iría irías iría iríamos iríais irían	vaya vayas vaya vayamos vayáis vayan	fuera fueras fuera fuéramos fuerais fueran	ve (tú), no vayas vaya (usted) vamos, no vayamos id (vosotros), no vayáis vayan (Uds.)
oír oyendo oído	oigo oyes oye oímos oís oyen	oía oías oía oíamos oíais oían	oí oíste oyó oímos oísteis oyeron	oiré oirás oirá oiremos oiréis oirán	oiría oirías oiría oiríamos oiríais oirían	oiga oigas oiga oigamos oigáis oigan	oyera oyeras oyera oyéramos oyerais oyeran	oye (tú), no oigas oiga (usted) oigamos oíd (vosotros), no oigáis oigan (Uds.)

Irregular Verbs (continued)

Infinitive Present Participle Past Participle	Indicative					Subjunctive		Imperative
	Present	Imperfect	Preterit	Future	Conditional	Present	Imperfect	Commands
poder pudiendo podido	puedo puedes puede podemos podéis pueden	podía podías podía podíamos podíais podían	pude pudiste pudo pudimos pudisteis pudieron	podré podrás podrá podremos podréis podrán	podría podrías podría podríamos podríais podrían	pueda puedas pueda podamos podáis puedan	pudiera pudieras pudiera pudiéramos pudierais pudieran	
poner poniendo puesto	pongo pones pone ponemos ponéis ponen	ponía ponías ponía poníamos poníais ponían	puse pusiste puso pusimos pusisteis pusieron	pondré pondrás pondrá pondremos pondréis pondrán	pondría pondrías pondría pondríamos pondríais pondrían	ponga pongas ponga pongamos pongáis pongan	pusiera pusieras pusiera pusiéramos pusierais pusieran	pon (tú), no pongas ponga (usted) pongamos poned (vosotros), no pongáis pongan (Uds.)
querer queriendo querido	quiero quieres quiere queremos queréis quieren	quería querías quería queríamos queríais querían	quise quisiste quiso quisimos quisisteis quisieron	querré querrás querrá querremos querréis querrán	querría querrías querría querríamos querríais querrían	quiera quieras quiera queramos queráis quieran	quisiera quisieras quisiera quisiéramos quisierais quisieran	quiere (tú), no quieras quiera (usted) queramos quered (vosotros), no queráis quieran (Uds.)
saber sabiendo sabido	sé sabes sabe sabemos sabéis saben	sabía sabías sabía sabíamos sabíais sabían	supe supiste supo supimos supisteis supieron	sabré sabrás sabrá sabremos sabréis sabrán	sabría sabrías sabría sabríamos sabríais sabrían	sepa sepas sepa sepamos sepáis sepan	supiera supieras supiera supiéramos supierais supieran	sabe (tú), no sepas sepa (usted) sepamos sabed (vosotros), no sepáis sepan (Uds.)
salir saliendo salido	salgo sales sale salimos salís salen	salía salías salía salíamos salíais salían	salí saliste salió salimos salisteis salieron	saldré saldrás saldrá saldremos saldréis saldrán	saldría saldrías saldría saldríamos saldríais saldrían	salga salgas salga salgamos salgáis salgan	saliera salieras saliera saliéramos salierais salieran	sal (tú), no salgas salga (usted) salgamos salid (vosotros), no salgáis salgan (Uds.)

Irregular Verbs (continued)

Infinitive / Present Participle / Past Participle	Indicative						Subjunctive		Imperative
	Present	Imperfect	Preterit	Future	Conditional		Present	Imperfect	Commands
ser / siendo / sido	soy / eres / es / somos / sois / son	era / eras / era / éramos / erais / eran	fui / fuiste / fue / fuimos / fuisteis / fueron	seré / serás / será / seremos / seréis / serán	sería / serías / sería / seríamos / seríais / serían		sea / seas / sea / seamos / seáis / sean	fuera / fueras / fuera / fuéramos / fuerais / fueran	sé (tú), no seas / sea (usted) / seamos / sed (vosotros), no seáis / sean (Uds.)
tener / teniendo / tenido	tengo / tienes / tiene / tenemos / tenéis / tienen	tenía / tenías / tenía / teníamos / teníais / tenían	tuve / tuviste / tuvo / tuvimos / tuvisteis / tuvieron	tendré / tendrás / tendrá / tendremos / tendréis / tendrán	tendría / tendrías / tendría / tendríamos / tendríais / tendrían		tenga / tengas / tenga / tengamos / tengáis / tengan	tuviera / tuvieras / tuviera / tuviéramos / tuvierais / tuvieran	ten (tú), no tengas / tenga (usted) / tengamos / tened (vosotros), no tengáis / tengan (Uds.)
traer / trayendo / traído	traigo / traes / trae / traemos / traéis / traen	traía / traías / traía / traíamos / traíais / traían	traje / trajiste / trajo / trajimos / trajisteis / trajeron	traeré / traerás / traerá / traeremos / traeréis / traerán	traería / traerías / traería / traeríamos / traeríais / traerían		traiga / traigas / traiga / traigamos / traigáis / traigan	trajera / trajeras / trajera / trajéramos / trajerais / trajeran	trae (tú), no traigas / traiga (usted) / traigamos / traed (vosotros), no traigáis / traigan (Uds.)
venir / viniendo / venido	vengo / vienes / viene / venimos / venís / vienen	venía / venías / venía / veníamos / veníais / venían	vine / viniste / vino / vinimos / vinisteis / vinieron	vendré / vendrás / vendrá / vendremos / vendréis / vendrán	vendría / vendrías / vendría / vendríamos / vendríais / vendrían		venga / vengas / venga / vengamos / vengáis / vengan	viniera / vinieras / viniera / viniéramos / vinierais / vinieran	ven (tú), no vengas / venga (usted) / vengamos / venid (vosotros), no vengáis / vengan (Uds.)
ver / viendo / visto	veo / ves / ve / vemos / veis / ven	veía / veías / veía / veíamos / veíais / veían	vi / viste / vio / vimos / visteis / vieron	veré / verás / verá / veremos / veréis / verán	vería / verías / vería / veríamos / veríais / verían		vea / veas / vea / veamos / veáis / vean	viera / vieras / viera / viéramos / vierais / vieran	ve (tú), no veas / vea (usted) / veamos / ved (vosotros), no veáis / vean (Uds.)

Stem-Changing and Orthographic-Changing Verbs

Infinitive / Present Participle / Past Participle	Indicative					Subjunctive		Imperative
	Present	Imperfect	Preterit	Future	Conditional	Present	Imperfect	Commands
almorzar (z, c) almorzando almorzado	almuerzo almuerzas almuerza almorzamos almorzáis almuerzan	almorzaba almorzabas almorzaba almorzábamos almorzabais almorzaban	almorcé almorzaste almorzó almorzamos almorzasteis almorzaron	almorzaré almorzarás almorzará almorzaremos almorzaréis almorzarán	almorzaría almorzarías almorzaría almorzaríamos almorzaríais almorzarían	almuerce almuerces almuerce almorcemos almorcéis almuercen	almorzara almorzaras almorzaras almorzáramos almorzarais almorzaran	almuerza (tú) no almuerces almuerce (usted) almorcemos almorzad (vosotros) no almorcéis almuercen (Uds.)
buscar (c, qu) buscando buscado	busco buscas busca buscamos buscáis buscan	buscaba buscabas buscaba buscábamos buscabais buscaban	busqué buscaste buscó buscamos buscasteis buscaron	buscaré buscarás buscará buscaremos buscaréis buscarán	buscaría buscarías buscaría buscaríamos buscaríais buscarían	busque busques busque busquemos busquéis busquen	buscara buscaras buscara buscáramos buscarais buscaran	busca (tú) no busques busque (usted) busquemos buscad (vosotros) no busquéis busquen (Uds.)
corregir (g, j) corrigiendo corregido	corrijo corriges corrige corregimos corregís corrigen	corregía corregías corregía corregíamos corregíais corregían	corregí corregiste corrigió corregimos corregisteis corrigieron	corregiré corregirás corregirá corregiremos corregiréis corregirán	corregiría corregirías corregiría corregiríamos corregiríais corregirían	corrija corrijas corrija corrijamos corrijáis corrijan	corrigiera corrigieras corrigiera corrigiéramos corrigierais corrigieran	corrige (tú) no corrijas corrija (usted) corrijamos corregid (vosotros) no corrijáis corrijan (Uds.)
dormir (ue, u) durmiendo dormido	duermo duermes duerme dormimos dormís duermen	dormía dormías dormía dormíamos dormíais dormían	dormí dormiste durmió dormimos dormisteis durmieron	dormiré dormirás dormirá dormiremos dormiréis dormirán	dormiría dormirías dormiría dormiríamos dormiríais dormirían	duerma duermas duerma durmamos durmáis duerman	durmiera durmieras durmiera durmiéramos durmierais durmieran	duerme (tú), no duermas duerma (usted) durmamos dormid (vosotros), no durmáis duerman (Uds.)
incluir (y) incluyendo incluido	incluyo incluyes incluye incluimos incluís incluyen	incluía incluías incluía incluíamos incluíais incluían	incluí incluiste incluyó incluimos incluisteis incluyeron	incluiré incluirás incluirá incluiremos incluiréis incluirán	incluiría incluirías incluiría incluiríamos incluiríais incluirían	incluya incluyas incluya incluyamos incluyáis incluyan	incluyera incluyeras incluyera incluyéramos incluyerais incluyeran	incluye (tú), no incluyas incluya (usted) incluyamos incluid (vosotros), no incluyáis incluyan (Uds.)

Stem-Changing and Orthographic-Changing Verbs (continued)

Infinitive / Present Participle / Past Participle	Indicative Present	Imperfect	Preterit	Future	Conditional	Subjunctive Present	Subjunctive Imperfect	Imperative Commands
llegar (g, gu) / llegando / llegado	llego, llegas, llega, llegamos, llegáis, llegan	llegaba, llegabas, llegaba, llegábamos, llegabais, llegaban	llegué, llegaste, llegó, llegamos, llegasteis, llegaron	llegaré, llegarás, llegará, llegaremos, llegaréis, llegarán	llegaría, llegarías, llegaría, llegaríamos, llegaríais, llegarían	llegue, llegues, llegue, lleguemos, lleguéis, lleguen	llegara, llegaras, llegara, llegáramos, llegarais, llegaran	llega (tú), no llegues, llegue (usted), lleguemos, llegad (vosotros), no lleguéis, lleguen (Uds.)
pedir (i, i) / pidiendo / pedido	pido, pides, pide, pedimos, pedís, piden	pedía, pedías, pedía, pedíamos, pedíais, pedían	pedí, pediste, pidió, pedimos, pedisteis, pidieron	pediré, pedirás, pedirá, pediremos, pediréis, pedirán	pediría, pedirías, pediría, pediríamos, pediríais, pedirían	pida, pidas, pida, pidamos, pidáis, pidan	pidiera, pidieras, pidiera, pidiéramos, pidierais, pidieran	pide (tú), no pidas, pida (usted), pidamos, pedid (vosotros), no pidáis, pidan (Uds.)
pensar (ie) / pensando / pensado	pienso, piensas, piensa, pensamos, pensáis, piensan	pensaba, pensabas, pensaba, pensábamos, pensabais, pensaban	pensé, pensaste, pensó, pensamos, pensasteis, pensaron	pensaré, pensarás, pensará, pensaremos, pensaréis, pensarán	pensaría, pensarías, pensaría, pensaríamos, pensaríais, pensarían	piense, pienses, piense, pensemos, penséis, piensen	pensara, pensaras, pensara, pensáramos, pensarais, pensaran	piensa (tú), no pienses, piense (usted), pensemos, pensad (vosotros), no penséis, piensen (Uds.)
producir (zc) / produciendo / producido	produzco, produces, produce, producimos, producís, producen	producía, producías, producía, producíamos, producíais, producían	produje, produjiste, produjo, produjimos, produjisteis, produjeron	produciré, producirás, producirá, produciremos, produciréis, producirán	produciría, producirías, produciría, produciríamos, produciríais, producirían	produzca, produzcas, produzca, produzcamos, produzcáis, produzcan	produjera, produjeras, produjera, produjéramos, produjerais, produjeran	produce (tú), no produzcas, produzca (usted), produzcamos, producid (vosotros), no produzcáis, produzcan (Uds.)
reír (i, i) / riendo / reído	río, ríes, ríe, reímos, reís, ríen	reía, reías, reía, reíamos, reíais, reían	reí, reíste, rio, reímos, reísteis, rieron	reiré, reirás, reirá, reiremos, reiréis, reirán	reiría, reirías, reiría, reiríamos, reiríais, reirían	ría, rías, ría, riamos, riáis, rían	riera, rieras, riera, riéramos, rierais, rieran	ríe (tú), no rías, ría (usted), riamos, reíd (vosotros), no riáis, rían (Uds.)

Stem-Changing and Orthographic-Changing Verbs (continued)

Infinitive / Present Participle / Past Participle	Indicative					Subjunctive		Imperative
	Present	Imperfect	Preterit	Future	Conditional	Present	Imperfect	Commands
seguir (i, i) (ga) siguiendo seguido	sigo sigues sigue seguimos seguís siguen	seguía seguías seguía seguíamos seguíais seguían	seguí seguiste siguió seguimos seguisteis siguieron	seguiré seguirás seguirá seguiremos seguiréis seguirán	seguiría seguirías seguiría seguiríamos seguiríais seguirían	siga sigas siga sigamos sigáis sigan	siguiera siguieras siguiera siguiéramos siguierais siguieran	sigue (tú), no sigas siga (usted) sigamos seguid (vosotros), no sigáis sigan (Uds.)
sentir (ie, i) sintiendo sentido	siento sientes siente sentimos sentís sienten	sentía sentías sentía sentíamos sentíais sentían	sentí sentiste sintió sentimos sentisteis sintieron	sentiré sentirás sentirá sentiremos sentiréis sentirán	sentiría sentirías sentiría sentiríamos sentiríais sentirían	sienta sientas sienta sintamos sintáis sientan	sintiera sintieras sintiera sintiéramos sintierais sintieran	siente (tú), no sientas sienta (usted) sintamos sentid (vosotros), no sintáis sientan (Uds.)
volver (ue) volviendo vuelto	vuelvo vuelves vuelve volvemos volvéis vuelven	volvía volvías volvía volvíamos volvíais volvían	volví volviste volvió volvimos volvisteis volvieron	volveré volverás volverá volveremos volveréis volverán	volvería volverías volvería volveríamos volveríais volverían	vuelva vuelvas vuelva volvamos volváis vuelvan	volviera volvieras volviera volviéramos volvierais volvieran	vuelve (tú), no vuelvas vuelva (usted) volvamos volved (vosotros), no volváis vuelvan (Uds.)

Appendix 3

Spanish to English Glossary

This vocabulary includes all words presented in the text, except for proper nouns spelled the same in English and Spanish, diminutives with a literal meaning, typical expressions of the Hispanic countries presented in the *Enfoque cultural,* and cardinal numbers (found on page 14). Other cognates and words easily recognized because of the context are not included either.

The number following each entry corresponds to the **capítulo** in which the word was first introduced. Numbers followed by "r" signal that the item was presented for recognition rather than as active vocabulary.

A

a *at, to* P
abajo *below, under* 4r
el/la abogado/a *lawyer* 9
abordar *to board* 12r
abrazar(se) (c) *to embrace* 13
el abrazo *hug* 4r
el abrigo *coat robe* 6
abril *April* Pr
abrir *to open* 12r
la abuela *grandmother* 4
el abuelo *grandfather* 4
abundar *to abound* 13
aburrido/a *bored* 6r; *boring* 1
acabar(se) *to complete, to finish; to run out of* 9r
el acceso *access* 15
el accesorio *accessory* 5
el aceite *oil* 10
la aceituna *olive* 3r
el achiote *paprika* 10r
acompañar *to accompany* 8
aconsejable *advisable* 11r
aconsejar *to advise* 5r
el acontecimiento *event* 13r
acostar(se) (ue) *to put to bed; to go to bed* 4
la actividad *activity* 1r
activo/a *active* Pr
el actor/la actriz *actor/actress* 9
actual *present, current* 14
actualmente *at the present time* 9
actuar *to act* 13
la adaptación *adjustment, adaptation* 14
adaptar *to adapt* 11r

Adelante. *Come in.* 5r
el adelanto *advance* 15, 15r
adelgazar *to lose weight* 10r
el ademán *gesture* 15r
además *besides* 11r
el aderezo *salad dressing* 10
adinerado/a *well-off* 8r
adiós *good-bye* Pr
adivinar *to guess* 6r
¿adónde? *where (to)?* 3
adornado/a *decorated* 8
la aduana *customs* 12
la aerolínea/línea aérea el asiento *airline seat* 12
el/la aeromozo *flight attendant* 12r
el aeropuerto *airport* 12
afeitar(se) *to shave; to shave (oneself)* 4
el afiche *poster* 4r
afirmar *to affirm* 7r
afortunadamente *fortunately* 4r
afuera *outside* 4r
las afueras *outskirts* 5
la agencia de viajes *travel agency* 12
el/la agente de viajes *travel agent* 12
agosto *August* Pr
agradable *agreeable* 11r; *nice* 2
agregar *to add* 10
el/la agricultor/a *farmer* 9
agrio/a *sour* 10
el aguacate *avocado* 10, 10r
agudo/a *sharp, acute* 11r
el águila *eagle* 14r
el/la ahijado/a *godchild* 4
ahora *now* 1
ahorrar *to save* 6r
los ahorros *savings* 9r

el aire acondicionado *air conditioning* 5
el ají *chile pepper* 10r
el ajo *garlic* 10, 10r
al *to the (contraction of a+el)* 3
la alacridad *alacrity* 13r
al aire libre *outdoors* 3
la alberca *swimming pool* 5r
el albergue juvenil *youth hostel* 13r
el alcalde *mayor* 14r
la alcoba *bedroom* 5r
al lado (de) *next to* P
alegrarse (de) *to be glad (about)* 11; *to be happy* 4r
alegre *happy, glad* 2
alegremente *happily* 4r
la alegría *joy* 8
alemán/alemana *German* 2
alérgico/a *allergic* 11r
el alfiler *pin* 15r
la alfombra *carpet, rug* 5
al fondo *at the back, in the rear* 13
la álgebra *algebra* 11r
algo *anything* 13r; *something* 1
alguien *everyone* 13r; *someone* 13r
algún/alguno(s)/alguna(s) *any* 13r; *any, some* Pr; *several* 13r
algunas veces *sometimes* 13r
alguna vez *ever* 13r; *sometime* 13r
aliviar *to relieve* 12r
el alivio *relief* 15r
allí *there* 4r
el alma *soul* 15r
el almacén *department store; warehouse* 6
la almeja *clam* 10r

la almohada *pillow* 5
almorzar (ue) *to have lunch* 4
el almuerzo *lunch* 3, Pr
¿Aló? *Hello? (on the telephone)* 3r
el alojamiento *lodging* 11r, 12
el alquiler *rent* 5
alquilar *to rent* 3
alternativo/a *alternative* 1r
alto *loudly* Pr
alto/a *tall* 2
el/la alumno/a *student* 1
el ama/o de casa *housewife, homemaker* 9
amarillo/a *yellow* 2
ambicioso/a *ambitious* Pr
a menos que *unless* 14r
el/la amigo/a *friend* P
la amistad *friendship* 13, 13r
el amor *love* 13
amplio/a *ample* 14
añadir *to add* 10
el analfabetismo *illiteracy* 14
analfabeto/a *illiterate* 14
anaranjado/a *orange* 2
la anatomía *anatomy* 1r
ancho/a *wide* 6
andar *to go* 14r
el anillo *ring* 6
animado/a *lively* 8
el año *year* P
anoche *last night* 6r
el Año Nuevo *New Year's Day* 8r
el año pasado *last year* 6r
la ansiedad *anxiety* 12r
ante(a)noche *night before last* 6r
anteayer *day before yesterday* 6r
el antepasado *ancestor* 8
antes *before* 6r, 8
antes (de) que *before* 14r
el antibiótico *antibiotic* 11
antiguo/a *old* 1
antipático/a *unpleasant* 2
la antropología *anthropology* 1
el anuncio *ad, advertisement* 9
apagar *to extinguish, to turn off* 9
el apagón *blackout* 8r
el apartamento *apartment* 5
a petición *on demand* 5r
el apio *celery* 10r
la aplicación *application* 15r
apoyar *to support* 7r
aprender *to learn* 1
apropiado/a *appropriate* 6r
aprovechar *to take advantage* 7
el apunte *note* 1

aquel/aquella *that (over there)* 5r
el árbitro *umpire, referee* 7
el árbol *tree* 7
el arete *earring* 6
argentino/a *Argentinian* 2
el armario *cabinet* 5r; *closet, armoire* 5
el aro *earring* 6r
el arpa *harp* 13r
el/la arquitecto/a *architect* 9, 9r
la arquitectura *architecture* 1, 5
arrepentirse (ie) *to regret* 7r
arrogante *arrogant* Pr
el arroz *rice* 3
el arte *art* 1r
la artesanía *handicrafts* 6
el/la artesano/a *craftsman/woman* 9; *craftsperson* 9
los artes plásticas *plastic arts* 1r
el artículo de belleza *beauty item* 11
el/la artista *artist* 9r
asar *to roast* 10r
asegurar *to assure* 7r
el aserrín *sawdust* 8
el asiento *seat* 12
el asiento de pasillo *aisle seat* 12
el asiento de ventanilla *window seat* 12
asistir *to attend* 1
la aspiradora *vacuum cleaner* 5
el astronomía *astronomy* 1r
asumir *to assume* 12r
asustado/a *scared* 12r
atar *to bind* 13r
aterrizar (c) *to land* 15
el ático *attic* 5r
atlético/a *athletic* Pr
la atmósfera *atmosphere* 7
atractivo/a *attractive* Pr
atrás *back, behind, backwards* 6r
a través de *through* 13
atreverse *to dare* 7r
aun *event* 14r
aunque *although* 14r; *even if* 14r; *even though* 14r
el auto *car* 2
el autobús/bus *bus* 12
la autopista *freeway* 12
el autorretrato *self-portrait* 13
el/la auxiliar de vuelo *flight attendant* 12, 12r
avanzar *to advance* 15r
a veces *sometimes* 1r; *at times* 13r
la avenida *avenue* Pr

a la venta *for sale* 6r
averiguar *to find out* 5r
las aves *poultry, fowl* 10
el avión *plane* 12
ayer *yesterday* 6r
ayudar *to help* 5, 5r
la azafata *flight attendant* 12r
el azar *chance* 13r
el/la azúcar *sugar* 10
azul *blue* 2

B

el bailarín/la bailarina *dancer* 13
bailar *to dance* 1
la bajada *slope* 7r
bajar *to download* 15
bajo/a *short (in stature)* 2
el balón *ball* 7r
el baloncesto/el básquetbol *basketball* 7
la bañadera *bathtub* 5r
la banana *banana, plantain* 10
el banano *banana, plantain* 10r
bañar(se) *to bathe; to take a bath* 4
el banco *bank* 9
el banco de peces *shoal; school of fish* 15
la banda ancha *broadband* 5r
la bandeja *tray* 10
la bañera *bathtub* 5, 5r
el baño *bathroom* 5
barato/a *inexpensive, cheap* 6
la barbacoa *barbecue pit; barbecue (event)* 5
el barco *ship/boat* 12
barrer *to sweep* 5
el barrio *neighborhood* 5
basar *to base* 13r
básicamente *basically* 4r
el básquetbol *basketball* 7
bastante *enough* Pr; *rather* P
la basura *garbage, trash* 5
la bata *robe* 6
el bate *bat* 7
el batido *milkshake, smoothie* 10r
batir *to beat* 10, 10r
el baúl *trunk* 12
el bautizo *baptism, christening* 4
beber *to drink* 1
la bebida *drink* 3
el béisbol *baseball* 7
las bellas artes *fine arts* 1r
beneficiar *to benefit* 6r
besar *to kiss* 11r

el **beso** *kiss* 4r
la **biblioteca** *library* 1; *library cafe, coffee shop cafeteria* 1
el/la **bibliotecario/a** *librarian* 9, 9r
la **biblioteca virtual** *virtual library* 15
la **bicicleta** *bicycle* 3r
bien *well* P
bienes raíces *real estate* 5r
bien parecido *good-looking* 2r
bilingüe *bilingual* 2
el **billete** *ticket (Spain)* 12r
la **billetera** *wallet* 6
la **bioquímica** *biochemistry* 1r
el **bisonte** *bison* 13r
el **bistec** *steak* 3
blando/a *soft* 13
la **blusa** *blouse* 6
blanco/a *white* 2
la **boca** *mouth* 11
la **boda** *wedding* 3
la **bodega** *wine cellar* 5
la **bola** *bowling ball* 7r
el **boleto** *ticket* 12r
el **boliche** *bowling* 7r
el **bolígrafo** *ballpoint pen* P
boliviano/a *Bolivian* 2
el **bolo** *bowling ball* 7r
la **bolsa/el bolso** *purse* 6
el/la **bombero/a** *firefighter* 9
bonito/a *pretty* 2
el **laboratorio** *laboratory* 1, Pr
el **borrador** *eraser* P
el **bosque** *forest* 15
el **bosque tropical** *rain forest* 15
la **bota** *boot* 6
la **botella** *bottle* 10
el **bowling** *bowling* 7r
el **brazo** *arm* 6r, 11
la **broma** *joke* 10r
brujo/a *broke* 2r
el **buceo** *snorkeling* 12r
buenas noches *good evening* P
buenas tardes *good afternoon* P
¡Buena suerte! *Good luck!* 1
buen mozo *good-looking guy* 2r
¡Bueno! *Hello? (on the telephone)* 3r
bueno/a *good* 1; *well (health); physically attractive* 6r
buenos días *good morning* P
la **bufanda** *scarf* 6, 6r
el **burgués** *middle class* 13r
el **bus** *bus (Puerto Rico, Cuba)* 12r
el **buscador** *search engine* 15
buscar *to look for* 1
la **butaca** *armchair* 5, 7r

C

el **cabello** *hair* 11
la **cabeza** *head* 6r, 11
la **cabuya** *ammunition* 2r
cada *each* 7
cada... horas *every . . . hours* 11
la **cadera** *hip* 11
caer *to drop* 8r
caer bien *to like* 6r
caer mal *to dislike* 6r
caer(se) *to fall* 11
café *brown* 2r
el **café** *cafe, coffee shop* 1; *coffee* 3
la **cafetería** *cafeteria* 1
caigue *lazy (Bolivia)* 13r
la **caja** *box* 6r
la **caja fuerte** *safe* 12
el/la **cajero/a** *cashier* 9
el/la **cajero/a** *cashier* 9r
el **cajero automático** *ATM* 12
el **calcetín** *sock* 6
el **calcio** *calcium* 10r
la **calculadora** *calculator* P
el **cálculo** *calculus* 1r
callado/a *quiet* 2
la **calefacción** *heating* 5
el **calendario** *calendar* Pr
el **calentamiento** *warming* 15
la **calidad** *quality* 6r, 13
caliente *hot* 3
callarse *to keep quiet* 14r
la **calle** *street* 5, Pr
calmar *to calm, alleviate* 11r
el **calor** *heat* 5r
el **calzado** *footwear* 6
calzar *to wear a shoe size* 6r
el **calzoncillo** *boxer shorts* 6
la **cama** *bed* 5
la **cámara** *camera* 9r
el **camarero/la camarera** *server, waiter/waitress* 3
el **camarón** *shrimp* 10
cambiar *to change, to exchange* 6
el **cambio** *change* 4r, 14
el **cambur** *banana, plantain* 10r
caminar *to walk* 1; *walk* 3r
el **camino** *road; way* 8
el **camión** *bus (Mexico)* 12r
la **camioneta** *bus (Guatemala)* 9r
la **camisa** *shirt* 6
la **camisa de manga corta** *short-sleeved shirt* 6r
la **camiseta** *T-shirt* 6

el **camisón** *nightgown* 6
la **campaña de publicidad** *publicity campaign* 15r
el **campeonato** *championship* 7; *tournament* 7r
el **campeón/la campeona** *champion* 7
el/la **campesino/a** *peasant* 10
el **campo** *countryside* 9
canadiense *Canadian* 2
el **canal** *channel* 7r
cancelar *to cancel* 12
el **cáncer** *cancer* 11
la **canción** *song* 3
la **canela** *cinnamon* 10r
el **cangrejo** *crab* 10r
cansado/a *tired* 2
cantar *to sing* 3
la **cantidad** *quantity* 9r
la **capa de ozono** *ozone layer* 15
el **capítan** *captain* 3r
la **capitanía general** *administrative unit of the Spanish Empire* 3r
el **capó** *hood* 12
la **cápsula** *capsule* 15
la **cara** *face* 4r, 11; *expression* 15r
el **cargador de celular (del móvil)** *cell phone charger* 5r
cariños *love (closing)* 3r
caritativo/a *charitable* 13r
carmelita *brown* 2r
el **carnaval** *carnival* 8
la **carne** *meat* 10
la **carne de res** *beef/steak* 10
la **carne molida/picada** *ground meat* 10
el **carnet de conducir** *driver's license* 15r
caro/a *expensive* 6, 6r
el/la **carpintero/a** *carpenter* 9
la **carrera** *major* 1r; *race* 7
la **carreta** *cart, wagon* 8
la **carretera** *highway* 12
el **carro** *car* 2
la **carroza** *float (in a parade)* 8
el **cartero/la cartera** *mail carrier* 12
la **casa** *house, home* 1
casado/a *married* 2
la **casa editorial** *editorial house* 13r
casar(se) *to get married* 4
castaño/a *brown* 2r
el **catarro** *cold* 11
la **cebolla** *onion* 10

la ceja *eyebrow* 11
la celebración *celebration* 3
celebrar *to celebrate* 3
el cementerio *cemetery* 8
la cena *dinner, supper* 3
cenar *to have dinner* 3
el centro *downtown, center* 5
el centro comercial *shopping center* 6
el centro de entrenamiento *training resort* 7r
el centro de salud *hospital* 11
el/la ceramista *potter* 9
cerca *near* 3r
cerca de *close to, near* 3
el cerdo *pork* 10
el cereal *cereal* 3
el cerebro *brain* 11
la cereza *cherry* 10
cerrar (ie) *to close* 4r
la certeza *certainty* 13r
la cerveza *beer* 1r, 3
el césped *lawn* 5
el cesto *wastebasket* P
el cesto/la cesta *basket, hoop* 7
el ceviche *dish of marinated raw fish* 3
las chanclas *flip-flops* 9r
la chancona *nerd (Peru)* 3r
chao *good-bye* Pr
la chaqueta *jacket* 6
chau *good-bye* Pr
el/la chef *chef* 9
el cheque *check* 9r
el/la chico/a *boy/girl* P
el chile *chile pepper* 10r
chileno/a *Chilean* 2
la chimenea *fireplace* 5
la chivita *bus* 1r; *bus (Colombia)* 12r
el choclo *corn* 10r
el/la chofer (chófer) *driver; chauffeur* 9
la chuleta *chop* 10
el chunche *thing (Costa Rica)* 12r
los churros *fried dough* 10
el ciclismo *cycling* 7
el/la ciclista *cyclist* 7, 7r
la ciencia *science* 1
las ciencias políticas *political science* 1
cien/ciento *hundred* 3r
el/la científico/a *scientist* 9, 9r
cierto/a *true* Pr
el cilantro *cilantro* 10r
el cine *cinema* 13r; *movies* 1r, 3

el/la cineasta *filmmaker* 13r
la cintura *waist* 11
el cinturón *belt* 6
el/la cirujano/a *surgeon* 11r
la cita *date* 6r
citar *to quote* 14r
la cita textual *quotation* 7r
la ciudad *city* 3
el ciudadano *citizen* 14r
clarear el día *dawn* 13r
¡claro! *of course!* 3
la clase turista *coach class* 12r; *tourist class* 12
el/la cliente/clienta *client* 6r, 9
climatizado/a *air-conditioned* 15
la clínica, el centro *clinic* 11
la clonación *cloning* 15
el clóset *closet* 5r
la cobija *blanket* 5r
el coche *car* 2
cocido/a *cooked* 3r
la cocina *kitchen* 5; *stove* 5r
la cocina fusión *fusion cuisine* 10r
cocinar *to cook* 5
el/la cocinero/a *cook* 5r
codiciado/a *sought after* 13r
el código *code* 15r
el codo *elbow* 11
el cognado *cognate* Pr
colapsar *to collapse* 9r
el colectivo *bus (Argentina)* 12r
el colesterol *cholesterol* 10r
colocar *to place* 5r
colombiano/a *Colombian* 2
los colores *colors* 2
el collar *necklace* 6
el comedor *dining room* 5, 5r
comenzar (ie) *to begin* 8
comer *to eat* 1
cómico/a *comic* Pr
la comida *food; meal; dinner, supper* 3
la comida chatarra *junk food* 10r
el comienzo *beginning* 7r, 8
el comino *cumin* 10r
¿cómo? *how/what?* 1r
la cómoda *dresser* 5
cómodo/a *comfortable* 9r
¿Cómo es? *What is he/she/it like?* P
¿Cómo está? *How are you (formal)?* P
¿Cómo estás? *How are you (informal)?* P

¡Cómo no! *Of course!* 9
¿Cómo se dice...? *How do you say...?* Pr
¿Cómo se escribe...? *How do you spell...?* Pr
¿Cómo se llama usted? *What's your name? (formal)* P
¿Cómo te llamas? *What's your name? (familiar)* P
¿Cómo te va? *How is it going?* 1
el/la compañero/a *partner, classmate* 1
la compañía de danza *dance company* 13
la compañía de teatro *theater company* 13
la compañía/empresa *company* 9
la comparsa *group dressed in similar costumes* 8
cómplice *complicit* 14r
el comportamiento *behavior* 9r
comprar *to buy* 1
comprender *to understand* 1
el compromiso *engagement* 8r
la computación *computer science* 1r
la computadora *computer* P
la computadora portátil *laptop* P
la comunicación *communication* 1r
comunicar *to communicate* 14r
comunicarse *to reach out to* 14r
con *with* 1
con cariño *affectionately* 4r
el concejo municipal *city council* 14r
la concha *shell* 8r
la conclusión *conclusion* 14r
la concordancia *agreement* 6r
el concurso *contest* 5r
el condimento *seasoning* 10
conducir *to drive* 15r
conectar *to connect* 15r
conectarse *to connect* 15
la conexión *connection* 12r
la confianza *trust* 14
el conflicto *conflict* 1r
congelar(se) *to freeze* 7
conmigo *with me* 7
conocer (zc) *to know* 3; *to meet* 13r
el conocimiento *knowledge* 15
con permiso *pardon me, excuse me* Pr
el/la consejero/a vocacional *career counselor* 9r
el consenso *consensus* 13r

la conservación *preservation* 15

construir (y) *to build* 15; *to construct* 12r

el consultorio *office (of doctor, dentist, etc.)* 9

consumir *to consume* 10r

la contabilidad *accounting* 1r

el/la contable *accountant* 9r

el/la contador/a *accountant* 9r

con tal (de) que *provided that* 14r

contaminado/a *polluted, contaminated* 7

contar *to count* 6r; *to tell* 7r

contemporáneo/a *contemporary* 1r

contento/a *happy, glad* 2

contestar *to answer* Pr

contigo *with you (familiar)* 7

continuar *to continue* 15r

contraer *to contract* 11r

contrario/a *opposing* 7, 7r

el contraste *contrast* 4r

el/la contratista *contractor* 9

contribuir (y) *to contribute* 15

conversador/a *talkative* 2

conversar *to talk, to converse* 1

la copa *(stemmed) glass* 10

la Copa Mundial *World Cup* 7r

el corazón *heart* 11, 11r

la corbata *tie* 6

el cordero *lamb* 10

el coroto *thing (Venezuela)* 6r

el correo *mail* 12

correr *to run* 1

la correspondencia *correspondence* 9r

la corrida (de toros) *bullfight* 8

cortar *to cut; to mow (lawn)* 5

la cortina *curtain* 5

corto/a *short (in length)* 2

la cosa *thing* 6

cosechar *to harvest* 9

costarricense *Costa Rican* 2

costar (ue) *to cost* 4

la costilla *rib* 10

la costumbre *custom* 8

creativo/a *creative* Pr

creer *to believe* 5

la crema *cream* 10

claro *of course* 4r

el crucero *cruise* 12

la clase *class* Pr

el cuaderno *notebook* P

la cuadra *city block* 12

el cuadro *picture, painting* 5

¿cuál(es)? *which?* 1r

¿Cuál es la fecha? *What is the date?* Pr

cuando *when* 14r

¿cuándo? *when?* 1r

¿cuánto/a? *how much?* 1r

¿Cuánto cuesta? *How much is it?* 1

¿cuántos/as? *how many?* 1r

el cuarto *bedroom* 5r; *room; bedroom* 5

el/la cuate *friend (Mexico)* 8r

cubano/a *Cuban* 2

cubista *cubist* 13

la cuchara *spoon* 10

la cucharada *spoonful* 10r

la cucharita *teaspoon* 10

el cuello *neck* 11

la cuenca *river basin* 15

la cuenta corriente *checking account* 9r

el cuento *story* 13

el cuero *leather* 6r

el cuerpo *body* 6r

el cuidado *care* 5r

cuidadosamente *carefully* 4r

cuidar(se) (de) *to take care of* 11

el culantro *cilantro* 10r

el cumpleaños *birthday* 3

cumplir *to fulfill* 7r

curar *to cure* 11

la curiosidad *curiosity* 12r

el currículum *résumé* 9

D

dañino/a *harmful* 10r

la danza *dance* 13r

dar *to give, to hand* 6

dar de comer *to feed* 9r

dar un paseo *to take a walk* 8

los datos *data* 14

de *of, from* 2

debajo (de) *under* P

deber *should* 1

debido a *due to* 15

débil *weak* 2

decepcionado/a *disappointed* 6r

decir (g, i) *to say, to tell* 4

la decisión *decision* 13r

el dedo *finger* 11

de estatura mediana *average, medium (height)* 2

la deforestación *deforestation* 15

de ida y vuelta *round trip* 12

dejar *to leave* 9

del *of the (contraction of de + el)* 2

delgado/a *thin* 2

la democracia *democracy* 14

de moda *stylish* 6r

de nada *you're welcome* Pr

denunciar *to denounce* 13

el departamento *apartment* 5r

el dependiente/la dependienta *salesperson* 1

el deporte *sport* 7

el/la deportista *athlete* 7r

la depresión *depression* 1r

deprimido/a *depressed* 11

¿de quién? *whose?* 2

la derecha *right* 4

el derecho *right* 14

derecho *straight* 12r

derretir *to melt* 10r

desamparado/a *homeless* 14r

la desaparición *disappearence* 15

desarmar *to disassemble* 9r

desarrollar(se) *to develop* 8r

el desarrollo *development* 13

desayunar *to have breakfast* 4

el desayuno *breakfast* 3

descansar *to rest* 3

descomponer(se) *to break* 9r

describir *to describe* 6r

la descripción *description* 1

el descubrimiento *discovery* 15

descuidado/a *careless* 9r

desde *since* 13

desear *to desire* 5r; *to wish, to want* 2

desechable *disposable* 15r

el desempleo *unemployment* 14

el desfile *parade* 8

el deshielo *thaw, thawing* 15

despacio *slowly* Pr

la despedida *closing* 4r

despedir (i) *to fire* 9r

despedir(se) (i) *to say goodbye* 7r

despegar (u) *to take off (airplane)* 15

despertar(se) (ie) *to wake (someone up)* 4

la despidida *farewell* Pr

el desplazamiento *movement, displacement* 14

después *after, later* 3

después (de) que *after* 14r

destacado/a *outstanding* 13

destacarse *to stand out* 14

el destino *destination* 12r

la desventaja *disadvantage* 5

el **detalle**   *detail* 12r
detener   *to stop* 9r
detrás (de)   *behind* P
devolver   *to return* 6r, 15r
el **día**   *day* P
diabético/a   *diabetic* 11r
el **Día del Amor y la Amistad**   *Valentine's Day* 8r
el **Día de Acción de Gracias**   *Thanksgiving* 8r
el **Día de la Independencia**   *Independence Day* 8r
el **Día de la Independencia de México**   *Mexican Independence Day* 8r
el **Día de las Brujas**   *Halloween* 8r
el **Día de los Enamorados**   *Valentine's Day* 8r
el **Día de los Muertos**   *Day of the Dead* 8r
el **Día de la Madre**   *Mother's Day* 8r
el **Día del Padre**   *Father's Day* 8r
el **día feriado**   *legal holiday* 8
el **día festivo**   *holiday* 8
dialogar   *to talk* 14r
el **diccionario**   *dictionary* 1
diciembre   *December* Pr
dictatorial   *dictatorial* 14
el **diente**   *tooth* 10r, 11
el **diente de ajo**   *clove of garlic* 10r
la **dieta**   *diet* 3r
difícil   *difficult* 1
difícilmente   *difficultly* 4r
difundir   *to spread, to disseminate* 15
difunto/a   *dead* 8
¿**Diga?, ¿Dígame?**   *Hello? (on the telephone)* 3r
digitalmente   *digitally* 13r
dinámico/a   *dynamic* Pr
el **dinero en efectivo**   *money in cash* 6
dirigir (j)   *to direct* 13
dirigirse (j)   *to address* 4r
la **discoteca**   *dance club* 1
disculparse   *to apologize* 7r
discutir   *to argue* 7
la **diseminación**   *dispersal, dissemination* 15
el **diseñador**   *designer* 5r
el **diseño**   *design* 1r
el **diseño gráfico**   *graphic design* 1r
disfrazarse   *to wear a costume* 8
disfrutar   *to enjoy* 10
disponible   *available* 5r
el **dispositivo**   *device* 5r
distinguir   *to distinguish* 13
la **distribución**   *layout* 5r

la **diversificación**   *diversification* 14
las **diversiones**   *leisure activities* 3
divertido/a   *fun, funny* 1r; *funny, amusing* 2
divertirse (ie, i)   *to have a good time* 8
divorciado/a   *divorced* 4
el **lado**   *side* 4r
doblar   *to turn* 12
doblar   *to fold* 5, 5r
el **documento adjunto**   *attached document* 15; *attachment* 15
el **dólar**   *dollar* 3r
doler (ue)   *to hurt, ache* 11
el **dolor**   *pain* 11
doméstico/a   *domestic* 5r
el **domingo**   *Sunday* Pr
dominicano/a   *Dominican* 2
dónde   *where?* Pr
¿**Dónde está... ?**   *Where is . . . ?* P
dorar   *to brown* 10r
dormir(se) (ue)   *to sleep; to fall asleep* 4
dormir (ue) la siesta   *to take a nap* 4
el **dormitorio**   *bedroom* 5r
el **drama**   *drama* 1r
la **droga**   *drug* 1r
la **ducha**   *shower* 5
duchar(se)   *to give a shower to; (to take a shower)* 4
la **duda**   *doubt* 13r
dudoso/a   *doubtful* 13r
el **dulce**   *candy/sweets* 10
duplicar   *to double* 10r
durante   *during* 3; *for (time)* 3r
durar   *to last* 7
el **durazno**   *peach* 10r
el **DVD**   *DVD; DVD player* P

E

la **economía**   *economics* 1
económicamente   *economically* 5r
ecuatoriano/a   *Ecuadorian* 2
el **edificio**   *building* 5
eficaz   *efficient* 12r
la **eficiencia**   *efficiency* 14
eficiente   *efficient* Pr
el/la **ejecutivo/a**   *executive* 9
el **ejercicio aeróbico**   *aerobic exercise* 11r
él   *he* P
elaborar   *to produce* 9
la **elección**   *election* 14r
el/la **electricista**   *electrician* 9r
el **electrodoméstico**   *appliance* 5

elegante   *elegant* Pr
elegir (i, i)   *to choose, to elect* 14
ellos/ellas   *they* 1
el **elote**   *corn* 10r
el/la **tenista**   *tennis player* 7
el **embarque**   *departure* 12r
la **emergencia**   *emergency* 9r
la **emigración**   *emigration* 14
el/la **emigrante**   *emigrant* 14
emigrar   *to emigrate* 9
empezar (ie)   *to begin, to start* 4
el/la **empleado/a**   *employee* 9
en   *in* P
en la actualidad   *at the present time* 13
en busca de   *in search of* 15
el **encaje**   *lace* 13r
en cambio   *on the other hand* 4r
encantado/a   *pleased/nice to meet you* P
encantar   *to delight, to love* 6
encargar   *to order* 9r
encauzar   *to channel* 7
encender (ie)   *to turn on* 15
encerrar (ie)   *to lock up* 8
encontrar (ue)   *to find* 6
en contraste   *in contraste* 4r
en cuanto   *as soon as* 14r
la **encuesta**   *Surveys/Polls* 14
la **encuesta de opinión**   *opinion poll* 14r
la **energía solar**   *solar energy* 15
enérgico/a   *energetic* 14
enero   *January* Pr
enfadarse   *to get angry* 7
enfermarse   *to become sick* 11
la **enfermedad**   *illness* 11
el/la **enfermero/a**   *nurse* 9
enfermo/a   *sick* 11
enfocarse (qu)   *to focus* 15
enfrente (de)   *in front of* P
el **enlace**   *link* 15
enojado/a   *angry* 2
enojar(se)   *to get angry* 7r
¿**En qué puedo servirle(s)?**   *How may I help you?* 6
en realidad   *in fact, really* 9
la **ensalada**   *salad* 3
enseguida   *immediately* 6
entender (ie)   *to understand* 4
enterar   *to find out* 7r
enterrar   *to bury* 8r
entonces   *then* 8

entrar (en) *to go in, to enter* 6
entre *between, among* P
entregar *to deliver* 5r
el entrenador/la entrenadora *coach* 7
el entrenamiento *training* 7r
entretenerse *to have fun* 5r
la entrevista *interview* 9
entrevistar *to interview* 7r
en vez de *instead of* 14
enviar *to send* 9
el equipaje *luggage* 12
el equipo *team; equipment* 7
el equipo deportivo *sports equipment* 7
eres *you are (familiar)* P
la ermita *hermitage* 8r
es *you are (formal), he/she is* P
la escala *stopover* 12
la escalera *stairs* 5
el escaparate *store window* 6
la escena *scene* 13
la escena retrospectiva *flashback* 13r
escribir *to write* 1, 6r, Pr
el escritorio *desk* P
el escritor/la escritora *writer* 13
escuchar *to listen (to)* 1
la escuela *school* 6r
el escultor/la escultora *sculptor* 13
ese/a *that (adjective)* P
el eslogan *motto* 12r
eso *that* 5r
los espaguetis *spaghetti* 3
la espalda *back* 11
el español *Spanish* Pr
español/a *Spanish* 2
la especialidad *specialty* 9
el/la especialista *specialist* 11r
las especias *spices* 10
el espejo *mirror* 5
el espejo retrovisor *rearview mirror* 12
la esperanza de vida *life expectancy* 14
esperar *to wait for* 9
las espinacas *spinach* 10
el espíritu *spirit* 8r
la esposa *wife* 4
el esposo *husband* 4
el esquí *skiing, ski* 7
esquiar *to ski* 7
la esquina *corner* 12, 12r
está *he/she is, you are (formal)* P
está despejado *it's clear* 7
el estadio *stadium* 7r
la estadística *statistics* 1

el estado de ánimo *mood* 5r
Estados Unidos *United States* 2r
estadounidense *U.S. citizen* 2
esta noche *tonight* 3r
está nublado *it's cloudy* 7
estar *to be* 1, Pr
estar de acuerdo *to agree* 11r
estar de moda *to be fashionable* 6
estar en forma *to keep in shape* 7r
estás *you are (familiar)* P
este/a *this* 1
el estilo *style* 5, 5r
Estimado/a *Dear* 3r
esto *this* 5r
el estómago *stomach* 11
estornudar *to sneeze* 11
estrecho/a *narrow, tight* 6
la estrella *star* 13
la estructura *structure* 1r
el/la estudiante *student* P
estudiar *to study* 1
el estudio *to show* 7r
estudioso/a *studious* 1
la estufa *stove* 5
estupendo/a *fabulous* 3; *stupendous, marvelous* 10r
el evento *event* 7
evidente *evident* 12r
evitar *to avoid* 10r
el examen *test* 1
examinar *to examine* 11
excelente *excellent* 1
la excentricidad *eccentricity* 15r
exigir *to demand, exact, require* 14r
el éxito *success* 10r, 13, Pr
la experiencia *experience* 9
el experto *expert* 7r
explicar *to explain* 6r, 15r
exponer (g) *to exhibit* 13
la exportación *export* 14
la exposición *exhibit* 12r
expresion *expression* P
la extinción *extinction* 15
extinguido/a *extinct* 15r; *extinguished* 15
extrovertido/a *extroverted* Pr

F

fabuloso/a *fabulous, great* 3
fácil *easy* 1
fácilmente *easily* 4r
facturar *to check in (luggage)* 12

la facultad *school, department* 1
la falda *skirt* 6
falso/a *false* Pr
la falta *lack* 4r
la familia *The family* 4
famoso/a *famous* 10r
el/la farmacéutico/a *pharmacist* 11
la farmacia *pharmacy* 1r, 11
fascinar *to fascinate, to be pleasing to* 6
favorito/a *favorite* 1
febrero *February* Pr
la fecha *date* Pr
felicidades *congratulations* 3
las felicitaciones *congratulations* 11r
felicitar *to congratulate* 11r
feo/a *ugly* 2
el festival *festival* 8
la festividad *festivity; holiday* 8
la fibra *fiber* 10r
la ficha *note card* 7r
la fiebre *fever* 11
la fiesta *celebration* 8; *party* 3, 7r
la figura de autoridad *authority figure* 6r
fijarse *to check out* 3r; *to take note* 14r
¡Fíjate qué noticia! *How about that!* 3r
la filología *philology* 1r
la filosofía *philosophy* 1r
finalmente *finally, at last* 6r
el Fin de Año *New Year's Eve* 8r
el fin de semana *weekend* 1
firmar *to sign* 9r
la física *physics* Pr
la fisiología *physiology* 1r
la flor *flower* 2
fluir *to flow* 10r
fomentar *to encourage* 13r
el fondo *background* 8r
el/la fontanero/a *plumber* 9
la forma *shape, form* 13
la foto(grafía) *photo(graph)* 4
el fracaso *failure* 13
fracturar(se) *to fracture, to break* 11
francés/francesa *French* 2
la frazada *blanket* 5r
frecuentemente *frequently* 4r
el fregadero *kitchen sink* 5
freír (i) *to fry* 10, 10r

la frente *forehead* 11
la fresa *strawberry* 10
el frijol *bean* 3
el frío *cold* 5r
frío/a *cold* 3
frito/a *fried* 3, 3r
la fruta *fruit* 3, 10
el fruto de pasión *passion fruit* 10r
la fuente *bowl* 10r; *source* 15
fuerte *strong* 2
fumar *to smoke* 11
la fundación *founding* 13
el fútbol *soccer* 7
el fútbol americano *football* 7r

G

las gafas *glasses* 13r
las gafas de sol *sunglasses* 6r
la galleta *cookie* 10
la gamba *shrimp* 10
el ganado *cattle* 10r
el ganador *winner* 5r
ganar *to win* 5r, 7
la ganga *bargain* 6r
el garaje *garage* 5
la garganta *throat* 11
gastar *to spend* 6
gemelo/a *twin* 4, 4r
generalmente *generally* 4r
generoso/a *generous* Pr
genéticamente *genetically* 15, 15r
la gente *people* 8
la geografía *geography* 1
el/la gerente (de ventas) *(sales) manager* 9
el gimnasio *gymnasium* 1
globalizar *to globalize* 11r
la gobernación *administrative unit of the Spanish Empire* 3r
el gobernador *governor* 3r
gobernar (ie) *to govern* 14
el gobierno *government* 11
el gol *goal* 7
el golf *golf* 7
golpear *to knock* 7r
gordo/a *fat* 2
la gorra *cap* 6, 6r
grabar *to record* 13r
gracias *thanks, thank you* Pr
gracioso/a *funny* 15r
gradualmente *gradually* 15r

graduarse *to graduate* 14r
gráfico/a *graphic* 15r
grande *big* 1
la grasa *fat* 10r
grave *serious* 11; *seriously ill* 6r
la gripe *flu* 11
gris *gray* 2
el grupo *group* 14r
la guagua *bus (Puerto Rico, Cuba)* 12r
el guajolote *turkey* 10r
el guante *glove* 6
la guantera *glove compartment* 12
guapo/a *good-looking, handsome* 2
guardar silencio *to keep silent* 14r
guatemalteco/a *Guatemalan* 2
la guía *guide* 6r
la guitarra *guitar* 3, 8r
el/la guitarrista *guitar player* 13
gustar (le) *to be pleasing to, to like* 6; *to like* 2r

H

la habitación *bedroom, room* 5
la habitación doble/sencilla *double/single room* 12
el/la habitante *inhabitant* 14
hablar *to speak* 1
hace *ago* 4r; *since* 6r
hace fresco *it's cool* 7
hacer *to do, to make* 3r
hacer cola *to stand in line* 12, 12r
hacer la cama *to make the bed* 3
hacerse *to become* 14r
Hace sol. *It's sunny.* Pr
el hacha *hachet* 13r
la hambre *hunger* 5r
la hamburguesa *hamburger* 3
la harina *flour* 10
hasta *including; until* 13
Hasta luego. *See you later.* Pr
Hasta mañana. *See you tomorrow.* Pr
Hasta pronto. *See you soon.* Pr
hasta que *until* 14r
hay *there is, there are* P
el hecho *fact* 6r
la heladería *ice creamery* 6r
el helado *ice cream* 3, 6r
heredar *to inherit* 14r
el/la herencia *inheritance* 14r

la herida *wound* 11r
el/la herido/a *injured person* 9r
herido/a *wounded, injured* 9r
la hermana *sister* 4
la hermanastra *stepsister* 4
el hermanastro *stepbrother* 4
el hermano *brother* 4
el herrero *blacksmith; ironworker* 9
hervir (ie, i) *to boil* 10
el hielo *ice* 7
la hierba *herb* 10
el higo *fig* 10r
la hija *daughter* 4
el hijo *son* 4
el hijo único/ la hija única *only child* 4
hinchar *to swell* 11r
la hinchazón *swelling* 11r
la hipótesis *hypothesis* 13r
hispano/a *Hispanic* 2
la historia *history* 1
hola *hi, hello* P
el hogar *home* 4r
la hoja *leaf* 5
el hombre *man* 3
el hombre/la mujer de negocios *businessman/woman* 9
el hombro *shoulder* 11
hondureño/a *Honduran* 2
la honestidad *honesty* 14
la hora *time; hour* Pr
el horario *schedule* Pr
hornear *to bake, to microwave* 10r
el (horno) microondas *microwave (oven)* 5
horrible *horrible* 15r
el hospital *hospital* 11
el hotel *hotel* 12
hoy *today* P
hoy en día *nowadays* 8
Hoy es... *Today is . . .* Pr
el hueso *bone* 11
el huevo *egg* 3
las humanidades *humanities* 1
humano/a *human* 11

I

la idea *idea* 10r
idealista *idealistic* Pr

la iglesia   *church* 8
la igualdad   *equality* 14
igualmente   *likewise* P
imaginar   *imagine* 3r
el imperfecto   *imperfect* 6r
el impermeable   *raincoat* 6
implementar   *to implement* 14r
importante   *important* Pr
imposible   *impossible* 6r
la impresora   *printer* 5r
impulsivo/a   *impulsive* Pr
inapropiado/a   *inappropriate* 6r
el incendio   *fire* 9
increíble   *incredible* 4r
independiente   *independent* Pr
indicar   *to indicate* 7r
la infancia   *childhood* 6r
infantil   *children's* 14
la infección   *infection* 11
influir   *to influence* 13r
la información   *information* 7r
la informática   *computer
    science* 1
la infraestructura   *infrastructure* 15
el/la ingeniero/a   *engineer* 9
el iniciado   *apprentice* 13r
la inmigración   *immigration* 14
el inodoro   *toilet* 5
inolvidable   *unforgettable* 13
el inspector   *inspector* 12r
la instrucción   *instruction* 14r
el instrumento   *instrument* 3
inteligente   *intelligent* Pr
el intercambio   *exchange* 15
interesante   *interesting* 1, Pr
interesar   *to interest* 6
internacional   *international* 7r
el/la intérprete   *interpreter* 9;
    performer, artist 13
la intimidad   *intimacy* 4r
introvertido/a   *introverted* Pr
la inundación   *flood* 15
la investigación   *research* 7r
investigar   *to study,
    research* 11r
el invierno   *winter* 6r
la invitación   *invitation* 3r, 8
invitar   *to invite* 8
la inyección   *injection* 11
el ipod   *iPod* 5r
ir   *to go* 3r, Pr
ir de compras   *to go
    shopping* 6
ir de tapas   *to go out for
    tapas* 1r

ir(se)   *to go away, to leave* 7
la izquierda   *left* 4

J

el jabón   *soap* 5
jamás   *never* 13r; *(not) ever* 13r
el jamón   *ham* 3
japonés/japonesa   *Japanese* 2
el jardín   *garden* 5
los jeans   *jeans* 6
el jefe/la jefa   *boss* 9
joven   *young* 2, 8r
el/la joven   *young man/woman* 3
la joya   *piece of jewelry* 6
el/la joyero/a   *jeweller* 9
jubilarse   *to retire* 14r
el juego/partido   *game* 7
el jueves   *Thursday* Pr
el/la juez   *judge* 9
el jugador/la jugadora   *player* 7
jugar (ue)   *to play (a game,
    sport)* 4
jugar (ue) a los bolos   *to bowl* 7
el jugo   *juice* 3
el juguete   *toy* 5r, 6
julio   *July* Pr
junio   *June* Pr
la junta directiva   *board of
    directors* 14r
juntos/as   *together* 4
el juramento   *oath* 13r

L

ella   *she* P
el labio   *lip* 11
laboral   *labor-related* 13r
la consola   *game station* 5r
lácteo/a   *dairy (product)* 10
el lago   *lake* 7
lamentar   *to be sorry* 11r
la lana   *wool* 6r
la langosta   *lobster* 10
lanzar   *to throw* 7r
el lápiz   *pencil* P
el lavabo   *bathroom sink* 5
la lavadora   *washer* 5
la lavandería   *dry cleaner* 6r
lavar en seco   *dry clean* 6r
la lección   *lesson* 1r
la leche   *milk* 3
la leche de coco   *coconut
    milk* 10
la lechuga   *lettuce* 3

la lectura   *reading* Pr
leer   *to read* 1, 7r, Pr
leer por encima   *to skim* 15r
las legumbres   *legumes* 10
lejano/a   *distant* 14r
lejos (de)   *far; (far from)* 3r, 5
la lengua   *language* 1r;
    tongue 15r
lentamente   *slowly* 4r
las lentejas   *lentils* 10
los lentes de contacto   *contact
    lenses* 2
levantar   *to raise* Pr
levantar la mano   *to raise one's
    hand* Pr
levantar(se)   *to raise; to
    get up* 4
la librería   *bookstore* 1
el libro   *book* 1r, 6r, P
la licuadora   *blender* 10r
ligero/a   *lightweight* 15r
el limón   *lemon* 10
el limpiaparabrisas   *windshield
    wiper* 12
limpiar   *to clean; to tidy up* 5
lindo/a   *pretty, attractive* 2r
el lío   *mess* 3r
la lista   *list* 10r
listo/a   *clever* 6r; *smart;
    ready* 2
la literatura   *literature* 1, 13r
el living   *living room* 5r
llamar   *to call* 7r
la llanta   *tire* 12
la llave   *key* 12
la llegada   *arrival* 12r
llegar   *to arrive* 1
llenar   *to fill (out)* 9
lleno/a   *full* 12
llevar   *to wear, to take* 6
llevarse bien   *to get along
    well* 13r
llover (ue)   *to rain* 7
la lluvia   *rain* 7
la lluvia de ideas   *brainstorming* 7r
loco/a   *crazy* 11r
el/la locutor/a   *radio announcer* 9
lógicamente   *logically* 4r
lograr   *to achieve* 4r
el logro   *achievement* 4r
lo importante   *the important
    thing* 9
Lo siento.   *I'm sorry (to hear
    that).* Pr
lo siguiente   *the following* 13r

los recursos *resources* 15
Lo vamos a pasar muy bien. *We are going to have a good time.* 3r
la lucha *fight* 14
luchar *to fight* 14r
el lucro *non-profit* 14r
luego *later* 3; *then* 4r
el lugar *place* 1
el lujo *luxury* 12r
el lunes *Monday* Pr

M

machacar *to crush* 10r
la madera *wood* 9
la madrastra *stepmother* 4
la madre *mother* 4
la madrina *godmother* 4
magnífico/a *great* 6
el maíz *corn* 10
mal *bad* P
la maleta *suitcase* 12, 12r
el maletero *trunk* 12
el maletín *briefcase* 12r
malo/a *bad* 1; *ill* 6r
la mamá *mom* 4
la mañana *morning* P, Pr
mañana *tomorrow* P
mandar *to send* 9
mandar saludos *to say hello* 5r
el mandato *command* 9r
manejar *to drive* 12
la mano *hand* 6r, 11, Pr
la manta *blanket* 5, 5r
la manteca/la mantequilla *butter* 10
el mantel *tablecloth* 10
mantener (g, ie) *to maintain* 8
mantenerse en contacto *to stay in touch* 5r
la manzana *apple* 10
la manzanilla *chamomile* 11r
el mapa *map* P
maquillar(se) *to put makeup on (someone)*; 4
el mar *sea* 3
el maracuyá *passion fruit* 10
la maravilla *marvel* 3r
maravilloso/a *marvelous* 8
la marca *brand* 7r
el marcador *highlighter* 5r; *marker* P
la margarina *margarine* 10
los mariscos *shellfish* 10
marrón *brown* 2, 2r
marroquí *Moroccan* 2

el martes *Tuesday* Pr
marzo *March* Pr
más *more* Pr
más o menos *more or less* P
más tarde *later* 3r; *much later* 4r
las matemáticas *mathematics* Pr
el material *material* 6r
mayo *May* Pr
la mayonesa *mayonnaise* 10
mayor *old* 2
la mayoría *majority* 14
el/la mecánico/a *mechanic* 9r
el médano *dune* 7r
el/la mediador *mediator* 13r
la media hermana *half-sister* 4
las medias *stockings* 6r
la medicina *medicine* 1, 11
el/la médico/a *medical doctor* 9
la medida *measure* 12r
el medio ambiente *environment* 15
el medio hermano *half-brother* 4
los medios de transporte *means of transportation* 12
me gusta(n) *I like* 2
Me gustaría... *I would like . . .* 6
la mejilla *cheek* 11
mejor *better* 11r
mejorar *to improve* 14
el melocotón *peach* 10r
la melodía *melody* 8, 13
el melón *melon* 10
los menonitas *Mennonites* 13r
el/la menor *the youngest* 4
menos *minus* Pr
el mensaje *message* 14r, 15
mentir *to lie* 11r
la mentira *lie* 7r
el menú *menu* 3r
el mercado *market* 6
el mes *month* P
la mesa *table* 10, P
metal *metal* 2r
meter *to insert* 15
meter un gol *to score a goal* 7
el metro *subway* 12
el metro cuadrado *square meter* 5r
mexicano/a *Mexican* 2
mi amor *my love (term of endearment)* 3r
mi cielo *term of endearment* 3r
el micro *bus (Chile)* 12r
el miedo *fear* 5r
mientras *while* 3, 8

el miércoles *Wednesday* Pr
la migración *migration* 14
migrar *to migrate* 11r
mil *thousand* 3r
mil gracias *many thanks* 7r
el/la millonario/a *millionaire* 15r
millón *million* 3r
mirar *to look (at)* 1
mi(s) *my* P
mi vida *my life (term of endearment)* 3r
la mochila *backpack* P
moderno/a *modern* 1r, Pr
módico/a *moderate* 12r
molestar(le) *to bother* 11
molido/a *ground* 10
montar (en bicicleta) *to ride (a bicycle)* 1
morado/a *purple* 2
moreno/a *brunette* 2
morir *to die* 6r
la mortalidad *mortality* 14
la mostaza *mustard* 10
el mostrador *counter* 12, 12r
mostrar (ue) *to show* 6
el motor *motor* 12
mover (ue) *to move* 11r
muchas veces *often* 1r
mucho *much, a lot (adv.)* 2
mucho/a *many (adj.)* 2
mucho gusto *pleased/nice to meet you* P
mudarse *to move* 5r
los muebles *furniture* 5
muerto/a *dead* 8; *dead (atmosphere); deceased* 6r
la mujer *woman* 3
la mujer de negocios *businesswoman* 9
la multa *fine/ticket* 15r
mundial *world, worldwide* 7
la muñeca *wrist* 11
el mural *mural* 13
el/la muralista *muralist* 1r, 13
el músculo *muscle* 11
el museo *museum* 12r
la música *music* 1r, 3; *Music* 8
muy *very* P

N

el nacimiento *birth* 7r
nacional *national* 7r
las nacionalidades *Nationalities* 2

nada *nothing* 13r

nadar *to swim* 3

nadie *nobody, no one* 13r

la naranja *orange* 3

naranja *orange (color)* 2r

la nariz *nose* 11

natal *native* 10r

la naturaleza *nature* 15

la nave *ship* 15r

la Navidad *Christmas* 8r

necesario/a *necessary* 11r

el negocio *business* 1r

negrita *bold* 4r

negro/a *black* 2

el nervio *nerve* 11

nervioso/a *nervous* 2, Pr

nevar (ie) *to snow* 7

la nevera *refrigerator* 5r

ni... ni *neither . . . nor* 13r

nicaragüense *Nicaraguan* 2

la nieta *granddaughter* 4

el nieto *grandson* 4

la nieve *snow* 6r, 7

nigeriano/a *Nigerian* 2

ningún/ninguno/ninguna *no; no one; not any* 13r

el niño/a *child* 4

el nivel *level* 14

no *no* Pr

la noche *night* Pr

la Nochebuena *Christmas Eve* 8r

la Nochevieja *New Year's Eve* 8r

No comprendo. *I don't understand* Pr

¡No me digas! *Really!* 4r

nominar *to nominate* 13

no obstante *however* 11r

normalmente *normally* 4r

norteamericano/a *North American* 1

No sé. *I don't know* Pr

nosotros/nosotras *we* 1

nostálgico *nostalgic* 14r

la nota *note* 1

la noticia *news* 3r, 4

la novela *novel* 13

el/la novelista *novelist* 13, 15r

la novia *fiancée, girlfriend* 4

noviembre *November* Pr

el novio *fiancé, boyfriend* 4

nuevo/a *new* 2

el número *size* 6r

nunca *never* 1r; *(not) ever* 13r

O

o *or* 13r

o... o *either . . . or* 13r

el objeto *object* 6r

la obra *work* 13

el/la obrero/a *worker, laborer* 9r

obtener *to obtain* 10r

obvio/a *obvious* 13r

el ocio *free time* 11r

octubre *October* Pr

la ocupación *occupation* 9r

ocupado/a *busy* 4

ocurrir *to occur* 10r

odiar *to hate* 8r

la oficina *office* 1, Pr

ofrecer (zc) *to offer* 9

el oído *(inner) ear* 11

Oiga, por favor. *Listen, please.* 1r

¡Oigo! *Hello? (on the telephone)* 3r

oír *to hear* 3r; *to listen* 1r

oír hablar *to hear about* 7r

ojalá que... *I/we hope that . . .* 11r

el ojo *eye* 2

las Olimpiadas *Olympics* 7r

olvidar *to forget* 10r

el ómnibus *bus (Peru)* 12r

la operación *surgery* 11r

la opinión *opinion* 14r

optimista *optimistic* Pr

el ordenador *computer* 1r

ordenar *to clean* 5

la oreja *ear* 6r; *(outer) ear* 11

la organización *organization* 14r

organizar *to organize* 7r

oro *gold* 2r

la orquesta *orchestra* 8

la oscuridad *dark* 15r

oscuro/a *dark* 2

el otoño *fall, autumn* 6r

otra cosa *something else* 6r

otra vez *again* Pr

otro/a *other* 4r; *other, another* 3

la oveja *sheep* 10

el OVNI *UFO* 15r

¡Oye! *Listen!* 1r

P

palabra *word* P

el/la paciente *patient* 11

paciente *patient (adj.)* Pr

el padrastro *stepfather* 4

el padre *father* 4

los padres *parents* 4

el padrino *godfather* 4

pagar *to pay (for)* 6

la página *page* Pr

el país *country, nation* 3

el paisaje *landscape* 13

la palabra *word* 6r

la palabra clave *key word* 6r

el paladar *palate* 13r

el palo *golf club* 7

las palomitas de maíz *popcorn* 10r

la palta *avocado* 10r

el pan *bread* 3

la panadería *bakery* 6r

panameño/a *Panamanian* 2

el pan dulce *bun, small cake* 10

la pantalla *screen* P

los pantalones *pants* 6

los pantalones cortos *shorts* 6

las pantimedias *pantyhose* 6

el pan tostado *toast* 3

el pañuelo *handkerchief* 6

el papá *dad* 4

la papa *potato* 3

las papas fritas *French Fries* 3

el penalti *penalty* 7r

el pendiente *earring* 6r

la pendiente *slope* 7r

pensar de *to think of/about (opinion)* 4r

pensar en *to think of/about* 4r

pensar (ie) *to plan to* 4; *to think* 4

el pepino *cucumber* 10

pequeño/a *small* 1

la pera *pear* 10

perder (ie) *to lose* 7

perderse (ie) *to get lost* 12

la pérdida *loss* 15

perdón *pardon me, excuse me* Pr

el perejil *parsley* 10r

perezoso/a *lazy* 2

perfeccionista *perfectionistic* Pr

perfectamente *perfectly* 4r

perfecto/a *perfect* 10r

el periódico *newspaper* 3; *periodical, newspaper* 1r

el/la periodista *journalist* 9, 9r

el permiso de conducir *driver's license* 15r

pero *but* 1

el perro *dog* 4, 11r

la persona *person* P

el personaje principal *main character* 13

la perspectiva *perspective* 11r

las pertenencias *belongings* 12r

peruano/a *Peruvian* 2

la pesa *weight* 10r

la pesadilla *nightmare* 12r

el pescado *fish* 3, 10

pesimista *pessimistic* Pr

la pestaña *eyelash* 11

el petróleo *petroleum* 15r

picado/a *chopped* 10r; *ground* 10

picar *to chop* 10r

picar(se) *to itch* 11r

el pie *foot* 2r, 5r, 11

la piel *skin* 10r

la piel de gallina *goosebumps* 15r

la pierna *leg* 2r, 6r, 11

el/la piyama *pajamas* 6

la pileta *swimming pool* 5r

el pimentón *paprika* 10r

la pimienta *pepper* 10

la pimienta roja *red pepper* 10r

el pimiento (verde) *(green) pepper* 10

la piña *pineapple* 10

el pintor/la pintora *painter* 13

la pintura *painting* 13

la piscina *swimming pool* 5, 5r

el piso *floor; apartment* 5

pitar *to whistle* 7

la pizarra *chalkboard* P

la placa *license plate* 12

el placer *pleasure* 7r

el plan *plan* 7r

el planeta *planet* 15

plástico *plastic* 2r

el plátano *banana, plantain* 10

el plato *plate, dish* 10

la plaza *city square* 13r

el/la plomero/a *plumber* 9

planchar *to iron* 5

la planta baja *first floor, ground floor* 5

la población *population* 14

pobre *poor* 2

la pobreza *poverty* 14

poco *few, little* 4r; *a little* 4r

polaco/a *Polish* 2

poco a poco *little by little* 4r

poco después *a little later* 4r

poder (ue) *to be able to, can* 4

el poema *poem* 13; *poema* 1r

la poesía *poetry* 13

el/la poeta *poet* 13

el/la policía *policeman/woman* 9

políglota *polyglot, multilingual* 14

el pollo *chicken* 3

el pomelo *grapefruit* 10

poner *to put* 3r

poner la mesa *to set the table* 3

ponerse en marcha *to go into effect* 15r

ponerse (g) *to become* 14r; *to put on (clothes)* 6r

popular *popular* Pr

la popularidad *popularity* 7r

popularizar (c) *to popularize* 13

por *by; for; along; through; in (time)* 3r

el porcentaje *percentage* 14

por ciento *percent* 3r

por cierto *by the way* 9

por ejemplo *for example* 3r

por eso *that is why* 3r

por favor *please* Pr

por fin *finally, at last* 3r, 15r

por lo menos *at least* 3r

por la mañana *in the morning* 3r

por la noche *in the evening* 3r

el poroto *bean* 10r

por otro lado *on the other hand* 4r

porque *because* 1r

¿por qué? *why?* 1r

por supuesto *of course* 3r

por la tarde *in the afternoon* 3r

por teléfono *by telephone* 3r

portugués/portuguesa *Portuguese* 2

por último *finally, at last* 4r

por un lado *on the one hand* 4r

posible *possible* 13r

la posición *position* P

potente *powerful* 15r

practicar *to practice* 1

preceder *to precede* 14

el precio *price* 6, 6r

precioso/a *beautiful* 6

preferir (ie) *to prefer* 4

la pregunta *question* Pr

premiar *to reward* 9r

el premio *award, prize* 13

preocupar(se) *to concern; to be concerned, worried* 11r

preparar *to prepare* 5

el preparativo *preparation* 8

la presentación *introduction* P

presente *here (present)* Pr

presidencial *presidential* 14r

el presidente/la presidenta *president* 14

prestar *to lend* 6r

el pretérito *preterit* 6r

prever *to foresee, to predict* 13r

la primavera *spring* 6r

la primera clase *first class* 12, 12r

primero/a *first* 4r

el primo/a *cousin* 4

la prisa *speed, haste* 5r

probable *probable* 13r

probar *to try* 10r

probarse (ue) *to try on* 6

el problema *problem* 1r, 13r

la procesión *procession* 8

producir *to produce* 15r

el producto *product* 10

el profesor/la profesora *professor, teacher* P

el programa *program* 1r

el progreso *progress* 14r

prohibir *to prohibit* 11r

el promedio *average* 8r, 14

prometedor/a *promising* 13

promocionar *to advertise* 6r

el pronóstico del tiempo *weather forecast* 7r

propio/a *own* 9

la propuesta *proposal* 7r

la proteína *protein* 10r

el proveedor de comida *caterer* 9r

el proveedor de salud *health care provider* 11

la proximidad *proximity* 14

próximo/a *next* 3r

la (p)sicología *psychology* 1, Pr

el/la (p)sicólogo/a *psychologist* 9

el/la (p)siquiatra *psychiatrist* 11r

el plato *dish, plate* 5

la publicidad *publicity* 6r

el pueblo *village* 5

la puerta *door* P

la puerta (de salida) *gate* 12

puertorriqueño/a *Puerto Rican* 2

el puesto *position* 9

el pulmón   *lung* 11
la pulsera   *bracelet* 6
el punto culminante   *climax* 13r
el punto de vista   *point of view* 11r
el pupitre   *student desk* P
la playa   *beach* 1
la plaza   *plaza, square* 1

Q

¿qué?   *what?* 1r
¡Qué bárbaro!   *Great!* 7r
¡Qué bien/bueno!   *That's great!* 4r
¡Qué casualidad!   *What a suprise/coincidence!* 1r
quedar   *to arrange to meet* 8; *to fit; to be left over* 6
¿Qué día es hoy?   *What day is it?* Pr
¿Qué fecha es hoy?   *What is the date?* Pr
¿Qué hay?   *Hello? (on the telephone)* 3r
¿Qué hora es?   *What time is it?* Pr
¡Qué increíble!   *How incredible!* 1r
la queja   *complaint* 13r
quejarse   *to complain* 7r
¡Qué lástima!   *What a pity!* 1
querer (ie)   *to want* 4
querido/a   *dear* 3r
Querido/a   *Dear* 3r
el queso   *cheese* 3
el queso crema   *cream cheese* 10
¿Qué tal?   *What's up, What's new? (informal)* P
¿Qué te/le(s) pasa?   *What's wrong (with you/them)?* 11
¿Qué te parece?   *What do you think?* 3
¿Qué tiempo hace?   *What is the weather like?* Pr
¿Quién es... ?   *Who is . . . ?* P
¿quién(es)?   *who?* 1r
la quijada   *jawbone* 13r
Quisiera...   *I would like . . .* 6
quitar(se)   *to take away; to take off* 4

R

el radiador   *radiator* 12
el/la radio   *radio* 5
el/la radiólogo/a   *radiologist* 11r
rallar   *to grate* 10r

rápidamente   *quickly* 4r
rápido/a   *fast* 3
la raqueta   *racquet* 7
el rasgo   *feature, trait* 12r
la razón   *reason* 5r
la realidad   *reality* 13r
realizar (c)   *to carry out* 14
realmente   *of course* 9; *in fact, really* 9; *really* 4r
reaparecer   *to reappear* 11r
la rebaja   *sale* 6
rebajado/a   *marked down* 6
la recámara   *bedroom* 5r
la recepción   *front desk* 12
la receta   *prescription* 11; *receipt* 10r; *recipe* 10
recetar   *to prescribe* 11
recibir   *to receive* 14r
reciclado/a   *recycled* 15
reclamar   *to claim* 12r
recoger (j)   *to pick up* 5
la recomendación   *recommendation* 15r
recomendar (ie)   *to recommend* 10
recopilar   *to compile* 14r
recordar(se) (ue)   *to remember* 4r, 8
recorrer   *to cover, to travel* 12; *to travel, to cover (distance)* 7
el recuerdo   *memory* 13; *souvenir* 6
la red   *net* 7; *network* 5r
reducir   *to reduce* 11r
reflejar   *to reflect* 5r, 13
el refrán   *proverb* 12r
el refresco   *soda; soft drink* 3
el refrigerador   *refrigerator* 5, 5r
regalar   *to give (a present)* 6
el regalo   *gift* 3r; *present* 6
regar (ie)   *to water* 5
regatear   *to haggle* 6r
el régimen   *regime* 14
la región   *region* 15r
regular   *fair* Pr
regularmente   *regularly* 4r
reír (i)   *to laugh* 7r
religioso/a   *religious* Pr
el relleno   *filling* 10r
relleno/a   *filled* 3r
el reloj   *clock* P
el remedio   *remedy, medicine* 11
el renacimiento   *rebirth* 8r
el rendimiento   *performance* 9r
repetir (i)   *to repeat* 4r
repoblar   *to reforest* 15; *to repopulate* 15r
el reproductor de CDs   *CD player* 5r

el reproductor de DVDs   *DVD player* 5r
la reputación   *reputation* 7r
la reseña   *review* 13r
la reserva natural   *nature preserve* 15
reservar   *to make a reservation* 12
respetar   *to respect* 13r
respirar   *to breathe* 11
responder   *to respond* 15r
responsable   *responsible* Pr
el restaurante   *restaurant* 1r
el resultado   *the result* 7r
resumir   *to summarize* 4r
relativamente   *relatively* 4r
el reto   *challenge* 15
retornar   *to return* 11r
retratar   *to portray* 13
la reunión   *meeting, gathering* 3
reunirse   *to get together, to meet* 8
revisar   *to inspect* 12
la revista   *magazine* 3
la revista de corazón   *gossip magazine* 13
el rey/la reina   *king/queen* 8
largo/a   *long* 2
el riachuelo   *creek* 4r
rico/a   *delicious (food)* 6r; *rich, wealthy* 2, 6r
el riel   *rail* 15, 15r
la risa   *laughter* 12r
el robo   *robbery* 10r
el robot   *robot* 15
rociar   *to spray* 8r
el rocoto   *pepper* 3r
rodear   *to surround* 13
la rodilla   *knee* 11
rojo/a   *red* 2
romántico/a   *romantic* Pr
romper   *to break* 15r; *to tear* 15r
la ropa   *clothes* 6
la ropa de estar en casa   *loungewear* 6r
la ropa deportiva   *sportswear* 6r
la ropa formal   *formalwear* 6r
la ropa informal   *casualwear* 6r
la ropa interior   *underwear* 6, 6r
rosa   *pink* 2
rosado/a   *pink* 2
el rotulador   *marker* P
rubio/a   *blond* 2
la ruda   *rue (herb)* 11r
la rueda   *wheel* 12
el ruido   *noise* 5r, 8

la telenovela *soap opera* 11r
el televisor *television set* P
el tema *theme* 13
temer *to fear* 11
temprano *early* 4
tender (ie) *to hang (clothes)* 5
el tenedor *fork* 10
tener (g, ie) *to have* 4
tener... años *to be . . . old* 5r
tener calor *to be hot* 5r
tener cuidado *to be careful* 5r
tener dolor de... *to have a(n) . . .
    ache* 11
tener éxito *to be successful*
    10r, 13
tener frío *to be cold* 5r
tener hambre *to be hungry* 5r
tener mala cara *to look terrible* 11
tener miedo *to be afraid* 5r
tener prisa *to be in a hurry,
    rush* 5r
tener que *to have to* 4r
tener razón *to be right, correct* 5r
tener sed *to be thirsty* 5r
tener sueño *to be sleepy* 5r
tener suerte *to be lucky* 5r
Tengo... años. *I am . . . years old.* 2
tengo/tienes *I have/you have* 1
el tenis *tennis* Pr
el/la tenista *tennis player* 7r
la tensión (arterial) *(blood)
    pressure* 11
la terapia *therapy* 13r
tercero/a *third* 5r
terminar *to finish* 14r
el termómetro *thermometer* 11
la terraza *deck* 9r; *terrace* 5
el terrorismo *terrorism* 14r
el testamento *will* 14r
la tía *aunt* 4
el tiempo *time; weather* Pr;
    weather 7
el tiempo libre *free time* 3
la tienda *store* 6
tiene *he/she has; you (formal)
    have* 2
la tierra *land, soil* 15
tímido/a *timid* Pr
la tina *bathtub* 5r
la tintorería *dry cleaner* 14r
el tío *uncle* 4
típico/a *typical* 3
titular(se) *to be called* 13
el título *motto* 12r; *title* 4r
la tiza *chalk* P
la toalla *towel* 5

el tobillo *ankle* 11
tocar (un instrumento) *to play
    (an instrument)* 3
todas las semanas *every
    week* 1r
todavía *still, yet* 10
todo *everything* 13r
todo/a *every* 1r
todos/as *all* 13r; *everybody* 2, 13r
todos los días *every day* 1r
todos los meses *every month* 1r
tomar *to take; to drink* 1
tomar apuntes/notas *to take notes* 1
tomar asiento *to take a
    seat* 9r
tomar el sol *sunbathe* 1r; *to
    sunbathe* 3
el tomate *tomato* 3
el tono *tone* 14r
tonto/a *silly, foolish* 2
torcer(se) (ue) *to twist* 11
el torneo *tournament* 7r
el toro *bull* 8
la toronja *grapefruit* 10
torpe *clumsy* 6r
la tos *cough* 11
toser *to cough* 11
tostar *to toast* 10r
la tostada *toast*
tóxico/a *toxic* 1r
trabajador/a *hardworking* 2
trabajar *to work* 1
el trabajo *work* 5, 9
el trabajo de campo *fieldwork* 13r
la tradición *tradition* 8
tradicional *traditional* Pr
tradicionalmente *traditionally* 4r
traducir (zc) *to translate* 7
traer *to bring* 3r
el tráfico *traffic* 15r
el tráfico de drogas *drug
    trafficking* 14
el traje *suit* 6
el traje de baño *bathing suit* 6
el traje de chaqueta *suit* 6
el traje pantalón *pantsuit* 6
tranquilo/a *tranquil* Pr
tranquilamente *tranquilly* 4r
transitar *to cross; to move back and
    forth* 12r
el tratamiento médico *medical
    treatment* 11
tratar *to treat* 11; *to be about* 13;
    to try 5r
el trayecto *route* 12
el tren *train* 12

triste *sad* 2, 14r
tropezarse *to stumble* 15r
tú *you (familiar)* P
tu(s) *your (familiar)* P
último/a *last* 8

U

la uña de gata *cat's claw
    (herb)* 11r
una semana atrás *a week
    ago* 6r
una vez *once* 12, 13r
unificar (qu) *to unify* 15
la universidad *university* 1
un poco *a little* 4
un/una *a, an* P
urgente *urgent* 11r
uruguayo/a *Uruguayan* 2
usar *to use* 2
usted *you (formal)* P
ustedes *you (plural)* 1
útil *useful* P
la uva *grape* 10

V

las vacaciones *vacation* 3
la vacante *opening* 9
vacío/a *empty* 12
la vainilla *vanilla* 10
valer *to be worth* 6
los vaqueros/jeans *jeans* 6
el vaso *glass* 10
Vaya. *Go.* Pr
la vecina *neighbor* 5r
el/la vecino/a *neighbor* 5r
el vegetal/la verdura *vegetable* 3
vegetariano/a *vegetarian* 12r
la velocidad *speed* 12
la vena *vein* 11
¡Ven/Anda, anímate! *Come on, cheer
    up!* 3r
el/la vendedor/a *salesperson,* 9;
    seller 6r
vender *to sell* 6, 6r
venezolano/a *Venezuelan* 2
venir (g, ie) *to come* 4
la venta *sale* 9r
la ventaja *advantage* 5
la ventana *window* 1r, P
la ventanilla *window* 12r
el ventilador *fan* 5
ver *to see* 1
el verano *summer* 6r
verbos *verbs* P

Appendix 4

English to Spanish Glossary

A

a un/una
a little later poco después
a lot (of) mucho/a (adj.); mucho (adv.)
to abound abundar
above sobre
access el acceso
accessory el accesorio
to accompany acompañar
according to según
accountant el/la contador/a (contable)
accounting la contabilidad
to ache doler (ue)
to achieve lograr
achievement el logro
to act actuar
active activo/a
activity la actividad
actor el actor
actress la actriz
ad, advertisement el anuncio
to adapt adaptar
adaptation la adaptación
to add agregar; añadir
to address dirigirse
adjustment la adaptación
advance el adelanto
to advance avanzar
advantage la ventaja
to advertise promocionar
advisable aconsejable
to advise aconsejar
aerobic exercise el ejercicio aeróbico
affectionately con cariño
to affirm afirmar
after después; después (de) que
afternoon la tarde
again otra vez
ago hace
to agree estar de acuerdo
agreeable agradable
agreement la concordancia
air-conditioned climatizado/a
air conditioning el aire acondicionado

airline la aerolínea/línea aérea
airport el aeropuerto
aisle seat el asiento de pasillo
alacrity la alacridad
algebra la álgebra
alive vivo/a
all todos/as
allergic alérgico/a
to alleviate calmar
along por
already ya
also también
alternative alternativo/a
although aunque
always siempre
ambitious ambicioso/a
ammunition la cabuya
ample amplio/a
amusing divertido/a
anatomy la anatomía
ancestor el antepasado
and y
angry enojado/a
ankle el tobillo
to answer contestar
Antarctica la Antártida
antes before
antes (de) que before
anthropology la antropología
antibiotic el antibiótico
anxiety la ansiedad
any, some algún/alguno/alguna
anything algo
apartment el apartamento; el departamento; el piso; la vivienda
to apologize disculparse
apple la manzana
appliance el electrodoméstico
application la aplicación; la solicitud
to apply (for) solicitar
apprentice el iniciado
appropriate apropiado/a
April abril
architect el/la arquitecto/a
architecture la arquitectura
area la zona
Argentinian argentino/a
to argue discutir

arm el brazo
armchair la butaca
arrival la llegada
to arrive llegar
arrogant arrogante
art el arte
artist el/la artista; el/la intérprete
as según
as much . . . as tanto ... como
as soon as as en cuanto
to ask for pedir (i)
to assist ayudar
to assume asumir
to assure asegurar
astronomy el astronomía
at a
at times a veces
athlete el/la deportista
athletic atlético/a
ATM el cajero automático
atmosphere la atmósfera
attached document el documento adjunto
to attend asistir
attic el ático
attractive atractivo/a; bonito/a; bueno/a; guapo/a; lindo/a
August agosto
aunt la tía
authority figure la figura de autoridad
available disponible
avenue la avenida
average el promedio
avocado el aguacate; la palta
to avoid evitar
award, prize el premio

B

back al fondo, atrás; la espalda
background el fondo
backpack la mochila
backwards atrás
bad mal; malo/a
bakery la panadería
ball el balón/la pelota
ballpoint pen el bolígrafo

banana el banano; el cambur; el plátano; la banana
bank el banco
baptism, christening el bautizo
barbecue pit; barbecue (event) la barbacoa
bargain la ganga
to base basar
baseball el béisbol
basement el sótano
basically básicamente
basket (hoop) el/la cesto/a
basketball el baloncesto/el básquetbol
bat el bate
to bathe; to take a bath bañar(se)
bathing suit el traje de baño
bathroom el baño
bathroom sink el lavabo
bathtub la bañera; la tina; la bañadera; la bañera
to be estar; ser
to be able to, can poder (ue)
to be afraid tener miedo
to be called titular(se)
to be careful tener cuidado
to be cold tener frío
to be crazy (Cuba) estar trocá
to be fashionable estar de moda
to be glad (about) alegrarse (de)
to be happy alegrarse
to be hot tener calor
to be hungry tener hambre
to be in a hurry (Colombia) estar de afán
to be in a hurry, rush tener prisa
to be lucky tener suerte
to be . . . old tener … años
to be pleasing to, to like gustar
to be right, correct tener razón
to be sleepy tener sueño
to be sorry lamentar; sentir(se) (ie, i)
to be successful tener éxito
to be thirsty tener sed
to be worth valer
beach la playa
bead la cuenta
bean el frijol; el poroto
to beat batir
beautiful precioso/a
beauty item el artículo de belleza
beauty salon, barbershop la peluquería
because porque
to become hacerse; poner(se)
to become sick enfermarse
bed la cama

bedroom el cuarto; el dormitorio; la habitación; la alcoba; la recámara
beef/steak la carne de res
beer la cerveza
to begin comenzar (ie)
to begin, to start empezar (ie)
beginning el comienzo
behavior el comportamiento
behind atrás; detrás (de)
to believe creer
belongings las pertenencias
below abajo
belt el cinturón
to benefit beneficiar
besides además
better mejor
between, among entre
bicycle la bicicleta
big grande
bilingual bilingüe
to bind atar
biochemistry la bioquímica
birth el nacimiento
birthday el cumpleaños
bison el bisonte
black negro/a
blackout el apagón
blacksmith; ironworker el herrero
blanket la manta; la cobija; la frazada
blazer, jacket el saco
blender la licuadora
blond rubio/a
(blood) pressure la tensión (arterial)
blouse la blusa
blue azul
to board abordar
board of directors la junta directiva
boarding pass la tarjeta de embarque;
boat el barco
body el cuerpo
to boil hervir (ie, i)
bold negrita
Bolivian boliviano/a
bone el hueso
book el libro
bookstore la librería
boot la bota
bored aburrido/a
boring aburrido/a
boss el jefe/la jefa
to bother molestar(le)
bottle la botella
to bowl jugar (ue) a los bolos
bowl la fuente
bowling el boliche; el bowling

bowling ball el bolo; la bola
box la caja
boxer shorts el calzoncillo
boy el chico
boyfriend el novio
bra el sostén
bracelet la pulsera
brain el cerebro
brainstorming la lluvia de ideas
branch (business) la sucursal
brand la marca
bread el pan
to break descomponer(se); fracturar(se); romper
breakfast el desayuno
to breathe respirar
briefcase el maletín
to bring traer
broadband la banda ancha
broke brujo/a
brother el hermano
to brown dorar
brown marrón
brunette moreno/a
to build construir (y)
building el edificio
bull el toro
bullfight la corrida (de toros)
bumper el parachoques
bun, small cake el pan dulce
to bury enterrar
bus el autobús, el bus
business el negocio
businessman/woman el hombre/la mujer de negocios
busy ocupado/a
but pero
butter la manteca/la mantequilla
to buy comprar
by por
by telephone por teléfono
by the way por cierto

C

cabinet el armario
cafe, coffee shop el café
cafeteria la cafetería
calcium el calcio
calculator la calculadora
calculus el cálculo
calendar el calendario
to call llamar
to calm, alleviate calmar
camera la cámara
Canadian canadiense
to cancel cancelar

cancer   el cáncer
candy/sweets   el dulce
cap   la gorra
capsule   la cápsula
captain   el capítan
car   el auto; el carro; el coche
care   el cuidado
career counselor   el/la consejero/a
   vocacional
carefully   cuidadosamente
careless   descuidado/a
carnival   el carnaval
carpenter   el/la carpintero/a
carpet, rug   la alfombra
carrot   la zanahoria
to carry out   realizar (c)
cart, wagon   la carreta
cashier   el/la cajero/a
casualwear   la ropa informal
caterer   el/la proveedor/a de comida
cattle   el ganado
CD player   el reproductor de CDs
to celebrate   celebrar
celebration   la celebración; la fiesta
celery   el apio
cell phone   el teléfono celular; el
   teléfono móvil
cell phone charger   el cargador de
   celular; el cargador del móvil
cemetery   el cementerio
cereal   el cereal
certain   seguro/a
certainly   seguramente
certainty   la certeza
chair   la silla
chalk   la tiza
chalkboard   la pizarra
challenge   el reto
chamomile   la manzanilla
champion   el campeón/la campeona
championship   el campeonato
chance   el azar
to change   cambiar
change   el cambio
channel   el canal
charitable   caritativo/a
charming   simpático/a
chauffeur   el/la chofer (chófer)
cheap   barato/a
check   el cheque
to check in (luggage)   facturar
to check out   fijarse
checking account   la cuenta corriente
cheek   la mejilla
cheese   el queso
chef   el/la chef
cherry   la cereza

chest   el pecho
chicken   el pollo
chicken breast   la pechuga de pollo
child   el niño/ la niña
childhood   la infancia
children's   infantil
Chile   Chile
chile pepper   el ají; el chile
Chilean   chileno/a
cholesterol   el colesterol
to choose   elegir (i, i)
chop   la chuleta
to chop   picar
chopped   picado/a
chore   la tarea
Christmas   la Navidad
Christmas Eve   la Nochebuena
church   la iglesia
cilantro   el cilantro; el culantro
cinema   el cine
cinnamon   la canela
citizen   el ciudadano
city   la ciudad
city block   la cuadra
city council   el concejo municipal
city square   la plaza
to claim   reclamar
clam   la almeja
class   la clase
classmate   el/la compañero/a
classroom   el salón de clase
to clean   limpiar; ordenar
clever   listo/a
client   el/la cliente/clienta
climax   el punto culminante
clinic   la clínica, el centro
clock   el reloj
clone   la clonación
cloning   la clonación
to close   cerrar (ie)
close to, near   cerca de
closet   el armario; el clóset
closing   la despedida
clothes   la ropa
clove of garlic   el diente de ajo
clumsy   torpe
coach   el/la entrenador/a
coach class   la clase turista
coat   el abrigo
coconut milk   la leche de coco
code   el código
coffee   el café
cognate   el cognado
cold   el catarro; el frío; frío/a
to collapse   colapsar
Colombian   colombiano/a
colors   los colores

to comb (someone's hair)   peinar(se)
to come   venir (g, ie)
Come in.   Adelante.; Pase(n).
Come on, cheer up!   ¡Ven/Anda,
   anímate!
comfortable   cómodo/a
comic   cómico/a
command   el mandato
to communicate   comunicar
communication   la comunicación
company   la compañía/empresa
to compile   recopilar
to complain   quejarse
complaint   la queja
to complete, to finish; to run out of
   acabar(se)
complicit   cómplice
computer   la computadora; el
   ordenador
computer science   la informática; la
   computación
conclusion   la conclusión
conflict   el conflicto
to congratulate   felicitar
congratulations   las felicidades; las
   felicitaciones
to connect   conectar(se)
connection   la conexión
consensus   el consenso
to construct   construir
to consume   consumir
contact lenses   los lentes de
   contacto
contaminated   contaminado/a
contemporary   contemporáneo/a
contest   el concurso
to continue   continuar
to contract   contraer
contractor   el/la contratista
contrast   el contraste
to contribute   contribuir (y)
convenience store   la tienda de
   conveniencia
to converse   conversar
to cook   cocinar
cook   el/la cocinero/a
cooked   cocido/a
cookie   la galleta
corn   el choclo; el elote; el maíz
corner   la esquina
correspondence   la correspondencia
corridor, hall   el pasillo
to cost   costar (ue)
Costa Rican   costarricense
cough   la tos
to cough   toser
council   el concejo

to count contar
counter el mostrador
country, nation el país
countryside el campo
cousin el primo/la prima
to cover recorrer; tapar
crab el cangrejo
craftsperson el/la artesano/a
crazy loco/a
cream la crema
cream cheese el queso crema
creative creativo/a
credit card la tarjeta de crédito
creek el riachuelo
to cross cruzar; transitar
cruise el crucero
to crush machacar
Cuban cubano/a
cubist cubista
cucumber el pepino
cumin el comino
cup la taza
to cure curar
curiosity la curiosidad
current actual
curtain la cortina
custom la costumbre
customs la aduana
to cut cortar
cycling el ciclismo
cyclist el/la ciclista

D

dad el papá
dairy (product) lácteo/a
to dance bailar
dance la danza
dance club la discoteca
dance company la compañía de
    danza
dancer el bailarín/la bailarina
dangerous peligroso/a
to dare atreverse
dark la oscuridad; oscuro/a
data los datos
date la fecha; la cita
daughter la hija
dawn clarear el día
day el día
day after tomorrow pasado mañana
day before yesterday anteayer
Day of the Dead el Día de los
    Muertos
dead difunto/a; muerto/a
Dear Estimado/a; Querido/a
dear querido/a

December diciembre
decision la decisión
deck la terraza
decorated adornado/a
deforestation la deforestación
delicious rico/a
to delight encantar
to deliver entregar
to demand exigir
democracy la democracia
to denounce denunciar
department, school la facultad
department store el almacén
departure la salida
depressed deprimido/a
depression la depresión
to describe describir
description a descripción
design el diseño
designer el diseñador
to desire desear
desk el escritorio
destination el destino
detail el detalle
to develop desarrollar(se)
development el desarrollo
device el dispositivo
diabetic diabético/a
dictatorial dictatorial
dictionary el diccionario
to die morir
diet la dieta
difficult difícil
difficultly difícilmente
digitally digitalmente
dining room el comedor
dinner la comida
dinner, supper la cena
to direct dirigir (j)
disadvantage la desventaja
disappearence la desaparición
disappointed decepcionado/a
to disassemble desarmar
discovery el descubrimiento
discreetly sigilosamente
dish, plate el plato
dishwasher el lavaplatos
to dislike caer mal
dispersal, dissemination la
    diseminación
displacement el desplazamiento
disposable desechable
distant lejano/a
to distinguish distinguir
diversification la diversificación
divorced divorciado/a
to do hacer

dog el perro
dollar el dólar
domestic doméstico/a
Dominican dominicano/a
door la puerta
to double duplicar
double/single room la habitación
    doble/sencilla
doubt la duda
doubtful dudoso/a
to download bajar
downtown, center el centro
drama el drama
dream el sueño
dress el vestido
to dress; to get dressed vestir(se) (i)
dresser la cómoda
to drink beber
drink la bebida
to drink tomar
to drive conducir; manejar
driver el/la chofer (chófer)
driver's license el carnet de conducir;
    el permiso de conducir
to drop caer
drug la droga
drug trafficking el tráfico de drogas
dry clean lavar en seco
dry cleaner la lavandería; la
    tintorería
to dry (oneself) secar(se)
dryer la secadora
due to debido a
dune el médano
during durante
DVD el DVD
DVD player el reproductor de DVDs
dwelling la vivienda
dynamic dinámico/a

E

each cada
eagle el águila
ear el oído; la oreja; la oreja
early temprano
earring el arete
easily fácilmente
Easter la Pascua
easy fácil
to eat comer
eccentricity la excentricidad
economically económicamente
economics la economía
Ecuadorian ecuatoriano/a
editorial house la casa editorial
efficiency la eficiencia

efficient   eficaz; eficiente
egg   el huevo
either . . . or   o … o
elbow   el codo
to elect   elegir (i, j)
election   la elección
electrician   el/la electricista
elegant   elegante
to embrace   abrazar(se) (c)
to emerge   surgir (j)
emergency   la emergencia
emergency exit   la salida de
   emergencia
emigrant   el/la emigrante
to emigrate   emigrar
emigration   la emigración
employee   el/la empleado/a
empty   vacío/a
to encourage   fomentar
energetic   enérgico/a
engagement   el compromiso
engineer   el/la ingeniero/a
to enjoy   disfrutar
enough   bastante
to enter   entrar (en)
entertainment   la diversión
environment   el medio ambiente
equality   la igualdad
equals   son
equipment   el equipo
eraser   el borrador
even if   aunque
even though   aunque
evening   por la noche
event   el acontecimiento; aun; el
   evento
ever   alguna vez
every   todo/a
every day   todos los días
every . . . hours   cada … horas
every month   todos los meses
every week   todas las semanas
everybody   todos/as
everyone   alguien
everything   todo
evident   evidente
to exact   exigir
to examine   examinar
excellent   excelente
to exchange   cambiar
exchange   el intercambio
exchange rate   la tasa de cambio
excuse me   con permiso, perdón
executive   el/la ejecutivo/a
to exert effort   fajar(se)
to exhibit   exponer (g)
exhibit   la exposición

expensive   caro/a
experience   la experiencia
expert   el experto
to explain   explicar
export   la exportación
expression   la cara; expresion
extinct   extinguido/a
extinction   la extinción
to extinguish, to turn off   apagar
extinguished   extinguido/a
extroverted   extrovertido/a
eye   el ojo
eyebrow   la ceja
eyelash   la pestaña

F

fabric   la tela
fabulous   fabuloso/a
face   la cara
fact   el hecho
failure   el fracaso
fair   regular
to fall   caer(se)
fall   el otoño
false   falso/a
family   la familia
famous   famoso/a
fan   el ventilador
far (from)   lejos (de)
farewell   la despedida
farmer   el/la agricultor/a
to fascinate   fascinar
fast   rápido/a
fat   gordo/a; la grasa
father   el padre
Father's Day   el Día del Padre
favorite   favorito/a
fear   el miedo; el susto
to fear   temer
feature, trait   el rasgo
February   febrero
to feed   dar de comer
to feel   sentir (se) (ie)
festival   el festival
festivity; holiday   la festividad
fever   la fiebre
few   poco
fiancé(e)   el/la novio/a
fiber   la fibra
fieldwork   el trabajo de campo
fig   el higo
fight   la lucha
to fight   luchar
to fill (out)   llenar
filled   relleno/a
filling   el relleno

film   la película
filmmaker   el/la cineasta
finally, at last   finalmente; por fin;
   por último
to find   encontrar (ue)
to find out   averiguar; enterar(se)
fine arts   las bellas artes
fine/ticket   la multa
finger   el dedo
to finish   terminar
to fire   despedir (i)
fire   el incendio
firefighter   el/la bombero/a
fireplace   la chimenea
first   primero/a
first class   la primera clase
first floor   la planta baja
fish   el pescado
flashback   la escena retrospectiva
flight   el vuelo
flight attendant   el/la auxiliar de
   vuelo; el/la aeromozo/a; la
   azafata
flip-flops   las chanclas
float (in a parade)   la carroza
flood   la inundación
floor   el piso; la planta
flour   la harina
to flow   fluir
flower   la flor
flu   la gripe
to fly   volar (ue)
flying   volador/a
to focus   enfocarse (qu)
to fold   doblar
to follow   seguir (i)
following   siguiente
food   la comida
foot   el pie
football   el fútbol americano
footwear   el calzado
for   durante (time); para; por
for example   por ejemplo
for sale   a la venta
forehead   la frente
to foresee   prever
forest   el bosque
to forget   olvidar
fork   el tenedor
form   la forma
formalwear   la ropa formal
fortunately   afortunadamente
to fracture   fracturar(se)
free time   el ocio; el tiempo libre
freeway   la autopista
to freeze   congelar(se)
French   francés/francesa

French fries las papas fritas
frequently frecuentemente
Friday el viernes
fried frito/a
fried dough los churros
friend el/la amigo/a
friendly simpático/a
friendship la amistad
from de
front desk la recepción
fruit la fruta
to fry freír (i)
to fry lightly sofreír
to fulfill cumplir
full lleno/a
fun divertido/a
funny divertido/a; gracioso/a
furniture los muebles
furrier el/la peletero/a
fusion cuisine la cocina fusión

G

game el juego; el partido
game station la consola
garage el garaje
garbage la basura
garden el jardín
garlic el ajo
gas station la tienda de gasolina
gate la puerta (de salida)
generally generalmente
generous generoso/a
genetically genéticamente
geography la geografía
German alemán/alemana
gesture el ademán
to get along well llevarse bien
to get angry enfadarse; enojar(se)
to get good/bad grades sacar
  buenas/malas notas
to get into subir
to get lost perderse (ie)
to get married casar(se)
to get together reunirse
to get up levantar
gift el regalo
girl la chica; la chica
girlfriend la novia
to give dar
to give (a present) regalar
glad alegre; contento/a
glass la copa; el vaso; el vidrio
glasses las gafas
to globalize globalizar
glove el guante
glove compartment la guantera
to go andar; ir

Go. Vaya.
to go away ir(se)
to go in entrar (en)
to go into effect ponerse en marcha
to go out salir
to go shopping ir de compras
to go straight seguir (i) derecho
to go to bed acostarse
to go up subir
goal el gol
godchild el/la ahijado/a
godfather el padrino
godmother la madrina
gold oro
golf el golf
golf club el palo
good bueno/a
good afternoon buenas tardes
good-bye adiós; chao; chau
good evening buenas noches
good-looking bien parecido
good-looking guapo/a
Good luck! ¡Buena suerte!
good morning buenos días
goosebumps la piel de gallina
gossip magazine la revista de
  corazón
to govern gobernar (ie)
government el gobierno
governor el gobernador
gradually gradualmente
to graduate graduarse
granddaughter la nieta
grandfather el abuelo
grandmother la abuela
grandson el nieto
grape la uva
grapefruit el pomelo; la toronja
graphic gráfico/a
graphic design el diseño gráfico
to grate rallar
gray gris
Great! ¡Estupendo!
great fabuloso/a; magnífico/a
green verde
green pepper el pimiento verde
greeting el saludo
grill la parrilla
ground molido/a; picado/a
ground floor la planta baja
ground meat la carne molida/picada
group el grupo
Guatemalan guatemalteco/a
to guess adivinar
guide la guía
guitar la guitarra
guitar player el/la guitarrista
gymnasium el gimnasio

H

hachet el hacha
to haggle regatear
hair el cabello; el pelo
hairdresser el/la peluquero/a
half-brother el medio hermano
half-sister la media hermana
Halloween el Día de las Brujas
hallway el pasillo
ham el jamón
hamburger la hamburguesa
to hand dar
hand la mano; la mano; la mano
handicrafts la artesanía
handkerchief el pañuelo
handsome guapo/a
to hang (clothes) tender (ie)
to happen pasar
happily alegremente
happy alegre; contento/a
hardworking trabajador/a
harmful dañino/a
harp el arpa
to harvest cosechar
hat el sombrero
to hate odiar
to have tener (g, ie)
to have a good time divertirse (ie, i);
  pasar bien
to have a(n) . . . ache tener dolor de...
to have breakfast desayunar
to have dinner cenar
to have fun divertirse (ie);
  entretenerse
to have lunch almorzar (ue)
to have to tener que
he él
he/she is es
head la cabeza
health la salud
health care provider el proveedor de
  salud
health center el centro de salud
healthy saludable
to hear oír
to hear about oír hablar
heart el corazón
heat el calor
heating la calefacción
height la estatura
hello hola
Hello? (on the telephone) ¿Aló?;
  ¡Bueno!; ¿Diga?; ¿Dígame?;
  ¡Oigo!; ¿Qué hay?
to help ayudar
her su(s)
herb la hierba

here (present) presente
hi hola
high-heeled shoe el zapato de tacón
highlighter el marcador
highway la carretera
hiker el senderista
hip la cadera
his/her/their su(s)
Hispanic hispano/a
history la historia
holiday el día festivo
home el hogar
homeless desamparado/a
homemaker el ama/o de casa
homework la tarea
Honduran hondureño/a
honesty la honestidad
hood el capó
horrible horrible
hospital el hospital; el sanitorio
hot caliente
hotel el hotel
hour la hora
house, home la casa
housewife el ama/o de casa
housing la vivienda
How about that! ¡Fíjate qué noticia!
How are you (formal)? ¿Cómo está?
How are you (informal)? ¿Cómo estás?
How do you say . . . ? ¿Cómo se dice … ?
How do you spell . . . ? ¿Cómo se escribe … ?
How incredible! ¡Qué increíble!
How is it going? ¿Cómo te va?
how many? ¿cuántos/as?
How may I help you? ¿En qué puedo servirle(s)?
how much? ¿cuánto/a?
How much is it? ¿Cuánto cuesta?
how/what? ¿cómo?
however no obstante
hug el abrazo
human humano/a
humanities las humanidades
hundred cien/ciento
hunger la hambre
to hurt doler (ue)
husband el esposo
hypothesis la hipótesis

I

I yo
I am soy
I am . . . years old. Tengo … años.
I don't know No sé.

I don't understand No comprendo.
I have/you have tengo/tienes
I like me gusta(n)
I/we hope that . . . ojalá que …
I would like . . . Me gustaría …
I would like . . . Quisiera …
ice el hielo
ice cream el helado
ice creamery la heladería
idea la idea
idealistic idealista
if si
ill malo/a
ill person el/la enfermo/a
illiteracy al analfabetismo
illiterate analfabeto/a
illness la enfermedad
I'm sorry (to hear that) lo siento
imagine imaginar
immediately enseguida
immigration la inmigración
imperfect el imperfecto
to implement implementar
important importante
impossible imposible
to improve mejorar
impulsive impulsivo/a
in boldface en negrita
in contrast en contraste
in fact in en realidad/realmente
in front of enfrente (de)
in search of en busca de
in (time) por
inappropriate inapropiado/a
including hasta
incredible increíble
Independence Day el Día de la Independencia
independent independiente
to indicate indicar
inexpensive barato/a
infection la infección
to influence influir
information la información
infrastructure la infraestructura
inhabitant el/la habitante
to inherit heredar
inheritance el/la herencia
injection la inyección
injured herido/a
injured person el/la herido/a
to insert meter
to inspect revisar
inspector el inspector
instead of en vez de
instruction la instrucción
intelligent inteligente
interesante en

to interest interesar
interesting interesante
international internacional
interpreter el/la intérprete
interview la entrevista
to interview entrevistar
intimacy la intimidad
introduction la presentación
introverted introvertido/a
invitation la invitación
to invite invitar
iPod el ipod
to iron to planchar
to itch picar(se)
it's clear está despejado
it's cloudy está nublado
it's cool hace fresco
It's sunny. Hace sol.
it's sunny hace sol

J

jacket la chaqueta
January enero
Japanese japonés/japonesa
jawbone la quijada
jeans los jeans; los vaqueros/ jeans
jeweller el/la joyero/a
jewelry, piece of la joya
job el trabajo
jogging suit la sudadera
joke la broma
journalist el/la periodista
joy la alegría
judge el/la juez
juice el jugo
July julio
June junio
junk food la comida chatarra

K

to keep in shape estar en forma
to keep quiet callarse
to keep silent guardar silencio
key la llave
key card la tarjeta magnética
key word la palabra clave
king el rey
to kiss besar
kiss el beso
kitchen la cocina
kitchen sink el fregadero
knee la rodilla
to knock golpear
to know conocer; saber
knowledge el conocimiento

L

labor-related laboral
laboratory el laboratorio
laborer el/la obrero/a
lace el encaje
lack la falta
lake el lago
lamb el cordero
to land aterrizar (c)
land la tierra
landscape el paisaje
language la lengua
laptop la computadora portátil
to last durar
last último/a
last night anoche
last year el año pasado
late tarde
later después; luego; más tarde
to laugh reír (i)
laughter la risa
laundry room la lavandería
lawn el césped
lawyer el/la abogado/a
layout ladistribución
lazy perezoso/a
leaf la hoja
to learn aprender
least at por lo menos
leather el cuero
to leave dejar; ir(se)
left la izquierda
leg la pierna
leg (animal) la pata
legal holiday el día feriado
legumes las legumbres
leisure activities las diversiones
lemon el limón
to lend prestar
lentils las lentejas
lesson la lección
lettuce la lechuga
level el nivel
librarian el/la bibliotecario/a
library la biblioteca
license plate la placa
to lie mentir
lie la mentira
life expectancy la esperanza de vida
lightweight ligero/a
to like caer bien; gustar
likewise igualmente
link el enlace
lip el labio
list la lista
to listen oír

Listen! ¡Oye!
Listen, please. Oiga, por favor.
to listen (to) escuchar
literature la literatura
little a poco; poco; a un poco
little by little poco a poco
to live vivir
lively animado/a; vivo/a
living room el living; la sala; el salón
lobster la langosta
to lock up encerrar (ie)
lodging el alojamiento
logically lógicamente
long largo/a
to look, appear ver(se)
to look (at) mirar
to look for buscar
to look terrible to tener mala cara
to lose perder (ie)
to lose weight adelgazar
loss la pérdida
loudly alto
loungewear la ropa de estar en casa
love el amor
Love (closing) Cariños
luck lasuerte
luggage el equipaje
lunch el almuerzo
lung el pulmón
luxury el lujo

M

magazine la revista
mail el correo
mail carrier el/la cartero/a
main character el personaje principal
to maintain mantener (g, ie)
major la carrera
majority la mayoría
to make hacer
to make a reservation reservar
to make the bed to hacer la cama
man el hombre
manager el/la gerente
many mucho/a (adj.)
many . . . as as tanto(s)/a(s) ... como
map el mapa
March marzo
margarine la margarina
marked down rebajado/a
marker el marcador; el rotulador
market el mercado
married casado/a
marvel la maravilla
marvelous estupendo/a;
  maravilloso/a

material el material
mathematics las matemáticas
May mayo
mayonnaise la mayonesa
mayor el alcalde
meal la comida
meaning el significado
means of transportation los medios de
  transporte
measure la medida
meat la carne
mechanic el/la mecánico/a
mediator el/la mediador
medical doctor el/la médico/a
medical treatment el tratamiento
  médico
medicine la medicina
to meet conocerse; reunir(se)
meeting, gathering la reunión
melody la melodía
melon el melón
to melt derretir
memory el recuerdo
Mennonites los menonitas
menu el menú
mess el lío; el majarete
message el mensaje
metal metal
mexican mexicano/a
Mexican mexicano/a
Mexican Independence Day el Día de
  la Independencia de México
to microwave hornear
microwave (oven) el (horno)
  microondas
middle class el burgués
to migrate migrar
migration la migración
milk la leche
milkshake, smoothie el batido
million millón
millionaire el/la millonario/a
minus menos
mirror el espejo
moderate módico/a
modern moderno/a
mom la mamá
Monday el lunes
money in cash el dinero en efectivo
month el mes
mood el estado de ánimo
more más
more or less más o menos
morning la mañana
Moroccan marroquí
mortality la mortalidad
mother la madre

Mother's Day　el Día de la Madre
motor　el motor
motto　el eslogan; el título
mouth　la boca
to move　mover; mudarse
movement　el desplazamiento
movies　el cine
to mow (lawn)　cortar
Mr.　el señor (Sr.)
Ms, Miss　la señorita (Srta.)
Ms., Mrs.　la señora (Sra.)
much　mucho/a (adj.); mucho (adv.)
much later　más tarde
multilingual　políglota
mural　el mural
muralist　el/la muralista
muscle　el músculo
museum　el museo
music　la música
must　tener que
mustard　la mostaza
my　mi(s)

N

napkin　la servilleta
narrow　estrecho/a
national　nacional
nationality　las nacionalidad
native　natal
nature　la naturaleza
nature preserve　la reserva natural
near　cerca (de)
necessary　necesario/a
neck　el cuello
necklace　el collar
neighbor　el/la vecino/a
neighborhood　el barrio
neither　tampoco
neither . . . nor　ni ... ni
nephew　el sobrino
nerve　el nervio
nervous　nervioso/a
net　la red
network　la red
never　jamás; nunca
nevertheless　sin embargo
new　nuevo/a
New Year's Day　el Año Nuevo
New Year's Eve　el Fin de Año; la
　Nochevieja
news　la noticia
newspaper　el periódico
next to　al lado (de); próximo/a
Nicaraguan　nicaragüense
nice　agradable; majo/a; simpático/a
niece　la sobrina

Nigerian　nigeriano/a
night　la noche
night before last　ante(a)noche
nightgown　el camisón
nightmare　la pesadilla
no　ningún/ninguno/ninguna; no
no one　nadie
nobody　nadie
noise　el ruido
to nominate　nominar
none　ningún/ninguno/ninguna
normally　normalmente
North American　norteamericano/a
nose　la nariz
nostalgic　nostálgico
not　tampoco
not any　ningún/ninguno/ninguna
(not) ever　jamás; nunca
note card　la ficha
notebook　el cuaderno
nothing　nada
novel　la novela
novelist　el/la novelista
November　noviembre
now　ahora
nowadays　hoy en día
nurse　el/la enfermero/a

O

oath　el juramento
object　el objeto
to obtain　obtener
obvious　obvio/a
occupation　la ocupación
to occur　ocurrir
October　octubre
of　de
of course　claro; por supuesto;
　realmente; cómo no
to offer　ofrecer (zc)
office　la oficina
office (of doctor, dentist, etc.)　el
　consultorio
often　muchas veces
oil　el aceite
old　antiguo/a; mayor; viejo/a
olive　la aceituna
Olympics　las Olimpiadas
on, above　sobre
on demand　a petición
once　una vez
one hand　por un lado
onion　la cebolla
only (adv.)　sólo
only child　el hijo único/la hija única
to open　abrir

opening　la vacante
opinion　la opinión
opinion poll　la encuesta de opinión
opposing　contrario/a
optimistic　optimista
or　o
orange　anaranjado/a, naranja (adj.);
　la naranja
orchestra　la orquesta
to order　encargar; pedir (i)
organization　la organización
to organize　organizar
other　otro/a
other, another　otro/a
other hand　en cambio; por
　otro lado
outdoors　al aire libre
outside　afuera
outskirts　las afueras
outstanding　destacado/a
own　propio/a
ozone layer　la capa de ozono

P

package　el paquete
page　la página
pain　el dolor
painter　el/la pintor/a
painting　el cuadro; la pintura
pajamas　el/la piyama
palate　el paladar
Panamanian　panameño/a
pants　los pantalones
pantsuit　el traje pantalón
pantyhose　las pantimedias
papaya　la papaya
paprika　el achiote; el pimentón
parade　el desfile
Paraguayan　paraguayo/a
pardon me　con permiso, perdón
parents　los padres
parsley　el perejil
to participate　participar
partner　el/la compañero/a
party　la fiesta
passenger　el/la pasajero/a
passion fruit　el fruto de pasión
passive　pasivo/a
passport　el pasaporte
past　pasado/a
pastry　el pastel
patient　paciente; el/la paciente
patriotic　patriótico/a
to pay (for)　pagar
peach　el durazno; el melocotón
pear　la pera

peasant el/la campesino/a
pedestrian area la zona peatonal
pediatrician el/la pediatra
pen el bolígrafo
penalty el penalti
pencil el lápiz
people la gente
pepper la pimienta
percent por ciento
percentage el porcentaje
perfect perfecto/a
perfectionistic perfeccionista
perfectly perfectamente
performance el rendimiento
performer el/la intérprete
periodical el periódico
person la persona; la persona
perspective la perspectiva
Peruvian peruano/a
pessimistic pesimista
petroleum el petróleo
pharmacist el/la farmacéutico/a
pharmacy la farmacia
philology la filología
philosophy la filosofía
photo(graph) la foto(grafía)
physics la física
physiology la fisiología
to pick up recoger (j)
picture el cuadro
pie la tarta
pill la pastilla
pillow la almohada
pin el alfiler
pineapple la piña
pink rosado/a, rosa
to place colocar
place el lugar
plan el plan
to plan to pensar (ie) + infinitive
plane el avión
planet el planeta
plastic plástico
plastic arts los artes plásticas
plate, dish el plato
to play (a game, sport) jugar (ue)
to play (an instrument) tocar (un instrumento)
player el/la jugador/a
plaza la plaza
please por favor
pleased/nice to meet you encantado/a; mucho gusto
pleasure el placer
plumber el/la plomero/a; el/la fontanero/a
plus y

poem el poema
poet el/la poeta
poetry la poesía
point of view el punto de vista
policeman/woman el/la policía
Polish polaco/a
political science las ciencias políticas
poll la encuesta
polluted contaminado/a
poor pobre
popcorn las palomitas de maíz
popular popular
popularity la popularidad
to popularize popularizar (c)
population la población
pork el cerdo
port el deportes
to portray retratar
Portuguese portugués/ portuguesa
position el puesto
possible posible
poster el afiche
potato la papa
potter el/la ceramista
poultry, fowl las aves
poverty la pobreza
powerful potente
position la posición
to practice practicar
to precede preceder
to predict prever
to prefer preferir (ie)
preparation el preparativo
to prepare preparar
to prescribe recetar
prescription la receta
present actual; el regalo
present time actualmente; en la actualidad
preservation la conservación
president el presidente/la presidenta
presidential presidencial
preterit el pretérito
pretty bonito/a; lindo/a
price el precio
printer la impresora
prize el premio
probable probable
problem el problema
procession la procesión
to produce elaborar; producir
product el producto
professor el/la profesor/a
program el programa

progress el progreso
to prohibit prohibir
promising prometedor/a
proposal la propuesta
protein la proteína
proverb el refrán
provided that con tal (de) que
proximity la proximidad
psychiatrist el/la (p)siquiatra
psychologist el/la (p)sicólogo/a
psychology la (p)sicología
publicity la publicidad
publicity campaign la campaña de publicidad
Puerto Rican puertorriqueño/a
purple morado/a
purse la bolsa/el bolso
to put poner (g)
to put to bed acostar
to put makeup on oneself maquillar(se)
to put one's clothes on poner(se) (g) la ropa

Q

quality la calidad
quantity la cantidad
queen la reina
question la pregunta
quickly rápidamente
quiet callado/a
quotation la cita textual
to quote citar

R

race la carrera
racquet la raqueta
radiator el radiador
radio el/la radio
radio announcer el/la locutor/a
radiologist el/la radiólogo/a
rail el riel
to rain llover (ue)
rain la lluvia
rain forest el bosque tropical
raincoat el impermeable
to raise one's hand levantar la mano
rate la tasa
rather bastante
to reach out to comunicarse
to read leer
reading la lectura
ready listo/a
real estate bienes raíces
reality la realidad
really in en realidad/realmente

Really! ¡No me digas!
to reappear reaparecer
rearview mirror el espejo retrovisor
reason la razón
rebirth el renacimiento
receipt la receta
to receive recibir
recipe la receta
to recommend recomendar (ie)
recommendation la recomendación
to record grabar
recycled reciclado/a
red rojo/a
red pepper la pimienta roja
redhead pelirrojo/a
to reduce reducir
to reflect reflejar
to reforest repoblar
refrigerator el refrigerador; la nevera
regime el régimen
region la región
to regret arrepentirse (ie)
regularly regularmente
relative el pariente; el/la pariente
relatively relativamente
relief el alivio
to relieve aliviar
religious religioso/a
remedy, medicine el remedio
to remember recordar(se) (ue)
to rent alquilar
rent el alquiler
to repeat repetir (i)
to repopulate repoblar
reputation la reputación
to require exigir
to research investigar
research la investigación
resources los recursos
to respect respetar
to respond responder
responsible responsable
to rest descansar
restaurant el restaurante
result el resultado
résumé el currículum
to retire jubilarse
to return devolver; retornar; volver (ue)
review la reseña
to reward premiar
rib la costilla
rice el arroz
rich, wealthy rico/a
to ride (a bicycle) montar (en bicicleta)
right el derecho; la derecha

right? ¿verdad?
ring el anillo
river basin la cuenca
road el camino
to roast asar
robbery el robo
robe la bata
robot el robot
romantic romántico/a
roof el tejado
room la habitación
room; bedroom el cuarto
round trip de ida y vuelta
route el trayecto
routine la rutina
rug la alfombra
ruins las ruinas
to run correr

S

sad triste
safe la caja fuerte
salad la ensalada
salad dressing el aderezo
salary el sueldo
sale la rebaja; la venta
(sales) manager el/la gerente (de ventas)
salesman, saleswoman el/la vendedor/a
salesperson el dependiente/la dependienta
salt la sal
Salvadorian salvadoreño/a
sandal la sandalia
sandwich el sándwich
Saturday el sábado
to sauté saltear
to save ahorrar
savings los ahorros
sawdust el aserrín
to say decir (g, i)
to say goodbye despedir(se) (i)
to say hello mandar saludos
scared asustado/a
scarf la bufanda
scene la escena
schedule el horario
school la escuela
school, department la facultad
science la ciencia
scientist el/la científico/a
to score a goal meter un gol
screen la pantalla
sculptor el escultor/la escultora
sea el mar

search engine el buscador
seasoning el condimento
seat el asiento
security la seguridad
sedentary sedentario/a
to see ver
see you later hasta luego
see you soon hasta pronto
see you tomorrow hasta mañana
seed la semilla
to seem parecer (zc)
self-portrait el autorretrato
to sell vender
seller el/la vendedor/a
seminar el seminario
to send enviar; mandar
sentimental sentimental
September septiembre
serious grave; serio/a
to serve servir (i)
server el/la camarero/a
to set the table poner la mesa
several algún/alguno(s)/alguna(s)
shape la forma
sharp agudo/a
to shave (oneself) afeitar(se)
she ella
sheep la oveja
sheet la sábana
shell la concha
shellfish los mariscos
ship la nave, el barco
shirt la camisa
shoe el zapato
shopping las compras
shopping center el centro comercial
short (in length) corto/a
short (in stature) bajo/a; chaparro/a
short-sleeved shirt la camisa de manga corta
shorts los pantalones cortos
should deber
shoulder el hombro
to show mostrar (ue)
shower la ducha
shrimp el camarón; la gamba
sick enfermo/a
side el lado
to sign firmar
signal la señal
significant other la pareja
silence el silencio
silly, foolish tonto/a
simply simplemente
since desde; hace
sincere sincero/a
to sing cantar

single   soltero/a
sister   la hermana
to sit down   sentarse (ie)
size   el número; la talla; el tamaño
to skate   patinar
ski   el esquí
to ski   esquiar
skiing   el esquí
to skim   leer por encima
skin   la piel
skirt   la falda
sleep   el sueño
to sleep (to fall asleep)   dormir(se)
   (ue)
slipper   la zapatilla
slope   la bajada; la pendiente
slowly   despacio; lentamente
small   pequeño/a
smallpox   la viruela
smart   listo/a
to smoke   fumar
snack   la merienda
to sneeze   estornudar
snorkeling   el buceo
to snow   nevar (ie)
snow   la nieve
so that   para que
soap   el jabón
soap opera   la telenovela
sober   sobrio/a
soccer   el fútbol
social   social
society   la sociedad
sociology   la sociología
sock   el calcetín
soda   el refresco
sofa   el sofá
soft   blando/a; suave
soft drink   el refresco
soil   la tierra
some   algún/alguno(s)/alguna(s)
someone   alguien
something   algo
something else   otra cosa
something foolish   la babada
sometime   alguna vez
sometimes   algunas veces; a veces
son   el hijo
song   la canción
to soon as   as tan pronto (como)
sorcerer   el brujo
soul   el alma
to sound   sonar
soup   la sopa
sour   agrio/a
source   la fuente
souvenir   el recuerdo

spaghetti   los espaguetis
Spanish   español/a; el español
to speak   hablar
specialist   el/la especialista
specialty   la especialidad
speed   la velocidad
speed, haste   la prisa
to spend   gastar
to spend (time)   pasar
spice   la especie
spinach   las espinacas
spirit   el espíritu
to sponsor   patrocinar
spoon   la cuchara
spoonful   la cucharada
sports equipment   el equipo
   deportivo
sportswear   la ropa deportiva
to spray   rociar
to spread, to disseminate   difundir
spring   la primavera
square   la plaza
square meter   el metro cuadrado
stadium   el estadio
stairs   la escalera
to stand in line   hacer cola
to stand out   destacarse
star   la estrella
to start   empezar
statistics   las estadísticas
to stay in touch   mantenerse en
   contacto
steak   el bistec
steering wheel   el volante
step   el paso
stepbrother   el hermanastro
stepfather   el padrastro
stepmother   la madrastra
stepsister   la hermanastra
still   todavía
stockings   las medias
stomach   el estómago
to stop   detener
stopover   la escala
store   la tienda
store window   el escaparate
story   el cuento
stove   la cocina; la estufa
straight   derecho
strawberry   la fresa
street   la calle
to stroll   pasear
strong   fuerte
structure   la estructura
student   el alumno/a; el/la estudiante
student desk   el pupitre
studious   estudioso/a

to study   estudiar; investigar
to stumble   tropezarse
stupendous   estupendo/a
style   el estilo
stylish   de moda
subsidize   subvencionar
subway   el metro
success   el éxito
sugar   el/la azúcar
to suggest   sugerir (ie, i)
suit   el traje; el traje de chaqueta
suitcase   la maleta
to summarize   resumir
summer   el verano
sun   el sol
to sunbathe   tomar el sol
Sunday   el domingo
sunglasses   las gafas de sol
sunrise   la salida del sol
supermarket   el supermercado
supper   la comida
to support   apoyar; sustentar
surely, certainly   seguramente
surgeon   el/la cirujano/a
surgery   la operación
to surprise   sorprender
surprise   la sorpresa
surrealist   surrealista
to surround   rodear
survey   la encuesta
to survive   sobrevivir
sweater   el suéter
sweatshirt; jogging suit   la sudadera
to sweep   barrer
to swell   hinchar
swelling   la hinchazón
to swim   nadar
swimming pool   la piscina; la alberca
symbol   el símbolo
symptom   el síntoma

T

T-shirt   la camiseta
table   la mesa
tablecloth   el mantel
to take   llevar; tomar
to take a nap   to dormir (ue) la siesta
to take a seat   tomar asiento
to take a walk   dar un paseo; pasear
to take advantage   aprovechar
to take away   quitar(se)
to take care of   cuidar; cuidar(se) (de)
to take note   fijarse
to take notes   tomar apuntes/notas
to take off   quitar(se)
to take off (airplane)   despegar (u)

to take out   sacar (qu)
to talk   conversar; dialogar
talkative   conversador/a
tall   alto/a
tamale   el tamale
tapas   las tapas
task   la tarea
tea   el té
teacher   el/la profesor/a
team; equipment   el equipo
to tear   romper
teaspoon   la cucharita
technician   el/la técnico/a
technology   la tecnología
telephone   el teléfono
television set   el televisor
to tell   contar (ue); decir (g, i)
tennis   el tenis
tennis player   el/la tenista
tennis shoe   la zapatilla de deporte
terrace   la terraza
terrorism   el terrorismo
test   el examen
thanks, thank you   gracias
Thanksgiving   el Día de Acción de
   Gracias
that   ese/a (adj.); eso (pron.)
that is why   por eso
that (over there)   aquel/aquella
That's great!   ¡Qué bien/bueno!
thaw, thawing   el deshielo
theater   el teatro
theater company   la compañía de
   teatro
their   su(s)
theme   el tema
then   entonces; luego
therapy   la terapia
there   allí
there is, there are   hay
thermometer   el termómetro
they   ellos/ellas
thin   delgado/a
thing   la cosa
to think   pensar (ie)
to think of/about   pensar en
to think of/about (opinion)   pensar de
third   tercero/a
thirst   la sed
this   este/a; esto
thousand   mil
throat   la garganta
through   por; a través de
to throw   lanzar
Thursday   el jueves
ticket   el billete; el boleto, el pasaje
tie   la corbata

tight   estrecho/a
time   la hora; el tiempo
timid   tímido/a
tire   la llanta
tired   cansado/a
title   el título
to   a; para
toast   el pan tostado/la tostada
to toast   tostar
today   hoy
Today is . . .   Hoy es …
together   juntos/as
toilet   el inodoro
tomato   el tomate
tomato sauce   la salsa de tomate
tomorrow   mañana
tone   el tono
tongue   la lengua
tonight   esta noche
too   también
tooth   el diente
toothpaste   la pasta de dientes
tourist class   la clase turista
tournament   el campeonato; el torneo
toward   para
towel   la toalla
toxic   tóxico/a
toy   el juguete
tradition   la tradición
traditional   tradicional
traditionally   tradicionalmente
traffic   el tráfico
train   el tren
trainer   el/la entrenador/a
training   el entrenamiento
training resort   el centro de
   entrenamiento
tranquil   tranquilo/a
tranquilly   tranquilamente
to translate   traducir (zc)
trash   la basura
to travel   viajar
travel agency   la agencia de viajes
travel agent   el/la agente de viajes
tray   la bandeja
to treat   tratar
to treat, to be about   tratar
tree   el árbol
trips   el viaje
true   cierto/a; verdad
trunk   el baúl; el maletero
trust   la confianza
truth   la verdad
to try   probar; tratar
to try on   probarse (ue)
Tuesday   el martes
turkey   el pavo

to turn   doblar
to turn on   encender (ie)
twin   gemelo/a
to twist   torcer(se) (ue)
typical   típico/a

U

UFO   el OVNI
ugly   feo/a
umbrella   el paraguas
umpire, referee   el árbitro
uncle   el tío
under   abajo; debajo (de)
to underline   subrayar
to understand   comprender;
   entender (ie)
underwear   la ropa interior
unemployment   el desempleo
unforgettable   inolvidable
to unify   unificar (qu)
United States   Estados Unidos
university   la universidad
unless   a menos que
unpleasant   antipático/a
until   hasta que
urgent   urgente
Uruguayan   uruguayo/a
U.S. citizen   estadounidense
to use   usar
useful   útil

V

vacation   las vacaciones
to vacuum   pasar la aspiradora
vacuum cleaner   la aspiradora
Valentine's Day   el Día de los
   Enamorados; el Día del Amor y
   la Amistad
vanilla   la vainilla
vegetable   el vegetal, la verdura
vegetarian   vegetariano/a
vein   la vena
Venezuelan   venezolano/a
verbs   verbos
very   muy
veterinarian   el/la veterinario/a
video game   el videojuego
view   la vista
village   el pueblo
vinegar   el vinagre
virtual library   la biblioteca virtual
virtually   virtualmente
to visit   visitar
vitamin   la vitamina
voice   la voz
volleyball   el vóleibol; el volibol

W

waist   la cintura
to wait for   esperar
waiter/waitress   el/la camarero/a
waiting area   la sala de espera
to wake (someone up); to
   despertar(se) (ie)
to wake up   despertar(se)
to walk   caminar
wallet   la billetera
to want   querer (ie)
warehouse   el almacén
warming   el calentamiento
to wash (oneself)   lavar(se)
washer   la lavadora
wastebasket   el cesto
water   el agua
to water   regar (ie)
way   el camino
we   nosotros/nosotras
We are going to have a good time.   Lo
   vamos a pasar muy bien.
weak   débil
to wear   llevar
to wear a costume   disfrazarse
to wear a shoe size   calzar
weather   el tiempo; el tiempo
weather forecast   el pronóstico del
   tiempo
wedding   la boda
Wednesday   el miércoles
week   la semana
week ago   a una semana atrás
weekend   el fin de semana
weight   la pesa
well   bien; bueno/a
well-off   adinerado/a
what?   ¿qué?
What a pity!   ¡Qué lástima!
What a suprise/coincidence!   ¡Qué
   casualidad!
What day is it?   ¿Qué día es hoy?
What do you think?   ¿Qué te parece?

What for?   ¿para qué?
What is he/she/it like?   ¿Cómo es?
What is the date?   ¿Cuál es la fecha?;
   ¿Qué fecha es hoy?
What is the weather like?   ¿Qué
   tiempo hace?
What time is it?   ¿Qué hora es?
What's new?   ¿Qué tal?
What's up?   ¿Qué tal?
What's wrong (with you/them)?   ¿Qué
   te/le(s) pasa?
What's your name? (familiar)   ¿Cómo
   te llamas?
What's your name? (formal)   ¿Cómo se
   llama usted?
wheel   la rueda
when   cuando
when?   ¿cuándo?
where?   ¿dónde?
Where do we meet?   ¿Dónde
   quedamos?
Where is . . . ?   ¿Dónde está... ?
where (to)?   ¿adónde?
wherever   donde
which?   ¿cuál(es)?
while   mientras
to whistle   pitar
white   blanco/a
who?   ¿quién(es)?
Who is . . . ?   ¿Quién es... ?
whose?   ¿de quién?
why?   ¿para qué?; ¿por qué?
wide   ancho/a
wife   la esposa
wild   silvestre
will   el/la testamento
to win   ganar
wind   el viento
window   la ventana; la ventanilla
window seat   el asiento de
   ventanilla
windshield wiper   el limpiaparabrisas
wine   el vino
wine cellar   la bodega

winner   el ganador
winter   el invierno
to wish, to want   desear
with   con
without   sin; sin que
woman   la mujer
wood   la madera
wool   la lana
word   la palabra
work   la obra
to work   trabajar
work   el trabajo
worker   el/la obrero/a
workshop   el taller
World Cup   la Copa
   Mundial
world, worldwide   mundial
to worry   preocupar(se)
wound   la herida
wounded   herido/a
wrist   la muñeca
to write   escribir
writer   el escritor/la escritora

Y

year   el año
yellow   amarillo/a
yes   sí
yesterday   ayer
yet   todavía
yogurt   el yogur
you are (familiar)   eres; estás
you are (formal)   es; estás
you (familiar)   tú (familiar); vos
   (Argentina)
you (formal)   usted (formal)
you (plural)   ustedes (plural)
young   joven
young man/woman   el/la joven
your (familiar)   tu(s)
you're welcome   de nada
youth hostel   el albergue juvenil
yucca   la yuca

Credits

Text Credits

Photo Credits

Language Functions Index

Subject Index